D0947200

HAZLITT
The Mind of a Critic

William Hazlitt,
drawing by William Bewick, 1825.
National Portrait Gallery, London

HAZLITT
The Mind of a Critic

David Bromwich

New York   Oxford
OXFORD UNIVERSITY PRESS
1983

Copyright © 1983 by Oxford University Press, Inc.

A version of chapter 10 appeared in *The Yale Review*.

Library of Congress Cataloging in Publication Data

Bromwich, David, 1951-
William Hazlitt, the mind of a critic.

Includes bibliographical references and index.
1. Hazlitt, William, 1778-1830—Philosophy.
2. Hazlitt, William, 1778-1830—Knowledge and learning.
3. Criticism—England—History—19th century.
4. Romanticism—England.   I. Title.
PR4773.B76   1984   824'.7   83-13452
ISBN 0-19-503343-4

Printing (last digit): 9 8 7 6 5 4 3 2 1

Printed in the United States of America

To my mother and father

PREFACE

This book could have been called "The Mind of an Interpreter," for the critic belongs to a more general category, and only does what the rest of us cannot help doing. But the critic differs from other interpreters in his degree of self-consciousness. He knows that the imagination grasps as a whole what it has first construed from a selection of parts; and that we are always making new stories for the sake of those elements in life that interest us most. "The world's contents," says William James, "are *given* to each of us in an order so foreign to our subjective interests that we can hardly by an effort of the imagination picture to ourselves what it is like. We have to break that order altogether. . . . We break it into histories, and we break it into arts, and we break it into sciences; and then we begin to feel at home." Hazlitt would have agreed with this, and I have tried to show how he agreed. The most unsatisfying thing about the account that emerges is that it gives little evidence of development. Here the fault is Hazlitt's as much as mine; his life as a writer has few turning points and no reversals. He knew this about himself, and apologized many times for the consequent want of picturesque interest. Still, if a man's imaginings be sufficiently comprehensive and his nature sufficiently undogmatic, he has an excellent chance of surviving. The sort of evidence I do give may be read as a test of the assertion.

Instead of narrating Hazlitt's career, either to pursue one theme or trace a rising and falling arc, I offer a story about his genius in relation to the literature he cared for and the age in which he lived. Two opening chapters are devoted to his early *Essay on Human Action* and other matters which might seem preliminary to criticism. They did not seem so to Hazlitt—he thought his early writings explained all the rest—and I have come around to his view. I suspect nevertheless that chapters 1 and 2, because more closely argumentative, will feel more difficult to some readers than anything that follows them. Those who want to hear directly about Hazlitt's criticism are invited

to move from the Introduction to chapter 3, and turn later to the discussions of action and association. Chapters 3 and 4 deal with Hazlitt's anti-professional view of both art and criticism, the dialogue he
presents between the sympathetic claims of the drama and the egotistical claims of poetry, and the way he undermines that opposition
by his appreciations of Rousseau and Wordsworth. Chapters 5, 6, and
7 explore three aspects of Hazlitt's concern with expression: the first
showing how an idea of nature as chosen rather than given leads him
to employ words like "ideal" and "imitation" while thoroughly revising their eighteenth-century meanings; the second contrasting his
respect for history with Coleridge's wish to transcend it, and bringing
out the consequences for their critical practice; and the third illustrating the uses of personality for a writer who supposes that criticism
is the work of our beliefs, and not the reward of a willing suspension
of disbelief. Chapter 8 seeks to exemplify Hazlitt's own rhetorical
power, in the texture of his quotations and in his lifelong contest
with Burke; chapter 9 isolates his analyses of two rival conceptions of
rhetorical power, in the articles on *Coriolanus,* and on Byron and
Pope. Two closing chapters offer a brief character of the essays in
which Hazlitt most strikingly reforms "the egotistical sublime," and
then register the strength of his influence on the parallel efforts of
Keats.

My larger aim throughout has been to help foster a new understanding of the romantic movement, by calling attention to a neglected side of it. What counts as romantic if Hazlitt counts will be
historical rather than apocalyptic; will value language centrally, but
language for its use by a community; and will esteem genius as it
typifies what may occur in all communication, where our sympathies
and powers are in question. If I am right, not only Hazlitt and Keats
but much of Wordsworth and much of Shelley have to be seen in this
perspective, before we can make sense of the continuity they recognized between themselves and the Enlightenment. In keeping with
the same emphasis, I have made the boundaries fluid rather than
fixed between criticism and its neighbors in Hazlitt's thinking, metaphysics, poetry, and politics. And, since I do not think even a great
mind's argument with itself is interesting in itself, I have defined
him partly by comparison with other writers. The procedure grew
out of a conviction that criticism matters to us because it relates to
life, and that in exploring what the relation means there is nothing
to be gained by invoking the idea of mimesis, or imitation at whatever remove, in any of its ancient or modern versions.

The term "critic" is of course far too vague. It has to cover *The*

Life of Milton, The Spirit of the Age, and *The Stones of Venice,* works as different from each other as "The Vanity of Human Wishes," "Tintern Abbey," and "The Waste Land." We would not think we had gone any distance toward describing the latter three by saying they were all poems. We feel much more complacent about describing the former as all works of criticism; and this confirms the suspicion that our dealings with prose are appallingly crude. There are two ways of solving the problem. We can invent more sophisticated prose-genres to ease our conscience. Or we can join the works of prose and poetry that survive, by appreciating both as great writing. This I think is the less tiresome way, and stretches of the book can be read as an experiment in looking at prose as something no less written than poetry. But it is intended also as a study of argument. I do not believe that prose any more than poetry becomes literary at the point where persuasion stops.

Years in the company of a skeptic can lead to some curious results, and on a good many questions I feel clearer-sighted than I ever wished to be before I studied Hazlitt. Thus I agree that criticism is as creative as poetry, without supposing that modern critics who say so have gained much for themselves. A confusion where these issues are debated comes from invoking two qualities that seem indistinguishable in great writing, and drawing the inference that each therefore entails the other. The qualities are interpretative vividness and the expressive power of utterance. To survive, a writer must have both, yet the matter is sometimes discussed as if, with the right luck, the first would carry double weight for the critic. The truth is that you will do well among your contemporaries by putting together the sort of interpretations they admire, breaking up the world in a manner they find congenial. If you have written without power, you will be dismissed by posterity as a sign of the times. If you have written with power—which, in our best figure for eloquence, *carries conviction*—your interpretation itself will be subject to change, but you will remain interesting. And that is all. The ideas that we of the twentieth century inherit—Nietzsche's conception of rhetoric, for example—are as right for us as Wordsworth's were for Hazlitt, and Corneille's were for the Lisideius of the "Essay of Dramatic Poesy." They make us good citizens of our age. It is academic to trust that they will do more, or fear that they will do worse.

Hazlitt thought of prose as a democratic art. I share the sentiment, and accordingly have tried to produce a readable book. The audience is limited by the nature of the subject, and it would be silly to suppose that one could remedy this by writing down, and explaining everything. Nobody will look at a study of Hazlitt who has not read something by him; and such a reader will be familiar with Johnson, Byron, and others who figure largely here. But to address the expert means to write for an audience of perhaps five hundred, and I have kept steadily in view those who care for Hazlitt without knowing a great deal about him. A large part of my task has been to exhibit seriously the whole range of his eloquence. The longer quotations are identified by volume and page number in P. P. Howe's edition of the works (*The Complete Works*, 21 vols. (London, 1930-1934)); but I hate a book with starts and stops on every page, and have eschewed the modern practice of giving a parenthetical volume-and-page reference for the slightest allusions. Cribbers have my blessing, but in some instances, to locate a phrase or a sentence, they may simply have to read Hazlitt. Anything not immediately relevant to the narrative has been dispatched to the limbo of notes, and the notes are placed where they can offer no distraction. I have modernized Hazlitt's sometimes archaic spelling whenever his practice elsewhere gives precedent for the change.

Grants from the National Endowment for the Humanities, and the Committee on Research in the Humanities of Princeton University, enabled me to complete the book in agreeable circumstances. I should like to acknowledge the assistance of the staffs of the Beinecke Library of Yale University; the Huntington Library; the British Library; Dr. Williams's Library; Keats Memorial House in Hampstead; the Poetry/Rare Book Collection of the University Libraries, State University of New York at Buffalo; and the Rare Book and Special Collections, Princeton University Library. Individual debts are harder to measure and harder to number than institutional ones, and a few names must represent many others. I owe much to two late scholars of Hazlitt: P. P. Howe, whose Centenary Edition, with its notes and index, made my work less daunting every step of the way; and J. R. Caldwell, from whose indispensable study, *John Keats' Fancy*, I learned what was at stake in a consideration of Hazlitt and Keats together. Hans Aarsleff, Irving Howe, and Richard Rorty gave comments on large sections of a near-final draft, which lightened the work of revision and improved the result. For advice on individual chapters, and on logistics and organization, I thank Jonathan Arac, Maria DiBattista, John Hollander, A. Walton Litz, Thomas McFarland, Edward Mendelson, and Michael Seidel. When I needed primary evidence to check a surmise, Gordon N. Ray called my attention to, and kindly allowed me to examine, the copy of Flaxman's

Lectures on Sculpture with Hazlitt's annotations, which I have used in several places. To Harold Bloom I am grateful for the encouragement that first made this project seem worthwhile, and for seeing it through its early stages as a Yale doctoral dissertation; and to the editorial staff of the Oxford University Press in New York, for watching over the progress of the manuscript at a later period. Marilyn Walden prepared the typescript, and Marc Wortman assisted in correcting proofs. Finally I owe most to Ross Borden, who read every page, helped me to shape a final draft, and has been made to assist without his consent from my feeling that he is at once a collaborator in the book and its ideal reader; and to Georgann Witte, whose interest all along has strengthened mine.

D.B.

CONTENTS

CHRONOLOGY

1778   Born April 10 in Maidstone, Kent.

1783–87   With family in America.

1788–92   Childhood in Wem, Shropshire.

1793–95   Student in dissenting academy, the New College at Hackney; meets Godwin; composes "Project for a New Theory of Civil and Criminal Legislation," as a voluntary tutorial exercise; leaves Hackney, Summer 1795, having determined not to become a minister.

1796–97   Companionship with Thomas Holcroft, Joseph Fawcett, and other radicals of the generation before; first reading of Burke and Rousseau; inconclusive work on a proof of the natural disinterestedness of the mind.

1798   Hears Coleridge preach in Shrewsbury; visits him and Wordsworth and in Nether Stowey and Alfoxden.

1799–
1804   "My initiation in the mysteries of art," at Orleans exhibition in London, Winter and Spring 1799; residence in Paris, to study and copy old masters in the Louvre (chiefly Titian); career as a painter, from portraits commissioned in Manchester, Liverpool, Keswick, and Grasmere.

1805   Publication of his proof in its final form, as *An Essay on the Principles of Human Action.*

1806–11   In London, political controversy and miscellaneous book-making: "Free Thoughts on Public Affairs" (1806); an abridgement of Abraham Tucker's seven-volume treatise on human nature and theology (1807); *The Eloquence of the British Senate,* specimens with notes (1807); letters in reply to Malthus including three published in Cobbett's *Political Register* (1807); and an English Grammar (1809).

Marriage to Sarah Stoddart, a friend of the Lambs, 1808; birth of his son, William Hazlitt, Jr., 1809.

1812–13   Parliamentary reporter and all-purpose column filler for *The Morning Chronicle.* First series of lectures, on English philosophy (1812).

1814–16   Sees Kean as Shylock (January 26, 1814); begins contributing to *Edinburgh Review* (February 1815); dramatic criticism for *The Morning Chronicle* and *The Champion;* articles for *The Examiner* on politics, theatre, literature, and painting, to relieve Leigh Hunt during his confinement in prison, and continued afterwards. *Life of Holcroft* (1816).

1817–18   *The Round Table; Characters of Shakespeare's Plays; Lectures on the English Poets; A View of the English Stage.*

1819   *Political Essays,* with extensive attacks on the anti-revolutionary writings of Coleridge and Southey; *A Letter to William Gifford,* in reply to three years of libellous assaults; *Lectures on the English Comic Writers.*

1820   Meets Sarah Walker. *Lectures on the Age of Elizabeth.*

1821   *Table-Talk.*

1822–23   Obtains divorce in order to marry Sarah Walker, and is rejected by her. *Characteristics,* a collection of aphorisms; *Liber Amoris,* an autobiographical romance, presented as letters and dialogues without narrative or commentary (anonymous, but immediately understood to be Hazlitt's).

1824–25   Marriage to Isabella Bridgwater, an admirer of his books; *The Spirit of the Age.* European tour; meetings in Paris and Fiesole with two new friends, Stendhal and Walter Savage Landor.

1826–27   *Notes of a Journey through France and Italy; The Plain Speaker.* Separation from his second wife; return to Paris for research on Napoleon.

1828–30   *The Life of Napoleon* (4 vols.), conceived as a reply to Walter Scott's *Life of Napoleon* (9 vols.), in the hope of paying debts and leaving behind one great work; *Conversations of James Northcote* (1830). Dies September 18, 1830.

My ideas, from their sinewy texture, have been to me in the nature of realities.

A Farewell to Essay-Writing

HAZLITT
The Mind of a Critic

INTRODUCTION

Hazlitt's reputation today is puzzling. He is cherished as an essayist, and honored as a name even by those who have scarcely read him. Yet writers can be lost track of by thoughtless selection as well as complete omission, and Hazlitt has suffered both sorts of neglect at different times. The result has been a refinement and a diminishment of our idea of him. Three or four specimens of his writing, repeated in as many generations of anthologies, have sketched a figure in the minds of most readers—sprightly, debonair, essentially worldly—that blends into the atmosphere of Robert Louis Stevenson's hearty compliment: "though we are mighty fine fellows nowadays, we cannot write like Hazlitt." The figure we have come to know is indeed something like Stevenson. And once we have him before us, we can think of celebrated lines that confirm his reality. "Reader, have you ever seen a fight?" This is that Hamlet the Dane, whom we read of in our youth." "To be young is to be as one of the Immortal Gods." His ease is admirable, and it makes admiration easy. Even in a melancholy fit he stays on the best terms with everything. "This," he seems to say, "is how we wrote once, when all topics were grateful to the pen; this is how the world stood with us, when even our self-knowledge kept us warm." The Hazlitt who speaks these lines has held the stage for almost a century, and made us cosy in our seats; but, reader, I never cared for him much; and to make his future a little uncomfortable, I have written a book about someone else.

The Hazlitt I care for is fiercer and less reconciled. Once discovered he is hard to forget, and some dubious critical tactics have been required to suppress him. Early in this century, for example, a scholar undertook to characterize Hazlitt's style by listing a few words. They were: "brilliance, buckle, lake, lamp, library, lustre, mariner, masquerade-dress, bosom, brow, dew-drops, garden, glass, spring, sun, pale, paste, cottage, glittering, smooth, soft, stamped, stripped, trembles, laugh, wandered, winged."[1] The list would please the compiler only if it seemed all of a piece. From its consistency he could infer that the tact and particularity which made these words "modern" had come at the expense of a certain weight, a dignity of abstract statement: with a minimum of effort he could then gratify the common wisdom about style, which holds that the virtues of sensory vividness and discursive generality are seldom found together. This is not too much to surmise from a single list, if the list is representative. But it happens that the page in question belongs to Hazlitt's lecture on Pope. He is in fact describing the qualities that he regards as distinctively Popean, to explain his judgment that "within this retired and narrow circle how much, and that how exquisite, was contained. . . . It is like looking at the world through a microscope." Hence the remarkable unity of the list, the charm and even daintiness of the prose one imagines it fairly to represent. A great many estimates of Hazlitt's achievement are founded on this sort of evidence. Nevertheless any reader will follow a received view until he discovers a sufficiently imposing obstacle in its way.

Mine was a paragraph on *The Merchant of Venice.*

Shylock is *a good hater;* "a man no less sinned against than sinning." If he carries his revenge too far, yet he has strong grounds for "the lodged hate he bears Anthonio," which he explains with equal force of eloquence and reason. He seems the depositary of the vengeance of his race; and though the long habit of brooding over daily insults and injuries has crusted over his temper with inveterate misanthropy, and hardened him against the contempt of mankind, this adds but little to the triumphant pretensions of his enemies. There is a strong, quick, and deep sense of justice mixed up with the gall and bitterness of his resentment. The constant apprehension of being burnt alive, plundered, banished, reviled, and trampled on, might be supposed to sour the most forbearing nature, and to take something from that "milk of human kindness," with which his persecutors contemplated his indignities. The desire of revenge is almost inseparable from the sense of wrong; and we can hardly help sympathising with the proud spirit, hid beneath his "Jewish gaberdine," stung to madness by repeated undeserved provocations, and labouring to throw off the load of obloquy and oppression heaped upon him and all his tribe by one desperate act of "lawful" revenge, till the ferociousness of the means by which he is to execute his purpose, and the pertinacity with which he adheres to it, turn us against him; but even at last, when disappointed of the sanguinary revenge with which he had glutted his hopes, and exposed to beggary and contempt by the letter of the law on which he had insisted with so little remorse, we pity him, and think him hardly dealt with by his judges.

(IV, 320)

Such a passage of course says nothing final about the play. The man who wrote it appears as a skeptic for whom skepticism is not a disease to be cured. He seeks no unity, offers no "resolution of tensions."

Trampled, brooding, and *indignities* had replaced *trembles, glittering,* and *dew-drops.* This gave me a jolt: the pages that follow are a record of its effects. I have listened to the author who "can hardly help sympathising," to whom sympathy means anger at an injustice and scorn for its apologists; who wonders, "Why should one not make a sentence of a page long, out of the feelings of one's whole life?"; who says of a "person" obviously himself, that he is "the last to quit his seat in your company, grapples with a subject in conversation right earnestly, and is, I take it, backward to give up a cause or a friend." He is the most restless of the English romantics, the most dangerous to his enemies, and in one sense the most shocking, since his familiarity of manner recommends him to those who would not knowingly welcome the products of a new school. That he is also shockable gives his work its delicacy and its depth. In English there is no one even roughly comparable to him: in French there is Stendhal. The Hazlitt of the Victorians, however, and of their followers almost to our own day, I neither wish nor expect to supplant. He is another character with the same name, who multiplies the lights and shadows that hold our interest in any given essay, whether it is called "On the Pleasure of Painting" or "On the Pleasure of Hating."

By his earliest writings Hazlitt came to be known above all as a champion of embattled causes: republicanism, democracy, and the freedoms of conscience and the imagination for which he sometimes reserved a single word, *expression.* To this role he was fitted equally by precept and conviction. He was a Dissenter, connected by tradition with Bunyan and Defoe, and son of the Reverend William Hazlitt, who supported the American Revolution, took his family with him to New England, and during a short stay gave a decided impetus to the founding of the first Unitarian church in the country. With this lineage Hazlitt could command the full eloquence and moral gravity of Dissent, without its principled bigotry. It is important not to simplify any conversion by supposing that the old energies must have escaped into a substitute faith; but for Hazlitt the loss of belief in God did unquestionably coincide with an awakened receptivity to art. The change is visible in two annotations to Flaxman's *Lectures on Sculpture,* where the conjunction occurs by chance, and with characteristic abruptness. Hazlitt comes to an apparently harmless phrase about those who believe in "a one Omnipotent" and comments in the margin, *"a lie";* he comes to a phrase about usefulness being "always a property of beauty," and objects that usefulness is *"always a bad reason"* for exalting art.[2] Most liberal-minded Dissenters would tolerate art—beyond the general principle of toleration, which might be conceded here with a certain distrust— on the ground that it instructs us in the love of God and our fellow men, and is so far a useful aid to morality. But Hazlitt rejected the new criterion of value along with the being invoked to justify it. He affirmed the difference this made when he wrote, "In one sense, Shakespeare was no moralist at all." Yet his rebellion from the religion of his fathers seems to have been as unanxious as such events can be, and at no point did he cease to admire a fortitude that for him was salvageable from its parent creed. Among the penny-a-line articles of his last year is an affectionate obituary for Joseph Priestley, the chemist, metaphysician, and scholastic hero of modern Dissent: "We should like to have seen a tilting-bout on some point . . . between the little Presbyterian parson and the great Goliath of modern Calvinism, Mr. Irving; [Dr. Priestley] would have had his huge Caledonian boar-spear, his Patagonian club out of his hands in a twinkling with his sharp Unitarian foil."

That foil by rights was Hazlitt's, too. For he was first celebrated not only as a critic but as a lecturer—and a lecturer, in the early decades of the century, was often a minister who had lost his complacency. This much at least of the minister remained in Hazlitt, that he sought to improve, by contending with, the unregenerate part of his audience. Those who were impenetrable by wit might be roused by other means. So when, as sometimes happened, his delivery was unexpectedly interrupted, he made it a practice to stare at those persons from whom any unbidden murmur had proceeded, and repeat with double force the passage that had given offense, or deliver the stunning blow to which it had been only a prelude. A nice instance of this occurred in his lecture on the periodical essayists. He had reached the peroration on Johnson which contained all his favorite anecdotes from Johnson's life, among them, "last and noblest, his carrying the unfortunate victim of disease and dissipation

on his back up through Fleet Street." Here, by the most convincing
biographical account, "he was interrupted not only by a buzz of
protest from some members of his audience, who felt that he was
introducing into his lecture matter unfit for 'Saintly' ears, but by
tittering from others, to whom the grotesque element in that sad
elephantine progress up Fleet Street made an immediate appeal."
Hazlitt took an ominous pause, went back, "with an air of determination and iron firmness," to read again the sentence that had occasioned the jeers, and spoke his conclusion as he had written it, slowly
enough for the reprobate to measure each word—"An act which re-
alises the parable of the good Samaritan!"[3]

At the Surrey Institution, where most of his lectures were given,
he attracted an audience of the self-taught and the self-improving:
middle class, and many of them Dissenters or Quakers. Even those
with literary pretensions had come largely of the same stock. A fair
example of the kind, on its more self-conscious and respectable side,
was Crabb Robinson, who prided himself on being the intimate of
Coleridge, and in the winter of 1818 scurried back and forth between Hazlitt's and Coleridge's lectures on poetry, comparing them
with the instinct of an expert consumer and all the while piquing
himself on his new accessions of knowledge. In *The Making of the
English Working Class*, E. P. Thompson, by whose studies of the
period I have been influenced at several points, concluded that Hazlitt was a middle-class Radical. It is perhaps a necessary discrimination, for it helps us to feel the contrast between Hazlitt's readers in
The Examiner and Cobbett's in the *Political Register*. But the well-
documented personality of Crabb Robinson must not be allowed to
define the limits of Hazlitt's audience in manners any more than in
politics; and to do justice to Hazlitt's situation the label needs to be
bigger even if that makes it more clumsy. "Middle-class Radical"
somehow fails to suggest the—from Robinson's point of view—altogether unrespectable atmosphere in which Hazlitt moved. "Hazlitt's
style," Thompson adds, "with its sustained and controlled rhythms,
and its antithetical movement, belongs to the polite culture of the
essayist."[4] Again, the contrast with the styles of working-class culture
can hardly be ignored: but "polite" in the one case, like "middle
class" in the other, hems him in too conveniently. How many readers, who had once got the polite middle-class Radical fixed in their
minds, would pick him out in the incident sketched above? Or in
another, from a different set of lectures—the speaker permitting himself a small ironic apology for his neglect of Hannah More, "a cele-

brated modern poetess, and I believe still living. She has written a great deal which I have never read"; his audience greeting that momentary assumption of superiority with the cry, "More pity for you!"; after which the lecture continues as before. Hazlitt's radicalism, the whole tenor of his criticism, was at home in the meeting-house as well as in the journals. More than this can I think be claimed for just one of his contemporaries, Blake, to whose *Songs,* when Robinson read him a few aloud, Hazlitt responded with immediate sympathy. "They are beautiful," Robinson reports him as saying, "and only too deep for the vulgar. He has no sense of the ludicrous, and, as to God, a worm crawling in the privy is as worthy an object as any other, all being to him indifferent. He is ruined by vain struggles to get rid of what presses on his brain—he attempts impossibles."[5] Hazlitt attempted possibles. He wrote for those who could understand him as he was; he had many shared aims but, it must be admitted, few shared words with working-class revolutionaries—he was poor at "accommodation"; in this sense alone it is fair to consider him a middle-class Radical.

Hazlitt's lectures on philosophy, poetry, comedy, and the Elizabethan Age, fill not quite three volumes of the twenty in his collected works; familiar essays and the *Life of Napoleon* account for another seven; of what remains the vast bulk is simply, or far from simply, journalism. Hazlitt wrote with such continuous and unexampled vehemence, fires stoked and ablaze for the strictest of deadlines, that his legend has joined and helped to keep alive the journalist's romance, from which the novice at the worst of times gets some encouragement. What makes for the romance? In part an ideal of independence, which is never altogether marred by the realities of shifting employment; and the sense that writing has its place in a larger cultural conversation, where the merits of everything are to be warmly debated, where indeed a thing's value lies partly in the discussion it provokes. The unhappier features of the romance were sketched by Virginia Woolf in an essay on Lockhart's criticism. Posterity may have gibbeted Lockhart for his ridicule of Keats, and yet "No one who sees him swinging in the wind can help a shudder and a sigh lest the same fate may one of these days be his. After all, new books of poems still appear."[6] But even for what we may consider his mistakes, Hazlitt cannot serve as a salutary warning, because he never tries to close off part of the conversation. He conveys, better than any other writer of any age, the charge and retreat of its battles, the skirmishes and stray shots, and trials of valor. Desertions are reported with unmerciful accuracy, and when the reporter cannot give his own name, he writes a letter with the signature SEMPER EGO AUDITOR. All this is carried off in a style that cannot be parodied, the style of a man who has listened to those whom he regards as his equals. It makes the great difference between Hazlitt and sages like Carlyle and Ruskin, whose every word carries the injunction, "Now, attend!" but whom we can hardly picture in the attitude of attending to someone else. And there is another difference: Hazlitt is angry without being a scold. Often, in the daily round of talk, he won arguments without wishing to reform his opponents altogether, or to make them over as disciples. Why should he put on a different face in his prose?

"Brow-hanging, shoe-contemplative, *strange,*" Coleridge called him—one of two interesting remarks he made about Hazlitt, in a lifetime of abuse. The other was: "He sends well-headed and well-feathered Thoughts straight forwards to the mark with a Twang of the Bow-string."[7] In several casual self-portraits, Hazlitt acknowledged both elements of his character but insisted on their coherence, and in "A Farewell to Essay-Writing," answering some good-natured criticisms by Leigh Hunt, his last words of apology were thoroughly unrepentant.

> Both from disposition and habit, I can *assume* nothing in word, look, or manner. I cannot steal a march upon public opinion in any way. My standing upright, speaking loud, entering a room gracefully, proves nothing; therefore I neglect these ordinary means of recommending myself to the good graces and admiration of strangers (and, as it appears, even of philosophers and friends). Why? Because I have other resources, or, at least, am absorbed in other studies and pursuits. . . . If my ideas, which I do not avouch, but suppose, lie below the surface, why am I to be always attempting to dazzle superficial people with them, or smiling, delighted, at my own want of success?
>
> What I have here stated is only the excess of the common and well-known English and scholastic character. I am neither a buffoon, a fop, nor a Frenchman, which Mr. Hunt would have me to be. He finds it odd that I am a close reasoner and a loose dresser. I have been (among other follies) a hard liver as well as a hard thinker, and the consequences of that will not allow me to dress as I please. (XVII, 317)

His sociability was of the intense and not the expansive kind. He liked the unrestricted company of the coffee-houses, and the more select groups presided over by Charles Lamb, for the possibility of a choice encounter. But it is impossible to imagine him, like Macaulay, employing all the arts of self-promotion, till the invitation to dine at Holland House is at last received. He was meant for other scenes, and he knew it. He always hears the duns at the door, as he dispatches twelve new table-talks in the post, hands over to his creditors the fifty pounds he has received in advance, and, with his moments of peace thus dearly purchased, goes off to play rackets, a game in which he excels at volleys.

He admired those contemporaries who seemed to resemble him in their indifference to public opinion, with the originality and unfaltering self-esteem that this implied. Chief among them were the "idols," Edmund Kean and Napoleon, to whom he administered frequent correctives as an earnest of his attachment, but of whom no one else was allowed to speak ill, on penalty of being thought lukewarm and demoted in Hazlitt's opinion to the mob of the genteel. Kean and Napoleon were alike in respects that are not generally understood. They had arrived on the scene with no remembered apprenticeship; they were physically unimpressive, and did not indemnify their defects by exhibiting the graces of a discipline: they scorned the correct models in acting and fighting, and together seemed to embody the very type of the irregular genius in a democratic age, getting their ends by force and cunning, but always open to the charge of vulgarity. In *The Spirit of the Age,* however, Hazlitt passes over them lightly. It may be that he grew more disappointed than he liked to admit, with the later performances of both men. But these omissions are also in keeping with a melancholy that pervades the book. Only those who have read it through can know that there is finally no lift even in the phrase, since for Hazlitt "the spirit of the age" is something that has been defeated. The evil work was done, as we learn in his panoramic asides, by oppression at home and wars abroad, by government spies and government critics. Miraculously, out of such sentiments, he made the most generous of all his books. Indeed, "generous" is a word that recurs so often in discussions of *The Spirit of the Age* that one may wonder if it really means anything. I think it is the right word but an unrewarding sort of praise until one sees what Hazlitt had to be generous *about.*

To consider only the most celebrated of the full-length portraits, those of Bentham, Godwin, Coleridge, Wordsworth, and Byron: Bentham had been Hazlitt's landlord, and by no means a sympathetic one; Godwin had based his reply to Malthus on Hazlitt's book of that title, without a word of acknowledgment, and had then asked Hazlitt to review it; Wordsworth and Coleridge, in the changed political climate a decade after their last sight of Hazlitt, had done their worst to blacken his name, to have him excluded from "polite company" as well as polite journals, by retailing ever more extravagant versions of a mortifying episode from his past, when a country jilt in Keswick rebuffed his advances, roused a mob of villagers to pursue him after he *"smote* her on the *bottom,"*[8] and obliged him to flee the district to avoid a ducking (aided, in a detail Coleridge honed to a fine pathos, by "all the money I had in the world, and the very Shoes off my feet,"[9] by which he meant his pocket money and a pair of old boots); Byron, once a sponsor of *The Liberal*—the vehicle for several of Hazlitt's liveliest essays—had responded to the warm solicitations of jealous friends, and withdrawn support from the magazine as a thing tainted by the cockneyism of Hazlitt and Hunt. Such were the involved relations between Hazlitt and those about whom he determined to write a book. But what reader without knowing them before has ever guessed their extent? The poise and exuberance of the writing, its freedom from malice, and from any particle of vanity, seem to rule such matters out of consideration: from the book alone we might suppose that Hazlitt knew none of his subjects, and that this explained his freedom from the personal motive. He knew them all, and yet he was free. So, in *The Spirit of the Age,* we encounter Byron as "a solitary peak," who "reminds us of the fabled Titans"; Coleridge, as the honorable exile from the comfort and commerce of all professions, "having no abiding place nor city of refuge"; Wordsworth, as the great original whose genius is "a pure emanation of the Spirit of the Age"; Godwin, as the sincere voice of a reasoning eloquence; and Bentham, as the prophet not without honor save in his own country.

Twenty years of steady writing, from which many of these portraits had been gradually built up, were interrupted twice to disastrous effect. The battle of Waterloo—the conquest, as Hazlitt would later call it, of a single tyrant by tyranny itself—staggered his faith in mankind. For weeks, Benjamin Haydon tells us in his *Autobiography,* Hazlitt walked the streets alone and spectral, hardly able to greet his friends; thereafter any disproportion between his bitterness and its supposed cause would have been referred by those nearest him to a day in June, 1815. But of this little more can be said, as Hazlitt has left no distinct record of it. Another and more private catastrophe, however, seems to have touched him as deeply. Hazlitt possessed, as he knew, not only a subtle and wide-ranging but a morbidly susceptible imagination, liable to seize upon out-of-the-way particulars and dwell on them till they became "a kind of substance in my brain." For most of two years, in his early forties, he abridged the whole routine of his life to think about love, and at last to torment himself as his thoughts darkened. He had become infatuated with the serving girl who brought him his tea in a lodging house, and who startled him one day by sitting in his lap. This was Sarah Walker, nineteen years old and a flirt. "She is not good or bad," wrote Hazlitt, in the only clear view of her character ever granted him; "she is defective in [certain] faculties that belong to human nature, and acts upon others."[10] Yet for her sake he made a wreck of his life. With friends and acquaintances, almost indifferently, he carried on a desperate correspondence about his pursuit of her; those whom he met on ordinary business might find themselves detained for hours with the tale of his woes; he tried every possible means to resolve Sarah's character into that of angel or demon, going so far as to test her faithfulness by laying a trap in the shape of a hired seducer; but when, after humiliating delays and contrivances, he procured a divorce from his wife and proposed marriage to Sarah, he was flatly rejected. Of all this we have an almost daily record, in the diaries of Hazlitt and of his wife, in his correspondence, and in his verbatim transcriptions of meetings with Sarah, which with the correspondence and some brief stretches of narrative he published in 1823, as soon as he was certain of his loss, under the title *Liber Amoris; Or, the New Pygmalion*. Of the many, usually scandalized, contemporary comments on the book, the truest is De Quincey's: "There was no indelicacy in such an act of confidence, growing, as it did, out of his lacerated heart. It was an explosion of frenzy. He threw out his clamorous anguish to the clouds, and to the winds, and to the air; caring not who might listen, who might sympathise, or who might sneer. Pity was no demand of his; laughter was no wrong: the sole necessity for *him* was—to empty his overburdened spirit."[11] The book is crowded with scenes for its dearth of characters—the same scene, coaxed into mocking repetitions—and sadly gifted with self-doubt.

My decision to consider Hazlitt's critical and moral writings in separate sections implies no assurance that the subjects in his mind were clear of each other, or that it would be a good thing if they were. In what first presents itself as a political essay, for example, he can gravely repeat Coleridge's discovery that Caliban was the first

Jacobin, and then use it as a pretext for recounting the plot of *The Tempest,* to prove that Caliban "is strictly the legitimate sovereign of the isle, and Prospero and the rest . . . usurpers." He also moves in the opposite direction: his discussion of *Coriolanus* in the *Characters of Shakespeare's Plays* might with equal plausibility have been included in *Political Essays*. But whatever the form in which he casts any given article, Hazlitt remains a rare instance of the speculative thinker who is also a representative observer—who can give a report on what lies directly before him which has the effect of prophecy. I despaired of ever seeing this quality locked into a phrase, until I came across Brecht's words about Karl Kraus: "When the age laid hands on itself, he was the hands."[12]

In criticism, where Hazlitt would seem to have made his largest claim on us, he has come to be regarded impatiently. He is found wanting in theory, though prolific of "impressions"; welcomed into our reading lists, and read for the analogies he provides to critics of a more imposing dignity. We live at a time of immense sophistication in criticism, yet the state of our dealings with Hazlitt might suggest other thoughts than the consoling one that we have advanced beyond him. We operate on a narrower basis, with better-defined targets, perhaps. Yet Hazlitt's decline and our progress did not take place overnight. A. C. Bradley's *Oxford Lectures on Poetry* (1909) mention him frequently in company with the romantic poets, as a critic who made his share of mistakes, but still a writer of genius with whom it was dangerous to disagree. A few years later, T. S. Eliot receives him with some show of embarrassment, as a poor relation of the responsible critic, guilty of "crimes against taste," and worth the trouble of decapitating only because there is still a price on his head.[13] Once he had been disposed of Hazlitt could be treated generously, and in *Literary Criticism: A Short History* W. K. Wimsatt describes him as "a kind of Addisonian spokesman for the romantic age, a very knowledgeable educator who blurted out secret meanings in quite plain prose."[14] This is a compliment, though a strange one, given Hazlitt's low opinion of Addison. In any case Hazlitt, the spokesman and educator, has been deprived of the name of critic. What had happened, between 1909 and 1957, to make that possible, was the rise of academic criticism.

Of our modern, exclusive, and professional criticism, with its love of method and yearning for system, the true father is Coleridge.

Its distinctive marks are a concern for the activity of reading, and a want of interest in the common reader. We have grown used to the consequences, and may have stopped our complaints about the widening distance between the world of journalism, where new literature is fostered or starved, and the world of scholarship, where old literature is interpreted and canonized. But the depth of taste that we find in Johnson and Hazlitt, and not less in Goldsmith and Lamb, was communicable long before criticism became a profession. Hence the eighteenth- and nineteenth-century interest in projects for "the diffusion of taste": we no longer hear the phrase because what can now be diffused is technique. To identify Coleridge as the first technical critic is doubtless a convenience. It is also a plausible deduction from his style: he addresses those who seek instruction in the mysteries; the process, it is assumed, will be exhausting, even at times repellent; yet such is the nature of instruction. There can be in his criticism, as Madame de Staël said of his conversation, "no idea of dialogue." If, in sections of this book, an argument with Coleridge is audible as a persistent undertone, that is because I have wondered how much Hazlitt really sacrificed when he incorporated in his writings an idea of dialogue. Coleridge's limitations may remind us of our own; Hazlitt's are irretrievable. But it is wrong to suppose that we have much in common with either of them. Coleridge distrusted temperament as a guide to judgment, Hazlitt endorsed it; but both knew its power, and we have tried to rid ourselves of such knowledge.

When Keats attended Hazlitt's lectures on poetry at the Surrey Institution, he went to hear not criticism but Hazlitt. Yet as he listened—as he revolved in his mind, along with certain phrases and ideas, some conception of the energies which the speaker himself appeared to exemplify—he began to think in a new way about poetry. His letters bear witness to his sense of the change; again and again they associate it with Hazlitt. Yet this is a sort of occurrence about which we have everything to learn. Keats praised a sentence of Hazlitt's as "a Whale's back in the Sea of Prose." We have lost the tact for such appreciation. Criticism now warns us against reducing poetry to statement, or against elevating it into statement, but we are baffled by the suggestion that critical prose be read as anything but statement. The audiences of Emerson, Ruskin, and Pater, like that of Hazlitt, went to criticism for something more than durable precepts; they searched out the intensities of the critic, his "sensations." Reading could lead to further sensations; it did not end in a "view." Compared with other masters of critical prose, Hazlitt seems at once stronger and subtler, infinitely finer in his modulations, and more stark in his shadings. We do not say of his description of a thing, "He has taken it up, and submerged it in his medium, and converted it into a Hazlitt-thing." Poetic statements, William Empson has said, "differ . . . from prosaic ones in imposing the system of habits they imply more firmly or more quickly."[15] More firmly or more quickly; not more subtly or more completely. Prose too has its way with us in the end, and the better we come to know its by-roads and clearings, the longer we want to pause at the intervals it affords, and the less paradoxical it appears that the difference between poetry and prose should be a difference only of degree.

But Hazlitt's style is familiar to us in a way we feel almost too closely to understand. For it is still modern. The fact may be concealed through whole passages which seem to exist for the sake of a clenching epigram in Bacon's style: "Prosperity is a great teacher; adversity is a greater. Possession pampers the mind; privation trains and strengthens it." Yet a look at the context of such sayings generally reveals what different and unsententious motives underlie the conduct of Hazlitt's prose. In the foregoing sentences, from an essay "On the Want of Money," he had been imagining the easy freedoms of "a man of rank and fortune" in letters, who is not obliged to pursue anything to the point of pedantry, or sink his pretensions deeply in the subject he writes on. The epigram occurs inconspicuously, in mid-paragraph, and is meant not to close the argument in favor of the imagined noble writer (someone like Byron), but to open it to the claims of a writer who has nothing to recommend him but his work (someone like Hazlitt). The argumentative valor and surprise of gestures like this prepare us for those aphorisms—chiefly collected in *Characteristics,* though a good anthology might be made from his earlier books—in which Hazlitt seems a precursor of Nietzsche, condensing into three lines the sort of psychological observation that issues in entire novels: "When the imagination is continually led to the brink of vice by a system of terror and denunciations, people fling themselves over the precipice from the mere dread of falling."

His prose is extraordinarily varied. It is also extraordinarily responsive, and he knew that he owed something of that quality to the luck of his birth. A writer who came of age as Hazlitt did, about 1800, found himself at a confluence of the Augustan and romantic idioms: Hazlitt was only more resourceful than others in feeling what this could mean. He could *choose* to retain the eighteenth-century pattern of balance and antithesis. In fact, Hazlitt carries on the inherited mode wherever it suits him, comfortably for any stretch of sentences, though as a rule he breaks it up before a paragraph is done. He also strives to create effects of an oratorical grandeur, like Burke's, with a fierceness that once it comes into his tone will have come to stay. He can be grave and clever, irritable and above dispute in the quick succession of his moods as his sentences move straight to the mark. The pace and consistency, the head-on stubbornness and willing imperfection of a man talking to you about what concerns him most are his constant strengths, and I know of no other writer in English who combines them.

The Augustan style was worth rebelling against because in Hazlitt's time it still existed as an almost palpable force: Johnsonian periods kept up a steady humming in the ear, an echo, as it would seem to Ruskin a generation later, "as of thunder answering from two horizons." So the deftness of Hazlitt's new cadences, the sinewy assurance with which they shoot clear of the jagged straits they like to negotiate, is figured against the roundness and fluency, the enlightened challenge to all idiosyncrasy of a prose which was still a live option even when it was firmly refused. When one encounters certain striking passages in which Hazlitt seems to look ahead to the great achievements of the realistic novel—

> It is not the contrast of pig-styes and palaces that I complain of, the distinction between the old and new; what I object to is the want of any such striking contrast, but an almost uninterrupted succession of narrow, vulgar-looking streets, where the smell of garlick prevails over the odour of antiquity, with the dingy, melancholy flat fronts of modern-built houses, that seem in search of an owner. A dunghill, an outhouse, the weeds growing under an imperial arch offend me not; but what has a green-grocer's stall, a stupid English china warehouse, a putrid *trattoria,* a barber's sign, an old clothes or old picture shop or a Gothic palace, with two or three lacqueys in modern liveries lounging at the gate, to do with ancient Rome?   (X, 232)

—one has to recall, as part of the background, the different movement that still served him in advancing a different sort of narrative:

> Mr. Williams has made the *amende honorable,* for his country, to the offended genius of art, and has stretched out under the far-famed Calton Hill, and in the eye of Arthur's Seat, fairy visions of the fair land of Greece, that Edinburgh belles and beaux repair to see with cautious wonder and well-regulated delight. . . . There played the NINE on immortal lyres, and here sit the critical but

admiring Scottish fair, with the catalogue in their hands, reading
the quotations from Lord Byron's verses with liquid eyes and
lovely vermilion lips—would that they spoke English, or any thing
but Scotch! (XVIII, 170-71)

The jolt, the spill, the alarming career down the page which suddenly stops, command interest partly by their contrast with the
steady chiming of the well-regulated instrument that may resume
control of the address at any time.

Readers of Hazlitt may seem peculiarly drawn to questions about
influence and originality. The truth is that he never lets one forget
them for long. Apart from the fragment on progress in the arts—an
essay which he took the trouble to revise, reprint, and even quote
approvingly but without attribution as the opinion of "a contemporary critic"—his further speculations on the subject have a way of
surfacing at apparently unapt moments and usurping the privilege
of other topics. A list of such moments would cover half of his writings on art; none is more striking than the sudden descent with
which he brings to a close his *Lectures on the English Poets:* "I have
felt my subject gradually sinking from under me as I advanced, and
have been afraid of ending in nothing. The interest has unavoidably
decreased at almost every successive step of the progress, like a play
that has its catastrophe in the first or second act." The first act had
been Shakespeare, the second Milton; after them, the flood: this is
the lament of a baffled survivor.

Originality, as Hazlitt uses the word, is inseparable from such
other words as *imagination, power,* and *sublimity.* In his first book,
An Essay on the Principles of Human Action, Hazlitt proposed that
the imagination, naturally out-going, and so not naturally selfish,
was the governing faculty of the mind. Being disinterested, however,
it was not *a priori* good or evil; and its distinctive activity, the projection of a possible future, could lead with equal plausibility to
sympathy or self-sympathy, to the sort of action we call altruistic or
egoistic. There is thus a moral ambiguity implicit in every exertion
of power to which the imagination moves us. The power of poetry
which Hazlitt loved, and the power of tyranny which he hated, were
not easy for him to confine within discrete categories, and he sometimes resigned himself to supposing that they were the same power.
One of his commentators, John Kinnaird, puts the idea of power at
the center of Hazlitt's thought; and though my understanding of it
differs from Kinnaird's, it has seldom been far from my own concerns in discussing Hazlitt's criticism and politics.[16] A name that does

not mislead us for the single aspect under which all power was comprehended by Hazlitt is the sublime. It was indeed the Burkean sublime of terror, of astonishment, and of privation—but still an experience as properly identified with the witness as with the participant. This conclusion is only a beginning; but it does show why Hazlitt's love of power was acceptable to himself.

By the strength of his speculations Hazlitt was equipped to be the most complex romantic exponent of an expressive poetics. The metaphysical sanction he required for this came from Hume's *Treatise of Human Nature:* "the memory, senses, and understanding [are] all of them founded on the imagination, or the vivacity of our ideas."[17] What Hazlitt learned from that sentence and others, might be summed up in the phrase, *ideas travel.* Hence, the expressive and affective moments of art could be interpreted as a single extended movement of sympathetic imagining—the listener is moved as the speaker was himself moved. This was an empiricist's, not a pantheist's, community of feling. Nevertheless it is commonly assumed that Hazlitt took his critical preconceptions from Coleridge. The honor of having been the first to say so goes to Coleridge himself: the person best situated to judge the truth of his claims was Charles Lamb, who regarded them as important chiefly to the history of spleen. Reason enough for doubting them can be found in the works of Hazlitt and Coleridge; and one ought in any case to be wary of confusing personal gratitude with intellectual debt. Coleridge begins as an enthusiastic associationist, names his son after the founder, then makes significant rumblings at so "necessitarian" a doctrine, and imagines he has disproved it. Hazlitt reads Hartley once, advances his objections, and keeps to them: he argues as a thinking disciple of Hume.

Coleridge despised Hume, without giving clear evidence that he had read or understood him. "The subject of my meditations," he writes, "has been the Relations of Thoughts to Things; in the language of Hume, of Ideas to Impressions."[18] This mistranslation is characteristic. It occurs in a letter to Sir Humphry Davy, two years after Coleridge had met the young Hazlitt and conversed with him, freely and scornfully, on the same subject of Hume. Hazlitt for his part had no use for a philosophy, German idealist or Scottish common-sense, which proposed and disposed of things-in-themselves: he tells us once and for all, "I never could make much of the subject of real relations in nature." To this, if we imagined it as part of a dialogue, Coleridge would mildly reply that he has *"completely ex-*

tricated the notions of time and space," seen how to deduce the five senses from one, and thus enabled himself to "solve the process of life and consciousness." Perhaps Hazlitt's admission that Coleridge was the only person from whom he ever learned any thing does not give away much after all.

Hazlitt's politics were in accord with his criticism. They are not, however, the self-conscious, the refined or anxious, politics of a literary man. For all his confessed hates, and his relish in saying that hatred with him was a more rooted passion than love, he speaks less against kings and aristocrats than on behalf of those whom they traduce. If an essay like "What Is the People?" moves with a high disdain far beyond the apprehension of the people themselves, he is capable of a humbler and not less persuasive eloquence. Reading in *The Statesman's Manual* of the dangers of nurturing a "Reading Public," he remembers how a friend once observed, "on seeing a little shabby volume of *Thomson's Seasons* lying in the window of a solitary ale-house, at the top of a rock hanging over the British Channel—'*That is true fame!*' If [Coleridge] were to write fifty Lay-Sermons, he could not answer the inference from this one sentence, which is, that there are books that make their way wherever there are readers, and that there ought every where to be readers for such books."[19]

The *Life of Napoleon* Hazlitt planned as his crowning work. Even his steadiest admirers have found it hard going (Lamb said he "skipped all the battles"); but from the reader who perseveres it earns a sympathetic hearing. Considered as an apology, it is honest at its own expense, and by no means an exercise in hero-worship. But it was beyond Hazlitt's endurance not to be placed on the winning side once in his life—the side of the great man against the contemptible multitude of his foes. It was equally beyond him to suppress his doubts, which appear throughout the *Life,* and still more in the journalistic work that followed. He confesses himself unhappy with the side-squint of envy that prevents a new audience from enjoying *The Beggar's Opera,* and reflects, "In a word, the French Revolution has spoiled all, like a great stone thrown into a well, 'with hollow and rueful rumble' and left no two ideas in the public mind but those of high and low." He was, as he wished to be, "proud up to the point of equality." He was not a leveller but an anti-exclusionist,[20] and would therefore have seen an egotism worse than Napoleon's in the story of how Wordsworth received Keats's "Hymn to Pan" with killing praise: "A very pretty piece of paganism." We honor Leigh Hunt as Wordsworth's opposite, because he "waged battles for Keats even before Keats was apprenticed as apothecary."[21] Much the same might be said of Hazlitt.

One area of his achievement I am sorry to have left comparatively unexplored is his criticism of painting. My excuse for drawing the line here is the same as Hazlitt's for losing at rackets: "Sheer incompetence." At describing a painting, whether Poussin's *Orion* or West's *Death on the Pale Horse,* I think he has few rivals and no superior; his strictures on the neo-classicism of Reynolds are comparable to Blake's, and comparably dazzling, but more inclined to argue and so a truer settler of the question. The terms of his criticism also look ahead: Sir Kenneth Clark has called him "the best English critic before Ruskin."[22] If at present Hazlitt attracts less attention than either Ruskin or his successors, Pater and Wilde, one reason may be that he refused to link his name with the fortunes of a single contemporary. A sentence on Turner, which he pretends to quote from a passer-by at an exhibition, is characteristic (though elsewhere he extols Turner as the most gifted living painter): "pictures of nothing, and very like." As seldom in looking at pictures as in reading poems can he strike the attitude of interested championing which has come to seem appropriate to an *avant-garde.*

This study, it will by now be plain, falls into a somewhat mixed genre. It is certainly in no sense a biography; yet I wanted to display and place in context a great many passages, and not expand to the limit my thoughts about a few: that labor, requiring a different sort of patience, is for those who come to their author at a much later stage, when the whole range of his work is better known than Hazlitt's is today. Occasionally too, when an anecdote solicited entrance into the argument, I have admitted it. I suspect there are readers who look on this as a dereliction from more exacting modes of discourse. Yet the well-placed anecdote was a favorite device of Hazlitt's: he recalls, for example, an evening at Lamb's, where, before a genial company, Coleridge injured the pride of "a gentleman of the last age," Thomas Holcroft.

> C—— was riding the high German horse, and demonstrating the Categories of the Transcendental philosophy to the author of the Road to Ruin; who insisted on his knowledge of German, and German metaphysics, having read the *Critique of Pure Reason* in the original. "My dear Mr. Holcroft," said C——, in a tone of infinitely provoking conciliation, "you really put me in mind of a sweet pretty German girl, about fifteen, that I met with in the

Hartz forest in Germany—and who one day, as I was reading the Limits of the Knowable and the Unknowable, the profoundest of all his works, with great attention, came behind my chair, and leaning over, said, What, *you* read Kant? Why, *I* that am German born, don't understand him!" This was too much to bear, and Holcroft, starting up, called out in no measured tone, "Mr. C————, you are the most eloquent man I ever met with, and the most troublesome with your eloquence!" P———— held the cribbage-peg that was to mark him game, suspended in his hand; and the whist table was silent for a moment. I saw Holcroft down stairs, and, on coming to the landing-place in Mitre-court, he stopped me to observe, that "he thought Mr. C———— a very clever man, with a great command of language, but that he feared he did not always affix very precise ideas to the words he used." After he was gone, we had our laugh out, and went on with the argument on the nature of Reason, the Imagination, and the Will.   (XII, 37-38)

The story is amusing enough; yet it makes a point which could not be trusted to emerge in any other way. Hazlitt had a qualified admiration for Holcroft; he edited, and wrote narrative and critical sections to complete, Holcroft's autobiography; on most days he would have spoken more affectionately of Holcroft than of Coleridge. Yet the story is given at the older man's expense, with none of its cruelty extenuated ("we had our laugh out"). And at the end Hazlitt goes upstairs to rejoin the company—what are we to make of that? It would not do for him to say, "I then felt myself to be, in spite of all the old allegiances, a member of Coleridge's generation; *this was an affirmation of the fact!*" Some such statement is offered nevertheless, in simple retrospect, and without the need of italics. Yet Holcroft is granted his parting sentence, and his judgment of Coleridge lingers on the scene as a vivid though gentle portent: a decade later Hazlitt would be repeating it, and signing his own name. Now, do we prefer the passage he wrote, or the closely reasoned page he might have given us on Holcroft's earnestness, Coleridge's eloquence, and his own divided loyalties? Whatever our choice, the answer should not be that in telling the story he somehow retreated into the shallows of criticism.

"Hazlitt," says Elisabeth Schneider, "had taken the eighteenth century with him when he entered the nineteenth."[23] The remark is worth developing because it explains a quality of fair-mindedness toward his immediate predecessors which sets him apart from the romantic movement as a whole. Boswell's *Life of Johnson* came out in 1791, in Hazlitt's fourteenth year, and its subject, buoyant and somber, and embellished by the oral traditions of London, dominated his youthful imaginings of the literary life. Indeed Hazlitt was among the first to admit a preference—kept up or at least confessed by most readers, until very recently—for Boswell's hero to the author of Johnson's prose. This gives a clue to his own intellectual deportment. Without Johnson's compulsion to talk for victory, he continued the practice of addressing most interlocutors with strict formality, as "Sir," punctuating his short verdicts with frequent repetitions of the word. He was famous for sharp retorts even to the closest of friends, when he saw truth made the plaything of headstrong humors. And, apart from the inherited manner, two Johnsonian assumptions emerge again in their full force with Hazlitt: that truth is not private but submits naturally to the medium of social exchange; and that whatever fills the mind, by supplying it with an interest, ought not to be scorned.

I have dealt with the eighteenth-century heritage as a matter of particular instances, but with Hazlitt it is one of those determinants of style that can be too easily overlooked. Thus it appeared strange to those who knew him a little, that he should seek out and delight in the company of James Northcote, the biographer of Sir Joshua Reynolds, in whose presence Hazlitt caught the still vivid tone of Johnson's circle and heard its livelier gossip. This fondness for Northcote is a delicate thing. When Hazlitt came to write his "Boswell Redivivus," he set up the fading society-painter as the Johnson of the piece. One of Hazlitt's friends, visiting the studio to hear them talk, was surprised to find Hazlitt saying all the good things: in the published *Conversations of James Northcote,* by William Hazlitt, these were usually refined into epigrams and then credited to Northcote. But the author warned in his introductory note: "I have feigned whatever I pleased. I have forgotten, mistaken, mis-stated, altered, transposed a number of things." It is a suitably romantic homage to the classic whom Hazlitt could not help sympathizing with as "the prince of biographers."

He could not belong wholeheartedly to any one age however all-disposing its spirit. The critic of an intellectual movement who was himself, in his practice, committed to the premises of that movement, he had the faculty of holding two opposed ideas in his mind at the same time. And that is the stumbling-block he puts in the way of all who take satisfaction in knowing a critic's "stance": for, though never an obscure writer, he is often an ambivalent one. Some of his essays are deliberately constructed as arguments with himself; but even when they are not, turning at random to a page in his own voice, we are likely to find him arguing with propulsive force one side of a question against which he is happy to argue somewhere else. It is not skittishness, or mere versatility, but the unpredictable outcome of sympathy, of what he was content to call "a certain morbid interest in things." In this light the steadiness of principle of which he was justly proud looks like an effort to unite his warring impulses, and his assurance at the end—in the last words, "Well, I've had a happy life"—may have been in proportion to his initial despair at the undertaking. But if Hazlitt could not have predicted the extent of his struggle, and the toll it would exact, his idea of the imagination took exhaustive account of its necessity. This idea, propounded lucidly, after long reflection, and in the spirit of disinterested action that he never tired of praising in others, is what we ought most to honor in reading him. For it freed him to imagine other things.

CHAPTER I

IMAGINATION

HAZLITT'S CONVERSATION WITH COLERIDGE

In January 1798, William Hazlitt walked ten miles to Shrewsbury to hear Coleridge preach. Coleridge had been entrusted with the spiritual charge of a Unitarian congregation, and this was to be the first performance of his duties. Before the second fell due, he would decide not to accept the position after all, preferring the annuity offered him by Tom Wedgwood, and suggesting that he would in any case have been too heretical to remain long among Unitarians. But in the meantime, on that Sunday, he had changed Hazlitt's life. When two days later he called on Hazlitt's father, as a courtesy owed the minister of a neighboring congregation, William was summoned downstairs and into Coleridge's presence, where "half-hoping, half-afraid," he "listened for a long time without uttering a word." The scene is recalled in a well-known essay, "My First Acquaintance with Poets"; and the circumstances of its appearance are as remarkable as the essay itself, though less well known. In January 1817, having published a dry account of one of Coleridge's rampantly allegorical attacks on "the spirit of Jacobinism," Hazlitt followed it with a letter to the editor from an imaginary correspondent, who refused to believe that the subject of the account could be the same Coleridge he had heard speak nineteen years before: "upon peace and war; upon church and state—not their alliance, but their separation—on the spirit of the world and the spirit of Christianity, not as the same, but as opposed to one another." This letter Hazlitt then expanded into "My First Acquaintance with Poets," with its gift to Coleridge of a lost early portrait. It was signed SEMPER EGO AUDITOR—a phrase that touches the common motive for Hazlitt's constancy in friendship and implacability in battle. He was always listening for the truth.

Of their first meeting Coleridge himself recalled "conversing with W. H.'s forehead" for two hours; Hazlitt had accorded him perfect attention, staring at the floor and bent on catching every word. Even when young he was not apt to strike a pose, or put a guest at ease. He attended closely because he was competent in a great many of the topics of Coleridge's talk. Over dinner he ventured an observation—that "the speaking of [Burke] with contempt might be made the test of a vulgar democratical mind"—which he was glad to hear Coleridge pronounce "just and striking." Coleridge also mentioned the poems of a contemporary, "Mr. Wordsworth," who "strides on so far before you, that he dwindles in the distance." The next morning Hazlitt accompanied Coleridge on his way back to Shrewsbury, hearing his talk once again, remarking how he veered from one side of the road to the other, thinking him unjust to Hume but accurate in his praise of Berkeley, and interested to learn that Joseph Butler, the author of *The Analogy of Religion,* had published a book of sermons which showed him "a genuine reader of nature and of his own mind." Hazlitt at length broached a metaphysical discovery of his own, concerning "the *Natural Disinterestedness of the Human Mind.*" He tried to give Coleridge some account of the argument, but without success; he tried on his return home, with the example of Coleridge's sermon still vividly in mind, to write two pages of the argument, again without success. Yet he took heart from Coleridge's firm prediction that when he did get words for his ideas, the world would hear of it, for "You have guts in your brains."

Indeed, Hazlitt's researches in what was then called metaphysics, to which we have a revealing if somewhat fragmentary index in his *Lectures on English Philosophy,* would interest us even if his discovery had never come to light, for he described his writings as the thoughts of a metaphysician expressed with the tact of a painter. He had learned from Rousseau the lustre as well as the language of impressions, even before he saw, under the spell of Coleridge's words, "the progress of human happiness and liberty in bright and never-ending succession, like the steps of Jacob's ladder"—before he met Wordsworth, and heard him say, "How beautifully the sun sets on that yellow bank," and thought to himself, "With what eyes these poets see nature!" He had grappled with Burke, the antagonist of Dissenters on the Test and Corporation Acts, as on the French Revolution,[1] and could pride himself on having "played . . . with his forked shafts unhurt, because I had a metaphysical clue to carry off the noxious particles." He had taken the measure of Godwin, among companions and in an atmosphere where Godwin's ideas were advanced in the most practical way conceivable,[2] and yet had found them slack, and not at all answerable to things-as-they-are. Above all, though he owed his scholarship in the New College at Hackney to the declared intention of becoming a minister, he had surprised his tutors and disappointed his father, strayed from the church and vowed to pursue the one calling in the world that seemed to him more independent than a Dissenting minister's. "I myself have been a *thinker*," he would affirm at a low point of his career, in defiance of his meanest attackers. That his moment of self-discovery should have coincided with his delight in the revived genius of English poetry—as he heard it in the conversation of Coleridge, and later the same year in the recitations of verse by Wordsworth and Coleridge together—is a decisive fact about Hazlitt's development. The beginnings of his intellectual manhood remain inextricable from the sort of encouragement poets on first acquaintance seem to afford, more by example than by precept; and when, in the essay "On Living to One's-Self," he alludes to Wordsworth's Immortality Ode, his act of quotation evokes the memory of a shared enterprise, and has almost the effect of invention.

> For many years of my life I did nothing but think. I had nothing else to do but solve some knotty point, or dip in some abstruse author, or look at the sky, or wander by the pebbled sea-side—
> "To see the children sporting on the shore,
> And hear the mighty waters rolling evermore."
> (VIII, 92)

THE "MODERN" PHILOSOPHY

The *Lectures on English Philosophy* reveal the character of Hazlitt's long metaphysical apprenticeship. In a Prospectus he announced his interest in three problems above all others: the supposed distinction between our knowledge of mental and of physical facts; the "natural disinterestedness" of the mind; and personal identity. Except on the first of these subjects we can find deeper speculations elsewhere in Hazlitt's work, and even on the first, his Prospectus, with the compression suitable to a polemic against more than a century of intellectual dispute, is superior to the lectures themselves. "It will be the writer's object," Hazlitt promised his audience, "besides reporting the opinions of others, to act as a judge," and to lay the groundwork for "a system more conformable to reason and experience . . . than the one which has been generally received by the most knowing persons who have attended to such subjects within the last century; I mean the material, or *modern,* philosophy." He would question the not always explicit tenets of that philosophy, that "all thought is to be resolved into *sensation,* all morality into the *love of pleasure,* and all action into *mechanical* impulse."

Hazlitt saw the second and third points of doctrine as following naturally from the first, and therefore concentrated his analysis on "a wrong definition of the word *experience,* confining it to a knowledge of things without us; whereas it in fact includes all knowledge, relating to objects either within or out of the mind, of which we have any direct and positive evidence." He accepts Hume's use of "idea" to denote an impression grown less distinct, but he is more skeptical than Hume when he wonders if, having once become conscious of ideas, we can ever reduce them to their origin in sensations and thus resolve mental into physical experience.

> Physical experience is indeed the foundation and the test of that part of philosophy which relates to physical objects. . . . But to say that physical experiment is either the test, or source, or guide, of that other part of philosophy which relates to our internal perceptions, that we are to look in external nature for the form, the substance, the colour, the very life and being of whatever exists in our minds, or that we can only infer the laws which regulate the phenomena of the mind from those which regulate the phenomena of matter, is to confound two things essentially distinct. Our knowledge of mental phenomena from consciousness, reflection, or observation of their correspondent signs in others is the true basis of metaphysical inquiry, as the knowledge of *facts* is the only solid basis of natural philosophy. To argue otherwise is to assert that the best method of ascertaining the properties of air is by making experiments on mineral substances. It is assuming the very point in dispute (namely, the strict affinity between mind and matter, insomuch that we may always judge of the one by the other). (II, 114)

The resolution not of thought into sensation, but of thought into more thought, is necessary because we want a knowledge that goes beyond our experience of physical objects. Such knowledge we owe to a capacity for abstraction: the point needs to be stressed particularly in the face of efforts to portray Hazlitt as a thoroughgoing enemy of abstraction.³ After all, an idea may come to be valued more than the impression from which it started; in this sense, Hazlitt only declared as a philosopher what he could not deny as a lover of art. He would write of his return to some favorite paintings at Burleigh House:

> The *Rembrandts* disappointed me quite. I could hardly find a trace of the impression which had been inlaid in my imagination. I might as well
>
> "Hunt half a day for a forgotten dream."
>
> Instead of broken wrinkles and indented flesh, I saw hard lines and stained canvas. I had seen better Rembrandts since, and had learned to see nature better. Was it a disadvantage, then, that for twenty years I had carried this fine idea in my brain, enriching it from time to time from my observations of nature or art, and raising it as they were raised; or did it much signify that it was disturbed at last? Neither. The picture was nothing to me; it was the idea it had suggested. The one hung on the wall at Burleigh; the other was an heir-loom in my mind. Was it destroyed, because the picture, after long absence, did not answer to it? No. There were other pictures in the world that did, and objects in nature still more perfect. This is the melancholy privilege of art; it exists chiefly in idea, and is not liable to serious reverses.   (X, 64-65)

In a lecture devoted to the *Essay concerning Human Understanding* Hazlitt criticizes Locke for having taken his whole system from Hobbes and added to it chiefly equivocation, so that what remained for Hume was to clear away the resulting confusion. Further, Locke's attack on innate ideas obscured an issue of much greater consequence. For, granted that we have no distinct idea of a thing we have never seen, we still need to explain the quickness and competence with which we respond to a thing we are seeing for the first time. To initiate a sort of answer not found in Locke's *Essay*, Hazlitt offers a conjecture about what may be innate.

> I do not know that Mr. Locke has sufficiently distinguished between two things which I cannot very well express otherwise than by a turn of words, namely, an innate knowledge of principles, and innate principles of knowledge. His arguments seem to me conclusive against the one, but not against the other, for I think that there are certain general principles or forms of thinking, something like the moulds in which any thing is cast, according to which our ideas follow one another in a certain order, though the

knowledge, *i.e.* perception of what these principles are, and the forming them into distinct propositions is the result of experience.

(II, 165)

One may be reminded of the similar doubts that Blake expressed. Like Hazlitt's in this respect, Blake's objections to Locke arose not from hatred of empiricism but from a principled refusal to see thoughts reduced to sensations. "Mental Things are alone Real; what is call'd Corporeal, Nobody Knows of its Dwelling Place." When Blake adds that "Innate Ideas are in Every Man, Born with him; they are truly Himself," he does not urge a return to the philosophy of the schoolmen, but wonders how we can fail to distinguish between "knowledge of principles" and "principles of knowledge."[4]

As a thinker committed to the procedures of empirical philosophy but convinced that the tradition ought to be revised—arguing always from experience, and drawing his illustrations from ordinary life; but unwilling to resolve mental into physical phenomena, when he came to define experience itself—Hazlitt was fond of quoting a motto from Kant: *"the mind alone is formative."* To him this meant that the end of philosophy was not a sophisticated calculus of pleasure and pain, with each new stimulus as it arrived being entered in the mind's copious ledger. It was rather an inquiry into that governing faculty of the mind which permits us to choose among pleasures, and teaches us to value some experiences more than others. In searching for a principle of action we require something far other than a machine for quantifying sensations: we turn from sense-experience, and ask what it is that binds our ideas to a coherent purpose.

The mind alone is formative: Hazlitt wished to trace the process through which accidental impulses were directed by a single organizing power. This is one instance where he may have picked up a phrase from Coleridge, and used it as he pleased. That he read Kant at all is more than we know; if he did, it was likely to have been Willich's volume of selections;[5] but the phrase was a device to cheer himself with, as he embarked on his own quest.

LOCKE'S IDEA OF POWER

An issue which Hazlitt believed empiricism had never addressed in the "true metaphysical spirit" was the idea of power; and though he mentions it only briefly, in the lecture "On Liberty and Necessity," he speaks with impressive authority; he had thought long and was confident of his solution.

We derive the idea of power from having performed some action, and felt that we ourselves caused it, and trusted to our feeling. Hume was obliged to deny the idea, by his argument on causation: no matter how many times an action, B, happens after and apparently as a result of some other action, A, and no matter how useful we find the assumption of cause in predicting the result, we cannot fully satisfy ourselves that the repeated conjunction of A and B proves the existence of cause-and-effect, because what we witness is not the operation of a law. So that when we see a heavyweight boxer knock out his opponent, we may think, "That was an exertion of power," yet in truth we can only say, "A fist appeared to fly out, and a head to recoil." Hazlitt thought this argument could be disposed of by recalling what we know from introspection. We have an idea of power because when we reach out our arms, and desire our hands to move, we feel that they do move, and are certain it is from our own power. Such an idea, he adds, in a characteristic aside, would have been weaker in Hume than in other men: having no "strong passions, or great muscular activity," Hume could discard the idea of power "with the least compunction," in keeping with his character as an "easy, indolent, good-tempered man, who did not care to stir out of his armchair."

But Hazlitt did find the idea of power in Locke. It is only by making power "an original idea derived from within, like the sense of pleasure and pain, and quite distinct from the visible composition and decomposition of other objects," that Hazlitt believes "we can avoid being driven into an absolute scepticism with regard to cause and effect." And this Locke had done. Chapter XXI of the *Essay concerning Human Understanding,* "Of Power," begins by enumerating the powers of the mind: the will, the ability to prefer an action; and freedom, the ability to perform an action. When we speak therefore of a free or unfree will, we make one power a predicate of another; and language no more allows us to do this, than it allows us to make "squareness" a predicate of "virtue." Once an action has been proposed to my mind, I am free to choose whether I shall perform it, "So that in respect of Actions, within the reach of such a power in him, a Man seems as free as 'tis possible for Freedom to make him."[6] But I am not free to choose whether I shall exert my will at all. In the illustration Locke employs, "a Man that is walking, to whom it is proposed to give off walking, is not at liberty. . . . He must necessarily prefer one, or t'other of them; walking or not walking."[7] This inherent limitation of the will is expressed by the law: *"a Man is not at liberty to will, or not to will, because he cannot forbear willing."*[8] He is free to act or not act; he must will.

The will in all its choices is determined by desire, a feeling that Locke suggests may be described with greater precision as uneasiness. I feel a *present uneasiness* in the want of something and I act so as to supply the want. This holds true even of the "greater good," the long-term benefit that I expect from prudent action. I act in conformity with prudence only when the benefit not yet achieved forms a present uneasiness in my mind. "For good, though appearing and allowed never so great, yet till it has raised desire in our Minds, and thereby made us *uneasie* in its want, it reaches not our *wills.*"[9] The larger part of mankind feel uneasiness, through most of their lives, in the want of something other than a remote good.

> Thus any vehement pain of the Body; the ungovernable passion of a Man violently in love; or the impatient desire of revenge, keeps the *will* steady and intent; and the *will* thus determined never lets the Understanding lay by the object, but all the thoughts of the Mind, and powers of the Body are uninterruptedly employ'd that way, by the determinations of the *will,* influenced by that topping *uneasiness,* as long as it lasts; whereby it seems to me evident, that the will, or power of setting us upon one action in preference to all other, is determin'd in us, by *uneasiness:* and whether this be not so, I desire every one to observe in himself.[10]

Having established the precedence of uneasiness over every other feeling as a motive of action, Locke must account for the sense of freedom which men nevertheless recognize as part of their experience. This sense he proposes to explain by a power in the mind to suspend its engagement with present uneasiness, and calmly weigh its reasons for acting or not acting in response to a given want.

> There being in us many *uneasinesses* always soliciting, and ready to determine the *will,* it is natural, as I have said, that the greatest, and most pressing should determine the *will* to the next action; and so it does for the most part, but not always. For the mind having in most cases, as is evident in Experience, a power to *suspend* the execution and satisfaction of any of its desires, and so all, one after another, is at liberty to consider the objects of them; examine them on all sides, and weigh them with others. In

this lies the liberty Man has; and from the not using of it right comes all that variety of mistakes, errors, and faults which we run into, in the conduct of our lives, and our endeavours after happiness; whilst we precipitate the determination of our *wills,* and engage too soon before due *Examination.* To prevent this we have a power to suspend the prosecution of this or that desire, as every one daily may Experiment in himself. This seems to me the source of all liberty; in this seems to consist that, which is (as I think improperly) call'd *Free will.* For during this *suspension* of any desire, before the *will* be determined to action, and the action (which follows that determination) done, we have opportunity to examine, view, and judge, of the good or evil of what we are going to do; and when, upon due *Examination,* we have judg'd, we have done our duty, all that we can, or ought to do, in pursuit of our happiness; and 'tis not a fault, but a perfection of our nature to desire, will, and act according to the last result of a fair *Examination.*[11]

Locke's argument for the power of "suspension" has the effect of overturning his previous assertions, in the effort to square them with the common sense of mankind. He has asserted that the will has no choice but to respond to present uneasiness; and from our observation of its power in response, the necessity of its preferring one state over another, we derived an idea of power. But he now asserts that the will may at any time be suspended, so that we ignore the solicitations of uneasiness in order to "examine, view, and judge." From our observation of the mind's power to suspend the first sort of response, it would seem that we derive a second idea of power. Which idea, and indeed which power, is sovereign? Locke cannot say because he does not acknowledge that they are in conflict.

Locke had proposed a supplementary idea of power too complex for his argument about "uneasiness" to explain or support. Yet the complexity was intrinsic to his subject, and had to be met by every thinker after him who sought to explain the operations of the mind. In reflecting on Locke's chapter, Hazlitt must have wondered whether a single idea could ever hold together our opposite experiences of power: as the response of the will to an immediate want; and as the suspension of the will, for the sake of comparing several future courses. Present uneasiness may be sufficient to explain those actions in which the will "never lets the understanding lay by" its object. But to explain certain actions, such as those involving a sacrifice of our own interest for the sake of another's, we have to suppose a different motive. We are at once interested and disinterested beings. The will-in-action yields an idea of interested, and the will-in-suspense an idea of disinterested, power.

The coherence of Locke's argument might still be defended in the following way. "Locke was not describing the two sorts of power that move men to act, but tracing a *sequence* of motives which men in society tend to follow, and we can test the accuracy of his description simply by observing them. In that sequence the response to uneasiness is supplanted by the weighing of ends and results to determine right conduct. If men, obedient to their desires, always pursued their short-term interests, society would be a chaos; but the truth is that they quite regularly suspend the pursuit of these, and society works. By the intervention of the reason, which allows them to reflect on their long-term interests, they bring moral conduct into accord with the law of nature."[12] This is a persuasive apology for Locke's decision to connect the two ideas as he does. But it only defers the task of justifying them as a theory of action, by justifying them instead as a theory of the state. The trouble with his chapter on power is that it does present itself as a theory of action, it splits into two theories, and both work as total explanations. A phrase like "intervention of the reason" may adequately describe the phenomenon of ordinary men becoming good citizens; it may suggest the function a picked body of representatives is supposed to perform in a well-managed state. But it begs the question of how, and at what promptings, an individual moves from satisfying a sensation of uneasiness to suspending consideration of his immediate wants. In what we read as two stages of one continuous process, Locke offers first a theory of action, and then a theory of right action. All we learn about the transition is that it is not impossible for an agent who can be explained only by the first to become an agent who can be explained only by the second.

A final passage from Locke will show why Hazlitt, after reading "Of Power," sought to derive from the will-in-suspense a single idea of power both disinterested and active, and therefore proper to the imagination. Motion and thinking, Locke observes, are actions, and yet certain actions are properly denominated *passions,* that is, effects of passive power. When a substance is given the first impulse of its motion from without, its power is passive. Only when it is able to set itself in motion is its power active.

> So likewise in *Thinking,* a Power to receive *Ideas,* or Thoughts, from the operation of any external substance, is called a *Power* of

thinking: But this is but a *Passive Power,* or Capacity. But to be able to bring into view *Ideas* out of sight, at one's own choice, and to compare which of them one thinks fit, this is an *Active Power.* This reflection may be of some use to preserve us from mistakes about *Powers* and *Actions,* which Grammar, and the common frame of Languages, may be apt to lead us into: Since what is signified by *Verbs* that Grammarians call *Active,* does not always signify *Action; v.g.* this Proposition, I see the Moon, or a Star, or I feel the heat of the Sun, though expressed by a *Verb Active,* does not signify any *Action* in me whereby I operate on those Substances; but the reception of the *Ideas* of light, roundness, and heat, wherein I am not active but barely passive, and cannot in that position of my Eyes, or Body, avoid receiving them. But when I turn my Eyes another way, or remove my Body out of the Sun-beams, I am properly active; because of my own choice, by a power within my self, I put my self into Motion. Such an *Action* is the product of *Active Power*.[13]

More in these sentences lay ready to explore than Locke himself seems to have realized. For the doubleness of his idea effects a paradoxical turn on the words "active" and "passive." If the power to receive and then act upon, but not to create motions or thoughts, is defined as passive; and the power to create motions or thoughts from within is defined as active; it follows that the will-in-action is really a passive power, since it must always respond to the stimulus of present uneasiness; whereas the will-in-suspense is an active power, since by its own choice it turns away from all present uneasiness, as surely as Locke in his illustration turns away from the sun. This distinction between the will-in-action and the will-in-suspense, and between passive and active power, helped others to generate ideas of the imagination of which Locke would certainly have disapproved. Nevertheless he is at their source. The imagination, having once been linked to the will-in-suspense, could be called an active power. We shall see what Hazlitt made of the possibility. But there are Lockean resonances even in Coleridge, who speaks of bringing "the whole soul of man into activity"; and in Wordsworth, who admits, a decade after having recommended the cultivation of a "wise passiveness," that wisdom comes of an active imagination, which must learn, do, and suffer by the power it alone has, and not depending on the nourishment it receives or fails to receive from without.[14]

ABRAHAM TUCKER AND *THE LIGHT OF NATURE PURSUED*

For half a century after the appearance of Locke's *Essay* the implications of "active power" remained dormant, and Locke's simpler theory of action was admitted as satisfactory. Men were supposed to act so as to relieve present uneasiness, to repel pain and receive pleasure. The sum total of a life's pursuit of pleasures was taken to reveal a commitment to long-term pleasure, or prudence. Locke found support even where it might not have been looked for, in the psychological writings of David Hartley. The association in our minds of pleasure with what is good, and pain with what is bad, Hartley took to have profound consequences for morality and religion. One of his aims was to justify the ways of Locke to God; and from the premise that men seek to increase their pleasant associations and limit their painful ones, and the corollary that the pleasures of life naturally predominate over the pains, he reached a tolerable conclusion: "Since God is the source of all good, and consequently must at last appear to be so, *i.e.* be associated with all our pleasures . . . the idea of God, and of the ways by which his goodness and happiness are made manifest, must, at last, take place of, and absorb all other ideas."[15] The process of association thus had a tendency "to reduce the state of those who have eaten of the tree of knowledge of good and evil, back again to a paradisiacal one."[16]

To thinkers who came of age about 1800, Hartley's psychology seemed a bringer of lucid consolation; and his influence survived to a later period, among many who never submitted to it systematically: one may detect it, for example, in Leigh Hunt's affirmation that "the very pains of mankind struggle towards pleasures."[17] Yet for all his subtlety, Hartley went not a step beyond Locke in exploring the motives of action. What he finally explained was the machinery by which we estimate pleasures and pains. It remained to ask why our pursuit of short-term interests so often appears to us in retrospect both selfish and imprudent. And that question would return any consideration of the pleasure-pain calculus to what could be discerned anyway in the background, in the older language of Hobbes which Locke had glossed over: "I put for a general inclination of mankind, a perpetual and restless desire of power after power, that ceaseth only in death."[18] This view, if more awesome, was not more satisfactory.

Eighteenth-century metaphysics has a larger and a stranger history than many accounts reveal, and opposition to the Hobbesian idea of power came from some unexpected quarters. Throughout the middle years of the century, a new theory of action was expanding to fill the leisure of a British country gentleman writing under the name of Edward Search. The name was an allegorical compliment paid to himself by Abraham Tucker, the author of *The Light of Nature Pursued,* of which three volumes were published in 1768 and another four posthumously in 1777. Tucker ought to interest us partly because Hazlitt repeated the compliment—he knew of nothing "in the shape of a philosophical treatise that contains so much good sense so agreeably expressed"—but also because his admiration for Tucker had a measurable effect: among Hazlitt's earliest published works is a very thorough abridgement of *The Light of Nature Pursued.*[19]

Tucker, though a passionate disciple of Locke, saw that in the realm of motives a good deal of work was still needed. To begin with, he attacked the quantitative definition of prudence as the largest possible mass of short-term pleasures successfully realized. How well do we know our own good, how well *can* we know it, when "inclination and humour so mimic the garb and gestures of reason that we take them for her very self"?[20] Thus the Lockean prudent man, that monster of compelled valor and relieved uneasiness, began to wear a human look. Tucker's next step was to expose a weakness at the source of Locke's theory, which sprang from "laying too much stress upon etymology":

> Selfishness being derived from Self, they learnedly infer that whatever is done to please one's inclinations must fall under that appellation, not considering that derivatives do not always retain the full latitude of their roots. Wearing woolen cloaths or eating mutton, does not make a man sheepish, nor does employing himself now and then in reading render him bookish: so neither is everything selfish that relates to oneself.[21]

Tucker was a convivial spirit who liked to toy with an adversary; but in contesting the Lockean polarity of uneasiness and satisfaction he is at his coolest: here the very scope of human experience is in question, and for all his modesty he feels himself on surer ground than Locke. He treats the linking of satisfaction with persistence in a course of action, and of uneasiness with deviation, as the *Essay's* main argument on the subject—fairly enough, since as we have seen

Locke's mechanical theory of action and his rational theory are blind to each other's implications, and therefore mutually exclusive. Tucker replies with two counter-examples: the fugitive who hides from his pursuers in a gully, and stays there, though he feels nothing but uneasiness at his situation; and the group of young people dancing, who learn that fireworks may be seen in a neighbor's garden, and disperse at once to look out the window, though in dancing they felt nothing but satisfaction. Doubtless Locke could have met the objection by refining uneasiness and satisfaction into several degrees of each. But this is precisely Tucker's point. For where would we stop refining? And on what grounds would we keep calling every new motive simply a degree of uneasiness or satisfaction?

In disclosing the flexibility of our motives and the comprehensiveness of the faculty by which we must choose among actions, Tucker was on his way to discovering the imagination which Hazlitt, in his more systematic fashion, had determined to furnish with an irrefutable "proof" of its own existence. A disinterested action, says Tucker, or a disinterested view of an action, is possible only because of "a common principle of thought, a superintending faculty, which alone perceives the relations of things, and enables us to comprehend their connexions, forms, masses." Tucker refers to it indifferently as either the understanding or the imagination: in the longer and wider views afforded us by this faculty, our feats of sympathy and of attachment to an unselfish good appear equally natural.

"Where," the admirer of Hazlitt's essays may now ask, "in all this controversy, is the flavor of Hazlitt himself? I see a great deal of philosophic atmosphere, a great many things leading up to 'natural disinterestedness' and 'the imagination.' But Hazlitt after all had little in common with any of these thinkers, and if you name the big ideas, he refutes you himself with his remark about the too metaphysical subtlety of Hume—he was the first to bring questions of theory back to questions of temperament." Yet much of Hazlitt's own temperament was formed by the anticipation of close combat in this atmosphere. He very unjustly, and in more than one place, speaks of his own first manner of writing as "dry." The truth is that he was drenched in doctrine, though even in his early writings he sought refreshment elsewhere, and strained against the limits of philosophic decorum. The result is often a tension which the modern reader finds distressing, but which Hazlitt's contemporaries would have left unremarked. A thinker was simply a man who had thoughts, and if he read philosophy he would write in the tradition of Hobbes and Hume, for there was no other. And why should he not publish his thoughts?—having no specialist available to tell him, "You, Sir, are better fitted to be an Essayist." With less formal training than Hazlitt, and a far less extensive acquaintance among philosophers of standing reputation, Tucker had published his thoughts for the world's inspection. Indeed, it is as a parallel case to Hazlitt that he interests us most.

He is an enormously appealing figure, as all who read him have felt, and his work, at twice the length, still makes a lively supplement to Locke's *Essay*. Yet Tucker seems to have emerged rather haplessly from the wrong age of the world—an angel, pendant from a reasonable chain. The direction of his posthumous influence was such as to confine his thoughts still further: even the exuberance of his theodicy would at last be absorbed into the mechanistic deism of Paley—if a watch, then a watchmaker; if a grand design, then a grand and *awful* designer.[22] In a single long and memorable chapter of his work, however, he slipped his fetters and sailed into a different air. Elsewhere he wrote to confute, while hoping faithfully to modify, Locke's principles: here he writes in a temper that would have baffled Locke to his inmost being. The chapter is called "The Vision." Hazlitt described it as Tucker's "boldest and most successful flight," and "that by which our author's reputation as a man of genius must stand or fall." I offer the following brief account of the chapter because none yet exists, and because I agree with Hazlitt that it is extraordinary. I will suggest later the sort of clue I think it gives to the residue of faith that could survive in as thoroughgoing a skeptic as Hazlitt.

THE VISION

Two preliminary chapters, on the "Vehicular State" and the "Mundane Soul," serve as introduction to the vision proper. The Vehicular State recommends itself to Tucker as a compromise between the philosophic materialist's doubt that any remnant of mind can be preserved when the body has perished, and the orthodox Christian's faith that the soul can indeed be preserved because it is not mere matter. As a settled Lockean, Tucker argues that the soul, if endued with sensation, memory, and consciousness, necessarily is material, for matter cannot leave impressions on an immaterial substance: the alternative supposition, that phantasmal images are impressed on an immaterial soul, is insulting to God because it involves him in a superfluous act of creation, there having been no need at all for the material world.[23] Tucker's hypothesis, which "nobody can disprove," is "that the spirit, upon quitting her present mansion, does not go out naked, nor entirely disengaged from matter, but carries away with her an integument from among those wherewith she was before invested."[24]

The integument forms the posthumous vehicle: "extremely small," to ensure that the souls of the dead will not crowd all space, the vehicle is composed entirely of its owner's sensations and compacted experience, with a shell around it "consisting all of muscle and fibre, tough and strong, but extremely flexible and obedient to the Will." Availing himself of Boerhaave's discovery of animalcules, and perhaps compounding this with memories closer to hand of Tristram Shandy's homunculus, Tucker next proposes that the vehicle is the mature form of the "little animalcule" that has made its way "into the ovum through the fresh wound of the calyx or stalk newly broken off from the ovary." For the duration of life the vehicle clings to the medullary fibers of the brain. Upon the body's death it finds itself at liberty. But an earthly residue is still present in the vehicle, from all those combinations or associations of ideas and feelings that belong to an individual life: Tucker calls them "terrene concretions." They appear to be encrusted on each vehicle in proportion with the influence of those "vicious courses" of action that tend to "endamage the little ethereal body." This notion of a choice between virtue and vice in our earthly state, with more than earthly consequences, is to be contrasted with Hartley's belief that every increase in the sheer quantity of associations tends irresistibly to the growth of virtue, reducing our state back again to a paradisiacal one.

Tucker writes both of the charms and the disappointments of life among the "vehicular people," whose defective solidity may, he thinks, be compensated for by "greater sagacity and agility." The vehicular people possess language, and the means of transportation from place to place, though "it would be in vain to conjecture what are their common employments and amusements." Each vehicle's destiny has been worked out almost before it reaches the vehicular state, by the quantity and nature of its terrene concretions: we decide "our future fortunes by our present behavior, and fit ourselves unknowingly for the several parts we are to act upon the next stage by practicing those assigned us in this." When at last each vehicle has been purged of its imperfections, the fibers that enclose it "open and let loose the enclosed spirit, which will then fly off naked and alone."

At this point the spirit is ready to join the Mundane Soul, the vast spirit of nature that lives and works as "one no otherwise than as the sea is one, by a similitude and contiguity of parts, being composed of an innumerable host of distinct spirits as that is of aqueous particles: and as rivers continually discharge into the sea, so the vehicular people upon the disruption of their vehicles discharge and incorporate into that ocean of spirits." That the Mundane Soul is "one" rather than many follows from a law central to Tucker's metaphysics: only the imagination can form compounds. Whatever belongs to nature as opposed to the imagination must therefore be single or unified. The Mundane Soul, with all the surface variations that lend it the appearance of a compound entity, is in fact "a new Being," a second and created god "dependent on [the first] for its existence and faculties, and produced from everlasting by his almighty power and good pleasure." The parts of the Mundane Soul are so interconnected as to convey perceptions instantaneously from one distant region of nature to another. Nothing, observes Tucker, is so quick as thought, and the parts of the Mundane Soul communicate with each other—it would be more correct to say: the Mundane Soul communicates with itself—by thinking. It is the sole cause of action in the visible world, and has at its command the laws of Gravitation and Cohesion, and all the other laws that have been or are to be found, so that Tucker can write of it, paraphrasing Pope: "All are but parts of one stupendous Whole whose body nature is and God, not the Almighty but this created god we have been speaking of, the soul." Yet in Tucker's representation, the powers of this god are indistinguishable from those of the prior God on whom it is said to depend.

For the Mundane Soul is "immortal, unchangeable, completely intelligent, wise, and happy." And though Tucker insists that it has only "as full an insight into the divine nature as is possible for created Being," there can be no doubt that when, in a climactic passage, he describes this god in action, its dependent status has been all but forgotten, and what is described is the creating God of nature, the highest degree of Lockean Imaginative Man.

Having given the fullest explication I could of that exalted Being the universal soul, the head and principal of creatures, let us now consider how well he may deserve the glorious things said of him in former times. And first we need not scruple to admit him for maker of the world, that is, the agent employed in executing that stupendous work: for penetrating into every pore of material substance, being all intelligence and activity throughout, he might discern all the particles in Chaos, if ever there was one, know what they were severally fit for, assort them into elements, and of them compose habitable earths. Upon the word given Let there be light, he might twist the sevenfold rays and dart them about in all directions, or upon a second word collect the main body of them into a Sun. He might give the heavy planets their tangential motion by one strong and exactly poised stroke. He might gather the waters from the dry land, having first scooped the capacious bed of ocean and raised the equatorial parts lest the diurnal rotation should cast the sea above them. He might give the earth a twirl as easily as a child twirls round his whirlagig to produce the vicissitudes of day and night. He might thrust the poles askance twice ten degrees and more that summer and winter, seed-time and harvest should never fail. He might draw out strings of viscous juices from the ground, and perforating them into tubes and interlacing them artfully together, compose therewith the tree yielding fruit after his kind and the herb after his kind whose seed is in itself. He might form the dust of the earth into animal organizations with proper members for walking or flying or creeping or swimming as soon as the breath of life should be breathed into them: and extracting the finer particles from the grosser might work them into mental organs and sensories fit for the reception of perceptive spirits who should be created for them to begin the race of men upon earth.[25]

That Tucker has no trouble assimilating his point of view to a Christian one is hardly the most striking feature of this paean to the creative powers of a "created Being." For he narrates the story of creation, numbers its phases, and evokes, as the fullness of God's will, a busy commerce with sensory organs, and diurnal rotation, and sevenfold rays, conceding every detail of the master plan to the physics required by the age of Locke, yet abating not a jot of what the story demands in fervor and wonder. In no thinker can the union of extravagant mysticism with extravagant common sense have been more complete.[26]

One day, Tucker says, having diverted himself with thoughts of the Vehicular State and the Mundane Soul, conversed about necromancy and the deeds of Orpheus, and at last fallen asleep, he felt his rest disturbed as if by a blow—"something broke on a sudden in my head, in the manner I have heard described in an apoplectic fit." With the sensation of letting go of something "like a stick," he loses all control of his muscles, nerves, and sense-perceptions generally, and slides into a trance, from which he is awakened by "something brushing along nimbly beside me." The stick he seemed to let go of was, he now realizes, "that part of my human composition to which I had been vitally united," which "being carried on with the annual motion of the earth after the rate of about nine hundred miles in a minute, had departed from me on my quitting my hold." In letting go he has accidentally become a vehicle, a "defunct."

He devotes his first energies to forming himself "a set of optics." And his first use of them discloses "a kind of sack or bag filled out like a bladder with air, uniform everywhere excepting that from one place there came out an arm which held me, and from another a longish neck with a head upon it, having a meagre lank-jawed face, very like the prints I have seen before some editions of Locke's works." It is the vehicle of the venerable Locke. Hailed by name (Ned Search), Tucker at once forms "a complete ear, with drum and everything required for the auditory function," and prepares to be instructed: he has been told to look on carefully if he wishes to acquire the faculty of speech. The fibers of Locke's vehicle are in constant motion as he speaks, and Tucker "can liken them to nothing so well as the little wrinkles continually changing their form in the skin on top of warm milk set in the window to cool, only they moved much quicker, and with more tremulous motion." He finds this motion hard to imitate; but Locke frightens him into speech, by assuming the shape of a lion and roaring at him: after prodigious struggles, an "O!" escapes from Tucker's vehicle. The rest of language, and elocution, quickly follow. Tucker owns a debt to Locke on earth which has now been augmented in the Vehicular State, and thanks his benefactor profusely. But Locke explains his solicitude for a disciple: in the history of philosophy all thinkers are divided into two sects; at first all were lovers of wisdom, with Pythagoras as their great exemplar; but with the advent of the Sophists they split into warring camps—on the one hand, those who were "always inquisitive, always improving, sensible their greatest wisdom lay in the knowledge of their ignorance"; on the other, those who "set up for oracles" and "issued their ipse dixits like the edict of an emperor." These are the Searches and the Knowals, and notwithstanding some reservations about Tucker's manner thus far in *The Light of Nature Pursued,* Locke can recognize in him the spirit of a fellow Search: "Since I discern the attentive prying eye, the modest brow, the serenely serious countenance, and the flexible neck of the Searches, and find you here in the helpless condition of a new-born babe, it raises a kind of paternal instinct towards you." Tucker confesses his "filial reverence and dependence" to Locke, and apologizes for his criticisms of Locke's *Essay.*

Locke proceeds to explain the intricacies of the Vehicular State. The vehicles are tiny, agile, in love with "gamboling," and capable of "all the pranks of a Proteus." A thousand of them might creep into a single grain of corn. The "river of stones" by which Tucker felt himself barraged on his awakening into the State was doubtless a single ray of light apprehended in its myriad particles. Now, every vehicle enters the State with some admixture of terrene concretions, and the goal of all vehicular existence is to clear them away. By the concretions, "by the condition a new comer appears in," other vehicles know "what have been his courses of behavior, his way of living, the company he has consorted, or objects he has conversed with." Those in whom the concretions are extraordinarily fixed or encrusted have no real hope of leaving the State, and live in despair. For the rest, Locke proposes that Tucker gather information in his own way, by surveying the vehicular haunts with Locke as his guide. All that he sees will be recorded, and preserved for the bodily memory that awaits him on earth, by Aulus Gellius, the collector of the *Attic Nights* and another Search.

In a man like Tucker the form assumed by selfish concretions is a too-implicit faith in metaphysics: before he can join the Mundane Soul he must realize the barrenness of all such speculation. He is therefore brought into the company of Professor Stahl. The admired Professor speaks an incomprehensible jargon, and wearies his listener with the acrimony of the schools. Meanwhile Tucker formulates to himself a most telling objection to the course of modern philosophy. Hartley, he says, by grounding the spiritual in the physiological, and Berkeley, by creating a material world of no use to the spiritual, have completely severed ethics from metaphysics, and cannot have reflected "that their doctrines must be utterly subversive of all religion, morality, and even common prudence." When, however, Tucker tries to cloak his thoughts in Stahl's language, the effort is misunderstood as a cruel parody and he is rebuffed. Yet he maintains his cheerful Search-disposition: Stahl, he concludes, "is a bar's length more profound than Pythagoras"; to which Locke replies that "Pythagoras had his reasons for being profound; but this man is profound because he cannot help it."

One more conversation with his guide, and Tucker is far enough advanced in wisdom to "discharge and incorporate" into the Mundane Soul. He finds it a region of never-ending activity. Entering into the moving power of nature, and helping to perform all the tasks that make nature one continuous process, he is conscious of owing his existence to a still higher power. But as in the earlier chapter, his emphasis falls upon the Mundane Soul itself; of the almighty God he writes: "We discerned his Will written in legible characters upon the face of his creation, and applied ourselves industriously to fulfill it." One notes the astonishing claim buried in the phrase, "we applied ourselves"—something only an active power can do—as well as the force of what Tucker leaves unsaid: from the point of view of man, the Mundane Soul *is* the "legible character" of God. The feeling goes far beyond anything one can find in other works where the countenance of nature is interpreted as the all-sufficient clue and analogy to God. On the contrary Tucker's is a thoroughly heterodox vision. But he invents a special device for subduing it to the conditions of orthodoxy: an illusion, having nothing to do with the Mundane Soul, is sent to the recording vehicle Gellius, to be fixed in the memory that will remain with Tucker on earth. How, by this curious scheme, the vision of the Mundane Soul ends up in his work anyway, we are never quite allowed to see.

As we read "The Vision" we are struck chiefly by the profusion of detail with which an empiricism of thoughts and sensations has been articulated. But the chapter doubtless appealed to Hazlitt for a very different reason. Implicitly in "The Vision," and explicitly in what Hazlitt called his chapters on "consciousness," Tucker elaborated Locke's argument that the mind was fitted to outward things. In Tucker's view it operated, however, not by a passive accumulation of sense-impressions, but by the faculty that organized those impressions into a consistent mass, and gave them meaning. That the mind was not mechanical; that it acquired a knowledge of "truth" and "the good" in the course of organizing its impressions of nature; that sense-experience without the aid of some higher faculty, could not account for the combining of impressions in one

way rather than another: these were conclusions for which an English philosopher after Hobbes could not easily have found words,
so entirely did they contradict a view which gave the more primitive
activities of the mind priority to, and "greater distinctness" than,
the more refined. Tucker offered reasons for asserting that the relation of the mind to the senses must be that of master to servant—
reasons, together with a passionate belief in the value of the assertion.

The detail and elaboration of this argument belong to another
phase of Tucker's work and are not our concern here. But in judging his visionary system we must bear in mind the constraint under
which he labored for the greater part of his life, as a philosopher
committed to the premises of Lockean empiricism. We feel in "The
Vision" that he has released the pent-up energies of years and volumes of thought: it is as if the single conviction to which Tucker
unswervingly held—that what man knows of divinity, he knows
through nature, and what he knows of nature is from the imagination alone—could only have been divulged allegorically, with nature swollen into the Mundane Soul, and the imagination reified
as the tiny spiritual vehicle. This tendency to guard himself with
highly visible escape clauses emerges again in the juxtaposition of
his experience of the Mundane Soul with the illusory vision sent to
Gellius. Why Tucker found such expedients desirable is an interesting question. The age of Locke's greatest influence, and of Hume's
Treatise and *Enquiries,* was also the age of Young's *Night Thoughts,*
of the sublime odes of Gray and Collins, of Akenside's *Pleasures of
the Imagination.* In their beliefs concerning the significance of the
imagination, empirical philosophy and pre-romantic poetry were far
apart. Tucker, though in a fugitive work and by roundabout means,
was making an unexampled effort to bring them closer together.

Hazlitt drew most from Tucker in viewing the imagination as a
dynamic but unified faculty. Impressions, ideas, or trains of association vastly different from each other, could never be brought into
conjunction were it not for some single comprehensive power, which
"alone is formative" in a way that Kant had not intended. As Tucker
put it: "I can see no more reason to suppose one faculty for apprehending, another for judging, and another for reasoning, than to
suppose one faculty for seeing blue, another for yellow and another
for scarlet."[27] In estimating Hazlitt's debt to Tucker one has to confront a large piece of conflicting evidence, in the form of Tucker's
near-idolatry of Locke, to which may be opposed the title of an article published by Hazlitt as late as 1826: "Mr. Locke a Great Pla-

giarist." But this does not affect the clue Tucker provides to the spirit in which Hazlitt undertook his *Essay on Human Action*. For that essay too, as Hazlitt tells us near the end of it, had its inception in a kind of day-dream of the afterlife; and both the plot and moral of Hazlitt's dream seem to recall Tucker's vision. Where Tucker, however, makes it an amusing gift to the reader after much sober speculation, Hazlitt was willing to regard his own work of fancy as itself a sufficient motive of speculation. Somehow—and here may be the profoundest effect of those talks with Coleridge—he had acquired daring.

> There are moments in the life of a solitary thinker which are to him what the evening of some great victory is to the conqueror and hero. . . . I remember I had been reading a speech which Mira-baud (the author of the System of Nature) has put into the mouth of a supposed atheist at the Last Judgment; and was afterwards led on by some means or other to consider the question whether it could properly be said to be an act of virtue in any one to sacrifice his own final happiness to that of any other person or number of persons, if it were possible for the one ever to be made the price of the other. Suppose it were my own case—that it were in my power to save twenty other persons by voluntarily consenting to suffer for them: why should I not do a generous thing, and never trouble myself about what might be the consequence to myself the Lord knows when? (I, 46-47)

Such dreams have passed before the eyes of many an idler. But for Hazlitt, some time near the beginning of a new century, they led to the grasp of an uncharted principle of action.

AN ESSAY ON HUMAN ACTION

In his *Essay* Hazlitt sets out to prove that our interest in others is the same in kind, and proceeds from the same motives, as our interest in ourselves.

We know the past by memory, and the present by consciousness: we are acquainted with impressions connected with our past and present objects, and therefore know them as we cannot know those of other minds.[28] *But it is future objects alone that determine a man's voluntary actions, and he can no more have a direct interest in his own future sensations than in another man's.*

The imagination, by means of which alone I can anticipate future objects, or be interested in them, must carry me out of myself into the feelings of others by one and the same process by which I am thrown forward as it were into my future being, and interested in it. I could not love myself, if I were not capable of loving others. Self-love, used in this sense, is in its fundamental principle the same with disinterested benevolence. (I, 1-2)

Since of our own minds we can know but the past and present objects, and of another's we can know neither—and since the objects to which we owe any interest either in ourselves or in others, all lie in the future—the imaginative "projection" required by the love of others is no different from that required by the love of ourselves. Hazlitt makes this argument on the first page of his *Essay:* what follows is a protracted and subtle effort to meet all possible objections.

He recognizes as his chief opponents the "school" of Hobbes and Mandeville. But one ought here to distinguish, as Hazlitt does not, between the psychological egoism of Hobbes, which holds that men cannot help acting in their own interests, and the ethical egoism of Mandeville, which follows the Hobbesian proposition as far as it goes, but adds the formula "private vices, public benefits," with the apparent conclusion that it is a good thing men act always in their own interests. Arguments of the latter sort have seldom been developed systematically. Yet Hazlitt is concerned lest a plausible but inadequate principle of action (in theory) so deeply impress the minds of those who give it credence that they come (in practice) to exclude every other. This after all is the commonest way in which our routine beliefs affect our conduct. An "absolute interest," says Hazlitt, if it were as undifferentiated as the egoist maintains, would admit a man suffering on the rack to feel only as much pain as a man anticipating the same torture a year in advance. And yet,

we have no instinctive secret sympathy with our future sensations by which we are attracted either consciously or unconsciously to our greatest good; we are for the most part indifferent to it, ignorant. We certainly do not know, and we very often care as little [as we know] what is to happen to ourselves in the future: it has no more effect upon us in any way, than if it were never to happen. Were it not for this short-sightedness, and insensibility, where would be the use, and what would become of the rules of personal prudence? (I, 3)

The egoists, psychological and ethical, fail to show how a man "can be said to have an interest in what he does not feel."

But a second argument has often been used to support the claims of self-interest. It is that we shall, even if we do not now, have an interest in our own future feelings, of a kind that we cannot have in the feelings of others. And this is a justification of egoism which many who do not admire selfish acts nevertheless find persuasive. The objection to it, Hazlitt insists, must be the objection to any assumption of the "absolute, metaphysical identity of my individual being." For we cannot identify ourselves with our future by means of sensations or associations: the self is the repository only of past and present experience. We naturally give credence to the idea of an extended self, and we assume that the phrase "self-love," as well as having reference to the feelings of something we choose for the present to call "the self," is perfectly translatable into the love of an actual being in the future. Yet if we do come to feel a genuine and lively interest in what is after all only a name, this is "the work of time, the gradual result of habit, and reflection." No matter how thoroughly the change is worked, or how many through habit and reflection come to believe that they act on behalf of a real future self, any personal identity extending beyond the past and present remains nothing more than a "distinct idea."

Hazlitt now considers the most important group of writers who have preceded him in the revolt against Hobbesian egoism, and expounded their own principles of action. He evidently has in mind, though he does not name them, Adam Smith and such scholars of the affections as Shaftesbury and Hutcheson. They account for all unselfish impulses as originating in "habit, or the constant connection between the pleasures and pains of others, and our own, by means of which we come at last to confound our own interests with theirs." By associating *un*selfish impulses with habit they adopt an opposite emphasis to Hazlitt's, and point the way to a society of benevolence grounded in calculation, a moral economy of expedience. They deduce the obligation to practice virtue from the prudence of being seen to be amiable, so that the habit of concern for others prevents us from attending to the short-run advantages we might otherwise pursue for ourselves, and we end by securing our own happiness anyway. This is the school of "propriety," and of that freedom from self-interest which comes of attachment to the generality of interests. Hazlitt ironically states its credo: "we ought to cultivate sentiments of generosity and kindness for others out of . . . selfishness." This is meant as caricature, and before judging the degree of truth it embodies we owe a fair hearing to the "sentimental" school.

Shaftesbury in his *Inquiry concerning Virtue and Merit* had asserted the naturalness of the benevolent affections while taking note
of the palpable rewards they could be relied on to bring. Generosity
is pleasurable in itself, yet by acting with love and esteem toward
others we expect to gain their love and esteem in return: Shaftesbury's benevolence is a Caliban that need only look in the mirror
to find Mandeville's egoism. Hutcheson sought to refine this ethic
of "private virtue, public benefits" by arguing for the disinterestedness of the benevolent affections. But he still regarded benevolence
primarily as a social good, derived from habit, and desirable as it
promoted the harmony of the "system" of affections. Adam Smith
was the first in this tradition to offer a theory of benevolence that
could not be disposed of as the disguise of a trimming expedience.
From the premise that we always act with a view to propriety, always asking ourselves "What ought to be done in this situation, by
any person toward any other person," Smith in his *Theory of Moral
Sentiments* elaborated the device of the "impartial spectator" or
"man in the breast." The witness of an action, according to Smith,
feels in direct sympathy with the agent, and in indirect sympathy
with the object. When it comes his turn to act, the witness will conduct himself so as to evoke the gratitude of his own object, and the
respect of the observer he would be if he could witness his own action from the outside.

Why does Hazlitt refuse to take encouragement from such a
view? One may detect a sarcasm in his phrase about the vanity of
confirming "habit into principle," and the phrase indeed contains
Hazlitt's rejection of a whole way of thinking. He was concerned
with inborn principles—he had objected to Locke's refutation of innate ideas on just this point—and the notion of a principle inculcated by training would have seemed to him a play on words. He
wanted to prove the natural disinterestedness of the mind rather
than its artificial benevolence, yet the sentimental school was unable to suppose a benevolence which failed to serve the interest of
something. As for the general system of the affections, and the invisible hand of propriety, they were postulates quite as unprovable
as a continuous personal identity.[29]

If such interests are chimerical, we may still wonder why an
identification with our own future interest roots itself so tenaciously
in our minds. Hazlitt has called such identification the gradual
work of reflection, and specifically of our reflection on the things to
which we are accustomed. In the lives of most people these stay

close to home. The common objects of our thought master us little by little, and we find that we are insensibly accommodated to a pattern of action centered on ourselves. That, as it becomes ever more narrowly circumscribed, may at last define "selfishness." There is no metaphysical necessity in it, but our progress does appear to be in this direction, and the rule of habit thus implies the loss of disinterestedness. We require as a motive of action only that the idea of a particular good be "sufficiently vivid" to excite in us "an emotion of interest." But let enough of those vivid particulars evoke objects associated with ourselves, and we shall be tempted to combine the several and occasional interests into a total, undying, and irresistible one.

In the present conditions of society the temptation can be resisted only by a deliberate effort. And because Hazlitt is reluctant to trust the fate of disinterestedness to such efforts, or to the legal and political artifices in which they sometimes result, he offers another motive of action besides the vivid idea of a particular future good. There is, he decides, "something in the very idea of good, or evil, which naturally excites desire or aversion." This second motive, however, cannot be placed on the same level with the first, or proved by empirical argument. It ramifies in much of Hazlitt's subsequent writing, and may claim an importance of its own. But it is not strictly necessary except to an argument for natural benevolence; and Hazlitt set out to prove something more modest: natural disinterestedness.

To establish the natural disinterestedness of the mind, he needed only to refute the idea of personal identity, and propose the vividness of a possible good as a sufficient motive of action. He would have discovered both elements of this proof developed separately in Hume's *Treatise*. Personal identity, for Hume, is a fiction we impose on the mind in order to bind together discontinuous perceptions: it comes from our unfounded belief that ideas must be related to each other by causation and resemblance; whereas "identity is nothing really belonging to these different perceptions, and uniting them together; but is merely a quality, which we attribute to them, because of the union of their ideas in the imagination, when we reflect upon them."[30] As for "vividness" and our indifference whether it comes from within or without, Hume employs a slightly different word, "vivacity," but his argument plainly resembles Hazlitt's. An idea, he asserts, by being repeated often enough or endowed with a local vivacity, may acquire the force of an impression, so that by assigning the appropriate degree of vivacity to different ideas the imagination carries us beyond the immediate objects of sense. In this way it sometimes happens that the imagined sensations of another person have more vivacity than our own.

> 'Tis certain, that sympathy is not always limited to the present moment, but that we often feel by communication the pains and pleasures of others, which are not in being, and which we only anticipate by the force of imagination. For supposing I saw a person perfectly unknown to me, who, while asleep in the fields, was in danger of being trod under foot by horses, I shou'd immediately run to his assistance; and in this I shou'd be actuated by the same principle of sympathy, which makes me concern'd for the present sorrows of a stranger. The bare mention of this is sufficient. Sympathy being nothing but a lively idea converted into an impression, 'tis evident, that, in considering the future possible or probable condition of any person, we may enter into it with so vivid a conception as to make it our own concern; and by that means be sensible of pains and pleasures, which neither belong to ourselves nor at the present instant have any real existence.[31]

But "the bare mention of this" strikes Hume's characteristic note. What was immediately observable he accepted as conclusive. That may be why he never brought the skeptical refutation of personal identity and the movement from "vivacity" to sympathy, into a single view of the imagination as a principle of action. It took Hazlitt to join them. In doing so he seems to have performed a simple logical maneuver, and yet taken a step inconceivable to Hume. For throughout Hume's *Treatise,* and notwithstanding the force of his own arguments, "imagination" retains something of the sense of "morbidly roving fancy," its primary meaning for Hobbes and Locke.

How different a faculty the imagination had become for Hazlitt is plain from his illustration. A child who is burned by a fire suffers, not because he thinks "It is I whom the fire is burning," but because the sensation is painful. His thought of himself, when he removes his hand from the flame, is a consequence of his having felt pain: he does not feel pain as a consequence of having thought of himself. And his future aversion from fire may be traced to an association of fire not with the idea of himself but with the idea of pain. So too, the child may one day sympathize with others in danger of suffering comparable pains, and yet he can do this without projecting himself into their past sensations. Thus our sympathetic response has the same principle as our self-interested one: both draw

equally on our own past experience; and in both our future aversion can be explained only as an act of the imagination. The imagi
nation supervises the work of the reason, which compares ideas, and
of the memory, which transforms past impressions into ideas. Without the imagination, we would have no foresight, and therefore no
sense of "self-motion" or self-interest—nothing, that is, to prevent us
from causing a repetition of pain. Without the imagination, the
memories of former sensations could by no means be connected
with each other, or projected into the future with any grasp of their
consequences. We could be neither reliably selfish nor reliably sympathetic.

Imagination, the same power that carries the child out of the paths
of memory, at times carries him out of the present entirely. He "projects himself forward, and identifies himself with his future being," so
that he "considers his future sensations as affecting that very same conscious being in which he now feels such an anxious and unavoidable
interest": the imagination in this way gives us our only idea of personal identity, and our sympathy is excited in proportion as we witness
sufferings in others that we ourselves have endured. We are not affected by a pain, *though it threaten us,* which we have never felt, as we
are by the threat of a pain to another *which we have felt.* The child's
feeling of an identity of interests between his past and present, and his
future being, "is itself the strongest instance that can be given of the
force of the imagination." Yet the imagination, as it enlivens our
idea of identity, refuses to draw a circle around that idea. For the
self is constantly changed by external events, and the future is end-
lessly unique. "In this sense," Hazlitt observes, "the individual is
never the same for two moments together."[32] We cannot be affected
by something we have never felt; we have never felt the effect of a
future event; we cannot therefore act mechanically with respect to
the future: we must act imaginatively.

One may now return to the question of Hazlitt's which I quoted
in commenting on Tucker, about the atheist's speech at the Last
Judgment. Do we have such knowledge of our own future interest
that we can justifiably feel regret for having failed to act on its behalf? The answer given by the *Essay* is that we have no such knowledge, and no obligation can be derived from it. *The disinterestedness of the imagination* means that human nature is not predisposed
to favor certain interests over others. It may end by favoring self-
interest or benevolence, but it can point to no metaphysical sanction
in doing so. What we take an interest in are simply the objects of

our interests. An example from common speech—not used by Hazlitt—will make the point more clearly. If I say, "I am interested in this," I am saying something different from "I am interested in me." Otherwise the word *interesting* would be superfluous. Indeed, to make sense of the sentence "I am interested in me," we have to suppose the subject in a manner standing outside of himself. Thus our habitual usage fails to support the identity of all interest with self-interest.

But Hazlitt makes a very different argument, and an unnecessarily risky one, when he writes that there may be an object such that "I am supposed to be interested without being sensible of it," an object "in itself *interesting* to me" in the sense that "I can and must necessarily be interested the moment it is known to me."

> To go farther than this, and say that the mind as the representative of truth is or ought to be interested in things as they are really and truly interesting in themselves, without any reference to the manner in which they immediately affect the individual, is to destroy . . . the foundation of every principle of selfishness, which supposes that all objects are good or bad, desirable or the contrary, solely from their connection with self. (I, 31)

The sliding from "is" to "ought," the echo of Godwin's "things as they are," the pulpit eloquence of "can and must," are uncharacteristic of Hazlitt, but if we mistake this for his central argument we will end as some critics have, with the charge that he recanted it later in life and yet never admitted having done so.[33] He is making use for the moment of a distinction between "having an interest" and "being interested," to justify a leap from the principle of natural disinterestedness to that of natural benevolence. But this second principle is disabling. Were our interest in a thing the simple consequence of its being "really and truly interesting" in itself, then there could be no virtue in unselfishness: our course of action would be entailed by the meaning of "interest." This seems to me the only flaw in Hazlitt's *Essay,* and it is after all a misplaced fragment of an altogether different argument.

As he goes on to define personal identity Hazlitt offers the metaphor of a stream of thought.

> The size of a river as well as its taste depends on the water that has already fallen into it. It cannot roll back its course, nor can the stream next the source be affected by the water that falls into it afterwards. Yet we call both the same river. (I, 40)

A footnote expands upon this, introduces a related metaphor, and pursues it through one of those lucid expositions of a single image in which Hazlitt rivals and at times surpasses Bacon.

> Suppose a number of men employed to cast a mound into the sea. As far as it has gone, the workmen pass backwards and forwards on it, it stands firm in its place, and though it recedes farther and farther from the shore, it is still joined to it. A man's personal identity and self-interest have just the same principle and extent, and can reach no farther than his actual existence. But if a man of a metaphysical turn, seeing that the pier was not yet finished, but was to be continued to a certain point and in a certain direction, should take it into his head to insist that what was already built and what was to be built were the same pier, that the one must afford as good footing as the other, and should accordingly walk over the pier-head on the solid foundation of his metaphysical hypothesis—he would argue a great deal more ridiculously, but not a whit more absurdly than those who found a principle of absolute self-interest on a man's future identity with his present being. But say you, the comparison does not hold in this, that the man *can* extend his thoughts (and that very wisely too) beyond the present moment, whereas in the other case he cannot move a single step forwards. Grant it. This will only shew that the mind has wings as well as feet, which of itself is a sufficient answer to the selfish hypothesis.   (I, 40)

At such moments one finds, even in this early *Essay,* an ease and grace which lovers of the parabola-shaped career have denied to Hazlitt's work until the following decade,[34] in essays of a smaller sort.

The principle of natural disinterestedness was a serious departure from what had preceded it in moral philosophy, and when at last the *Essay* was published, Hazlitt felt that his discovery had entered the public domain. With those who persisted in the errors he had exposed, he was not charitable: they baffled him by remaining at the mercy of that exploded dualism, self-love and benevolence, after he had spent half his youth freeing himself from it and making his freedom available to others. His remonstrances with Coleridge for having failed ever to adhere to a principle are too easily put down to the political falling-out between them after 1800. For he was also exasperated at Coleridge's failure to understand *this* principle. Coleridge had begun as a philosopher in the sentimental tradition, and then transferred his allegiance to idealism, without stopping to register the advance that Hazlitt made. Nor do his earlier speculations in this area afford anticipations of Hazlitt. His "Moral and Political Lecture" of 1795 is worth putting into evidence:

> We turn with pleasure to the contemplation of that small but glorious band, whom we may truly distinguish by the name of thinking and disinterested Patriots. These are the men who have encouraged the sympathetic passions till they have become irresistible habits . . . by the long continued cultivation of that moral taste which derives our most exquisite pleasures from the contemplation of possible perfection, and proportionate pain from the perception of existing *depravation*. . . . Calmness and energy mark all their actions, benevolence is the silken thread that runs through the pearl chain of all their virtues. Believing that vice originates not in the man, but in the surrounding circumstances; not in the heart, but in the understanding; [a man like this] is hopeless concerning no one—to correct a vice or generate a virtuous conduct he pollutes not his hands with the scourge of coercion; but by endeavouring to alter the circumstances removes, or strengthening the intellect disarms, the temptation.[35]

Coleridge here is very much in the eighteenth-century tradition of writing on the affections. Certain feelings, for which we may "cultivate a taste," ought to be encouraged instead of others, and we may thus confirm habit into a principle. His ambition is to promote the benevolence of the mind, for which disinterestedness is a pleasant synonym. The reference to a taste for virtue is thoroughly Shaftesburian, and in keeping with the aristocratic image of the virtuous man as a *virtuoso* to whom benevolence is an attainment on a par with scholarship, or the possession of a work of art.

Hazlitt's disinterestedness, on the other hand, is what every man owns at birth, displays in the morbid or unrefined sympathies of childhood, but as an adult must be taught to cherish if he is to maintain it even in principle. Against its survival are arrayed the multitude of plausible occasions for interpreting it into non-existence, and the curious paradox by which we flatter ourselves that when we expose disinterestedness as at bottom an expression of self-interest, our analysis has itself been disinterested. The advantage of allowing this principle the largest conceivable scope ought to be plain for those to whom the idea of genius is sacred. For the disinterested mind simply feels more than the selfish, and sees more. It is that in others by which we measure our own capability and find the range of our own experience; and the more easily we ourselves have given up the principle, the more dwarfed we feel in the comparison.

In *The Eloquence of the British Senate,* an anthology Hazlitt compiled not long after the *Essay,* he praised Cromwell for speaking like a man with his hand on his sword. That is a kind of praise common in Hazlitt, and yet peculiar to him. He was not averse to thinking of philosophy too as a mode of action, and if we have followed the argument of the *Essay* closely, we are in possession not so much of a key to conduct as a weapon of criticism. There was in Hazlitt's time, and to a smaller extent still is, a cant of egoism among the adepts of moral philosophy. But there has always been a more pervasive and insidious cant of common life, which alludes triumphantly to the rise of selfishness, the narrowing of the soul's prospects and contraction of its sympathies, as if these things were inextricable from the very processes of human growth and decay. This makes for a language of apology so transparent that we sometimes forget it *is* apology, and has a motive. Those who speak the language do not say, "All men are selfish; now let me have my bit." They say instead, "Generosity and idealism are the privilege of youth; as I grow older I resign myself to the conditions of life." Hazlitt, without failing to reckon with the circumstances that make disinterested conduct so rare as to be praised extravagantly, shows why self-interest cannot be taken for granted, or allowed an honorable place among the conditions of life. He knew that the effect of his book might be to put the apologists more on guard. But perhaps also it would embolden those who dissent from things as they are.

That Hazlitt could imagine the holder of a fixed principle as untainted by self-regard may be surmised from his admiration for his father. This is a large conclusion to draw from evidence so limited and unique; yet one becomes more sure of it looking at Hazlitt's portrait of him. "My father," he recalled in his essay "On the Pleasure of Painting," "was willing to sit as long as I pleased . . . and besides his satisfaction in the picture, he had some pride in the artist, though he would rather I should have written a sermon than painted like Rembrandt or like Raphael!" The figure is sedate, justified, and without a particle of vanity; and the painting itself was a confession of gratitude for his father's example. Hazlitt's own dedication to a principle which he had seen others make good throughout their lives was also a pledge of vigilance, and the steady adherent of anything will often strike comically defensive postures.

Hazlitt was aware of these in his own conduct, and savored their comedy; yet he preferred such "drawbacks" to the deftest versatility; and he was right. His *Essay* had an early admirer, Mr. Scarlett (afterwards Lord Abinger), who communicated to Hazlitt his high opinion of the work, and appeared ready to open a connection of "considerable advantage and eventual emolument" to its author. Hazlitt would thus have acquired a patron, and some relief from the pressures of book-making—if only his father had not at that juncture "inculcated upon his son the idea that his new correspondent had sinister designs upon his liberty of action."[36] One might interpret Hazlitt's compliance as simple obedience to orders; but there remains the fact that he never referred to the incident in all his writings, either for amusement or regret, and it was left for his grandson to mention as a tradition in the family. This too reveals something of what he meant by disinterestedness.

CHAPTER II

INTEREST, HABIT, ASSOCIATION

HABITUAL FEELINGS AND THE LOVE OF POWER

Hazlitt's principle of disinterested imagination makes unselfish action seem possible, but not necessary; it establishes a structure of motives more flexible than any that egoism can allow; and by depriving us of our reasons for selfish action, it might be supposed to take away the lustre of our rationalizations. His principle thus dispels the authority or "realism" in which the Hobbesian pessimist cloaks himself. Yet it gives no cause for optimism. Indeed, the *Essay* seems to say that however natural disinterestedness may be, it is not likely ever to become common. For habit is a stern and selfish master. It engenders reflection on self-interest more than on the interests of others, because at any given moment it is *my* situation that comes to appear most vivid to *my* imagination. This once again is only likely, and not an inheritance entailed on us by virtue of our humanity. But habit makes inroads upon every life: we endure these as an apparently inevitable erosion of the capacity for disinterested action. Habit makes us repetitive, repetition makes us narrow, and our narrowness ends in self. Thus "habitual" has its place alongside "irritable," among the many aids to criticism that render Hazlitt's judgments of character so extraordinarily compressed—another word that implies egotism, to be used when he wanted to make the charge quietly and make it stick.

Yet even without Hazlitt's proof we would feel that selfishness, however frequent its displays, is not an essential fact of our nature, because we can remember a time when it was not habitual. In writing of childhood as the time of keener and less efficiently disposed perceptions, Hazlitt was already a disciple of Wordsworth, and in his way a master of Wordsworth's subject. By 1805, when the *Essay* was published, he would have been familiar with such poems as "We are Seven" and "Anecdote for Fathers," and possibly with stanzas I–IV of the Immortality Ode. At any rate he quotes from the Ode in later years almost as often and impressively as from *Hamlet* and *Paradise Lost,* and by the evidence of the *Essay* alone one might guess that he would come to read Wordsworth's great poem as a palinode, in which the glory of vision yields reluctantly to the claims of the "philosophic mind."

The love of self in childhood, Wordsworth and Hazlitt are agreed, has no taint of habitual selfishness. This is a condition to which an abstract principle cannot possibly return us. *That we once lived in it* nevertheless matters a great deal to Hazlitt, and in reading the *Essay* one wonders how he would describe a fully achieved disinterestedness beyond childhood. In fact, when he does speak of the quality in adults, he makes its possessors look strangely like children; the compliment though heartfelt is often ambiguous; so that, beside his portrait of his father, and to qualify it in some degree, one has to set a celebrated passage on the heroes of Dissent, from the *Reply to Malthus.* Similar passages may be found in the essays "On the Tendency of Sects" and "On Court-Influence."

> Happy are they, who live in the dream of their own existence, and see all things in the light of their own minds; who walk by faith and hope, not by knowledge; to whom the guiding-star of their youth still shines from afar, and into whom the spirit of the world has not entered! They have not been "hurt by the archers," nor has the iron entered their souls. They live in the midst of arrows, and of death, unconscious of harm. . . . Evil impressions fall off from them, like drops of water. The yoke of life is to them light and supportable. The world has no hold on them. They are in it, not of it; and a dream and a glory is ever about them. (I, 284)

This is a sort of language Hazlitt reserves for two subjects especially: his own childhood, and his father's whole existence. Nothing, he tells us in another place, had prepared the Reverend Mr. Hazlitt for the visit of a poet—"My father's life was comparatively a dream; but it was a dream of infinity and eternity, of death, the resurrection, and a judgment to come!" In the longer passage one feels the strain much more: it is poised on the brink of an irony that is never quite formulated.

Happy are they, at once lovely and improbable. There is a strong implication that they are too innocently good ever to be good fighters—unlike the author of the *Reply to Malthus,* whose principled hatred in that work is equalled only by his logical acumen; unlike all those who have been hurt by the archers, but not hurt into selfishness. "Evil impressions" after all are as real as good ones: before we alter any state of things we must know it. Some trace of the grit if not the iron of this world enters into the fortitude we need for our battle against it. In admitting this we make no compromise but only grant the place in any moral scheme of the common experience of mankind. It was here that Godwin had gone badly wrong. Hazlitt saw him as having proposed an extreme reduction of the speculative morality of Dissent, to the point where he became "the first whole-length broacher of the doctrine of Utility": those who know nothing of evil and those who think unimaginatively of the greatest good for the greatest number, were thus related to each other, and liable to a common defect of policy. What both lack is the gravity of habitual feelings.

Here I find a dilemma at the heart of Hazlitt's thinking about the imagination, which has broad consequences for the shape of his career, and leads to the famous double-topics for essays: "On Genius and Common Sense," "On Paradox and Common-Place," "On Vulgarity and Affectation." In forming sympathies we begin with what we know best because we know it from habit. We have a self, a family, a neighborhood, and move outward gradually to a community, and at last to mankind. Habit drives us back into our selves, and yet habitual feelings alone lend to all our sympathies a more than speculative character.

Hazlitt's description of those on whom "the world has no hold" should be compared with two passages from his later writings. The question before Hazlitt, in the ninth of his *Conversations of Northcote,* is why Godwin should seem "shocking on paper and tame in reality":

> It is easy enough to be accounted for; he is naturally a cold speculative character, and indulges in certain metaphysical extravagances as an exercise for the imagination, which alarm persons of a grosser temperament, but to which he attaches no practical consequences whatever. . . . Persons of a studious, phlegmatic disposition can with impunity give a license to their thoughts, which they are under no temptation to reduce into practice. The sting is taken out of evil by their constitutional indifference, and they look on virtue and vice as little more than words without meaning or the black and white pieces of the chess-board, in combining which the same skill and ingenuity may be shewn.   (XI, 235-36)

In this way Godwin is credited with an imagination, but one that is "indifferent" rather than "disinterested." As we observe this instance of a mind so speculative that it has come unmoored from the objects of its speculation, we may think it no bad thing that our sympathies work outward from ourselves. Godwin supposes that we can make all things well if only we extend our view to all things at once. Hazlitt replies that we ought to begin with the little that we have, and build by steady increments from that, remembering as we do that all is not impossible. In the meantime, from the rule of habit we derive at least one consolation in good faith, and different from Wordsworth's: in proportion as our feelings are personal, they are deep, inwoven, and not to be overthrown except by death. Sympathies close to home may by extension and analogy produce sympathies more remote. And from its very tenacity, our self-interest—as long as we refuse to treat it as an end—may become the basis of self-sacrifice. If we count habitual feelings among the circumstances of all conduct, without dignifying them with the name of a principle, we have done what we can to guard against their exclusiveness.

Another such passage belongs to Hazlitt's dialogue on "The New School of Reform," the two speakers of which are named Rationalist (a devotee of Benthamite Utilitarianism) and Sentimentalist (Hazlitt). Again the debate is serious enough to require two speakers, but again the persuasive words are on one side.

> I am afraid such a speculative morality will end in speculation, or in something worse. Am I to feel no more for a friend or a relative (say) than for an inhabitant of China or the Moon, because, as a matter of argument, or setting aside their connection with me, and considered absolutely in themselves, the objects are, perhaps, of equal value? Or am I to screw myself up to feel as much for the Antipodes (or God knows who) as for my next-door neighbours, by such a forced intellectual scale? The last is impossible; and the result of the attempt will be to make the balance even by a diminution of our natural sensibility, instead of an universal and unlimited enlargement of our philosophic benevolence. The feelings cannot be made to keep pace with our bare knowledge of existence or of truth; nor can the affections be disjoined from the impressions of time, place, and circumstances, without destroying their vital principle. (XII, 189)

Even the benevolent man cannot breathe the pure air of a principle, a duty, a categorical imperative. For it is accustomed objects that lead him to these exalted ones.

Habit is among the ideas Hazlitt is most inclined to treat in a dialectical spirit. We must be careful if we speak at all of "habitual sympathies," for each new act of sympathy presupposes an original act of the imagination; but every such act in turn presupposes the existence of our own habitual feelings, because it is to them we refer in imagining the interests of others. *Abstraction* is a second complex idea and *power* a third. We formulate a principle only by an effort of abstraction—in the case before us, by abstracting the idea of interest from ourselves. No great result is ever attained by the imagination, whether in art or in action, but by means of some such effort. And yet an utterly abstract principle, when the work of arriving at it is complete, may behave as if it were detached from its own source. As for the idea of power, we recognize it in two forms: as a "perpetual and restless desire" for something immediately present to us (Locke's will-in-action); and as an unexpected stopping to consider our ends, with the aid of the imagination (Locke's will-in-suspense). Here the ambiguities are plain enough in common usage, where power can denote either force or capability. The connection between these two versions of habit, abstraction, and power begins with Hazlitt's use of "vividness."

Thus, in the *Lectures on English Philosophy* we are informed that only the vividness of the particular case, of suffering, despair, or insulted virtue, and not "the cause of humanity" or of myself, can inspire sympathy: "A total alteration in the situation of the individual produces a total change in my feelings with respect to him, which could not be the case, if my compassion depended wholly on my sense of my own security, or the general condition of human nature." Vividness alone draws us out of ourselves in spite of the rise and fall of our own interests. But there are times when we find it difficult to separate the vividness of the object from the power defining it: the ambiguity is neatly displayed by a note on Burke in *The Eloquence of the British Senate.*

> Burke understood metaphysics, and knew their true boundaries: when he saw others venturing blindly upon this treacherous ground, and called out to them to stop, shewing them where they were, they said, This man is a metaphysician. General unqualied assertions, universal axioms, and abstract rules serve to embody our prejudices; they are the watch-words of party, the strong-holds of the passions. It is therefore dangerous to meddle with them.

Solid reason means nothing more than being carried away by our passions, and solid sense is that which requires no sense to understand it.[1]

Power is passion, and derives its strength for the spectator from its vividness, which is the opposite of generality. But somehow "general unqualified assertions" can also become "the strong-holds of the passions": these strongholds Hazlitt obviously believes ought to be broken down, and given a thorough airing. "Solid reason," however, of which he approves, itself "means nothing more than being carried away by our passions." The passage is difficult. If we take "solid reason" to belong to the character of Burke, the question must be how, thus unreflecting, thus carried away, he is in a position to show others the treacherous ground on which *they* venture.

At any rate warm feeling partakes of power, but not the power of calculated self-interest, and it is the latter that Hazlitt opposes resolutely. Of the "exclusive patriots" who glorify their country as a stalking-horse for their own concerns, he observes in "Free Thoughts on Public Affairs": "They have neither grand and elevated views, nor the warm, genuine feelings of nature. They have no *principles* of action. Irresolute, temporizing, every thing is with them made a subject of selfish calculation." That essay, along with the "Illustrations of Vetus," revolves around a series of comparisons between the vivid sentiment of the familiar that supplies the context of action for the true patriot, and the calculating spirit, at once selfish and coldly detached, which distinguishes the party man even when he calls for war. But the party man too may summon eloquence to his cause: his power will then demand a suppression of all unselfish impulses, and sweep along every opposing tendency:

> Modesty, impartiality, and candour, are not the virtues of a public speaker. He must be confident, inflexible, uncontrolable, overcoming all opposition by his ardour and impetuosity. We do not *command* others by sympathy with them, but by power, by passion, by will. Calm inquiry, sober truth, and speculative indifference, will never carry any point. (VII, 300)

These lines were written of Chatham in a fit of generosity: the memory of his eloquence had driven from Hazlitt's mind any further alternative to the bare choice between power and "speculative indifference." But when one allows such a passage the full complexity of Hazlitt's argument, its meaning is less bleak: one feels that for a moment, as Hazlitt remembered Chatham's finest speeches, the power of eloquence concentrated his passions on a single object, and called them away from all others. A sufficiently urgent appeal seemed to reduce disinterestedness to mere speculative indifference. If, however, we adhere to "principles of action," then the power of a speech, and indeed of a whole ministry, will sway us only for the moment.

Power, then, like habit, works into the momentum of good and evil indifferently. Our attraction to power serves in concert with the whole system of our passions, so that even the caprices it may end in, the departures it may cause from the true course we would rather have followed, are to be valued as proceeding from our inmost nature. This is more than can be said for the motives of action recommended by Utilitarianism.

> A calculation of the mere ultimate advantages, without regard to natural feelings, and affections, may improve the external face and physical comforts of society, but will leave it heartless and worthless in itself. In a word, the sympathy of the individual with the consequences of his own act is to be attended to (no less than the consequences themselves) in every sound system of morality; and this must be determined by certain natural laws of the human mind, and not by rules of logic or arithmetic.
>
> The aspect of a moral question is to be judged very much like the face of a country, by the projecting points, by what is striking and memorable, by that which leaves traces of itself behind, or "casts its shadow before." . . . We must have some outstanding object for the mind, as well as the eye, to dwell on and recur to— something marked and decisive to give a tone and texture to the moral feelings.   (XII, 50)

In the need for objects really worthy of our attention to be apparently worthy of it before we can act with respect to them, and in the rejection of "logic or arithmetic" as motives, in favor of "projecting points" that are "striking or memorable," one can find a basis for the reconciliation Hazlitt always sought between power and disinterestedness. His difficulty all along has been that power is employed universally in executing an action, whereas disinterestedness comes into play far from universally in choosing the perceptions that lead to action. But at the fount of all our actions, and involved in every perception, is the response of the affections, or what Hazlitt sometimes calls "sentiment." And if we balance sentiment, as the initiative moment of any action, against power as the performative moment, we may regard power as no more necessarily confined to selfish actions than imagination is to selfish interests.

For we are dealing with two closely related impulses. We are deceived into thinking them one, and wondering if Hazlitt does not admit the prevalence of selfishness, only because both proceed along the same continuum.

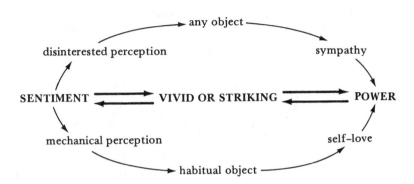

Along the top line, or high road: "Sentiment (whatever is salient among our affections) disposes us to the disinterested perception of any object, and accordingly to unselfish action, from which we abstract the ideal of sympathy, by our sense of imaginative power." Along the bottom line: "Sentiment (whatever is salient among our affections) disposes us to the mechanical perception of an habitual object, and accordingly, to selfish action, from which we abstract the ideal of self-love, by our sense of instrumental power." Here are the disinterested and the self-interested man, and a reading of the common humanity of their actions. Yet involuntarily we sometimes contract both schemes into a third: power becomes the cause of passion and the striking thing carries us away. Hazlitt believed that poets, who delight in reversing cause and effect, were especially liable to this contracted or even preposterous view of action; that the moral indifference implied in his eulogy to Chatham, they carried into their poetry all the time; that the meaning of "the imagination" was therefore as peculiarly double as the meaning of "power"; and that all who had thus short-cut their understanding would show the consequences in actual life.

Concerned with the immediate task of representation, poetry naturally seeks out action on the largest possible scale, and where power is most visible: as, for example, when a king heroically defies his ten thousand petitioners. It throws all its weight on the arbitrary side of a question, and becomes a force in tipping the scales of actual life toward established power. It transforms selfish action into the swift spell of "power defining an object," while disinterested action is ruled out of the question, since we do not associate it with visible displays of power. We can *see* power working out its way on a field of battle, as Wordsworth knew when he shocked a generation of admirers with his paean to the "Almighty God":

> But Thy most dreaded instrument
> In working out a pure intent
> Is Man—arrayed for mutual slaughter,
> —Yea, Carnage is thy daughter.[2]

The anti-Napoleonic "Ode: 1815" from which these lines were eventually deleted, refers us to an imagination "restless in her pride," the imagination not so much of the hero of *The Prelude* as of the heroes of *Coriolanus* and *Henry V*. Was it Wordsworth's awareness of dwindling powers that plotted this direction for his later poetry? Or did the fault lie rather in his neglect of conscious "principles of action"—a neglect that began in his earliest work, and caught up with him? Readers of his poetry several generations later, sensitive to the poignance of his apologies for the shape of his career, are likely to recoil from what they take to be the crudeness of the second possibility. But Hazlitt wants us to take it seriously. He wonders at what depth beliefs about human nature may affect our commitment to principles that become motives of action, and how far even in the subtlest movements of our affections "thinking makes it so." Let us first grant the propriety of the question. For when we turn to the post-revolutionary decade or so of Wordsworth's career—a period in which he and Hazlitt were not thinking of entirely different faculties when they used the word "Imagination"—we still find assumptions which Hazlitt would never have granted, and to which some of his later antagonism may be traced. Such assumptions are partly buried, and in any case impossible to recover, but we glimpse their tendency as early as "Tintern Abbey," where a kind of fatalism mars every stride into the future. Wordsworth's curious literal-mindedness led him at times to regard all associations as constituting a steady reservoir of experience, which, since it could be tapped, could also be depleted. Once he had granted himself this metaphor, the logic of associations was destined to have unhappy consequences for his faith in the imagination; and the possibility of returning to the worn channels of custom and habit took on a lively certainty in the fear of going dry. Hazlitt's insight here remains implicit but it is unmistakable. "Nutting," and the "spots of time" in *The Prelude,* like many similar episodes of Wordsworth's poetry, are to be read as confessions of a partial sympathy, deficient and entirely self-regarding until it was enforced as a principle by a sudden apprehension of power. Wordsworth was disposed *by his beliefs about the imagination* to resign himself to a change of heart as his reliance on memory deepened, and his interests grew circumscribed.[3]

But this summary of an argument Hazlitt carried through two decades—with the attendant shifting moods of his own mind—does an injustice both to him and to his subject. How seldom, after all, his vigilance on the score of principles issued in that pace-setting and relentless vehemence by which we recognize the professional moralist, and dismiss him. How little he wished to be a chastening influence on Wordsworth's poetry, or a "humanizing" influence on his life. It was part of Hazlitt's strength to interpret the fate of genius as catastrophic; but in his sketch of Wordsworth in *The Spirit of the Age* another possibility is allowed. We are made aware that a movement of the imagination which spared us the "Ode: 1815" might also have deprived us of the Immortality Ode.

> He exemplifies in an eminent degree the power of *association;* for his poetry has no other source or character. . . . Every one is by habit and familiarity strongly attached to the place of his birth, or to objects that recal the most pleasing and eventful circumstances of his life. But to the author of the *Lyrical Ballads* nature is a kind of home; and he may be said to take a personal interest in the universe. There is no image so insignificant that it has not in some mood or other found the way into his heart: no sound that does not awaken the memory of other years.—
> "To him the meanest flower that blows can give
> Thoughts that do often lie too deep for tears."
>
> (XI, 89)

These sentences register Hazlitt's ambivalence, in the true sense of a double weight fully felt on both sides. Habit too commonly restricts us to an interest in pleasing and eventful circumstances of one kind only: yet Wordsworth "may be said to take a personal interest in the universe," so that he makes the universe personal to him, and his personality of consequence to us; the thousand feelings, "links in the chain" that bind him to an idea of nature, bind us no less to him. Many of Hazlitt's descriptions of Wordsworth are also descriptions of himself, and they show the tug of habitual feelings in his own life, the tightening circle into which he too might have been drawn. What kept him from Wordsworth's fate, however, was not only the original bias of his mind, but also his engagement with the doctrines of Hartley, culminating in the forty-page appendix to his *Essay*. This piece of sustained philosophical criticism explains better than anything else why Hazlitt did not think himself an associationist.

ASSOCIATION

Locke was the first writer to broach the principle of association in its modern form, but for Locke association was an aberrant function of the mind: it carried overtones of the accidental delusion, the misfire, everything that comes to us today in popular usage as *bad associations*. It was a strange phenomenon, far from universal, but nevertheless significant, for it gave evidence of an irreducibly personal residuum in the workings of each mind. Hume made the principle universal, and Hartley put it on a sound mechanical basis, with enough detail and regularity to dignify a science. Hazlitt's distinction, I believe, is that he proposed a credible synthesis of Hartley and Locke, by finding in association both a reliable indicator of the mind's interconnections, and a clue to the unexpected turn on things wrought by a powerful personal bias. To him the process seemed necessary in Hartley's sense as well as personal in Locke's. Association, he tells us, by itself is indeed mechanical, and can therefore be methodized, but it is not association we are looking at when we discern the individual qualities of a mind. It is rather the power, hardly separable from temperament, that guides every choice we make among ideas, the power of imagination.

An impression or idea, Hazlitt supposes, is perceived by every part of the brain at once, or in close succession. It *must* reach all parts of the brain in order to be sure of reaching the appropriate part to effect a given association. By writing in this way, Hazlitt asks us to imagine the mental operations parcelled out to different areas of the brain as physiologically distinct, like the squares on a map. He is taking the simplification for granted in order to defeat Hartley on his own ground, and guards himself by noting that to show the absurdity of Hartley's physiological language it is enough to speak it. Fortified by a notion of the vibrations and "vibratiuncles" by which sensations are carried, Hartley believed that an impression affected only those parts of the brain nearest it. But how does any impression, when new to the mind, know where to find its true "seat" or destination?

The overarching faculty that permits the mind's simultaneous awareness of disparate things, is consciousness. But the doctrine of vibrations "all along goes on the supposition of the most exact distinction and regular arrangement of the *places* of our ideas."[4] This, Hazlitt argues, is to generate new entities without reason. Given the infinite number of associations possible among our ideas, we can hardly suppose that they are somehow isolated from each other. Such an assumption would imply their being associated always in a fixed series, a possibility that does not fit what we know of our powers of instant recognition and association. Even if our ideas *were* associated in an inviolable order, how could we believe that the effect of one would not be felt by all the rest? "It is like supposing that you might tread on a nest of adders twined together, and provoke only one of them to sting you."

We have the inescapable testimony of experience that the senses themselves are not easily separable from each other. From Hazlitt's illustration it is clear that the experience on which he most securely founds his case is poetry, and especially Wordsworth's poetry.

> If from the top of a long cold barren hill I hear the distant whistle
> of a thrush which seems to come up from some warm woody shel-
> ter beyond the edge of the hill, this sound coming faint over the
> rocks with a mingled feeling of strangeness and joy, the idea of the
> place about me, and the imaginary one beyond will all be com-
> bined together in such a manner in my mind as to become insepa-
> rable. (I, 56)

The elaborating and yet lucid syntax, and relaxed but sufficient punctuation, nicely exemplify Hazlitt's argument from experience: that to the mind all impressions are mingled, and never cease to carry traces of each other.

Hartley's doctrine of vibrations asserts that only ideas collected at a common place or time can be associated, or call up each other. Further, a combination of ideas cannot occur in which the order of place and the order of time do not correspond in exactly the same way as in every other combination of the same ideas. This in turn is a consequence of Hartley's belief that the contiguity of objects makes them fit for association. But neither rule comes near exhausting the mind's capacity for, and freedom of, association. We know this again from experience, in respect to which we are all poets because we constantly remake our ideas of things, and place them in a new relation to accord with our present need. The mind neglects precise distinctions of place and time; it works as if it were a simple entity: all associations seem to "belong absolutely to the same place or internal seat of consciousness." The reason for this ought to interest a metaphysician, and yet Hartley neglects it: "I think Hartley constantly mistakes tracing the *order* of palpable effects, or overt acts of the mind for explaining the causes of the connection between them, which he hardly ever does with a true metaphysical feeling."

In addition to the natural comparison of the adders twined together, Hazlitt now offers an artificial one, more in keeping with Hartley's own metaphors but equally destructive of his argument. The mind is like a supremely well-organized building: "By touching a certain spring, all obstacles are removed, the doors fly open, and the whole gallery is seen at a single glance." Not only similars, but opposites as well, illuminate this indoor scene, by reminding us of each other.

> The very opposition of our feelings as of heat and cold frequently produces a transition in the mind from the one to the other. This may be accounted for in a loose way by supposing, that the struggle between very opposite feelings producing a violent and perturbed state of mind excites attention, and makes the mind more sensible to the shock of the contrary impression to that by which it is preoccupied, as we find that the body is more liable to be affected by any opposite extremes, as of heat and cold, immediately succeeding, and counteracting each other. Be this as it may, all things naturally put us in mind of their contraries, cold of heat, day of night, &c.   (I, 61)

It therefore seems reasonable to Hazlitt to propose three relations by which ideas are connected in the mind: association (by which he means what Hartley called "contiguity"), similarity, and contrast. Yet Hazlitt admits that his own scheme, though better than Hartley's, is little more than a "faint approach to a satisfactory account of the matter." To illustrate the elastic quality of all association, he inquires what is meant when anyone says that X's face reminds him of Y's. Surely it does not mean that he fancied he saw one man's nose on another man's face.[5]

We are now at the center of Hazlitt's argument. The real difficulty, he tells us, in accounting for the operations of the mind—a
difficulty which Hartley, and disciples such as Mackintosh, are prevented by their theory from acknowledging—occurs not "in connecting the links in the chain of previously associated ideas, but in arriving at the first link,—in passing from a present sensation to the
recollection of a past object." Memory may supply the past object
but can never provide for the leap from present to past. The first
link, which makes possible all the rest,

> can never be by an act of association, because it is self-evident that
> the present can never have been previously associated with the past.
> Every beginning of a series of associations, that is every departure
> from the continued beaten track of old impressions or ideas re-
> membered in regular succession therefore implies and must be ac-
> counted for from some act of the mind which does not depend on
> association.   (I, 64)

Association on Hartley's view is an habitual relation between two or
more ideas. The great weakness of this theory is its tendency to deal
with received patterns only, and never with causes. Hazlitt's criticism, though he does not say so, would apply with equal force to
Hume, since if ideas differ from impressions not in kind but merely
in the degree of their distinctness, it is not clear by what means we
move from a new impression to the desired ideas already in our
stock.

We are asked at this juncture to contemplate an illustration more
obviously "compound" than those offered before. Hazlitt casts his
mind over the impressions associated with the lectures on philosophy which he heard Mackintosh give at Lincoln's Inn Hall. He can
understand how his *thinking* of Lincoln's Inn Hall brings back his
impressions of Mackintosh lecturing there (this Hartley's theory
takes care of), but not how his actually *seeing* it today brings back
the memory of having seen it yesterday (since for this we need to
know what connects the "first link" with previous associations).
Hazlitt tries to account for such a mental event—theoretically impossible, but well known to all of us—by postulating a special susceptibility of the mind at particular moments. Even so modest a
claim will require us to look at association itself as "only a particular
and accidental effect of some more general principle." And we can
observe other effects of the same principle which are not less important than association, effects such as reasoning, abstraction, wis-

dom, morality, sympathy, foresight ("imagination" in its simplest meaning)—in short everything "that is essential, or honorable to the human mind." If association is the governing principle of the mind, the existence of these other capacities must be denied: for they are all, what association does not allow them to be, synthetic.[6]

The defense of abstract ideas, which appears at greater length in the *Lectures on English Philosophy,* is offered here as the pivot on which Hazlitt's dismissal of Hartleyan associationism must turn, before it can justify the imagination of the *Essay.* Consider, Hazlitt says, the idea we have of the equality of two lines. Is it arrived at by association? Better still, consider "a heap of mites in a rotten cheese lying as close together as they can stick." The heap contains no "idea" of "the intricate involutions of that little, lively, restless tribe," and evidently the same involutions do not add up to the "idea" of the heap. We hardly think this model of sensation-without-thought an adequate image of the mind. Yet in this heap each mite has greater mobility than Hartley allows to an association. Are we to consider the human brain even less complex than the mite-infested heap?

The example is sufficiently striking to yield an epigrammatic formula inspired by Kant's "the mind alone is formative": *"one brain is one power."* But the statement for Hazlitt implies no larger allegiance. Of the sort of metaphysics from which he abstained, he tells us in this discussion: "I never could make much of the subject of real relations in nature"; and he would have made nothing of the categories very different from Hartley's which were being refined elsewhere even as he wrote, to perfect an idealist vocabulary for the subject of real relations in the mind. His guide all along has been Rousseau more than Kant, and he now quotes a passage from *Emile* in which Rousseau wonders how, unless we are governed by a faculty neither subordinate to nor mechanically connected with sensations, we can account for the common human experience of *making an error.*

> Qu'on donne tel ou tel nom à cette force de mon esprit qui rapproche et compare mes sensations; qu'on l'appelle attention, méditation, réflexion, ou comme on voudra; toujours est-il vrai qu'elle est en moi et non dans les choses, que c'est moi seul qui la produis, quoique je ne la produise qu'à l'occasion de l'impression que font sur moi les objets. (I, 72)

> Whatever name one gives to that power of mind which relates and compares my sensations; whether one calls it attention, meditation,

reflection, or what you will; the fact remains that it is in me and not in things, that it is I alone who supply it, even if I supply it only when objects make an impression on me. [my translation]

"One brain is one power" acquires, in view of this passage, a second sense inextricable from the first, as a formula for the mental process that draws our associations into a coherent mass.

Whatever we choose to make of "real relations in nature," objects in nature cannot be related to each other by the same "inward conscious principle" to which objects are submitted in the mind. This principle binds even as it relates. Objects, as they exist in nature, can at best resemble objects of the mind before they have been submitted to this principle, or as they are present to different minds. Yet, as far as Hartley and his school are concerned, objects of the mind are themselves no more intimately related to each other than objects in nature, or of different minds. When several biases urge us in several directions, how do we decide which to follow? Hartley cannot tell us. He allows no "comprehensive idea of things to check any immediate, passing impulse." Again, why do we sometimes desire one thing more than another? One may recall Tucker's critique of Lockean "satisfaction"; but there is above all a common-sense objection to Hartley's reductive account of motives: that the ideas of some things clearly suggest themselves as sufficient causes of action. In his lectures Mackintosh had denied the very existence of feelings of benevolence, because they could not be explained by the laws of association; Hazlitt comments: "It is a maxim which these gentlemen seem to be unacquainted with that it is necessary to strain an hypothesis to make it fit the facts, not to deny the facts because they do not square with the hypothesis."

Concerning habit the associationist psychology can of course have little to say. It is evident that we may learn from association how to perform any action precisely as we did on the last try. But the circumstances of action are in constant flux, and association cannot account for the minute adjustments of habit that make it appropriate to each new context. Rousseau pointed out that a strict relation between our perceptions and their objects would leave no room for error; and to this Hazlitt adds that mechanical association leaves no room for *unprecedented* success. Hartley can explain only the element of pure repetition in human action. The endless modifications without which action would be impossible are an immense blank space in his theory.

Even if association were discovered to underlie every action's purpose as well as its execution, it would not help us to understand the enormous observable variety in the modes of execution. Hazlitt gives the example of a child running in pursuit of his favorite toy, in a direction he has never taken before. The child may successfully avoid some obstacle in his path. Because he is afraid of the blow, says the associationist. But what if he has never met with such an accident before? In that case he must have been moved by the idea of a pain which he has never yet experienced. He *"constructs* an artificial idea . . . beyond his actual experience,"* by applying the idea of pain that exists in his mind to an entirely new object.

> To suppose that the mechanical tendencies impressed on the muscles by any particular series of past objects can only require to be unfolded to produce regular and consistent action is like supposing that a hand-organ may be set to play a voluntary, or that the same types will serve without any alteration to print a column of a newspaper and a page of Tristram Shandy.[7]   (I, 78)

In all action, the means necessary to a given end are employed, not because they have been associated with the same end in the past, but because they are seen to be indispensable to the attainment of that end in the present. We select for ourselves what we need from the objects we encounter—both objects of the past (in memory) and objects of the present (in the moment of perception). This capacity for modification serves us, among other instances, when we make the transfer of affections involved in passing from self-love to sympathy.

Having drawn together his criticisms of "the selfish philosophy" and associationism, by showing where both require and do not propose an idea of the imagination, Hazlitt has accomplished what he set out to do. He still intends, he says, to prove that "the love of good or happiness" is accompanied by two other principles of comparable strength, the love of truth and the love of power: to inquire into these principles will be the work of another book. He was never able to write it, but of the claim he would have made for the principle of power I have marked the broader outlines in sorting through his remarks on habit. As for the love of an abstraction like truth, one may wonder why it should have proved a necessary principle to a critic of the imagination in art. Here the answer must emerge from the tenor of remarks outside the *Essay* and its appendix.

ABSTRACTION

Hartley's scheme of advancement-through-association was graduated in seven degrees: sensation, imagination, ambition, self-interest, sympathy, theopathy, and morality. The order itself is a clue to his falling back on the older meaning of imagination as image-making, or "decaying sense." To Hazlitt, a worse offense was the complacency with which Hartley portrayed the mind as moving from crude sense-experience to the ideal, by a curriculum of tiny quantitative accessions. How abstraction might alter the whole character of experience was left for others to explore as a secondary issue. I have already noticed Hazlitt's respectful use of the word when he writes of moral judgment; a second non-pejorative use appears in his remarks on the acquisition of knowledge: with these examples in view one concludes that for "abstraction" the common modern senses are not a safe guide to Hazlitt's meanings. The problem arises at all only because Hazlitt is often read as what he is not, a typical commentator on a new school of poetry. Every new school from Wordsworth to Eliot has wanted to believe that its productions were somehow more concrete, more vivid, more striking than those of its predecessor, and therefore less abstract. But the author of *An Essay on the Principles of Human Action* had a richer understanding both of the word and of the process it describes, than the author of the Preface to *Lyrical Ballads*.

In the most famous of all attacks on abstract ideas, Berkeley had defied his readers to imagine triangle-ness, without forming to themselves the image of a particular triangle. Hazlitt in his *Lectures on English Philosophy* changed the example and gave a pointed reply: "Those who say that we cannot conceive of an army of men without conceiving of the individuals composing it, ought to go a step further, and affirm that we must represent to ourselves the features, form, complexion, size, posture, and dress, with every other circumstance belonging to each individual." He took this example seriously enough to generalize from it.

> The same reasoning by which it has been attempted to prove that we have no abstract ideas, would prove that we have no particular ones. Perfect and absolute distinctness would require not only knowledge of all the individual objects in a class, but of all the parts of each object, which is impossible. . . . To deny that we can have any knowledge or conception of things without clearly

apprehending every different circumstance belonging to them, is
to exclude all ideas from the mind. It is only by passing over their
differences, taking them in the gross, and attending to the general
effect of a number of undistinguished, and undistinguishable impressions that we ever arrive at those just notions of objects, on
which all our after-knowledge is built. The knowledge of every
finite being rests in generals: and the only difference between abstract and particular, is that of being more or less general, of leaving out more or fewer circumstances.   (II, 117)

We never experience a sensation without linking it to a complex of
associations: insofar as the work of the mind is progressive, therefore, it is the work of abstraction. This process, Hazlitt says in his
lecture "On Abstract Ideas," "is a consequence of the limitation of
the comprehensive faculty, and mixes itself more or less with every
act of the mind of whatever kind." It is a limitation in the same
sense in which any order is a limitation of chaos.

He still makes use of certain pejorative overtones: even in 1812
they were hard to avoid entirely, and besides they had their value.
But he commonly employs a special sense of the word, without
connotations of dryness, sterility, or mere system. Thus Hobbes is
praised as an author who "not only threw out the first hints" of the
modern philosophy, but "by a very high kind of abstraction . . .
carried it to perfection at once." Two decades later, in the *Life of
Napoleon,* he has not changed his view: "The natural tendency of
the human mind . . . is from the concrete to the abstract." The
context for this last comment is Hazlitt's disdain for the invention of
the Legion of Honor as a badge of merit, in an age when internal
worth is all that concerns us. The streets of Paris and London were
once filled with signs over every shop; these had their uses, which
wore out with the rise of literacy; the mind of man was thus enlarged, and we prefer not to see it diminished again. Why indeed
did Napoleon, having conquered Egypt, encourage his soldiers to
pin hieroglyphics to their breasts? By the defect of an unabstracting
mind.[8]

As an observer of politics, Hazlitt was ready to say with Burke: "I
cannot stand forward, and give praise or blame to any thing which
relates to human actions and human concerns on a simple view of
the object, as it stands stripped of every relation, in all the naked-
ness and solitude of metaphysical abstraction."[9] That Hazlitt was
nevertheless able to conceive of a thing as abstract and not stripped
of every relation, may be inferred from his comment on Shallow and

Silence, where he speaks of "an *atmosphere* of abstraction." It is a phrase that brings together the vocabularies of metaphysics and criticism, and shows them to be pertinent even "in the meanest circumstances."

COALESCENCE

Usually when a critic speaks of the atmosphere of a story, he means the special quality or temper that pervades it, from the author's selection among possible elements. That is why having "a point of view" can entail creating "a world."[10] The argument may be summed up in the following way. If, owing to the work of abstraction, we choose from a multitude of associations a few representative ones, and make them carry the atmosphere of those we exclude, then we have the ability to suggest by implication what we do not record by exhaustive inventory. Hazlitt's preference of the relation of "contrast" to that of "contiguity" is thus at the heart of his criticism. Joined by contiguity, our associations are like points on a line; joined by contrast, they are like points on a circle: a shape asserts itself more deftly, with the suggestion of completeness or comprehensiveness. It is the difference between a hot day reminding us of another hot day, and a heat that suggests its opposite, cold, with the attendant circumstances of light and shade. By imagination we make relevant parts serve as the abstract of a whole. This happens even in our most casual acts of perception: as when sweetness, whiteness, and a granular texture, yield the "whole" we call sugar; or when, in Tucker's phrase, "yellowness, hardness, and valuableness in commerce" yield the "whole complex of gold."[11] The process by which we find such combinations and determine their propriety, Hartley and his successors referred to as coalescence.

Hazlitt would have objected to our use of a different word, "selection," that it takes for granted the thing to be proved, namely the consciousness of a choice. He speaks instead of "elective affinity"; and his broadest speculations on this subject, in the essay "On Genius and Common Sense," imply a parallel between the suggestive association and the individual artist: what the former does for the circle of associations in one mind, the latter does for the community of minds that constitute nature.

> Nature has a thousand aspects, and one man can only draw out one of them. Whoever does this, is a man of genius. One displays

her force, another her refinement, one her power of harmony, another her suddenness of contrast, one her beauty of form, another
her splendour of colour. Each does that for which he is best fitted
by his particular genius, that is to say, by some quality of mind in
which the quality of the object sinks deepest, where it finds the
most cordial welcome, is perceived to its utmost extent, and where
again it forces its way out from the fulness with which it has taken
possession of the mind of the student. The imagination gives out
what it has first absorbed by congeniality of temperament, what it
has attracted and moulded into itself by elective affinity, as the
loadstone draws and impregnates iron.   (VIII, 47)

All this, particularly the analogy with physical laws, is familiar to
the reader of Tucker's "Vision," where the mind-nature relation is
between the individual Vehicle and the Mundane Soul.[12] But Hazlitt gave no credence to the notion of a material "integument" which
had led Tucker to predicate a soul of nature. When Hazlitt spoke
of nature he always meant our idea of nature, the community of all
our associations—even if he never felt duty-bound to enforce the
pedantry of the distinction. Similarly, when he spoke of "objects,"
he meant objects of the mind.[13]

Isolate a particular object, treat it as the focus of all associated
thoughts and feelings, or the anchor without which all would drift
and therefore perish, and you initiate a discourse of the symbol.[14]
Hazlitt's criticism moves in the opposite direction, from the particular to its atmosphere in the mind: poetry, he says, "describes the
flowing, not the fixed."

This conviction was adapted to his critical practice, most unexpectedly in certain demonstrations of his prowess as a physiognomist.
He liked to read faces and could discern a character stamped boldly
in every feature; even the lack of expression might be a clue. In this
branch of criticism, abstraction and coalescence are names for the
metonymy of wit. When Northcote calls *Tom Jones* "a masterpiece,
as far as regards the conduct of the fable," Hazlitt divines its secret
in a portrait of the author: "Do you know the reason? Fielding had
a hooked nose, the long chin. It is that introverted physiognomy that
binds and concentrates." He follows the same method in the bold
sketch of Coleridge for "My First Acquaintance with Poets":

His forehead was broad and high, light as if built of ivory, with
large projecting eyebrows, and his eyes rolling beneath them like a
sea with darkened lustre. "A certain tender bloom his face o'er-

spread," a purple tinge as we see it in the pale thoughtful complexions of the Spanish portrait-painters, Murillo and Velasquez. His mouth was gross, voluptuous, open, eloquent; his chin good-humoured and round; but his nose, the rudder of the face, the index of the will, was small, feeble, nothing—like what he has done. It might seem that the genius of his face as from a height surveyed and projected him (with sufficient capacity and huge aspiration) into the world unknown of thought and imagination, with nothing to support or guide his veering purpose, as if Columbus had launched his adventurous course for the New World in a scallop, without oars or compass. (XVII, 109)

The extraordinary assurance of both judgments may indicate a motive for Hazlitt's violent rejection of phrenology. Here was a new pretender to exactitude in the cartography of the mind, prepared to reduce human nature to a science, yet dispensing with the *marks* of individuality, and content if it could remove them to a place where they would never be seen. Hazlitt's descriptions, on the contrary, tell us only what he saw, with the extravagance of belief and not of system. In these passages a whole character is made to emerge from a few "projecting points"; and we feel that the whole of Hazlitt's character has been brought into play as well.

MEANINGS OF DISINTERESTEDNESS

Other uses of the word "disinterestedness" have done much to obscure what it meant in the *Essay,* and as a help in clarifying this I want to contrast Hazlitt with two apparently congenial thinkers who also make it their central term, Godwin and Matthew Arnold. A formula Godwin repeated with slight variations throughout *Political Justice* was that *understanding is virtue.* "A vicious conduct" could therefore only be "the result of narrow views," and vice itself was "unquestionably no more than an error of judgment."[15] Right judgment would necessarily produce virtuous conduct. But the man for whom understanding is virtue can bring no interests of his own to bear on the choice to act one way or another. Such interests, though part of his mores, are entirely separate from his moral life. The uprooting of sentiments which Godwin's disinterestedness required was of course a simple consequence of referring all moral choices to the standard of utility; but the very isolation of the useful from the interesting which that standard presumed Hazlitt saw as perverse. He believed "disinterestedness" meant not excluding all interests but being open to an unpredictable plurality of them.

This might seem a lesson sufficiently attractive to anyone wary of utilitarianism. Nevertheless Arnold, an anti-utilitarian in most respects, takes up a position in literary criticism not unlike Godwin's in moral philosophy. As Godwin thought we could agree in our understanding of actions and our definition of virtue, so Arnold thinks we can agree in our understanding of literature and our definition of a great work, by excluding our interests. To Godwin, interests were sentimental, irrational, and ultimately selfish; to Arnold, they are philistine, parochial, and ultimately destructive of culture. *Understanding is taste* seems to me a fair translation of his credo: there is a way of seeing the object rightly, and we can find it by removing from our judgments everything connected with ourselves. Hazlitt, who rejected virtue in Godwin's sense, would I think have rejected culture in Arnold's sense. For by leaving no room for personal interest, both ideals teach us that in every situation there is exactly one right move to make.

The only writer I have found who employs the vocabulary of interests as Hazlitt did is William James in his *Psychology*. I do not think James had read Hazlitt's *Essay*. When he comes to reinvent a large portion of its argument in his chapters on "Habit" and "Association"—and again when he recovers Hazlitt's metaphor as the title of another chapter, "The Stream of Thought"—he feels no need to speak of the mind's *dis*interestedness. He argues instead that we are richer for having a diverse organization of interests. But I will return to James, and in the meantime suggest only a paraphrase of his theory of action, with an application to morals that he did not venture: we feel the claims of a great many interests, and yet we act selectively on behalf of a few, whether belonging to ourselves or others; so that the difference between the ordinary man and the good man is traceable not to the latter's renunciation of interests but to his persistence in making them flow into more than one channel.

To make sense of Godwin's proposition that understanding is virtue, one has to recognize that he defines virtue as an intelligible property of a thing which remains constant over time. Further, the measure we use in judging a thing's function can be extended without change to our estimates of human action. If the virtue of any object consists in "certain beneficial qualities which really belong to that object," then "a knife is as capable as a man of being employed in the purposes of virtue, and the one is no more free than the other as to its employment. . . . The man differs from the knife, just as the iron candlestick differs from the brass one; he has one more way of being acted upon. This additional way in the man is motive, in the candlestick is magnetism."[16] So properties, or virtues, which are calculated with precision for one thing, may be calculated with no less precision for twenty, or two million. In reducing morals to a science, Godwin was eager to publish every implication of his leading principle; but he gave particular attention to this one, by inventing the phrase *moral arithmetic.* "Twenty, other things equal, is twenty times better than one. He that is not governed by the moral arithmetic of the case, or who acts from a disposition directly at war with that arithmetic, is wrong."[17] If thus to act is to act rightly, and to act otherwise is the result simply of miscalculation—"wrong," and not wicked—then Godwin has adequate grounds for his conclusion that "Man is in reality a passive, and not an active being."[18]

Hazlitt's reply, in his *Essay* and elsewhere, is that we do in fact often judge from a disposition at odds with moral arithmetic, and can hardly help doing so, since we are beings for whom other things never are equal. We enter every situation with interests of our own, and these influence us in making judgments. A late essay "On the Causes of Popular Opinion" confronts Godwin's idea of disinterestedness without quite naming it: by a rapid sequence of illustrations, it shows why our attachment to a few objects would not be weakened even by the conscious application of moral arithmetic. The essay starts off as a dialogue, and the speaker clearly identified with Hazlitt takes his most vivid example from a poem founded on the affections.

> Michael is an old shepherd, who has a son who goes to sea, and who turns out a great reprobate by all the accounts received of him. Before he went, however, the father took the boy with him into a mountain-glen, and made him lay the first stone of a sheep-fold, which was to be a covenant and a remembrance between them if anything ill happened. For years after, the old man used to go to work at this sheep-fold—
>
> > "Among the rocks
> > He went, and still look'd up upon the sun,
> > And listen'd to the wind"—

and sat by the half-finished work, expecting the lad's return, or
hoping to hear some better tidings of him. Was this hope founded
on reason—or was it not owing to the strength of affection which,
in spite of everything, could not relinquish its hold of a favourite object, indeed the only one that bound it to existence?

(XVII, 309)

Hazlitt is certain that "The understanding takes a tincture from outward impulses and circumstances, and is led to dwell on those suggestions which favour, and to blind itself to those objections which
impugn, the side to which it personally and morally inclines." He
thus brings the category of the moral into close relationship with
our interests, habits, and associations. The unstated conclusion is
that society, in order to be reformed on Godwin's principles, would
have to understand moral conduct in a light wholly unfamiliar to
the individual mind.

This is the kind of opposition that Wordsworth offered in *The
Prelude;* but his was not an available example to Hazlitt, when he
wrote against *Political Justice* in the early 1800s; and it needs to be
remembered that Godwin's better-known contemporaries adopted a
very different tone of attack. Malthus for his part granted the connection of justice with calculable utility, but thought the two could
be shown to conflict if the earth's supply of food were ultimately
limited. In this way he advanced the case against distributive justice
by appearing as a stricter utilitarian than Godwin: for, with the
population steadily pressing against the limits of the means of subsistence, a just distribution of goods would require everyone to be
miserable; though the condition would be shared it would be unhappy. The reader was invited to choose between an unequal division of happiness, with much for a few and little for the rest, and an
equal division of unhappiness to all. Because the moral arithmetic
of the case told entirely for preserving a degree of happiness, the
very possibility that this choice would some day become actual was
sufficient to nullify Godwin's proof that utility, the good of mankind, and a disinterested justice were inseparable.

Now, having first disposed of Godwin's utilitarianism, Hazlitt
published several letters in reply to Malthus's anti-utopian paradox.
The letters kept returning to a practical objection: Malthus's discovery held no present-day consequences for the reform of society,
since the choice between unequal happiness and universal misery
would not become actual until all the usable lands of the earth were
under active cultivation. Whatever therefore its long-term impor-

tance, nothing about the *Essay on the Principle of Population* could warrant its immediate employment as "a gospel preached to the poor." A one-sentence parody of the *Essay* quoted by a Unitarian writer for the *Monthly Repository* sums up the logic of Hazlitt's *Reply to Malthus*: "the world will be filled with misery a thousand years hence; and therefore we ought to begin to be miserable in good time."[19]

But Malthus's was an avoidable though clever misreading of *Political Justice*. For Godwin had not consistently defined the good which utilitarian calculations were supposed to pick out as "the greatest happiness for the greatest number"; and, even where he implied such a definition, he did not consistently present happiness as synonymous with physical well-being. One cannot be sure that the prospect of all mankind starving together would afford the slightest embarrassment to Godwin's ideas of utility and justice; at any rate Malthus's reliance on the greatest-happiness principle gives an emphasis to physical well-being which Godwin cannot be shown to endorse; for that emphasis came from Malthus's deference to a version of the social contract: society is bound by a commitment to the survival of as many of its members as is compatible with the happiness of some. Here Godwin escapes the trap laid for him in still another direction, by refusing to credit any form of contract. He has, and wishes to make, no defense against the critic who observes that to prohibit every contract is altogether to cease thinking in terms of society. He supposes that we are good without respect to society, and that contracts, like all social rules, by confining us to precedent only obstruct our inquiry into the moral arithmetic of a given case. This is true even of promises. If good and right, they will be kept anyway by our adherence to justice. "But," Godwin imagines someone asking, "if promises be not made, or when made not fulfilled, how can the affairs of the world be carried on?" The answer is, "By rational and intelligent beings acting as if they were rational and intelligent."[20] Without promises, we can still decide how to act by bestowing "a steady attention upon the quantities of convenience or inconvenience, of good or evil, that might arise from our conduct."[21] By the end of *Political Justice* Godwin is ready to defy not only the claims of society but of common sociability. The same ideal that has set him against habit as a kind of prejudice and therefore of obscurantism, leads him to denounce conformity of any sort—habit being only the conformity of the individual to his past, and social harmony the conformity of individuals to each other's desires. In music he favors solo performances and deplores concerts, "everything that is usually understood by the term co-operation" being "in some degree an evil."[22]

There remain two sorts of occasion for which any action we contemplate is likely to emerge as the unified effort of some corporate body or society—occasions when deliberate conformity seems necessary to the achievement of any result. They are, the reformation of a widespread abuse, and the punishment of a crime. About the first of these Godwin is equivocal. He acknowledges that a significant group can shape the attitudes of an individual as much as the individual himself can, and even if his theory admits no such influence as beneficial, he knows that in effecting a momentous change nothing else will do. "Large bodies of men, when once they have been enlightened and persuaded, act with more vigour than solitary individuals. They animate the mutual exertions of each other, and the unified forces of example and shame urge them to perseverance."[23] Still Godwin can fairly claim that when the enlightenment has become general, there will be no further need for society or for corporate bodies of any description. On the question of punishment he is much more straightforward: "No two crimes were ever alike; and therefore the reducing them explicitly or implicitly to general classes, which the very idea of example implies, is absurd."[24] This seems to echo Hume's argument that the derivation of "ought" from "is" is not founded on the nature of things, and can only be justified by social norms; but, unlike Hume, he refuses to admit that such norms themselves are worth having.[25] So regular punishments have no place in his system; and yet, Godwin does not oppose capital punishment: "It is right that I should inflict suffering, in every case where it can be clearly shown that such infliction will produce an overbalance of good. But this infliction bears no reference to the mere innocence or guilt of the person upon whom it is made."[26] One can justify on utilitarian grounds the punishment of an innocent man, and even the taking of his life.

It is on this question of capital punishment that the difference between Godwin and Hazlitt emerges most starkly. An essay "On the Punishment of Death"—written by Hazlitt in 1812, and commissioned by the Society for the Diffusion of Knowledge upon the Punishment of Death—opposes capital punishment for crimes of theft, and defends it for the crime of murder, but for reasons Godwin would have thought unsound. "There is a natural and home-felt connection between the hardened obduracy which has shewn itself insensible to the cries of another for mercy and the immediate burst of indignation which dooms the criminal to feel that he has no claims on the pity of others." For the want of some such home-felt connection, Hazlitt dismisses the punishment of life-imprisonment as likely to be worse than useless: "Those punishments are the best which require the least previous familiarity with objects of guilt and misery to make them formidable, which come least into contact with the mind, which tell at a distance, the bare mention of which startles the ear, which operate by an imaginary instead of an habitual dread, and which produce their effect once for all, without destroying the erectness and elasticity of social feeling by the constant spectacle of the degradation of the species." In that sentence Hazlitt outlines a moral basis for a criminal code radically opposed to the standard of utility. His consistency brings out by contrast the moderate utilitarianism which we—the disciples of Godwin and Bentham—take for granted in our own commonplaces about deterrence.[27] Hazlitt flatly rejects the very idea of deterrence as bad moral reasoning: to ask which of two punishments inspires greater fear he sees as a pointless undertaking, for he believes criminals are deterred not by the severity of punishments in themselves, but by the way punishments are associated with the general disapprobation of society. Punishment is an action by which the members of a society confirm to themselves the sentiments that they hold in common: only when the associated sentiments have weakened or vanished is it right for the punishment to be revised. The criminal too is sensible of this fact, and though a life in prison may seem to him less endurable than death, he will abhor death as the greater punishment, because he knows it to be the penalty that expresses the community's utmost abhorrence. The following three sentences appear italicized in Hazlitt's essay:

> *It is not the calculation of consequences, but their involuntary and irresistible impression on the mind that produces action. The laws to prevent crimes must appeal to the passions of men, and not to their reason: for crimes proceed from passion, and not from reason. If men were governed by reason, laws would be unnecessary.*
>
> (XIX, 325)

This reminds us that the actions of a society, as much as those of an individual, depend on how the imagination is employed. Indeed our motives are always in some sense other-regarding and therefore social: they no more proceed from our knowledge of utility (the intrinsic properties of an action) than they do from our knowledge of identity (the intrinsic properties of a self). Hazlitt's argument on interest makes it possible even for a society to embody the principle of disinterested action. At least, if it is responsive to many interests, and settled in its service to none, we are making sense when we praise it as disinterested.

Interests for Hazlitt were not independent of prejudices. He remarks to Northcote in the *Conversations:* "We cannot set aside those prejudices which are founded on the limitation of our faculties or the constitution of society; [but] we need not lay them down as abstract or demonstrable truths. . . . The language of taste and moderation is, *I prefer this, because it is best to me;* the language of dogmatism and intolerance is, *Because I prefer it, it is best in itself."* Arnold wanted to be able to say something different from either of these: "I prefer it because, and only because, it is best in itself." His disinterestedness required him to bring no interests to his consideration of the object, and this meant he would also be free of prejudices. Actions properly understood, in Godwin's view, had a reason-giving force to the moral agent; and objects properly understood, in Arnold's view, have a reason-giving force to the critic. When one realizes this, there is nothing mysterious about his statement that the discipline of the critic is to see the object "as in itself it really is." Our interested judgments are wonderfully various but all wrong, each in its separate way, and we can improve them only by submitting to the corrective guidance of disinterestedness. It seems to me pertinent that Arnold is the great user of the word in its substantive form. Hazlitt preferred the adjective that could suit itself to this or that occasion: a certain estimate of character or approach to an issue might be disinterested. But he frequently alludes to the idea where every form of the word is absent, as when he makes it a "test of the sense and candour of anyone belonging to the opposite party, whether he allowed Burke to be a great man."

The great obstacle in the way of any modern reader's understanding what Hazlitt meant is the confusion of "disinterested" with "uninterested." The disinterested man is still looking at what he judges; the uninterested one has gone on to something else. But there is a second confusion, also of recent origin, and less easily recognized; for the over-educated reader, in rescuing "disinterested" from its use as a careless synonym for "uninterested," sometimes displays his prize as a distinguished-sounding synonym for "impartial" or "detached." The truth is that a disinterested investigator, a disinterested judge, a disinterested historian, need not be detached: he may begin on one side, and end on the opposite one—or even on the same. Indeed it is unimaginable that he should be strictly neutral (human nature being what it is) except when he is also uninterested. Thus the over-educated reader falls into an error comparable to the one he revolts from. All that an attitude of disinterestedness ought to mean for the person who holds it, is that his final judgment is the result of what he sees, hears, and feels as the merits of the case. He has no vested interest in what he undertakes to judge, and his thoughts are not swayed by tormenting fears or habitual associations. But he will feel stirrings within him even as he makes his judgment. A biographer of Cromwell may, for example, end by approving of his protagonist or by condemning him, and still be disinterested. But ten disinterested biographers are not expected to emerge with the same finding: to wish that they could betrays a poor insight into both our nature and our reasons for caring about biography.

An important source of this second confusion has been Arnold's essay, "The Function of Criticism at the Present Time." Arnold remembered disinterestedness from his reading of Hazlitt and the eighteenth-century moralists. He liked the word, and proposed that English culture needed more of the principle—thinking about the word would lead to acting on the principle. He provides, in the course of the essay, a touchstone of disinterested thinking, and predictably enough it is from Burke. He singles out for praise Burke's "return upon himself," and quotes the final turn of *Thoughts on French Affairs* in which Burke considers that a new system of things may have entered the world, and reflects that if this is so the record of his protests will matter little to posterity. Arnold does not allow for the dark-beyond-dark irony that many have felt in reading the passage; but he uses it very effectively, and it gives him a new meaning of disinterestedness: it is now the characteristic virtue, not of the member of the opposite party who still recognizes Burke's greatness, but of the member of no party at all. Culture stands apart from a world of passions, and returns upon itself. With Arnold we are well on the way to the complaint against a modern political columnist: "You are too resolute in your defense of X. Try to be more disinterested."

Arnold in this essay does not speak of "objectivity" and "subjectivity." Yet those terms were on his mind and had already come into play in the "Preface" of 1853, where he spoke of "the calm, the

cheerfulness, the disinterested objectivity" of the classics, as opposed
to "the dialogue of the mind with itself" of the moderns. By 1864,
when "The Function of Criticism" was first published, disinterestedness had won out over objectivity as the master-term. It had the
right touch of mystery. When, however, Arnold makes it a point
against the romantics that "they did not know enough," a further
confusion is introduced. He means that they were not sufficiently
disinterested in his new sense. But to Hazlitt this use of *know* would
have been incomprehensible, unless it were taken to mean "see, hear,
and feel one's way into this or that situation." Doubtless it is a limitation not to go out of oneself; but for Hazlitt's meaning of disinterestedness, the alternative was to imagine other selves; for Arnold's
it is to enter the condition of selflessness. The motive for this change
is clear from the "Preface." In full revolt against his own poetry,
Arnold needed to avoid the romantic vocabulary of impressions (a
vocabulary well suited to the particular occasions of poetry besides
his own). That is why he summed up seeing, hearing, feeling, and so
forth, with the single cover-sense, knowing: the "best ideas" would
come when correctly summoned. His criticism, it must be added, betrays no awareness of the genealogy of ideas in impressions, a piece
of knowledge that had entered English criticism through Hume's
philosophy, and by Hazlitt's persistence as a revisionist of Hume.

Wherever Godwin and Arnold show us the phenomenon of disinterestedness, a great shifting of gears is heard, and what we see is something outside the routines of ordinary life. But with Hazlitt the distinction between interested and disinterested conduct is a matter of
degree only. It is a way of looking at action that makes a disinterested judgment unexceptionally human, and no less praiseworthy for
that. This I believe is the element of his thinking that James did
most to extend later in the century, with one important change.
When Hazlitt wrote about the choice of objects of attention which
goes on steadily all our lives, his metaphor was elective affinity. When
James wrote about the same process thirty years after *The Origin of
Species,* his metaphor was natural selection.

James represents motives as arising from the emphasis we give
to certain interests for the sake of a purpose dominant at a given
moment. But that purpose in turn must have emerged from the total
drift of all our past moments: it is always changing—we cannot in-
spect a single mind twice, and find quite the same purpose within—

yet it has a satisfying continuousness. Thought then is personal, changing, and continuous, and to this list James adds two more elusive characteristics: "It always appears to deal with objects independent of itself," and "It is interested in some parts of these objects to the exclusion of others."[28] By his choice of words James is exempted from the idealist-realist debate. We think about objects of which our impressions give an imperfect account, because we have no need for the whole of any object. How in that case do we make an imaginative whole of what our senses present to us only as parts? A short answer would be, by means of imagination. The longer one that James proposes both in *Psychology* and more elaborately in *Radical Empiricism,* in a revision of many earlier conjectures about the process of coalescence, is "substitution." He is justified in giving it a different name because in his discussion the process makes a larger class of effects than it did for Tucker and Hazlitt. It not only combines aspects of objects with each other, but objects of vastly disparate sorts, and partial glimpses of events from different times. Thus it covers a good deal of the work to which Hazlitt referred by an additional word, "abstraction."

Of the mind's necessary bias, James writes: "Experience is remoulding us every moment, and our mental reaction on every given thing is really a resultant of our experience of the whole world up to that date."[29] This is his chief reason for asserting that no "brain-state" can ever be precisely repeated: "Something like it may recur; but to suppose *it* to recur would be equivalent to the absurd admission that all the states that had intervened between its two appearances had been pure nonentities, and that the organ after their passage was exactly as it was before."[30] Hazlitt's various criticisms of Hartley proceeded from a consideration of the same absurdity. Far from absorbing ideas mechanically and exhaustively, we gather those we want for the sake of certain aspects, and in a single gesture of experience interpret them as a whole. That gave the appropriateness to Hazlitt's image of thought as a large gallery opened and lit up in an instant. We may experience it first as a gallery, only later as a succession of furniture pieces; but neither experience is essentially prior to the other, and neither is less unified. In confirming our sense of the mind's adaptability, James remarks with special emphasis: "*There is no manifold of coexisting ideas; the notion of such a thing is a chimera. Whatever things are thought in relation are thought from the outset as a unity, in a single pulse of subjectivity, a single psychosis, feeling, or state of mind.*"[31]

James's treatment of self-interest and its connection with other interests, in his chapter on "The Consciousness of Self," is close to both the letter and spirit of Hazlitt's *Essay*. He concedes that our idea of personal identity is a strong influence on action; but then he adds, in two sentences that get a paragraph to themselves: *"We see no reason to suppose that self-love is primarily, or secondarily, or ever, love for one's mere principle of conscious identity. It is always* love for something which, as compared with that principle, is superficial, transient, liable to be taken up or dropped at will."[32] The *something* is the interesting object of the moment, which we choose in keeping with tendencies common to most experience. The body first, according to James's ranking, friends next, and finally spiritual dispositions, are *"the supremely interesting* OBJECTS *for each human mind."*[33] But the ranking too is open to reverses, and there is no simple way of telling by what sort of action we will decide these objects are best served.

> If the zoological and evolutionary point of view is the true one, there is no reason why any object whatever *might* not arouse passion and interest as primitively and instinctively as any other, whether connected or not with the interests of the me. The phenomenon of passion is in origin and essence the same, whatever be the target upon which it is discharged; and what the target actually happens to be is solely a question of fact. I might conceivably be as much fascinated, and as primitively so, by the care of my neighbor's body as by the care of my own. The only check to such exuberant altruistic interests is natural selection, which would weed out such as were very harmful to the individual or to his tribe. Many such interests, however, remain unweeded out—the interest in the opposite sex, for example, which seems in mankind stronger than is called for by its utilitarian need; and alongside of them remain interests, like that in alcoholic intoxication or in musical sounds, which, for aught we can see, are without any utility whatever. The sympathetic instincts and the egoistic ones are thus co-ordinate. They arise, so far as we can tell, on the same psychologic level. The only difference between them is, that the instincts called egoistic form much the larger mass.[34]

With allowances for the change of vocabulary imposed by James's understanding of Darwin, this seems to me an excellent summing-up of the *Essay on Human Action*. Because he thought such interests, built up constantly and imperceptibly, formed a clue to whatever experience with all its circumferences might hold beyond the experience of each central self, James felt a lifelong admiration for Gustav Fechner's speculations on the World Soul, which in his description sound extraordinarily like Tucker's on the Mundane Soul.[35]

An ascent from the disinterestedness of the imagination to the mind's freedom was beyond James's scope as a psychologist, and yet his own criticisms of mechanical association allow him to affirm that freedom as securely as Hazlitt did in his "Remarks on the Systems of Hartley and Helvetius." All we know of the mind, writes James, is confined to *"effects of interested attention and volition,"* and he admits that though there may be such a thing as "mental spontaneity," it can have the power only of *"selecting* amongst those which the associative machinery has already introduced or tends to introduce." But here James turns upon himself, and asks why that should not be enough. "If it can emphasize, reinforce, or protract for a second either one of these, it can do all that the most eager advocate of free will need demand; for it then decides the direction of the next associations by making them hinge upon the emphasized term; and determining in this wise the course of the man's thinking, it also determines his acts."[36] As for the causes of interested attention, he has demonstrated that they may be as varied as the objects of our world.

LATER SOUNDINGS

Near the end of his life, Hazlitt said he believed in the "theoretical benevolence and practical malignity" of mankind. What had failed him, however, to make this new credo plausible, was not his proof of disinterestedness but his faith in benevolence: it is important to keep the two issues separate. More than once, he had shown to his satisfaction that the possibility of disinterested conduct exists in all men, and he would never stop measuring them by so natural a standard. In noting later that the world was not filled with displays of a consistent and principled benevolence, he was recording the testimony of his senses.

Because we are ill-acquainted with benevolence, we do not understand it; and when we see it, we may not be entirely sure that we like it. On this state of affairs Hazlitt commented at length, in a passage of acute psychological analysis that he contributed to the *Life of Thomas Holcroft.* He was trying here to account for the mixed feelings with which we greet the altruism of Enlightenment Romance. Holcroft in *Anna St. Ives* produced one of the nobler speci-

mens of the genre: Hazlitt found himself admiring the book and
thoroughly approving of its sentiments, yet troubled by a want
of sympathy for the characters; a response that brought back his
favorite questions about the remoteness of our ideals and the familiarity of our habitual feelings, illiberal and destructive as the latter
often are.

> It was Mr. Holcroft's business to make his characters not only con-
> sistent, but interesting and amiable: and he has done nearly all
> that was possible to accomplish this end. But it seems as if the
> difficulty of the undertaking, from the very nature of it, was too
> great to be overcome. For in spite of all the appeals that are made
> to reason, and though we strive ever so much to suspend our in-
> vidious prepossessions, yet the old adage of "A faultless monster,
> which the world ne'er saw," continually obtrudes itself upon us, and
> poisons our satisfaction. It is true, our dislike may be irrational,
> but still it is dislike. That which, if left in generals, we might be-
> lieve and admire, if brought to a nearer view, and exhibited in all
> its circumstances of improbability, we begin to distrust, and for
> that reason to hate: *quod sic mihi ostendis, incredulus odi.* Perfect
> virtue, the pure disinterested love of justice, an unshaken zeal for
> truth, regardless of all petty consequences, a superiority to false
> modesty, a contempt for the opinion of the world, when reason and
> conscience are on our side, all these are fine things, and easily
> conceived, while they remain, what they are, the pure creatures of
> the understanding, mere abstract essences, which cannot kindle too
> warm a glow of enthusiasm in the breast. But when these airy
> nothings are made reluctantly to assume a local habitation and a
> name, called Frank, or Anna; when they are personified in the son
> of a knavish steward, or the daughter of a foolish baronet; . . .
> when they are mounted on horse-back, or seat themselves in a post-
> chaise, or walk arm in arm through the streets of London, or
> Paris,—the naked form of truth vanishes under all this pitiful
> drapery, and the mind is distracted with mean and contradictory
> appearances which it knows not how to reconcile. . . . [In *Anna
> St. Ives,* we admire the hero's actions] but we do not love the man:
> his motives we respect, but with his feelings we have little sym-
> pathy. Indeed he is a character who does not stand in need of our
> sympathy; "A reasoning, self-sufficient thing, an intellectual all in
> all." He is himself a being without passions; and in order to feel
> with him, we must ourselves be divested of passion.[37] (III, 129–30)

Hazlitt is describing the tension, common enough in our feelings
about real as well as imaginary characters, between admiration for

an abstract moral principle, because it is moral, and suspicion of it because it is abstract. The actions of which we approve in theory are not necessarily those in which we take the most delight, nor as a rule those by which we choose our friends.

The revealing phrase about Holcroft concerns his obliviousness to "habitual feelings of nature and probability": *feelings* in this instance means *expectations*. When asked to believe in imaginary characters who embody a single relentless ethical principle, we feel just as we would if in life we were asked to sympathize with a generous action performed from "pure duty" instead of affection. We may admire the working out of the principle, in either case, but it will be a cold admiration. Do we then find Holcroft's characters unbelievable because they are unsympathetic, or unsympathetic because they are unbelievable? There ought to be nothing inherently unsympathetic in moral perfection. If there were, the prospects for the betterment of mankind would be a great deal narrower than Hazlitt ever reckoned them to be. But we are unfitted, by all we have seen of life, for believing in a principle of action that walks, talks, and is neatly personified in a work of art. Belief, where art is concerned, requires the animation of passions we share, and in this sense forms the basis of all sympathy. Our disbelief removes every trace of sympathy. Perfected Man may be without rooted affections, and without the need for them. But until we know him better, the characters of fiction, if indeed they are characters and not spectral shapes, must conform to our mixed state. The creatures of art make their appeal to the creatures of life, and "we do not like our friends the worse because they sometimes give us the opportunity to rail at them heartily. Their faults reconcile us to their virtues."[38]

To feel the tension in Hazlitt's own thinking between the undoubted possibility and the doubtful probability of the triumph of disinterestedness in actual life, it is enough to watch him carefully throughout his career. One need not postulate a sudden intellectual crisis, in line with the emotional crisis recorded in *Liber Amoris,* to account for a reluctant shift that may seem to end in a settled pessimism. The metaphor implied by "tension" is at all events far more accurate than that implied by "change of heart." In the essay "On Old English Writers and Speakers," Hazlitt observes:

> There appears to be no natural necessity for evil, but that there is a perfect indifference to good without it. One thing exists and has a value set upon it only as it has a foil in some other; learning is set off by ignorance, liberty by slavery, refinement by barbarism.

> . . . I could make the world good, wise, happy to-morrow, if,
> when made, it would be contented to remain so without the alloy
> of mischief, misery, and absurdity: that is, if every possession did
> not require the principle of contrast, contradiction, and excess, to
> enliven and set it off and keep it at a safe distance from sameness
> and insipidity.   (XII, 322)

This was written in 1824, but its sense clearly depends on the associative relation of contrast which Hazlitt had found essential to all
acts of the mind as early as his 1805 strictures on Hartley. In employing contrast more widely, and making it serve his observations
on society, Hazlitt betrayed no principle.

Again, to set off the hopeful tone of the *Essay* with a tone of near
resignation, one need only look into the *Life of Holcroft,* published
some years later.

> The whole of the *modern* philosophy (as far as relates to moral
> conduct), is nothing more than a literal, rigid, unaccommodating
> and systematic interpretation of the text (which is itself pretty old
> and good authority) "Thou shalt love thy neighbour as thyself,"
> without making any allowances for the weaknesses of mankind, or
> the degree to which this rule was practicable; and the answer to
> the question, "Who is our neighbour," is the same, both in the
> sacred records, and in the modern paraphrase, "He who most wants
> our assistance." I have mentioned this coincidence (I hope without
> offence), to shew that the shock occasioned by the extreme and
> naked manner of representing the doctrine of universal benevo-
> lence, did not, and could not, arise from the principle itself, but
> from the supposition that this comprehensive and sublime prin-
> ciple was of itself sufficient to regulate the actions of men, without
> the aid of those common affections, and mixed motives, which our
> habits, passions, and vices, had taught us to regard as the highest
> practicable point of virtue.   (III, 134)

By speaking of "the modern philosophy" Hazlitt once more calls attention to the line of descent that begins with Godwin and ends in
James Mill. The opening sentence is an ironic sally against Godwin's
attackers: it is they, in their corruption, who find the gospel "literal,
rigid, unaccommodating." Yet Hazlitt is also impatient with Godwin,
and at last more forbearing than ironic toward those who cannot
follow his perfectibilities. "Common affections, and mixed motives":
these are what Godwin cannot see or understand; and *common* is
required by the context to mean "shared" instead of "low." Our
affections receive their bias before philosophy enters on the scene,

from our "habits, passions, and vices." In mixed tones the passage insists on the reality of mixed motives, without holding up either for praise or blame the world in which those motives play so large a part. This world was not the subject of Hazlitt's *Essay;* but the *Essay* has not left us unprepared for it.

Hazlitt's later writings expand his speculations on habit, to make sense of the decline of those "generous and aspiring impulses" that nourish disinterested motives. The impulsive child of the *Essay,* whose interest is at first drawn out by any object, and then narrowed by force of habit, is portrayed again in the *Life of Holcroft,* but the means by which he is torn away from a naïve disinterestedness now appear to Hazlitt more painful, and more assured of success.

> We should be tempted to assert, that men do not become what by nature they are meant to be, but what society makes them. The generous feelings, and higher propensities of the soul are, as it were, shrunk up, seared, violently wrenched, and amputated, to fit us for our intercourse with the world, something in the manner that beggars maim and mutilate their children, to make them fit for their future situation in life.   (III, 155)

Here the struggle long familiar to Hazlitt's mind, between Adam Smith on the one hand, and Rousseau and Wordsworth on the other, seems to have been won by the latter. Habit is completely identified with the social self, sympathy with the natural self, and so far from there being a habit of sympathy, the two terms are understood as exclusive after all. The final metaphor, with its strong hint that the accommodations exacted by society are unnatural, and that the privation we suffer is a kind of death (the loss of our shape, our limbs, our senses), shows how fiercely Hazlitt was able to contemplate the imagined contest, and how he could appall himself with the result. Yet victories such as habit attains for one long moment in the *Life of Holcroft,* are with Hazlitt always temporary. They may be reversed in a subsequent paragraph, or on a different field of battle, at the prompting of some new and equally passionate observation.

Nowhere does he consider opposite tendencies more fully than in the book of aphorisms, *Characteristics,* which he published in the aftermath of his disastrous infatuation with the "lodging-house decoy" Sarah Walker. This is where Herschel Baker finds evidence of a change of heart.[39] But it seems to me that *Characteristics* is chiefly remarkable for the steadiness with which it refuses to consolidate all its unhappy views into an attitude toward mankind. If Hazlitt's statements on either side of a question are keener than ever before, his reason may lie in the nature of aphoristic writing: "There is a peculiar *stimulus,* and at the same time a freedom from all anxiety, in this mode of writing. A thought must tell at once, or not at all. There is no opportunity for considering how we shall make out an opinion by labour and prolixity."[40]

Characteristics revolves around a fixed group of contrasting motives and qualities. But it has scarcely the effect we should look for, if it were done in retraction of the *Essay;* for Hazlitt sets vanity against modesty, vice against virtue, calculation against impulse, the head against the heart, more often than he sets self-love against benevolence. He is unwilling to play the trick of *resolving* benevolence into self-love, even if the selfish traits are admitted to have a dangerous prevalence that they were denied in his earlier work. The admission itself is the real basis of the charge that he lost hope.

How true is the charge? The book certainly has sayings which would be at home in Hobbes or Mandeville:

> Reflection makes men cowards. There is no object that can be put in competition with life, unless it is viewed through the medium of passion, and we are hurried away by the impulse of the moment.
> (IX, 201)

> It makes us proud when our love of a mistress is returned: it ought to make us prouder that we can love her for herself alone, without the aid of any such selfish reflection. (IX, 202)

> Friendship is cemented by interest, vanity, or the want of amusement: it seldom implies esteem or even mutual regard. (IX, 226)

Such passages suggest that a close attention to the motives of men will oblige us to admit vanity as a motive of friendship, and pride as a motive of love, and selfish prudence as a consideration more influential than passion in the conduct of human affairs. "The seat of knowledge," Hazlitt observes, "is in the head; of wisdom, in the heart. We are sure to judge wrong, if we do not feel right." It may appear that he has changed from the force of his own observation that men do act from the head, and do judge wrong: thinking is helpless where feeling is corrupt. But to end here would belie a premise to which Hazlitt constantly recurs in his aphorisms, that our bad motives are also mixed motives.

> Envy, among other ingredients, has a mixture of the love of justice in it. We are more angry at undeserved than at deserved good-fortune.
> (IX, 169)

So too, our self-indulgent vices protect us from more devastating ones.

> Profound hypocrisy is inconsistent with vanity: for the last would betray our designs by some premature triumph. Indeed, vanity implies a sympathy with others, and consummate hypocrisy is built on a total want of it. (IX, 224)

Neither what is selfish nor what is selfless in our motives now seems to Hazlitt of much practical consequence. For in their first state our motives are almost always double.

> Those people who are fond of giving trouble like to take it; just as those who pay no attention to the comforts of others, are generally indifferent to their own. We are governed by sympathy, and the extent of our sympathy is determined by that of our sensibility. (IX, 226)

Thus sympathy includes sympathy with ourselves: those who attend wisely to their own interests will *if they choose* attend wisely to the interests of others. At least, the two forms of attention are more often found together than apart. With this coincidence in mind Hazlitt is in a position to return to the *Essay*'s understanding of habit:

> The secret of our self-love is just the same as that of our liberality and candour. We prefer ourselves to others, only because we have a more intimate consciousness and confirmed opinion of our own claims and merits than of any other person's. (IX, 170)

It is only our being accustomed to ourselves that weights the balance of action toward ourselves. But the relation between self-regard and attention to others cannot be represented adequately by the figure of a balance, since the weight on one side must in this case entail weight on the other, and they must either remain fixed or go down together.

The findings of the *Essay* might even be supposed to gain a new authority in *Characteristics*, by the detection of sympathy in what appear to be our most selfish or vicious actions.

> The error in the reasonings of Mandeville, Rochefoucault, and others, is this: they first find out that there is something mixed in the motives of all our actions, and they then proceed to argue, that they must all arise from one motive, *viz.* self-love. They make the exception the rule. It would be easy to reverse the argument, and prove that our most selfish actions are disinterested. There is honour among thieves. Robbers, murderers, &c. do not commit those actions, from a pleasure in pure villainy, or for their own

benefit only, but from a mistaken regard to the welfare or good opinion of those with whom they are immediately connected.

(IX, 184)

The aphoristic strategy here is remarkable. The aim of any romantic aphorist is first to invert or twist the proverbial wisdom on some topic, so as to discover truth under an unfamiliar aspect; and then to subject the aphorism itself to a further inversion or twist, so as to reveal the truth it carries as provisional also. One can see this happening in Nietzsche's, "A people is a detour of nature to get to six or seven great men.—Yes, and then to get around them."[41] The genius is in the second turn. But Hazlitt, though he commonly shows us the possibility of some such turn, and makes us share the pause while he estimates its brilliance, seldom allows himself the pleasure of completing it. Preserving the aphorist's detachment from common valuations and therefore, apparently, from the common equipment-for-living we extract from sayings, he uses this attitude to restore the proverbial wisdom on his chosen topic, as if that were the last imaginable gift of an aphorism. Hence, "There is honour among thieves."

A test case for Hazlitt's belief that our motives cannot all be reduced to self-interest or benevolence, is the character of a hypocrite. For the hypocrite puts a face of disinterested concern on actions that are really self-serving, and gains a reputation for moral probity only by concealing his service to vice. The Hobbesian wisdom about him is plain: he enforces, as a conscious practice, what the rest of us are compelled to do in any case; the chief difference is that we shall never cause our neighbors discomfort by being unmasked, since we are hypocrites only to ourselves. La Rochefoucauld summed up this view of the matter, "Hypocrisy is the homage that vice pays to virtue." But, recalling such summary dismissals as he came to write his own aphorism about the same character, Hazlitt observed a distinction. If what we see of a man is that he does not practice what he preaches, we do not know enough to call him a hypocrite; and if we withhold our judgments of such men, the character is much less widespread than La Rochefoucauld had supposed.

> It does not follow that a man is a hypocrite, because his actions give the lie to his words. If he at one time seems a saint, and at other times a sinner, he possibly is both in reality, as well as in appearance. A person may be fond of vice and of virtue too; and practise one or the other, according to the temptation of the moment. A priest may be pious, and a sot or bigot. A woman may be modest, and a rake at heart. A poet may admire the beauties of nature, and

be envious of those of other writers. A moralist may act contrary to his own precepts, and yet be sincere in recommending them to others. These are indeed contradictions, but they arise out of the contradictory qualities in our nature. A man is a hypocrite only when he affects to take a delight in what he does not feel, not because he takes a perverse delight in opposite things.   (IX, 206)

This reasoning, which came naturally to a reader well acquainted with characters like Falstaff, Edmund, Angelo, and Cleopatra, leads to the further suggestion that the man who preaches vice may actually be worse than the man who practices it, since a professed concern for morality is the first concession we make to the feelings that cement persons into a society. The presence of *any* hypocrisy may testify less therefore to the blindness than to the acknowledged strength of virtue.

If we still feel that Hazlitt's emphasis falls unwarrantably on examples of vice, it must be remembered that in *Characteristics* he is writing about man as he is in society, and has vowed to do so "in the manner of" La Rochefoucauld. Only once does he fall so thoroughly into this manner that the author of the *Essay* seems to have been left behind. "Vice," he tells us, "is man's nature: virtue is a habit— or a mask." On Hazlitt's earlier view, self-love and benevolence are both parts of our nature, either of which may become stronger through habit. To call virtue a habit, and a habit only, instead of one innate potentiality among others in man, which will emerge or not depending on whether we encourage it or "sear it away"—to speak thus is pointed, but imperfectly worthy of the principled metaphysician he wished to be. To call virtue a "mask" goes still further. It is calling hypocrisy the homage that vice pays to virtue.

Immediately after saying this, Hazlitt regrets it and attributes his lapse to the very structure of aphoristic thinking, by which he has been seduced into falsehood: "The foregoing maxim shews the difference between truth and sarcasm." This may mean, of course, only that the maxim is a truth, and any milder estimate of human nature merely a sarcasm; or that in the maxim itself, truth and sarcasm make a compound. The more one ponders Hazlitt's self-criticism, however, the more convinced one becomes that he felt a division within the aphoristic sentence. At some point it stopped being truth, and the author was left alone with the trophies of a cynical frolic. We certainly feel some such break at the dash in "habit—or a mask." It enforces too sharp a distinction between nature and habit. If some virtues have to be encouraged, we must not assume that they are less "natural" on that account. At the same time, as Hazlitt must have realized, the presence of any distinction at all between nature and habit—and it is a distinction we acknowledge by our very use of the words—takes the edge off the first part of the aphorism. By our recognition that vicious actions grow habitual more easily than virtuous ones, we are not entitled to regard the former as wholly natural, or the latter as wholly artificial.

Here are Hazlitt's final reflections on the good of resolving benevolence into self-love, or any one passion or interest into any other:

> Self-love, in a word, is sympathy with myself, that is, it is I who feel it, and I who am the object of it: in benevolence or compassion, it is I who still feel sympathy, but another (not myself) is the object of it. If I feel sympathy with others at all, it must be disinterested. The pleasure it may give me is the consequence, not the cause, of my feeling it. To insist that sympathy is self-love because we cannot feel for others, without being ourselves affected pleasurably or painfully, is to make nonsense of the question; for it is to insist that in order to feel for others properly and truly, we must in the first place feel nothing. *C'est une mauvaise plaisanterie.*
>
> (IX, 185)

"If I feel sympathy with others at all, it must be disinterested": about the truth of this insight Hazlitt remains unshaken. In return for a sympathetic action, or a *display* of sympathetic feeling, I may expect to receive gratitude, or some palpable good to myself. But from the sympathetic feeling itself, before I display it or convert it into action, I gain nothing. I can hardly choose to stop having such feelings, though the pleasure I derive from them is often mingled with, or overbalanced by, pain. "Sympathy" is a useful word, and has remained in the language, because it names something complex, relating to the self and others, and to pain not less than to pleasure.[42]

That Hazlitt never recanted his metaphysical discovery is what must be remembered most steadily as one observes the progress of his career. This adherence to a principle was the leading trait of his character, and of his intellect; so it was perceived by himself, and by his friends and antagonists. To explain much of what is said about him by Wordsworth and Coleridge, and some of Hazlitt's criticism of them, one has to see that he refused to change his mind, with respect either to this moral principle or the political allegiances that followed from it, when to do so would have been opportune and thoroughly pardonable. Unless one holds this trait in view, it will be difficult to see how he could become not only a literary preceptor but something of a personal hero for Keats. He was the sworn adherent of a cause, with the unalterable resoluteness and contempt for wavering allies that the dissenters of all ages have found necessary if they were to pursue an undeviating course.

Hazlitt's discovery is sufficiently plain and sufficiently profound to attract and retain the allegiance of a subtle mind. Its qualifications, not so much in what it asserts of the imagination, as in what it reluctantly admits of habit and the love of power, may seem in retrospect as important as its central argument. Indeed, it is these that show us why Hazlitt was so well equipped to become a critic of the "egotistical sublime," and why he was able, almost alone in his time, to leave us a sustained discussion of the achievements and limitations of what came to be called romanticism, and yet to do so from a point of view sympathetic to romanticism. Already, in parts of the *Essay*, Hazlitt had begun to recognize that power is no less at home in the mind than sympathy. It was left for him to explain what an uneasy companionship power and sympathy make. Now and then, in his later writings, they seem to inhabit entirely different and exclusive portions of the mind, as if there were two distinct faculties that went by the same name of imagination. Yet even when Hazlitt spoke of the love of power as a necessary, at times a defining, attribute of the poetic imagination, he was prevented by his first principle from ever putting aside the claim of sympathy. Genuine poetry without power is a contradiction in terms, whereas poetry can indeed subsist on the narrowest of sympathies, and can find strength in doing so. But in that case it forfeits something of its stature.

Hazlitt retraced the argument of the *Essay* in his Preface to Tucker, in a *New Monthly Magazine* dialogue "On Self-Love and Benevolence,"[43] and again in the *Table-Talk* essay "On the Past and Future." But the most stirring avowal of his pride in the *Essay* occurs at the end of "A Letter to William Gifford." The passage is all the more striking because the "Letter" for the most part sustains a grandly impersonal tone. Gifford was worth Hazlitt's attention only in his official role as editor of the Tory *Quarterly Review:* "the *Government Critic*," as Hazlitt called him, "a character nicely differing from that of a government spy—the invisible link, that connects literature with the police." But this Government Critic had damned *The Round Table* and Hazlitt's books on Shakespeare and the English poets, with all the threadbare rhetorical stances, of derision, bewilderment, fake humility, and slander, which Peacock catalogued in "An Essay on Fashionable Literature." Leigh Hunt was able to respond to such tactics by writing "Ultra-Crepidarius," a mock epic in which Gifford appears as a curmudgeonly *shoe,* envious of Venus's slipper and anxiously inquiring into its pedigree. Hazlitt's reaction was bound to be stronger: less willing than Hunt to be identified with a party of his own, he was more vulnerable to the stings of party malice. From the opening sentence of his "Letter to William Gifford": "You have an ugly trick of saying what is not true of any one you do not like; and it will be the object of this letter to cure you of it"—to the opening paragraph of "Mr. Gifford" in *The Spirit of the Age,* where Hazlitt's opinion of so many other Tories seems to have mellowed:

> Mr. Gifford was originally bred to some handicraft: he afterwards contrived to learn Latin, and was for some time an usher in a school, till he became a tutor in a nobleman's family. The low-bred, self-taught man, the pedant, and the dependant on the great contribute to form the Editor of the *Quarterly Review.* He is admirably qualified for this situation, which he has held for some years, by a happy combination of defects, natural and acquired; and in the event of his death, it will be difficult to provide him a suitable successor. (XI, 114)

—there is never any mellowing toward Gifford. He was the spokesman of a single interest, and his career had become to Hazlitt a living allegory of the spite, rancor, and servility of prostituted intelligence.

At the end of his letter Hazlitt makes an effort to explain his principles to the man who has waded so far into opposite ones: his summary of the old argument is curious for its movement from satire to confession. Before rehearsing the *Essay* for Gifford, however, he wonders how Wordsworth and Coleridge can ever have reconciled themselves to their new allies in the *Quarterly.* He concludes that in the poets the love of power has at last conquered the love of truth. Yet, with characteristic generosity, he mentions their eagerness for "honours, places, and pensions" as the one infirmity of genius, and accounts for his different conduct by the intellectual pride to which years of thinking had brought a lesser and more constant mind.

> The spirit of poetry is, as I believe, favourable to liberty and humanity, but not when its aid is most wanted, in encountering the shocks and disappointments of the world. Poetry may be described as having the range of the universe; it traverses the empyrean, and

looks down on nature from a higher sphere. When it lights upon the earth, it loses some of its dignity and its use. Its strength is in its wings; its element is the air. Standing on its feet, jostling with the crowd, it is liable to be overthrown, trampled on, and defaced; for its wings are of a dazzling brightness, "sky-tinctured," and the least soil upon them shews to disadvantage. Sullied, degraded as I have seen it, I shall not here insult over it, but leave it to Time to take out the stains, seeing it is a thing immortal as itself. "Being so majestical, I should do it wrong to offer it but the shew of violence."—The reason why I have not changed my principles with some of the persons here alluded to, is, that I had a natural inveteracy of understanding which did not bend to fortune or circumstances. I was not a poet, but a metaphysician; and I suspect that the conviction of an abstract principle is alone a match for the prejudices of absolute power. The love of truth is the best foundation for the love of liberty. In this sense, I might have repeated—

> "Love is not love that alteration finds:
> Oh! no, it is an everfixed mark,
> That looks on tempests and is never shaken."

Besides, I had another reason. I owed something to truth, for she had done something for me. Early in life I had made (what I thought) a metaphysical discovery; and after that, it was too late to think of retracting. My pride forbad it: my understanding revolted at it. I could not do better than go on as I had begun. I too, worshipped at no unhallowed shrine, and served in no mean presence. I had laid my hand on the ark, and could not turn back!

(IX, 50–51)

CHAPTER III

WHY THE ARTS
ARE NOT PROGRESSIVE

PREDILECTIONS

Hazlitt's great years as a writer for periodicals, roughly from 1815 to 1820, owed much to the receptiveness of three journals: *The Morning Chronicle, The Examiner,* and *The Edinburgh Review.* The first, a daily, generally liberal in tone, could tolerate a writer like Hazlitt because it could absorb him; when after a time his personality began to be unmistakable from one article to the next, he became a liability; but by then he was ready to move out of the *Chronicle's* orbit. The *Examiner* and the *Edinburgh Review,* from supporting him through several phases of their own existence, notwithstanding lapses of months or years, may be said once they encountered him never to have quit his company. The *Examiner* had a weekly circulation of almost ten thousand for certain issues, but, as the liveliest resource of the liberal and republican middle class, it exerted an influence beyond what numbers can suggest. A writer in its columns was allowed space for a paragraph about *Comus,* and could expect his readers to be unpedantically informed about Cromwell, the history of the masque, and utilitarian discussions of chastity. The editors were Leigh Hunt and his brother John: to the latter Hazlitt dedicated *Political Essays,* describing him as "a friend in need, a patriot without an eye to himself; who never betrayed an individual or a cause he pretended to serve—in short, that rare character, a man of common sense and common honesty."

The *Edinburgh Review* occupied a very different place in Hazlitt's intellectual economy. It brought him glamor; and he claimed, with less irony than one may at first suppose: "To be an Edinburgh Reviewer is, I suspect, the highest rank in modern literary society." Almost from its founding, the *Edinburgh* had become a clearinghouse for what De Quincey fastidiously called "Whiggism in its relations to liteɪature." It was read on three continents, and had a gift which it never quite reduced to a principle, of finding out uncommon talents before the public had heard of them: Stendhal, when still unknown in any other capacity, could be read in the *Edinburgh* among its European correspondents. Hazlitt's notes to the editor, Francis Jeffrey, in search of new assignments, and to his successor Macvey Napier, are surprisingly in the key of humble-servant requests. But he never sounded them for their opinions, and there would have been an irony detectable even to Napier, in his writing as late as 1829: "The only reason why I presume to think my articles may *do* for the *Edinburgh* . . . is that they make perhaps a variety. If not so good, they are different from others, and so far, are the better for being worse." As for Jeffrey, he served Hazlitt not only as editor but as legal counsel, and in the years between Hazlitt's first article for the magazine and his deathbed request for a final loan from Jeffrey to "consummate your many kindnesses," relations between them grew strained only once, when Jeffrey reviewing *The Spirit of the Age* suggested that the author was too brilliant to be taken quite seriously.

If Hazlitt was content to appear in any publication that let him say what he pleased, he nevertheless rated these two as peculiarly suited to him. To adapt a remark of Johnson's, one may say that though he wrote for the *Edinburgh* like a man who remembered he was writing for the *Edinburgh,* he wrote for the *Examiner* like one who lets thoughts drop from his pen as they rise into his mind.

In 1812, when his reviews and comments started appearing in the *Morning Chronicle,* the taste of the public had the assurance of a finished fact. One went to Benjamin West for paintings, sound historical paintings, meant to crowd the mind and cover a wall; to Fanny Burney for prose romances; and to Rogers and Scott for poetry. How secure the consensus seemed, to all but the most confident rebels against it, may be surmised from one of Byron's journal entries for 1813, a diagram of the modern *Gradus ad Parnassum* which accords with what we know of the age and much that we have preferred to forget about Byron (see page 106). This was seriously intended. Scott, in Byron's view, "is undoubtedly the Monarch of Parnassus, and the most *English* of bards. I should place Rogers next," though as "the last of the *best* school." A little more of this and Byron is done, hardly troubled by the murmur of doubt which he thinks he should record: "I have ranked the names upon my triangle more upon what I believe popular opinion, than any decided opinion of

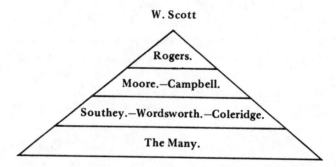

W. Scott

Rogers.

Moore.—Campbell.

Southey.—Wordsworth.—Coleridge.

The Many.

my own."[1] No *decided opinion:* it is the sort of hesitation most readers have felt at most times. Today we might propose a different triangle, with Wordsworth at the pinnacle, Keats in a penultimate chamber to himself, followed at no great remove by Shelley, Coleridge, and Byron. We have had a century and a half to reconstruct the diagram.

Hazlitt reached conclusions similar to ours, but with less effort and much less hesitation, undeterred by what he believed to be the state of public opinion. He dealt out verdicts with a relish of decision that might have seemed impossible after Johnson's death. But, in this respect more elusive even than Johnson, he appears to have worked without a plan. He had no notion of fitting out a splendid role for himself to play; for he never wished to mold the minds of readers. He left the record of his own impressions, and they would do. So he wrote of Benjamin West's paintings, that beyond "the negative and instrumental parts of the art" they were "nothing."

> Perhaps in the entire body of Mr. West's productions, however meritorious the design and composition often are, there is not to be found a single instance of exquisite sentiment, or colour, or drawing; not one face or figure, hand or eye, which can be dwelt upon as an essence of its kind; as carrying truth, or beauty, or grandeur, to that height of excellence to which they have been sometimes carried, and beyond which the mind has no wish or conception that they should go. (XVIII, 30–31)

Of Fanny Burney:

> Her characters, whether of refinement or vulgarity, are equally superficial and confined. The whole is a question of form, whether that form is adhered to, or violated. It is this circumstance which takes away dignity and interest from her story and sentiments, and makes the one so teazing and tedious, and the other so insipid.

. . . The author appears to have no other idea of refinement than that it is the reverse of vulgarity; but the reverse of vulgarity is fastidiousness and affectation.   (XVI, 22)

Of Rogers's poetry, that "his verses are poetry, chiefly because no particle, line, or syllable of them reads like prose"; and of Scott's, that it "has all the good qualities that the world agree to understand," including "neither depth, height, nor breadth . . . neither uncommon strength, nor uncommon refinement of thought, sentiment, or language. It has no originality."

These passages belong to the first five years of Hazlitt's journalism: he spoke, from the first, for genius, and he had a distinct advantage over friends and rivals alike: he was fearless.

But it was an age in which a man of Hazlitt's convictions required some such quality to survive—that, or an insouciance equal in practice to any bravery. After Waterloo, the Tory style of attack favored in *Blackwood's Magazine* and other strongholds of self-amused merciless invective, coarsened beyond what any earlier generation had known, to the brink of one continuous libel. So when Leigh Hunt followed his own advice to Hazlitt and lay low, he had to watch in silence while his reputation was buried under a heap of epithets: "eunuch," "Cockney," "You exquisite idiot. . . . You deserve, sir, for this parenthesis, to be hung up by the little finger till you are dead!"[2] Hunt, to his credit, kept quiet as he had resolved to do; Hazlitt, to his, did not. Described as "a mere ulcer, a sore from head to foot, a poor devil, so completely flayed, that there is not a square half-inch of healthy flesh on his carcass,"[3] he found himself in a mood to reply. His occasion was supplied by the appearance of "eight queries," addressed to him by the so-called "young men" of *Blackwood's,* but signed only "Z," all contributing to forge an analogy between Hazlitt's loose morals as a writer (plagiarism) and as a man (anything). The reply came swiftly:

Before I answer your questions, give me leave to tell you my opinion of the person who asks them. I think then that you are a person of little understanding, with great impudence, a total want of principle, an utter disregard to truth or even to the character of common veracity, and a very strong ambition to be picked up and paid as a cat's-paw. If I were in the habit of using the words, Liar, Fool, Coxcomb, Hypocrite, Scoundrel, Blackguard, &c, I should apply them to you, but this would be degrading them still lower unnecessarily, for it is quite as easy to prove you the *things* as to call you the *names*.   (IX, 3)

Instead of publishing this, however, Hazlitt decided to retain his counsel, pointing out those statements which "seem to me particularly actionable" from having been written with the clear intent to deprive him of employment. At the threat of protracted litigation John Murray withdrew his backing from *Blackwood's,* and Hazlitt won a settlement out of court. Had the contest been fought in words alone, he would have won still more decisively.

From the point of view of the Tory press, Hazlitt was important because by 1818 he was among the most widely esteemed independent critics. He himself saw no vast importance in what he wrote, piece by piece; and this reluctance to urge his own claims has come down to us as one more illustration of a journalist's disenchantment: somehow the work does not add up. Yet the truth is that Hazlitt was an exception to this rule, and was so perceived by his contemporaries, not only among the sympathetic "circle" of Bewick, J. H. Reynolds, and the friends of Keats, but also in the daily notations of Crabb Robinson, whose entry into Lake-school society demanded a cooling of his friendship with Hazlitt, and even a resolution to end all relations with him, frequently broken by surreptitious and well-chaperoned visits to the excommunicant. We may take Robinson to typify the hostile part of Hazlitt's usual audience; intelligent, innocent of cleverness, always lamenting the author's waste of God-given powers and always curious to see what he would do next. In both reading and conversation, Robinson sought out the edifying figures of his own party, in the hope of forming, at least to his diary's satisfaction, some comparison unfavorable to Hazlitt. With opportunities as remote from each other as those afforded by Coleridge and Scott, he was still disappointed. Something about Hazlitt's tone stayed in the mind.

In six months at the *Morning Chronicle* Hazlitt tells us he produced seventy columns "on every conceivable subject," while the paper's circulation grew impressively. But there were scrapes with James Perry, the editor, who liked to take credit for having written the articles he published, and found Hazlitt's work troubling to his reputation; the morning's clear paragraphs were too often irreconcilable with the genial sentiments Perry had expressed at dinner the evening before, to a favorite actress or manager. Perry of course took advantage of the situation when he could, and in *A View of the English Stage* Hazlitt recalls his own pleasure at having met "Miss Stephens coming out of the Editor's room, who had been to thank him for his very flattering account of her"; but in the *Table-*

Talk essay "On Patronage and Puffing," he adds: "Poor Perry! what bitter complaints he used to make, that by *running-a-muck* at lords and Scotchmen I should not leave him a place to dine out at! The expression of his face at these moments, as if he should shortly be without a friend in the world, was truly pitiable." Careless of his own prospects as a diner-out, Hazlitt left the *Chronicle* at what proved to be a fortunate time, with Hunt's *Examiner,* John Scott's *Champion* and later the *London Magazine,* ready to take up the slack.

Yet he brought controversy wherever he went. It is characteristic that, after a particularly vigorous sally which ended in his being knocked to the floor by Charles Lamb's brother, he rose to offer a handshake with simple cordiality, neither to apologize nor to protest: "I am a metaphysician, and nothing but an *idea* hurts me." By friends who understood his energies, he was acknowledged to have "great impartiality of assault,"[4] in person as well as in print; a mixed virtue that became intolerable when the characters of Hunt and Shelley were turned into neat abstracts for his table-talks. Hunt, chiding him for this abuse of friendship and disservice to the radical cause, "this dog-in-the-manger philosophy, which will have neither one thing nor t'other"[5]—even Hunt *in extremis,* failed to stimulate regrets: "I have always spoken well of you," Hazlitt wrote him back, "to friend or foe, *viz* I have said you were one of the pleasantest and cleverest persons I ever knew; but that you teazed any one you had to deal with out of their lives."[6] *Extravagances of stomach,* Hunt called such moods in Hazlitt, and by his choice of words forgave them.

THE COCKNEY SCHOOL

Because they were men of genius, possessed sympathies as perfect as rival gifts could make them, and never joined "the unclean side" in politics, Lamb and Hunt were the company Hazlitt liked best. "The present," he would write, near the end of his life, "is an age of talkers, not of doers; and the reason is, that the world is growing old." He was thinking of Coleridge: but during Hazlitt's great decade, his mentor was to be found holding forth at Highgate, to a more youthful circle of admirers. We are too apt to remember Coleridge as he appeared in his earlier years, and as Hazlitt more than anyone else has fixed him in our minds—"sounding on his way," heedless of the new channels of thought he made for those who took him as their guide; a figure who "in digressing, in dilating, in passing from subject to subject" appeared "to float in air, to slide on ice." But to recover the perspective of 1820, we have to set beside this Coleridge the very different figure who now appeared regularly before a gathering of the faithful and the curious—the Coleridge of whom Thomas Carlyle wrote: "The moaning singsong of that theosophico-metaphysical monotony left on you, at last, a very dreary feeling." A lifetime of monologue had taken its toll, and the prose that Hazlitt found a willful contrivance had become a sad necessity.

In contrast, Lamb and Hunt were expansive. Their talk met the highest expectations of those not in want of oracular wisdom; and Hazlitt enjoyed their different styles of address as a set-off to his own. Mr. Leigh Hunt "improves upon acquaintance," he wrote in *The Spirit of the Age.* "The author translates admirably into the man." Hazlitt did not always think so, but he could always remind himself that Hunt's "high animal spirits, and the *vinous* quality of his mind, produce an immediate fascination and intoxication in those who come in contact with him, and carry off in society whatever in his writings may to some seem flat and impertinent." Still, Hunt's "teazing" has not been forgotten, even if it can be met with equanimity: "We have said that Lord Byron is a sublime coxcomb: why should we not say that Mr. Hunt is a delightful one?" The history of a friendship is contained in that sentence. The more complicated but finally deeper affection that Hazlitt felt for Lamb receives its fullest expression in the same book. Lamb is praised for excelling "in familiar conversation almost as much as in writing, when his modesty does not overpower his self-possession. He is as little of a proser as possible; but he *blurts* out the finest wit and sense in the world."

Lamb, Hazlitt, and Hunt perhaps do not make a critical school between them, but if they did one might praise it as the least moralistic school that ever was. For Hazlitt, the sufficient moral of *The Beggar's Opera* was "the *vulgarity* of vice." In the same key Lamb noted that "there is scarce one of [Hogarth's] pieces where vice is most strongly satirised, in which some figure is not introduced upon which the moral eye may rest satisfied"—but, "A little does it, a little of the *good* nature overpowers a world of *bad*." Both critics were thus saved from the consolidating pieties of the Regency years. They owed their strength in part to an early acquaintance with the theatre, and familiarity with its artifices. The comic actors of "the last

age," when performing Congreve or Wycherley, had always revealed
the distance between themselves and their roles, and delighted an
audience which understood this distance to be the essence of comedy. Since then a new audience had taken charge, and it was scandalized. "I must," wrote Lamb, "conclude the present generation of
playgoers more virtuous than myself, or more dense." Hazlitt blamed
"those *do-me-good*, lack-a-daisical, whining, make-believe comedies
of the next age" after Farquhar, on the heels of which came modern
sentimentality. Hunt joined his friends but without their intimate
knowledge of a gone era, and for his part believed that the theatre's
moral vigilance and emotional feebleness were associated with the
style of acting which he immortalized as "clap-trapping." But whatever the cause assigned, all three critics were unhappy with the loss
of a resilience any living art demands of its audiences. "We would
indict our dreams," Lamb wrote—if we could be sure that they had
no tendency to improve us.

In our time Hunt's reputation has sunk lower than either Hazlitt's or Lamb's. But though he helped to mar his fortunes in his
own lifetime, by publishing rather diffusely and, in his memoirs of
Byron, recklessly, he is due for a serious revival. The risks he took
to protect his independence are not less admirable from having
been calculated for dramatic effect: refusing to accept free tickets
for the theatrical performances he was to review; describing the
Prince Regent as "a violator of his word, a libertine over head and
ears in debt and disgrace, a despiser of domestic ties, the companion
of gamblers and demireps, a man who has just closed half a century
without one single claim on the gratitude of his country or the respect of posterity";[7] and, on the verge of the trial for libel that soon
followed, addressing the judge, Lord Ellenborough, in print, with a
lecture on the deportment proper to his station. By the time Hazlitt
first visited Hunt in prison, he must already have felt bound to him
by many loyalties; and he agreed to take over a great share of the
writing, in more than one department, that was necessary to keep
the *Examiner* afloat. To the republican cause Lamb of course contributed an occasional squib or jest: but when one thinks of Hazlitt,
the most dependable of all the "Wednesday-evening men" at Lamb's,
breaking his routine again and again to revisit Hunt in prison and
buoy his spirits, one realizes how far Hazlitt alone served to unite
the other two.

Among them there was a nice parcelling out of allegiances. Hazlitt and Hunt shared *The Examiner;* Hunt and Lamb, the comic

temperament with its master-trait, puns; Lamb and Hazlitt, a suspicion of the exclusionist taste already being inculcated by "the Lake school." Important as the last point of accord may seem, it indicated no profound affinity of temperament. For Lamb derived himself from a recondite ancestry—from Thomas Browne, Robert Burton, and unpredictable others: in a phrase or sentence he can summon the exuberance of Shakespeare's prose as well. Hazlitt concluded that his friend had a fine tact for the "blind alleys" of literature, then reframed the epigram as a compliment: "His style runs pure and clear, though it may often take an underground course, or be conveyed through old-fashioned conduit-pipes."

It is Hunt who yields the more satisfying comparison with Hazlitt's own prose. Their shared predecessors among eighteenth-century authors, however, would not have sufficed to link them in the public mind, without a shared fondness for the types and haunts of London, with which both maintained an ease of commerce that never relaxed into quaintness. Like Hazlitt in "The Fight," Hunt could stamp a scene forever on the mind, as part of the unending mock epic of actual life: gradually the mockery fades and an unforced dignity remains. We feel in such scenes, what ought to be less surprising than it is, the work of a democracy of the affections. On his way to the Neate-Hickman fight, Hazlitt—as he reminds us obliquely—had been brooding on Sarah Walker's rejection of him; until the "tall English yeoman" he found at an inn, "making a prodigious noise about rents and taxes, and the price of corn now and formerly," dismissed someone who wanted to call off a bet, saying "Confound it, man, don't be *insipid!*"—at which, from the blackness of self-sorrows Hazlitt was roused. "Thinks I, that is a good phrase." His comment after the fight to P. G. Patmore, who had displayed a copy of *La Nouvelle Héloïse* in his pocket, shows Hazlitt at his usual distance both from vulgarity and affectation.

> The delight Hazlitt expressed [was] at meeting with the work under *such* circumstances, and at the sort of feeling which *he* must have for it who could make it his companion to such a scene as we had just left. "Why, then," he said, "you actually had the 'Nouvelle Héloise' in your pocket all the while you were watching those fellows this morning, mauling and hacking at each other, like devils incarnate! Well, I confess, that's a cut above me. I can 'applaud the deed'; but to have done it is beyond me. In putting the book into my pocket, I should have had some silly scruples— some indelicate feelings of delicacy, come across me, and I should

have left it at home. It's the highest thing I remember—a piece of real intellectual refinement, by G-d! and I congratulate you upon it."[8]

He was never more cheerful than in pointing out refinement where it might not have been supposed to lie; as when he ends his great essay on genius, "The Indian Jugglers," with an epitaph for John Cavanagh, "the famous hand fives-player."

> He was a fine, sensible, manly player, who did what he could, but that was more than any one else could even affect to do. His blows were not undecided and ineffectual . . . wavering like Mr. Coleridge's lyric prose, nor short of the mark like Mr. Brougham's speeches, nor wide of it like Mr. Canning's wit, nor foul like the *Quarterly,* nor *let* balls like the *Edinburgh Review.* Cobbett and Junius together would have made a Cavanagh. (VIII, 87)

Lighter in his graces and better equipped than Hazlitt to sound the by-ways of common emotions, Hunt is also less bold. He slides from the center of a paradox that interests him, to the punch line of a joke that interests his audience. His is an art of deflection. The closest he comes to the passage quoted from "The Indian Jugglers" is an essay "On the Graces and Anxieties of Pig-Driving," where the difference from Hazlitt—a touch of mischief not without archness—can be felt even in his title. The pig-driver has a mean occupation or what is esteemed so, but Hunt uses his observations of one man, Jenkins, to fashion a heroic counter-example.

> He was a born genius for a manoeuvre. Had he originated in a higher sphere he would have been a general, or a stage-manager, or, at least, the head of a set of monks. Conflicting interests were his forte; pig-headed wills, and proceedings hopeless. To see the *hand* with which he did it! How hovering, yet firm; how encouraging, yet compelling; how indicative of the space on each side of him, and yet of the line before him; how general, how particular, how perfect! No barber's could quiver about a head with more lightness of apprehension; no cook's pat up and proportion the side of a pasty with a more final eye. The whales, quoth old Chapman, speaking of Neptune,
>
> "The whales exulted under him, and knew their mighty king."
>
> The pigs did not exult, but they knew their king. Unwilling was their subjection, but "more in sorrow than in anger." They were too far gone for rage. Their case was hopeless. They did not see why they should proceed, but they felt themselves bound to do so;

forced, conglomerated, crowded onwards, irresistibly impelled by fate and Jenkins.[9]

At the end of the piece we feel less certain of the author's breadth of sympathies than we did at the beginning. A great many details have been harnessed, and beautifully knotted and cinched, until the eulogy almost exists for its own sake. The style is a miracle of small pleasures. The essayist has spent much time learning to be exquisite, in just the right degree.

Yet this impression is true for only one of Hunt's moods. His fund of "animal spirits" was always ready to supply the needs of essay-writing, and when, with Keats's help, he composed an essay "Descriptive of a Hot Day," he could borrow from a stock of images that had crossed his vision but a moment before, without any time to be cast into molds.

> Now delicate skins are beset with gnats; and boys make their sleeping companion start up, with playing a burning-glass on his hand; and blacksmiths are super-carbonated; and cobblers in their stalls almost feel a wish to be transplanted; and butter is too easy to spread; and the dragoons wonder whether the Romans liked their helmets; and old ladies, with their lappets unpinned, walk along in a state of dilapidation; and the servant maids are afraid they look vulgarly hot; and the author, who has a plate of strawberries brought him, finds that he has come to the end of his writings.[10]

He can be the most spontaneous of essayists, and in this respect a fit rival for Hazlitt, who often prepared himself for writing *in* writing, as for a chore but with perfect panache. Title written, the rest had better follow.

On Living to one's-self

> "Remote, unfriended, melancholy, slow,
>   Or by the lazy Scheldt or wandering Po."

> I never was in a better place or humour than I am at present for writing on this subject. I have a partridge getting ready for my supper, my fire is blazing on the hearth, the air is mild for the season of the year, I have had but a slight fit of indigestion to-day (the only thing that makes me abhor myself), I have three hours good before me, and therefore I will attempt it. It is as well to do it at once as to have it to do for a week to come.   (VIII, 90)

Implicit in such passages, though with all solemnity charmed away, is a conviction that one's work, to deserve the name *essay,* must propose a trial of some sort: above all of the writer's susceptibility, of the keenness with which he exhibits the links between his ideas and impressions. Memory is viewed as the residuum of the essayist's personality, without which his invention cannot advance a jot: the work of the essayist is so to station himself that the segregate elements of experience are released together, and can test each other's truths. Judged by this standard, Hazlitt and Hunt are innovators, while Lamb confines himself to the researches of the antiquarian. Introducing himself as a loller about town, with a tolerable regimen of sedentary topics, he has an air of dallying and asking our indulgence in just those matters that he would have us regard with a serious sympathy. It must be added that Lamb's criticism is one long triumph of the powers that he allows to languish in his essays. His reply, for example, to Southey's advice that he join all sensible men in ostracizing Hazlitt, moves with a singleness of resolve that no admirer of the Elia-manner could have predicted.

> I stood well with [Hazlitt] for fifteen years (the proudest of my life), and have ever spoke my full mind of him to some, to whom his panegyric must naturally be least tasteful. I never in thought swerved from him, I never betrayed him, I never slackened in my admiration of him, I was the same to him (neither better nor worse) though he could not see it, as in the days when he thought fit to trust me. At this instant he may be preparing for me some compliment, above my deserts, as he has sprinkled many such among his admirable books, for which I rest his debtor; or, for any thing I know, or can guess to the contrary, he may be about to read a lecture on my weaknesses. He is welcome to them (as he was to my humble hearth), if they can divert a spleen, or ventilate a fit of sullenness. . . . Protesting against much that he has written, and some things which he chooses to do; judging him by his conversation which I enjoyed so long, and relished so deeply; or by his books, in those places where no clouding passion intervenes—I should belie my own conscience, if I said less, than that I think W. H. to be, in his natural and healthy state, one of the wisest and finest spirits breathing. So far from being ashamed of that intimacy, which was betwixt us, it is my boast that I was able for so many years to have preserved it entire; and I think I shall go to my grave without finding, or expecting to find, such another companion.[11]

This affirmation restored a trust which for a time appeared to have weakened on both sides. Lamb writes as a defender who cannot be shamed out of friendship—even, a little, as a protector affording Hazlitt some temporary shelter. That he should need to do so tells us how far Hazlitt had placed himself outside any literary set that might have provided him not with a temporary success but with the secure tenure in journalism which great gifts alone could never promise to achieve. Coleridge and Wordsworth, Byron and Shelley, all had gathered about themselves a following of the awe-struck or the thoroughly entertained. With the first pair Lamb never let his loyalties expire; with the second Hunt, at least until the fall-ing-out over Byron's lordly indifferences in the management of *The Liberal*, kept up his cordial terms of dependence without constraint. It is irrelevant to ask whether Hazlitt avoided this sort of friendship or was robbed of it. Anyway it was not to be his. He did not seek through Lamb to renew contact with Wordsworth's circle, in cir-cumstances where, had he done so in a spirit of moderate humility, all might have been forgiven. Nor did he seek through Hunt to im-prove his acquaintance with Shelley, or procure an introduction to Byron. He kept clear of these rewarding intimacies, both from the shyness of an inveterate pride, and because he valued the advantage from which an outsider alone could view the comings and goings of the literary world.

THE ACADEMY AND THE PROFESSION OF GENIUS

From the first Hazlitt's name in criticism was identified with his pre-occupying theme: the decline of the arts.

> The greatest poets, the ablest orators, the best painters, and the finest sculptors that the world ever saw, appeared soon after the birth of these arts, and lived in a state of society which was, in other respects, comparatively barbarous. Those arts, which depend on individual genius and incommunicable power, have always leaped at once from infancy to manhood, from the first rude dawn of invention to their meridian height and dazzling lustre, and have in general declined ever after. This is the peculiar distinction and privilege of each, of science and of art; of the one, never to attain its utmost summit of perfection, and of the other, to arrive at it almost at once. Homer, Chaucer, Spenser, Shakespeare, Dante, and Ariosto (Milton alone was of a later age, and not the worse for it), Raphael, Titian, Michael Angelo, Correggio, Cervantes, and Boccaccio—all lived near the beginning of their arts—perfected, and all but created them. These giant sons of genius stand, in-deed, upon the earth, but they tower above their fellows, and the

long line of their successors does not interpose any thing to obstruct their view, or lessen their brightness. (XVIII, 6)

Men of genius may in any age triumph from a new "point of view" by revealing what once seemed hidden to art; but even those who surpass their predecessors in ingenuity cannot equal them in scope or grandeur.

In the sciences progress is generally supposed to accompany refinement. Hazlitt followed the advanced minds of his age in thinking so, and published "Why the Arts are not Progressive?" with this passage at its center, to expose the weak foundations of any analogy with the arts. The superiority of Raphael to Sir Joshua Reynolds, of Shakespeare to Pope and even, more nicely, of Congreve to Sheridan, had for him the force and clarity of an axiom. Yet this was a discovery about the nature of art *in general:* to reduce the perception to a code of laws would be absurd, though the hope that some such codification could retard the process of decline was an unspoken assumption of much eighteenth-century criticism. Passages of Reynolds's *Discourses,* for example, might be taken to imply as much. Once we understand man as part of nature and subject to nature's laws, there seems to be no reason why knowledge of those laws should not lead to improvement in every sphere of life. The error here, according to Hazlitt, lies in supposing that the genius of art has anything to do with knowledge.

The poet's wish to "think into the human heart"[12]—the painter's, to "excite the sympathies of mankind, and make the Human Form expressive of all that the Human Mind can exert or feel"[13]— these are not subject to laws. Nor can an earnest creator ascend to mastery by experimental degrees. Art proceeds by sudden accessions of power, and that power decreases as we move from its source. For the optimistic analogy of the chemist's laboratory Hazlitt substitutes the following. A company of explorers find themselves in a valley, and take up positions on a hillside overlooking it. Those who arrive first naturally occupy the choicest positions; the next party, the "niches" a little lower down; and so forth. The valley is the imaginative given of any art, everything which the artist must animate with a context and a name. But the task becomes harder to perform as the hillside grows more populous and the settlers begin to worry about their neighbors, till at last they hardly look into the valley at all, or only in sidelong glances: they are too busy regarding those who dwell above them, knowing that *they* see all.

Hazlitt seldom wrote about the history of the arts without in some way alluding to this trope, though he never expanded it as fully as I have done. I think the advantage of doing so is to make one see why the decline seemed to him irreversible, and also why an artist of great originality could seem to ignore it. Milton alone, Hazlitt says, was able to invest with power even his consciousness of his own situation below the heights. So Hazlitt leaves us with the suggestion that there may now and then arise a capable genius before whose energies the pattern of decline is suspended. But as yet this remains only a suggestion.

A second analogy, less important to Hazlitt than that of the terraced *gradus,* compares the estate of the arts with a tract of once fertile land, which with unintermitted cultivation gradually loses its richness, until it can yield nothing. For this he was indebted to Hume's essay "Of the Rise and Progress of the Arts and Sciences." Hume too had proposed a distinction between the fruits of repeated effort in the arts and in the sciences; after three mild observations, about the merits of various forms of government in fostering the arts, his essay offered an unpleasant fourth: *"That when the arts and sciences come to perfection in any state, from that moment they naturally, or rather necessarily decline, and seldom or never revive in that nation, where they formerly flourished."*[14] The praise and glory, Hume adds, on which genius relies for encouragement, are never quickly or gratefully enough bestowed, when every new production must submit to be compared with a large number of acknowledged masterpieces. The artist finds on the contrary that "the posts of honor are all occupied." Or, as Leigh Hunt was informed by an insufficient encourager of his first poems, "the shelves are full!"

Hume's interest in the national basis of the arts led him to suppose the decline of poetry might in some cases be limited by the boundaries of language. Thus, to use an illustration he may well have pondered, the imagination of Milton was curbed by the example of Shakespeare but spurred by that of Ovid. Nevertheless Hume reached a conclusion as pessimistic as Hazlitt's: "the arts and sciences, like some plants, require fresh soil; and however rich the land may be, and however you may recruit it by art or care, it will never, when once exhausted, produce any thing that is perfect or finished in the kind."[15] With Hume's essay in mind, and the record of comparable doubts that assailed Dryden, Johnson, and others, one may feel Hazlitt's bold remarks have dwindled into a commonplace.

Yet in such eighteenth-century speculations, as W. J. Bate remarked in *The Burden of the Past and the English Poet,* there was often a reserve of self-confidence. Johnson could make a sustained comparison between Pope and Dryden, to Dryden's advantage for both elevation and originality, and still conclude with the question: "if Pope be not a poet, where is poetry to be found?" And there was at least room for the plausible assertion—in Dryden's "Essay of Dramatic Poesy," with its tactics for survival distributed among four speakers—that the late-born genius could retire from his ruined estate to the flourishing life of the hot-house, and methodize himself into immortality.

With Hazlitt's generation that reserve had vanished. New books destined for the reading public came under the heading of "fashionable literature"—a phrase with a double edge. Perhaps they would survive, perhaps not; but all they could claim with assurance was: "Once, we were fashionable." Given the opinions of this public, and the truckling to their supposed opinions by authors and reviewers, a work that dared to be singular might struggle heroically short of a second edition, only to be cast into Byron's limbo of "the many."

The situation was scarcely better in painting. Yet when Hazlitt wrote his first articles against the Royal Academy to clear a path for original work, he numbered among his allies Benjamin Robert Haydon, of the "new historical school" of painters. Men like Haydon had a remedy. They rested their hopes on the encouragement of modern works in the mass. Of course, the best way to assure that what was encouraged would be really valued, was to provide the arts with a national or institutional basis: organized government patronage would revive the genius of English painting. Whenever Haydon announced this feature of his program, he found Hazlitt in his way, and soon the alliance was at an end. Hazlitt laid it down flatly that "Professional Art is a contradiction in terms. Art is genius, and genius cannot belong to a profession." His provocation in this instance came not from Haydon but from the *Catalogue Raisonné* of the British Institution (1816), and the aids-to-appreciation of Benjamin West's paintings that had been approved and in part dictated by West himself, in his role as President of the Royal Academy. Occasionally, when reviewing Haydon's work, Hazlitt would strike a more conciliatory note; but his skepticism on the larger question could not be concealed. Both the Academy and its rivals were certain that if a great age had been, a greater might yet be. Hazlitt denied this claim, and for proof described their paintings.

In setting at defiance the clamor and enthusiasm of a new school as well as the hallowed pretensions of an established one, he lost many admirers besides Haydon. But he pursued his criticisms masterfully, deliberately, with a curious persistence. Here, even more than in his political writings, Hazlitt's motives were at once public and personal, and took their authority from his refusal to separate those realms. He had sought for a brief period, in the early years of the century, to make a career for himself in painting, with some success in portraits. But on seeing his likeness of Wordsworth, Southey said it showed the poet "At the gallows—deeply affected by his deserved fate—yet determined to die like a man," while to Coleridge he wrote that Hazlitt "does show you at your trial, and you certainly had stolen the horse; but then you stole it cleverly."[16] The intermittent failures must have been all the more dispiriting because he had taken up portraits only to get some independence, before involving himself in larger projects. Yet the landscapes of Claude, or the allegories of Poussin, seemed always beyond his reach. It may be that Hazlitt's attack on programs for the invigoration of the arts eased his own renunciation, and helped him to make peace with his ambitions. He was sharing the bad tidings; and he did not tire of repeating them. The aim after all was to teach others a habit of suspicion he had learned for himself.

He returned to the subject of "Why the Arts are not Progressive?" in three further essays, each time with a slightly different emphasis. His review of the *Catalogue Raisonné* deals with "the principle of universal suffrage" as applied to matters of taste. That principle in the wrong context signalled a tacit conspiracy between the more tractable among the candidates for fame and the more corporate-minded among their judges, together plotting the euthanasia of the idea of genius. Of the remaining essays, "On Modern Comedy" and "The Periodical Press," the first became well-known in Hazlitt's lifetime, from its inclusion in *The Round Table*. It argues that when the comic types of society have once been captured by art, arrested in motion, and fixed unforgettably in the minds of spectators, society itself becomes alert to those qualities (whether vicious or hobby-horsical) that are apt to be ridiculed: we want at all costs to avoid seeing ourselves singled out as *instances*. In this way manners are refined and the stock of comedy attenuated, and "comedy naturally wears itself out." Are we to conclude that art improves society to the detriment of art? This seems to be implied in the concluding chapter of *Lectures on the English Comic Writers,* where he says there are few recent comedies because there were once many. So direct a link between the fortunes of art and the understandings of society would make an anomaly in Hazlitt's criticism, were it offered as the whole solution to the problem: but the essay "On Modern Comedy" hints at another possibility. The argument—that the follies of imaginary characters put real characters on good behavior—is extended to tragedy as well. Yet in rephrasing it Hazlitt alters its meaning. "Shakespeare, with all his genius, could not have written as he did, if he had lived in the present times. Nature would not have presented itself to him in the same freshness and vigour." He seems here to have advanced, beyond the notion of a withdrawal of objects-for-imitation, to that of a crisis of naming. Even Shakespeare could do nothing with the materials presented to him today, because so much has already been done in art, and life would only remind him of art. The parson who has read all about Parson Adams, and is too guarded ever to become the model for another, thus has his counterpart in the artist who when he does see an unguarded caricature sitting beside him in a coach, mutters to himself cheerlessly, "What a charming *convention.*" Decadence is this degree of self-consciousness grown proud of itself: with Hazlitt's speculation begins the movement in thought that one day will make it possible for Wilde to point out a Turner sky. Of course, it is no good telling someone in this predicament that he had better imitate Homer simply by imitating nature; the result will nevertheless sound like Homer, or Shakespeare, or some other artist who worked with an undepleted stock, and that is the problem.

Thus extended, Hazlitt's argument about comedy may seem congenial to us after all. But we cannot dismiss his earlier and cruder formulation with the assurance that history has proved it false. He said that an artificial state of manners perplexed the freedoms required for social comedy. And indeed, the comedy of society around which related genres are clustered was never again so perfect as in *The Way of the World* and *Joseph Andrews.* The distance between high and low remains vast, the subject of tragedy no less than comedy; but fewer levels intervene, and to the side a narrowing preserve of eccentricity; a smaller number of fashions hold sway, with proportionably greater force. These are the original terms in which Hazlitt reflected on his situation. They may sound abstract in the extreme, but they become less so in his discussion of "The Periodical Press." He had in mind, chiefly, the reviews, those utilitarian grottoes to which one retired for amusement and standards.

To such publications Thomas Love Peacock addressed "An Essay on Fashionable Literature." He was there concerned to defend Coleridge from a particularly malicious attack in the *Edinburgh Review,* and for good measure added some barbs to catch Gifford. With the same topics in view, Hazlitt felt he could not make an honest survey unless he remarked how even fashion finds itself perpetually in arrears. To the decline of the arts Peacock devoted a separate essay, "The Four Ages of Poetry," but for Hazlitt this had become inseparable from the rise of fashionable literature; and "The Periodical Press" starts by diagnosing the conditions in which the two tendencies merge. Hazlitt sets himself two questions: *"Whether Periodical Criticism is, upon the whole, beneficial to the cause of literature?";* and *"Whether Shakespeare could have written as he did, had he lived in the present day?"* He satisfies his audience's need to extort from the times some promise of fortitude by displaying the prodigious exertions of Scott and Byron, impossible to thwart—after which he announces himself ready for the worst.

> We will content ourselves with announcing a truism on the subject, which, like many other truisms, is pregnant with deep thought,—*viz. That periodical criticism is favourable—to periodical criticism.* It contributes to its own improvement—and its cultivation proves not only that it suits the spirit of the times, but advances it. It certainly never flourished more than at present. . . . And what, it may be asked, can be desired more than to have the perfection of one thing at any one time? If literature in our day has taken this decided turn into a critical channel, is it not a presumptive proof that it ought to do so? Most things find their own level; and so does the mind of man. If there is a preponderance of criticism at any one period, this can only be because there are subjects, and because it is the time for it. We complain that this is a Critical age; and that no great works of Genius appear, because so much is said and written about them; while we ought to reverse the argument, and say, that it is because so many works of genius *have appeared,* that they have left us little or nothing to do, but to think and talk about them—that if we did not do that, we should do nothing so good—and if we do this well, we cannot be said to do amiss!   (XVI, 212)

The sentence in italics, with its splendid irony, is qualified and then refuted in an uncharacteristic way; a concession perhaps to the *Edinburgh Review* banner under which, with his commission for the article, Hazlitt had consented gratefully to march. This may also

account for his willingness to identify refinement with enlightenment—a Scottish equation which he was elsewhere at pains to disprove. But what he does not qualify is the abiding sense of oppression, that we live in the shadow of great things; and with it, a lesson
read out of *Rasselas:* all distractions carry their sufficient meaning in
their use, to rescue us from idleness and despair. Even closer to
Hazlitt's purpose, however, was another familiar eighteenth-century
text, Dryden's poem to Congreve.

> Our Age was cultivated thus at length;
> But what we gain'd in skill we lost in strength.
> Our Builders were, with want of Genius, curst;
> The Second Temple was not like the First.

Those lines would have reverberated in the memory of Hazlitt's audience, as, long after the catastrophe, he went on to describe the
subtler complacencies of the present.

> When the edifice is raised and finished in all its parts, we have
> nothing to do but to admire it; and invention gives place to judi-
> cious applause, or, according to the temper of the observers, to
> petty cavils. While the niches are empty, every nerve is strained,
> every faculty is called into play, to supply them with the master-
> pieces of skill or fancy: when they are full, the mind reposes on
> what has been done, or amuses itself by comparing one excellence
> with another. . . . "We are nothing, if not critical." Be it so: but
> then let us be critical, or we shall be nothing.   (XVI, 212–13)

He writes here as Nietzsche's "monumental historian," the man
for whom at every instant modern works must be weighed in the
scales with their predecessors, and be seen to kick the beam; who
says to his listeners, "See, the great thing is already here!" and to
himself, "Let the dead bury the—living."[17] To this situation any
remedy must itself be catastrophic. Hazlitt had been impressed, in
conversation, as he recalls in "A Reply to Z," by the special pathol-
ogy of Wordsworth's repression of the past—how he could declare of
Milton, that "the only great merit of the Paradise Lost was in the
conception or in getting rid of the horns and tail of the Devil, for
as to the execution, he thought he could do as well or better himself"; or of Shakespeare, that "there was something in [him] that he
could not make up his mind to, for he hated those interlocutions
between Lucius and Caius." But such triumphant lies were true on

pragmatic grounds, for whoever believed them would survive in his own mind the comparison with his masters, and in the end might live to merit it. Besides, Wordsworth had only enforced in his opinions, and to free himself, what others must wish to accomplish in fact, once and for all. Hazlitt continues: "We can hardly expect a new harvest till the old crop is off the ground. If we insist on absolute originality in living writers or artists, we should begin by destroying the works of their predecessors." The monumental critic need not in principle oppose all acts of destruction. Yet he remains a melancholy preserver of past things because he respects the truths of monuments, such as they are. Redirecting Hazlitt's analysis very slightly, one may conclude that this sort of historian occupies the foreground in a critical age, and sets its tone. "No doubt, nature is exceedingly various; but the capital eminences, the choicest points of view, are limited; and when these have once been seized upon, we must either follow in the steps of others, or turn aside to humbler and less practicable subjects."

It is remarkable that Hazlitt should have lodged these sentiments in the prefatory remarks of an article destined for the *Edinburgh Review*. The ideal reader of that journal could be expected to chime in with The Honourable Mr. Listless of *Nightmare Abbey:* "Modern books are very consolatory and congenial to my feelings. There is, as it were, a delightful north-east wind, an intellectual blight breathing through them; a delicious misanthropy and discontent, that demonstrates the nullity of virtue and energy, and puts me in good humour with myself and my sofa." Literature was a craving, the satisfaction of which would produce reliably tranquil states. And the same result with quicker comfort might be achieved by reviews themselves, authoritative scanners of books never to be read. There were bound to appear, in any given issue, numberless confessions of humility by the reviewers or editors, but it was above all the assured authority of modern criticism that recommended it to Mr. Listless, by putting him in a good humor and soothing his complacency. Into his life Hazlitt now dropped a pinch of disquiet.

But he did more than tell disturbing truths. He told them in a disturbing way, that called attention to the uneasiness of the critic himself as a mark of his sincerity. Consider his use of the phrase, "we are nothing if not critical." It comes from Iago's description of himself to Desdemona—"For I am nothing if not critical"—in its context, a smart repartee but with a hidden warning. Hazlitt liked the tag enough to use it again as the epigraph for *A View of the English Stage*. This reliance on a borrowed self-portrait was meant to excite suspicion: how *does* Iago resemble the critic? Some Polonius-like answers present themselves. Cunning, persuasive, in dread of being passed over; though apparently modest, yet ready on an instant to command any situation in which the traditional powers have weakened; gifted with "honesty" and capable of producing "ocular proof" should the argument require it: so far the description fits them both. The immediate points of comparison, however, become tedious on further reflection; they remind us that there was an element of jesting here, and of conscious perversity: the point for Hazlitt was to advertise his sympathy with upstart pride.

Yet he was also acknowledging a kind of resentment that lurks in the most gracious acceptance of a secondary relation to the arts. He himself had sometimes been chargeable with shifting his ground of argument to cover his own retreat from an earlier position, in a manner that could seem to the by-stander merely petulant or motiveless. One example will serve. In "Whether the Arts Are Promoted by Academies" he quarreled with those philanthropists who urged the British Institution to keep the old masters on permanent exhibition. It would, said Hazlitt, be desolating for any young artist to be tried by his predecessors in a tribunal holding session every time he glanced upward, and incorruptibly severe in its verdicts.

> The student who has models of every kind of excellence constantly before him, is not only diverted from that particular walk of art, in which, by patient exertion, he might have obtained ultimate success, but, from having his imagination habitually raised to an overstrained standard of refinement, by the sight of the most exquisite examples in art, he becomes impatient and dissatisfied with his own attempts, determines to reach the same perfection all at once, or throws down his pencil in despair. Thus the young enthusiast, whose genius and energy were to rival the great Masters of antiquity, or create a new æra in the art itself, baffled in his first sanguine expectations, reposes in indolence on what others have done; wonders how such perfection could have been achieved,—grows familiar with the minutest peculiarities of the different schools,—flutters between the splendour of Rubens and the grace of Raphael, finds it easier to copy pictures than to paint them, and easier to *see* than to copy them, takes infinite pains to gain admission to all the great collections, lounges from one auction room to another, and writes newspaper criticisms on the Fine Arts————.
> (XVIII, 41–42)

"And finds no end, in wand'ring mazes lost"; for Hazlitt had been just such an artist.

He concluded that the British Institution would do better not to hang many great paintings. Yet when the Academy had achieved its aim, and having once set up the masterpieces itself began to deplore them—because Academicians were "forced into a hasty competition every year with works that have stood the test of ages"—Hazlitt ridiculed the same argument which not two months earlier he had justified with his own character, ending in the pathos of the broken career and the speechless triple-dash. Confronted with the institutional pathos of the *Catalogue Raisonné* he now announces: "It is for that very reason [the despair of competing with Raphael and Rubens] that it was proper to exhibit the works at the British Institution, to shew to the public, and by that means to make the Academicians feel, that securing the applause of posterity and a real rank in the Art, which that alone can give, depended on the number of pictures they finished, and not on the number they began." The contradiction is perhaps sufficiently explained by the different exigencies of the two occasions: the Academy first maintaining that new art would be fostered by the study of great exemplars, with Hazlitt's answer that it would only be staggered by them; the Academy on second thought preferring not to place its works in competition with so many veterans, with Hazlitt's answer that these alone provided the standard by which Academicians should wish to be judged. This would make him in both instances an heroic apologist for art against that faith in the results of diligence which leads to a mercenary professionalism.

Yet the explanation is not entirely satisfying; for his vehemence on both sides of the question remains extraordinary. When one turns to the essay on "English Students at Rome," one finds the personal poignance that elsewhere is lost in the shock and counterpoint of scorn.

> What minor pencil can stand in competition with the "petrific mace" that painted the Last Judgment? What fancy can expand into blooming grace and beauty by the side of the Heliodorus? What is it *we* could add, or what occasion, what need, what pretence is there to add anything to the art after this? Who in the presence of such glorious works does not wish to shrink into himself, or to live only for them? . . . If the artist has a genius and turn of mind at all similar, they baulk and damp him by their imposing stately height: if his talent lies in a different and

humbler walk, they divert and unsettle his mind. If he is contented to look on and admire, a vague and unattainable idea of excellence floats before his imagination, and tantalises him with equally vain hopes and wishes. If he copies, he becomes a mechanic; and besides, he runs another risk. He finds he can with ease produce in three days an incomparably finer effect than he could do with all his efforts, and after any length of time, in working without assistance. He is therefore disheartened and put out of countenance, and returns with reluctance to original composition. . . . When I was young, I made one or two studies of strong contrasts of light and shade in the manner of Rembrandt with great care and (as it was thought) with some success. But after I had copied some of Titian's portraits in the Louvre, my ambition took a higher flight. Nothing would serve my turn but heads like Titian—Titian expressions, Titian complexions, Titian dresses; and as I could not find these where I was, after one or two abortive attempts to engraft Italian art on English nature, I flung away my pencil in disgust and despair.   (XVII, 138–39)

In such passages it may appear that Hazlitt favored nothing short of the eugenic decimation of candidates for fame. The charge is at least so far warrantable that one can imagine him applauding the remark of a modern novelist: "Everywhere I'm asked if I think universities stifle writers. My opinion is that they don't stifle enough of them."[18] And yet, his impatience at pretenders springs from a common impulse with his anxiety for those who do stand a chance of surviving. That their apprenticeship should be braced, not pampered, or cozened into quiescence—on this he never slackened. He believed that genius should take pride in the number of obstacles thrown in its path (all except poverty), as by negotiating them it tested its strength. Criticism itself could hope to become one such obstacle by urging the importance of a still greater one: the presence, whether recognized or not, of predecessors to whom the artist gravitates half-unwillingly. Such pilgrimages, the critic can remind us, are to be undertaken alone, without the mutual rewards and comforts of fellow-sufferers. Whether the arts should be promoted by academies is really a secondary question. His larger concern is whether, by consenting to an efficient commercial understanding between the artist and his public, we do not risk choking all communication between the artist and his true peers living or dead, and therefore between the genius and the practice of art.

What then is to be done with the public? "The good old Latin style of our forefathers, if it concealed the dullness of the writer, at

least was a barrier against the impertinence, flippancy, and ignorance of the reader. . . . The perfection of letters is when the highest ambition of the writer is to please his readers, and the greatest
pride of the reader is to understand his author." This, from the
Round Table essay "On Pedantry," is only the plainest instance that
might be given of Hazlitt's ambivalence. It seems a narrow defile
between "pleasing" the audience and wheedling with it, and one
may feel that Hazlitt's anger at the introduction into letters of "a
species of universal suffrage" is always partly feigned. The same
public after all had created the profession of authorship as Hazlitt
knew it, free from that other commerce of flattery and insolence
which thrived in the institution of patronage. But the public is
blamed not for giving scope to abuses worse than these but for disappointing the hopes it might have led a democrat to form.

> The real patron is anxious to reward merit, not to encourage
> gratuitous pretensions to it; to see that the man of genius *takes
> no detriment,* that another Wilson is not left to perish for want;—
> not to propagate the breed, for that he knows to be impossible.
> But there are some persons who think it as essential to the interests
> of art, to keep up "an airy of children,"—the young fry of embryo
> candidates for fame,—as others think it essential to the welfare of
> the kingdom to preserve the spawn of herring fisheries. In general,
> public, that is, indiscriminate patronage is, and can be nothing
> better than a species of intellectual seduction; by administering
> provocatives to vanity and avarice, it is leading astray the youth
> of this nation by fallacious hopes, which can scarcely ever be
> realized.   (XVIII, 43)

By this means the public incorporates, though with a broader distribution of favors, all the insincerity, the courtly pliability and un-
dependable enthusiasm of the old system, with a new claim to be
advancing "the march of intellect."

If the young artist could be persuaded to paint or write for the
public but care only for the judgment of his peers, including those
greater than himself, he would be better situated to create great
works than either those like Byron who define immortality as the
indefinite extension of fashion, or those like Wordsworth who consider the public as objects of total dismissal followed by total conquest.[19] Of the former solution enough has been said, and the latter
begs an all-important question with its slogan, "Create the taste by
which you will be judged"; for others have conspired to create *your*

taste and it is open to any reader to consult those others. Neverthe-less Byron and Scott, having started from an outsize awe of fashion, were creating, as even Hazlitt in his *Edinburgh Review*ish moods had to acknowledge, works of enormous vigor. Wordsworth and Coleridge were creating works of great originality. And no artist of Hazlitt's third sort had yet arisen. What had altered most with the progress of the arts, and perhaps here the public did give the death-blow, was that such an artist even when blessed with a long and productive life could never again feel himself to be an undisputed center of forces, as Shakespeare or Raphael had been, in whom the impulses of the past and present converged irresistibly and with equal momentum.

CHARACTERS, DRAMATIC AND LYRIC

To the question why such responsiveness should no longer be avail-able to the highest genius, Hazlitt gave an answer that closely antic-ipates T. S. Eliot's speculations on the "dissociation of sensibility." "A thought," writes Eliot, "to Donne was an experience; it modified his sensibility"; but "in the seventeenth century a dissociation of sensibility set in from which we have never recovered." Hence the predicament of the nineteenth century in which there are "poets, and they think; but they do not feel their thought as immediately as the odour of a rose." Eliot adds that a general satisfaction with the "poetic functions" Milton and Dryden had "performed . . . so mag-nificently well," may have prevented their successors from seeing that "the magnitude of the effect concealed the absence of others."[20] Beyond its immediate service as a tactic in the war against Donne's rivals, this remark is mysterious: we are not told what the functions and effect were, or what must be done to restore the absent ones. Yet the perception of so clear a missed opportunity yields Eliot an open sequence to which certain later works, his own in particular, may attach themselves without the opprobrium of repeating a func-tion already well performed.[21]

Hazlitt is at once more deeply pessimistic and more matter-of-fact. At some point in history, he believes, the elective affinities by which the artist draws his likeness from nature, lost their boldness, and became strained, peripheral, or "personal" in a highly special-ized sense. He gives a picture of the age before the fall in *The Elo-*

quence of the British Senate, in one of those scattered notes on forgotten parliamentary orators which he rightly feared would be too
good for their setting.

> The distinctive character of the period of which we are now
> speaking [the seventeenth century] was, I think, that men's minds
> were stored with facts and images, almost to excess; there was a
> tenacity and firmness in them that kept fast hold of the impressions
> of things as they were first stamped upon the mind; and "their ideas
> seemed to lie like substances in the brain." Facts and feelings went
> hand in hand; the one naturally implied the other; and our ideas,
> not yet exorcised and squeezed and tortured out of their natural
> object, into a subtle essence of pure intellect, did not fly about like
> ghosts without a body, tossed up and down, or up-borne only by
> the ELEGANT FORMS of words, through the *vacuum* of abstract
> reasoning, and sentimental refinement.   (I, 147)

The phrase, "facts and feelings went hand in hand," foreshadows
Eliot's nostalgia for the thought that is itself an experience. But elsewhere, with his idea of "extinction of personality"—a hopeful formula
for the poet who requires some assistance in filling the vacuum—Eliot
speaks as a meliorist of decline. He implies that the situation has
always been essentially the same: an asectic routine has been required of the poets of every age to assure their humility. "The existing monuments form an ideal order among themselves, which is
modified by the introduction of the new (the really new) work of art
among them," and with the postulation of an ideal order we put
aside all thoughts of decline.[22] Such an order must be temporal if
the new work is to be felt as "really new"; and yet Eliot writes as if
the situation of the artist were outside history. We may leave his
celebrated early essays with the suspicion that he had seen the worst
history can disclose to a new poet, and was on the verge of saying
what he saw. But what outweighed every other consideration was
the need to supply heartening views to a generation.[23]

Let us return for a moment to *impersonality.* Though Hazlitt
would not have understood Eliot's use of the idea, Eliot took it from
Keats's "negative capability," and must in the first instance have
meant it as a rephrasing of Keats. How did so much get lost in translation? To begin with, Keats picked a somewhat misleading phrase for
what he meant: he would have cared most about capability, but it
was *negative* that stayed with Eliot. What enforced the shift of meaning, however, was the mediating influence of Arnold. For Eliot's
impersonality is closely related to Arnold's disinterestedness: they

involve analogous distortions of an idea original with Hazlitt. Arnold names the distinctive trait of a full ethical freedom, the sympathetic acknowledgment of others, and interprets it as the negation of personality to be found in the ideal critic. Eliot names the distinctive trait of a full aesthetic freedom, the sympathetic imagining of others, and interprets it as the negation of personality to be found in the ideal poet. Theirs is a negative freedom which guards against the abuse of established rights. But Hazlitt had regarded the whole question from the point of view of a society in which rights were just being invented, for the critic and poet among others, and the claims could still be very large.

To adapt Hazlitt's usual comparison, the poet not confined to his own personality has the same advantage over the poet thus confined that the house on a cliffside with windows on all sides has over the cubicle with a narrow grating that looks into a dirty alley. It is the advantage simply of priority: there comes a time when there can be no more houses like that. As in the history of a person, so in the history of poetry, "shades of the Prison-House" close round us; and though the change may be beyond our power to stop, we must regard ourselves as if we were responsible for it. The state from which we fell will then at least be kept in sight as an available ideal.

The part of this truth Hazlitt considered hardest for modern poets to admit was the superiority of the dramatic to the lyric mode. The dramatic poet sees more generously and therefore sees more. Wordsworth, Coleridge, Keats, Shelley, and Byron all shared this perception at times, and strove to meet its demands. The results were variously unsatisfactory: even the most powerful work of genius among them, Wordsworth's *The Borderers,* is diminished by comparison with the play that influenced it, *Othello;* and in the end it piques our curiosity as an original interpretation of Iago, from a poet who otherwise has little of interest to say about Shakespeare. At any rate, for these poets the ambition to write dramatic works had nothing to do with a timeless hierarchy of genres or with the opportunities for modification within an ideal order. It was rather one feature of a common intimation of historical decline, to which the alternative postures of defiance (as in Wordsworth's "Essay Supplementary") and ironic acceptance (as in Byron's worship of Pope) could never be wholly convincing even to the poets themselves. Shakespeare was inescapable for them, and at times their uncertainty reduced itself to a feeling that they needed his universality because their own had become doubtful.

Hazlitt writes about the particular causes of the decline of tragedy since Shakespeare, in a theatre chronicle of 1820 for the *London
Magazine.*

> We participate in the general progress of intellect, and the large
> vicissitudes of human affairs; but the hugest private sorrow looks
> dwarfish and puerile. In the sovereignty of our minds, we make
> mankind our quarry; and, in the scope of our ambitious thoughts,
> hunt for prey through the four quarters of the world. In a word,
> literature and civilization have abstracted man from himself so far,
> that his existence is no longer *dramatic;* and the press has been the
> ruin of the stage, unless we are greatly deceived.   (XVIII, 305)

Without this progressive abstraction there can be no steady movement toward a principle of disinterestedness. On the other hand,
the imagination of Shakespeare has the "gross" disinterestedness of
childhood which requires no principle to keep it alive. And apparently, the decline of drama from the time of Shakespeare resembles
the fall from childhood in the course of an individual life. That
freedom lost, one may choose principled disinterestedness or habitual selfishness: in the latter case one will simply have agreed to live
with less; in the former, one's sympathies, though still wide, can no
longer have the impulsive ease they seem to have had in childhood.
Wordsworth and his school, their talents pressed into service for the
drama but their genius at liberty only in the lyric, had universal
sympathies in them. But in their thinking about poetry these emerged
with all the narrowness of system. Some such disabling refinement
Hazlitt found inseparable from the progress of the mind. The same
passage continues:

> If a bias to abstraction is evidently, then, the reigning spirit of
> the age, dramatic poetry must be allowed to be most irreconcile-
> able with this spirit; it is essentially individual and concrete, both
> in form and in power. . . . It is not enough for [characters] to de-
> claim on certain general topics, however forcibly or learnedly—this
> is merely oratory, and this any other characters might do as well,
> in any other circumstances: nor is it sufficient for the poet to fur-
> nish the colours and forms of style and fancy out of his own store,
> however inexhaustible; for if he merely makes them express his
> own feelings, and the idle effusions of his own breast, he had better
> speak in his own person. . . . Within the circle of dramatic char-
> acter and natural passion, each individual is to feel as keenly, as
> profoundly, as rapidly as possible, but he is not to feel beyond it,
> for others or for the whole. Each character, on the contrary, must

be a kind of centre of repulsion to the rest; and it is their hostile interests, brought into collision, that must tug at their heart-strings, and call forth every faculty of thought, of speech, and action. They must not be represented like a set of profiles, looking all the same way, nor with their faces turned round to the audience; but in dire contention with each other. . . . The poet, to do justice to his undertaking, must not only identify himself with each, but must take part with all by turns, "to relish all as sharply, passioned as they";—must feel scorn, pity, love, hate, anger, remorse, revenge, ambition, in their most sudden and fierce extremes—must not only have these passions rooted in his mind, but must be alive to every circumstance affecting them, to every accident of which advantage can be taken to gratify or exasperate them.   (XVIII, 305-306)

The *reasoning* propensities of romantic heroes and villains seemed to Hazlitt thoroughly in keeping with their deficiency of natural passion: for a representative instance he referred, both in this article and elsewhere, to a passage in Coleridge's *Remorse* where Ordonio gives the following argument for murdering his brother.—This is no worse than a reptile killing a reptile, after which one beast the less disfigures the face of nature. Besides, even if it is considered a crime against nature, the effects are such as to compensate the injury ten thousand times over. For sentient beings will breed from the corpse; and does this not mean I beget many lives at the sacrifice of one death?—It is ingenious in a high degree, but, Hazlitt comments, "This is a way in which no one ever justified a murder to his own mind." His criticism would apply with somewhat less force to the reasonings of Falkland in *Caleb Williams* and of Oswald in *The Borderers*. But when one contrasts with these the varied company of Shakespeare's reasoners, Iago and Macbeth, Richard III and Edmund, Shylock and Ulysses and the gravediggers of Elsinore, how oddly restricted seems the play of motives. Shakespeare registered the properties, and therefore all the minute veerings and listings of an imagined being. This may make us churlish about his successors:

But surely it is hardly to be thought that the poet should feel for others in this way, when they have ceased almost to feel for themselves; when the mind is turned habitually out of itself to general, speculative truth, and possibilities of good, and when, in fact, the processes of the understanding, analytical distinctions, and verbal disputes, have superseded all personal and local attachments and antipathies, and have, in a manner, put a stop to the pulsation of the heart—quenched the fever in the blood—the madness in the brain;—when we are more in love with a theory than a mistress, and would only crush to atoms those who are of an opposite party to ourselves in taste, philosophy, or politics. . . . Therefore, we have no dramatic poets. (XVIII, 306)

It greatly simplifies Hazlitt's procedure in the *Characters of Shakespeare's Plays* to identify him as the first "character critic." Characters gave him an easy way to divide chapters into paragraphs; but he is sufficiently bold in avoiding the inference that the plays are about character: he appears to regard them on the contrary as "imitations of action," the agent in each case being the single "passion" guided on its course through the play by the intentions of its several characters. John Kinnaird nicely sums up this part of his critical enterprise:

> "Passion" emerges in his essays on the tragedies as an elemental "force" which, while it emanates only from within the characters and can be understood only through a knowledge of them as individuals, becomes more powerful than the several wills and minds through which it moves; it seems to acquire a life and momentum of its own, as Hazlitt expressly suggests when he speaks of the "sea," the "storm," the "tide" of tragic passion in Shakespeare. . . . The "character" critic, at least as defined by current legend, is interested in emotion as inward state of mind, as the motivation of unique and separate individuals, but Hazlitt's interest is in "passion" as the energy of human *conflict*—as the dynamism of "circumstance," a force generated by sympathies and antagonisms, by the motives of individuals as they exist only in combination with one another and in response to some extraordinary challenge to the generic resources of "the human soul."[24]

This interpretation of the book accords with Hazlitt's earlier argument against the reductive schools of moral philosophy. Faced with the conflict of passions that Shakespeare alone understood in its whole range—the conflict within a single character so often mirroring what we expect to see only between plain antagonists—we recognize everything in human nature that cannot be reduced to calculated self-interest (as in Mandeville) or principled disinterestedness (as in Godwin).

Kinnaird goes on to suggest an inventive reading of Iago which he claims to have taken from Hazlitt. He believes Hazlitt identified Iago with the creative spirit of the drama, so that Iago's situation, tactics, and temperament are a key to Hazlitt's idea of how a poet looks at his material. Poets and Iagos are united on the ground of their common "will to power," and Hazlitt could not help admiring Iago's "penetrating indifference of mind," since it represents

> what might be called the amorality of the tragic intelligence—the knowledge and resentment of passional "weakness" and the impulse, born from that weakness, not only to "know the worst" about human nature but to "contend" with it, however perversely, "to the utmost." So understood, Iago's will to power over weakness proves strangely akin, in principle, to the striving of Othello's mind for "command" over its agony, as well as to our own "admiration" of that evil when we go to witness it on stage. Iago's will to power is also akin, ultimately, to the poet's delight in creating both the torment and the tormentor.[25]

The surprise of this is partly absorbed by "strangely akin," "akin, ultimately," and the other qualifications. That Kinnaird is uncomfortable with his own interpretation of Hazlitt appears also in the unannounced shading from Iago's "will to 'mischief,' " on an earlier page, to his will to power.[26] But on this view, however one hedges it, Iago stands as an artist-figure *in* the play.

Was Hazlitt's idea of passion leading all along to this? If so, Shakespeare becomes one more romantic poet, with the romantic fondness for associating a character with himself. It is no small sacrifice for our ideas of sympathy and genius, and we may wonder what we get in return. I think in fact Kinnaird has misread Hazlitt. But the steps he took in doing so, and the pressure he felt to make Hazlitt timely at whatever cost, illustrate the special difficulties of dramatic criticism in an age of the lyric. By turning Shakespeare into an egotistical poet Kinnaird has turned Hazlitt's book on him into a properly romantic critical act. But it was a troubling book in its own day and has remained so ever since, to readers who do not imagine they have done with his idea of power when they call it "the will to power." That phrase was domesticated long ago, and it now gives us the satisfaction of any thoroughly digested fact. But the truth is that Hazlitt did not associate the poetic power of Shakespeare with individual characters: one face "turned round towards the audience," as the poet's spokesman, seemed to him as poor a thing as "a set of profiles, looking all the same way." To say that Iago "represents" the poet only sounds sweeter. It still means that Shakespeare contented himself, on this occasion, with personifying his genius in one exceptionally interesting profile; and nothing in Hazlitt's criticism prepares us to hear this, much less to hear it said as praise.

The error begins with the assumption that "penetrating indifference" was meant as a compliment to Iago. It is true Hazlitt thought this the salient quality of Iago's mind, but indifference was hardly a quality he admired. Throughout his work that word denotes an alienation from every natural sentiment and rooted affection. In a sketch of Kean which was later incorporated into the chapter on *Othello,* he writes:

> The character of Iago . . . belongs to a class of characters common to Shakespeare, and at the same time peculiar to him, namely, that of great intellectual activity, accompanied with a total want of moral principle, and therefore displaying itself at the constant expence of others, making use of reason as a pander to will— employing its ingenuity and resources to palliate its own crimes, and aggravate the faults of others, and seeking to confound the practical distinctions of right and wrong, by referring them to some overstrained standard of speculative refinement.   (V, 213)

This is the language in which Hazlitt had criticized Malthus: the "modern philosopher" like Iago refers all questions to "some overstrained standard of speculative refinement," and uses reason (high-sounding arguments, with the appearance of a high motive) as a pander to will (the interest of a person, sect, or class). As for "the amorality of the tragic intelligence," Hazlitt does say, in his chapter on *Measure for Measure,* that Shakespeare was "in one sense, no moralist at all." But there is not a word about amorality, and, so that there could be no mistaking his purpose, he added that Shakespeare was "a moralist in the same sense in which nature is one." He meant that Shakespeare could be moral without laboring to be so. Again, to the degree that he resembles an artist, the motive for Iago's art is resentment, and that was not a quality Hazlitt looked for in works of genius. He would have maintained that an artist of Shakespeare's class can never resent in his art: to do so would imply irritability, a disposition that returns us to habitual trains of thought and limits the scope of the imagination. One sort of art, Pope's in *The Dunciad* perhaps, can be nourished by resentment. But this is a long way from the "poet's delight" which Hazlitt found in Shakespeare.

Nevertheless, a curious suggestion of fellow-feeling remains in his description of Iago as "an amateur of tragedy in everyday life"; in his original sketch for the *Examiner* he also said: "For our own part, we are a little of Iago's counsel in this matter [of Desdemona's fidelity]." The insight into Desdemona was a grand exercise in perversity: it caused a stir in theatrical circles, for a week or two, and stimulated Hunt to write a gallant defense of the lady. Hazlitt later withdrew his allegation against her, and no trace of the aberrant passage appears in the *Characters of Shakespeare's Plays*.[27] The more sober phrase about Iago as an "amateur of tragedy" may be taken to indicate that Iago allows no distinction between real and fictional beings, and lays snares for creatures of flesh and blood with all the relish usually reserved to the artist in dealing with creatures of the imagination. This does not make him an artist-figure in the play. He is a shaky scaffolding for any argument about the will to power; and much as his sketch of Iago differs from Coleridge's, Hazlitt would have agreed that the obscurity of motives for which Iago is remarkable from beginning to end is the source of all his fascination. Such obscurity is not an attribute of will in Nietzsche's sense but of power, in a sense peculiar to Hazlitt and untranslatable. To him, our fascination with power in life and in poetry is always unconscious, and unpredictable in the working out of its effects. If he had thought it could be reduced to a question of will, he might have viewed the matter with less perplexity and less dismay.

Instead of the artist's will to power, Hazlitt speaks of the display of power that draws our interest to a distinct character in a play. The rest of his sketch, which has echoes in all his writings on poetry, leaves the full meaning of power unresolved.

Some persons more nice than wise, have thought the whole of the character of Iago unnatural. Shakespeare, who was quite as good a philosopher as he was a poet, thought otherwise. He knew that the love of power, which is another name for the love of mischief, was natural to man. He would know this as well or better than if it had been demonstrated to him by a logical diagram, merely from seeing children paddle in the dirt, or kill flies for sport. We might ask those who think the character of Iago not natural, why they go to see it performed—but from the interest it excites, the sharper edge which it sets on their curiosity and imagination? Why do we go to see tragedies in general? Why do we always read the accounts in the newspapers, of dreadful fires and shocking murders, but for the same reason? Why do so many persons frequent executions and trials; or why do the lower classes almost universally take delight in barbarous sports and cruelty to animals, but because there is a natural tendency in the mind to strong excitement, a desire to have its faculties roused and stimulated to the utmost? Whenever this principle is not under the restraint of humanity or the sense of moral obligation, there are no excesses to which it will not of itself give rise, without the assistance of any other motive, either of passion or self-interest. Iago is only an extreme instance of the kind; that is, of diseased intellectual activity, with an almost perfect indifference to moral good or evil, or rather with a preference of the latter, because it falls more in with his favourite propensity, gives greater zest to his thoughts and scope to his actions. Be it observed, too (for the sake of those who are for squaring all human actions by the maxims of Rochefoucault), that he is quite or nearly as indifferent to his own fate as to that of others; that he runs all risks for a trifling and doubtful advantage; and is himself the dupe and victim of his ruling passion—an incorrigible love of mischief—an insatiable craving after action of the most difficult and dangerous kind. Our Ancient is a philosopher, who fancies that a lie that kills, has more point in it than an alliteration or an antithesis; who thinks a fatal experiment on the peace of a family a better thing than watching the palpitations in the heart of a flea in an air-pump; who plots the ruin of his friends as an exercise for his understanding, and stabs men in the dark to prevent *ennui*. Now this, though it be sport, yet it is dreadful sport.[28]   (V, 213–14)

Evidently he had been thinking of Burke's observation in the *Enquiry into the Sublime and Beautiful:* if at a theatrical performance the audience learned of a hanging taking place in the next street, the theatre would be emptied at once. Iago competes with the hanging, and yet his poetry of action is completely artificial: it is the real-life counterpart of alliteration and antithesis; as an artist, he is a contriver of farces who spoils his own plot. His genius is therefore the opposite of Shakespeare's. It presents all things in a distorting medium, and only when we look at the whole play of which his poetry is one part, do we find those involuntary movements of the imagination by which Hazlitt recognized the greatest art.[29] The touch of nature that is absent from Iago's portrait of Desdemona can be found in Shakespeare's portrait of her. Besides, what we feel in watching Iago himself is not admiration but helpless absorption; we are drawn not so much by the evil actions as by the energy shown in their performance. Iago's peculiar genius is finally to be understood as the exuberance of one part of Shakespeare's mind—not as an allegorical representation of the whole of it. Because he never lost sight of this distinction between the poetry of a play and that of a single character in it, Hazlitt was able to hold firmly to his preference of the dramatic to the lyric mode.

Individuality, a completeness of character not assimilable to the poet himself, becomes for Hazlitt the great mark of Shakespeare's strength. He sets, against the representations of "general nature" which Johnson found in the plays, his own discovery of particular natures, the sum of all these being perhaps the "great creating Nature" about which we are instructed in Act IV of *The Winter's Tale.* Hazlitt's language of praise may seem to lead away from the universality of the plays by making them incorrigibly plural, but again this reduces itself to a question about the developing sense of a word. Universality can denote many things, none of them very precise, though few critics would wish on that account to let it go unused as a name for a value. Johnson took it to mean that Shakespeare's characters were representative of whole classes, and typical enough to be universally understood. But the word can also accommodate Hazlitt's polemic against general nature, in which case it must mean that Shakespeare individuates over such a range, and with an intensity so great in each character, that his imagination comprehends universal variety. In this sense it is a feeling that we build up unconsciously, by the work of abstraction and coalescence. Indeed the associations by which a poet manages the trick may be so personal that they seem, in the light of all our previous expectations of poetry, and all our knowledge of its decorums, oddly artificial. This is a paradox until we see it worked out in practice, with a poem equally famous for its artifice and its passion.

Hazlitt's essay on "Lycidas" was written for *The Round Table* but plainly draws on a larger stock of ideas from his thinking about Shakespeare. "Passion," Johnson had said, "picks no berries from the myrtle and ivy, nor calls upon Arethuse and Mincius, nor tells of 'rough satyrs and fauns with cloven heel.' Where there is leisure for fiction there is little grief." To these strictures Hazlitt objects that the poem's language and allusions have a lustre for us, its machinery however archaic seems to us more than machinery, when we take into account the speaker with whom we are to sympathize. It is Milton himself.

> Habit is a second nature; and, in this sense, the pedantry (if it is to be called so) of the scholastic enthusiast, who is constantly referring to images of which his mind is full, is as graceful as it is natural. It is not affectation in him to recur to ideas and modes of expres-

sion, with which he has the strongest associations, and in which he
takes the greatest delight.   (IV, 33)

It is a splendid defense. A criticism that admitted the personal origin
of associations has now been augmented by one that insists on their
personal value. That Hazlitt wrote in full awareness of the parallel
with his philosophical thinking is underscored by his reference to
habit. Having begun with the self, we value things by how they
accord with the self: we come to prefer unselfishness, too, for self-
centered reasons. As in his *Essay* Hazlitt had argued for sympathetic
over selfish action while refusing to distinguish in kind between their
motives, so in his writings on Shakespeare he values the dramatic
over the lyric mode while giving reasons that make the distinction
uncertain.

Other distinctions too grow less plausible as a result. Thus the
first chapter of Hazlitt's *Lectures on the Age of Elizabeth* invests the
dramatic poet with a motive that must once have seemed appropriate to the lyric poet alone.

> All the disposeable materials that had been accumulating for a
> long period of time, either in our own, or in foreign countries,
> were now brought together, and required nothing more than to be
> wrought up, polished, or arranged in striking forms, for ornament
> and use. To this every inducement prompted, the novelty of the
> acquisition of knowledge in many cases, the emulation of foreign
> wits, and of immortal works, the want and the expectation of such
> works among ourselves, the opportunity and encouragement af-
> forded for their production by leisure and affluence; and, above all,
> the insatiable desire of the mind to beget its own image, and to
> construct out of itself, and for the delight and admiration of the
> world and posterity, that excellence of which the idea exists only
> in its own breast, and the impression of which it would make as
> universal as the eye of heaven, the benefit as common as the air
> we breathe.   (VI, 186-87)

"To beget its own image" means for the mind to follow the lyric
impulse till it is spent: the phrase itself returns us to the language
of Shakespeare's sonnets rather than his plays. But this image by its
excellence leaves, as an "impression" for those who encounter it, a
"benefit as common as the air we breathe": the egotistical idea survives its rebirth as a sympathetic impression, and becomes universal.
Once again the difference between lyric and dramatic poetry has
been reduced to a matter of reference. With the lyric we are conscious of the person for whom certain associations were linked; with

the drama we forget the person and his situation and glory in a feeling common as the air; but when we interrogate ourselves on the subject we realize that the movement of mind in both cases was essentially the same.

"The natural impression of any object or event, by its vividness exciting an involuntary movement of imagination and passion, and producing, by sympathy, a certain modulation of the voice, or sounds, expressing it": that was Hazlitt's definition of poetry, in the lecture "On Poetry in General"; and it describes what happens in the reader as much as in the poet. The movement, that is, in creation as in re-creation, is from the vivid impression, to an involuntary sympathetic excitement that completes itself in the act of expression, or "voicing." From this description it looks as if the advantage of drama lies simply in leaving us doubtful how the associations worked for the poet himself. That the same steps were taken before, we cannot but suppose; only, the dramatic poet invents a middle-man whose name is not William Shakespeare, or the "Lycidas" that Johnson regretted as a transparent disguise, "easy, vulgar, and therefore disgusting," but rather Leontes, or Hamlet, or Angelo; it is this middle-man, whom we have named "character," that draws off the noxious particles of egotism. Characters allow the reader to share that unconscious power of the imagination to which Hazlitt had traced the largest exertions of the mind. Yet Shakespeare is an ego *in his work* to the same degree that Wordsworth is, even if we do not see the wheels turning; just as the benevolent man too has his rooted affections, no matter how much he tempts us to suppose a more-than-personal idea of disinterestedness. I think Hazlitt was able to read Shakespeare a good deal in the spirit of Stephen's disquisition in *Ulysses*—the work of another respecter of character, whose interest in Shakespeare's plays did not require their author to disappear. It would be in keeping with Hazlitt's skepticism, and with his psychological subtlety, to regard the whole of the *Characters of Shakespeare's Plays* as a sketch of the single unnamed character, Shakespeare. That book's straightforward procedure, taking the characters flatly, one-by-one as they come, was the only way to hold together the enormous claim being made for Shakespeare, with the empirical definition of poetry which put Shakespeare alongside others. The method is psychological anatomy: this is the naming of the parts for Shakespeare's mind, and evidently we do need all the names he gave us. For every later poet we need only a few—usually fewer than the poet thinks.

SHAKESPEARE AND MILTON

Hazlitt commonly lets his praise of Shakespeare pivot on the words "imitation of nature" or some version of them. By "imitation" he meant something very distinct from Augustan usage: "the greatest difficulty of imitation," he says in the *Round Table* essay on the subject, "is the power of imitating expression"; he glosses this in the lecture "On Poetry in General," with the judgment, "Poetry then is an imitation of nature, but the imagination and the passions are a part of man's nature." To put it another way, imitation presumes the psychological understanding granted to any far-reaching sympathy, and all sympathy begins at home. This needs to be reaffirmed because Hazlitt occasionally neglects the precision of his own idea. In writing about Shakespeare he can describe the great effects as if they came because Shakespeare just copied what he saw: there lay his superiority; others have only been poorer, more involuted or distracted, copyists. These deviations are a result of Hazlitt's too literal acceptance of the figure about "points of view" which he had proposed in "Why the Arts are not Progressive?" In its deeper sense, as an image expressing the origin, diffusion, and gradual exhaustion of the ideas and language of genius, the figure implies no belief about "real relations in nature" which could give stability to the imitative act itself. Hazlitt thus makes an unreliable ally for the mimetic schools of criticism which have emerged since the eighteenth century. True, he can imply that Shakespeare wrote of what was *there,* whereas poets ever after have interposed themselves. But we are reminded in his review of A. W. Schlegel that he takes this too as figurative speech, for Shakespeare himself appears there as the disruptive modern whose "truth," unlike that of the Greeks, depends on his seeing with all the associations that clung to the objects of his mind, and first made them "romantic."[30]

The review of Schlegel is Hazlitt's most ambitious effort to define Shakespeare's genius; and its interest in associations rescues Shakespeare from the irrecoverable past to which his uniqueness as an imitator seemed to consign him. Indeed, in positing an original nature as the storehouse of objects-for-imitation, Hazlitt has to drive it further and further into the past: first Shakespeare, then the Greeks. He asserts a doctrine of imitation grounded in real nature only when for the moment he has no interest in the object about which the doctrine is said to hold true. By the end of his *Essay* Hazlitt had grown suspicious of any action that did not proceed from sentiment. In his criticism, for similar reasons, he is reluctant to grant poetry a convincingly impersonal origin, except in asides that turn out to be of no use to his practice as a critic. Out of a conflict never openly acknowledged in his pages, we get the suggestion of a "romantic" Shakespeare who nevertheless is without egotism. This author remains superior to every poet after him because his associations refer us to more than a single character. And yet he is the first modern, because his associations owe their existence not to the fidelity of his imitation but to impressions that began by having a meaning peculiar to one mind. The romantic Shakespeare also qualifies the notion of a poetic fall from natural disinterestedness and universal sympathy by making that fall appear less sudden and perhaps less unfortunate.

Most of Hazlitt's doubts about mimesis have eluded his commentators because they are conveyed in metaphors where he speaks with apparent satisfaction of the process of imitation. This is nowhere more true than in "Why the Arts are not Progressive?", with its two central images: of the imitator as Antaeus; and of his imitation as reflection.

> The arts hold immediate communication with nature, and are only derived from that source. When that original impulse no longer exists, when the inspiration of genius is fled, all the attempts to recal it are no better than the tricks of galvanism to restore the dead to life. The arts may be said to resemble Antaeus in his struggle with Hercules, who was strangled when he was raised above the ground, and only revived and recovered his strength when he touched his mother earth.   (XVIII, 5)

Simple mimesis would require art to derive its strength from the objects it has in view. Even in the figure of Antaeus, however, Hazlitt restores priority to the viewing mind: its strength comes from itself, though it flows in only when the mind is rightly situated. A less complex figure would have served for Hazlitt's point about mimesis; but evidently he wants us not so much to accept a mimetic account of art, as to realize the difficulties it must contain before it can tally with our experience of genius. These loom larger in the passage that follows concerning the "reflection" practiced by great art.

> The arts of painting and poetry are conversant with the world of thought within us, and with the world of sense without us— with what we know, and see, and feel intimately. They flow from

the sacred shrine of our own breasts, and are kindled at the living lamp of nature. The pulse of the passions assuredly beat as high, the depths and soundings of the human heart were as well understood three thousand years ago, as they are at present; the face of nature and "the human face divine," shone as bright then as they have ever done. It is this light, reflected by true genius on art, that marks out its path before it, and sheds a glory round the Muses' feet, like that which circled Una's angel face,

> "And made a sunshine in the shady place."

Nature is the soul of art. There is a strength in the imagination that reposes entirely on nature, which nothing else can supply. There is in the old poets and painters a vigour and grasp of mind, a full possession of their subject, a confidence and firm faith, a sublime simplicity, an elevation of thought proportioned to their depth of feeling, an increasing force and impetus, which moves, penetrates, and kindles all that comes in contact with it, which seems not theirs, but given to them.   (XVIII, 9)

The argument depends on what it means for an imagination to be strong, and to repose on its object. Now, the "strength in the imagination" may refer either to how it is sustained from the outside, or to its consciousness of its own power. Its repose may be either an involuntary or voluntary state of rest, as an invalid may repose in a bed or a free man on a grassy mound. The passage, in spite of its declared purpose, moves toward the second meaning, and so connects imitation with an active power that can never simply mirror what lies before it. The arts "flow from the shrine of our own breasts," a shrine rendered sacred by "the living lamp of nature" which burns there. But is this a lamp *of* nature or *on* nature? If "nature is the soul of art" meant what it seems to say, then the artist to make his work natural would require nothing but a mirror. Even the mirror we do find in the passage, however, is of a special sort, and has all the properties of a lamp. It does not reproduce but enhances and transfigures the light it reflects; it sheds a more than natural "glory round the Muses' feet," and makes " 'a sunshine in the shady place.' " As for the "lamp of nature" introduced before, which alone can illuminate the "world of thought within us"—who holds up the lamp in that triumphant final cadence? Is it not the artist's own energy of mind that "moves, penetrates, and kindles all that comes in contact with it"? The qualification admitted at the end—that the mind's objects seem as if "given" to it—has a perfunctory sound after so much activity. Though it shines upon nature, the lamp has come to represent the power that begins in man.

Hazlitt's metaphors have led him where he might have preferred not to go, to the point where an idea of art as imitation must be absorbed into an idea of art as second nature. Beyond this point Shakespeare's naturalness can no longer be set against the egotism of modern poetry: imitation becomes a fiction that has a strictly honorific value as praise, and egotism a term of reproach no less applicable to Shakespeare than to Wordsworth. Hazlitt would have liked to preserve something more of imitation-as-reflection; his inability to do so bears witness to his honesty. For nature like benevolence was an ideal Hazlitt wanted us to hold sacred, and yet his assertion of simple mimesis was no better warranted than the assertion of natural benevolence into which he had lapsed at one point in the *Essay*. Both were meant as an emphatic record of a felt value: that the good is its own justification; that genius once had a qualitatively larger scope. But both lead to a denial of the active power of imagination. That is why Hazlitt could never give them a greater role in his thinking, and why even the rhetoric in which he asserts them frequently contains their refutation. Having banished the possibility of egotism, in theory, from an ideally early poetry associated with the name of Shakespeare, he could not help readmitting it when he came to write of Shakespeare's poetry in detail. Here, and through the whole range of its concerns, Hazlitt's criticism has two voices. The first voice, emphatic and persuasive, seeks to restore values that were in danger of slipping into total eclipse, while the second, antithetical and observant, remains aware of all that qualifies the truth of those values.

By the time Hazlitt's *Lectures on English Poetry* arrive at Milton, even the rhetorical uses of imitation-as-reflection have vanished. With Milton, to be moved is to be conscious of the poet who seeks to move us. We not only feel that the associations he brings to an object must be personal, we see how they are personal in each instance. Yet this does not diminish our appreciation: "He strives hard to say the finest things in the world, and he does say them. . . . The power of his mind is stamped on every line." Power, in Shakespeare's plays, had seemed to Hazlitt a property of dramatic action, or an idea that we abstract from the play itself: at any rate, energy of mind was a quality we could admire without crediting it to an agent. In our experience of Milton all this has changed. Now, power belongs to the author, and the knowledge that our idea of power is connected with him serves in turn to enhance an idea of him which exceeds anything we find in his work. Hazlitt continues to be interested in the character of the poetry rather than the poet's character. But poetry has become entirely a matter of individual expression, and we look to the poet not for edification on the score of reality or morals, but for the beauties or sublimities of poetic expression.

Since by "Milton" the lecturer meant chiefly *Paradise Lost,* his doubts about imitation open a new question about the energies of drama. How far, in our awe of *Paradise Lost,* can we distinguish what this feeling owes to Milton from what it owes to Satan? Of the power exhibited by Satan in the poem, Hazlitt observes:

> The sense of his punishment seems lost in the magnitude of it; the fierceness of tormenting flames is qualified and made innoxious by the greater fierceness of his pride; the loss of infinite happiness to himself is compensated in thought, by the power of inflicting infinite misery on others. Yet Satan is not the principle of malignity, or of the abstract love of evil—but of the abstract love of power of pride, of self-will personified, to which last principle all other good and evil, and even his own, are subordinate. From this principle he never once flinches. His love of power and contempt for suffering are never once relaxed from the highest pitch of intensity. His thoughts burn like a hell within him; but the power of thought holds dominion in his mind over every other consideration.   (V, 64)

Power, Hazlitt has already told us, is the leading characteristic of Milton's poetry; he now adds that Milton realized power as a principle of being when he imagined a single character, Satan; from this, and his whole treatment of the poem, it seems to follow that the dramatic power of Satan and the lyric power of Milton derive from the same source. *Paradise Lost* is superior to later and smaller masterpieces of egotism by reason of its dramatic form: this draws off the irritables that would otherwise cling to the poet's representation of himself. Yet between Milton and Wordsworth there is a difference only of degree.

With Milton English poetry took a decisive inward turn that prepared the way for the new poetry Hazlitt first heard at the turn of the century, examples of which—"The Rime of the Ancient Mariner," "Peter Bell," certain lines from "Christabel" and *The*

Borderers—were so stamped on his mind that years later he could quote accurately from memory against the revised public record. The poetry of egotism had joined his other "habitual attachments"; yet its mastery seemed to him comparatively artless; what was inspiring about Milton was the art with which he had met the challenge of great predecessors. For he no less than the Lake poets had felt oppressed by a sense that all the niches were filled, that he had chosen to write his epic an age too late. In the light of this his achievement seems especially heroic. His work was a beautiful sublimation of the lyric motive, and he did not accomplish it by recurring to familiar sentiments or unfamiliar fancies. On the contrary, "The quantity of art in him shows the strength of his genius: the weight of his intellectual obligations would have oppressed any other writer." Shakespeare had intuitions that defeated all the pretensions of learning; but "Milton's learning has the effect of intuition." A vivid recognition of the art, learning, and conscious power Milton employed in his dealings with poetic tradition, licensed Hazlitt for his speculations on the imperfect sympathies Milton may have felt for God.

Art, learning, and conscious power: these were the weapons Satan too was bound to employ, in the battle against his own predecessor.

> Milton was too magnanimous and open an antagonist to support his argument by the bye-tricks of a hump and cloven foot. . . . He relied on the justice of his cause, and did not scruple to give the devil his due. Some persons may think that he has carried his liberality too far, and injured the cause he professed to espouse by making him the chief person in his poem. Considering the nature of his subject, he would be equally in danger of running into this fault, from his faith in religion, and his love of rebellion; and perhaps each of these motives had its full share in determining the choice of his subject.   (V, 65)

From Hazlitt's remarks elsewhere one may conclude that Milton could not well have carried his liberality too far. Shelley and Blake admired Satan in a dialectical spirit, as the ironic inversion or proper bane of the Christian God. But Hazlitt admired him more simply, as a hero who wagered everything to win his freedom and to defy arbitrary power. Of all the romantics he comes closest to Empson's position in *Milton's God;* a poem, he would have agreed, that shows the inner workings of a terrific and barbarous religion, cannot help making us despise what it sets out to justify.[31] That is his logic in telling us Milton "would be equally in danger of running into this fault, from his faith in religion, and his love of rebellion." An honest attempt to defend an inhuman faith must always end in rebellion against it. Hazlitt went the whole length with this interpretation, and liked to quote Satan in defense of the causes for which he himself fought: "And what else is not to be overcome?" He quoted here from memory, of course, and by restoring the natural order to Milton's "is else" turned the moment into a small triumph of prose.

To any reader familiar with the attacks on Wordsworth which Hazlitt carried through several published books, and two decades of periodical criticism, some troubling questions now present themselves. Why, of all the egotists whom he knew as contemporaries, did he elect to praise only Napoleon for exhibiting a freedom from worldly vanity, and antagonism to arbitrary power? On the subject of egotism and poetry, was he at liberty when he wrote of Milton and in fetters when he wrote of Wordsworth? Or does he adopt a sliding scale according to which some egotisms are better than others?

A fuller discussion of Hazlitt's complex attitude toward Napoleon must be deferred to chapter 8, but some obvious analogies with Satan emerge from a few sentences in his Preface to the *Life*.

> He was nothing, he could be nothing but what he owed to himself. . . . He did many things wrong and foolish; but they were individual acts, and recoiled upon the head of the doer. They stood upon the ground of their own merits, and could not urge in their vindication "the right divine of kings to govern wrong". . . . [Apart from a hatred of tyranny] there were two other feelings that influenced me on this subject; a love of glory, when it did not interfere with other things, and the wish to see personal merit prevail over external rank and circumstance. I felt pride (not envy) to think that there was one reputation in modern times equal to the ancients, and at seeing one man greater than the throne he sat upon.   (XIII, ix-x)

Satan too is self-made, owing nothing to the system of places and pensions celebrated in hosannahs by all but the rebel angels; he is proud, and inspires the pride of self-worth in others; he is human in both his fallibility and his dignity as a moral agent: Napoleon then, like Satan, and like the poet who sympathizes with him, is at least a sublime egotist. Beside them Wordsworth seemed a petty one.

Hazlitt reached this verdict on the evidence of Wordsworth's personal manner ("All I remember of his conversation turned upon extreme instances of self-will and self-adulation") but also, as Words-worth played Abdiel to George III's God, on the evidence of his politics. For us it may seem absurd to weigh such allegiances in the balance with the revolutionary poetry of Wordsworth's great decade. But Hazlitt lacked the benefit of our detachment, and what he did have may be harder for us to recover than detachment. He registers the strangeness of a moment when the humanities of Wordsworth's ballads, of his great odes, and even of "Tintern Abbey," began to appear suspect, as they were mediated by the statements of a public man with whom the poet shared a name. Doubtless it was cruel to submit Wordsworth's poems to this test; it was also the only way to rescue them at all. From any other point of view—that dictated by philosophic radicalism, or fashionable literature—they were private and perhaps mad. Besides, we have to remember that when Hazlitt looked for some larger poetic achievement to measure against Words-worth's tergiversations in politics, he could not point to *The Pre-lude*. The ambitious poem by which Wordsworth chose to be known in his lifetime was *The Excursion*.

CHAPTER IV

THE EGOTISTICAL SUBLIME

WORDSWORTH AND ROUSSEAU

Wordsworth, chastened by the reign of terror in France, and returning to swell the war-whoop in England, came to exemplify all that Hazlitt most distrusted about "poetic versatility" and the imagination's affinity for power; and Hazlitt left a full record of those satiric epiphanies which cooled his distrust into loathing: digressions on the spirit of poetry, and its opposition to the spirit of humanity, that reach their climax in the years 1815–1820 in articles written for the *Examiner*. As he opened his lecture on "the living poets" his audience must have expected the worst. And yet, Hazlitt began it by praising Wordsworth as "the most original poet now living." He has "produced a deeper impression, and on a smaller circle, than any other poet in modern times has done, or attempted": modern times, for Hazlitt, would have included every poet from Pope onward; and apart from the restriction, *on a smaller circle,* he admits only one reservation. Wordsworth "cannot form a whole." So in *The Excursion,* in spite of "noble materials . . . the poem stands stock-still." The general application of this criticism to Wordsworth's genius he explains by observing that Wordsworth "is totally deficient in all the machinery of poetry." He then quotes all of "Hart-Leap Well," with the warning, right for an interested propagandist who must be willing to bully a little, that "those who do not feel the beauty and the force of it, may save themselves the trouble of inquiring farther."

Only after all this does Hazlitt adopt the derisive nickname, "the Lake school," which had been invented by reviewers as a tax on the efforts of mutual promotion by Wordsworth, Southey, and Coleridge.

A thorough adept in this school of poetry and philanthropy is jealous of all excellence but his own.[1] He does not even like to

150

share his reputation with his subject. . . . He tolerates only what
he himself creates; he sympathizes only with what can enter into
no competition with him, with "the bare trees and mountains
bare, and grass in the green field." He sees nothing but himself
and the universe. He hates all greatness and all pretensions to it,
whether well or ill-founded. His egotism is in some respects a madness; for he scorns even the admiration of himself, thinking it a
presumption in any one to suppose that he has taste or sense
enough to understand him.   (V, 163)

There follows an impressive list of Wordsworth's dislikes, including
"all science and all art," everything from Voltaire and Newton to
"conchology" and "the dialogues in Shakespeare." This is the part
of Hazlitt's lecture that is usually remembered. But if he meant to
advertise the power of Wordsworth's achievement as a thing attained
in spite of egotism, the choice of "Hart-Leap Well" was subversive
of his design. For the poem is a subtle instance of the appropriation
by an egotistical poet of a subject he seems to hold at a distance—a
demonstration of just how Wordsworth refuses "to share his reputation with his subject," and makes us admire him for refusing.

"Hart-Leap Well" is written for more than one voice; and Hazlitt, who was a skilled performer of verse, would have impressed it
on his audience that the voice which emerges at the end is Wordsworth's own.

> "The pleasure-house is dust:—behind, before,
>   This is no common waste, no common gloom;
>   But Nature, in due course of time, once more
>   Shall here put on her beauty and her bloom.
>
> "She leaves these objects to a slow decay,
>   That what we are, and have been, may be known;
>   But at the coming of the milder day,
>   These monuments shall all be overgrown.
>
> "One lesson, Shepherd, let us two divide,
>   Taught both by what she shews, and what conceals,
>   Never to blend our pleasure or our pride
>   With sorrow of the meanest thing that feels."

The story is of a knight who builds a pleasure-house to com-
memorate his successful hunt for the "gallant brute" that died by
the well. But the telling is elliptical; only the Shepherd's later em-
bellishments complete it; and only with the arrival of a third presence on the scene, Wordsworth's own, do the story and the ruins

take on their proper meaning: nature has destroyed the pleasure house by "slow decay," to rebuke man's restless impulse to mingle his own pleasure and pride with the suffering of meanest things. The durability of monuments, a reader of Wordsworth may suppose, is conquered by the durability of human sympathies. True enough, Hazlitt replies by his choice of poems, but the means employed to perfect this moral are egotistical. The subject, the story, are nothing: they try to give an account of themselves but remain inarticulate until Wordsworth speaks for them.[2]

Thus, in the *Lectures,* Hazlitt concedes the power of Wordsworth's egotism only by indirection. Elsewhere he makes the concession allegorically, by imputing to Rousseau certain qualities that seemed to him equally prominent in Wordsworth. But in a single plain sentence Hazlitt himself gives us the license for this easy transition: "we see no other sort of difference between them, than that the one wrote in prose and the other in poetry." Owing to distance of several kinds, Hazlitt was able to praise Rousseau with a warmth that never entered his tone in writing of Wordsworth: if politics made it hard for him to acknowledge Wordsworth's greatness, he could go on about Rousseau's, and allow no sort of difference between the genius of their works; the reader might draw his own inferences. Yet he portrayed Rousseau from several points of view, not all of them sympathetic. A representative sample of these may lend perspective to the less openly expressed shifts in his attitude toward Wordsworth. But the passages I will be quoting illustrate not the development of a single view but the constant revision and integration of more than one. As is often the case with Hazlitt, the conclusive judgments, offered at different stages of his life, contradict without appearing to exclude each other.

I begin with a little known passage from the review of Sismondi's *De la Litterature du Midi de L'Europe,* the second of Hazlitt's contributions to the *Edinburgh Review.* Whoever, he suggests, will compare the beauty of the young woman shrouded in her bower and listening to the song of the nightingale, in Chaucer's "The Flower and the Leaf," with a similar passage in Rousseau, the description of the Elysée in *La Nouvelle Héloïse,* may see how far the self-consciousness of the modern writer has impaired even his powers of observation. For the comparison shows

> the difference between good writing and fine writing; or between
> the actual appearances of nature and the progress of the feelings
> they excite in us, and a parcel of words, images and sentiments

thrown together without meaning or coherence. We do not say
this from any feeling of disrespect to Rousseau, for whom we have
a great affection; but his imagination was not that of the poet or
the painter. Severity and boldness are the characteristics of the
natural style; the artificial is equally servile and ostentatious.

(XVI, 55)

Nothing is said in favor of the artificial style; it has only the fineness
of finery. Still, "we have a great affection" for Rousseau. So far the
causes of his affection are as obscure as his motive would be for
thinking Wordsworth original, had the reader been shown nothing
but the satirical comment on the Lake poets.

A more balanced judgment may be found in the "Character of
Rousseau," which matches praise and blame as subtly as the Wordsworth lecture.

His genius was the effect of his temperament. He created nothing, he demonstrated nothing, by a pure effort of the understanding. His fictitious characters are modifications of his own being,
reflections and shadows of himself. His speculations are the obvious exaggerations of a mind, giving loose to its habitual impulses, and moulding all nature to its own purposes. Hence his
enthusiasm and his eloquence, bearing down all opposition. Hence
the warmth and the luxuriance, as well as the sameness of his
descriptions. Hence the frequent verboseness of his style; for passion lends force and reality to language, and makes words supply
the place of imagination. Hence the tenaciousness of his logic, the
acuteness of his observations, the refinement and the inconsistency
of his reasoning. . . . Hence his excessive egotism, which filled
all objects with himself, and would have occupied the universe
with his smallest interest. (IV, 89)

"Passion" has now become Rousseau's element, and his whole justification. While his singularity is perhaps to be regretted there is
also something admirable in it. He is a self-sympathizer; but within
the limits of his exclusive mode of feeling, we cannot doubt his
sincerity, or persuade ourselves to resist his spell. Everything he tells
us is colored by the exaggerating power of a mind turned in upon
itself, yet for Hazlitt the imagination is necessarily an exaggerating
faculty; so Rousseau's failure to accomplish anything "by a pure
effort of the understanding" serves only to recommend him to those
who care for something more than understanding; and it is just such
readers Hazlitt has been courting, or hoping to create, in all his
essays for *The Round Table*. Rousseau substitutes words for things,

but his words become our things, so long as we are reading him.
His passion, concentrated as it is, cannot help being infectious. Hazlitt recognizes the danger that in the process reason may be made a
pander to the will (in this case the will of the writer). He qualifies
his enthusiasm accordingly, without altering his conviction that
"passion," so far as it refuses to act in the service of petty self-interest, is an unmixed good no matter how egotistical its origins.

Sometimes he prefers to admit no qualification at all. Throughout his rhapsody on the march of intellect, in the sixteenth of his
Conversations of Northcote, one feels that egotism has become his
ally against a common enemy—power, "turretted, crowned, and
crested"—and for this contest, the egotistical imagination is assim-
ilated to a new and *principled* freedom. The march of course leads
to the French Revolution, and egotism is the weapon every soldier
has been issued along the way. With a pride unusual in these conversations, Hazlitt acknowledges the speech as his own, and climbs
swiftly to the defiance of its liberating questions: to abridge him
here would be unthinkable.

> Before we can take an author entirely to our bosoms, he must be
> another self; and he cannot be this, if he is "not one, but all man-
> kind's epitome." It was this which gave such an effect to Rous-
> seau's writings, that he stamped his own character and the image
> of his self-love on the public mind—*there* it is, and there it will
> remain in spite of every thing. Had he possessed more comprehen-
> sion of thought or feeling, it would only have diverted him from
> his object. But it was the excess of his egotism and his utter blind-
> ness to every thing else, that found a corresponding sympathy in
> the conscious feelings of every human breast, and shattered to
> pieces the pride of rank and circumstance by the pride of internal
> worth or upstart pretension. When Rousseau stood behind the
> chair of the master of the *château* of ———, and smiled to hear
> the company dispute about the meaning of the motto of the arms
> of the family, which he alone knew, and stumbled as he handed
> the glass of wine to his young mistress, and fancied she coloured at
> being waited upon by so learned a young footman—then was first
> kindled that spark which can never be quenched, then was formed
> the germ of that strong conviction of the disparity between the
> badge on his shoulder and the aspirations of his soul—the deter-
> mination, in short, that external situation and advantages are but
> the mask, and that the mind is the man—armed with which, im-
> penetrable, incorrigible, he went forth conquering and to conquer,
> and overthrew the monarchy of France and the hierarchies of

the earth. Till then, birth and wealth and power were all in all, though but the frame-work or crust that envelopes the man; and what there was in the man himself was never asked, or was scorned and forgot. And while all was dark and groveling within, while knowledge either did not exist or was confined to a few, while material power and advantages were every thing, this was naturally to be expected. But with the increase and diffusion of knowledge, this state of things must sooner or later cease; and Rousseau was the first who held the torch (lighted at the never-dying fire in his own bosom) to the hidden chambers of the mind of man—like another Prometheus, breathed into his nostrils the breath of a new and intellectual life, enraging the Gods of the earth, and made him feel what is due to himself and his fellows. Before, physical force was every thing: henceforward, mind, thought, feeling was a new element—a fourth estate in society. What! shall a man have read Dante and Ariosto, and be none the better for it? Shall he be still judged of only by his coat, the number of his servants in livery, the house over his head? While poverty meant ignorance, that was necessarily the case; but the world of books overturns the world of things, and establishes a new balance of power and scale of estimation. Shall we think only rank and pedigree divine, when we have music, poetry, and painting within us? Tut! we have read *Old Mortality;* and shall it be asked whether we have done so in a garret or a palace, in a carriage or on foot? Or knowing them, shall we not revere the mighty heirs of fame, and respect ourselves for knowing and honouring them? This is the true march of intellect, and not the erection of *Mechanics' Institutions,* or the printing of *twopenny trash,* according to my notion of the matter, though I have nothing to say against them neither. (XI, 278-79)

By the end of this speech, all Hazlitt's doubts about egotism seem to have vanished. Any author whom we love *must* ·be another self. Besides, Rousseau's want of comprehension now looks like a virtue, since anything less single-minded than the exclusive idea of himself would only have diverted him from his object—an object that is the greatest imaginable for any human mind, the discovery of "a corresponding sympathy" in the minds of others. By that sympathy the world of books overturns the world of things. If we ask why the power of egotism, instead of merely teaching by example and so producing more egotism, now draws out a corresponding sympathy in the reader, the answer is that it is only with the egotism of another person that we sympathize in any case: we cannot sympathize with his sympathy. Rousseau overthrew "all the hierarchies" when he made inward feeling the measure of anyone's worth, and did so from the unshakable conviction of his own. Hazlitt's familiar image of the lamp of nature appears once again, but now as the Promethean fire kindled by man's imagination of himself, and kept alive by his ability to repose on the strength of his own aspirations. The triumph of words over things, and of the individual over the arbitrary power of despotism, is thus implicit in Rousseau's use of egotism. He sought and found a sympathetic response to the confessed privacy of his experience. After that, the march of intellect could not be stopped.

So far has Hazlitt come, with all he implies about the egotistical imagination in his lecture on Wordsworth and the associated remarks on Rousseau, that the distinction between the imagination's repose on nature and its repose on itself can no longer be maintained: the movement is exactly parallel to that of "Why the Arts are not Progressive?" Of course, "nature" may still be a useful slogan to combat the intrusions into poetry of a preening fashionability; and we may prefer the dramatic mode, and regard Shakespeare as somehow beyond all challenge. Yet if we are asked to account for the power of Shakespeare's poetry, we must resort to the same explanation that serves us in accounting for the power of Milton's or Wordsworth's: we can only say, Wordsworth looked into himself; Milton looked into himself; Shakespeare looked into himself. This extended movement of Hazlitt's thought can be summed up by saying that an unidealizing view of the imagination rescues from complete pessimism his unidealizing view of progress in the arts. If the history of art is mostly a history of diminishing returns, that is because the example of the great dead presses down on the memory of the living; yet tradition has no more determining force in the life of a poet than do "habitual trains of thought" in the life of a moral agent; we can never be sure when, by an act of vivid imagining, some one may not succeed in revising the precedents that define him. There are times for Hazlitt—looking at the Immortality Ode or "Michael," and comparing it with *The Rape of the Lock*—when he can regard even Wordsworth in this light.

This may be an unduly hopeful note on which to part from some of the gloomier pages bequeathed to us by nineteenth-century criticism. It will make a sufficiently dry conclusion to point out that the loss and gain entailed on literary history by Hazlitt's analysis have emerged with equal probability from a coherent idea of genius. Rhetorically he urges the claim of the "natural" or sympathetic artist. But he knows that this sort of genius differs from the egotist only in his choice of strategy, never in the work his imagination performs. The strengths of art are to be cherished for themselves, because they draw from each other by strange additions and none can offer a promise of transcending history. Hazlitt's tolerance would stand less in need of apology if it were a commoner trait among critics.

"Talent," one reader of Hazlitt has reminded us, "may frolic and juggle; genius realizes and adds."[3] It was the talent rather than the genius for egotism that Hazlitt distrusted above all: the swagger of the man with a knack. That quality, with something too of a morbid restiveness which played havoc with the juggler's reflexes, he detected in Byron from his first reading of *Childe Harold's Pilgrimage;* and after quoting the stanzas in the fourth canto which describe the falls of Velino, he remarked: "There is here in every line an effort at brilliancy, and a successful effort; and yet, in the next, as if nothing had been tried, the same thing is attempted to be expressed again with the same labour as before, the same success, and with as little appearance of repose or satisfaction of mind." Once he had read a good many of the Waverley novels Hazlitt liked to set Byron against Scott, whose works showed invention, and the repose of a thousand truths in as many characters: in *The Spirit of the Age* it would seem right to praise Scott simply by reeling off their names. This was repeating the contrast between Shakespeare and Wordsworth; and it is in the special sense I have explored that Hazlitt declares the secret of Scott's mastery in three words: *"absence of egotism."* In fact, the case against Byron could be made out with more propriety than that against Wordsworth, since Byron had ventured much farther onto Shakespeare's ground. When we finish a play by Shakespeare, we feel that we have seen a piece of the earth; with Byron, it is a carefully wild exotic preserve, and on every tree the tag: "Imported from Byronland."

I think Hazlitt was projecting his final estimate of Byron's dramatic powers when he engaged with Jeffrey to review *Sardanapalus.* But the way to a satisfying conclusion has been blocked by Jeffrey himself, for the published review was absorbed into his works instead of Hazlitt's: it seems to have been one of those instances in which the editor revised a contribution so extensively that he came to think it his own. The following passage, however, I believe to be entirely Hazlitt's.

Close the play, and we meet with [Hamlet] no more—neither in the author's other works, nor any where else. A common author who had hit upon such a character, would have dragged it in at every turn, and worn it to very tatters. Sir John Falstaff, again, is a world of wit and humour in himself. But except in the two parts of Henry IV, there would have been no trace of such a being, had not the author been "ordered to continue him" in the Merry Wives of Windsor. He is not the least like Benedick, or Mercutio, or Sir Toby Belch, or any of the other witty and jovial personages of the same author—nor are they like each other. Othello is one of the most striking and powerful inventions on the stage. But when the play closes, we hear no more of him. The poet's creation comes no more to life again, under a fictitious name, than the real man would have done. Lord Byron in Shakespeare's place, would have peopled the world with black Othellos! What indications are there of Lear in any of his [other] plays? . . . None. It might have been written by any other man, he is so little conscious of it. He never once returns to that huge sea of sorrow; but has left it standing by itself, shoreless and unapproachable.[4]

There is, among other qualities, a prodigality in genius, a self-forgetfulness that sometimes looks like forgetfulness. The object of the poet's gaze is interesting while it interests him: it can be taken up with the sudden and transfiguring intensity that Hazlitt called "gusto" only because the poet knows that once put away, or overlooked, it may never again pass before him.

THE EXCURSION

Hazlitt's most substantial consideration of Wordsworth's poetry was his review of *The Excursion,* which appeared in three installments in *The Examiner,* between August 21 and October 2, 1814. It was the first serious discussion of Wordsworth's poetry by a critic who could claim to be neither an advocate set up by the poet himself nor a spokesman for fashionable literature. Jeffrey, whose article for the *Edinburgh Review* appeared a month later, for all his acuteness still wrote as a critic of the latter sort: every student of the period knows his opening line, "This will never do," and the tone of efficient scrupulosity that goes with it. Such is the tone that has dominated the intellectual journalism of the past 150 years. Yet Jeffrey's review appeals to no standard more exacting than the reader's expectation that he shall be entertained. Hazlitt's review, on the contrary, begins by granting that Wordsworth's poetry is something new in the world. And it was Hazlitt's review, far more than Coleridge's discussion of Wordsworth in the *Biographia Literaria,* which showed the first generation of readers *what* was new about the poetry.

Wordsworth himself seems to have understood the importance of Hazlitt in this respect, though his resentment in the end outweighed his gratitude: *Hazlitt, a younger man whom he knew,* had dared to speak of him critically. An anecdote, not yet canonical, about Wordsworth's reading aloud of the review, may be worth repeating here. Hazlitt tells it in the "Reply to Z," and must have heard the details through the *Blackwood's* critic John Wilson, who was with Wordsworth at the time. A critic for the *Examiner* might have been relied on to deprecate the poem on political grounds alone, and, by his high-handedness both within literary society and without, Wordsworth had supplied certain of the contributors with a more personal reason for aversion. He would therefore have been anxious at the prospect of any report on the poem from that quarter—but let Hazlitt tell the story.

Some time in the latter end of the year 1814 Mr. Wordsworth received an *Examiner* by the post, which annoyed him exceedingly both on account of the expence and the paper. "Why did they send that rascally paper to him, and make him pay for it?" Mr. Wordsworth is tenacious of his principles and not less so of his purse. "Oh," said Wilson, "let us see what there is in it. I dare say they have not sent it you for nothing. Why here, there's a criticism upon the Excursion in it." This made the poet (*par excellence*) rage and fret the more. "What did they know about his poetry? What could they know about it? It was presumption in the highest degree for these cockney writers to pretend to criticise a Lake poet." "Well," says the other, "at any rate let us read it." So he began. The article was much in favour of the poet and the poem. As the reading proceeded, "Ha," said Mr. Wordsworth, somewhat appeased, "there's some sense in this fellow too: the Dog writes strong." Upon which Mr. Wilson was encouraged to proceed still farther with the encomium, and Mr. Wordsworth continued his approbation; "Upon my word very judicious, very well indeed." At length, growing vain with his own and the *Examiner*'s applause, he suddenly seized the paper into his own hands, and saying "Let me read it, Mr. Wilson," did so with an audible voice and appropriate gesture to the end, when he exclaimed, "Very well written indeed, Sir, I did not expect a thing of this kind," and strutting up and down the room in high good humour kept every now and then wondering who could be the author, "he had no idea, and should like very much to know to whom he was indebted for such pointed and judicious praise"—when Mr. Wilson interrupting him with saying, "Oh don't you know; it's Hazlitt, to be sure, there are his initials to it," threw our poor philosopher into a greater rage than ever, and a fit of outrageous incredulity to think that he should be indebted for the first favourable account that had ever appeared of any work he had ever written to a person on whom he had conferred such great and unmerited obligations.

(IX, 6)

Only the first installment of the "Character of Mr. Wordsworth's New Poem, The Excursion" could have struck Wordsworth as very favorable. But for us the difficulty of recovering the whole feeling of the review is aggravated by the many revisions Hazlitt made before allowing it to be printed in *The Round Table;* these were done several months later, and by then he had doubtless heard of, and otherwise felt reverberations from, Wordsworth's reception of the piece; he had seen, too, the vindictiveness of Wordsworth's odes against Napoleon, which though they might seem to follow naturally from the political retreat of *The Excursion,* no critic could have predicted solely on the evidence of that poem. The paragraph on Wordsworth's politics, however, Hazlitt left as it stood. What he reworked for *The Round Table* was his tone, in the light of subsequent doubts concerning Wordsworth's politics and pastoralism: without actually strengthening these, Hazlitt makes them a good deal more prominent.

He accomplished the revision both by verbal changes and logical transpositions. In the *Examiner* he had regretted Wordsworth's pretence of story-telling, and wished he could have "given to his work the form of a philosophic poem altogether": in *The Round Table,* "philosophic" has become "didactic." Again, he had tried to convey the limitations of Wordsworth's poetry by distinguishing between imagination and sentiment, between "richness of invention and depth of feeling." The greatest poets have both; Young and Cowley have imagination or fancy,[5] with too little of the common sentiments of mankind; while Wordsworth is preeminently the poet of feeling without invention. But a long passage introducing these categories is omitted from *The Round Table,* so that Hazlitt may circumscribe Wordsworth's genius more thoroughly. Where he wrote that Wordsworth's "imagination broods over that which is 'without form and void,' and 'makes it pregnant' "—plainly introducing a comparison with Milton—he now omits "imagination" in favor of "understanding," and thus implies the question: "What troubles will beset a long poem written in the age of Locke?" Even more decisive is the reframing of his conclusion. The last sentence in the *Examiner* had been: "It is not in our power to add to, or take away from, the pretensions of a poem like the present, but if our opinion or wishes could have the least weight, we would take our leave of it by saying— *Esto perpetua!*" The new conclusion for *The Round Table* comes from the first paragraph in the *Examiner;* and taken not as a qualification when praise is understood to follow, but as a summing-up when all praise is done, its effect is severe.

> If the skill with which the poet had chosen his materials had been equal to the power which he has undeniably exerted over them, if the objects (whether persons or things) which he makes use of as the vehicle of his sentiments, had been such as to convey them in all their depth and force, then the production before us might indeed "have proved a monument," as he himself wishes it, worthy of the author, and of his country. Whether, as it is, this very original and powerful performance may not rather remain like one of those stupendous but half-finished structures, which have been suffered to moulder into decay, because the cost and labour attending them exceeded their use or beauty, we feel that it would be presumptuous in us to determine. (IV, 124-25)

By assigning his doubts a determinate position at the end of the review, Hazlitt did an injustice to the spirit in which he had conceived it. For this reason among others the earlier version seems to me preferable, and I shall be quoting it without further reference to *The Round Table.*

A challenge is laid down in the opening sentence which the rest of the review must try to meet: "In power of intellect, in lofty conception, in the depth of feeling, at once simple and sublime, which pervades every part of it and which gives to every object an almost preternatural and preterhuman interest, this work has seldom been surpassed." This is Longinian praise, yet we feel a remoteness from our sympathies in an interest "almost preternatural and preterhuman." By going on to describe the mountain landscape in which Wordsworth moves by elective affinity, Hazlitt tells us how a work that is cold to the touch may be great.

> The Poem of the *Excursion* resembles the country in which the scene is laid. It has the same vastness and magnificence, with the same nakedness and confusion. It has the same overwhelming,

oppressive power. It excites or recals the same sensations which those who have traversed that wonderful scenery must have felt. We are surrounded with the constant sense and superstitious awe of the collective power of matter, of the gigantic and eternal forms of Nature, on which, from the beginning of time, the hand of man has made no impression. Here are no dotted lines, no hedge-row beauties, no box-tree borders, no gravel walks, no square mechanic enclosures. All is left loose and irregular in the rude chaos of aboriginal nature. . . . Such is the severe simplicity of Mr. Wordsworth's taste, that we doubt whether he would not reject a druidical temple, or time-hallowed ruin, as too modern and artificial for his purpose. He only familiarises himself or his readers with a stone, covered with lichens, which has slept in the same spot of ground from the creation of the world, or with the rocky fissure between two mountains caused by thunder, or with a cavern scooped out by the sea. His mind is, as it were, coeval with the primary forms of things, holds immediately from nature; and his imagination "owes no allegiance" but "to the elements." (XIX, 9-10)

At this distance we are struck by what Hazlitt's first readers could not easily have known—the extent to which he was reviewing not *The Excursion* but all of Wordsworth's poetry leading up to it. When for example he evokes those "gigantic and eternal forms" on which "the hand of man has made no impression," he is recalling Wordsworth's claim in the Preface to *Lyrical Ballads,* to have chosen subjects from rustic life "because in that condition the passions of men are incorporated with the beautiful and permanent forms of nature." So the entire Wordsworthian program for poetry receives a fairer hearing than might have been expected. And the imaginative power Hazlitt admits him to possess is, from one point of view, the greatest he would admit for any poet: among those primeval shapes Wordsworth discourses as freely, as unserviceably, as Satan stalking *his* subject in *his* Chaos. But there is also a suggestion of puritanical self-denial in the "severe simplicity" of Wordsworth's taste: the same faculty that keeps him to his regimen will understandably put others out of patience. Why should he not furnish us with livelier matter for so long a journey?

He might do so, if it were an excursion into the country. But Hazlitt says in effect: you may search all England and not find a place like this. In his opening metaphor the vehicle has finally displaced the tenor; nothing but Wordsworth's mind has quite this look. The main argument of the review begins only after Hazlitt has interpreted the country, and the peculiar virtues ascribed to it, as a fiction of the probable-but-impossible sort. Some of his objections are therefore delayed: only in the final installment do we get the passage beginning, "All country people hate each other. . . . There is nothing good to be had in the country, or, if there is, they will not give it to you." It continues splendidly and exorbitantly, a long-delayed revenge for the country-jilt episode; for at that point Hazlitt felt he could afford to widen the attack. The key phrase of the paragraph just quoted—"his mind . . . holds immediately from nature"—had already made his position clear, by indicating both the intensity and the limitations of Wordsworth's power.

From this phrase Hazlitt derives his interpretation of the whole poem as a psychological romance. And since everything we know about the poet leads us to expect that his talk will be about politics, the intensity of nature-instruction comes to be a measure of the repression of politics. In observing the inward turn of Wordsworthian romance, Hazlitt stresses repeatedly what the poem is not, as if the exclusions were deliberate. He was convinced that they were, and would use his conviction later in the review to open up the subject of politics. But for the time being the issue is held in suspense.

> The *Excursion* may be considered as a philosophical pastoral poem—as a scholastic romance. It is less a poem on the country than on the love of the country. It is not so much a description of natural objects, as of the feelings associated with them, not an account of the manners of rural life, but the result of the Poet's reflections on it. He does not present the reader with a lively succession of images or incidents, but paints the outgoings of his own heart, the shapings of his own fancy. He may be said to create his own materials; his thoughts are his real subject. . . . He sees all things in his own mind; he contemplates effects in their causes, and passions in their principles. He hardly ever avails himself of striking subjects or remarkable combinations of events, but in general rejects them as interfering with the workings of his own mind, as disturbing the smooth, deep, majestic current of his own feelings. Thus his descriptions of natural scenery are not brought home distinctly to the naked eye by forms and circumstances, but every object is seen through the medium of innumerable recollections, is clothed with the haze of imagination like a glittering vapour, is obscured with the excess of glory, has the shadowy brightness of a waking dream. The object is lost in the sentiment, as sound in the multiplication of echoes.[6]   (XIX, 10)

The dangers of this situation to the poet himself emerge in the next paragraph: "An intense intellectual egotism swallows up every thing. . . . The power of his mind preys upon itself." Still, as we see Wordsworth's universe through his eyes, it hardly seems possible that we should wish to look elsewhere: without him it would remain for us so much inanimate matter. Wordsworth "may be said to create his own materials," he is original, and for Hazlitt that marks an end of our search. The attitude here may remind us of Johnson's in the *Life of Swift*—another work by a critic temperamentally allied to his subject, in writing about whom the critic betrays a severity of reproach in proportion to the acuteness of his self-knowledge. For both Johnson and Hazlitt, all objections are silenced by the praise of originality. Even the words, "He sees all things in his own mind," would have had a special force for Hazlitt, from their inversion in the "Character of Rousseau": "He sees himself in all things." Though he would later profess to find no essential difference between them, it appears from this contrast that Wordsworth alone has got the epigram right, and with it the sublime perspective of egotism. For Rousseau "No matter what he looks at, it is himself that he sees"; for Wordsworth: "He looks into himself, and there finds all of nature." This of course had also been Dryden's praise of Shakespeare, repeated with small modifications by Pope, Johnson, and Hazlitt. It shows how generous his view of Wordsworth could become, and how far in practice his worries about egotism could be suspended or made to seem only the worries one always has about poets.[7]

Only once does Hazlitt describe the tedium of the poem in Jeffrey's style; but even here, the tone never slips into mere decorous impatience, and the objection takes into account the strangeness of Wordsworth's genius, as well as the use to which a "philosophic" age puts all poetic gifts. Most of the passage was omitted from *The Round Table,* but it anticipates, more nearly than anything else in Hazlitt's first decade of journalism, the treatment of both Wordsworth and Coleridge in *The Spirit of the Age.*

> There is in his general sentiment and reflections on human life a depth, an originality, a truth, a beauty, and grandeur, both of conception and expression, which place him decidedly at the head of the poets of the present day, or rather which place him in a totally distinct class of excellence. But he has chosen to encumber himself with a load of narrative and description, which, instead of assisting, hinders the progress and effect of the general reasoning. Almost all this part of the work, which Mr. Wordsworth has in-

woven with the text, would have come in better in plain prose as notes at the end. Indeed, there is something evidently inconsistent, upon his own principles, in the construction of the poem. For he professes, in these ambiguous illustrations, to avoid all that is striking or extraordinary—all that can raise the imagination or affect the passions—all that is not every way common, and necessarily included in the natural workings of the passions in all minds and in all circumstances. Then why introduce particular illustrations at all, which add nothing to the force of the general truth, which hang as a dead weight upon the imagination, which degrade the thought and weaken the sentiment, and the connection of which with the general principle it is more difficult to find out than to understand the general principle itself? It is only by an extreme process of abstraction that it is often possible to trace the operation of the general law in the particular illustration, yet it is to supply the defect of abstraction that the illustration is given. (XIX, 11-12)

To acquit Hazlitt of any charge of complicity with *Edinburgh* taste, one need only compare the nuance of these lines with the self-possessing flippancy of Jeffrey as he frames an apparently similar complaint: "What Mr. Wordsworth's ideas of length are, we have no means of accurately judging; but we cannot help suspecting that they are liberal, to a degree that will alarm the weakness of most modern readers." As Jeffrey explains Wordsworth's autobiographical plan, the long poem of which *The Excursion* forms a part will cover the whole of Wordsworth's life up to the time when the poem was conceived, and "the quarto before us contains an account of one of his youthful rambles in the vales of Cumberland, and occupies precisely the period of three days; so that, by the use of a very powerful *calculus,* some estimate may be formed of the probable extent of the entire biography." It is a neat jibe, though frankly addressed to just that "weakness of most modern readers"—a weakness baffled by Spenser no less than Wordsworth—with which it affects to sympathize from an attitude of well-earned strength. Reduced to a single phrase, Hazlitt's paragraph also identifies a simple enough fault: "How much better it would be if he took out the plot, and then the characters!" But Hazlitt is saying something important about Wordsworth's ambivalent view of romance, and about the poem's elusiveness in relation to its declared genre. From his inmost moral being Wordsworth distrusts the *episode,* the "illustration"—all that dissolves the soul in pleasure, as Hazlitt said of *The Faerie Queene,* and holds it "captive in the chains of suspense"—so that as the narrator of several distinct stories he operates under constraint. He cannot bear to defer his moral, and yet morality is real to him only in its pure state, as exhortation. When we compare the illustrative tale with its parent truth we find that they are mismatched, or that any match would be improbable: they have wills of their own and prefer to stand alone. In *The Excursion* the two great impulses of romance, to tell a story and to give instruction, have thus separated out completely. Born an age too late, Wordsworth at every moment disappoints one of the aims his title had appeared to unite: excursus and excursion leave no room for each other.

"A single letter from the pen of Gray," Hazlitt says in an article written much later, "is worth all the pedlar-reasoning of Mr. Wordsworth's Eternal Recluse [the Wanderer], from the hour he first squats himself down in the sun to the end of his preaching. In the first we have the light unstudied pleasantries of a wit, and a man of feeling;—in the last we are talked to death by an arrogant old proser, and buried in a heap of the most perilous stuff and the most dusty philosophy." Hazlitt could think himself into such dismissals as easily as Jeffrey: but not when the poem was before him, and his duty was to present it to its first readers. His recognition of all Wordsworth's liabilities as a narrator leads him instead to question the narratability of Wordsworth's sort of poetry; and his conclusion is that the poem would have been more satisfying had it been more straightforwardly egotistical. In the end therefore Hazlitt says what his mind-landscape trope had only implied, that egotism is the wrong name for what troubles him in Wordsworth's poetry. Yet a look at a representative "illustration" may be necessary to explain his justification for sounding troubled at all.

The reader unfamiliar with *The Excursion* needs to be told here that its three main characters are the Wanderer, the Poet, and the Solitary: the first an old man who by slow accretions of experience has become a sage; the second a stand-in for Wordsworth, but several years younger than the author of the poem; the third a pretender-sage whose wisdom has been distorted by resentment, and whose experience is vexed by alternations of crisis and disappointment. The poem is a battle for the Solitary's soul, with everything in his own life conspiring to draw him into despair, and only the Wanderer fighting to redeem him. The contest has for its spectator one person, the Poet, and there are occasional suggestions that his great choices in life will be influenced by the outcome. What excitement the story possesses is owing to the self-doubt one imagines as a motive for the Poet's questions, and even for the answers supplied by the Solitary and the Wanderer. The three days' discourse, in nine books of about one thousand lines each, is varied beginning in Book V by the appearance of another character, a Pastor, whose function in the scheme of "Despondency" and "Despondency Corrected" is to administer routinely from tradition the comforts that the Wanderer has gathered and can impart through inspiration alone.

In Book VI the Pastor, walking among the gravestones of a mountain churchyard, recounts several of the histories they bring to mind. This survey appears to be mildly cautionary in intent: the cases he selects—a disappointed lover, a prodigal son, a pair of zealots, "flaming Jacobite / And sullen Hanoverian"—all illustrate some sort of restlessness of spirit being subdued to the love of nature and the uses of a community, even if this means a community of two. Against so exclusive a concern with those who have offered "obeisance to the world" the Solitary protests—too sharply, as Wordsworth informs us by temporarily renaming him the Skeptic, but still with a propriety that extends beyond this moment in *The Excursion*. He wonders why the destinies of those whom the community of men have cast out should not make equally fit matter for a tale, the more incumbent upon our sympathies because the more easily ignored. In saying this he has the sanction of Gray's Churchyard Elegy, and of Wordsworth in other places than *The Excursion*, so that he must be granted his eloquence.

> Say why
> That ancient story of Prometheus chained
> To the bare rock, on frozen Caucasus;
> The vulture, the inexhaustible repast
> Drawn from his vitals? Say what meant the woes
> By Tantalus entailed upon his race,
> And the dark sorrows of the line of Thebes?
> Fictions in form, but in their substance truths,
> Tremendous truths! familiar to the men
> Of long-past times, nor obsolete in ours.
> Exchange the shepherd's frock of native grey
> For robes with regal purple tinged; convert
> The crook into a sceptre; give the pomp
> Of circumstance; and there the tragic Muse
> Shall find apt subjects for her highest art.
> (*Excursion*, VI, 538-552)

The Pastor is kept from such tales, of "grievous crimes / And strange disasters," by the constraints of his office; but the Poet now gives a different reason for passing them by, in keeping with Wordsworth's argument in the "Essay upon Epitaphs." A churchyard is a place where the memory of a community is preserved, and the record of each individual life is confirmed and given value by its association with others. If in rural districts the record is scant, this ought only to confirm the proper modesty of the storyteller. "Temptation here is none to exceed the truth. . . . And who can blame, / Who rather would not envy, men that feel / This mutual confidence; if from such source, / The practise flow,—if thence, or from a deep / And general humility in death?" About their own lives they are silent. Let us remember them therefore with the moral which the very presence of a graveyard seems to imply: we all go to the same end, and our last moments are necessarily moments of acceptance.

Grateful for this help, the Pastor affirms his intention to supply only such narratives as excite the genial affections; but he is not entirely satisfied with the Poet's reassurance, and confesses having felt a scruple about his own work as a moralist.

> And yet there are,
> I feel, good reasons why we should not leave
> Wholly untraced a more forbidding way.
> For, strength to persevere and to support,
> And energy to conquer and repel—
> These elements of virtue, that declare
> The native grandeur of the human soul—
> Are oft-times not unprofitably shown
> In the perverseness of a selfish course.
> (*Excursion*, VI, 660-668)

The "more forbidding way" alludes, among other things, to the errant path of romance, in which the wanderer must be lost to be saved; the central lines of the passage, with their weird shift to the optative mood, register the dangers that lie in the way: the echo of Satan rousing his troops is very odd, and unless one has in mind Wordsworth's larger anxiety about the genre of the poem it can feel as if for the moment he had lost control.

The Pastor now points to the burial-place of a woman who even in death appears to refuse all connection with her neighbors. In life she was tall, dark, and saturnine, "surpassed by few / In power of mind, and eloquent discourse," with a serious and self-communing imagination, that required only the solitude of nature for support: indeed, in one of her characteristic attitudes, akin to the youthful Wordsworth—

> her head not raised to hold
> Converse with heaven, nor yet deprest towards earth,
> But in projection carried, as she walked
> For ever musing.
>
> *(Excursion,* VI, 679-682)

But one aim of *The Excursion* is to make those elements of Wordsworth himself which correspond to the "Matron" here described, submit to a new control. So a strength that might be admirable in other settings—for example, a novel by George Eliot or Charlotte Brontë—is resolved into a peculiarly destructive compound of "ruling passions."

> Two passions, both degenerate, for they both
> Began in honour, gradually obtained
> Rule over her, and vexed her daily life;
> An unremitting, avaricious thrift;
> And a strange thraldom of maternal love,
> That held her spirit, in its own despite,
> Bound—by vexation, and regret, and scorn,
> Constrained forgiveness, and relenting vows,
> And tears, in pride suppressed, in shame concealed—
> To a poor dissolute Son, her only child.
>
> *(Excursion,* VI, 706-715)

The marriage, we are told somewhat mysteriously, "opened with mishap," but there is no time for further explanations, because the life and this account of it both close suddenly. The Matron dies, "vexed and wrought upon" to the end, attended by her husband's sister, whose command of the household deepens her despair.

> "And must she rule,"
> This was the death-doomed Woman heard to say
> In bitterness, "and must she rule and reign,
> Sole Mistress of this house, when I am gone?
> Tend what I tended, calling it her own!"
>
> *(Excursion,* VI, 752-756)

By this time she has become more interesting to us than any inference Wordsworth can possibly draw from her way of life. A poet more settled in his task, Frost in "Home Burial," or Wordsworth in Book I of this poem, would let the picture answer for itself: but here the life must be grimly appraised, and tagged with its lesson. *She would not subdue herself to the conditions of life.* Yet we are told that the Pastor by happy accident, still on the right path, happened to pass near the window of her bedroom in the moments near her death; she looked at a shining star and was glad it would outlast her: this is then read back into the story as its clarifying episode, the much sought-for token of the Matron's acceptance of her human lot. "With a sigh . . . yet, I believe, not unsustained / By faith in glory. . . . She, who had rebelled, / Was into meekness softened and subdued."

Thus Wordsworth in pursuit of a moral. We know that the episode interested Hazlitt since he quotes the lines about those tragedies that await our discovery even in the humblest life. And in this instance we share his bewilderment at illustrations, "the connection of which with the general principle it is more difficult to find out than to understand the general principle itself." Still, with the rest of the poem in view, and the gravity of its concern for "Despondency Corrected," the moral of the Matron's tragedy may easily enough be guessed. She withdrew herself from the life and affections of a community, and Wordsworth, in response, would prefer to have excluded her from the poem. He tells us so in the words of the Poet, the character most nearly allied with himself. The Pastor by an extravagance of sympathy points out her gravestone nevertheless, and gives her story, making the gesture of forgiveness which the Poet had hoped to forestall. We are perhaps meant to treat the curious exchange as part of Wordsworth's own education in charity; but the poem as a whole offers no clear assurance on this score. In the end we may have to regard *The Excursion* itself as one enormous "illustration," the connection of which with its own moral remains uncertain throughout. For Wordsworth, who would teach the good of community, can envision only a community that derives its chief sustenance from those negative powers which ought to define but a small part of its value: the power, for example, to exclude, or to withhold sympathy from those it includes for the purpose of correction.

Yet the poem makes an honest picture of its uncertainties. The skeptical and utopian arguments of the Solitary are allowed to emerge persuasively enough for us to feel their intoxication, until we hear them answered by the Wanderer; and even then, we may recall them vividly enough to suppose that the Wanderer has the best of the debate only because his words are always the last. Wordsworth seems to have felt so acutely the strength of the Solitary's arguments that he took the trouble to discredit their advocate beforehand, by exhibiting the unhappy life in which they took root, and to which presumably they must always lead. So the most anxious moment of the poem, for Wordsworth, and the most awkward for the reader, is the moralized biography of the Solitary with which the Wanderer is kept busy through the opening of Book II—interpreting the Village Wake he has glimpsed from a distance as a sure sign of the Solitary's death; pronouncing his eulogy with the mingled satisfaction and regret that befits the fulfillment of a predictable fate; plucking the rain-drenched copy of Voltaire from the mossy nook, and giving back a sermon on the desolation of a life parched by skepticism. After that, the Solitary's refusal to be already dead is an anti-climax eight books long. To the reader it presents the constant irritation of any unresolved irony, though doubtless it was beyond the reach of Wordsworth's self-knowledge to have analyzed the Wanderer's motives for prematurely dismissing his friend into eternity.

In calling this an honest confusion and not just heartlessness, we adopt Hazlitt's insight: that *all* the characters are really Wordsworth; but we must invent for ourselves the corollary: that Wordsworth is cruel to them in proportion as they bring to mind elements of himself which he now wants to banish. Certain characters, however, remain stubbornly attractive in spite of the narrator's disapproval, because too much was invested in them for Wordsworth to complete his task with the severity it required. At such moments as these, when the poet loses his moral claim on the reader, the pretence of drama vanishes and the poem has to be salvaged as a monologue broken arbitrarily into separate voices. Hazlitt's defense of Wordsworth starts from the need to apologize for just such moments; yet his review is a moral as well as a critical act, involving the recognition of a permanent dignity both in Wordsworth's isolation, and in the political ideals he had deserted. These emphases, both unexpected in 1814, were unimaginable in combination, and the excitement one can still feel about the review comes from seeing how they are brought together. In setting about his task Hazlitt took heart from the memory of comparable feats of generosity which he had seen performed by the Reverend Joseph Fawcett, a poet and lecturer of his father's generation, about whom he wrote in *The Life of Thomas Holcroft:* "He was one of the most enthusiastic admirers of the French Revolution; and I believe that the disappointment of the hopes he had cherished of the freedom and happiness of mankind, preyed upon his mind, and hastened his death." The description may remind us a good deal of Wordsworth's Solitary, for whom Fawcett was in fact generally taken to have been the model. Hazlitt would have had Fawcett often in his mind as he read the poem.

The dissent from Wordsworth's politics, to which Hazlitt devotes the second part of his review, is above all a protest against Wordsworth's portrait of the Solitary. Oppressed by private loss, as the Wanderer describes him—having seen his wife and two children die young and communed with their memory till he prayed for his own death—the Solitary is revived by the new and public energies of the French Revolution. But this "righteous cause," says the Wanderer, "Was served by rival advocates that came / From regions opposite as Heaven and Hell." Men like the Solitary, who confuse political design with personal compensation, will always demand most of their fellows and suffer the worst disappointments.

> An overweening trust was raised; and fear
> Cast out, alike of person and of thing.
> Plague from this union spread, whose subtle bane
> The strongest did not easily escape;
> And He, what wonder! took a mortal taint.
> How shall I trace the change, how bear to tell
> That he broke faith with them whom he had laid
> In the earth's dark chambers, with a Christian's hope!
> An infidel contempt of holy writ
> Stole by degrees upon his mind; and hence
> Life, like that Roman Janus, double-faced;
> Vilest hypocrisy—the laughing, gay
> Hypocrisy, not leagued with fear, but pride.
>
> (*Excursion*, II, 241-253)

In the passage that follows, the Wanderer's denunciation of the Solitary as an infidel cannot quite erase our impression that Wordsworth objects to his revolutionary zeal on different grounds altogether. What troubles Wordsworth is that the Solitary has dared to hope; in searching for a good beyond his sufferings he has somehow been false to them. That is the real meaning of "breaking faith" with the memory of his wife and children. However, for Wordsworth to interpret the story in this way would have meant giving up the political and religious debates, and admitting that his whole interest lay elsewhere. In choosing instead to speak through the Wanderer—sanctioned by a piety not his own—he found a license for the triumphant scorn with which he concludes his account of the Solitary's life. The words are not his, they are spoken by a man assured, as Wordsworth could not be, that *these* hopes were wrong to entertain: but even so we may feel there is something indecent in the tone.

> The glory of the times fading away—
> The splendour, which had given a festal air
> To self-importance, hallowed it, and veiled
> From his own sight—this gone, he forfeited
> All joy in human nature; was consumed,
> And vexed, and chafed, by levity and scorn,
> And fruitless indignation; galled by pride;
> Made desperate by contempt of men who throve
> Before his sight in power or fame, and won,
> Without desert, what he desired; weak men,
> Too weak even for his envy or his hate!
> Tormented thus, after a wandering course
> Of discontent, and inwardly opprest
> With malady—in part, I fear, provoked
> By weariness of life—he fixed his home,
> Or, rather say, sate down by very chance,
> Among these rugged hills; where now he dwells,
> And wastes the sad remainder of his hours,
> Steeped in a self-indulging spleen, that wants not
> Its own voluptuousness;—on this resolved,
> With this content, that he will live and die
> Forgotten,—at safe distance from "a world
> Not moving to his mind."
>
> (*Excursion*, II, 293–315)

Those final phrases about the Solitary, with certain others later in the poem, that speak of his "one bare dwelling; one abode, no more," link him with a type of Wordsworthian character especially fit for redemption: Margaret for example, in the first book of *The Excursion*, dying in the place that has witnessed the death of her hopes, "Last human tenant of these ruined walls"; or Wordsworth in the "Elegiac Stanzas on Peele Castle," as he describes himself, "Housed in a dream, at distance from the Kind." But the general tendency of the passage is to find its subject easily deplorable. His conversion, we feel, would make an unendurable trial and had better be spared: to which end the Wanderer quickly moves by supposing him dead.

Let us see how far we can square Wordsworth's portrait of the

Solitary with some passing remarks about Joseph Fawcett in Hazlitt's *Table-Talk* essay "On Criticism." The point of this exercise is to test Wordsworth's generosity to a rival, by which his claim to the title of dramatic poet must finally be judged.

> I have sometimes thought that the most acute and original-minded men made bad critics. They see every thing too much through a particular medium. . . . Men who have fewer native resources, and are obliged to apply oftener to the general stock, acquire by habit a greater aptitude in appreciating what they owe to others. . . . I might take this opportunity of observing, that the person of the most refined and least contracted taste I ever knew was the late Joseph Fawcett, the friend of my youth. He was almost the first literary acquaintance I ever made, and I think the most candid and unsophisticated. . . . "That is the most delicious feeling of all," I have heard him exclaim, "to like what is excellent, no matter whose it is." In this respect he practised what he preached. He was incapable of harbouring a sinister motive, and judged only from what he felt. There was no flaw or mist in the clear mirror of his mind. . . . Most men's minds are to me like musical instruments out of tune. Touch a particular key, and it jars and makes harsh discord with your own. They like Gil Blas, but can see nothing to laugh at in Don Quixote: they adore Richardson, but are disgusted with Fielding. Fawcett had a taste accommodated to all these. He was not exceptious. He gave a cordial welcome to all sorts, provided they were the best in their kind. . . . A heartier friend or honester critic I never coped withal. He has made me feel (by contrast) the want of genuine sincerity and generous sentiment in some that I have listened to since, and convinced me (if proof were wanting) of the truth of that text of Scripture—"That had I all knowledge and could speak with the tongues of angels, yet without charity I were nothing!" I would rather be a man of disinterested taste and liberal feeling, to see and acknowledge truth and beauty wherever I found it, than a man of greater and more original genius, to hate, envy, and deny all excellence but my own—but that poor scanty pittance of it (compared with the whole) which I had myself produced! (VIII, 224-25)

For those who could see beyond the speeches to the man, Fawcett seemed the very pattern of a disinterested sympathy. Indeed it was Fawcett, as Hazlitt reminds us in another place, who bound the *Rights of Man* and *Reflections on the Revolution in France* into one volume, saying that together they made a good book. How then do we judge the poet who can see here only the fixities of the ideologue?

In one sense this is a false problem, for we need not suppose that Hazlitt and Wordsworth were describing the same man. But we have to remember that Hazlitt supposed they were; that he doubtless took the Solitary to represent what Wordsworth would have done with any man like Fawcett; and that these considerations entered into his thinking about the poem. In the review itself he was showing Wordsworth a Fawcett-like generosity. Instead of dwelling on Wordsworth's defects of sympathy, he would take the "best of that kind" of poetry, and interpret the Solitary as a partial portrait of Wordsworth. The whole poem would then become egotistical but great of its kind: the political sermons could be met head-on, having so to speak fallen out of solution, and no longer enjoying the protection of dramatic immunity. Years after writing the review, Hazlitt still cannot summon memories of Fawcett without setting him against Wordsworth; and in the paragraph I quoted from "On Criticism," he deploys the whole established arsenal of anti-egotistical tropes. The dense particular medium of Wordsworth's mind discovers its contrary in the unmisted mirror of Fawcett's. Again, as in the lecture-cadenza on the Lake poets, we are warned of the tendency in "original-minded men" to insist on some "exclusive excellence." A special irony is reserved for Wordsworth's pretensions as a sage, and this would touch most of all the Wordsworth of *The Excursion:* it is Fawcett, the figure of generous common sense, and not Wordsworth, the hoarder of a single interest raised to the intensity of genius, who can draw more often on what Hazlitt calls "the general stock" of ideas—that is, the ideas shared by a community. The implication is that men like Fawcett and not Wordsworth, men reluctant to discard even the most far-fetched vision of utopia as the wreckage of their youth, are likelier some day to advance from the "one abode, no more!" that houses poets and fanatics, and to form part of a living community.

Wordsworth's view of the Solitary provoked the most famous section of the review: Hazlitt's defense of the French Revolution. This has occasionally been dismissed as a fit of spleen. With the facts before us, however, we can now understand it as the final move in a well-pondered strategy. The question of Wordsworth's politics had been opened by his neglect of dramatic artifice: no author above the battle would have granted one of his characters the same liberty, and steady advantage in dealing with another, which the Wanderer evidently has in all his speeches to the Solitary. The speeches revolve around Wordsworth's twin ideals of concern and retreat—an unstable combination throughout his poetry, and never more so than here. As for the double piety which emerges, Hazlitt distrusts it from the bottom of his soul. He begins his denunciation by quoting the Wanderer's eloquent summary of the fate of the revolution. Lamenting the darkness that has "overspread / The groaning nations" in the bloody aftermath, together with "that other loss, / The loss of confidence in social man"—the Sage, as Wordsworth calls him throughout this part, admits nevertheless that by "faith more firm . . . the Bad / Have fairly earned a victory o'er the weak." Hazlitt's reply winds deliberately into its strength, and then as deliberately uncoils.

> In the application of these memorable lines, we should perhaps differ a little with Mr. Wordsworth; nor can we indulge with him in the fond conclusion afterwards hinted at, that one day *our* triumph, the triumph of virtue and liberty, may be complete. For this purpose, we think several things necessary which are impossible. It is a consummation which cannot happen till the nature of things is changed, till the many become as the *one*, till romantic generosity shall be as common as gross selfishness, till reason shall have acquired the obstinate blindness of prejudice, till the love of power and of change shall no longer goad man on to restless action, till passion and will, hope and fear, love and hatred, and the objects to excite them, that is, alternate good and evil, shall no longer sway the bosoms and business of men. All things move not in progress, but in a ceaseless round; our strength lies in our weakness; our virtues are built on our vices; our faculties are as limited as our being; nor can we lift man above his nature more than above the earth he treads. (XIX, 17-18)

So far the modified hopes endorsed by the Wanderer have been accepted as solid sense, for they are in keeping with the *Essay on Human Action,* where Hazlitt admitted the common basis of good and evil actions. But in Wordsworth's injunction to choose, between the extremes of hope and despair, some "middle point, whereon to build / Sound expectations," he senses the deeper complacency of a man to whom many new oppressions will soon be thinkable. Hazlitt continues:

> But though we cannot weave over again the airy, unsubstantial dream, which reason and experience have dispelled—
>
> > "What though the radiance which was once so bright
> > Be now for ever taken from our sight,
> > Though nothing can bring back the hour
> > Of glory in the grass, of splendour in the flower":—

yet we will never cease, nor be prevented from returning on the wings of imagination to that bright dream of our youth; that glad dawn of the day-star of liberty; that spring-time of the world, in which the hopes and expectations of the human race seemed opening in the same gay career with our own . . . when, to the retired and contemplative student, the prospects of human happiness and glory were seen ascending, like the steps of Jacob's ladder, in bright and never-ending succession. The dawn of that day was suddenly overcast; that season of hope is past; it is fled with the other dreams of our youth, which we cannot recal, but has left behind it traces, which are not to be effaced by birth-day odes, or the chaunting of *Te Deums* in all the churches of Christendom. To those hopes eternal regrets are due; to those who maliciously and wilfully blasted them, in the fear that they might be accomplished, we feel no less what we owe—hatred and scorn as lasting. (XIX, 18)

In tone this is very close to the peroration of Hazlitt's lecture "On the Living Poets." The men now renouncing their early ideals once showed him the prospects of happiness "like the steps of Jacob's ladder": the phrase, associated in his mind with Coleridge's eloquence, reminds him in turn of a favorite sentence from *La Nouvelle Héloïse*, which he would use again to introduce "My First Acquaintance with Poets." *"Il y a des impressions que ni le temps ni les circonstances peuvent effacer."* Those words here find their echo in the suggestion of all that birthday-odes cannot efface. On the impulse of such memories even the sounding numbers of Wordsworth's great elegy are hitched into the lost cause, where for a moment, and without the lines that follow, they seem rightly to belong.

The figurative movement of the passage reveals Hazlitt's usual gift for a metaphysical skepticism and moral firmness which are sometimes supposed to exclude each other. What remains of the cause, after all, is only one's fidelity to the task of remembering. But it plays our memories false to exclaim with Wordsworth: "By a curious sequence of events, too sad to recount in their whole length, our fair seed-time was lost." There are, says Hazlitt, for this as for other human actions, particular agents responsible for the outcome. And they can be sought out, and punished, with words: we must not from a pretended charity relax our love of truth. Thus, to Wordsworth's nostalgia he opposes a narrower but more fully transitive quest for vengeance. The gesture is crude by comparison, and derives its great strength from its readiness to appear so. One may recall that Hazlitt when sufficiently roused was not above the Junius-like tactic of confronting an enemy with his grey hairs.[8] Something almost as abrupt is happening here. The ghost of Wordsworth's youth is visited upon the spectral impotence of his middle age, and Hazlitt personally assures him that the visitations will continue forever.

From much recent discussion of Wordsworth's poetry *The Excursion* has been excluded altogether. And yet, by a consensus so complete that it need never be articulated, we now recognize in Wordsworth's disenchantment the single attitude by which a poet is likeliest to survive his own dealings with politics, and to command our admiration in retrospect: the modern critic who has not learned this from Yeats will have come to know it more obliquely from Eliot or Auden. The result has been an oddly uncritical acceptance of Wordsworth's position—in the work of his most scrupulous commentators, one can feel that he has survived Hazlitt's challenge almost uncontested. That *The Excursion* should be shelved in favor of *The Prelude* is of course nothing against the apology both poems advance. *The Prelude,* with its sufficiently confessional disclaimers, would in any case be more congenial to modern taste. But, to repeat, it was *The Excursion* alone that Hazlitt and other contemporaries had to refer to, in framing their response to Wordsworth's account of his own political conversion. And only one modern defense of Wordsworth, E. P. Thompson's "Disenchantment or Default: A Lay Sermon," has relied chiefly on *The Excursion.*

In that essay Thompson pointed out that Wordsworth could claim to have been disenchanted by certain experiences, of which he tried to make an honest record: the modern reader, in contrast, is apt to use the accumulated moral capital of Wordsworth's disenchantment as a means of dignifying his own unchanging complacency. Thompson writes as an admirer of both Hazlitt and Wordsworth, but in examining the passage just quoted he finds Hazlitt's rhetoric uncharacteristically strained. Perhaps, in 1814, *these* ideals could no longer summon a language proved on the pulses of feeling; perhaps that is why Hazlitt's "we will never cease" has an urgency the preceding words seem not to have earned. But Thompson also looks beyond Hazlitt, to a moment of history when the rhetorical gestures associated with any ideal whatever must similarly have faltered.

How far is it possible for men to hold on to aspirations long after there appears to be no hope of inserting them into "the real world which is the world of all of us"? If the social context makes all insertion seem impossible—if all objective referents for these hopes are cruelly obliterated—if the attempt to live out the ideals appears to produce their opposite—if *fraternité* produces fratricide, *egalité* produces empire, liberty produces liberticide—then aspirations can only become a transposed interior faith. There may be a deepening of sensibility. But the dangers are also evident. This driving back into interior faith, this preoccupation with trying to "hold" and to meditate upon past states of feeling, is surely the clue not only to the increasingly self-preoccupied tone of Wordsworth's life, and style of life, as the Lake Poet, but also to the increasing failure of *observation* even in his nature poetry. . . . If there is a moral, it is not that he became a poorer poet because he changed his political views, but that his new "good views" were not held with the same intensity and authenticity.[9]

With this context understood, Thompson wonders how far Hazlitt may have resigned himself to displaying his refusal of "transposed faith" as a willed act of defiance.

How long could any man have stood a tension of that sort, at its full creative intensity, between a vision of the universal heart, and the marching and counter-marching of armies across Europe? There must be *some* objective referent for social hope, and it is one trick of the mind to latch on to an unworthy object in order to sustain such hope. Those who did not become apostates in this circle did not fare much better. Some, like James Losh, became cautious Whigs and exponents of the new political economy, whose cash equivalents opened up a distance between men immeasurably colder than that of Tory paternalism. Hazlitt preserved much of the early vision [in the passage quoted]. . . . But there is a curious arrest, a stasis, in this: the passage works by means of a tension between stale libertarian rhetoric ("glad dawn," "day-star," "golden era") pressed to the point of self-mockery, nostalgic rhythms, and sudden, muscular polemic. Hazlitt could maintain his affirmatives only by latching on to the hero figure of Napoleon, and by sustaining his aspiration out of a kind of whimsy fortified by rancor.[10]

In the literature of two centuries Thompson's is the most eloquent and sympathetic attack on the politics of Hazlitt's criticism: but the object of the attack is partly his own invention; the doubts that he supposes Hazlitt felt, and repressed for the sake of this review, were never as strong as we may wish them to have been.

For all Hazlitt's profound distrust of political economy, he would never have admitted that it opened up a distance between men "immeasurably colder" than what came before—that warm and proper distance of which we hear so much in Wordsworth's revisions for Book I of *The Excursion:* "rosy" children, "homely" fare, "the keen, the wholesome, air of poverty," to repeat only the paternalistic tagwords cited by Thompson. If we nevertheless assume that Hazlitt in his self-counsels must have shared some part of Wordsworth's nostalgia, we do so from the perspective of the 1840s and of all we now know about the effects of the First Reform Bill. But here, though his causeries against utilitarianism have something even of the eloquence of *Hard Times,* Hazlitt must be allowed to be a very imperfect prophet. He did not guess that the retrospective politics of *The Excursion* might one day appear as an alternative vision of community to be cherished in good faith. And we can trace his failure to see this to a date much later than the review; indeed, to a comment from 1830. Hazlitt had asked Macvey Napier, Jeffrey's successor at the *Edinburgh,* to review Southey's *Colloquies.* The book as it turned out was given to Macaulay to review, and he did so in a style, and with comments on Southey's literary gifts, closely modeled on Hazlitt's treatment of him in *Political Essays, The Spirit of the Age,* and the *Edinburgh* article on Coleridge's *Biographia.* It was, however, not Macaulay's style alone but his unromantic *laissez-faire* politics that pleased Hazlitt as he read the review, with its dismissal of Southey's paternalism, and endorsement of "leaving capital to find its most lucrative course, commodities their fair price, industry and intelligence their natural reward, idleness and folly their natural punishment."[11] With these phrases still in his ear Hazlitt could write to Napier: "I am not sorry I had not *Southey* as it is so ably done."[12]

Now, Macaulay's engagement with the *Colloquies* is similar in kind to Hazlitt's with *The Excursion,* and in the more than fifteen years given him to modify his views Hazlitt has not retreated an inch. I agree with Thompson that it would be more satisfying to his admirers if he had; but as there is no evidence on the point, I think it wrong to suppose his protest against Wordsworth can be reduced to whimsy fortified by rancor; or that he might in other circumstances have said a word in favor of Wordsworth's nostalgia as a decent choice among poor alternatives. We must recall that Hazlitt was arguing with Wordsworth not only about Wordsworth's past but his own. He could renew the same rhetoric, its stale figures beautifully refreshed, in a later essay like "On the Feeling of Immortality in

Youth," where he writes without the benefit of *The Prelude* (Book XI) but in a comparable strain.

> For my part, I set out in life with the French Revolution, and that event had considerable influence on my early feelings, as on those of others. Youth was then doubly such. It was the dawn of a new era, a new impulse had been given to men's minds, and the sun of Liberty rose upon the sun of Life in the same day, and both were proud to run their race together. Little did I dream, while my first hopes and wishes went hand in hand with those of the human race, that long before my eyes should close, that dawn would be overcast, and set once more in the night of despotism—"total eclipse!"   (XVII, 196-97)

In a very different strain, he approaches as nearly Wordsworth's "daring sympathies with power," when he writes elsewhere that on hearing news of Napoleon's victory at Austerlitz, "I walked out in the afternoon, and, as I returned, saw the evening star set over a poor man's cottage with other thoughts and feelings than I shall ever have again."

Hazlitt, then, as he contemplated a long poem which aimed to change men's minds about politics no less than poetry, was confronting Wordsworth's past with his own. The political claims of *The Excursion*—which he takes to be isolable from its grandeur of conception and its power of interesting us in a single self—are first scattered from coherence with the rest of the poem, and only then discredited. I have already compared this with the much simpler strategy followed by Jeffrey. It may now be worth adding De Quincey to the comparison. After all, he wrote of the poem at some length, in his essay "On Wordsworth's Poetry," and from reposing greater trust in the exclusive demands of Wordsworth's imagination, might be expected to regard it more sympathetically. But in fact it seems to have caused him boundless irritation. He catches a glimpse of the moral ambiguities disclosed by Wordsworth's relation to the Wanderer, and has doubts about any character who can have "found so luxurious a pleasure in contemplating a pathetic *phthisis* of heart in the abandoned wife," but he quickly trivializes the issue by putting to the Wanderer the rhetorical question, "Pray, amongst your other experiments, did you ever try the effect of a guinea?", and at last is sidetracked into one of his appalling jokes. A report from a neighborhood coroner, he says, would have found that Margaret's child died chiefly of "sloth, and the habit of gadding about."[13] It is beside such procedures as this that we come to value Hazlitt's undeviating seriousness. Nothing about the poem seems to him quaint or absurd. As for Wordsworth's politics, they are rejected not because they disagree with Hazlitt's, not because they have swerved from an ideal of progress—but because the revolutionary fraternity of the 1790s had been the only community Wordsworth ever lived in for long, by voluntary association; and now his strange choice of tactics, confessing bad motives in himself and inviting others to admit they shared them, has overturned Hazlitt's faith that he can fairly represent any community at all.

If Hazlitt had to resort to a language not quite his own in affirming the aims of a lost community, he could respond to Wordsworth's praise of an invented one with entirely characteristic vehemence. Indeed, for both Wordsworth and Hazlitt in this encounter, it is the negative moment of rhetorical performance, the *reprehensio,* which triumphs: Wordsworth on France is matched by Hazlitt on the country.

> The common people in civilised countries are a kind of domesticated savages. . . . They are taken out of a state of nature, without being put in possession of the refinements of art. The customs and institutions of society cramp their imaginations without giving them knowledge. If the inhabitants of the mountainous districts described by Mr. Wordsworth are less gross and sensual than others, they are more selfish. Their egotism becomes more concentrated, as they are more insulated, and their purposes more inveterate, as they have less competition to struggle with. The weight of matter which surrounds them, crushes the finer sympathies. Their minds become hard and cold, like the rocks which they cultivate. The immensity of their mountains makes the human form appear little and insignificant. Men are seen crawling between Heaven and earth, like insects to their graves. Nor do they regard one another more than flies on a wall. (XIX, 23-24)

Hazlitt's opening gambit, that *The Excursion* "resembles the country in which the scene is laid," looks different in the light of this conclusion. It is tempting to split the difference, and say that the poem presents a country of Wordsworth's imagining and the review a country of Hazlitt's: but that concession itself does far more to stagger Wordsworth's pretensions than Hazlitt's. For *The Excursion* is the poem in which Wordsworth steps forward decisively to address us as the poet of ordinary life. This claim holds up very well throughout the poem, largely owing to the way "The Ruined Cottage" shelters the remaining eight books; so that De Quincey could chide Hazlitt with some show of propriety, for contriving "the least plausible objection" ever brought against Wordsworth's poetry in the sentence: "One would suppose, from the tenor of [Wordsworth's] subjects, that on this earth there was neither marrying nor giving in marriage." But in putting it this way, all Hazlitt denies is that Wordsworth can make such actions as marriage—such communications between me and my neighbor, such bonds uniting mind with mind—actual to his readers with the force he commands in making solitude actual, and the power of one mind in solitude. De Quincey's strictures, it may be remarked, closely and rather surprisingly anticipate Thompson's. He too wants to restore to Wordsworth something of the dignity of his intentions in writing *The Excursion*. Hazlitt would have felt a good deal of sympathy with these efforts at rehabilitation, but for him the poet who expresses egotistical power, and the poet who represents the affections of a community, cannot dwell in the same body at the same time. He understands the depth at which the hope of fulfilling a double office has been experienced; yet he sees that Wordsworth will never cease to prize the lustre of a personal glory above all.

What may be called the received figure of Wordsworth for the second half of the nineteenth century and the first several decades of the twentieth—the Wordsworth evoked for us by Arnold's touchstone line, "Of joy in widest commonalty spread"—this poet, at his first annunciation, seemed to Hazlitt a hollow thing. The essence of Wordsworth's genius he took to be a sublimity whose only true occasion could be a history of the self. The assurance with which he maintained that estimate brings him closer to Bradley, and his successors in our own day, than to any nineteenth-century critic of Wordsworth; and it accounts for the feeling we can sometimes have as we read him, that he has mistaken his text and by uncanny transposition found a way to review *The Prelude* before its time. Yet he negotiated his task while also fulfilling a journalistic duty—for which he neither felt nor expressed the slightest degree of contempt—the duty to serve his readers as a generous guide to the complexities of voice that make the chief difficulty of *The Excursion*. We ought to consider finally the sort of tact Hazlitt can impart for our reading of passages he does *not* discuss: one such instance is the Solitary's renunciation of life and the energies of life, which closes the book entitled "Despondency."

> The tenour
> Which my life holds, he readily may conveive
> Whoe'er hath stood to watch a mountain brook
> In some still passage of its course, and seen,
> Within the depths of its capacious breast,
> Inverted trees, rocks, clouds, and azure sky;
> And, on its glassy surface, specks of foam,
> And conglobated bubbles undissolved,
> Numerous as stars; that, by their onward lapse,
> Betray to sight the motion of the stream,
> Else imperceptible. Meanwhile, is heard
> A softened roar, or murmur; and the sound
> Though soothing, and the little floating isles
> Though beautiful, are both by Nature charged
> With the same pensive office; and make known
> Through what perplexing labyrinths, abrupt
> Precipitations, and untoward straits,
> The earth-born wanderer hath passed; and quickly,
> That respite o'er, like traverses and toils
> Must he again encounter.—Such a stream
> Is human Life; and so the Spirit fares
> In the best quiet to her course allowed;
> And such is mine,—save only for a hope
> That my particular current soon will reach
> The unfathomable gulf, where all is still!
>
> > (*Excursion,* III, 967-991)

Without Hazlitt's aid we might hear in this only the lament of a materialism returning aridly on itself, and finding dearth in nature's sublimest scenes because it has brought nothing to them. What Hazlitt encourages us to hear besides, is how far these sentiments implicate Wordsworth himself, so that his own voice gives companionable relief to the Solitary's, and works for his vindication. The echoes of "Tintern Abbey," in the sound of the soft inland murmur, and of the Boy of Winander episode of *The Prelude*—in the concern for how reflection may procure or impede "Knowledge not purchased by the loss of power"—indeed indicate a closer kinship between poet and solitary than Wordsworth was prepared to acknowledge. Here as elsewhere Hazlitt testifies for the tale against the teller. And, so far as the passage and others like it, with their hints of what "perplexing labyrinths, abrupt / Precipitations, and untoward straits, / The earth-born wanderer hath passed," look forward to the romance of the egotistical sublime in *Alastor* and *Endymion*, Hazlitt has informed our sense of the connection, by all his doubts respecting the future of dramatic poetry. Of those doubts both his praise and blame of *The Excursion* were a fitting summation.

A NOMINALIST OF THE SUBLIME

Hazlitt's criticism as much as Wordsworth's poetry belongs to a time when terms like "the self" have moved to the center of literary discourse; and Hazlitt never affects to judge his own moment from a point outside it. Indeed, the historical character of his work emerges saliently in his use of Wordsworthian tags against Wordsworth himself; as if to say: "I still own the right to echo these great words of yours; you have lost it; for what confers the right is to have maintained a permanent relation to the childhood vision, to have seen in one's own life that 'though much is taken, much abides.' " The very idea of judging politics as an index of personal continuity is Wordsworthian. For Hazlitt does not assert that consistency is a virtue, the sort of trait one looks for in an ideal citizen; or that his unswerving loyalties are somehow more reasonable than Wordsworth's shifts and hesitations: both positions which might be argued from the premise on which Hume, Smith, and Burke could all have agreed, that society is nothing but the common affections of men, extending to form insensible but permanent bonds in space and time. Here Hazlitt's break with them is complete. He requires of the political actor not reason, not consistency for its own sake, but the steady adherence to a personal principle, which alone may foster something more than those alternate forays into petulance and irritability that supply our usual idea of personal identity. Even the history of one's politics is a history of the self, and it had better appear all to have been written by the same author.

In chapter 2 I mentioned the Immortality Ode for its importance to Hazlitt's later speculations on habit. His remarks on the poem now merit fuller scrutiny in the light of his intellectual relations to Wordsworth, the tenor of which seems to have depended so largely on the varied interpretation of a single text. His master-reading of the poem centers on the double contrast of past with future, and youth with age.

> [Mr. Wordsworth] has very admirably described the vividness of our impressions in youth and childhood, and how "they fade by degrees into the light of common day," and he ascribes the change

to the supposition of a pre-existent state, as if our early thoughts
were nearer heaven, reflections of former trails of glory, shadows
of our past being. This is idle. It is not from the knowledge of the
past that the first impressions of things derive their gloss and
splendour, but from our ignorance of the future, which fills the
void to come with the warmth of our desires, with our gayest
hopes, and brightest fancies. It is the obscurity spread before it
that colours the prospect of life with hope, as it is the cloud which
reflects the rainbow. . . . It is the delight of novelty, and the seeing no end to the pleasure that we fondly believe is still in store
for us. The heart revels in the luxury of its own thoughts, and is
unable to sustain the weight of hope and love.   (IV, 250)

Thus Hazlitt reads the fiction of a pre-existent state as an instance
of myth-making which serves the purposes of scientific induction: to
explain "the vividness of our impressions in youth and childhood."
That the fiction serves also to distract Wordsworth from his sorrow,
and consoles him by removing the past to a still more distant realm
where it may seem *never* to have been his to possess, this Hazlitt
does not see or care to see. Yet he understands the pathos of the
phrase, "The Child is father of the Man," at a depth inaccessible to
most of us.

The child, Hazlitt says, sees differently because he is ignorant of
the future. He can remain so only as long as he has no significant
past, no habitual interests or fears: his freedom from the past enables him to project his imagination into a future of infinite possibility. The man, on the other hand, clings to the past the more tenaciously for his fear that he can never recover it wholly. So he loses
his freedom and clothes the future with already familiar regrets.
These observations, of course, owe much to Hazlitt's writings on
human action, but what he sees for the first time, with the example
of Wordsworth and Wordsworth's poem before him, is that memory
can be but a precarious ally of the imagination's freedom. After
childhood and in all retrospective shapings of childhood, memory
takes for the mind's original bias a prudential flexibility that has
come into being with the accommodations of later life. Hazlitt would
have noticed an instance of such unconscious reshaping in the account given in *The Excursion* of the Wanderer's moral education.

Much as one may value Hazlitt in his role as interrogator, his
sympathy with Wordsworth's way of seeing is most striking where
his announced subject is not poetry. It is a sympathy implicit in the
pervasive concerns of his essays and the divisions within him that

they reflect. For Hazlitt was a critic of egotism in theory but an adept of it in practice, and in reading his prose we need never look far to discover an eloquent defense of his practice. To the extent that he recognizes this, his essays move incidentally toward a more forgiving view of Wordsworth. One feels some such change between two statements about Wordsworth from the essay "On Genius and Common Sense." First, that he is "the greatest, that is, the most original poet of the present day, only because he is the greatest egotist." And on the next page: "He has opened a new avenue to the human heart." The essay as a whole is one continuous attempt to demystify the idea of the man of genius. The genius makes his appeal to other men by means of a common rather than an exclusive faculty, and yet by this he shows them what they did not know. Hazlitt's section on common sense, or "tacit reason," begins with an appreciation of Goldsmith as the antithesis to Johnson, for "the fine tact, the airy, intuitive faculty with which he skimmed the surfaces of things, and unconsciously formed his opinions." And "Common sense," he adds, "is the just result of the sum-total of such unconscious impressions in the ordinary occurrences of life, as they are treasured up in the memory, and called out by the occasion. Genius and taste depend upon much the same principle exercised on loftier ground and in more unusual combinations."

Genius therefore can accomplish feats undreamed of by common sense, which, however, common sense is perfectly equipped to appreciate. Given the strength of the connection, it seems enough to call genius *"some strong quality in the mind, answering to and bringing out some new and striking quality in nature."* This is the definition that opens the way, later in the essay, for Hazlitt's special use of the phrase "elective affinity." Such affinities, we may now see, are between mind and mind as well as between mind and nature. Our stock of common sense enables us all to know the strong quality by which genius declares itself. But genius is "sufficiently exclusive and self-willed, quaint and peculiar. It does some one thing by virtue of doing nothing else." The formula, "answering to and bringing out," thus refers to a process by which genius selects and appropriates its objects, and persuades common sense to say of them: "This nature has become mine." Hazlitt's idea of affinity conceals no unexamined faith in nature-as-origin. His thinking begins at a point where such beliefs no longer matter, since nature is the name for a series of appropriations and displacements effected by genius. This becomes clearer if one sees that Hazlitt's use of "and" here im-

plies a genuine indifference to the alternatives. *Answering to and
bringing out* makes sense only if one assumes that all expression is
a mode of response, and that to respond is to evoke, to call out, to
make room for counter-speech. The truth Hazlitt asks us to recognize about the psychology of genius is this: what to an artist is simply expression, "Something I said," to his successor appears as invention, "Something you brought out of nothing." The artist, who
was only in quest of an answerable style, is always surprised by such
reactions, but without them criticism would be very dull.

By its near-alliance with common sense, and ascendency over it,
genius becomes an irresistible power and potentially a dangerous
one. It is rendered more formidable by an apparent similarity between the performances of genius in art and the mundane tasks of
the will in forming projects for the future. For there is a plausible
analogy between the two pairs, common sense : genius and past : future. Everyone has a future, few have genius, yet Hazlitt shows how
the egotistical genius, by the force of self-concern, converts us even
to the terms of his future. The means of effecting that conversion
make one theme of his essay "On the Past and Future"—among the
most Wordsworthian of all Hazlitt's writings, to judge not only by
its subject but by the sheer density of quotations.[14] As in his discussion of genius and common sense, he dwells at first on the be-
nign prevalence of the more available idea: the prospect of the next
six thousand years presents a blank, compared with the "mighty
scene" of the past six thousand.

> As far as regards the appeal to the understanding or the imagina-
> tion, the past is just as good, as real, of as much intrinsic and os-
> tensible value as the future: but there is another principle in the
> human mind, the principle of action or will; and of this the past
> has no hold, the future engrosses it entirely to itself. It is this
> strong lever of the affections that gives so powerful a bias to our
> sentiments on this subject, and violently transposes the natural
> order of our associations. We regret the pleasures we have lost,
> and eagerly anticipate those which are to come: we dwell with
> satisfaction on the evils from which we have escaped (*Posthaec
> meminisse juvabit*)—and dread future pain. The good that is past
> is in this sense like money that is spent, which is of no further use,
> and about which we give ourselves little concern. The good we
> expect is like a store yet untouched, and in the enjoyment of
> which we promise ourselves infinite gratification. What has hap-
> pened to us we think of no consequence: what is to happen to us,
> of the greatest. Why so? Simply because the one is still in our

power, and the other not—because the efforts of the will to bring any object to pass or to prevent it strengthen our attachment or aversion to that object—because the pains and attention bestowed upon any thing add to our interest in it, and because the habitual and earnest pursuit of any end redoubles the ardour of our expectations, and converts the speculative and indolent satisfaction we might otherwise feel in it into real passion.   (VIII, 25-26)

Notice the predominance of "will," "passion," "power," and, in a phrase combining them all, the violent transposition of habitual associations. We are again in Wordsworth's Ode, with its resolute anticipations founded on present disappointment. Here, "Another race hath been" means "Another race will be," and is interpreted in no other way. Or, to adopt Hazlitt's translation, the past is "of no consequence," placing no limit on the possible sequel.

But why should we grant the egotist so special and excessive an influence on our thoughts about the future? In part, for a reason Hazlitt alludes to but does not explain in speaking of "another principle in the human mind, the principle of action or will." The first principle is imagination, and to that Hazlitt devoted his *Essay on Human Action;* the second is power, on which he promised but never produced a companion-essay. But he comes closest to explaining this second principle in such conversions to the Wordsworthian mode of genius as "On the Past and Future" affords. Our reason for admitting Wordsworth's "transpositions" may be no different than our reason for granting any claim to personal power. Why for that matter should we have agreed to care for *his* past more than for anyone else's? All that can be said is that we have indeed been persuaded to do so, by Rousseau, Wordsworth, and others whose rhetorical enterprise is to allow no precedent and no imitator. Their example they insist that we take into ourselves and preserve, even as we employ it in forming our future. This involves a process of intense identification: Boswell's demand of Rousseau, "Will you, Sir, assume direction of me," marks no unusual disorder, any more than De Quincey's readiness at eighteen "to sacrifice even his life" for Wordsworth. Both gestures of fealty seemed appropriate to the younger men in the course of introducing themselves to their heroes. And so they were: Boswell and De Quincey understood their authors well enough, and were answered in kind (from Rousseau, a firm "I cannot"; from Wordsworth, "My friendship is not in my power to give"). The exchanges are troubling because they exhibit the splendid indifference of genius to those whom it has conquered.

The reader, an unwanted third party to this affair, misses perhaps a note of pride in the under-studies, but they knew better than to expect that. They were seeking to lose their way and themselves.

Of this process of identification Hazlitt is the most reliable witness who has ever survived to write criticism. He saw that the overruling of sense, the power in which the egotistical genius excels the rest of us, consisted in nothing other than an ability to deform the past. By such extortions the genius does make good his promise: to bring out some striking quality in himself which ever after we must honor as nature. Wilde's ironic claim at the end of this tradition, that "Things are because we see them," has to be modified very slightly to fit what happens in our reading of Rousseau or Wordsworth. These things are, for us, because they saw them for themselves.

A violent transposition of habitual associations, deforming the past, and projecting a future which the reader is persuaded to share: the entire process returns us to those dangers of the egotistical imagination which Hazlitt has always been willing to ponder. They also recall the worry that the unenchanted reader, having once got another past by proxy, may elect to share the glamor without the self-knowledge that comes of disenchantment. Hazlitt found this process no less morally ambiguous for being inextricable from the kind of poetry Wordsworth wrote. The shift of interest in his own "transposing" essays, from the principle of imagination to that of "action or will," implies that Wordsworth can be challenged only on his own ground, by supplying an alternative past and self to the poet's. Such tactics will of course also be regarded as figurative and deforming, though their employer may describe them as merely corrective: the aim in any case is counter-persuasion. Hazlitt became a disciple of Wordsworth's method to revise the interpretation of Wordsworth's story.

In short, his protest against Wordsworth, through all its varied occasions, could never be reduced to the simple objection that this was a poet who claimed too much for himself. From the first Hazlitt read him as a poet of the sublime. And with the idea of sublimity Hazlitt had inherited from Burke, decorum, and indeed morality as it is commonly understood, had no necessary connection. We need to recall once more the metaphor which he selected to describe Wordsworth's long poem—"one of those stupendous but half-finished structures, which have been suffered to moulder into decay." This belongs to the repository of tropes which since Longinus have counted as an index of sublimity. Fragmentary ruins exhibit the energies of mind that were once concentrated in a particular place; such energies are active "momently," their start and stop is sudden; and when they are done, we measure the height of the adventure by the sharpness of the break. Longinus compares the master of rhetorical effects, Cicero, to a rolling fire, but the orator who takes greater risks and attains true sublimity is Demosthenes, whom he compares to a thunderbolt. We trace the thunderbolt's work in the jagged rocks or shattered columns it leaves behind: stupendous monuments half-built and now standing alone. Longinus suggests also that to remain somehow unfinished is a predictable fate for works produced by the highest genius: "in the sublime, as in great fortunes, there must be something which is overlooked."[15]

Hazlitt read poetry for the values Longinus and Burke had taught him to cherish. These sufficiently distinguish him from Coleridge, with his demand for unity and the reconciliation of opposites. Temperamentally Hazlitt was better suited to diversity and the war of contraries; he no more wanted to be freed from conflict at the end of a work than at the beginning; on the popular critical theme of *unity,* his writings contain nothing markedly graver than the passage cited earlier on Fielding's physiognomy. It is odd that in literary criticism our unity-lovers should often have been the most resourceful inspectors of morality—though perhaps both concerns spring from the desire to award works a clean bill of health one way or another. Even in his own time, however, Coleridge was an extreme case. How plainly so may be surmised from the juxtaposition of two entries in Crabb Robinson's diaries. In May of 1812, after a lecture by Coleridge on the nature of comedy, Robinson held a conversation with the lecturer and Wordsworth. "Coleridge talked on the impossibility of being a good poet without being a good man, and urged the immorality of Goethe's works as a proof that he is not a good poet. This I demurred to." Two days later, "at Hammond's," he finds Wordsworth "demonstrating . . . some of the points of his philosophical theory. Speaking of his own poems, Wordsworth said he principally valued them as being *a new power* in the literary world. Hammond's friend, Miller, esteemed Wordsworth for the pure morality of his works. Wordsworth said he himself looked to the powers of the mind his poems call forth, and the energies they presuppose and excite, as the standard by which they are to be esteemed."[16]

The opposition here is starker than usual, but it helps us to see more clearly the differences—which talk about any "movement" can obscure—between what Coleridge and Wordsworth looked for in poetry. In the first of Robinson's entries, where one expects to hear that the immorality of Goethe's works is deducible from the flaws of his character and vice versa; or, more scrupulously, that the immorality of parts of Goethe's works has increased Coleridge's suspicion that he is an immoral man, and this larger impression in turn has provoked him to return to the works and discover a flaw more essential than it once seemed; he asserts instead that the immorality of the works proves the badness of—the works. Of course, Robinson may have garbled every word; but the *non sequitur* has the true Coleridgean ring. As for Wordsworth, his apparent change of heart between the 1802 *Preface* and this 1812 affirmation about "power"— the withdrawal of any claim for the poet's moral character—need not trouble us greatly. In the *Preface* despite many open disagreements about its argument, he was still writing with Coleridge over his shoulder. In front of Robinson (a kind of slow Boswell) he could speak more freely. Between these positions Hazlitt was never at a loss to choose. If at times he seems nostalgic for Coleridge's view of poetry, the reason is that he has said farewell to it. He would certainly have agreed with the dictum that Coleridge in a less ambitious mood was willing to settle for: that "poetry which excites us to artificial feelings makes us callous to real ones."[17] But (he would have added), so far and no further can moralism take us, without betraying the independence of criticism. In this debate therefore Hazlitt is of Wordsworth's party. He takes for granted that the self portrayed in a great poem, or implied by its action and characters, is not a datum submitted for moral judgment but a fiction. Being a fiction it leads back into life nevertheless.

Hazlitt respects the power of words not merely to supply the place of imagination but to communicate all that can be known of it. Words, as he writes in a great and little-known passage, are our only universals, the tools by which alone we hold fast to our realities. The declaration stands out abruptly, as it would anywhere, from the introductory sentences of an essay on "Sir Walter Scott, Racine, and Shakespeare."

> Words are a key to the affections. They not only excite feelings, but they point to the *why* and *wherefore*. Causes march before them, and consequences follow after them. They are links in the

chain of the universe, and the grappling-irons that bind us to it. They open the gates of Paradise, and reveal the abyss of human woe.

> "Four lagging winters and four wanton springs
> Die in a word; such is the breath of kings."

But in this respect, all men who have the use of speech are kings. It is words that constitute all but the present moment, but the present object. They may not and they do not give the whole of any train of impressions which they suggest; but they alone answer in any degree to the truth of things, unfold the dark labyrinth of fate, or unravel the web of the human heart; for they alone describe things in the order and relation in which they happen in human life.   (XII, 337)

The final phrases appear to revert from an expressive theory of language to a mimetic theory, according to which one would properly speak of the capacity of words to trace events rather than direct them. But that is evidently false to the rest of the passage; one may be misled only because the controlling metaphors are buried in "unfold" and "unravel": in their original sense, these are intentional actions, and it is this sense that Hazlitt restores. Words carry their own causes and consequences, potent enough to make competing words "of no consequence." The quoted lines come from Bolingbroke in *Richard II,* after the King on a whim has commuted his sentence from ten to six years' banishment. In this illustration words perform an action in the course of their saying. By alluding to the scene Hazlitt refuses to draw the line between literary language and matters of power and commandment, the domain of performative utterance. "How long a time lies in one little word!"—but "in this respect, all men who have the use of speech are kings."

Words stop short only before "the present moment . . . the present object," and in that moment, when for Wordsworth "the light of sense / Goes out, but with a flash that has revealed / The invisible world," Hazlitt locates the disjunction or privation of sublimity. It is as words break down, break off, that we feel their power most acutely, while being made aware also of something greater than words: what that is remains one of those things that can be shown but not said. Hazlitt at any rate declines to single out the rhetorical figures by which such moments are recognized, as Longinus had done in exemplifying *asyndeton, hyperbaton,* and so forth. Instead, he gives a master-image for all kindred deviations from sense: the abyss. Wordsworth, on hearing he had crossed the Alps, writes that he was caught unawares, emptied of the occasional eloquence he had stored up, "Halted without an effort to break through." The phrase expresses as well as any in Hazlitt's own work the relation he supposed between "the present moment" and the words that interpret it. In the presence of sublimity we feel a peculiar limitation on words, and for Hazlitt literary power derives from the reticences of a moment to which all words strive powerfully to return.

Hazlitt had a pronounced admiration for "the negative sublime,"[18] the sublime that registers the shock of breaking off, without any attempt to moralize or go beyond it. He would I think have preferred the bare majesty of the halt in Book VI of *The Prelude* to the still more celebrated passage that follows, in which Wordsworth says that the contesting elements before him "Were all like workings of one mind, the features / Of the same face, blossoms upon one tree," and by producing a single clear image from so many fragmentary signs, offers himself positive reassurance. In keeping with Hazlitt's preference was his esteem of *King Lear* above Shakespeare's other tragedies, for the several reasons listed in his *Characters of Shakespeare's Plays*.

> Four things have struck us in reading LEAR:
> 1. That poetry is an interesting study, for this reason, that it relates to whatever is most interesting in human life. Whoever therefore has a contempt for poetry, has a contempt for himself and humanity.
> 2. That the language of poetry is superior to the language of painting; because the strongest of our recollections relate to feelings, not to faces.
> 3. That the greatest strength of genius is shewn in describing the strongest passions: for the power of the imagination, in works of invention, must be in proportion to the force of the natural impressions, which are the subject of them.
> 4. That the circumstance which balances the pleasure against the pain in tragedy is, that in proportion to the greatness of the evil, is our sense and desire of the opposite good excited; and that our sympathy with actual suffering is lost in the strong impulse given to our natural affections, and carried away with the swelling tide of passion, that gushes from and relieves the heart. (IV, 271-72)

The third seems to me the consideration that applies most distinctly to *Lear,* as well as the one most consistent with Wordsworth's interest in "the powers of the mind" a poem calls forth. Shelley's *De-*

fence of Poetry—which also favors poetry as the superior art on the ground that only language is a totally human medium—offers a comparable estimate of the same play as "the most perfect specimen of the dramatic art," with comic episodes as "universal, ideal, and sublime" as the tragic. Hazlitt and Shelley arrived at their view while thinking about the poetic strengths of *sympathy* and *power*. To suggest the power of mind signalled by halts, breaks, sudden stops, one may recall Lear's cry, "I will have such revenges on you both / That the world shall—I will do such things— / What they are, yet I know not; but they shall be / The terrors of the earth." And, for the effortless out-going of sympathy, Lear's ministrations to Edgar: "Didst thou give all to thy daughters? And art thou come to this?"—lines Hazlitt quoted many times as giving the essence of Shakespeare's genius. In valuing genius by the criterion of sublimity, Hazlitt and Shelley arrive at a point where sympathy and power seem indistinguishable from each other, being absorbed into the larger category of "energies of mind." Is not Lear's violent transposition of his own fate with Edgar's a perfect instance of that "change of person" which according to Longinus outpaces the very mind that makes it? Nevertheless, though both Hazlitt and Shelley would like to believe, neither is finally persuaded by the hopeful Wordsworthian credo according to which power and sympathy coincide.

To exhibit this sort of energy, to sustain this pressure and strange release, nature must be seen to have more than "one mind." *King Lear* was after all the natural text for both critics to place at the center of their polemic against Wordsworth. It is a play in which power, and especially the power to curse, brings with it fancied causes and actual consequences which can never be retracted, and its greatness for them lay in a dramatic result that touched the limits of action and suffering. Wordsworth, as these critics recognized, was a true poet of the sublime, who wished for himself chiefly the power to bless. But that wish threatened the principle of his genius, since it was a wish for community, which it could only picture as retreat; and for energy drawn from the mind apart, which it served up as a sacrifice to the one mind and "same face" of nature. Hazlitt and Shelley ask whether the energies implicit in both parts of this program may not be realized without the sacrifice.

Shelley gave his answer in "Mont Blanc," where knowledge—that the mind's objects must dwell apart from it in order to excite the mind's own exertions—is purchased without the loss of power. All Hazlitt's criticism on this theme contains no such explicit piece of controversial eloquence, but he too wrote about Mont Blanc, in his *Notes of a Journey through France and Italy,* and the description is as searching and delicate for what it leaves unsaid as for what it records.

> Mont-Blanc itself was round, bald, shining, ample, and equal in its swelling proportions [to cliffs beside or fronting it]—a huge dumb heap of matter. The valley below was bare, without an object—no ornament, no contrast to set it off—it reposed in silence and in solitude, a world within itself. . . . There is an end here of vanity and littleness, and all transitory jarring interests. You stand, as it were, in the presence of the Spirit of the Universe, before the majesty of Nature, with her chief elements about you; cloud and air, and rock, and stream, and mountain are brought into immediate contact with primeval Chaos and the great First Cause. The mind hovers over mysteries deeper than the abysses at our feet; its speculations soar to a height beyond the visible forms it sees around it. As we descended the path on foot (for our muleteer was obliged to return at the barrier between the two states of Savoy and Switzerland marked by a solitary unhewn stone,) we saw before us the shingled roofs of a hamlet, situated on a patch of verdure near inaccessible columns of granite, and could hear the tinkling bells of a number of cattle pasturing below (an image of patriarchal times!)—we also met one or two peasants returning home with loads of fern, and still farther down, found the ripe harvests of wheat and barley growing close up to the feet of the glaciers (those huge masses of ice arrested in their passage from the mountains, and collected by a thousand winters,) and the violet and gilliflower nestling in the cliffs of the hardest rocks. (X, 292)

Here the mind soars above itself and reaches—we are not told what. Nor does the mind itself need to know. Its exertions are valued for their own sake, and there is no suggestion of transcendence: the first cause is whatever caused this. With no sense that he is making a remarkable transition, Hazlitt then proceeds to the common world in which other sights, and persons not less strange to him than the mountain, swing into view and demand utterance. With a will less divided than Wordsworth's, he teaches us to value, also for their own sake, these descents into the ordinary, to a place where flowers nestle in the rocks, where cattle-bells ring as they did a thousand years before, and laborers in the field must resume their daily circuit while we pursue our journey on to the next hamlet, and the next peak.

CHAPTER V

FROM IMITATION TO EXPRESSION

THE PARTICULAR AS IDEAL

"Let those who have a prejudice against Johnson read Boswell's Life of him," Hazlitt advised the audience of his *Lectures on the English Comic Writers;* "as those whom he has prejudiced against Shakespeare should read his Irene." In such statements Hazlitt appears to confess a simple preference for the man Samuel Johnson, over the writer and doctor. Part of his generosity is that he does allow for preferences: he regarded the lives of writers as in this respect no different from the lives of other notable men; they might make an interesting study for any number of reasons, and if certain incidents outshone all the works together, so much the better for the incidents. In keeping with Hazlitt's tolerance, many later estimates of Johnson, the great essays by Carlyle and Emerson for example, conclude that he remains vivid to us and chiefly memorable as an exemplary fellow-man. Yet Hazlitt himself did not mean to separate the man from his works quite as Emerson and Carlyle did; for his warning against Johnson's version of Shakespeare was made rather with the hope of distinguishing two elements in the critic. As a reader of Johnson, he prefers the humane and personal moralist to the licensed master of regulation, and the best means he can find of discrediting Johnson in the latter role is to remind us how seldom he seems to play it in the *Life,* and how much we love the character we do meet there.

A play like *Irene* was one product of the eighteenth-century critical practice of identifying the ideal in art with "general nature." In poetry, this led to the artificial diction Wordsworth hoped to repel forever with his *Preface:* when you mean "the morning sun," say "smiling Phoebus"; a step behind will be Fielding with his parody, "All nature wears one universal grin." In drama the results were equally flattening, but there they were part of a larger imaginative failure which could hardly be explained as a consequence of any single tenet of critical faith. About such of its causes as might be traced to doctrine, Boswell's *Life* has a nicely cautionary tale, which ends with a cheerful rebuke Goldsmith once made to Johnson. Goldsmith had spoken of the difficulty in writing fables, of getting the animals to talk in character, and gave as an example "the fable of the little fishes, who saw birds fly over their heads, and envying them, petitioned Jupiter to be changed into birds. The skill consists in making them talk like little fishes"; upon which, observing Johnson "shaking his sides, and laughing" as at nonsense, Goldsmith turned on his listener and said, "Why, Dr. Johnson, this is not so easy as you seem to think; for if you were to make little fishes talk, they would talk like WHALES." In this encounter Hazlitt's sympathies would have been entirely with Goldsmith, and by referring us to the great-whale tragedy *Irene* he does not so much disqualify Johnson from commenting on his superior in poetic drama, as indicate how far everything valuable that Johnson says about Shakespeare must have gone against the grain of precisely those doctrines with which he took visible pains to square his own dramatic practice.

When, in his *Preface to Shakespeare,* Johnson traces out the source of Shakespeare's strength at delineating character, he says much that is inconsistent with the idea of general nature; yet what he most wants to believe, and feels happiest saying, is that Shakespeare imagined his characters by first conceiving of them as representatives of a class: Brutus, the stoic, withdrawn from worldly passions, a poor judge of character in proportion as he is a faultless servant of principles; Falstaff, the very type of grossness and corruption, but pure in the respect he shows for no appetite but his own, and almost appeasing our censure with a power of wit that turns all obstacles into instrumentalities. By presenting such abstracts as the essence of character, Johnson aimed to justify Shakespeare to eighteenth-century taste; his effort was a success, and this might simply be counted a gain for Shakespeare; yet to Hazlitt the loss in dramatic and imaginative truth was beyond measure. Johnson, he says, "found the general species or *didactic* form in Shakespeare's characters, which was all he sought or cared for; he did not find the individual traits, or the *dramatic* distinctions which Shakespeare has engrafted on this general nature, because he felt no interest in them. Shakespeare's bold and happy flights of imagination were equally thrown away upon our author." In short there were rules about art, which the generation before Johnson's had made up, and he still abided by; his mistake was not that he held them in high esteem, but that he tried to make Shakespeare answerable to them.

"Rules are applicable to abstractions, but expression is concrete and individual." That sentence comes from Hazlitt's essay "On Genius and Common Sense," of which Burke rather than Johnson is the hero. Genius and common sense, as I pointed out in the last chapter, differ for Hazlitt in degree, genius commanding a larger field and making its observations more swiftly and completely. But it is the fault of common sense to set itself up as a judge of genius, without recognizing that there is any difference at all: it fortifies criticism with rules which are of interest only to itself. Hazlitt's essay goes on to exemplify the deftness of genius in making any observed particular *tell* with the force of generality.

> We know the meaning of certain looks, and we feel how they modify one another in conjunction. But we cannot have a separate rule to judge of all their combinations in different degrees and circumstances, without foreseeing all those combinations, which is impossible: or, if we did foresee them, we should only be where we are, that is, we could only make the rule as we now judge without it, from imagination and the feeling of the moment. . . . I once heard a person remark of another—"He has an eye like a vicious horse." This was a fair analogy. We all, I believe, have noticed the look of an horse's eye, just before he is going to bite or kick. But will any one, therefore, describe to me exactly what that look is? It was the same acute observer that said of a self-sufficient prating music-master—"He talks on all subjects *at sight*"—which expressed the man at once by an allusion to his profession. The coincidence was indeed perfect. Nothing else could compare to the easy assurance with which this gentleman would volunteer an explanation of things of which he was most ignorant; but the *nonchalance* with which a musician sits down to a harpsichord to play a piece he has never seen before. . . . When we thoroughly understand the subject, it is easy to translate from one language into another. Raphael, in muffling up the figure of Elymas the Sorcerer in his garments, appears to have extended the idea of blindness even to his clothes. Was this design? Probably not; but merely the feeling of analogy thoughtlessly suggesting this device, which being so suggested was retained and carried on, because it flattered or fell in with the original feeling. The tide of passion, when strong, overflows and gradually insinuates itself into all nooks and corners of the mind. (VIII, 40-41)

The impediment to Johnson's ever openly admitting these truths was a conception of taste which he shared with Reynolds.

Taste when highly cultivated, as we learn both from Johnson's *Rasselas* and from Reynolds's *Discourses,* prefers to avoid all particularities of expression; it directs our admiration to the ideal, and ideal form omits whatever is idiosyncratic or *pointedly* individual in human nature. So taste gives us a careful medium between any two extremes. But to this way of thinking Hazlitt saw one great objection, which he liked to frame as a series of interrogatives. Can we speak of ideal beauty as a compromise between perfect beauty and something else? Or of ideal virtue, except as the perfection of good conduct, its furthest extreme? And is it not the same with all other moral and physical qualities, which a countenance or language may express, and a painter or poet interpret? Hazlitt's different version of the ideal springs from a different conception of taste. For Johnson and Reynolds it had been the faculty that refined, and improved by moderating, the exuberances of genius. But for Hazlitt it teaches not the improvement but the appreciation of genius, whose works contain within themselves all the refinement that analysis exists to admire and explain.[1] In this sense genius in art presumes taste, as genius in life presumes common sense. A late essay collecting Hazlitt's "Thoughts on Taste" makes the distinction very clearly:

> Genius is the power of producing excellence: taste is the power of perceiving the excellence thus produced in its several sorts and degrees, with all their force, refinement, distinctions, and connections. In other words, taste (as it relates to the productions of art) is strictly the power of being properly affected by works of genius. . . . The eye of taste may be said to reflect the impressions of real genius, as the even mirror reflects the objects of nature in all their clearness and lustre, instead of distorting or diminishing them.
>
> (XVII, 57)

Having learned "the power of being properly affected," the critic's mistake is first to apply to all works a single standard of propriety, and second to suppose there must be something like identity between the power of admiring art and the power of creating it. In fact, the artist has less need of a mirror—even of the idea of a mirror, as a guide to the nature of his task—than does the critic. For when we look at a picture, we have before us no model of whatever we there find reflected. Whereas, in examining the productions of the critic, we have a model by which to check his account, in the form of the text itself. The mistake of the critic who starts with an idea of taste rather than an idea of genius is to transfer to the artist the mirror-metaphor that he may find helpful in his own speculations, and thereafter use it as a standard of representative adequacy.

The critic looks into his mirror and finds, as he is obliged to do, general ideas, and the characters of general nature. This happens in the eighteenth century. Does it follow that general nature is what every poet has in his poem, or ought to have? Not if one remembers how recent a produce of the mind certain ideas of nature are; not if one believes—against Reynolds and Johnson at their most orthodox— that great art falsifies any opposition between the particular and the general. These reservations were present to Hazlitt whenever he wrote criticism, and for the latter he had an important ally in Coleridge, who said of Lady Macbeth that "like all in Shakespeare" she was "a class individualised."[2] Hazlitt extends this view in his *Table-Talk* essay on Reynolds: "Titian's real excellence consisted in the power of generalising and of *individualising* at the same time: if it were merely the former, it would be difficult to account for [an error] pointed out by Sir Joshua. [He says in the *Discourses*,] 'Many artists . . . have ignorantly imagined they are imitating the manner of Titian, when they leave their colours rough, and neglect the detail.' " Finish, as Hazlitt reminds Reynolds with his own words, is one mark of great art, and it is no more incompatible with general effect than the absence of it is an earnest of sublimity.

In many of the *Discourses* Reynolds was seeking to divest of its prestige the popular notion of the unschooled genius, with which Burke's idea of sublimity as an obscure grandeur seemed to have forged a strong though accidental alliance. Yet Reynolds too had felt Burke's influence, and in his attempt to strike a balance for the accomplishment of the grand style he ended by proposing a curious formula: great effects were to be achieved by avoiding the clarity of individual form. But this would seem to require a deliberate lack of finish. Hazlitt kept up his salvoes against the implied equation, great = obscure, long after he had stopped reviewing academic painting: as late as *Characteristics*, one can find whole aphorisms very close in spirit to Blake's explosive comments on the *Discourses*.

> The greatest painters are those who have combined the finest general effect with the highest degree of delicacy and correctness of detail. It is a mistake that the introduction of the parts interferes or is incompatible with the effect of the whole. Both are to be found in nature. The most finished works of the most renowned artists are also the best.   (IX, 219)

That a picture is built up from individual forms now seems so self-evident that even the terms of the debate may be difficult to recover. But there was truth—the truth of a living art—on both sides: in the fiercer encounters between Reynolds and Hazlitt, individuality appears as one convenient index of the rival claims of an art founded on accommodation with the audience, which values propriety, and an art aimed at the conversion of the audience, which values power. These sorts of art of course do not behave as exclusively as the contrast requires; but never in history did their interests seem more exclusive than between 1790 and 1820; this was true in poetry as well as painting, for partisans of both the new and the old school. Reynolds's "middle forms"—making the portrait-nose look not too big and not too small, whatever it was on the actual face—need for their defense only one assumption, that the most important moment in the audience's contact with a new work is their first sight of it. It follows that their expectations had better not be shocked; and what they least expect is anything that deviates far from the norms of moderate life at its most refined. The Blake-Hazlitt protest is that such arguments ask us to believe life can somehow be rich without being various. In response, Blake paints his *Ghost of a Flea;* his answer was in fact complete when he thought of the title for that picture. Hazlitt for his part points to Hogarth, and wonders what general nature can make of him.

Thus the ideal can no longer be defined as at once grand and conventional. Rather, as Hazlitt observes in his review of Flaxman's *Lectures on Sculpture,* it "may be regarded as a certain predominant quality or character (this may be ugliness or deformity as well as beauty, as is seen in the forms of fauns and satyrs) diffused over all the parts of an object, and carried to the utmost pitch that our acquaintance with visible models, and our conception of the imaginary object, will warrant." All this is done without mirrors: what Hazlitt calls the "models," or earlier instances of the genre, are visible; but the only "object" of art is an imaginary one. With this definition the moral objections to a painter like Hogarth disappear: if Hazlitt is right that "The true artist will paint not material points, but *moral quantities,*" then Hogarth is a moralist in the same sense as Shakespeare. Moral quantities—we do feel the need of this, or some other phrase equally paradoxical—are the artist's sole means of representing the "passion" without which he would never have set out to paint the forms that evoke it. Hazlitt's *Champion* article on "The Ideal" widens the debate by remarking one unforeseen consequence of the doctrine of middle forms, its exclusion of the human passions themselves, which no matter what their character (rage, envy, pity, fear, love) are most expressive at the extremes.

> The ideal is that which answers to the idea of something, and not to the idea of any thing, or of nothing. Any countenance strikes most upon the imagination, either in a picture or in reality, which has most distinctness from others, and most identity with itself. The keeping in the character, not the want of character, is the essence of history. Without some such limitation as we have here given, on the general statement of Sir Joshua, we see no resting-place where the painter or the poet is to make his stand, so as not to be pushed to the utmost verge of naked commonplace inanity,—nor do we understand how there should be any such thing as poetry or painting tolerated. A *tabula rasa,* a verbal definition, the bare name, must be better than the most striking description or representation;—the argument of a poem better than the poem itself,—or the catalogue of a picture than the original work.

. . .

> If we are asked, then, what it is that constitutes historic expression or ideal beauty, we should answer, not (with Sir Joshua) abstract expression or middle forms, but consistency of expression in the one, and symmetry of form in the other.
>
> A face is historical, which is made up of consistent parts, let those parts be ever so peculiar or uncommon. Those details or peculiarities only are inadmissible in history, which do not arise out of any principle, or tend to any conclusion,—which are merely casual, insignificant, and unconnected,—which do not *tell.*

. . .

> All intellectual and impassioned faces are historical;—the heads of philosophers, poets, lovers, and madmen. Passion sometimes produces beauty by this means, and there is a beauty of form, the effect entirely of expression; as a smiling mouth, not beautiful in common, becomes so by being put into that action. (XVIII, 78–83)

At this point the whole theory of "a certain central form" is ready to be dismissed, because however fine the temperate mastery that it suggests, "it does not include many other things of much more importance in historical painting . . . namely, character, which necessarily implies individuality; expression, which is the excess of thought or feeling; strength or grandeur of form, which is excess also."[3] Haz-, litt maintains that all strength, all expression, all character, is ideal; that the ideal is to be sought precisely in the literal; that when it is said, for example, of Raphael's histories that the women in the streets of Rome seem to have walked out of the pictures in the Vatican, this is as it should be.

To explain our sense that the artist is at once "conversant" with a world within and without—our exhilaration at the swiftness of his conversational moves, from an energy of his own to the passion of individual form—Hazlitt invented for English the word *gusto,* of which I have more to say presently. But it is important to note here that seeing, making, and understanding seem, in the artist who has this quality, condensed into a single gesture of knowing and savoring. This is a reward of the genius unconscious of its power, and in commending it Hazlitt goes a step beyond Reynolds's prudential words to the studious.

> Sir Joshua has laid himself open to criticism, in saying that "a picture must not only be done well, it must seem to have been done easily." It cannot be said to be done well, unless it has this look. That is the fault of those laboured and timid productions of the modern French and Italian schools; they are the result of such a tedious, petty, mechanical process, that it is as difficult for you to admire as it has been for the artist to execute them. Whereas, when a work seems stamped on the canvas by a blow, you are taken by surprise; and your admiration is as instantaneous and electrical as the impulse of genius which has caused it. (XI, 222–23)

The language of things "stamped," struck off at a blow, making sparks fly by the effort or collision, is characteristic of Hazlitt: his vocabulary of the sublime is more purely Longinian than Burke's. For where Burke associates sublimity with an overwhelming of all our *capacities,* Hazlitt traces it to a simple but penetrating shock to our *expectations.*

As soon as we accept such a vocabulary, the interest we take in the power of genius will tell against Reynolds's argument for squaring genius with convention.

> Suppose there is no capacity in form to affect the mind except from its corresponding to previous expectation, the same thing cannot be said of the idea of power or grandeur. No one can say that the idea of power does not affect the mind with the sense of awe and sublimity. That is, power and weakness, grandeur and littleness, are not indifferent things, the perfection of which consists in a medium between both. Again, expression is not a thing

indifferent in itself, which derives its value or its interest solely from its conformity to a natural standard. Who would neutralise the expression of pleasure and pain? (VIII, 140–41)

What is hidden from Reynolds and his disciples is the origin of power in individuality. Admitting this, we may see a final weakness in the generalizing view of Shakespeare's characters. As Johnson conceives of the process that formed them, though there is room for Miranda, or for a character somewhat like her without the miracle of her individual speech and gestures, there ought to be none at all for Caliban or Ariel. Hazlitt asserts a truth that Johnson denied in principle, and could only affirm in spite of himself by the very range of his practice: that it is in the nature not simply of ideal form but of expression as such, to interest us most at the heights and depths of action and suffering.

THE ELGIN MARBLES

Hazlitt wrote a great deal about the works of painting and sculpture that appeared in his day, but two articles especially, on the Elgin Marbles and West's picture of *Death on the Pale Horse,* indicate how his objections to a grand style of middle forms led him to formulate a psychological and expressive idea of imitation. The Elgin Marbles review, published in two installments in *The London Magazine,* applauds these recoveries of the original grand style as giving such unembarrassed prominence to details of the human form that they might have been made from casts; and Hazlitt is quick to read the implications for his long-standing argument with Reynolds: "The Elgin Marbles give a flat contradiction to this gratuitous separation of grandeur of design and exactness of detail, as incompatible in works of art, and we conceive that, with their whole ponderous weight to crush it, it will be difficult to set this theory on its legs again." The new evidence seems to show that Hazlitt's way of seeing is better fitted than Reynolds's for sympathizing with the classics themselves; but Hazlitt finally sets against Reynolds's middle forms (which never did and never will exist) an ideal of *directly copied* individual forms (which differ in no respect from their models, except that they are presented to us as art): "It is evident to one who views these admirable remains of Antiquity (nay, it is acknowledged by our artists themselves, in despite of all the melancholy sophistry which they have been taught or have been teaching others for half a century) that the chief excellence of the figures depends on their having been copied from nature, and not from imagination."

Hardly anywhere else in Hazlitt's work does the word "imagination" appear in so subordinate and derisory a role: but he is in a reductive mood, and goes even further.

> Nature is consistent, unaffected, powerful, subtle: art is forgetful, apish, feeble, coarse. Nature is the original, and therefore right: art is the copy, and can but tread lamely in the same steps. Nature penetrates into the parts, and moves the whole mass: it acts with diversity, and in necessary connexion; for real causes never forget to operate, and to contribute their portion. Where, therefore, these causes are called into play to the utmost extent that they ever go to, there we shall have a strength and a refinement, that art may imitate but cannot surpass. But it is said that art can surpass this most perfect image in nature by combining others with it. What! by joining to the most perfect in its kind something less perfect?
>
> (XVIII, 154)

He seems to have forgotten everything he meant by saying poetry and painting were "an imitation of nature, but the imagination and the passions are a part of man's nature"—everything that a later writer of comparable sympathies, Leo Steinberg, meant by the slogan "the eye is a part of the mind." The distinction between natural model and imaginative object has vanished unaccountably here. For the old contrast that weighed one kind of nature (as seen by taste, unimaginatively) against another (as seen by genius, imaginatively), Hazlitt now substitutes a much simpler contrast that exalts nature at the expense of artifice. A dialectical insistence similar to Blake's, on the love genius has of painting "minute particulars," even to the extent of coming to know them by "servile copying," has ended in the grim assertion that originality is servility to nature: genius on this view would appear to be a euphemism for some of life's humbler crafts.

But this is an unusual moment, the full significance of which Hazlitt apparently does not recognize. For the main tendency of his skepticism about the dichotomies enforced by taste is the reverse: by asking how the mind interprets and creates expression in its varied objects, he means to give us in the end a more generous idea of what the imagination can do. That becomes plain in the next stage of his argument, when he moves from Reynolds's favorite dichotomy of grandeur vs. precision-of-detail to attack Burke's sublimity vs. beauty. Before Burke, the two qualities had been thought fully compatible: anyone who reads the *Enquiry into the Sublime and Beautiful* directly after Addison's "Pleasures of the Imagination" can see how great the change was; and those who have charted the history of Burke's influence agree on how thoroughly his division had won out by Hazlitt's day.[4] Beauty is soft, delicately and exquisitely formed, soothing to contemplate; sublimity is strong, violently and obscurely formed, taxing to contemplate. Burke paints the memorable picture of a spectator fondly taking in the beautiful thing, his hands at ease together behind his back, his legs slightly apart, his head tilted to one side; and the same spectator being possessed by the sublime thing, his hands rigid at his side, his whole body tense with apprehension, his legs stiff, head straight, and each particular hair standing on end. With the Elgin Marbles before him, Hazlitt wonders about the justice of this account: "As sublimity is an excess of power, beauty is, we conceive, the blending and harmonising of different powers or qualities together, so as to produce a soft and pleasurable sensation." It is not then a question of the presence or absence of power, and sublimity is not as remote from beauty as Burke supposed. But, so far, Hazlitt may seem merely to have returned the pleasure to sublimity, and thus returned the argument to the place where Addison had left it.

Pleasure, however, has no great importance in Hazlitt's discussions of art; it is the reach of the mind that interests him; and in the passage that follows, he expands his definition of the beautiful to make it a quality sometimes included in and sometimes introducing the sublime.

> There is no incompatibility between strength and softness, as is sometimes supposed by frivolous people. Weakness is not refinement. A shadow may be twice as deep in a finely coloured picture as in another, and yet almost imperceptible, from the gradations that lead to it, and blend it with the light. Correggio had prodigious strength, and greater softness. Nature is strong and soft, beyond the reach of art to imitate. Softness then does not imply the absence of considerable extremes, but it is the interposing a third thing between them, to break the force of the contrast. Guido is more soft than strong. Rembrandt is more strong than soft.
>
> (XVIII, 166)

In these sentences Hazlitt sounds to me particularly happy, as if he would conclude his strictures by saying—"And all this is possible to art, because all this the mind of man can compass. It may stand to reason that such and such sensations are never to be found together—

but then we find that they are, and that we understand them." He has thoroughly heeded Johnson's warning against the cant of reasoning from principles rather than perception.

As he thought about his perception in this instance, Hazlitt appears to have been provoked by two feelings that dominated him as a spectator: first, the humanity of the figures, inseparable from each detail, and then their sublimity. He was impressed by the endurance through time of a made thing, which seemed as intimate in its expressiveness as it was remote in the design of its expressions. That distance in time belongs now to its sublimity, that closeness in space to its beauty, and here again they work together. Yet for all the lessons he derives from the marbles, he does not recommend that they be adopted as a pattern for future sculptors. They are better left standing alone, and not quite absorbed by our later understandings, as simple imitation would make them. It was a way of regarding them congenial also to Haydon and Keats, and best captured perhaps in Keats's phrase about teasing the mind out of thought. To be teased is to be in a not wholly pleasurable state, between complacency and irritation. What we most need to be teased out of, what the marbles help us to be unhappy with, is the ideal of a taste always aware of the laws governing discrete sensations. It does not really matter whether those laws come from Reynolds or Burke—though temperamentally Hazlitt is much closer to Burke.[5] Either way we risk becoming confirmed admirers of our own habits of appreciation, unaware that they *are* habits and therefore unable to change them when we confront something new.

DEATH ON THE PALE HORSE

Hazlitt's article on West's painting, though briefer than that on the Elgin Marbles, offers a more considered explanation of the "moral quantities" he believed an artist ought to represent. It begins by acknowledging that there may be subjects in which an art of the visible is at a disadvantage: in such cases it is better to confess the disadvantage and work by indirection, than to translate all that remains elusive into a language of the visible. Ever since Burke's *Enquiry*, Death, especially in Milton's portrayal, had been cited as an unrivalled instance of sublime terror,[6] effecting "privation" of the senses of the viewer, with the suggestion of uncontrollable energies both immediate and yet obscure, so that the mind hovers between alternatives and makes of this void of solid sense a new terror all its own. In a fine paragraph, Coleridge had used the celebrated lines from *Paradise Lost* to indicate one possible ground of poetry's superiority over painting. The passage shows him in a frame of mind uncharacteristically close to Hazlitt, as it makes the experience of a terrible sublimity the highest mark of imagination, and speaks of a "reconciliation" of opposites without implying their resolution. Reconciliation in Coleridge's usual, spiritually affirmative sense appears to be far from the intended meaning here, though he still uses the word from habit; he is pointing rather to a state in which opposites continue to haunt the mind because neither will allow complete satisfaction to the other.

> As soon as [the mind] is fixed on one image, it becomes understanding; but while it is unfixed and wavering between them, attaching itself permanently to none, it is imagination. Such is the fine description of Death in Milton:—
>
> > "The other shape,
> > If shape it might be call'd, that shape had none
> > Distinguishable in member, joint, or limb,
> > Or substance might be call'd, that shadow seem'd,
> > For each seem'd either: black it stood as night;
> > Fierce as ten furies, terrible as hell,
> > And shook a dreadful dart: what seem'd his head
> > The likeness of a kingly crown had on."
> >
> > *Paradise Lost,* Book II
>
> The grandest efforts of poetry are where the imagination is called forth, not to produce a distinct form, but a strong working of the mind, still offering what is still repelled, and again creating what is again rejected; the result being what the poet wishes to impress, namely, the substitution of a sublime feeling of the unimaginable for a mere image. I have sometimes thought that the passage just read might be quoted as exhibiting the narrow limit of painting, as compared with the boundless power of poetry: painting can not go beyond a certain point; poetry rejects all control, all confinement.[7]

Coleridge's editor, T. M. Raysor, remarks that in such a passage Coleridge would have been working out of a critical tradition which derives from Kant's analytic of the sublime in the *Critique of Judgment,* and he quotes this sentence from Kant: "The beautiful in nature is a question of the form of an object, and this consists in limitation, whereas the sublime is to be found in an object even devoid of form, so far as it immediately involves, or else by its presence provokes, a representation of *limitlessness,* yet with a super-added thought of its totality."[8] But here Coleridge does without any such super-added thought. And though the mind's self-searching, to which Coleridge devotes these remarks, would seem to define Kant's sublime as opposed to Burke's, a similar quest might be reconstructed from Burke's use of the infernal episodes of *Paradise Lost,* and his interest in the mind of Satan with its "thoughts that wander through Eternity." With Hogarth's picture as a likely though unmentioned example, Coleridge notices the inadequacy to this subject of a painter's representative means, and the absurdity of the pretension to adequacy. But the conclusion about poetry's general superiority to painting came more easily to him than to Hazlitt because he was less responsive to pictures.

Hazlitt in making his own comparison of painting with poetry would have had in mind the moral quantities of Rembrandt and Correggio, to place beside the academic failures. So he judges West's picture against *what painting can do and has done* with subjects limitless to the imagination. Yet he offers this judgment without recourse to the Coleridgean distinction between understanding and imagination; for why should we assume that "the dryest and hardest image" conceivable, as Coleridge calls it, leads us to understand any more than it leads us to imagine Death?

> The moral attributes of death are powers and effects of an infinitely wide and general description, which no individual or physical form can possibly represent, but by courtesy of speech or by a distant analogy. The moral impression of Death is essentially visionary; its reality is in the mind's eye. Words are here the only things; and things, physical forms, the mere mockeries of the understanding. The less definite the conception, the less bodily, the more vast, unformed, and unsubstantial, the nearer does it approach to some resemblance of that omnipresent, lasting, universal, irresistible principle, which everywhere, and at some time or other, exerts its power over all things. Death is a mighty abstraction, like Night, or Space, or Time. He is an ugly customer, who will not be invited to supper, or to sit for his picture. He is with us and about us, but we do not see him. He stalks on before us, and we do not mind him; he follows us behind, and we do not look back at him. We do not see him making faces at us in our lifetime! we do not feel him tickling our bare ribs afterwards, nor look at him through the empty grating of our hollow eyes! Does

Mr. West really suppose that he has put the very image of Death upon the canvas; that he has taken the fear of him out of our hearts; that he has circumscribed his power with a pair of compasses; that he has measured the length of his arm with a two-foot rule; that he has suspended the stroke of his dart with a stroke of his pencil; that he has laid his hands on the universal principle of destruction, and hemmed him in with lines and lineaments, and made a gazing-stock and a show of him, "under the patronage of the Prince Regent" (as that illustrious person has taken, and confined, and made a show of another *enemy of the human race*)—so that the work of decay and dissolution is no longer going on in nature; that all we have heard or felt of death is but a fable compared with this distinct, living, and warranted likeness of him? Oh, no! There is no power in the pencil actually to embody an abstraction, to impound the imagination, to circumvent the powers of the soul, which hold communion with the universe. The painter cannot make the general particular, the infinite and imaginary defined and palpable, that which is only believed and dreaded, an object of sight. (XVIII, 137–38)

From a similar premise about the difficulty of such subjects, Hazlitt reaches a conclusion at odds with Coleridge's. For it is one feature of Coleridge's argument that stereotyped works of art are so because they appeal to the understanding, while great ones naturally appeal to the imagination: as if the artist had a choice before he set out upon a subject, and the understanding-artist chose wrongly. But Hazlitt sees the understanding as always at work mastering what is presented to it; sometimes it may be thwarted, but it cannot help busying itself even with the void of sense: there is an opening into the sublime whenever imagination takes the place of understanding. The artist can only show the point at which understanding stops by dealing in implication rather than fact—in "mighty abstractions" rather than conventional forms. Hazlitt verges here on an insight comparable to Lessing's in the *Laocoön,* about the consequences for representation of the differences in means that separate poetry from painting. As, in a poem, a beautiful woman would be revealed to better effect by the awe of her admirers than by a minute description, which is what only painting can give truly; so, in a picture, a fearful and obscure *idea* like Death conveys more than any portrait can, and death's implements, scythe, horse, and skull, are apt to make him ridiculous when rendered too palpable.

The distinction between imaginative object and natural model has thus come back in full force, to the advantage of the former.

Hazlitt's interest in the difference between words and pictures comes from no contempt for the human need to fashion allegories: revive an abstraction like Death, and all his terrors return—he "will not be invited to supper, or to sit for his picture." But this is just what West has made him do, by remaining faithful to the academic portrait-painter's decorum. To realize its inadequacy we need only attend to Hazlitt's rhetorical questions, like those questions God addressed to Job in correcting a similar wish to translate sublime intuitions into practical results. The parenthetic allusion to Napoleon caged at St. Helena brings out the element of social expedience in all such translations—a pragmatic containment of great ideas that is society's correlative of the rules of academic painting. The effort to turn Napoleon into a common prisoner is only an effort (but a poor one) to suppress the magnitude of awe and wonder that are naturally connected with his name, thanks to the victories he won against all odds, and the mighty abstraction we supposed as the cause for so strange an effect.

The review continues with a suggestion about the means by which a better translation might be achieved, and then a sinkingly literal description of the picture.

> The artist has represented Death riding over his prostrate victims in all the rage of impotent despair. He is in a great splutter, and seems making a last effort to frighten his foes by an explosion of red-hot thunderbolts, and a pompous display of allegorical paraphernalia. He has not the calm, still, majestic form of Death, killing by a look,—withering by a touch. His presence does not make the still air cold. His flesh is not stony or cadaverous, but is crusted over with a yellow glutinous paste, as if it had been baked in a pye. Milton makes Death "grin horrible a ghastly smile," with an evident allusion to the common Death's head; but in the picture he seems grinning for a wager, with a full row of loose rotten teeth; and his terrible form is covered with a long black drapery, which would cut a figure in an undertaker's shop, and which cuts a figure where it is (for it is finely painted), but which serves only as a disguise for the King of Terrors. We have no idea of such a swaggering and blustering Death as this of Mr. West's. He has not invoked a ghastly spectre from the tomb, but has called up an old squalid ruffian from a night cellar, and crowned him "monarch of the universal world." The horse on which he rides is not "pale," but white. There is no gusto, no imagination in Mr. West's colouring. As to his figure, the description [in the Descriptive Catalogue] gives an accurate idea of it enough. "His horse rushes forward with

the universal wildness of a tempestuous element, breathing livid
pestilence, and rearing and trampling with the vehemence of un-
bridled fury." The style of the figure corresponds to the style of
the description. It is over-loaded and top-heavy. The chest of the
animal is a great deal too long for the legs.   (XVIII, 138)

Hazlitt supposes that our dominant emotion is terror and this ought
to be, as it was for Burke, a terror of things that remain obscure,
never realizing themselves or satisfying our wish that they come to
rest in some palpable form. Yet West, instead of exiling us from the
detail we look for in ordinary representation, and refusing to supply
the connecting links, has given us a perfectly commonplace image of
Death and then sought to obscure it, as the phrases of his catalogue-
description seek to obscure the embarrassment of anything too blunt
in the sound of "horse." The embarrassment, and the method-mind-
ing arrogance that led to it, Hazlitt isolates in the image of West
measuring the figure of Death with the compass and a two-foot rule.
As a satiric emblem of the painter's situation, the image recalls
Blake's proverb of hell, "Bring out number weight & measure in a
year of dearth."

Probably it was Hazlitt's description that sent Keats to see West's
picture, and so provoked the letter on negative capability. "It is a
wonderful picture," says Keats, "when West's age is considered; But
there is nothing to be intense upon; no women one feels mad to kiss;
no face swelling into reality. The excellence of every Art is its intensity, capable of making all disagreeables evaporate, from their
being in close relationship with Beauty & Truth."[9] Despite a strong
temptation to interpret this in line with Hazlitt's criticism, I think
Keats's reservations about the picture have a different cause. The
chief fact to emerge from his comments is his growing impatience
with the Miltonic sublime—which can never give a "face swelling
into reality," though it may suggest the once-bold features of a face
dissolving from reality. The same impatience would lead him to give
up both *Hyperions* and write the odes and *Lamia,* so that in retrospect his criticism of West seems part of a larger movement from a
Miltonic to a Shakespearean ideal of poetic tact. Hazlitt, on the other
hand, wrote his strictures on West to confirm the sense even among
the general public that the Miltonic sublime was something rather
different from this, and to strengthen in his more advanced readers
the conviction that it could still make a living force in art. Wordsworth's poetry would have shown them how that could be so; and
West's painting must not make them despair, or invent false con-

trasts between the arts: in rejecting it they are rejecting neither painting nor sublimity.

For Hazlitt, a mode of execution was to blame. Hence his advice to painters elsewhere in the review, that they learn the art of "substituting hieroglyphics for words," or somehow adopting a symbolism that has the double power claimed by words, both to suggest and to evoke. But how can this be carried out in painting when "words are here the only things"? One notices in the phrase—as in the passage on how words alone approach "this present moment, this present object"—that Hazlitt's absorbing concern with words has a double focus, on the promise they give of presenting objects and the shock they give by making us more completely aware of our distance from objects. Words acknowledge the fragmentary character of their relation to anything they try to make present, and a sublime poet is always showing us how imperfectly they aim at embodiment. A sublime picture must find a way of doing this as well: Burke's "a clear idea is another name for a little idea" was a fair enough stricture against the artist who finds his way too quickly, or without a hint of the imagination's striving for a doubtful result. Keats's remark about no "face swelling into reality" laments West's failure to get effects which he should not have wanted anyway. But this is what imitation has come to, so late in the history of the ideal: a picture neither intensely vivid nor intensely obscure, neither adequately literal nor cunningly hieroglyphic, but fretting away at misplaced details and affording a half-hearted approximation of the bloody-bones sublime. The painter has invited us to dwell on the elements of "fine painting" where they can only appear as a vain set-off to the ghastliness of the subject; and Hazlitt's anger at the result belongs properly to the author of "On the Fear of Death" and "On the Feeling of Immortality in Youth," essays in which death comes to seem a brute fact as definitive of life as it was for Hobbes and Burke. With every involuntary offense against our moral ideas—and the solemnity of death has to do with many of them—the imagination sustains an injury. To give the extremes of passion, beyond the frigid compromise of middle forms, with a distinct view of whatever is most striking in the subject; and yet at times to steer away from whatever is distinct, and even from what is commonly called nature (the sum of the things that exist): these are the apparently contradictory functions Hazlitt associates with art. Still, to unite them all we really need is an understanding of art as "heterocosm" or another nature.

In the essay "On a Landscape of Nicolas Poussin," Hazlitt seems to endorse some such formulation:

> To give us nature, such as we see it, is well and deserving of praise; to give us nature, such as we have never seen, but have often wished to see it, is better, and deserving of higher praise. He who can show the world in its first naked glory, with the hues of fancy spread over it, or in its high and palmy state, with the gravity of history stamped on the proud monuments of vanished empire,—who, by his "so potent art," can recal time past, transport us to distant places, and join the regions of imagination (a new conquest) to those of reality,—who teaches us not only what nature is, but what she has been, and is capable of being,—he who does this, and does it with simplicity, with truth, and grandeur, is lord of nature and her powers; and his mind is universal, and his art the master-art!   (VIII, 169)

This has strong echoes of Sidney's "Apology for Poetry," with its praise of the poet's "high flying liberty of conceit" and the invention by which he "doth grow in effect another nature," making a golden world of our brazen one. The allusion to a master-art, *Architectonike,* also returns us to the "Apology." But Sidney's was a fully rhetorical culture, its limits drawn from within by the poet's ability to range freely in the zodiac of his wit. Tropes, figures, topics and commonplaces, a thorough possession of the five faculties of rhetoric, and the tact of decorum for each occasion: these made a single vast, adaptable, and all-absorbing strategy of persuasion, and in the end made the poet's identity the sum-total of his achieved persuasions. If Sidney has any anxiety, it is that words may establish their world and create "another nature" all too completely. Hazlitt's on the contrary was a dialectical culture, with Bacon more than Sidney as its hero.[10] His anxiety is that artists may no longer be of a "universal" mind, and the words of poetry may have ceased to surpass all others in taking the place of the object.

So Hazlitt remains Sidney's opposite in spite of the echoes. A universe created by art, and utterly self-sustaining, is foreign to his interests; and in the next paragraph he writes not of another nature but of a *second* nature. The change of a word registers the impact of two centuries of philosophy, but makes nonsense of the extension into criticism of correspondence-theories of truth, beginning with Hobbes's definition of poetry as a "semblance of truth." A second nature for Hazlitt modifies or complicates the truth of the first. *Not* to paint a picture that corresponds to what we see out there, *not* to feign a semblance of what we anyway accept as given, may be to imitate nature in the only interesting sense.

> There is nothing in this "more than natural," if criticism could be persuaded to think so. The historic painter does not neglect or contravene nature, but follows her more closely up into her fantastic heights, or hidden recesses. He demonstrates what she would be in conceivable circumstances, and under implied conditions. He "gives to airy nothing a local habitation," not "a name." . . . *His* art is a second nature; not a different one.   (VIII, 170)

The artist, far from giving us back our experience as we knew it, is the specialist of the contrary-to-fact-conditional *that matters:* range enough of them side by side and they make a satisfying plurality, with inward relations to each other; and this may be called without exaggeration a second nature. To have isolated a thing for certain of its powers or characteristics, and brought to light what was hidden, is to have invented it as something new. It is not a matter of those powers or characteristics having been always latent and at last simply realized. They were not talked about, from which it follows that they were not there as they have since come to be, until isolated in this way. "Isolated" may conceal, however, an unhappy metaphor: chosen, recombined, thrown into relief—anything else will do, except the suggestion that this second nature competes with the first as the strange with the familiar. That was just what had caused trouble for Sidney's "another nature," and what made Bacon confine poets to naming alone. Hazlitt rejects naming for the greater task of making "a local habitation," a setting dense with circumstance in which the redisposed elements of our experience play out their story. But a tacit redefinition of nature has been at work all along, to accord with his view of art. Nature is no longer the sum of the things that exist, but rather the sum of the things we could recognize as ours if they joined our experience. These make a number beyond reckoning, but a group each of whose members bears a family resemblance to the rest, since of all our experience the limits are set by the humanness of our imaginings. To house everyone we need exactly as many local habitations as there are geniuses of place.

My account of "second nature" shows how closely Hazlitt's idea of imitation borders on an idea of originality. The essay on Poussin, however, advances the phrase chiefly to launch another attack on the academic style, only later recalling Poussin's landscapes, in a careful montage from memory, to reveal how they become second nature to the mind that has once penetrated their hidden recesses. For a fuller argument about the relation between nature and the original genius who invents a point of view, one must turn to Hazlitt's essay "On Imitation."

IMITATION AND GUSTO

It could more appropriately have been called "On Invention" or "On the Realities of the Imagination," because it starts with this sentence: "Objects in themselves disagreeable or indifferent, often please in the imitation." Imitation, then, has ceased to refer to art's work of reflecting objects, nor can we suppose any surface-to-depth relation between the imitation and the character of the object imitated. Throughout this essay Hazlitt is proposing a radically unexpected definition of the artist's work, and of the reasons for our interest in it. Of course, the difference between copy and imitation is known to most modern readers from chapter 17 of the *Biographia Literaria,* where Coleridge's aim was to disencumber Wordsworth of the belief that poetry can ever take its language "from the mouths of men in real life"; he gave as a likelier cause of the pleasure afforded by Wordsworth's poetry "the apparent naturalness of the *representation,* as raised and qualified by an imperceptible infusion of the author's own knowledge and talent, which infusion does, indeed, constitute it an *imitation* as distinguished from a mere copy."[11] But Hazlitt's thinking goes beyond this, and encourages us to extend the meaning of "representation" also. His title, "On Imitation," was in one sense a throw-away, in another simply a good tactic. He might as well have said to Reynolds and Johnson, "Here is *your* name for the family of facts in whose presence we feel that art and life are both interesting, and have something to do with each other; and, to show how little the name matters to me, I take it over without protest. But by every word I write, by every appeal I can make to common experience, you will see what narrow limits you placed on the idea by explaining it through this word, and the word itself in the light of your mirror-metaphor."

In his opening paragraph Hazlitt points to a cause of our pleasure in imitation which he says has never been properly understood, that "by exciting curiosity, and inviting a comparison between the object and the representation, it opens a new field of inquiry, and

leads the attention to a variety of details and distinctions not perceived before." This suggests that neither art nor nature is subordinate: when we make our comparisons, we use both to learn about
both. And what we especially want to learn about a thing are its
"distinctions, connections, structure, uses"—a list which implies that
the artist's quest is purposive in the same way as the scientist's, and
his "field of inquiry" determined by similar motives. The affinity
between artist and scientist is a theme of Hazlitt's essay to which he
recurs with delicate insistence, as when a painter is described taking
satisfactions we ordinarily associate with a chemist.

> An entire new set of ideas . . . occupies the mind of the student,
> and overcomes the sense of pain and repugnance, which is the only
> feeling that the sight of a dead and mangled body presents to ordi-
> nary men. It is the same in art as in science. The painter of still
> life, as it is called, takes the same pleasure in the object as the spec-
> tator does in the imitation; because by habit he is led to perceive
> all those distinctions in nature, to which other persons never pay
> any attention till they are pointed out to them in the picture. The
> vulgar only see nature as it is reflected to them from art; the
> painter sees the picture in nature, before he transfers it to the can-
> vas. He refines, he analyses, he remarks fifty things, which escape
> common eyes; and this affords a distinct source of reflection and
> amusement to him, independently of the beauty or grandeur of
> the objects themselves, or of their connection with other impres-
> sions besides those of sight.   (IV, 73)

This praise of the painter's idea apart from whatever he can
"transfer to the canvas," recalls Sidney's notion of the poet's "fore-
conceit," and anticipates the expressive theorists of art, Croce and
Collingwood. But to place Hazlitt even in so distinguished a tradition is somewhat misleading. It gives no vivid sense of his originality,
and conceals his determination to make any argument tell in a contest about living art. In these sentences he was aiming—just as he
had done in the essay "On Genius and Common Sense"—to discredit
the belief that nature could be "methodized" by talent, and at the
same time to dispel the notion current since Young, that genius had
mysterious traffic with a nature from which others were shut out.
Here, the artist of genius is one who can collect all the materials and
marshal all the faculties he needs to execute his work, only more
rapidly than his fellows, with what Hemingway would call "a quicker
ratio to the passage of time." He is, finally, a good observer; he connects his observations, and savors the result, with an ease the wisest

appreciator can hardly match. In this sense too, art is perhaps his second nature.

Hazlitt now restates his initial paradox, and to the question, How can one derive pleasure from what *just is* unpleasant?, finds a tentative answer in keeping with his chemist-analogy. Experiments, which widen experience, will have formed the groundwork of the only kind of imitation that interests us, whether or not we are clever enough to reconstruct them in looking at the picture.

> Imitation renders an object, displeasing in itself, a source of plea-sure, not by repetition of the same idea, but by suggesting new ideas, by detecting new properties, and endless shades of difference, just as a close and continued contemplation of the object itself would do. Art shows us nature, divested of the medium of our prejudices. It divides and decompounds objects into a thousand curious parts, which may be full of variety, beauty, and delicacy in themselves, though the object to which they belong may be dis-agreeable in its general appearance, or by association with other ideas. . . . Art is the microscope of the mind, which sharpens the wit as the other does the sight; and converts every object into a little universe in itself. Art may be said to draw aside the veil from nature.   (IV, 73–74)

The painter might be described as a representative man, but for one special skill: he is a discoverer of *un*habitual associations, which seem part of our nature as soon as we learn them. Hazlitt is careful to exhibit such discoveries reaching across the art-nature boundary, lest we suppose that "new properties" are something only art can give to nature, or only nature to art. They are something either can tell us about itself or about the other: as, for example, the Elgin Marbles make us see repose as an expression of power; or a cozen-ing neighbor saying, "Put money in your purse," alters our under-standing of the character who says those words in a play. We are warned against separating aesthetic experience from the rest of ex-perience by Hazlitt's remark that "a close and continued contempla-tion of the object itself" may accomplish all that the painter does. At the same time, we are warned against setting up any given world prior to art, whether we call it life or experience or nature, by the concluding epigram, "Art may be said to draw aside the veil from nature." I take this to mean that there are aspects of nature that remain hidden from us until we have something in art to compare them with. Art, in that case, like any other influential creation of the mind, would be seen as a prejudice and a necessary one, itself brought into being by earlier prejudices. But this sense of art and prejudice is in keeping with a second epigram, "Art shows us nature, divested of the medium of our prejudices"; for prejudice there has a more limited meaning: it denotes the received ideas that we lay up all our lives, assent to as a matter of social conformity, and then give back to the world in a dry interval as if they were cherished convictions. What Hazlitt does *not* mean ever to exclude from our judgments of art are opinions, interests, concerns, biases—all those things which art helps to form, and of which we can never be divested in any case. Again, his concern to discourage us from interpreting art's "little universe" as "another nature" with laws all its own, is plain in the accompanying words, "Art is the microscope of the mind." Contemplating a second nature we find our gaze turning gradually inward, and in the end our knowledge of art modifies our self-knowledge.

It is possible to read "On Imitation" several times, with increasing confusion about Hazlitt's use of "nature." He moves back and forth through the range of available meanings, and only a reader's tact will decide just how the going definition is set by the tone of a particular passage. Nevertheless it seems fair to distinguish two main emphases. First, nature may be everything which we take for granted, and to which therefore our responses are conventional. The "rage for the *picturesque*" comes in here, because it is the most recent instance of an original taste being converted into a broadly intelligible routine. Once a mark of self-consciousness, it has become a token of fashionable pedantry, the vaguely necessary background against which tourists confirm each other's pretensions, in ten thousand letters in the manner of Gray and Walpole. Every writer, says Hazlitt, "teazes you almost to death with the frequency and insignificance of his discoveries." Yet he also speaks of a nature which may exist in contrast with the one for which a conventional vocabulary has been devised; a nature that is made each moment from the new ideas suggested and new properties detected by genius. In his most striking statement on imitation, where he tells why a painter's work should matter to the spectator, Hazlitt distinguishes between the same two meanings of nature, the first being now identified with the ideal as defined by Reynolds and Johnson.

> It is not to be denied that the study of the *ideal* in art, if separated from the study of nature, may have the effect . . . of producing dissatisfaction and contempt for everything but itself, as all affec-

tation must; but to the genuine artist, truth, nature, beauty, are almost different names for the same thing.

Imitation interests, then, by exciting a more intense perception of truth, and calling out the powers of observation and comparison: wherever this effect takes place the interest follows of course, with or without imitation, whether the object is real or artificial. The gardener delights in the streaks of a tulip, or "pansy freak'd with jet"; the mineralogist in the varieties of certain strata, because he understands them. Knowledge is pleasure as well as power. A work of art has in this respect no advantage over a work of nature, except inasmuch as it furnishes an additional stimulus to curiosity. (IV, 75)

I will be returning to this passage in a discussion of Keats's Grecian Urn, but so much nonsense has been written about truth and beauty that it seems necessary to take a preliminary view of the idea as Hazlitt presented it.[12] The modern notion of verifiability is of course very remote from this, and I think the trouble begins with the assumption that Keats must at any rate have been working up to it. He was doing nothing of the sort, as Hazlitt's "different names for the same thing" make plain. Hazlitt could frame his explanation so casually because these half-equations were on the verge of being commonplace. "Beauty" for him is close enough to what it remains for us; "nature" is the object becoming a little universe under the microscope of the mind; "truth" is everything that is the case, but "divested of the medium of our prejudices," as a camera lens may be wiped clean without losing the point-of-view of the eye composing the picture. Hazlitt understandably does not quit the theme until a final allusion has turned the argument against Johnson's great sentence on imitation, from *Rasselas*—that the poet's business is to "examine, not the individual, but the species; to remark general properties and large appearances; he does not number the streaks of the tulip." True, replies Hazlitt, unless one happens to meet a gardener, whose knowledge is power, and whose science has the effect of art by "exciting a more intense perception" and "calling out the powers of observation" in anyone who shares his pleasure. We are drawn out by power, and feel that our whole being is changed as we follow "of course" an interest not our own. As for the mineralogist, he might be any experimenter whose art seems strange at first, and out of the way. Let him stand for Wordsworth as he would appear to a critic first encountering the line, "And never lifted up a single stone."

"On Imitation" concludes with a skeptical turn against the faith that certain subjects can always be relied on for their intrinsic worth. If Hazlitt is right about the mind's dividing and decompounding and its "comparisons," then every critic is wrong who pretends to have found a reason for decorum in the nature of things. Imitation, on Hazlitt's view, becomes a matter not of exhaustively recording the essence of a thing but selectively portraying a mind in motion: the interest of a picture has everything to do with such ideas as a chosen object can suggest, and nothing to do with such ideas as a given object is supposed to transmit. The interest of a thing, that is, owes none of its force to the thing itself. So it is with the mathematician's "lines, points, angles, squares, and circles"; so too with the satirist's puffs, powders, patches, bibles, billets-doux.

> [Such things] are not interesting in themselves; they become so by the power of mind exerted in comprehending their properties and relations. People dispute for ever about Hogarth. The question has not in one respect been fairly stated. The merit of his pictures does not so much depend on the nature of the subject, as on the knowledge displayed of it, on the number of ideas they excite, on the fund of thought and observation contained in them. They are to be looked on as works of science; they gratify our love of truth; they fill up the void of the mind: they are a series of plates of natural history, and also of that most interesting part of natural history, the history of man.   (IV, 75)

We may now imagine two narratives, one a story and the other a history: let us call them *The Rake's Progress* and *Lord Rochester's Decay*. Hazlitt would recognize a simple difference between them by observing that one never happened and the other did. But this fact has no consequences for the kind of interest they afford, and it is only interest that leads us to a truth we care about. So in praising either for its truth, Hazlitt would claim to be using a language we all understand, and to need only one sense of "truth" to cover story and history. The different sense of truth in the phrase "what really happened," which would apply only to history, refers to a knowledge in most cases easily acquired, but it is hard to imagine what interesting questions could be answered by this knowledge and nothing more. When we have got it, after all, what have we got? A series of plates depicting the skeleton rather than the physiognomy of conduct—a history of man which would make far from the most interesting part of natural history. Story and history, art and science, pleasure and power, beauty and truth, have all, in the course of this essay, passed from their usual opposition into an unfamiliar alliance (which we find we knew all along), that makes them "almost different names for the same thing." At the rear of their procession comes Hogarth, the faithful painter of artificial life, now triumphant over West and the adepts of the grand style, and praised as a naturalist of the mind of man.

Two eighteenth-century critics, working like Hazlitt in the empiricist tradition, had preceded him in writing essays on taste in which imitation does not figure as mirror-work. Both Hume, in his essay "Of the Standard of Taste," and Burke, in the essay on taste that forms the Introduction to his *Enquiry,* admit that "Beauty is no quality in things themselves: it exists merely in the mind which contemplates them"; but that as "the senses are the great originals of all our ideas," we may expect as much conformity with each other in our ideas as in our sensations, and as much again in imagination as in our ideas.[13] Imagination might thus be seen as leagued with the rest of our experience, since all it can do is, in Burke's memorable phrase, "represent at pleasure" the images of things we have collected, though it does so "in a new manner, and according to a different order" from that of the great originals. This sounds like the experimental liberty that Hazlitt grants the imagination. Yet the pleasure Burke speaks of is always a "pleasure of resemblance," never a gain registered from the work of comparison. And Hume as well as Burke ends by setting judgment over imagination, in the belief that through judgment alone we detach ourselves from a particular state of mind, humor, culture, and history, everything which permits us to be "influenced by prejudice" and prevents us from enlarging our comprehension. "Cleared of all prejudice," we may acquire delicacy of taste. It is judgment then, and a judgment in which knowledge of existing resemblances is the ground-rule, which returns us to a law-governed idea of imitation, even in a critic like Hume who believes there is no right point of view in art.

The greatness of the earliest imitations is a puzzle to both critics. Burke confesses their superiority but then consoles himself with the thought that they may have stolen a march on posterity, from the untutored judgment of their first admirers: "The rude hearer is affected by the principles which operate in poetry and music even in their rudest condition; and he is not skillful enough to perceive the defects."[14] Hume for his part goes some way toward denying their superiority—and thus contradicting the thesis of his companion essay "Of the Rise and Progress of the Arts and Sciences"—by first drawing a distinction between fluctuating manners (in judging which we must beware of prejudice) and permanent morals (in judging which no human being can easily go wrong), and then discovering in the early stages of art a deformity owing to the "vicious manners" art must depict. This deformity he extends beyond manners into morals: "the want of humanity and of decency" in Homer and the Greek tragedians "diminishes considerably the merit of their noble performances."[15] With the ancients cleared away, we more readily believe that judgment can be improved by continual "practice" (Hume) and by ever "greater attention and habit in such things" (Burke), until, freed from prejudice entirely, it achieves a point of view that sums up all points of view. Taste for Hume and Burke comes to seem the master-craft of discrimination by which genius may be improved; and so, from a position very remote from Johnson's and Reynolds's they arrive at almost the same end.

Hazlitt admired Hume and Burke above all other writers of the past century, and from incidental remarks one may guess his disappointment at the stubborn loyalty with which, in spite of all their ambivalence, they adhered to the received vocabulary of taste. However, their successor in the psychology of taste, Archibald Alison, goes much further in the direction promised by Burke's interest in what "flatters the imagination"; and, though one cannot be certain Hazlitt read his *Essays on Taste,* they afford many anticipations which help to explain Hazlitt's thinking in the essay "On *Gusto.*"[16]

In accord with his predecessors Alison acknowledges the persuasive influence of habit on our associations, and therefore on our mode as well as our objects of imitation: "No man in general, is sensible to beauty, in those subjects in which he has not previous ideas."[17] He further strengthens the argument against the intrinsic value of objects by remarking how our tact is made subtler by the force of accumulated experience: "the more our ideas are increased, or our conceptions extended upon any subject, the greater the number of associations we connect with it, the stronger is the emotion of sublimity or beauty we receive from it."[18] It was at this juncture that Hume and Burke alike introduced judgment as a faculty which brings into conformity with social norms our sentiments respecting different objects. Burke had the livelier sense of how judgment might thwart individual imaginings, though he defended this as a necessary limitation: "the judgment is for the greater part employed in throwing stumbling blocks in the way of the imagination, in dis-

sipating the scenes of its enchantment, and in tying us down to the
disagreeable yoke of our reason."[19] But Alison holds that the errant
imagination cannot be judged errant except when it does not pre-
vail; if it does, its products enter into and modify our future definition of judgment; so that in the end, the opposition of imagination
to judgment is no help in talking about art. To the imagination
itself all our habits of mind contribute. And imitations, though they
bear a family resemblance to each other, are interesting because we
read in the expression of the object the expression of the mind that
chose it (ours as well as the artist's). Alison is thus the first to assert
that both the matter and manner of imitation are determined by
elective affinity.

> It is not, surely, that Nature herself is different, that so different
> effects are produced upon the imaginations of [men of great sen-
> sibility]; but it is because the original constitution of their minds
> has led them to different habits of Emotion,—because their imagi-
> nations seize only those expressions in nature, which are allied to
> their prevailing dispositions,—and because every other appearance
> is indifferent to them.[20]

Alison's achievement was to have taken seriously Hume's protest
against the transition from "is" to "ought"—which denied that we
can find a satisfactory way of deducing the correct moral judgment
of an action from a correct description of it—and then to have applied it consistently where Hume did not, to our judgments of art.
You cannot, says Alison, get from the indicative description of a
scene to the exclamatory one, or by any means judge the worth of
the latter, without entering into the associations of the individual
case, which always lead back to the particular situation of an experi-
encing mind. For example, we may call the sound of thunder sublime, "yet how different is the Emotion which it gives to the peasant
who sees at last, after a long drought, the consent of Heaven to his
prayers for rain,—to the philosopher, who, from the height of the
Alps, hears it roll beneath his feet,—to the soldier, who, under the
impression of ancient superstition, welcomes it, upon the moment of
engagement, as the omen of victory!"[21] Because all these emotions
seem to fall into a "natural" category, we make them share a name,
and suppose as a result that we have registered a fitness of our emotions to their objects. The relation, however, between any awful fact
and its sublimity, is a relation only between a sign proper to many
occasions, and the thing signified on a particular one. "Sign" and
"signified" are Alison's words: there may be times, he adds, when

we lose sight of the human peculiarity of the relation; and there are occurrences in nature—"the sound of Thunder, of a Whirlwind, of a Torrent, of an Earthquake"—so apparently limited in what they can mean to us that we suppose the sign inevitably linked with the thing signified, as in these instances with "the qualities of Power, or Danger, or Awfulness."[22] We realize that this is a wrong view of the matter only when a faulty or mistaken connection is brought plainly before us, as when the sound we took to be thunder turns out to have been the clatter of carriage wheels. Hearing the same sound we then cease to feel the same emotion, and recognize that we ourselves make the fitness between the two: if it were not so, the sound itself would continue to be sublime even after we were "undeceived." Neither the sound nor the category to which taste assigns it, but *how we construe it,* aided by a lifetime of such activity, alone rouses us to a certain feeling. Instead of an original fitness between mind and nature, or a standard that detaches our habits of judgment from prejudice or situation, Alison can thus maintain that the *expression of mind* which we project into nature is the sole cause of our emotions, whether in looking at nature itself or at imitations.

A fuller quotation from each critic will bring out how explicitly Alison broadens the skepticism of Hume, without ever proposing a new idealism of his own. Of the qualifications necessary to a right judgment of art, Hume remarks:

> Those finer emotions of the mind are of a very tender and delicate nature, and require the concurrence of many favourable circumstances to make them play with facility and exactness, according to their general and established principles. The least exterior hindrance to such small springs, or the least internal disorder, disturbs their motion, and confounds the operation of the whole machine. When we would make an experiment of this nature, and would try the force of any beauty or deformity, we must choose with care a proper time and place, and bring the fancy to a suitable situation and disposition. A perfect serenity of mind, a recollection of thought, a due attention to the object; if any of these circumstances be wanting, our experiment will be fallacious, and we shall be unable to judge of the catholic and universal beauty. The relation, which nature has placed between the form and the sentiment, will at least be more obscure.[23]

In speaking of a "relation, which nature has placed between the form and the sentiment" Hume falls back on the notion of a fitness not created by us, between the sign and the thing signified. His judge has a mind without expression, what might be called a moodless mind, as serenity implies a cloudless sky. This comes from having thought of taste as the work of rectification. Alison thinks of it rather as a process of continual testing, and his spectator can afford to have moods of his own, by which to estimate those that art presents. Taste in this sense is a faculty which the spectator shares with the artist, and which he applies as actively as the artist. His judgment of a work will depend on the sympathy between his expression of mind and the author's; and this holds equally for his estimate of certain works by the author of nature.

> The same degree of uniformity which is pleasing in a scene of Greatness or Melancholy, would be disagreeable or dull in a scene of Gaiety or Splendour. The same degree of variety which would be beautiful in these, would be distressing in the others. By what rule, however, do we determine the different Beauty of these proportions? Not surely by the Composition itself, else one determinate Composition would be permanently beautiful; but by the relation of this Composition to the Expression or Character of the scene by its according with the demand and expectation of our Minds; and by its being suited to that particular state of interest or of fancy, which is produced by the Emotion that the scene inspires. When this effect is accordingly produced, when the proportion either of uniformity or variety corresponds to the nature of this Emotion, we conclude that the Composition is good. When this proportion is violated, when there is more uniformity of Expression than we choose to dwell upon, or more variety than we can follow without distraction, we conclude that the Composition is defective, and speak of it either as dull or confused.[24]

The argument here may be weakened by its reliance on "uniformity" and "variety," which belong to the period vocabulary of the picturesque, yet what Alison says of them would apply no less to other qualities. The point in any case remains clear. He refuses to conceive of taste as the understanding of a universal and catholic beauty which nature establishes before we enter the scene, or for which civilization has set norms that we cannot hope to shake. Taste for Alison is the faculty that seeks expression in nature, as in imitations, "according with the demand and expectation of our Minds." Nor does he require our minds to repose in a moodless serenity. It is understood that we search out impressions in keeping with our previous bias, and that every new response to what "corresponds to the nature of this Emotion" will modify the emotion itself. Expression can be read at all, in a landscape or a painting, only because we are interpreters: the sort of reading we can make is always determined by our need to work outward from our own minds. Any value therefore which we discern in a composition, we must have been ready to project into it, and this means that taste is another name for the mind's characteristic composure. Genius is implicit in it and, like genius, it communicates its results with a relish of first finding; it does not receive, it explores; and its aim, far from "improving" those who listen, is to change them.

With this analysis of expression, Alison gives a satisfying clue to what Hazlitt meant by *gusto*—a word for taste, but one picked out for a few special implications which remove it as far as possible from the idea of taste as a passive and inculcated knowledge. Gusto is "power or passion defining any object," the power of at once recognizing and interpreting expression, which the artist shares with the critic. Works rich in sensuous detail and immediately appealing to the eye may nevertheless lack this quality. Claude's landscapes, perfect but without gusto, "do not interpret one sense by another." Again, with Vandyke's flesh-colour, "the eye does not acquire a taste or appetite for what it sees. In a word, gusto in painting is where the impression made on one sense excites by affinity those of another." The importance granted to a quality felt in all the senses, and by which they confirm each other, follows naturally from imitation's thousand hidden properties, which possess us in concert at the moment of their discovery. Gusto, taste that is made and found as if in a single gesture, belongs to a few select spirits and those who can cherish them: Titian, Correggio, Raphael, Michelangelo, Milton, Pope in his compliments, Dryden in his satires, Rubens "in his Fauns and Satyrs, and in all that expresses motion, but in nothing else." As Hazlitt refines his definition, he seems to feel its essence eluding him and grows more conscious of the "delicacy" of the subject. That it was suggested to him by reflections like Alison's—on the difference between false and true delicacy, and the home of the latter in any outward expression answering the expression of mind—Hazlitt's opening paragraph sufficiently attests.

> It is not so difficult to explain this term in what relates to expression (of which it may be said to be the highest degree) as in what relates to things without expression, to the natural appearances of objects, as mere colour or form. In one sense, however, there is hardly any object entirely devoid of expression, without some character of power belonging to it, some precise association

with pleasure or pain: and it is in giving this truth of character from the truth of feeling, whether in the highest or the lowest degree, but always in the highest degree of which the subject is capable, that gusto consists.   (IV, 77)

Gusto is a quality belonging to a picture, as much as to its creator and appreciator. In this sense it might be defined as expression intensely realized and widely diffused; the application to Hazlitt's remarks on the blind Elymas of Raphael would then be clear: to express blindness with double force, by covering the face itself, was to give the truth of character from the truth of feeling. (In the same way Hazlitt praises Milton for the "repeated blows" of his up-piling adjectives—"Or where Chineses drive / With sails and wind their *cany* waggons *light*.") The picture interprets one sense by another, sight in this instance by touch, with a directness that makes Hazlitt's reservations about Claude and Vandyke less extravagantly figurative than we may have supposed.

Hazlitt's idea is evocative enough of the "sensuous vividness" modern criticism values for *gusto* to have survived into our day with much of its force still available. What may eventually diminish its value is over-use, as a color-word for every nameless grace. So a critic who praises the gusto of the antithetical style in Johnson's "Vanity of Human Wishes," when what he means is strength, boldness, assurance that carries conviction,[25] is hastening the process of synonymization by which a language is made one word the poorer—the same process by which we have lost "empathy," "insight," and "suggestiveness." Keats, in all his uses of the word, is a better guide to its possibilities. He saw that it was a widening, to include the artist, of an idea of taste once confined to the critic; and in praising Hazlitt's "Letter to William Gifford," he turned instinctively to a gustatory figure: "The manner in which this is managed: the force and innate power with which it *yeasts and works itself up*—the feeling for the costume of society; is in a style of genius."[26] The italics are mine, but none will be necessary for a more modern illustration, from the advertising slogan that promises "real gusto in a great, light beer." This shows as tactful an understanding as one could wish: gusto is great in its effects, light in the visible pains by which it earns them. And I find here the suggestion that gusto is a property of the drinker as well as the beer, for he must know in himself what he seeks by assimilation. There is something generous in the appeal, which accords nicely with the belief that taste adds to our nature instead of correcting it.

CHAPTER VI

AGAINST AESTHETICS

RECONCILIATION AND DISSENT

As critics of eighteenth-century taste, Coleridge and Hazlitt are often in agreement, with a depth of shared feeling that quotations can barely suggest; and the break with general nature, to which I have stressed Hazlitt's contribution, might by others be credited to Coleridge as the sole original.[1] I remain convinced that Hazlitt, naturally a thinker for himself, had no need of Coleridge's guidance in a movement of revolt already alive on many fronts, but his own testimony here is partly against him. It affords the liveliest imaginable record of the way Coleridge's judgments took hold of anyone who once encountered them, and of their persuasiveness in revising the English poetic canon. Thus, a passage in *The Spirit of the Age* introduces a contrast between Godwin the well-employed talent and Coleridge the unserviceable genius; Hazlitt has just praised Godwin's "correct *acquired* taste" and now launches a different sort of encomium: "The alteration of his taste in poetry, from an exclusive admiration of the age of Queen Anne to an almost equally exclusive one of that of Elizabeth, is, we suspect, owing to Mr. Coleridge, who some twenty years ago, threw a great stone into the standing pool of criticism, which splashed some persons with the mud, but which gave a motion to the surface and a reverberation to the neighbouring echoes, which has not since subsided." This goes a long way to explain the praise of Coleridge in Hazlitt's lecture on the living poets, as "the only person I ever knew who answered to the idea of a man of genius." Yet Coleridge had an idealizing temperament, Hazlitt a skeptical one. We can measure the consequences in their habits of interpretation, and above all in the views they do *not* share of the function of criticism. On general questions of this sort Coleridge was always prepared to hold forth; Hazlitt, by reputation, never;

230

yet I believe Hazlitt was right in saying that his readers knew very well "where to have him," provided they read with tact. Before proceeding to some famous passages from both critics, I shall list four points of substantial disagreement; these make nothing more than convenient rubrics for a great many particular judgments, but they help to organize a daunting subject. The best beginning may be to think of Coleridge as the Affirmative Man and Hazlitt as the Negative—happy, when he can find some reason, to discredit even the working assumptions that he has received as critical truths.

(1) *To Coleridge, poetry's greatness is that it frees us from belief and practice by showing us a thing completely organized, beautiful in conformity to its own law, and therefore free of any rhetorical motive. To Hazlitt, its greatness is that it makes new channels for belief and practice, or immeasurably deepens the existing ones.* Although, for the reasons I sketched in chapter 1, he connects the imagination with Locke's will-in-suspense, nothing can be found in Hazlitt comparable to the idea of a willing suspension of disbelief. He would say our disbelief goes to make part of our belief, and beliefs are only the aggregate of powers that we bring to the reading or writing of a poem. We need no more suspend them to get the whole experience of a poem than we need disown our previous convictions when from the opposing bench we admire the force with which an orator like Burke makes his argument. Coleridge wants to enforce an absolute distinction between the work of persuasion and the play of art; whereas Hazlitt reads any such distinction as a denial that art can really change us.

The issue between them might be reduced to a central tenet of Kant's *Critique of Judgment,* that "The [separate] arts of speech are *rhetoric* and *poetry. Rhetoric* is the art of carrying on a serious business of the understanding as if it were a free play of the imagination; *poetry,* the art of conducting a free play of the imagination as if it were a serious business of the understanding."[2] To this Coleridge emphatically assents. Hazlitt wonders how it can be shown to be other than a pretty compliment to art, the result more of our wish for stability than of any felt difference between the way an impassioned listener responds to a speech or sermon and the way an impassioned reader responds to a poem. To take one vivid example: in praising *Coriolanus* Hazlitt pictures Shakespeare himself as simultaneously orator and poet, one who "seems to have had a leaning to the arbitrary side of the question, perhaps from some feeling of contempt for his own origin; and to have spared no occasion of baiting the rabble. What he says of them is very true: what he says of their betters is also very true, though he dwells less upon it." Hazlitt admires the play while preserving his disbelief and applauds Shakespeare for a performance he partly deplores. No such passage will be found in the whole range of Coleridge's criticism.

(2) *Coleridge is the first important critic in English to divest the common reader of authority and entrust the survival of great works to a specially trained clerisy.* Hazlitt, on the other hand, inherits the Johnsonian feeling about the common reader's taste and judgments, as the only measure of "duration" in literature. Coleridge's defection to the university-man's view was accomplished by stages, but in tracing his development one need not ignore the unforeseen effects of his own style. About these he spoke defensively almost from the first number of *The Friend,* though never without some consciousness of the justice of the complaint. Modern accounts of his prose—with its fatal disregard for the self-respecting or non-discipular majority of his potential audience—show a misplaced delicacy, as if so clear a fact were an affront to so great a man. But style is at any rate part of the story. Coleridge was a disaster with the new reading public; and though neither party is wholly to blame, the outcome might have been predicted from his own mixed qualities: a style idiosyncratically inventive, but given to bouts of petulance long drawn-out; a cherished wealth of scruples which made even Crabb Robinson fidget in his seat, displayed chiefly in elaborate prefatory disclaimers; genuine eloquence, that had attained its height early—in the *Consciones ad Populum* of 1795—but ended by submitting the reader for whole eras to its own counterfeit, in caressing swells of fustian.

To encounter his intelligence in prose was, to borrow Hazlitt's phrase, like booking voyage on a ship becalmed, "tedious, improgressive, and sickening." Yet Hazlitt may be challenged as a suspect witness since he too is on trial. Peacock, however, is impartial enough—the admirer of Malthus and friend of Shelley—and from Peacock's *Melincourt* one gets a fuller sense of the difficulty, in the portrait of Mr. Mystic.

> Tea and coffee were brought in. "I divide my day," said Mr. Mystic, *"on a new principle:* I am always poetical at breakfast, moral at luncheon, metaphysical at dinner, and political at tea. Now you shall know my opinion of the hopes of the world.—General discontent shall be the basis of public resignation! The materials of political gloom will build the steadfast frame of hope. The main point is to get rid of analytical reason, which is experi-

mental and practical, and live only by faith, which is synthetical and oracular. The contradictory interests of ten millions may neutralize each other. But the spirit of Antichrist is abroad:—the people read!—nay, they think!! The people read and think!!! The public, the public in general, the swinish multitude, the many-headed monster, actually reads and thinks!!!! Horrible in thought, but in fact most horrible! Science classifies flowers. Can it make them bloom where it has placed them in its classification? No. Therefore flowers ought not to be classified. This is transcendental logic. Ha! in that cylindrical mirror I see three shadowy forms:—dimly I see them through the smoked glass of my spectacles. Who art thou?— MYSTERY!—I hail thee! Who art thou?—JARGON!—I love thee! Who art thou?—SUPERSTITION! I worship thee! Hail, transcendental TRIAD!"[3]

The contempt that Coleridge felt *in advance*, even for his potential audience, can be heard in a sentence of *The Statesman's Manual* which Peacock seems to have been remembering: "From a popular philosophy and a philosophic populace, Good Sense deliver us!"— with the unhappy concession quickly attached, "Here, as in so many other cases, the inconveniences that have arisen from a thing's having become too general [large numbers now being literate], are best removed by making it universal."[4] This cannot be explained away as a decent wariness about those who read Gothic novels, take literature as a crude and violent stimulant, and crave in books the immediate effect of pornography or military music. Coleridge was disturbed by the prospect that such readers would multiply faster than their betters, but he is looking beyond them and, even were they to vanish, would reserve for literature the privilege of making no inroads on the mind of the amateur. Writing is for those who know how to welcome it, that is, as a kind of knowledge good in itself, which leads to nothing beyond itself. Coleridge's strictures here make an instance of what Nietzsche called the protective instinct of the ascetic ideal. It was in protest against this effort to dignify the literary idea as complete *and therefore without effect*, that Keats spoke out in a letter, "O for a Life of Sensations rather than of Thoughts," and talked hopefully of *Lamia* as a poem with "that sort of fire in it which must take hold of people in some way—give them either pleasant or unpleasant sensation."[5]

(3) *Coleridge views the mind of the poet, or the text of a poem, as the staging ground for a reconciliation of opposites. Hazlitt sees no reason why opposites should be reconciled, and never leads us to*

expect this as a formal property of great works. Indeed Coleridge's "reconcilement" has to work far beyond the context he builds for it in "On Poesy or Art," which already includes the poet's fusion of genius with judgment, the internal with the external, unconscious with conscious activity. The idea of transcending mere contraries was for him an answer to the riddles of conduct as much as a way of doing justice to the complexity of art. Coleridge, who in 1796 wrote the "Ode to the Departing Year" with its treasonous *vade retro* to England, and followed it hardly two years later in "France: An Ode" by announcing his disaffection with all politics; but then made up a good nick-name for Napoleon, "the Corsican Upstart," and took pride ever after in having roused the public to war: this Coleridge may decently have wished for a reconciliation of all the vagrant impulses that lead into or away from the text and link it with a world of actions. Hazlitt, in a less extravagant career, was securer in his purposes and did not wish for any tranquil retirement, or for a silencing victory. If the eloquence of a given work is completely on one side, he makes that nothing against it, but supposes the other side will find another voice.

Even where he might point to a reconciliation, Hazlitt is apt to record only a stalemate: in *Measure for Measure,* for example, where "the affections are at a stand; our sympathies are repulsed and defeated in all directions." But that play is a strange arena of contesting sympathies—all with a real claim on us, all equally incorrigible— and Coleridge takes no more satisfaction than Hazlitt in the outcome. A better test of reconciliation, and of its practical worth for each critic, is in the treatment of works they both admire. Hazlitt could admire power even in the service of a single dominant sympathy. Coleridge, before he can award praise, must have decided that the contending sympathies of action are replaced by a higher unity in contemplation. Thus, to return to *Coriolanus,* Hazlitt wrote of Shakespeare's gravity on "the arbitrary side of the question"—by which he meant the legitimist or aristocratic side—but Coleridge believes that Shakespeare can only have written honorably if he ended on no side: so he speaks of Shakespeare's "wonderful philosophic impartiality" in the play, and even singles out his "good-humored laugh at mobs." Raysor conjectures that this is a theft from Schlegel,[6] but stolen or not it is very wrong: it was something fiercer than laughter, and there was nothing good-natured about it. Yet to praise a work *for these reasons* seemed to Coleridge a necessary condition of establishing its greatness. Again, we have their verdicts on

Timon of Athens, starting from the same perception but leading to opposite conclusions. This play, according to J. P. Collier's lecture-notes, was "on the whole, a painful and disagreeable production" to Coleridge, "because it gave only a disadvantageous picture of human nature, very inconsistent with what, he firmly believed, was our great poet's real view of the characters of his fellow-creatures."[7] Where Shakespeare can by no means be thought impartial, Coleridge simply finds him insincere, and demotes the play on that ground since on any other it is great but repellent. No reconciliation is imaginable with so pure a strain of misanthropy: therefore *Timon* cannot be great.

By this route Coleridge's moralism sometimes ends in forging again the old connection betwen value and subject-matter. Hazlitt is less primly magisterial:

> *Timon of Athens* always appeared to us to be written with as intense a feeling of his subject as any one play of Shakespeare. It is one of the few in which he seems to be in earnest throughout, never to trifle nor go out of his way. He does not relax in his efforts, nor lose sight of the unity of his design. It is the only play of our author in which spleen is the predominant feeling of the mind. (IV, 210)

Why, asks Hazlitt, should he not be splenetic *and* "in earnest"? In *Timon,* Shakespeare treats mankind to the same good-humored laugh he directed against the mob in *Coriolanus,* and his greatness is to be found in the energy with which he sustains the effect.

(4) *Coleridge's thinking about literature revolves around an idea of the symbol.* (Versions of the idea have been attributed to Hazlitt, but never with much conviction.) A celebrated passage from *The Statesman's Manual* makes the distinction between symbol and allegory:

> Now an Allegory is but a translation of abstract notions into a picture-language which is itself nothing but an abstraction from objects of the senses; the principal being more worthless even than its phantom proxy, both alike unsubstantial, and the former shapeless to boot. On the other hand a Symbol . . . is characterized by a translucence of the Special in the individual or of the General in the Especial or of the Universal in the General. Above all by the translucence of the Eternal through and in the Temporal. It always partakes of the Reality which it renders intelligible; and while it enunciates the whole, abides as a living part of that Unity, of which it is the representative.[8]

Here the symbol is a particular through which we read the whole of reality, but which must fully represent the whole, not because we can see it so but because that is its nature. It is timeless and placeless, in the use we eventually make of it: a careful reader of Coleridge will speak not of symbolic action—which must always be connected with a time and place—but of symbolic contemplation. A poem therefore that is properly symbolic cannot be a scene of persuasion: what it reads out from itself it reads back in; it gives the quickest of tautologies, telling us what we knew before, but with a command of implication that enlarges our sense of what knowledge is. Coleridge seems to have conceived of the symbol as an expansion of the trope of synecdoche (a part standing for the whole).[9] A metaphor for Coleridge is *made,* and calls attention to its making; when we admire it, we have been persuaded of something new about the world; a synecdoche, in contrast, has the air of being *recovered.* If metaphor suggests the possibility of change in language, synecdoche suggests the sense of something "fitting and fitted" between mind and nature. Coleridge tells us it is to be preferred to metaphor, which he calls "a fragment of an allegory"; and if indeed an allegory is an extended narrative metaphor, one can see why he would have thought it an unworthy rival of the symbol. In allegory, poetry cannot be distinct from persuasion—for allegory to succeed means to convert the reader to its own terms, which he began by regarding as strange. With symbolism on the contrary the reader is shown that they were his terms all along.

Erich Auerbach wrote of this kind of symbolic relation: "to act upon the symbol is conceived as tantamount to acting on the thing symbolized." Yet Coleridge's symbol grants a knowledge (acting upon the symbol) so complete that it can never foster action (acting upon the thing symbolized). In this way it preserves intact the poetry-rhetoric opposition: the play of the imagination is unsullied by the business of the understanding. One need not believe in the contrast between symbol and allegory to see how much it meant to Coleridge, and what hopes for the autonomy of literature he reposed in it. On the other hand, one may applaud every recent effort to dispose of the symbol by illustrating its tendency to relapse into allegory: but it must be added that in practice Hazlitt calls our attention to this all the time.[10] It is true that his skepticism allowed him to proceed with a clearer conscience than Coleridge's faith, and that makes him a rather unspectacular entry in the contest of existential heroism which criticism is now and then supposed to afford. When Coleridge gives us an interpreter's allegory, it is in violation of his avowed critical stance; when Hazlitt does so, it is in keeping; for to read allegorically is to insist that poems are made from a particular situation, and to be used in others. Here another dictum from Kant's *Critique of Judgment* may be pertinent—the phrase in which the subjective activity of the poet is credited with a "purposiveness without purpose." Coleridge felt the attractiveness of this formula, as a promise of unconditioned knowledge, and of an impersonal power. Hazlitt would have liked the implication that artists do occasionally convince us that they are above the battle: when they do, it seems right to place their work beside certain achievements of the mind in actual life, about which we are driven to use words like truth and justice. But he could have made no sense of the words "without purpose" as applied to any human act: you *may* interpret poetry like that, he admits, for no pastime ought to be forbidden that is harmless to others; but in doing so you are making the poetry—and by gradual immersion, yourself—as uninteresting as possible.

AESTHETIC JUDGMENT

A large part of Hazlitt's protest against Coleridge in all four categories may be traced to a special and ambivalent version of idealism which Coleridge was building up almost from the start of his adult life. Berkeley had made the world we read in our ideas not a partial representation of the physical world but the only world we have or need. To a mind like Coleridge's, the appeal was that this left us fully in possession of our experience, no longer cut off from an aspect of it by the division between the primary qualities of objects themselves and the secondary qualities which our senses add to them. Another admirer of Berkeley's idealism, Yeats, in some journal-entries on romanticism and eighteenth-century metaphysics, noticed a sound poetic motive for appropriating an argument many have been prepared to dismiss as ingenious. Berkeley thought "that by showing that certain abstractions—the 'primary qualities'—did not exist he could create a philosophy so concrete that the common people could understand it"; and his achievement according to Yeats, after "Descartes, Locke, and Newton took away the world and gave us its excrement instead," was that he "brought back to us the world that only exists because it shines and sounds."[11] This I think was the reason for Coleridge's gratitude, as he himself makes plain in a metaphor similar to Yeats's near the end of "On Poesy or Art," where a world in which the body has grown separate from the mind is described as "almost of an excremental nature." When the mind itself contains the whole of a world that only exists because it shines and sounds, one can claim without vanity that for the first time one is seeing the object clearly, because for the first time one has a meta-physical theory which makes that possible. Nothing remains outside the mind as waste, potential for experience but never to be used, ex-crement-out-there which one sets against nourishment-in-here. In af-fording this satisfaction Berkeley and Kant do seem heroes of the same story. Coleridge was glad to find them so, and the revisions of-fered by Kant's successors in the next generation confirmed his sense that idealism was restoring man to unity with himself.

The most neatly illustrative example of such revisions is Schel-ling's common-sense proof that idealism affords us a surer reality than realism. Idealism, Schelling observed, identifies the phenome-nal world we know with all there is, whereas realism has to posit a separate world of constants, beyond our experience and rendering all we know illusory. Even the law of parsimony can thus be seen as favoring an idealist solution. Yet Coleridge, in advancing his own ar-guments, was almost unique in the emotional demands for which he held a philosophy answerable: unlike Schelling or Fichte, he wanted to insure the reality, stability, permanence, freedom from change and freedom from interest, of the very object he had disclaimed by removing it from consideration. The intensity of his demand emerges with peculiar vividness in two more passages of "On Poesy or Art." He speaks of poetry "impregnating" objects with an interest not their own, and so grants a distinct role, in the drama of creation, to the existence outside the mind of all its potential objects, which it may in a manner survey before it decides to confer on them a new interest. Alluding to this moment, when the mind holds the object at a distance, he speaks of the artist's need to "eloign himself from nature in order to return to her with full effect." Now for Hazlitt there is no such moment. The artist stands in a continuous construc-tive relation to the object he selects for portrayal: the ideal object all along is natural for him, and it becomes so for his audience; but it has no existence that can be referred to intelligibly apart from what he makes of it. One might have expected a similar result from Cole-ridge's idealism, but his view of creation evidently requires an eloign-ment—a separation between the artist and his object—followed later by a reconciliation. For the drama to work itself out, the object must have had *significant* being outside the creator's mind.

Coleridge's quest is for something that combines the properties of the imaginative object and the natural model: created yet secure, devoid of interest, and unitary in its coherence as in its self-containment. And this he finds in the poem-in-itself. It grows like a tree; each specimen that comes to fullness must be perfect of its kind; the beauty that it presents is without impulse, accident, or inclination. It has no aim but to be known, it was not made, and we violate its being when we make it do anything for us. Though Coleridge delights in tracing an author's footsteps through a poem, such investigations are against his principles. The organic metaphor was devised in the first instance to show that art can be vitally self-legislating only when it carries no stamp of human agency.

That metaphor, with the comfort and new questions that it brings, held comparatively little interest for Hazlitt, and the reason can be explained as a difference of disposition. One may call it (if one prefers him) a stronger or (if one prefers Coleridge) a plainer disposition. It could exalt sublime energies without wondering if they had been properly sublimated, and without linking the fate of art-objects with the task of sublimation. Yet the assertion of some such link has a claim to be called *the* idealist solution to the status of art; so that it may be asked how tenuous a loyalty Hazlitt owed to the movement of thought that extended from Kant and far beyond Coleridge. The question becomes especially interesting in the light of his early appeal to the Kantian motto, "the mind alone is formative." By this, as I have argued, he intended only a summary recognition of some organizing faculty for associations, in every kind of human activity, making, doing, and knowing. Having anticipated, he would have graciously endorsed, Max Müller's one-sentence version of Kant's first critique—"That without which experience is impossible, cannot be the result of experience."[12] This would have been enough in Hazlitt's view to reveal the conception of the mind for which Kant was superior to Hume; and he would remain superior so long as the consequences of the discovery were kept as modest and negative as possible, the way one finds them in William James's illustration: "Take a sentence of a dozen words, and take twelve men and tell to each one word. Then stand the men in a row or jam them in a bunch, and let each think of his word as intently as he will; nowhere will there be a consciousness of the whole sentence."[13] It is

the negative features of Kant's argument, those demonstrating the
limits of Hume's skepticism, that most appeal to Hazlitt. As for its
positive and system-building propensities, all that leads Kant to conceive of, refine upon, and leave hanging a "supersensible substrate"
for the judgment to get a purchase on if it can: for this Hazlitt finds
no use. "I never could make much of the subject of real relations in
nature." The remark, since it is all we have from him on the subject, has to serve as his final confession that he was baffled by any
further conjecture. It puts to an end all talk about the object, and
most talk about the subject. Instead, it is supposed that a seeing self
is what we begin with, and that its demands affect the way we encounter anything in life. But the world of action in which we operate remains the world Hume described; we are not obliged to shrink
it or to lop off several limbs of our vocabulary in recognition of
what we now know of the *apparent* otherness of what we see: we
will speak in whatever terms we find helpful.

So Hazlitt found in Kant a way out of what he would have
called metaphysics. This was the opposite of what Coleridge found,
and perhaps only available to a reader who had not investigated
Kant thoroughly. But it was for this reason that Willich's *Elements
of the Critical Philosophy* could seem liberating to an empiricist who
had no interest in radical skepticism. To escape radical skepticism
by pursuing idealism itself as a constructive philosophy struck Hazlitt as reading the Kantian moral backwards, even if Kant himself
went in for it; and his first and decisive step as a thinker was to deny
the separation between making, doing, and knowing as essentially
different sorts of activity which presume different relations between
the mind and what it confronts: the separation Kant had honored
by his presentation of the critical philosophy in three critiques.

With one passage from the *Critique of Judgment* Hazlitt would
have counted himself in perfect accord, though a knowledge of eighteenth-century English criticism would have made the argument less
boldly original in his eyes than it seemed to Kant's followers.

> What shows the principle of the *ideality* of the purposiveness in
> the beauty of nature, as that which we always place at the basis of
> an aesthetical judgment, and which allows us to employ, as a
> ground of explanation for our representative faculty, no realism of
> purpose, is the fact that, in judging beauty, we invariably seek its
> gauge in ourselves *a priori* and that our aesthetical judgment is
> itself legislative in respect of the judgment whether anything is
> beautiful or not. This could not be, on the assumption of the

realism of the purposiveness of nature, because in that case we must have learned from nature what we ought to find beautiful, and the aesthetical judgment would be subjected to empirical principles. For in such an act of judging the important point is not what nature is, or even, as a purpose, is in relation to us, but how we take it.[14]

The key phrases for Hazlitt would have been, "our [general] aesthetical judgment is itself legislative in respect of the [particular] judgment whether anything is beautiful or not," and "the important point is not what nature is . . . but how we take it." The passage as a whole says that we can produce convincing evidence of how little the object itself supplies us with any hints toward its correct interpretation, by recalling that in order to judge it we had to consult our previous idea of beauty-in-objects. And so on each occasion of judgment: we could not feel as we do, that we are applying standards which we ourselves know very well, if before judging we had to receive our standard anew from the object in question. "How we take it," the whole tone of our judgment as interpreters, determines "what nature is" for us, the perceptions we call to mind in assigning reasons for our judgment. But so far as Hazlitt concurs with this description of judgment, he reads Kant just as if he were Alison: *a priori* means "in keeping with memory and habit," and nothing more. That we should judge *a priori* in a graver sense, obedient to our idea of an object in which nature and reason coincide, and moved by none of the usual gusts of desire or inclination: this would have struck him as humanly absurd.

One can also imagine Hazlitt agreeing with Kant's definition of genius as "the innate mental disposition (*ingenium*) through which nature gives the rule to art"—a deduction from his general remark that "Nature is beautiful because it looks like art, and art can only be called beautiful if we are conscious of it as art while yet it looks like nature."[15] But again Hazlitt would have found no need to connect this with the mind's employment of *a priori* categories. After all, the definition was in one of its meanings as old as Longinus, who wrote: "art is perfect when it seems to be nature, and nature hits the mark when she contains art hidden within her."[16] Longinus presents his aphorism within a discussion of *hyperbata,* the sort of rhetorical inversions which may shock and convert the listener by placing the figurative conclusion of an argument first, and treating it literally; as when an orator says "Our fortunes lie on a razor's edge, men of Ionia" *before* giving the reasons that should lead to so bold an assertion. In cases like this a rhetorical figure, which ordinarily makes us conscious of artifice, seems to open up at one blast a reservoir of feeling which every member of a verbal community shares, but which all repress by common consent except at crisis-moments when it takes a figure of speech to reveal it. The uncanniness of the revelation—the sense we have that we are learning something we already knew, but have kept hidden—accounts for our reading of art *when perfect* as a nature that was there all along. In turn, as we reflect on such experiences, we may feel that here nature contained art "hidden within her": to account for the propriety, and what seems more than propriety—the realized and inevitable relation—between "the razor's edge" and the whole chain of causes and circumstances linked to it on this occasion, we say that both the trope and the scheme that placed it at the head of the argument are somehow sublimely natural.

As a theorist of the sublime Hazlitt will be found closest to Kant where Kant himself is most Longinian, in those sections of the *Critique of Judgment* where full justice is done to sublimity as "the echo of a great soul," or as a power by which we feel enthralled when "our soul is uplifted, . . . takes a proud flight, and is filled with joy and vaunting, as though it had itself produced what it has heard."[17] Kant's primary formula, *"the sublime is that, the mere ability to think which shows a faculty of the mind surpassing every standard of sense,"* is uncompromising enough to satisfy Hazlitt, along with its corollary, that "the sublime in nature is improperly so called" because "properly speaking, the word should only be applied to a state of mind."[18] On this view it makes no sense to speak of objects of the mind as themselves sublime. The consciousness we achieve of our own powers, in contemplating something that frustrates all our equipment of sensory cognition, and in finding we can still imagine our relation to it though that relation is beyond all measure, alone deserves to be called sublime.

Coleridge gravitates toward a later and teleological stage of Kant's argument, where the faculty of imagination, which Kant has acknowledged as sublime, is said to be in touch with something as good as real: the supersensible substrate of humanity. Kant offers this return to the object as the single conceivable solution of what he calls "the antinomy of taste." The antinomy arises in the following way. We can only argue, Kant observes, about concepts; but concepts pertain to the understanding rather than the imagination; so it appears we can only argue about works of art if they can be construed as a kind of quasi-concept. Kant's supersensible substrate of humanity is a concept presented directly to the judgment, which has the subjective purposiveness-without-purpose that distinguishes works of art from objects of our interested understanding.[19] This stage, unexpected in Kant's treatment of the aesthetic, and to a mind as pragmatic as Hazlitt's a revolting piece of sophistry, forms the point of departure for Coleridge's later criticism. For he agrees that our conversations about art have no coherence—because we cannot be sure we are all talking about the same thing—until we refer to a single concept.

The conclusion is plausibly deduced from Kant's premise that concepts alone make our experience available to us by the work of synthesis. But that premise itself exhibits what Richard Rorty has called "the paradoxical but unquestioned assumption which runs through the first *Critique*—the assumption that manifoldness is 'given' and unity is made."[20] Some such assumption also runs through Coleridge's many statements about the imagination's blending of the general and the particular, with his assurance that the mind can determine by rules, *independent of context,* what sort of thing is general and what particular. Hazlitt replies with a strong protest against any idea of the "given," when he finds the division of phenomena into depth and surface utterly context-dependent.

> What is *depth,* and what is *superficiality?* It is easy to answer that the one is what is obvious, familiar, and lies on the surface, and that the other is recondite and hid at the bottom of a subject. The difficulty recurs—What is meant by lying on the surface, or being concealed below it, in moral and metaphysical questions? Let us try for an analogy. *Depth* consists then in tracing any number of particular effects to a general principle, or in distinguishing an unknown cause from the individual and varying circumstances with which it is implicated, and under which it lurks unsuspected. It is in fact resolving the concrete into the abstract. Now this is a task of difficulty, not only because the abstract naturally merges in the concrete, and we do not well know how to set about separating what is thus jumbled or cemented together in a single object, and presented under a common aspect; but being scattered over a larger surface, and collected from a number of undefined sources, there must be a strong feeling of its weight and pressure, in order to dislocate it from the object and bind it into a principle. The impression of an abstract principle is faint and doubtful in each individual instance; it becomes powerful and certain only by the repetition of the experiment, and by adding the last results to our

first hazardous conjectures. We thus gain a distinct hold or clue to
the demonstration, when a number of vague and imperfect reminiscences are united and drawn out together, by tenaciousness of
memory and conscious feeling, in one continued act. So that the
depth of the understanding or reasoning in such cases may be explained to mean, that there is a pile of *implicit* distinctions analyzed from a great variety of facts and observations, each supporting the other, and that the mind, instead of being led away by the
last or first object or detached view of the subject that occurs, connects all these into a whole from the top to the bottom, and by its
intimate sympathy with the most obscure and random impressions
that tend to the same result, evolves a principle of abstract truth.

(XII, 355-56)

Hazlitt's concern with memory, feeling, and the "one continued act"
of interpretation, reminds the idealist system maker that his naming
of depth and surface is governed by his purpose in each case. This
need not prevent him from so naming them, and evolving an abstract principle for cases of a certain type. But art does not present
cases all of one type; we can never "well know how to set about separating what is thus jumbled or cemented together"; we do make the
necessary distinctions, with swiftness and tact as the occasion arises,
but we are impelled by "a strong feeling" of the "weight and pressure" urging us to the interpretation, and not by a concept drawn
from a supersensible substrate.

The concept, which insures consensus in matters of judgment as
in those of understanding, makes it possible for Coleridge to argue
consistently, whenever he writes about taste, as if any disagreement
with him proceeded from the inferior education or capacities of his
opponent. This is a fact about Coleridge which his readers have to
live with—however patronizing, it is an acceptable tone given his
view. But Hazlitt takes it for granted that intelligent dissent is possible in criticism as in politics, that his own judgments come from
the weight and pressure of his feelings, and that in the great majority of them he occupies some common ground with his readers,
judging merely by the circumstance that they continue to read him.
His bluntest confession of bias happens also to be a confession of his
debt to Coleridge, but everything about this passage conspires to tell
us where the debt stopped: Hazlitt expected his audience to start
with their own bias and end without having made it the same as his.
He opens his discussion of "the living poets" with an apology for
speaking at all about the present.

It was not my wish to go into this ungrateful part of the subject; but something of the sort is expected from me, and I must run the gauntlet as well as I can. Another circumstance that adds to the difficulty of doing justice to all parties is, that I happen to have had a personal acquaintance with some of these jealous votaries of the Muses; and that is not the likeliest way to imbibe a high opinion of the rest. Poets do not praise one another in the language of hyperbole. I am afraid, therefore, that I labour under a degree of prejudice against some of the most popular poets of the day, from an early habit of deference to the critical opinion of some of the least popular. I cannot say that I ever learnt much about Shakespeare, or Milton, Spenser or Chaucer, from these professed guides; for I never heard them say much about them. They were always talking of themselves and one another. Nor am I certain that this sort of personal intercourse with living authors, while it takes away all real relish or freedom of opinion with regard to their contemporaries, greatly enhances our respect for themselves. Poets are not ideal beings.   (V, 146)

With the aid of Kant's concept, the *poem* does become an ideal being for Coleridge. And the poet easily inherits much of its prestige. Hazlitt saw this as a danger of Coleridge's method, and avoided it by steering clear of method entirely. This was a choice as deliberate as the choices thinkers are always making.

MILL'S ESSAY ON COLERIDGE

In my first chapter I cited Coleridge's revulsion from the complete divorce of duty from sentiment in Kantian morality. But this, it must now be added, was uncharacteristic. In general Coleridge was ready to endorse Kant's deductions from the premise that man is "the only being which has the purpose of its existence in itself."[21] Man-as-subject created the aspects under which things could be known, and therefore the only aspects under which they could *be;* there was just one given, or uncreated, fact about his world: his own nature as a being defined by reason. What Coleridge took from Schelling as well as Kant was all that seemed to offer a steady certainty for each pole of the subject-object dialectic, and to gain this he was even intermittently willing to pay the price of Kant's "inhuman" sentiment-free morality. He was able to explore the dialectic while appearing to do justice to the subject's creativity, *and* to the aesthetic mood of certainty which demands a concept moored to a

supersensible substrate, *and* to the "it is" which gives brute resistance to every assertion of the "I am,"[22] because the hope of simultaneously fulfilling all three claims was in the nature of the game:
Coleridge was only its most eclectic, resourceful, and genuinely anxious player. Rorty makes this point nicely: "The result of running
together spirit as romantic self-transcending creativity (always liable
to begin talking in a way incommensurable with our present language) with spirit as identical with man's Glassy Esssence (with all
its metaphysical freedom from physical explanation), and with spirit
as the 'constitutor' of phenomenal reality, was the metaphysics of
nineteenth-century German idealism."[23]

The knotting together of this bundle of assurances licensed Coleridge's intolerance as a critic—an intolerance to which the Humean
vocabulary of sentiments would have offered resistance. Only his
claim to speak on behalf of a knowable power of creation, ideal of
reason, and reality of things, all unified by the word *spirit,* could
make the rewards seem high enough to outweigh the sacrifice, in
gaining credence for a taste that excluded whole periods of literary
production. No matter how much one values the result for practical
criticism, it is wrong to ally Coleridge's version of idealism with a
Burkean respect for tradition. Burke in this was of Hume's party, in
every reach of his speculations. Yet an impulse still exists to read
Coleridge as the legitimate heir of Burke—particularly among con-
servatives who want to trace a full lineage for themselves throughout the nineteenth century—and it draws powerful support from
John Stuart Mill's essay on Coleridge.

The essay owes much of its authority to our sense of Mill himself as a member of the opposite party giving Coleridge his due. In
this light of course his estimate is wonderfully generous. But Mill's
language shows that he was reading Coleridge as a simple successor
to Burke, and in its least ambivalent moments the essay might well
have been called "Burke."

> By Bentham, beyond all others, men have been led to ask them-
> selves, in regard to any ancient or received opinion, Is it true? and
> by Coleridge, What is the meaning of it? The one took his stand
> outside the received opinion, and surveyed it as an entire stranger
> to it: the other looked at it from within, and endeavoured to see it
> with the eyes of a believer in it; to discover by what apparent facts
> it was at first suggested, and by what appearances it has ever since
> been rendered continually credible. . . . Bentham judged a propo-
> sition true or false as it accorded or not with the result of his own

inquiries; and did not search very curiously into what might be meant by the proposition, when it obviously did not mean what he thought true. With Coleridge, on the contrary, the very fact that any doctrine had been believed by thoughtful men, and received by whole nations or generations of mankind, was part of the problem to be solved, was one of the phenomena to be accounted for. . . . He considered the long or extensive prevalence of any opinion as a presumption that it was not altogether a fallacy; that, to its first authors at least, it was the result of a struggle to express in words something which had a reality to them, though perhaps not to many of those who have since received the doctrine by mere tradition. The long duration of a belief, he thought, is at least proof of an adaptation in it to some portion or other of the human mind; and if, on digging down to the root, we do not find, as is generally the case, some truth, we shall find some natural want or requirement of human nature which the doctrine in question is fitted to satisfy: among which wants the instincts of selfishness and of credulity have a place, but by no means an exclusive one.[24]

Now all this would be truer of Burke on Bolingbroke, and indeed of Hazlitt on Godwin, than of Coleridge in any engagement of his long career. Even the passages that Mill quotes care less about the naturalization of beliefs through long duration, than about their special fitness as the reflection of some antecedent order or groundwork of all possible beliefs. To explain why the clerisy once acknowledged theology as its master-science, Coleridge says (and Mill cites him approvingly), "to divinity belong those fundamental truths which are the common groundwork of our civil and our religious duties, not less indispensable to a right view of our temporal concerns than to a rational faith respecting our immortal well-being."[25] Again, but much more provocatively, Mill quotes him on the Idea of the Constitution:

Our whole history . . . demonstrates the continued influence of such an idea, or ultimate aim, in the minds of our forefathers, in their characters and functions as public men, alike in what they resisted and what they claimed; in the institutions and forms of polity which they established, and with regard to those against which they more or less successfully contended; and because the result has been a progressive, though not always a direct or equable, advance in the gradual realization of the idea; and because it is actually, though (even because it is an idea) not adequately, represented in a correspondent scheme of means really existing—we speak, and have a right to speak, of the idea itself as actually exist-

ing; that is, as a principle existing; that is, as a principle existing
in the only way in which a principle can exist—in the minds and
consciences of the persons whose duties it prescribes, and whose
rights it determines. [This fundamental idea] is at the same time
the final criterion by which all particular frames of government
must be tried: for here only can we find the great constructive
principles of our representative system—those principles in the
light of which it can alone be ascertained what are excrescences,
symptoms of distemperature, and marks of degeneration, and what
are native growths, or changes naturally attendant on the progressive development of the original germ.[26]

Only the single reference to "the means really existing" is Burkean—
the rest reads like a parody of Burke's prudential defense of the English constitution. For Coleridge's idea *pre*exists any actual parties
by whom it might have been embodied—just the sort of metaphysical
sleight of hand that prompted Burke to write, "Nothing can be
colder than the heart of a pure-bred metaphysician."

It was probably the organic metaphor that misled Mill. When we
judge the right future course for a natural growth by its previous
roots and branchings, we are judging as Burke would have wished.
When, however, we deduce its past, present, and future by our complete knowledge of its essence, we are making the revision of Burke
that Coleridge proposes. Burke has in mind the observable shape of
the organism, and how by seeing we can deduce its nature; while
Coleridge presumes a knowledge of its genetic code, such as would
allow us to judge any moment of its growth as a fulfillment of or deviation from its given kind. The two metaphors are similar only in
that both have something to do with the maturing of a plant.

Gravitating in his early years to Unitarianism and philosophic
radicalism, because they seemed to afford some standard of thought
above mere habit and sentiment, Coleridge arrived at German idealism in the end for much the same reasons. His thinking in either
phase was hardly as Mill describes it. But Mill's tactical motive for
naming the subject of his tribute "Coleridge" is plain when one
considers the date of publication (1840). Partly freed from disciple-
ship to his father, yet still relying on the *Westminster Review* circle
as his main audience, he needed some figure at once special and elusive, to use as a plank on which to cross over from Benthamite utilitarianism to the more complex position he would associate elsewhere
with the teachings of Wordsworth. This was an order Burke could
never fill; to bring up his name would be to risk the appearance of

making too exclusively political a point; and it would alienate many persons in advance. But Coleridge was a figure sufficiently identified with Burke's politics, and otherwise sufficiently obscure to serve Mill's purpose. What Mill did not realize was how thoroughly Coleridge had adapted Burke's rhetoric to different ends. Later in the essay he regrets the German influence on Coleridge—as with the same resigned fellow-feeling, Pater would regret the impress of "a somewhat inferior theological literature"—but he made a mistake in thinking the Burkean sound of Coleridge's politics somehow separable from their practical inflexibility, and from the tendency of all idealist metaphysics to abstract speculation on the thing-in-itself from any interest in the history of things, including the history of thinking and feeling *about* them.

The chief point that I take Mill to have overlooked, when he said one could retain the feeling conservative in Coleridge without the metaphysician of reaction, is that Coleridge belonged finally to the movement of abstract right inaugurated by Rousseau, the movement through which the mind came to be regarded as a self-legislating source of cognitions, judgments, and duties. So in Coleridge's faith that unity and plurality at last yield "omneity," one may detect a queer echo of Rousseau's affirmation that the law of society resides in the general will as distinct from the mere majority or totality. Reduced to its essentials, the premise Coleridge shared with Kant was that the nature of morality follows from something universal, non-empirical, and non-historical.[27] For Burke on the contrary as for Hazlitt, the nature of morality is determined above all by what we have received from other or earlier minds. To imagine a Burkean response to Kant's procedure in philosophy is to imagine something like this, from Hazlitt's review of the *Biographia Literaria*:

> If the French theories of the mind were too chemical, this is too mechanical:—if the one referred every thing to nervous sensibility, the other refers every thing to the test of muscular resistance, and voluntary prowess. It is an enormous heap of dogmatical and hardened assertions, advanced in contradiction to all former systems, and all unsystematical opinions and impressions. [Kant] has but one method of getting over difficulties:—when he is at a loss to account for any thing, and cannot give a reason for it, he turns short round upon the inquirer, and says that it is self-evident. . . . He defines beauty to be perfection, and virtue to consist in a conformity to our duty; with other such deliberate truisms; and then represents necessity as inconsistent with morality, and insists

on the existence and certainty of the free-will as a faculty necessary
to explain the *moral sense,* which could not exist without it. This
transcendental philosopher is also pleased to affirm, in so many
words, that we have neither any possible idea, nor any possible
proof of the existence of the Soul, God, or Immortality, by means
of the ordinary faculties of sense, understanding, or reason; and he
therefore (like a man who had been employed to construct a machine for some particular purpose), invents a new faculty, for the
admission and demonstration of these important truths, *namely,
the practical reason;* in other words, the will or determination that
these things should be infinitely true because they are infinitely
desirable to the human mind,—though he says it is impossible for
the human mind to have any idea whatever of these objects, either
as true or desirable.   (XVI, 123-24)

It was in this language that Burke spoke of "whole nests of pi-
geon-holes full of constitutions ready-made, ticketed, sorted, and
numbered, suited to every season and every fancy: some with the
top of the pattern at the bottom, and some with the bottom at the
top," all under the keeping of the Abbé Sieyès, and all contrived
to stupefy the English understanding. Had he lived long enough
he could have extended the same language to Coleridge's *a priori*
changes of heart; and Hazlitt knew he was speaking with Burke's
sanction when he remarked that Coleridge went from an abstract
radicalism to an equally abstract conservatism. Some reserve clauses
of Coleridge's prose could be pointed out as exceptions to this, as
there are exceptions to any generalization about a subtle mind. But
one feels that it is an important part of the truth about his politics,
and *not* about Wordsworth's, which through every shift moved in
some steady relation to both a personal and a national history. One
cannot imagine Coleridge at any stage of his career becoming an impassioned advocate of reform, as opposed to revolution or reaction:
the sort of imaginative work it took to construct a speech like Burke's
on Economic Reform was simply outside his emotional range, or
what may come to the same thing, beyond the scope of his belief in
the attainability of *made things purified of a maker's will.* The essence of society, like the essence of poetry, he speaks of in the language of revelation, as a sudden glimpse of ourselves in the act of
seeing the things that are. Hazlitt is his natural rival, but in a secu-
lar language, and accordingly speaks of a society or a poem as re-
forming the nature of the objects we care about. Both can be criti-

cized, Hazlitt assumes, because they are nothing essentially but what their history makes them, and we too belong to their history.

The foregoing excursion into politics will seem out of the way if one assents to the Kantian and Coleridgean split between empirical prudence and the ideal morality of practical reason. But Hazlitt in his review of the *Biographia* found this separation so peculiar that he supposed it to have been constructed as a metaphysical "machine for some particular purpose," and certainly not for human use. This makes him just the sort of ally Mill was looking for, as a set-off to Bentham: much more persistently than Coleridge, he wrote about literature as a social institution. Mill's appreciation of the "seminal mind" of the age will never lose its importance, for histories much larger than the history of criticism, but in time it may come to be read more suspiciously, and as something of an allegory. He chose the right ground for unification but cast the wrong man in the heroic role of unifier.

TWO DEFINITIONS OF POETRY

Without pretending to have passed beyond politics, I want to compare the definitions of poetry that Coleridge and Hazlitt offer in the *Biographia* and *Lectures on the English Poets*. Great care seems to have been employed in both passages: for the strongest possible contrast I give them side by side.

Coleridge:

The poet, described in ideal perfection, brings the whole soul of man into activity, with the subordination of its faculties to each other, according to their relative worth and dignity. He diffuses a tone and spirit of unity that blends and (as it were) fuses, each into each, by that synthetic and magical power to which we have exclusively appropriated the name of imagination. This power, first put into action by the will and understanding, and retained under their irremissive, though gentle and unnoticed, controul (*laxis effertur habenis*) reveals itself in the balance or reconciliation of opposite or discordant qualities; of sameness, with difference; of the general, with the concrete; the idea, with the image; the individual, with the representative; the sense of novelty and freshness, with old and familiar objects; a more than usual state of emotion, with more than usual order; judgement ever awake and steady self-possession, with enthusiasm and feeling profound or vehement; and while it blends and harmonizes the natural and the artificial, still subordinates art to nature; the manner to the matter; and our admiration of the poet to our sympathy with the poetry.[28]

Hazlitt:

Poetry . . . is an imitation of nature, but the imagination and the passions are a part of man's nature. We shape things according to our wishes and fancies, without poetry; but poetry is the most emphatical language that can be found for those creations of the mind "which ecstasy is very cunning in." Neither a mere description of natural objects, nor a mere delineation of natural feelings, however distinct or forcible, constitutes the ultimate end and aim of poetry, without the heightenings of the imagination. The light of poetry is not only a direct but also a reflected light, that while it shews us the object, throws a sparkling radiance on all around it. . . . Poetry represents forms chiefly as they suggest other forms; feelings, as they suggest forms or other feelings. Poetry puts a spirit of life and motion into the universe. It describes the flowing, not the fixed. . . . The poetical impression of any object is that uneasy, exquisite sense of beauty or power that cannot be contained within itself; that is impatient of all limit; that (as flame bends to flame) strives to link itself to some other image of kindred beauty or grandeur. . . . It is strictly the language of the imagination; and the imagination is that faculty which represents objects, not as they are in themselves, but as they are moulded by other thoughts and feelings, into an infinite variety of shapes and combinations of power.   (V, 3-4)

Coleridge says three things about the imaginative work of a poet: it begins with diverse materials ("discordant qualities"); it imparts to these an original character ("magical . . . individual . . . novelty and freshness"); and it yields what can be experienced as a unified whole ("whole soul of man . . . spirit of unity . . . blends . . . fuses . . . sameness . . . order"). He says not one word about expression, nothing for example that would enable his reader to distinguish the ideal poet from the ideal painter or the ideal husband; but this may be excused if one grants poet as a generic term for artist. The confusions of the passage, in the mixed rhetoric of Kant and Schelling, "synthesis" and "reconciliation," down to the accidental spoiling of an antithesis between "the individual with the representative," where the representative ought to have come first to accord with "general" and "idea": all these have been unravelled in detail by Mary Warnock.[29] More perplexing still is the curious transition that Coleridge seems to have undergone in his sense of what he was actually defining. It is sometimes the poem, sometimes the poet, until by the end one feels that the poem is lost in the poet, and the poet in the ideal being.

Hazlitt's definition has come in for much heavier criticism, from readers who look on themselves as guardians of precision, but in his case the complaints seem to me misdirected. William Gifford pointed out that he made poetry mean (1) the text of the poem; (2) what readers feel that the poet had in mind; and (3) *materia poetica,* anything that could inspire the poet, or what is sometimes loosely called "sheer poetry." Gifford's charge that this is so broad-minded as to be useless has been repeated more recently by M. H. Abrams, and may therefore be worth confronting. It is true that Hazlitt favored the energies that produced a poem, and those that might result from it, over the text-in-itself, and spoke of the former as what one ought first to consult if one wanted to locate its interest. But he defended his procedure by implying—so far as one could imply anything to a man like Gifford—that he had thought a good deal about poetry and believed it wisest to let the motives of readers and poets count in one's idea of the activity, so that the affective and intentional meanings of the word (poetry as what we feel and poetry as what the poet drew from) together outvote the pedantic one (poetry as the words written on the page). The latter is in no danger of losing its claim on us since it is always the occasion for the other two.

Abrams, who is the politer of Hazlitt's critics, may now be quoted.

> On the premise that poetry expresses feeling, we find certain critics using the word "poetry" in a diffusive sense, not only for the language which exhibits feeling, but also for feelings which are not expressed in words, and even for objects and events which are merely typical occasions for feeling. William Hazlitt, for one, was subject to whirling off in this way, at those times when he gave his journalistic pen free rein.[30]

To which Hazlitt replied more than a century earlier, in "A Letter to William Gifford": "It is true I have used the word poetry in the three senses above imputed to me, and I have done so, because the word has these three *distinct* meanings in the English language, that is, it signifies the composition produced, the state of mind or faculty producing it, and, in certain cases, the subject-matter proper to call

forth that state of mind. Your objection amounts to this, that in reasoning on a difficult question I write common English, and this is
the whole secret of my extravagance and obscurity.—Do you mean
that the distinguishing between the compositions of poetry, the
talent for poetry, or the subject-matter for poetry, would have told
us what poetry *is?*"

In Hazlitt's opening statement that poetry "is an imitation of
nature, but the imagination and the passions are a part of man's
nature," expression and imitation are so cunningly mingled that we
feel no poem can signal where nature appears as itself, uncolored
by our desires. The "heightenings of the imagination" aim at bringing the reflected lights of many objects into what Coleridge would
have called a whole, but what Hazlitt describes simply as an emphatic relation which occupies our mind to the exclusion of all
others. His remark that poetry describes "the flowing, not the fixed"
comes very close to Coleridge's analysis of Miltonic sublimity in the
passage on Death which I quoted earlier; only, what Coleridge held
true of the sublime Hazlitt now applies to the sense of beauty and
power communicated by any poetic impression: it is "uneasy," because its object is unfixed; it is "impatient of all limit," and "strives
to link itself" by elective affinity with some kindred sense; it represents, in a fine associationist trope, objects "not as they are in themselves, but as they are moulded by other thoughts and feelings, into an
infinite variety of shapes and combinations of power." Throughout
this passage Hazlitt is rejecting the neat Burkean division between
the beautiful and the sublime: he speaks of "beauty or power,"
"beauty or grandeur," as almost different names for the same thing,
and calls the impression at once "uneasy" and "exquisite." At the
same time he makes even the Kantian language about "surpassing
every limit of sense" as appropriate for the beautiful as for the sublime. He seems to have realized with Alison that the same object in
different situations could be beautiful or sublime, without causing
us to feel that our point of view was radically unstable.

In the light of these definitions the vocabularies of praise which
Coleridge and Hazlitt work out for their criticism of Shakespeare
are more distinct than they first appear to be. Both stress Shakespeare's infinite variety, the motions of a sympathy so complete that
we feel him to be a "myriad-minded man," in Coleridge's grand
phrase. But Hazlitt went beyond this, when, borrowing a figure from
A. W. Schlegel, he observed: "The poet may be said, for the time, to
identify himself with the character he wishes to represent, and to

pass from one to another, like the same soul successively animating different bodies. By an art like that of the ventriloquist, he throws his imagination out of himself, and makes every word appear to proceed from the mouth of the person in whose name it is given." Coleridge as a rule was wary of this metaphor of ventriloquy, and offered a differently shaded account of Shakespeare's effects, first by calling him a "Proteus" among artists and then by contrasting his selflessness with Milton's egotism. The Tomalin report of the 1811–1812 lectures gives only a fragmentary paraphrase but that is enough.

> [Shakespeare], darting himself forth, and passing himself into all the forms of human character and human passion; the other attracted all forms and all things to himself into the unity of his own grand ideal.
>
> Shakespeare became all things well into which he infused himself while all forms, all things became Milton—the poet ever present to our minds and more than gratifying us for the loss of the distinct individuality of what he represents.[31]

The trouble with ventriloquy, from Coleridge's point of view, would seem to be that it gives too vivid a picture of the purposeful activity behind the scenes, and thus of the poet *who secretly remains himself* working on the audience to achieve a particular end. The advantage of Coleridge's description is that it excludes any presumption of unmasking the poet in his self-counsels, as he plots his next change of shape. Whatever Shakespeare may be, he is not a willing agent: these characters are things that happen to him. I have shown Hazlitt tempted by a similar conception, but finally assimilating Shakespeare's kind of activity to Milton's, from his strengthening conviction that dramatic form may be superior to lyric and yet not owe its power to an imagination different in kind. But Shakespeare has to supply Coleridge with the great instance of a triumph over any need for human agency. His works give evidence of nature herself as "the prime genial artist, inexhaustible in diverse powers."[32] With his forms as with nature's "each exterior is the physiognomy of the being within its true image reflected and thrown out from the concave mirror." This mirror, concave because only so will it appear rounded like a world, makes Shakespeare's essence identical with nature's, and therefore begs the question of who did the work.

Now the romantic revolt against the division of the mind into active and intellectual powers had begun as early as Godwin, and was continued through its many ramifications by Hazlitt as well as

Wordsworth and Coleridge, but of the four I think Coleridge was most prone to reinstitute some form of the division behind his own back, as a way of insuring the integrity of pure meditation. This will seem to his admirers an unfair reduction, or an incompetent translation of his active-passive distinction, but my understanding of these terms comes from one of the better known passages in the *Biographia Literaria,* where the purpose that Coleridge makes them serve is open to any reader's inspection. He is attacking what he takes to be both the idealism and mechanism of Hartley's account of the mind, and its irrelevance to Hartley's proof of God in Volume Two. He then mentions the laws of matter as the "limit and condition of the laws of mind," in order to set up the imagination as a mediating faculty between them, with powers not deducible from the Hartleyan scheme of association. All this is familiar to us from Hazlitt's *Essay* of a decade before, but Coleridge's language at this point has unhappy consequences for any idea of the imagination as necessarily active.

> Most of my readers will have observed a small water-insect on the surface of rivulets which throws a cinque-spotted shadow fringed with prismatic colours on the sunny bottom of the brook; and will have noticed how the little animal wins its way up against the stream, by alternate pulses of active and passive motion, now resisting the current, and now yielding to it in order to gather strength and a momentary fulcrum for a further propulsion. This is no unapt emblem of the mind's self-experience in the act of thinking. There are evidently two powers at work which relatively to each other are active and passive; and this is not possible without an intermediate faculty, which is at once both active and passive. (In philosophical language we must denominate this intermediate faculty in all its degrees and determinations the *imagination.* But in common language, and especially on the subject of poetry, we appropriate the name to a superior degree of the faculty, joined to a superior voluntary controul over it.)[33]

Recall Hazlitt's description of the men building a pier, and the mechanist's failure to show how the mind could imagine the unbuilt section except by actually walking across it on the strength of his own metaphysical hypothesis—a maneuver which must imply that the mind "has wings, as well as feet," just the conclusion we had been set to avoid. The bridge for Hazlitt represented the limit and condition of the laws of mind, as the stream does for Coleridge; but notice that it is essential to Coleridge's idea that he should imagine the mind fronting against the laws that condition it; whereas in Hazlitt's figure, either way we cross we are going with the bridge: it is a natural guide (itself man-made), not an obstacle, to our human purpose. Coleridge's mind is active only when it wills its opposition to laws, as their counter-force; and it can chart its course, like the water-insect, only by a kind of reflection that is independent of action because occurring at a different moment; when the mind thinks, it is "yielding" to the current "to gather strength and a momentary fulcrum." This is what I noted in Locke as the power of the will-in-suspense: Coleridge sees the attractiveness of the idea, and like Hazlitt connects it with imagination. But he refuses to by-pass the intellectual-active distinction by connecting imaginative power with reflection and action *in the same moment,* as known to us only through our interpretation of a single purpose. This refusal has its source in a Kantian reluctance to identify the pure reflection or dreamwork of the imagination with the will. The water-insect drifting with the current in spite of his own direction is an emblem of the mind's choicest intervals, when it receives its impulses in wise passiveness, and always with a will suspended.

What perplexes this view of Coleridge is that one cannot help knowing him to be the same man who schooled Wordsworth in the active power of the mind:

> Oh Lady! we receive but what we give,
> And in our life alone does Nature live.

Why should there have been so marked a falling away from this belief in Coleridge's criticism? If one is disposed to read careers as all of a piece, there are many ways of bringing Coleridge's earlier idea of active power into line with his later rhetoric of reconciliation. But the biographical evidence gives sufficient cause for supposing a crisis some time between 1800 and 1810—a crisis brought on partly by the sense that his life's work had been displaced, because Wordsworth was the poet of the imagination he had prophesied. He laid most stress on the active power of the imagination when he was grappling with Hartley, writing his great poems, and giving Wordsworth the benefit of all that he learned from both undertakings. By the time he and Hazlitt came to lecture across town from each other, Coleridge was a very different critic from the one whose Dejection Ode inspired Wordsworth to finish the Immortality Ode. As he seemed between 1810 and 1820—roughly, the years of his lectures on poetry and of the *Biographia*—Coleridge, the cultivator of passiveness, was inseparable from Coleridge the talker-*to,* the brilliant secondary man. No better picture exists of the way these features came together in his presence than the opening paragraphs of "Mr. Coleridge" in *The Spirit of the Age.*

> The present is an age of talkers, and not of doers; and the reason is, that the world is growing old. We are so far advanced in the Arts and Sciences, that we live in retrospect, and doat on past achievements. The accumulation of knowledge has been so great, that we are lost in wonder at the height it has reached, instead of attempting to climb or add to it; while the variety of objects distracts and dazzles the looker-on. What *niche* remains unoccupied? What path untried? What is the use of doing anything, unless we could do better than all those who have gone before us? What hope is there of this? We are like those who have been to see some noble monument of art, who are content to admire without thinking of rivalling it; or like guests after a feast, who praise the hospitality of the donor "and thank the bounteous Pan"—perhaps carrying away some trifling fragments; or like the spectators of a mighty battle, who still hear its sound afar off, and the clashing of armour and the neighing of the war-horse and the shout of victory is in their ears, like the rushing of innumerable waters.
>
> Mr. Coleridge has "a mind reflecting ages past"; his voice is like the echo of the congregated roar of the "dark rearward and abyss" of thought. He who has seen a mouldering tower by the side of a crystal lake, hid by the mist, but glittering in the wave below, may conceive the dim, gleaming, uncertain intelligence of his eye.   (XI, 28-29)

The bounty denied to Coleridge is that of Milton and Shakespeare, as the quotations from *Comus* and *The Tempest* recall, working in mingled measure with Hazlitt's prose to suggest their foreshortened offspring "Kubla Khan." The pleasures still allowed him are those of *The Castle of Indolence,* and Hazlitt leaves his rival the same reward—again by the gift of quotation, but now more pressingly and with a larger feeling of melancholy—in an essay "On the Qualifications Necessary to Success."[34]

> The man of perhaps the greatest ability now living is the one who has not only done the least, but who is actually incapable of ever doing any thing worthy of him—unless he had a hundred hands to write with, and a hundred mouths to utter all that it hath entered into his heart to conceive, and centuries before him to embody the

endless volume of his waking dreams. Cloud rolls over cloud; one train of thought suggests and is driven away by another; theory after theory is spun out of the bowels of his brain, not like the spider's web, compact and round, a citadel and a snare, built for mischief and for use; but like the gossamer, stretched out and entangled without end, clinging to every casual object, flitting in the idle air, and glittering only in the ray of fancy. No subject can come amiss to him, and he is alike attracted and alike indifferent to all—he is not tied down to any one in particular—but floats from one to another, his mind every where finding its level, and feeling no limit but that of thought—now soaring with its head above the stars, now treading with fairy feet among flowers, now winnowing the air with winged words—passing from Duns Scotus to Jacob Behmen, from the Kantean philosophy to a conundrum, and from the Apocalypse to an acrostic—taking in the whole range of poetry, painting, wit, history, politics, metaphysics, criticism, and private scandal—every question giving birth to some new thought, and every thought "discoursed in eloquent music," that lives only in the ear of fools, or in the report of absent friends. Set him to write a book, and he belies all that has been ever said about him—

> "Ten thousand great ideas filled his mind,
> But with the clouds they fled, and left no trace behind."
>
> (XII, 198-99)

English culture during the Regency years is itself, in Hazlitt's view of it, a Castle of Indolence, kept up by enchanters fluent in every kind of luxury, who will supply even genius with a comfortable cell provided it agrees to remain a curious item on display, and can be dismissed as a harmless extravagance.

Some deep reserve of Hazlitt's inheritance from Dissent has been touched in this judgment of what Coleridge made of his gift; and for all its gentleness the Godwin-Coleridge contrast in *The Spirit of the Age* concludes on the same note. "Mr. Coleridge has flirted with the muses as with a set of mistresses: Mr. Godwin has been married twice, to Reason and to Fancy, and has to boast no short-lived progeny by each." Both met their proper rewards, Godwin his pair of masterpieces and Coleridge his too rich florilegium of poetic and philosophical fragments: "Justice has, after all, been done to the pretensions of each; and we must, in all cases, use means to ends." *Use* is still on Hazlitt's mind when he compares the spider's web, "built for mischief and for use," with Coleridge's built only to shimmer in the light and tremble in the breeze. Work for use will be

militant against any establishment that sanctifies old usages for their
own sake; but Coleridge professed to find new reasons for them in
the nature of things; and at this point his politics again seem pertinent to the denial of agency implicit in his idea of the imagination.
At any rate that was the way Hazlitt read his career, with its movement from Unitarianism to Trinitarianism doubtless falling into
place also, as a subtext for the movement in defining imagination
from an active power to an "irremissive, though gentle and unnoticed, controul" over opposites. Hazlitt summed up his analysis in
the lecture "On the Living Poets," where he announced his intention to say "a few words of Mr. Coleridge," with the afterthought:
"there is no one who has a better right to say what he thinks of him
than I have." Awe still predominates over his other feelings about
Coleridge: "he is the only person I ever knew who answered to the
idea of a man of genius. He is the only person from whom I ever
learnt any thing." But he has this reservation: "There is only one
thing he could learn from me in return, but *that* he has not." This
must refer not only to the argument for disinterestedness which
Coleridge had admired without applying it to his own life, but also
to the link Hazlitt saw between the imagination and the many active
interests it brings into being.

CHAPTER VII

CRITICAL TEMPERAMENT

PUBLIC PERSONS

What most depressed Hazlitt's reputation in his own lifetime was the use of just such personal judgments as the reference to Coleridge in "On the Living Poets." Here a more restrained policy may seem the preferable one, and before going on to compare Hazlitt and Coleridge as readers I need to defend Hazlitt's practice. To do so will involve for the moment a somewhat larger cast of characters, but others must be allowed their say, and Hazlitt's dealings with them ought to be sampled for the continuous fidelity of detail as well as the occasional asperity. He often made essay-illustrations from the gossip of the day, or from episodes in the lives of his acquaintances, to which he was a privileged witness sworn (by tacit consent) to silence. The protests of the living usually proceeded from wounded vanity, which could always wear the disguise of simple incomprehension. Hazlitt, it was said, violated the common decencies of private life; Pope of course had not scrupled to work this way with his enemies, but it should be no one's way with his friends; if it were to be encouraged, society itself would disintegrate. The liveliest protest not open to the charge of disingenuousness, came from Leigh Hunt, who had been surprised by the open mention of himself and Shelley in two of Hazlitt's essays. The allusion to someone like Hunt as the darling of his own existence—self-regarding epicure of every selfless-seeming pleasure with a friend—is very long and besides of uncertain application: P. P. Howe says of it rightly, "Leigh Hunt recognised himself in this passage . . . and Hazlitt did not deny him the right to do so, if he chose." But since Hunt makes a point of taking Shelley's part rather than his own, the second passage is more rewarding to examine.

The author of the Prometheus Unbound . . . has a fire in his eye, a fever in his blood, a maggot in his brain, a hectic flutter in his speech, which mark out the philosophic fanatic. He is sanguine-complexioned, and shrill-voiced. As is often observable in the case of religious enthusiasts, there is a slenderness of constitutional *stamina,* which renders the flesh no match for the spirit. His bending, flexible form appears to take no strong hold of things, does not grapple with the world about him, but slides from it like a river—

> "And in its liquid texture mortal wound
> Receives no more than can the fluid air."

The shock of accident, the weight of authority make no impression on his opinions, which retire like a feather, or rise from the encounter unhurt, through their own buoyancy. He is clogged by no dull system of realities, no earth-bound feelings, no rooted prejudices, by nothing that belongs to the mighty trunk and hard husk of nature and habit, but is drawn up by irresistible levity to the regions of mere speculation and fancy, to the sphere of air and fire, where his delighted spirit floats in "seas of pearl and clouds of amber." There is no *caput mortuum* of worn-out, thread-bare experience to serve as ballast to his mind; it is all volatile intellectual salt of tartar, that refuses to combine its evanescent, inflammable essence with any thing solid or any thing lasting. . . . Curiosity is the only proper category of his mind, and though a man in knowledge, he is a child in feeling. (VIII, 148–49)

Hunt wrote a private letter in reply, in which he taxed Hazlitt with having betrayed the radical cause, and read him a humorless but sufficiently earnest lecture on the laudableness of never breaking ranks.

I think, Mr. Hazlitt, you might have found a better time, and place too, for assaulting me and my friends in this bitter manner. . . . In God's name, why could you not tell Mr. Shelley in a pleasant manner of what you dislike in him? If it is not mere spleen, you make a gross mistake in thinking that he is not open to advice, or so wilfully in love with himself and his opinions. His spirit is worthy of his great talents. Besides, do you think that nobody has thought or suffered, or come to conclusions through thought and suffering, but yourself? You are fond of talking against vanity: but do you think that people will see no vanity in that fondness—in your being so intolerant with everybody's ideas of improvement but your own, and in resenting so fiercely the possession of a trifling quality or so which you do not happen to number among your own? I have been flattered by your praises: I have been (I do not care what you make of the acknowledgement) instructed, and I thought bettered, by your objections; but it is one thing to be dealt candidly with or rallied, and another to have the whole alleged nature of one's self and a dear friend torn out and thrown in one's face, as if we had not a common humanity with yourself.[1]

Hazlitt, answering Hunt with his own letter of self-defense, admitted the justice of the charge but took shelter in a legalism: "You would not have cared one farthing about annoying me, and yet you complain that I draw a logical conclusion from all this and publish it to the world without your name."[2] It is an unsatisfying answer, and one can note in extenuation only that Hazlitt complains in this letter that he is tired. However, what he later calls the "general ground" of argument—his willingness to illustrate the characteristics of public men which are already to some extent public knowledge, by using his own observations to confirm them—receives a much more spirited defense.

Hazlitt's advantage here is that he does not affect to hold himself above personal concerns: these, he claims, work their way into any essayist's or critic's writing, and short of libel it is as well to speak of them openly.

I am fond of a theory as you know; but I will give up even that to a friend, if he shews that he has any regard to my personal feelings. You provoke me to think hard things of you, and then you wonder that I hitch them into an Essay, as if that made any difference. I pique myself on doing what I can for others; but I cannot say that I have found any suitable returns for this, and hence perhaps "my outrageousness of stomach."[3]

He then adds, though he apologizes for adding, "a parcel of small, old grievances" against some lesser lights of journalism.[4] On a more heated occasion, Crabb Robinson—whose new loyalty to the Lake poets made him a far more hostile audience than Hunt—confronted Hazlitt with the record of his indiscretions, and was treated to a stronger and more circumstantial defense of the practice. Robinson had taken the offensive by adverting to "the breach of confidence in the detail of conversation" with Wordsworth and Coleridge, and, as he reports, "Hazlitt then made a distinction. He said he would never take advantage of a slip in a man's conversation, and repeat what was not such a person's real opinion; but where what he had said was his notorious opinion not said to one person only, but gen-

erally, he thought such things might without injustice be repeated."[5]
The great majority of his personal allusions were certainly of this
kind. As for the "tergiversation" of Wordsworth, Coleridge, and
Southey, this so far from being a secret was a proof of good citizen-
ship vouchsafed by the poets themselves year after year to a grateful
public. Hazlitt's only discovery was that the apostasy to which these
writers pointed with pride, as a token of their common humanity
and continually ripening sincerity, could be written about also in
a tone of sad perplexity, or of mingled amazement and scorn.

Wordsworth's egotism, Coleridge's weakness of will, the overstrained idiosyncrasy of Shelley's radicalism and the preening humility of Hunt's connoisseurship, were in the public domain for somewhat different reasons. These belonged to the category of worst-kept
secrets, and gave the very grain and texture to anything written by
the authors in question. Hazlitt would take the liberty of bringing
out the notorious trait with an especially pungent anecdote which
then acquired a fame of its own. His favorite victim was Wordsworth,
who of all others could best defend himself; whereas believing, as he
told Robinson, that Coleridge was "a man without a will," and
armed with a quiver of fine-honed instances, he abstained from
launching any into the air: he saw the pathos of Coleridge's situation, and in attack confined himself strictly to matters of principle
or public conduct. Edmund Blunden notices what other readers have
too often missed, that "In Hazlitt's maltreatment of Coleridge there
is usually a strain of Olympian jest or secret admiration which makes
those papers seem amiable if they are compared with his white-lipped
fury against Wordsworth at the close of 1816."[6] One can lay it down
as a rule without exceptions, that Hazlitt's "breaches of confidence"
always tended to confirm the familiar impression of the author whom
they evoked, and that they were hitched into an essay only because
they were more vivid and memorable than anything else could be.

One story may indicate the sort of malice behind the scenes to
which his anger compelled him to respond, and his sense of fairness
obliged him to respond in public. After Hazlitt's qualified praise of
The Excursion, and probably as a deliberate revenge, Wordsworth
informed Robinson that he must always of course suffer unmerited
criticism from Hazlitt, since he had once come to his aid at an embarrassing moment. Because Wordsworth also retailed this story to
Haydon, we have a record of his exact words: "Some girl called him
a black-faced rascal, when Hazlitt enraged pushed her down, '& because, Sir,' said Wordsworth, 'she refused to gratify his abominable

& devilish propensities,' he lifted up her petticoats & *smote* her on the *bottom*." One may accept the accuracy of this without trusting its more extravagant implications: "Devils!" was also what Wordsworth said on being shown a picture of Cupid and Psyche. At all events Hazlitt, in this incident from many years before, had been so far discountenanced by the girl's refusal that he struck her, and soon found himself pursued by a small but determined mob, doubtless more aroused by his Jacobin politics than by the girl's offended honor. When he appeared before Wordsworth he was received cordially, and later assisted down byroads to the more sympathetic midlands. Wordsworth in this case had acted creditably. He loses credit for it by his failure to be content with a good deed done in stealth and discovered by accident. Instead he waited for his moment, picked out a notable diarist to flatter (and shock) with his account of Hazlitt's ingratitude, and slandered the character he had once taken extraordinary measures to save. In both the Haydon and Robinson versions of this story, there is the simple imputation of a bad motive. It amounts to an unmasking of Hazlitt's review on the system of La Rochefoucauld: my friend cannot forgive me for the terrible way he behaved in my presence; that explains his reluctance to endorse every word of my latest composition. A less paradoxical view of the incident would hold it likely for Hazlitt to have been still well disposed to Wordsworth, and not overcome by the resentful after-tremors of shame: the "white-lipped fury" comes only after he has found Wordsworth's story in wide circulation, and his old misfortune a source of mirth even among those who would not use it to injure him.

If it is still objected that criticism cannot be made from the stuff of mere biography, a reply even better than Hazlitt's comes from Johnson in *Rambler* 60.

> There are many who think it an act of piety to hide the faults or failings of their friends, even when they can no longer suffer by their detection; we therefore see whole ranks of characters adorned with uniform panegyrick, and not to be known from one another, but by extrinsick and casual circumstances. "Let me remember," says Hale, "when I find myself inclined to pity a criminal, that there is likewise a pity due to the country." If we owe regard to the memory of the dead, there is yet more respect to be paid to knowledge, to virtue, and to truth.[7]

The strength of Hazlitt's criticism comes from the ability to hold in tension, with his achieved verdict on a character, all those chance affections that tell against it. Thus his criticism of Southey in the "Letter to William Smith"—an uncompromising polemic for the most part, even by Hazlitt's standards—ends by recalling his encounter with Southey a few days earlier, and the more-than-Laureate reminiscences it brought, which he says were almost enough to make him forget his contempt for Southey's politics.

> We met him . . . the other day in St. Giles's, (it was odd we should meet *him* there) were sorry we had passed him without speaking to an old friend, turned and looked after him for some time, as to a tale of other times, sighing, as we walked on, *Alas poor Southey!* "We saw in him a painful hieroglyphic of humanity; a sad memento of departed independence; a striking instance of the rise and fall of patriot-bards!" In the humour we were in, we could have written a better epitaph for him than he has done for himself.
>   (VII, 208)

Hazlitt was prepared to write more completely in this humor when he undertook the sketch of Southey for *The Spirit of the Age.* But in the review of Southey's "Letter" he prefers to demystify the encounter, in a negative turn that is characteristic. "We went directly and bought his Letter to Mr. W. Smith, which appeared the same day as himself, and this at once put an end to our sentimentality." An inward questioner is on the watch for the unearned reprieves Hazlitt grants to old friends, as much as for the unearned condemnations he levels against those whom he "cannot like." In both cases his affections are withheld only for the moment, and to deepen the play of intelligence with which we receive them when their time has really come.

We now come to a test case involving Coleridge. Hazlitt went out of his way to review an advertisement for *The Statesman's Manual,* and in doing so referred to Coleridge as "the Dog in the Manger of literature, an intellectual Mar-Plot, who will neither let anybody else come to a conclusion, nor come to one himself." The accusation may seem enough to upset the poise I have been claiming for his interest in personality. It looks more like a triumph of restraint when one realizes that Coleridge had twice deprived Hazlitt of a patron, and hence of an opportunity to gain the freedom for his own researches which helped to establish Coleridge himself as a scholar. In 1803, Tom Wedgwood wrote to Coleridge asking whether Hazlitt would be a suitable walking companion for a trip he planned—and received in answer, first a high commendation, that Hazlitt was "a thinking, observant, original man"; then a qualification nicely calculated to repel enthusiasm, "addicted to women, as objects of sexual indulgence"; with the conclusion drawn for Wedgwood, that Hazlitt was "utterly unfit" to be his companion; all rounded with a solemn disclaimer in the poet's worst Micawberish style—"I have written, as I ought to do, to you most freely imo ex corde; you know me, both head and heart, and will make what deductions, your reason will dictate to you."[8] Probably Hazlitt never heard of this incident. But he told Robinson of another—unpleasant enough to serve double duty—in which Coleridge's tactics were unconcealed. At a dinner once with Sir George Beaumont, a dispute arose concerning the merits of Junius, the exemplar of high Whig satire in the age of Wilkes, who in his private character, as Philip Francis, used to chide Burke, "I wish you would let me teach you to write English."[9] With a lord beside him, Coleridge quickly denounced Junius as a Whig, while Hazlitt, "growing impatient of Coleridge's cant," opposed him resolutely and at length, forgetting that it was in his interest to appease Beaumont's prejudices. That night Coleridge went on to give an exceedingly sanctimonious exhibition of clerical versatility. The next day he called on Hazlitt to display his own copy of Junius, thoroughly scored in the margins and revealing him to be a warm admirer of the author. "But," added Hazlitt in recounting the episode, "Sir George Beaumont is a High Tory and was so offended with me, both for presuming to contradict and interrupt Coleridge and for being so great an admirer of Junius, that in disgust he never saw me afterwards. And I lost the expectation of gaining a patron."[10] With this in view he chose to describe Coleridge as an *"intellectual Mar-Plot,"* alluding to a feature of his literary character which would be known also to many unhappy subscribers to *The Friend.*

CALIBAN AND THE FRENCH REVOLUTION

Something remains to be said of Hazlitt and Coleridge as practical critics, especially in their judgments of the author they cared for most. The plays I have chosen are *Hamlet* and *The Tempest,* and I will quote famous comments from both writers. On *Hamlet* I think Coleridge the more original speculator. There is evidence in parts of Hazlitt's essay that he was consciously adopting an interpretation then widely current, and we have no reason to doubt that Coleridge made it so. But on *The Tempest* it is Hazlitt who writes both with greater justice and higher imagination. I mention my own estimate of these passages to exclude any impression that the aim is a comparison of quality. But in their finer as well as their more ordinary moments, each writer shows a consistent tendency. Coleridge reads a character—and often, the moral of a play—as part of a symbolic structure, with which one's active relation comes to an end when one has known it. Hazlitt never does offer a moral, and in reading any character is apt to make it a focus of allegorical possibilities for the reader, whose understanding can only be registered by its influence on his life. Two sketches of Hamlet's character, Hazlitt's and then Coleridge's ought to bring out this divergence, the more starkly because they appear in essays that take for granted many points of accord.

Hazlitt:

> Hamlet is a name; his speeches and sayings but the idle coinage of the poet's brain. What then, are they not real? They are as real as our own thoughts. Their reality is in the reader's mind. It is *we* who are Hamlet. This play has a prophetic truth, which is above that of history. Whoever has become thoughtful and melancholy through his own mishaps or those of others; whoever has borne about with him the clouded brow of reflection and thought himself "too much i' th' sun"; whoever has seen the golden lamp of day dimmed by envious mists rising in his own breast, and could find in the world before him only a dull blank with nothing left remarkable in it; whoever has known "the pangs of despised love, the insolence of office, or the spurns which patient merit of the unworthy takes" . . . whose bitterness of soul makes him careless of consequences, and who goes to a play as his best resource to shove off, to a second remove, the evils of life by a mock representation of them—this is the true Hamlet.   (IV, 232-33)

Coleridge:

> Anything finer than this conception, and working out of a great character, is merely impossible. Shakespeare wished to impress upon us the truth that action is the chief end of existence—that no faculties of intellect, however brilliant, can be considered valuable, or indeed otherwise than as misfortunes, if they withdraw us from or render us repugnant to action, and lead us to think and think of doing, until the time has elapsed when we can do anything effectually. In enforcing this moral truth, Shakespeare has shown the fullness and force of his powers: all that is amiable and excellent in nature is combined in Hamlet, with the exception of one quality. He is a man living in meditation, called upon to act by

every motive human and divine, but the great object of his life is defeated by continually resolving to do, yet doing nothing but resolve.[11]

These are visibly the same character, though to Coleridge's splendid final sentence Hazlitt seems to have added an implication of his own, by connecting Hamlet's "meditation" with his interest in the players: it is as if acting, for Hamlet, had temporarily replaced action. Yet to speak of his condition as temporal, or otherwise suggest that Hamlet wards off the myriad evils that stagger him with the impulse of the moment, is already to take Hazlitt's side in the debate. The purpose of all his tags and casual paraphrases is to make Hamlet's situation as circumstantial as it can be made. Hamlet's melancholy is no less unique for having emerged from his grappling with the monstrousness of other wills. To Coleridge's "This *is* Hamlet, defeated by continually resolving to do, yet doing nothing but resolve," Hazlitt replies, "But note, this also is how he appears to have been formed *by the events of the play.*" To make the point still more clearly he describes Hamlet, a little further into his essay, as "the sport of circumstances, questioning with fortune and refining on his own feelings, and forced from the natural bias of his disposition by the strangeness of his situation."

For Coleridge the situation is hardly more than a pretext. The "conception" of Hamlet's character is *given:* he is the profoundly good man of thought, lacking in one quality; he exists as a type, and has something to teach us. A. C. Bradley saw that the defects of this as a description of Hamlet were necessary to its astonishing success as a self-portrait of Coleridge, and objected to Coleridge's assurance that Hamlet had been defeated in the "great object" of his life. One might as warrantably question all that is implied in the phrase, "Shakespeare wished to impress upon us the truth that . . ."; and one's doubts will be stronger in proportion as one has studied poetry with Hazlitt, who teaches a thoroughgoing suspicion of critical statements cast in this form. It could still be urged in defense of Coleridge that his reading is properly allegorical, if that is what one wants: the contrast, Hazlitt (allegory) vs. Coleridge (symbol), will not work here, for Coleridge does give the play an instructive purpose. The difficulty I think is that his allegory is peculiarly static: it instructs, without engaging, the reader; nobody is going to say, "It is I who am Hamlet," while at the same time coming to know the dangers of inaction as Coleridge describes them. By judging Hamlet very plainly, but so as to rule out any further response to his experience, Coleridge makes him as unified a symbolic entity as the water-snakes of "The Rhyme of the Ancient Mariner": as they were horrible but fertile and part of the consonance of life, so this hero is admirable and yet foredefeated by his metaphysical yearnings. One cannot say of his eloquence that its "reality is in the reader's mind." By Coleridge's lights one ought to speak instead of the conception he embodies, and conclude that a right judgment of it may subsist even in a mind largely innocent of specific memories of the play.

On the morality of literature, Coleridge will usually be found a resolute guide, and Hazlitt an unsettling observer. Moralism is of course a general characteristic of Coleridge's stance: one hears the best of it in his early invective against Pitt and Napoleon, the worst in the rant against Unitarians that fills his second *Lay Sermon*. Fairly typical of his usual tone are such scattered remarks as his denunciation of Falstaff as "an open and professed liar: even his sensuality was subservient to his intellect, for he appeared to drink sack that he might have occasion to shew his wit"[12]—a judgment Coleridge felt would form an insufficient warning against similar behavior unless he added that Falstaff's wit was always more strained and artificial than Prince Hal's. He must be the only man of genius ever to have thought so; and Hazlitt makes the necessary point against all such strictures in his *Lectures on the English Comic Writers:*

> The severe censurers of the morals of imaginary characters can generally find a hole for their own vices to creep out at; and yet do not perceive how it is that the imperfect and even deformed characters in Shakespeare's plays, as done to the life, by forming a part of our personal consciousness, claim our personal forgiveness, and suspend or evade our moral judgment, by bribing our self-love to side with them. (VI, 33)

To learn where our self-love is implicated is for Hazlitt the task of justice as well as of charity.

Justice again is the undeclared subject of Hazlitt's defense of Caliban, and here at last the engagement between the two critics need not be plotted by a historian. In *The Courier* of February 9, 1818, Hazlitt read the following report of a lecture by Coleridge.

> The character of *Caliban,* as an original and caricature of Jacobinism, so fully illustrated at Paris during the French Revolution, he described in a vigorous and lively manner, exciting repeated bursts of applause. . . . He said, wherever Shakespeare had drawn

a character addicted to sneering, and contempt for the merits of others, that character was sure to be a villain. (XIX, 206)

Hazlitt's reply appeared in *The Yellow Dwarf* of February 14.

> Caliban is so far from being a prototype of modern Jacobinism, that he is strictly the legitimate sovereign of the isle, and Prospero and the rest are usurpers, who have ousted him from his hereditary jurisdiction by superiority of talent and knowledge. "This island's mine, by Sycorax my mother;" and he complains bitterly of the artifices used by his new friends to cajole him out of it. He is the Louis XVIII of the enchanted island in *The Tempest*. . . . His boast that "he had peopled else this isle with Calibans," is very proper and dignified in such a person; for it is evident that the right line would be supplanted in failure of his issue; and that the superior beauty and accomplishments of Ferdinand and Miranda could no more be opposed to the legitimate claims of this deformed and loathsome monster, than the beauty and intellect of the Bonaparte family can be opposed to the bloated and ricketty minds and bodies of the Bourbons, cast, as they are, in the true *Jus Divinum* mould! (XIX, 207)

The sincere compliment to Napoleon makes the rest of this seem not entirely feigned. But Hazlitt immediately adds, "This is gross. Why does Mr. Coleridge provoke us to write as great nonsense as he talks?"

More however was at stake than the divine right of kings. Both here and elsewhere, Coleridge understood Caliban to be coarse and therefore base. Hazlitt's sketch of Caliban in the *Characters of Shakespeare's Plays* is intended to clear away such confusions, and he follows Schlegel in noticing that Caliban speaks the most natural poetry of all the characters. His mind is " 'of the earth, earthy.' It seems almost to have been dug out of the ground, with a soul instinctively superadded to it answering to its wants and origin." On the other hand, vulgarity, the quality of Antonio and Sebastian, "is not natural coarseness, but conventional coarseness, learnt from others." Whatever one makes of Caliban, it is no use dismissing him as simply contemptible. The justice of his cause keeps returning even when he is offstage, in the promptings of Ariel and Miranda and even Prospero. He is, in Hazlitt's reading of the play, that without which there can be no Ariel. And Hazlitt derives from these two characters, and from the dialectic they create together, a morality not at all identical with the conventional one shared by Gonzalo, Sebastian, and Coleridge, yet profound enough to sustain a romance that has at heart the fate of humanity itself. "Shakespeare has, as it were by design, drawn off from Caliban the elements of whatever is ethereal and refined, to compound them in the unearthly mould of Ariel. Nothing was ever more finely conceived than this contrast between the material and the spiritual, the gross and the delicate." One may add that Ariel's rebuke to Prospero, about the pity he should feel for his captives, announces a justice complete enough to include Caliban among its beneficiaries.

> ARIEL: Your charm so strongly works 'em,
>   That if you now beheld them, your affections
>   Would become tender.
>
> PROSPERO: Dost thou think so, spirit?
>
> ARIEL: Mine would, sir, were I human.

Coleridge would see in this passage a suggestion of the inclusiveness and consequent unity of the human society framed by the play—Hazlitt, of the exclusiveness and consequent limitation of any society which has to learn its humanity from Ariel.

Here Coleridge's larger tendency, to praise in poetry a wholeness that he believes to be self-generated and self-legislating, joins with his apology for society as it is, which he sees as manifesting a given and essential order. In both movements of his thought, the reformative work of the mind on its object, whether society or a poem, is acknowledged under the heading of "secondary imagination," but then elided from his particular descriptions of praiseworthy objects. This may be thought to stretch the point; but in this stretch I am borne out by some curious notes of Coleridge's for a general lecture at Bristol, where he speaks of Shakespeare's "reverence of classes that are permanent elements of the social state, as physicians, priests, Kings. Even [when] worst, yet some palliation thrown in."[13] There seems to me to be no truth in this, and some part of certain falsehood. It exemplifies very vividly the ease with which a great author can be made to say something you wish he had said, because it accords with your own deeper meditations; something so general that almost anybody *might* be thought to have said it, but on which you have not carefully canvassed your author before attributing it to him; and which he turns out sometimes flatly to have contradicted. Can any meaning be assigned to Coleridge's statement, for example, as applied to the priest of *Hamlet?* To the King of *Henry VIII?* Yet these instances would necessarily have been present to Coleridge had he been thinking not about his need to find the order of society reflected within the unity of each play, but about the individual life and feeling of the plays themselves.

It was left to Hazlitt to interpret Caliban's coarseness and the justice of his protests as both alike irreducible. Coleridge reads him as one might read Jack Cade in *Henry VI:* a perfect type of the terrors of man in an unsocialized state—the sort of creature bred by anarchy who seems to breed anarchy in turn. His final understanding of Caliban is determined by a plain-minded view of the ending, with its closed circle of a redeemed humanity, and Caliban standing alone outside it. But Hazlitt, whose criticism is not a quest for unity, is in a position to go on asking after the play is done the very questions Caliban's existence had posed, questions that do after all linger in the mind. He can see Caliban as allied with Stephano and Trinculo in the "low plot," but also with Ariel (another prisoner of the island's new king), and even with Prospero (another ruler unjust by virtue of his desire to rule).

Yet Hazlitt's most brilliant stroke as an interpreter of Caliban occurs not in his chapter on the play itself but in the essay "What Is the People?"

Legitimate governments (flatter them as we will) are not another Heathen mythology. . . . They are indeed "Gods to punish," but in other respects "men of our infirmity." They do not feed on ambrosia or drink nectar; but live on the common fruits of the earth, of which they get the largest share, and the best. The wine they drink is made of grapes: the blood they shed is that of their subjects: the laws they make are not against themselves: the taxes they vote, they afterwards devour. They have the same wants that we have: and having the option, very naturally help themselves first, out of the common stock, without thinking that others are to come after them. With the same natural necessities, they have a thousand artificial ones besides; and with a thousand times the means to gratify them, they are still voracious, importunate, unsatisfied. . . . They live in palaces, and loll in coaches. In spite of Mr. Malthus, their studs of horses consume the produce of our fields, their dog-kennels are glutted with the food which would maintain the children of the poor. They cost us so much a year in dress and furniture, so much in stars and garters, blue ribbons, and grand crosses,—so much in dinners, breakfasts, and suppers, and so much in suppers, breakfasts, and dinners. These heroes of the Income-tax, Worthies of the Civil List, Saints of the Court Calendar (*campagnons du lys*), have their naturals and non-naturals, like the rest of the world, but at a dearer rate. They are real *bona-fide*

personages, and do not live upon air. You will find it easier to keep
them a week than a month; and at the end of that time, waking
from the sweet dream of Legitimacy, you may say with Caliban,
"Why, what a fool was I to take this drunken monster for a God!"

(VII, 263)

This conscious interest in opening up the play to its fiercer implications, instead of sealing it tight from them, is repeated in a passage
of the essay "On Vulgarity and Affectation," where Caliban is mentioned as a pure instance of what is *common,* and linked with the
national spokesman for liberty in the vulgate, William Cobbett.
Both characters are harsh, persistent, troublesome, truthful. Neither
is vulgar. "A thing is not vulgar because it is common. 'Tis common
to breathe, to see, to feel, to live. . . . Caliban is coarse enough, but
surely he is not vulgar. We might as well spurn the clod under our
feet, and call it vulgar. Cobbett is coarse enough, but he is not vulgar. He does not belong to the herd."[14] In Hazlitt's terms the herd
includes the vulgar of every class.

Written less than a month after the reply to Coleridge's lecture,
the paragraph from "What Is the People?" still has in view the general moral tendency to idealize society, and to preserve society's conquests just as they are. About this time Coleridge was proposing the
consolidation of a new and artificial class, a body of guardians maintained by the state for the cultivation and protection of knowledge.
Members of such a clerisy, like members of the clergy formerly,
would compose a little world of Prosperos. But now, against them
and in permanent opposition, Hazlitt sets the monster who claims
a right to know. A hero of satire, in a situation only legible as satire,
Caliban is a discoverer of society's laws; and like that other monster,
the people, he comes to respossess what was his. The allusion guides
our thinking so far, and yet it encourages certain readers to go further. By placing Caliban's final recognition in an essay addressed to
the people, Hazlitt asks them to pursue for themselves Stephano's
suggestion that "Thought is free." How long, when once they have
penetrated its mysteries, they will continue to tolerate a routine of
dinners, breakfasts, and suppers varied by suppers, breakfasts, and
dinners, the essay leaves as undecided as the play.

CHAPTER VIII

THE POLITICS OF ALLUSION

QUOTATION AND ALLUSION

A critic when he quotes is interrupting the text to which his chosen passage belongs, and exhibiting his power in relation to an author he cares for, at the same time that he acknowledges the author's mastery over him. His wish is to take possession of what he was possessed by. No interesting act of quotation therefore can imply a simple gesture of homage; the reader cannot help being interested in more than the accuracy of the result. In quoting one summons both a witness and a judge to the "tribunal of the soul" which Longinus speaks of, where every writer hopes to be judged great by his sympathy with the great writers who preceded him. Whatever fragment the critic picks out for emphasis will distort its parent text by presenting less than the whole of it, and so will shape the reader's understanding of everything it does not mention. Longinus's definition of sublimity, as "the echo of a great soul," admits, only more openly than other phrases about literary invention, the distance between any great work and a vivid memory of it. The distance and the change it brings about are necessary to appreciation, because according to Longinus we are unwilling as well as unable, when we have been moved by a work of literature, to see it steadily and see it whole. Once that is recognized, it may be added that there evidently is such a thing as having a genius for quotation.

Hazlitt often quoted from memory. His favorite lines, including those his memory had changed, he exhibited with the tacit understanding that they were to be read not merely as evidence of conscientiousness, but as a leading clue to every quality that ought to be searched out in *his* writing. Quotation in this sense, judged as a critical tactic, marks the pride not the humility of the writer who quotes: "Here you see what I have found, what I remember, what

I now prefer to think mine; part of my character—a great part of what makes me unique." De Quincey thought Hazlitt went too far in the direction of mere display, and called it dealing in borrowed tinsel.[1] But in making that objection he betrayed a protective concern for his own style, which was more elaborate than Hazlitt's, less sudden in its wit or grandeur: a style of amplification rather than sublimity. The distinction between these terms also comes from Longinus, and may help to explain Hazlitt's preferences both as a writer and as an observer of writing. Sublimity occurs as a break or rift in the routine progress of utterance, and the flowing-in of some higher utterance: the work of an instant, and gone in an instant. Amplification works more methodically and with better calculated results. By slow augmentation it may achieve something of comparable power—or rather, something of comparable energy, counted in its total sweep. So, with a grand enough subject, the rhetorical pattern of "The House that Jack Built" might arrive at a power equal to that of the single sentence, "Let there be light." But De Quincey trusted amplification as the only dependable source of eloquence: what he calls (praising himself) "rhythmus, or pomp of cadence, or sonorous ascent of clauses," he suspects is denied to Hazlitt, whose style he calls "(to borrow an impressive word from Coleridge) non-sequacious."[2] Putting the same observation in a light more favorable to Hazlitt, one might say his are the shorter, higher flights, though De Quincey stays longer on the wing. The effect of sublimity, "not persuasion but transport," as Longinus describes it, can hardly be sustained in a manner suitable to a Verrine Oration, or an oriental narrative like De Quincey's "Revolt of the Tartars."

Yet it was shrewd of De Quincey to link Hazlitt's extensive use of quotation with the bursts of eloquence that can seem the distinctive feature of his style. I have mentioned in Hazlitt's defense the Longinian belief that eloquence is the work of memory, a contest with the "souls" of earlier writers who impose themselves on the memory of their successor. But the contrast with De Quincey brings out Hazlitt's agreement with Longinus in a more general assumption: that power is measured by its striving to overcome resistance. Longinus could make oratory the pattern of all eloquence because his ideal community of speech was a republic, in which the speaker's power is freely given, the listener's assent may be withheld, and a rival example of eloquence may arise from any member of the community. He refused for the same reason to suppose that tyranny or oligarchy could ever foster great writing. Sublimity is known by its conversion of the audience, and for the conversion to be real the audience cannot have been bought, or chained to their seats. They must be an audience of equals. Longinus says much of this and implies the rest, in a commonly overlooked passage near the end of *On the Sublime*. Hazlitt confirms it when he writes, "The mind strikes out truth by collision." The phrase gains special force from its context, in his essay "On the Aristocracy of Letters."

> Learning is a kind of external appendage or transferable property—
>
> " 'T was mine, 'tis his, and may be any man's"—
>
> Genius and understanding are a man's self, an integrant part of his personal identity; and the title to these last, as it is the most difficult to be ascertained, is also the most grudgingly acknowledged. . . . Pedants, I will add here, talk to the vulgar as pedagogues talk to school-boys, on an understood principle of condescension and superiority, and therefore make little progress in the knowledge of men or things. . . . There can be no true superiority but what arises out of the presupposed ground of equality: there can be no improvement but from the free communication and comparing of ideas. Kings and nobles, for this reason, receive little benefit from society—where all is submission on one side, and condescension on the other. The mind strikes out truth by collision, as steel strikes fire from the flint! (VIII, 208)

This was Hazlitt's favorite metaphor of resistance, and he sometimes gave it a bolder emphasis by the cheerless thing he made of its opposite. In *The Spirit of the Age,* after paying his respects to the elegance, learning, and public spirit of Mackintosh's writings, he comes to the single defect which none of these qualities can lighten: "he strikes when the iron is cold." Again, in defending the remark that the French are a nation "void and bare of the faculty of imagination," he dwells on the irreconcilability of continuous finish with unexpected grandeur. Finish affords perfection of a kind; but where no roughness exists, the habitual response will soon find a home; in a nation that cares for Racine more than Shakespeare, there is a soft sediment of presumed understanding, into which even the language of common use pretty comfortably settles.

> The words *charming, delicious, indescribable,* &c. excite the same lively emotions in their minds as the most vivid representations of what is said to be so; and hence verbiage and the cant of sentiment fill the place, and stop the road to genius—a vague, flaccid, enervated rhetoric being too often substituted for the pith and marrow

of truth and nature. The greatest facility to feel or to comprehend will not produce the most intense passion, or the most electrical expression of it. There must be a resistance in the matter to do this—a collision, an obstacle to overcome. The torrent rushes with fury from being impeded in its course: the lightning splits the gnarled oak. (X, 116)

In figures like these Hazlitt represented the energy of mind that he honored in others and sought in himself.

Quotation belongs among the signs of such energy—not only because a writer discloses his own identity partly by declaring his affinities, and quotation is a way of doing so—but also from its resourcefulness as a weapon. Suppose I am embroiled in a controversy with X, the author of a celebrated but unreadable Lay Sermon; we both claim legitimate descent from a great Protestant poet, and know it will add to the respect others feel for us, to be considered his rightful heir. Now, if I can quote him, in his own voice, or what I convince you to be his true voice, more effectively than X, I will have won two battles at once: at the "tribunal of the soul," I am found adequate; and in the rhetorical contest with my rival contemporaries, I have prevailed for the moment. Any interpretation, of course—like Hazlitt's polemical reading of *The Tempest,* which I discussed in chapter 7—can effect a similar double conquest, but for different reasons. There the debate is manifest. (Why do they fight so about Caliban?—Because Caliban had long been a code-name for the lower classes.—But Coleridge only called him "Jacobin"; why then defend him from *that* charge, if the good of the lower classes is what you have at heart?—It looks as if Coleridge were really trying to attach his new anti-Jacobin allegory to the old fear of those classes, and get the combined force of two prejudices by employing a code-word; but it takes a reply like Hazlitt's to make us see this.) Yet with quotation the terms of the debate may themselves be suppressed. The advantage of quoting is simply the advantage of speed and wit—of a particularly compressed sort of interpretation which requires all the reader's ingenuity to unpack.

If one allows quotation the broad sense in which alone it matters to Hazlitt, it comes to seem closely related to echo and allusion. It is one means of advancing the writer's argument while evoking other strengths as the likeness of his own. And it gives the welcome to tradition without which any claim of originality is null. Hazlitt's ease in quoting for the sake of illustration has appeared plainly enough in the preceding chapters. The few examples that follow, of quotations not identified, but reshaped as allusions for the sake of argument, fall outside the range of what is normally called literary criticism. They suit my purpose the better for that. After all, one can feel the same doubts in reading a great many other eighteenth- and nineteenth-century critics, and everything Longinus says about the connection between memory and genius, quotation and invention, echo and original, has the aim of warning us that the line had better not be drawn anywhere.

Hannah More remarked of Burke: "How closely that fellow reasons in metaphor!"[3] Modern readers, if they find this a surprising thought, still know what kind of excellence it refers to—the intellectual rigor that impresses us, for example, in a sentence by Johnson on the beginning of Savage's life: "Born with a legal claim to honour and to affluence, he was in two months illegitimated by the parliament, and disowned by his mother, doomed to poverty and obscurity, and launched upon the ocean of life, only that he might be swallowed by its quicksands or dashed upon its rocks"; or in a sentence by Henry James, on a mother's shameless apology to the daughter she has neglected and now wishes to desert in good conscience: "She turned this way and that in the predicament she had sought and from which she could neither retreat with grace nor emerge with credit: she draped herself in the tatters of her impudence, postured to her utmost before the last little triangle of cracked glass to which so many fractures had reduced the polished plate of filial superstition."[4] *Close reasoning* here means the joining of discrete elements in a metaphor that houses them all: by elaboration (the quicksands—the rocks; the glass—the fractures), but also by the improvised movement that justifies the introduction of a metaphor in the first place ("doomed" by a strictly verbal parallel brings forth "launched"; "turned this way and that" makes room for "postured" and so for the imaginary mirror). All this we see, with a little conscious effort, and with pangs unknown to the nineteenth-century reader. What it means to have earned a different compliment—"How closely that fellow reasons in allusion"—may have passed beyond our grasp. But unless we try to make sense of Hazlitt's reasoning-in-allusion, we separate him from a virtue that he ranked very high, and possessed in a high degree: what he liked to call, quoting Dryden, the "o'erinforming power" of style.

I start with an illustration of reasoning loosely, taken not from

Hazlitt but from a biography of him. It should be plain at the outset
that there is nothing intrinsically fine about an allusion; used as a
make-weight in any rhetorical balance of fear, to lighten the pretensions of the reader by loading him down with a sense of the author's
learning, it is a harmless sort of bullying: among the academic vices,
it offers a more limited assault than shouting from the lectern, with
a more visible termination than footnotes in Sanskrit. The biographer in this instance, Herschel Baker, has been discussing the effect
of Burke's writings on the debate over the French Revolution, an
effect Hazlitt described as "tremendous, fatal, such as no exertion
of wit or knowledge or genius can ever counteract or atone for." Yet
Baker himself has a good deal of sympathy for Burke, and this is
important to my sense of the allusion's misfiring; for he writes of
Burke: "His sentence was for open war."[5] A careless reader can be
expected to go past it quickly, thinking it perhaps an allusion. But
the careful reader, who pauses long enough to recall the precise context of the allusion, will pause long enough also to construe its translation into the new setting and to ask what is gained. The original
speaker of the line is Moloch, in Book II of *Paradise Lost,* and he
says it in the course of another debate about war and revolution.
The fallen angels in Pandaemonium are wondering how to deport
themselves now that Heaven is lost: Belial wants them to plead for
God's mercy; Mammon, to make Hell inhabitable; but Moloch urges
a renewal of war against Heaven—"My sentence is for open war."

What has all this to do with Burke? How seriously does Baker
intend the comparison between Burke and Moloch, and how seriously can we take it? A scholar of anti-Jacobin sympathies, he probably did not mean to imply a likeness between Burke and the least
repentant of the crew assembled in Hell; on the contrary, with more
care for the parallels, he would doubtless have preferred to compare
the revolutionary metaphysicians of France with Satan, Moloch, and
the rest: if we regard Burke as a hero of legitimacy, and really want
to translate him into the scheme of *Paradise Lost,* we shall align him
with Abdiel. The wrong comparison occurred, however, because this
critic *as he wrote* was not aware just what his source did with the
words, "His sentence was for open war"; or if he knew, he chose not
to think about it. This sort of occurrence, multiplied many times,
gives us the "quotey" atmosphere that is so familiar a feature of modern criticism.

An example like this can remind us by negative instruction what
happens in a genuine allusion. It will be worked out closely enough

for the chosen text to resonate fully both in its original and in its adopted context. Always, the allusion thinks about what it is up to, and lets us see it thinking. Whether the author is conscious of his source may be a less important question than it seems: in either case the act of appropriation brings a new gravity to the new context. The tact is there, and the impression of choice. One is not looking at a chance ornament that the author lunged for with one hand while keeping his fingers crossed in the other. Allusion may therefore be our best evidence of a quality for which we have as yet no good name—a poor one which will serve for the moment is *rhetorical density*—in the command of which Hazlitt's only rivals in prose are Burke and Ruskin. So one can turn De Quincey's comment around, and see it as a resentful version of the praise Hazlitt awarded to Milton: "The quantity of art in him shews the strength of his genius." How richly Hazlitt himself merits this praise will emerge from any careful survey of his practice.

My first example comes from a long footnote midway through the essay "On Paradox and Common-place," on the propensity in all theoretical philosophers, all extreme partisans of a single theory, to react extravagantly against the errors into which their own extravagance has plunged them. The note follows this sentence: "Jacobins or Anti-Jacobins—outrageous advocates for anarchy and licentiousness, or flaming apostles of political persecution—always violent and vulgar in their opinions, they oscillate, with a giddy and sickening motion, from one absurdity to another, and expiate the follies of youth by the heartless vices of advancing age." So far, Hazlitt gives no quotation marks; yet we are aware already of Milton's fallen angels arguing to "no end, in wand'ring mazes lost," and, in much closer reach, Pope's vision of the Hags' Sabbath in the "Epistle to a Lady":

> At last, to follies Youth could scare defend,
> 'Tis half their Age's prudence to pretend;
> Ashamed to own they gave delight before,
> Reduc'd to feign it, when they give no more.

The sentence is quite casual—a passing move, nothing more—and its allusions seem contained in the compositional texture, without ambition for a life of their own. The comparisons with Milton and Pope are far from pointed; they are thought, and felt; not false, but not trying to be significantly true. In the footnote however, there is a sustained allusion, capped by a quotation, which convinces us without mere muscular display that this was the writer's only means of working his will.

> To give the modern reader *un petit aperçu* of the tone of literary conversation about five or six and twenty years ago, I remember being present in a large party composed of men, women, and children, in which two persons of remarkable candour and ingenuity were labouring (as hard as if they had been paid for it) to prove that all prayer was a mode of dictating to the Almighty, and an arrogant assumption of superiority. A gentleman present said, with great simplicity and *naïveté,* that there was one prayer which did not strike him as coming under this description, and being asked what that was, made answer, "The samaritan's—'Lord be merciful to me a sinner!'" This appeal by no means settled the sceptical dogmatism of the two disputants, and soon after the proposer of the objection went away; on which one of them observed with great marks of satisfaction and triumph—"I am afraid we have shocked that gentleman's prejudices." This did not appear to me at that time quite the thing, and this happened in the year 1794. Twice has the iron entered my soul. Twice have the dastard, vaunting, venal crew gone over it; once as they went forth, conquering and to conquer, with reason by their side, glittering like a faulchion, trampling on prejudices and marching fearlessly on in the work of regeneration; once again, when they returned with retrograde steps, like Cacus's oxen dragged backward by the heels, to the den of Legitimacy, "rout on rout, confusion worse confounded," with places and pensions and the Quarterly Review dangling from their pockets, and shouting "Deliverance for mankind," for "the worst, the second fall of man." Yet I have endured all this marching and countermarching of poets, philosophers, and politicians over my head as well as I could, like "the camomoil that thrives, the more 'tis trod upon." By Heavens, I think, I'll endure it no longer! (VIII, 152)

Here, in small, is the adventure of a generation of poets, philosophers, perfectibilitarians of every sort, Socratic and Pantisocratic, as they sally out to do battle with the enemy and return in defeat (which having changed sides they call victory), while Hazlitt stands watching at the center of the turbulence, somewhere between dissent and subordination, between paradox and commonplace. There are in fact several interlinked allusions; but the drama of this passage owes everything to an image which is made distinct in the quotation, "rout on rout, confusion worse confounded": a fragment of what old Chaos says to Satan about the War in Heaven.

> I know thee, stranger, who thou art,
> That mighty leading Angel, who of late
> Made head against Heav'n's King, though overthrown.
> I saw and heard, for such a numerous Host
> Fled not in silence through the frighted deep
> With ruin upon ruin, rout on rout,
> Confusion worse confounded.

The quotation gives us a picture of Hazlitt, neither so ancient nor so durable as Night, unable to tolerate the war-whoops and lesser noisemaking of the marchers and counter-marchers, who since they *back into* Hell can think it Heaven. But the grotesque power of his mockery—"places and pensions and the Quarterly Review dangling from their pockets"—suggests also an oblique homage to Pope, whose full-scale allusion to Milton appeared in *The Dunciad*. In this way Hazlitt gathers strength as he goes, by recognizing allies in the middle distance as well those he meant to salute from afar; or rather, his memory seems to do the work for him, as if, coming late in history, it had a certain itinerary to complete.[6]

Some readers may now be ready to protest. It does seem a very full tableau for a single quotation to sketch; if a footnote takes so much art, how can imaginative prose, especially a headlong energetic prose like Hazlitt's, ever get off the ground; for this (the protest concludes) is the under-song of writing, which only criticism troubles about. The objection sounds plausible. Yet apply it to a poetic allusion, which we recognize also as a critical act, and it loses its plausibility. The double standard says a great deal about our distance from Hazlitt. He wrote with an ease of reference we are now so far from taking for granted that when we see it in an older writer of prose, our daily practice gets in the way of our understanding. The impulse that makes us say, or want to say, "He couldn't have worked in all that," belongs to the same family of reflexes at whose bidding we write "the poet T. S. Eliot," to be certain of every reader's confidence. At the very least we want to identify all our quotations. But Hazlitt knew his audience better than that, and had no need to apologize for a strategy of allusion that prose and poetry can share. To quote or allude is, in certain circumstances, an act of invention. And the same goes for any argument from a received trope which modifies, extends, or subverts the trope itself.

A simple instance of this sort of argument may be taken from Hazlitt's debate with Southey over the reasonableness of timely conversions. Southey wrote in defense of his change of heart: "They [the Dissenters] had turned their faces towards the East in the morning, to worship the rising sun, and in the evening they were looking eastward still, obstinately affirming that still the sun was there. I, on the contrary, altered my position as the world went round." But for Hazlitt this metaphor was adaptable to different ends, and by directing it to them he could seem to observe the natural figurative logic of language itself. "It is not always," he replies, "that a simile runs on all-fours; but this does," and one can imagine him thinking here with a murmur of triumph, The Lord has delivered him into my hands: "The sun, indeed, passes from the East to the West, but it rises in the East again; yet Mr. Southey is still looking in the West—for his pension."

Open battles of so blunt a character will seldom tempt either side into the dramatic subtlety of allusion. But to a mind certain of the advantage it gets in arguing from a received trope, allusion will always seem an attractive way of crowding an argument and making implicit alliances by an act of invention that looks like an act of recovery. We all know this trick from our intimate experience of sarcasm in conversation; as when I say to a friend, "Our foreign policy works!" and he replies, "Yes, like the future." Hazlitt, playing with Southey's revolutionary sundown, was correcting a metaphor to make its interest flow all his way, without quite having to allude. Yet this kind of maneuver shares the spirit of allusion. How much so will appear from a similar effect in two sentences of Hazlitt's *Table-Talk* essay on "On Patronage and Puffing," where he imagines the late-won pride of an unhappy dependent. "You are not hailed ashore, as you had supposed, by these kind friends, as a mutual triumph after all your struggles and their exertions on your behalf. It is a piece of presumption in you to be seen walking on *terra-firma;* you are required, at the risk of their friendship, to be always swimming in troubled waters, that they may have the credit of throwing out ropes, and sending out life-boats to you, without ever bringing you ashore." One's first thought in reading this is that the situation it describes hardly answers to any Hazlitt could have experienced in his own life. A second thought is that it does, however, fit the life of Johnson; indeed it feels like a conscious allusion to his letter to Lord Chesterfield, which includes the phrase about a patron as "one who looks with unconcern on a man struggling for life in the water, and, when he has reached ground, encumbers him with help." Boswell's *Life,* which first printed the letter, was among Hazlitt's favorite books, even if it would have not have seemed to him in a class with Shakespeare or Wordsworth; not, that is, a book which he could properly introduce to readers without quotation marks. But though Boswell may have made a still deeper impression on him than he knew, I prefer to think of his passage as an improvised cadenza on the same metaphor, by a mind in love with metaphorical thinking, and having the letter as part of its accidental store. At any rate one can say that the Patronized Drowning Man is being employed in a way that agrees with Johnson, and with Johnson's context. The reverberations are full where those of Burke-as-Moloch are empty.

There is no clear way of distinguishing unconsicous allusion, or allusion that seems to do its work as part of an author's second nature, from *echo* in the sense of that word defined by John Hollander: "echo . . . represents or substitutes for allusion as allusion does for quotation."[7] In practice the first two often merge into a single effect since a reader can estimate how well an echo conceals its work of substitution only from his judgment of the "keeping" between the text and its new context; and nothing but the poetic intelligence every reader creates from the sum of his reading will decide whether a given allusion ought to be honored with the associations of artful distance that the idea of echo includes. As readers we do not sophisticate our guesswork beyond some such rule as this: we want to interpret a passage as echo when by its sound an unsuspected accompaniment is brought into being, which at last we come to think necessary. So, when Hazlitt criticizes the style of the *Rambler* in the style of the *Lives of the Poets,* we hear a profound echo of the later Johnson's manner, cadence, and sense. And when he ventures an echo of poetry it has the power of his best quotations. Consider the following sentence on Coleridge, part of a longer passage I have already quoted from *The Spirit of the Age:* "He who has seen a mouldering tower by the side of a crystal lake, hid by the mist, but glittering in the wave below, may conceive the dim, gleaming, uncertain intelligence of his eye." This presents a familiar array of Coleridgean effects; there, warns Hazlitt, you see what became of his flashing eyes, his floating hair; in their place now is the eye of the mariner, "dim, gleaming, uncertain," and fixed on whomever he encounters. Yet allusion gives the full measure of Hazlitt's genius under different conditions, where several quoted passages can be heard working in concert, all to a single purpose because they direct us to contexts generically allied with each other.

If, as Walter Benjamin argued, quotation always implies an interruption of context,[8] then this sort of composite allusion proceeds by a more complex and interscored series of tonal effects. A writer, gifted with the sense of perfect pitch, interrupts several melodies in which only an ear like his can detect the same signature; he makes of his own recoveries a style we are tempted to describe as pastiche, except that the result adds a new eloquence to what we have known before; with the result that his listening somehow improves ours, and at the same time compels our admiration for the power implied in any sustained act of attentiveness. In the following passage of an 1817 polemic against Southey, it seems to me that Hazlitt does all this. His interruptions have the effect of claiming not only the words but the character who first spoke them for the new context into which they are suddenly imported. The central device of the passage is the personified idea of Legitimacy ("Fine word, Legitimate," Hazlitt says in another place, quoting). The idea is unmasked as Duessa of *The Faerie Queene,* and yet she dominates the allusion very unexclusively. Among the other voices clearly audible are Hamlet in his first and third soliloquies, Leontes in one of his rages, and Timon, self-exiled from the community of men, hoarding his gold and hates. Modern criticism has of course drawn a good many connections among these characters, but none more inevitable than what Hazlitt tells of, as he writes and quotes, answers and listens. A pedant fully imbued with the De Quincean spirit of cavilling might object that the passage is *nothing but* a tissue of paraphrase and quotation. My point is that by the end, as between Hazlitt and the "sources" he gets for kin by serving them as a satisfactory host, we no longer know which is which, and no longer care to ask.

> [Mr. Southey's] engagement to his first love, the Republic, was only upon liking; his marriage to Legitimacy is, *for better, for worse,* and nothing but death shall part them. Our simple Laureate was sharp upon his hoyden Jacobin mistress, who brought him no dowry, neither place nor pension. . . . He divorced her, in short, for nothing but the spirit and success with which she resisted the fraud and force to which the old bawd Legitimacy was forever resorting to overpower her resolution and fidelity. He said she was a virago, a cunning gipsey, always in broils about her honour and the inviolability of her person, and always getting the better in them, furiously scratching the face or cruelly tearing off the hair of the said pimping old lady, who would never let her alone, night or day. But since her foot slipped one day on the ice, and the detest-

able old hag tripped up her heels, and gave her up to the kind keeping of the Allied Sovereigns, Mr. Southey has devoted himself to her more fortunate and wealthy rival: he is become uxorious in his second matrimonial connexion; and though his false Duessa has turned out a very witch, a foul, ugly witch, drunk with insolence, mad with power, a griping, rapacious wretch, bloody, luxurious, wanton, malicious, not sparing steel, or poison, or gold, to gain her ends—bringing famine, pestilence, and death in her train—infecting the air with her thoughts, killing the beholders with her looks, claiming mankind as her property, and using them as her slaves—driving every thing before her, and playing the devil wherever she comes, Mr. Southey sticks to her in spite of every thing, and for very shame lays his head in her lap, paddles with the palms of both her hands, inhales her hateful breath, leers in her eyes, and whispers in her ears, calls her little fondling names, Religion, Morality, and Social Order, takes for his motto,

> "Be to her faults a little blind,
> Be to her virtues very kind"—

sticks close to his filthy bargain, and will not give her up, because she keeps him, and he is down in her will. Faugh!

> "What's here?
> Gold! yellow, glittering, precious gold!
> ———The wappened window,
> Whom the spittle house and ulcerous sores
> Would heave the gorge at, this embalms and spices
> To the April day again."

The above passage is, we fear, written in the style of Aretin, which Mr. Southey condemns in the *Quarterly*. It is at least a very sincere style. . . . Why should not one make a sentence of a page long, out of the feelings of one's whole life.   (VII, 193-94)

"That sentence," remarked Keats, "about making a Page of the feelings of a whole life appears to me like a Whale's back in the Sea of Prose."[9] It is true Southey's line on sedition, which required that the rights of certain Englishmen be held in suspense, would have shut down the publications that kept Hazlitt a little ahead of his debts. He was fighting for life. Yet sentences like his are made out of a lifetime of reading; and who that has listened can say where reading ends and feeling begins?[10]

BURKE

Burke was the great soul whose echo returned constantly to Hazlitt's thoughts, presided over his inward debates on the idea of equality, and summoned his prose to its keener intensities. From the first he tried to acknowledge Burke's power in a way that would temper its authority. His veneration is for Burke's writings; his contest is with the figure that looms behind the writings; he can therefore imagine a great soul who is at once his judge and antagonist, but the latter only when he appears in a corruptible form outside his work. Two tactics were open to Hazlitt for making his engagement both fair-minded, and sometimes favorable to himself. He could read Burke as a "mighty opposite," to be struggled against sincerely because he serves as a touchstone of good faith to those who encounter him fairly. Or he could read him, not as a spokesman on certain topics, where he would always be unassailable, but as the inspired voice through whom a story is told, in his case a story about the love of power. In fact both tactics were helpful, at different times. But the first is perhaps the more pertinent to Hazlitt's early feelings about Burke since it employs him specifically as a touchstone of disinterestedness: "it has always been with me a test of the sense and candour of any one belonging to the opposite party, whether he allowed Burke to be a great man." Great, in this sentence, means greatly imaginative, as those alone can be whose success in power indemnifies us for their failures in knowledge.

The distinction between the literature of knowledge and the literature of power, familiar to scholars of romanticism from a great many sources,[11] was first ventured *in those terms* by Hazlitt, in some sentences of "Why the Arts are not Progressive?" which he cut from the *Round Table* version of that essay. "We judge of science by the number of effects produced—of art by the energy which produces them. The one is knowledge—the other power." But in the "Character of Mr. Burke," written several years earlier, by a man still in his twenties, the same contrast had already begun to emerge.

> There are two very different ends which a man of genius may propose to himself either in writing or speaking, and which will accordingly give birth to very different styles. He can have but one of these two objects; either to enrich or strengthen the mind; either to furnish us with new ideas, to lead the mind into new trains of thought, to which it was before unused, and which it was incapa-

ble of striking out for itself; or else to collect and embody what we already knew, to rivet our old impressions more deeply; to make what was before plain still plainer, and to give that which was familiar all the effect of novelty. In the one case we receive an accession to the stock of our ideas; in the other, an additional degree of life and energy is infused into them: our thoughts continue to flow in the same channels, but their pulse is quickened and invigorated. I do not know how to distinguish these different styles better than by calling them severally the inventive and refined, or the impressive and vigorous style. (VII, 303)

On the face of it this looks more like a comparison of wit and wisdom, or the novel and the familiar, than of knowledge and power: if we transpose it into the last vocabulary, both sides of the comparison evidently have their shares of both knowledge and power. In fact Hazlitt must have been thinking largely of eighteenth-century instances. To enrich the mind by furnishing it with new ideas and leading it into new trains of thought, would do as praise of works as different from each other as *The Rape of the Lock* and *Political Justice*. On the other hand, to strengthen the mind by collecting or embodying what we already knew, and riveting our old impressions more deeply, is the virtue at once of Gray's Churchyard Elegy and of Burke's pre-1789 speeches on American Taxation, on Conciliation with America, and on Economic Reform. Yet when we try to apply "inventive and refined" vs. "impressive and vigorous" to Burke's writings as a whole, we realize how completely he resists the exclusions these categories were meant to enforce. Hazlitt, because he knows this, has to add that Burke "united the two extremes of refinement and strength in a higher degree than any other writer whatever." But as soon as the admission is made, other categories with more efficient border-guards must seem better equipped to hold him.

"Refined" drops out of the description, and Burke appears as at once inventive, impressive, and vigorous, in the essay-digressions that Hazlitt cannot help devoting to him for the rest of his career. These are apt to occur anywhere, but the most memorable are in "On the Prose-Style of Poets," "On Reading Old Books," "Arguing in a Circle," and the review of Coleridge's *Biographia*. In all these places Hazlitt leaves no doubt that for him, Burke's is the style of power, the whole figure of his prose darting out always abruptly, in its sudden flexions, and alternately towering above the reader: "forked and playful as the lightening, crested like the serpent." But the play in

Burke's writing is always a play of contrasts; before him, and lacking these, the face of nature had never yet appeared so expressive. One side of the contrast emerges from Burke's willingness to be *not* always grand: "He delivered plain things on a plain ground; but when he rose, there was no end of his flights and circumgyrations." The same quality of dramatic variability is a master-clue to his pre-eminence as a genius of prose; for his style comes as near as possible to poetry without ever tipping over the verge.

> It has the solidity, and sparkling effect of the diamond: all other *fine writing* is like French paste or Bristol-stones in the comparison. Burke's style is airy, flighty, adventurous, but it never loses sight of the subject; nay, is always in contrast with, and derives its increased or varying impulse from it. It may be said to pass yawning gulfs "on the unstedfast footing of a spear": still it has an actual resting-place and tangible support under it—it is not suspended on nothing. It differs from poetry, as I conceive, like the chamois from the eagle: it climbs to an almost equal height, touches upon a cloud, overlooks a precipice, is picturesque, sublime—but all the while, instead of soaring through the air, it stands upon a rocky cliff, clambers up by abrupt and intricate ways, and browzes on the roughest bark, or crops the tender flower. (XII, 10)

We feel its power both from the refusal to be deterred even in the rockiest terrain, and in the mastery with which it covers so wide a range.

That the admiration we feel for such power might be disinterested, and never expose us to the practical effects of persuasion, was a dream of Hazlitt's youth, still enchanting when he proposed his test of candor in the "Character of Mr. Burke," but dismissed in the essays "On Reading Old Books" and "Arguing in a Circle," as impossible to any reader less strong-minded than himself. The metaphor he adopts in both places implies that the reading of Burke can serve as a homeopathic cure, and even strengthen the patient's convictions by introducing him early to the most virulent force that threatens them. But this only works where the resistance is high enough from the first, as it was in Hazlitt. "I did not care for his doctrines," he writes in "On Reading Old Books." "I was then, and am still, proof against their contagion; but I admired the author, and was considered as a not very staunch partisan of the opposite side, though I thought myself that an abstract proposition was one thing—a masterly transition, a brilliant metaphor, another." The separation, as "Arguing in a Circle" makes clear, is less easy to enforce for those whose contest with Burke is less spirited than his own. Burke's adamantine tropes, forged from the long practice of oratory, and tempered by one continuous allusion to Milton, which made Paris in 1789 the focus of an old anarchy sprung loose out of Pandaemonium—these, to other readers, would be literally death-dealing: so many young men would enlist, so many each year be pressed into their country's service, because of them.

> The madness of genius was necessary to second the madness of a court; his flaming imagination was the torch that kindled the smouldering fire in the inmost sanctuary of pride and power, and spread havoc, dismay, and desolation through the world. The light of his imagination, sportive, dazzling, beauteous as it seemed, was followed by the stroke of death. It so happens that I myself have played all my life with his forked shafts unhurt, because I had a metaphysical clue to carry off the noxious particles, and let them sink into the earth, like drops of water. But the English nation are not a nation of metaphysicians.   (XIX, 271)

The first sentence affords a striking anticipation of the passage from Hazlitt's *Conversations of Northcote* which I quoted in chapter 4, where he spoke of Rousseau as a kind of Prometheus. Burke looms up here as a similar figure, but belonging to the party of "pride and power" instead of humanity—a Prometheus, by ambition distorted into his opposite, and visible as such only to one who possesses "a metaphysical clue." In view of the resemblance it is not surprising that Hazlitt should sometimes have felt Burke's "jealousy of Rousseau was one chief cause of his opposition to the French Revolution." In a more savage mood he is capable of insisting on Rousseau as the *only* cause. But we should pause a little over Hazlitt's quick escape by way of metaphysics, for the passage and the concern it suggests are deeper than this lets them seem. What Burke, Rousseau, and Hazlitt all share is a fascination with the power words exert over their readers, in action, in feeling, and in the habits of reading and writing that have their event in these. Only a reader of a genius masterful enough to compete with that of the author he admires, can learn not to read him innocently, and thus not be influenced by him where he needs not to be. The area of choice is limited: if it were otherwise, there would be no fascination and no readers. Burke was able to mark the limit of Rousseau's effect on him, and at last to become Rousseau's antithesis in the same way that Hazlitt, "playing with his forked shafts unhurt," emerges intact from his contest with Burke and speaks of the "noxious particles" as a matter for concern to other persons. Only this sort of victory makes a writer bold enough to reduce the power of another writer to a question of style. And even so the victory can never be complete—something we cannot help seeing in Hazlitt's many returns to Burke, as to a case that may never be closed.

Read an author like Burke and you place yourself under his spell. You find, as Johnson observed in a different connection, that "the power of example is so great, as to take possession of the memory by a kind of violence, and produce effects almost without the intervention of the will";[12] that this power is as strong in the memory of texts as in the memory of events; and that it is never more persuasive than in the examples laid down for us by an interested historian. Such was the example of Marie Antoinette as Burke presented her in the *Reflections*.

> It is now sixteen or seventeen years since I saw the queen of France, then the dauphiness, at Versailles; and surely never lighted on this orb, which she hardly seemed to touch, a more delightful vision. I saw her just above the horizon, decorating and cheering the elevated sphere she just began to move in,—glittering like the morning-star, full of life, and splendor, and joy. Oh! what a revolution! and what an heart must I have, to contemplate without emotion that elevation and that fall! Little did I dream when she added titles of veneration to those of enthusiastic, distant, respectful love, that she should ever be obliged to carry the sharp antidote against disgrace concealed in that bosom; little did I dream that I should have lived to see such disasters fallen upon her in a nation of gallant men, in a nation of men of honour and of cavaliers. I thought ten thousand swords must have leaped from their scabbards to avenge even a look that threatened her with insult.—But the age of chivalry is gone.—That of sophisters, œconomists, and calculators, has succeeded; and the glory of Europe is extinguished for ever. Never, never more, shall we behold that generous loyalty to rank and sex, that proud submission, that dignified obedience, that subordination of the heart, which kept alive, even in servitude itself, the spirit of an exalted freedom. The unbought grace of life, the cheap defence of nations, the nurse of manly sentiment and heroic enterprize is gone! It is gone, that sensibility of principle, that chastity of honour, which felt a stain like a wound, which inspired courage whilst it mitigated ferocity, which ennobled whatever it touched, and under which vice itself lost half its evil, by losing all its grossness.[13]

It may have been impossible for a radical of Hazlitt's time to read this without thinking that pension prose had here done its finest, just as it is impossible for an American to celebrate it now, when it carries so peculiar a savor of the flowers the American South would choose to garland its catastrophe seventy years later. But while conscious that this was Burke at his most overstrained and sentimental, all his antagonists knew that it was the single passage they could not avoid confronting. It was the occasion of Paine's famous rebuke, that Burke pitied the plumage but forgot the dying bird. It caused Mary Wollstonecraft to exclaim, "Infatuated moralist!" And it brought from Mackintosh the splendid anti-rhetorical rejoinder, "Absolved from the laws of vulgar method, he can advance a groupe of magnificent horrors to make a breach in our hearts, through which the most undisciplined rabble of arguments may enter in triumph."[14]

Yet Hazlitt, alone of Burke's rivals, saw that an anti-rhetorical prejudice would be no help in defeating him. If the issue was power, then the power of rhetoric was naturally in league with whichever side could discover the most intensely vivid "example." One could not hope to defeat Burke by remarking that he broke all the rules of a game bounded by abstract principles. For it was never that. Radical principles too are built up from sympathy, and sympathy from the vivid and particular instance that demands to be taken to heart. Hazlitt thus is in a position to ask the hard question: not, Why does Burke give comfort to his new allies, the aristocracy, when he appeals to something other than their intelligence?; but, Why has he succeeded in converting those who need not be his allies since they have no clear interest in the affairs of France? It was Burke's effect on the latter that gave England a counter-revolutionary policy, from his ability to persuade moderate Whigs as well as Tories. But Hazlitt sees that Burke, with all his powers, can expect to reach even farther down than this; for curiously, of all who take up interests foreign to themselves, none are more generous than those who have nothing to their name. So, writing "On the Connexion between Toad-Eaters and Tyrants," Hazlitt recalls the sense in which even the love of power is disinterested; having begun a paragraph with the assertion "Man is a toad-eating animal," he continues:

> It is not he alone, who wears the golden crown, that is proud of it: the wretch who pines in the dungeon, and in chains, is dazzled with it; and if he could but shake off his own fetters, would care little about the wretches whom he left behind him, so that he might have an opportunity, on being set free himself, of gazing at this glit-

tering gew-gaw "on some high holiday of once a year." The slave, who has no other hope or consolation, clings to the apparition of royal magnificence, which insults his misery and his despair; stares through the hollow eyes of famine at the insolence of pride and luxury which has occasioned it, and hugs his chains the closer, because he has nothing else left.   (VII, 148)

The radical investigators of political justice, expert at disenchantment, suppose that once they have demonstrated to the slave that he acts a subordinate part in someone else's drama, they have done all that is necessary to assure his revolt. But in fact this part is the only one he knows, and he takes his satisfaction within it as well as he can. To ask him to project himself as the lead in a different drama is to suppose in the common slave an imagination he is no likelier to be possessed of than the common man. Burke's interest in the Queen, on the other hand—or any similar interest, as a reader encounters it—relieves him of responsibility for the first and imaginative moment of sympathy, by showing its workings in another mind. We may then, rich or poor, slaves or freemen, identify with her interests in spite of ourselves, or even in spite of our own, and yet feel that to do so is somehow an act of generosity. We feel this because we see the writer, Burke, who has the imagination we lack, carried away by emotions that evidently surprise even him.

Understanding this in a way others of his party did not, Hazlitt proposed, as the best answer to Burke, not disenchantment but enchantment *on a different principle*. To overthrow the Queen in the minds of readers as well as in fact, some hero or heroine from romance would have to be fitted to the cause of the people themselves. But it was absurd to prescribe a single work, let alone a whole literature, worked out on such a system. These could only emerge from the chance encounters of genius with its own sovereign but unpredictable sympathies; for only thus had the figure of Marie Antoinette been stamped upon Burke's mind, to be molded after sixteen years into tropes more unconquerable than herself. The majesty of Burke's writing, unlike the Queen herself, can vindicate every wish contrary to the event, and provide for every future myth: from "a thousand swords must have leaped from their scabbards," to "the glory of Europe is extinguished for ever." In a wonderfully sustained passage of "Arguing in a Circle," Hazlitt interprets all Burke's writings on the French Revolution as a deliberate effort to launch a counter-revolution, successful beyond anything else of their sort because they were works of power rather than knowledge.

> He contrived . . . to persuade the people of England that Liberty
> was an illiberal, hollow sound; that humanity was a barbarous
> modern invention, that prejudices were the test of truth; that rea-
> son was a strumpet, and right a fiction. Every other view of the
> subject but his ("so well the tempter glozed") seemed to be with-
> out attraction, elegance, or refinement. Politics became poetry in
> his hands, his sayings passed like proverbs from mouth to mouth.
> . . . Liberty from thenceforward became a low thing: philosophy
> was a spring-nailed, velvet-pawed tyger-cat, with green eyes, watch-
> ing its opportunity to dart upon its prey: humanity was a lurking
> assassin. (XIX, 271–72)

This, as Hazlitt reminds us by his constant reference to literary
devices, only shows the success of all the arts of persuasion working
in concert, but none of it is conceivable from a motive simply of
persuasion. He comes back therefore to the Queen, and her youthful
passage before the eyes of her infatuate, managed as nicely as if it
were a stage entrance. But the lesson of the meeting for Hazlitt is
that everything a monarch does must be theatrical, in that it takes
place at a level above the audience, who if addressed can never reply
in the currency of familiar exchange: any effort they make in that
direction will only be translated into the language of deference. Beyond his memory of the Queen, what then was Burke's motive for
reversing history? Pressed for a second or third answer, Hazlitt will
call it jealousy of Rousseau and the Encyclopaedists, who "had la-
mentably got the start of him"; as Mary Wollstonecraft, with more
complacency, had called it reluctance to share the celebrity of a
great cause with *anyone:* "had the English in general reprobated
the French revolution, you would have stood forth alone, and been
the avowed Goliath of liberty."[15] Hazlitt, as he proceeds with "Arguing in a Circle," suggests an analysis more in consonance with the
rest of his criticism. As a man of genius, Burke naturally sought to
communicate his strongest impression, to possess his reader at once
and utterly, and by doing so to render a powerful creature more powerful still by words.

> Half the business was done by his description of the Queen of
> France. It was an appeal to all women of quality; to all who were,
> or would be thought, cavaliers or men of honour; to all who were
> admirers of beauty, or rank, or sex. Yet what it had to do with the
> question, it would be difficult to say. If a woman is handsome . . .
> it is no reason why she should poison her husband, or betray a
> country. If, instead of being young, beautiful, and free of manners,

Marie Antoinette had been old, ugly, and chaste, all this mischief had been prevented. The author of the Reflections had seen or dreamt he saw a most delightful vision sixteen years before, which had thrown his brain into a ferment; and he was determined to throw . . . the world into one too. It was a theme for a copy of verses, or a romance; not for a work in which the destinies of mankind were to be weighed. Yet she was the Helen that opened another Iliad of woes; and the world has paid for that accursed glance at youthful beauty with rivers of blood. If there was any one of sufficient genius now to deck out some Castilian maid, or village girl in the Army of the Faith, in all the colours of fancy, to reflect her image in a thousand ages and hearts, making a saint and a martyr of her; turning loyalty into religion, and the rights and liberties of the Spanish nation, and of all other nations, into a mockery, a bye-word, and a bugbear, how soon would an end be put to Mr. Canning's present *bizarre* (almost afraid to know itself) situation! How gladly he would turn round on the pivot of his forced neutrality, and put all his drooping tropes and figures on their splendid war-establishment again!   (XIX, 272)

Had Canning been moved by one scruple the less or, what Hazlitt describes as the same thing, one Spanish heroine the more, he might have launched, with a believing heart, a patriotic war in defense of the true Spain and for the good of England. For that to happen only a myth-maker of Burke's stature was wanting. In the absence of one, however, Canning acted up to a principle really alien to his political instincts, heedless of the love of power that shaped his career; his present situation is *"bizarre* (almost afraid to know itself)" because he is too shallow a rhetorician to sway either himself or others with a power that takes the place of knowledge. His speeches may have—to recall for a moment Hazlitt's characterization from *The Eloquence of the British Senate*—"a certain ambitious tip-toe elevation." But that makes for a balance easily shaken, and a poor conformity of the body's parts with the design of the whole. "His eloquence is like a bright, sharp-pointed sword, which, owing to its not being made of very stout metal, bends and gives way, and seems ready to snap asunder at every stroke; and he is perpetually in danger of having it wrested out of his hands." It would take an eloquence crested like the serpent—capable of *glozing well,* in efforts at conversion that tempted the breach of every precedent among the listener's beliefs—to animate the "drooping tropes and figures" of a politician like Canning.

A maker of grand and influential tropes need never be praised for his consistency. In the review of the *Biographia* Hazlitt flatly states that "Mr. Burke, the opponent of the American War—and Mr. Burke, the opponent of the French Revolution, are not the same person, but opposite persons—not opposite persons only, but deadly enemies." Two views of Burke's change of allegiance have always been plausible. According to the first (widely held by reformers of Hazlitt's generation), some fatal turn of Burke's own sympathies must have been necessary to produce so determined an enmity to the French in so steadfast a friend of the American Revolution. To confirm this, Hazlitt felt it was enough to try the "vulgar and palpable test of comparison. Even Mr. Fox's enemies, we think, allow *him* the praise of consistency. *He* asserted the rights of the people in the American war, and continued to assert them in the French Revolution. He remained visible in his place; and spoke, throughout, the same principles in the same language." But suppose that the French Revolution presented a movement in human affairs entirely different from the American, that altered all one's surroundings and therefore the very meaning of what it was to stand in one place. This is a second plausible view, which Burke's writings fostered and which in turn has been put to excellent use in the defense of Burke. Here the American appears as a bourgeois revolution, a movement of national sovereignty that formed part of the design of a particular social class, but preserving after the break the same structure of loyalties, inherited sentiments and affections, which were all but nominally the most important links to its parent country, and indeed to the rest of Europe. The French Revolution was on this analysis a definitive break, not the reform of a society attained by art but its complete destruction, for the sake of a society still only ideal, and based on abstract rights. A weakness of the first view is that it ignores the extent to which two revolutions addressing their constituencies in the same language may really have meant different things. A weakness of the second—perhaps more important to recall, because this is essentially the modern view—is that it treats the French Revolution Burke knew in the *Reflections* as if its salient facts were the killing of a hereditary monarch and the ensuing terror. But England had itself survived regicide, with a constitution Burke professed to admire above all other artifices of human government; and besides, he wrote his book before the terror, and before the peace with France was a regicide peace.

These views have to be mentioned chiefly because at different times Hazlitt was convinced by versions of both. Yet the Burke we have heard him praise as a figure of power requires neither as an apology for the *Reflections*. Indeed, in another passage of his *Eloquence of the British Senate*—the passage I quoted in chapter 2, which concludes "Solid reason means nothing more than being carried away by our passions"—he had located Burke's greatness in a skeptical indifference to metaphysics and a contempt for thoroughly codified policy of any sort. Hazlitt there sees him as having no use for consistent principles, except as a response to some great challenge, and subject to revision by a great challenge of a different sort. Of course, this may leave Burke as only the most complex exponent of the "definitive break" view, but anyway it does not leave him a vulgar pragmatist. In the passage Hazlitt presents him as a *true* metaphysician, who recognized that the rules we construct and positions we occupy always presume our ability to separate differences of degree from differences of kind, while history is always changing what we interpret as a kind.

I cannot see how to reconcile this early skeptical questioning of "solid reason" with Hazlitt's later charge, that Burke was a court sycophant who opposed the revolution because he would rather be doing mischief than doing nothing; that it was never sympathy but only the premeditated decision to "palliate a falsehood," which drew him from old alliances; and that he sank into deserved neglect because he was rightly seen as a man whose reason had been bribed. As portrayed in *The Eloquence of the British Senate*, Burke seems on the contrary an entirely respectable ally of Hume, who also insisted that the proper work of reason was to make us act in accord with our passions. Yet Hazlitt's wish to read the *Reflections* as a conscious betrayal of what Burke knew to be the good cause, probably had its source not in his deeper impressions of the book but rather in a well-earned scorn for those who claimed legitimate descent from it, and a willingness to fight them with any weapon that came to hand. This emerges vividly in part of a note which he omitted from the essay "On Beauty," when he transferred it from the *Examiner* to *The Round Table*.

> [Burke] was at once a liar, a coward, and a slave; a liar to his own heart, a coward to the success of his own cause, a slave to the power he despised. See his Letter about the Duke of Bedford, in which the man gets the better of the sycophant, and he belabours the Duke in good earnest. It is not a source of regret . . . that he closed his eyes on the ruin of liberty, which he had been the principal means of effecting, and of his own projects, at the same time. He did not

live to see that deliverance of mankind, bound hand and foot into the absolute, lasting, inexorable power of Kings and Priests, which [Mr. Southey] has so triumphantly celebrated. He did not live to see the sending of the Liberales of Spain to the gallies, and the liberating of the Afrancesadoes from prison, for which our romantic Laureat, who sees so much farther into futurity than the Edinburgh Reviewers, thanks God. He did not live to read that Sonnet to the King which Mr. Wordsworth has written, in imitation of Milton's sonnet to Cromwell. There is a species of literary prostitution which has sprung up and spread wide in these days, more nauseous and despicable than any recorded in Juvenal. (XX, 405)

His tone for a moment expresses crude pleasure in the consummation of a revenge long delayed. Yet beneath this one hears an unmistakable lament for Burke, as the superior in genius and valor of those who succeeded him.

Burke's most sustained attack on the metaphysicians of revolution, the "grave, demure, insidious, spring-nailed, velvet-pawed, green-eyed philosophers, whether going upon two legs or upon four," appears in the "Letter to a Noble Lord," the work in which he defended himself against the charges levelled by the Duke of Bedford (an aristocratic opponent of the war government of Pitt): first that his pension was undeserved, and second, that it was inconsistent with his policies on Economic Reform. In this letter Burke is intent on substituting the tropes and figures that may dignify an individual, for the statistical records of woe that evoke our compassion for a people; and one hardly expects the sympathy with it that Hazlitt professes, in a note otherwise so unyielding in its bitterness. The "Letter" owed its effect to the picture it gave of a man alone, who from a titanic rage nursed on the fears of isolation and death, lashed out against his foes as if his long agony of life could be vindicated only by this final act. Here was power in its pure state, shorn of the petty vanities of a worldly throne. And yet by this reckoning, Hazlitt's praise of the "Letter" discredits every low name he calls Burke at the start of the passage, since these only amount to a less deferential version of the charges Burke was answering. If the "Letter" is a great work "in good earnest," then Burke's decision to throw his weight on the arbitrary side of the question can be traced to no venal motive or interest. It might even be said that he became a legitimist because it enabled him without a motive to say better things for the established order than it could say for itself. The several tones of Hazlitt's note, which never manage to harmonize with each other—a suggestion that Burke in his most infernal portrait of revolutionaries was most in earnest, but with the smart still lingering of a betrayal now twenty years old—may simply incline us to agree that Hazlitt was right to cut it, and to end his divagations in *The Round Table* on a point of elliptical violence that translates the Latin pronoun, *iste:* "This man,—but enough of him here." The very irresoluteness of the dismissal makes sense of another note, which Hazlitt appended to the "Character of Mr. Burke" in *Political Essays,* and which otherwise might be read as a specimen of detached and self-confident irony. "This character," he recalls, "was written in a fit of extravagant candour, at a time when I thought I could do justice, or more than justice, to an enemy, without betraying a cause." To Hazlitt both the extravagance and the justice had their cost.

THE THEATRE OF HISTORY

A quality Burke shared with the most imaginative of writers, and not with the republicans he was compelled to treat as allies through most of his career, was precisely the "love of power in the mind" that Hazlitt is always speaking of, which "when it comes to be opposed to the spirit of good, and is leagued with the spirit of evil to commit it with greediness, is wickedness." Essentially this is a Satanic disposition: "Power, be thou my object" begins as something different from, but by insensible gradations may be perverted to, "Evil, be thou my good." Hazlitt, who in the *Essay on Human Action* had promised a sequel on power, himself felt the force of *this* principle of action, in politics no less than in prose, and in the form of a Johnsonian demand for subordination as well as a Burkean respect for calendars that refuse to christen the day before yesterday "Year One." We can hardly exaggerate Hazlitt's interest in power; it was a theme he found early, and afterwards never sought in vain; and unless we remember that the interest had at times the shape of a fascination, his thousand-page apology for Napoleon, coming at the end of two decades of minute and personal care for his fortunes, will seem more baffling than it was to Hazlitt's friends.

Leigh Hunt, a political ally Hazlitt never charged with inconsistency except where Napoleon was involved, understood this simple allegiance of his friend's as an earnest submission to temperament, untouchable by the exigencies of reasoned argument. His comments on *The Plain Speaker* agree with Hazlitt in despising Napoleon's enemies, but not in therefore regarding Napoleon's victories as occasions for compelled idolatry. Hunt took particular exception to the strain of overwrought sentiment, so alien to Hazlitt at other times, with which he mingled every reference to his hero. For Napoleon, as Hunt observes in sentences meant for Hazlitt more than for other readers, was himself "a turncoat from the cause" of liberty, or at least one who "never entered sincerely into it," and "freedom will have gained more, after all, from the weakness of lesser men than it would from the strength of the greater one." These strictures bear directly upon Hazlitt's engagement with Burke: "Mr. Hazlitt's love of power [is] more on a par with his love of truth than he may chuse to discover."[16] He cites as evidence Hazlitt's extravagant fondness for Burke, and, in particular, his praise of the climactic paragraph of the "Letter to a Noble Lord." Here is the passage which Hunt thought could only be admired by a man in whom the love of power was strong:

Such are *their* ideas; such *their* religion; and such *their* law. But as to *our* country and *our* race, as long as the well-compacted structure of our church and state, the sanctuary, the holy of holies of that ancient law, defended by reverence, defended by power—a fortress at once and a temple—shall stand inviolate on the brow of the British Sion; as long as the British Monarchy—not more limited than fenced by the orders of the State—shall, like the proud Keep of Windsor, rising in the majesty of proportion, and girt with the double belt of its kindred and coeval towers; as long as this awful structure shall oversee and guard the subjected land, so long the mounds and dykes of the low, fat, Bedford level will have nothing to fear from all the pickaxes of all the levellers of France. As long as our Sovereign Lord the King, and his faithful subjects, the Lords and Commons of this realm—the triple cord which no man can break; the solemn, sworn, constitutional frank-pledge of this nation; the firm guarantees of each other's being, and each other's rights; the joint and several securities, each in its place and order, for every kind and every quality of property and dignity—As long as these endure, so long the Duke of Bedford is safe: and we are all safe together—the high from the heights of envy and the spoliations of rapacity; the low from the iron hand of oppression and the insolent spurn of contempt. Amen! and so be it: and so it will be,

"*Dum domus Aeneae Capitoli immobile saxum*
Accolet; imperiumque pater Romanus habebit."[17]

The grave testamentary oath would have earned Hazlitt's wonder for its sense of a mind's faculties stretched to the limit. Its oratorical power comes from a struggle between two dominant schemes, anaphora and asyndeton, the repetition of a few emphatic phrases and the scattering of many others, wide of the syntactical norm. For Burke's dashes, expressive of emotion almost beyond what the speaker can bear, Lear is certainly the prototype. Yet Burke stands always before us, conscious of his power, and turning from side to side in the pleasure of it, as he holds fast to those energies he himself has summoned, which seem bent on loosing all their fury unmastered. Our shock at the discovery of these two moods in a single frame, the impression of words existing at their final stress before they split apart in chaos, and yet the mind still commanding and sure of its conquest: these things make the question of sincerity almost impossible to ask. The parallel cadences, "defended by reverence, defended by power—a fortress at once and a temple," have the force of law, and, framed at every juncture by the incantation, "As long as"—the only available reprieve from the death-sentence of "Such, such, such"—the entire passage seems to have the inviolability of prayer.

But Hunt did not find it so. "We are aware," he comments, "of the sympathies to be found in remote ideas, and the wit and the fine wisdom thence to be adduced; but we do not think . . . that Mr. Burke has done it; and we think he fails, partly because he substitutes the love of power for that of truth, and partly because he has a real reverence for those very sophistications and petty lordly authorities which we are called upon, in his pages, at once to think great and little."[18] This refers explicitly to the contrast between the proud Keep of Windsor and "the low, fat, Bedford level," double emblem of the great and beleaguered class whom Burke professes to defend in spite of itself. The queer intrusion of satire even here need not be deplored as out of keeping with Burke's design. But at all events the justice of Hunt's criticism is less important than his discovery that on certain subjects, Hazlitt cannot be trusted to display his taste "in its usual state of independence." When he sits down to read Burke, as much as when he rises to knock down an enemy of Napoleon, his love of truth deserts him. Here is his response to the same passage:

> Nothing can well be more impracticable to a simile than the vague and complicated idea which is here embodied in one; yet how finely, how nobly it stands out, in natural grandeur, in royal

state, with double barriers round it to answer for its identity, with "buttress, frieze, and coigne of 'vantage" for the imagination to "make its pendant bed and procreant cradle," till the idea is confounded with the object representing it—the wonder of a kingdom; and then how striking, how determined the descent, "at one fell swoop," to the "low, fat, Bedford level!" Poetry would have been bound to maintain a certain decorum, a regular balance between these two ideas; sterling prose throws aside all such idle respect to appearances, and with its pen, like a sword, "sharp and sweet," lays open the naked truth! The poet's Muse is like a mistress, whom we keep only while she is young and beautiful, *durante bene placito;* the Muse of prose is like a wife, whom we take during life, *for better for worse.* Burke's execution, like that of all good prose, savours of the texture of what he describes, and his pen slides or drags over the ground of his subject, like the painter's pencil. The most rigid fidelity and the most fanciful extravagance meet, and are reconciled in his pages. I never pass Windsor but I think of this passage in Burke. (XII, 12)

The associative logic of "usurpation" by which words take the place of things, is the common source of Hazlitt's several counts of praise: the idea's displacement by "the object representing it" and Windsor's displacement by the figure of Burke. One may find a consolation in all this, for a man of Hazlitt's politics, by noting that the power he seeks out is restless, and always moving on to something else. Yet the truth is that for Hazlitt it stops at a man whose power is eloquence, whereas for other readers it may go on until it reaches one whose power is action.

Napoleon gave Hazlitt his adventure among the others. The curious feature of all his writings about the Napoleonic system is that they are closer in spirit to Burke's praise of monarchy than the political context ever strictly requires. It was open to Hazlitt, in his *Life of Napoleon,* to go forward in sequence, giving for each instance of vanity or deceit the most credible apology he could unfold, as has been usual among defenders of Napoleon, Cromwell, Stalin, and all tyrants some of whose enemies were also tyrants. But he chose instead to lay before his reader the starkest and most general apology conceivable, with the help of Burkean assumptions about human nature which few readers could have deduced from his Preface to the *Life.* The apology, which occurs at the start of his chapter on "The Establishment of Empire," has an air of briskly unpacking stilettos, truncheons, and every manner of small arms and trick security, at the border of a small country swarming with banditti; but the country is human nature, and Hazlitt in twenty years of writing has supplied us with no hint of the need for such precautions.

> There is something in the form of monarchy that seems vastly adapted to the constitution and weaknesses of human nature. It . . . puts a stop by a specific barrier to the tormenting strife and restless importunity of the passions in individuals, and at the same time happily discharges the understanding of all the labour and turmoil of its concern for the public good. The crown, the emblem of precedence and sovereignty, for which all are contending, is snatched from the reach of all to be placed on the brow of a baby yet unborn; the troublesome differences of right and wrong, which produce such infinite agitation of opinion and convulse the bosom of states, are set at rest by the maxim that the king can do no wrong; and a power whose origin is lost in the distance of time and that acts upon no other warrant than its own will, seems in a manner self-existent, and baffles alike resistance or censure. Once substitute the lineal distinctions of legitimacy and illegitimacy for those of right and wrong; and the world, instead of being turned upside down, runs on in a smooth and invariable course. That a thing *is,* is much easier to determine than whether *it is good or bad.*   (XIV, 235)

Did monarchy appeal to Burke too by this ability to set a term for debates that gave no promise of concluding themselves? Power simplifies; it gives its own scale of values at once, with no enervating halt or question; it supplies an order of rank with which the mind rests content. Some resistance can be felt in Hazlitt's prose even as he describes the convenience of the result: if Burke makes the aristocracy appear both great and little, Hazlitt writes of subordination as an *apparent* need of mankind, the more fortunate the more he thinks it a necessity. But the passage certainly seeks to baffle a reader's own censure. And in the pages that follow Hazlitt will work to the top of his bent to extol the glories of a coronation-scene.

In these pages I have referred to two of Burke's treatises on power, the *Enquiry into the Sublime and Beautiful* and the *Reflections on the Revolution in France,* and it may now be asked what connected them, both for Burke himself and for Hazlitt. So far as I know, the only place where Hazlitt brought the two into deliberate conjunction was his chapter on the French Revolution in the *Life of Napo-*

leon. There he begins by observing the extraordinary conceit that was required to make the overthrow of the Bourbons appear anything less than simply necessary: "A crazy, obsolete government was metamorphosed into an object of fancied awe and veneration, like a mouldering Gothic ruin, which, however delightful to look at or read of, is not at all pleasant to live under. Thus the poetry and imagination of the thing were thrown into the scale of old-fashioned barbarism and musty tradition, and turned the balance." Even so, the reversal was only possible to a man of violent imaginings, like Burke:

> No one could have performed this feat but the celebrated author of *The Sublime and Beautiful,* with his metaphysical subtlety and poetical flights. Mr. Pitt has been hailed by his flatterers as "the pilot that weathered the storm"; but it was Mr. Burke who, at this giddy, maddening period, stood at the prow of the vessel of the state, and with his glittering, pointed spear *harpooned* the Leviathan of the French Revolution, which darted into its wild career, tinging its onward track with purple gore.   (XIII, 51–52)

Yet this still leaves uncertain the precise character of the poetry that the *Enquiry* and the *Reflections* have in common. I can suggest what it was only by observing that Hell seemed to Burke a place of sublimity, especially that wandering Hell, the mind of Satan; and after 1789, he never thought of the Revolution except as a strange irruption of the demonic into human history, which had naturalized Hell.

> The Revolution harpies of France, sprung from Night and Hell, or from that chaotic Anarchy which generates equivocally "all monstrous, all prodigious things," cuckoo-like, adulterously lay their eggs, and brood over, and hatch them in the nest of every neighbouring state. These obscene harpies, who deck themselves in I know not what divine attributes, but who in reality are foul and ravenous birds of prey, (both mothers and daughters), flutter over our heads, and souse down upon our tables, and leave nothing unrent, unrifled, unravaged, or unpolluted with the slime of their filthy offal.[19]

As an argument for the practical terror of sublimity, Burke had speculated in the *Enquiry* that at any theatrical performance, news of a hanging in the next street would empty the theatre: the two sorts of performance appealed to the same faculties, and the second gave the stronger jolt. But now, in Paris during the terror, every street was in a sense the theatre of practice Burke had mentioned.

Something had happened in actual life to place his theory in a ghastly new light; friends one had met a decade ago might be found hanging from lamp-posts; and the audience was there just as Burke had said they would be. It was farcical, grotesque, anything (Burke would have argued) but sublime. The *Reflections,* when one reads it beside the *Enquiry,* and in the scheme of Burke's career, looks like a deliberately repressive work. The darkness of chaos and the sublimity of Hell are now before his eyes, with the onrush of multi-tudes, and Burke responds with unrelenting mockery. The picture of this revolution as the sublime grotesque of actual life was in the end drawn by Carlyle; but it was a temptation Burke knew, and knew that he must refuse; with his refusal came renunciation of an idea of sublimity that drew no line between art and life. The stage was now littered with real corpses, and the worst fault of the revo-lutionaries was their failure to *realize* the events in which they took part. They would not make a full stop, in passing from the sort of terror at home in poetry, to a historical scene in which terror ought never to be domesticated. When he began to write like this, Burke had entered a new phase, and our sense of the difference is only heightened by the savage irony with which he descends again and again to remark how cheaply the revolutionaries have lent themselves to the theatrical momentum of politics.

In the fourth of his *Letters on a Regicide Peace,* Burke recalls a conversation with David Garrick, which had begun with his asking why the audience at a theatre always laughed when senators came on stage, whatever the play might be. Garrick's explanation was that only the lowest of the profession ever played those parts, and some-how the audience were alert to this fact.

> They knew that they were no other than candle-snuffers, revolu-tionary scene-shifters, second and third mob, prompters, clerks, exe-cutioners, who stand with their axe on their shoulders by the wheel, grinners in the pantomime, murderers in tragedies, who make ugly faces under black wigs,—in short, the very scum and refuse of the theatre; and it was of course that the contrast of the vileness of the actors with the pomp of their habits naturally ex-cited ideas of contempt and ridicule.
>
> So it was at Paris on the inaugural day of the Constitution for the present year. The foreign ministers were ordered to attend at this investiture of the Directory;—for so they call the managers of their burlesque government. The diplomacy, who were a sort of strangers, were quite awe-struck with the "pride, pomp, and cir-

cumstance" of this majestic senate; whilst the *sans-culotte* gallery instantly recognized their old insurrectionary acquaintance, burst out into a horse-laugh at their absurd finery, and held them in infinitely greater contempt than whilst they prowled about the streets in the pantaloons of last year's constitution, when their legislators appeared honestly, with their daggers in their belts, and their pistols peeping out of their side-pocket-holes, like a bold, brave banditti, as they are.[20]

The incongruity between mask and face has converted the dignified spectacle of tragedy into "horse-laugh" farce. Burke's task as a critic is no longer to show the parallel between art and life but to open up the distance between them so that the work of satire can be done. This means in practice: to reveal the Jacobin stage as a perfect copy of the sort of spectacle Garrick had understood, which can entertain the pit and at the same time draw their hoots and hisses. It is left to his readers to supply the missing link in the argument, that the Revolution affords but the depraved caricature of a senate which we could contemplate with the awe proper to a sublime idea.

Now Hazlitt was aware of the theatrical element in Burke, and of how it drew him to metaphors like these; some remarks in his review of the *Biographia Literaria* suggest that he saw the critic of the sublime and the critic of the Terror as the same man after a strange alteration: "He constructed his whole theory of government . . . not on rational, but on picturesque and fanciful principles; as if the King's crown were a painted gewgaw, to be looked at on gala-days; titles an empty sound to please the ear, and the whole order of society a theatrical procession. His lamentation over the age of chivalry, and his projected crusade to restore it, is about as wise as if any one, from reading the Beggar's Opera, should take to picking of pockets." When, in the *Life of Napoleon,* Hazlitt comes to write his own descriptions of the Terror, the theatrical metaphor remains, but the mode is apocalyptic with no hint of satire.

The sun of Liberty was in eclipse, while the crested hydra of the Coalition glared round the horizon. The atmosphere was dark and sultry. There was a dead pause, a stillness in the air, except as the silence was broken by a shout like distant thunder or the wild chaunt of patriotic songs. There was a fear, as in the time of a plague; a fierceness as before and after a deadly strife. It was a civil war raging in the heart of a great city as in a field of battle, and turning it into a charnel-house. The eye was sleepless, the brain heated. Sights of horror grew familiar to the mind, which

had no other choice than that of being either the victim or the exe-
cutioner. What at first was stern necessity or public duty, became a
habit and a sport; and the arm, inured to slaughter, struck at
random and spared neither friend nor foe. The soul, harrowed up
by the most appalling spectacles, could not do without them, and
"nursed the dreadful appetite of death." The habit of going to the
place of execution resembled that of visiting the theatre. Legal
murder was the order of the day, a holiday sight, till France became one scene of wild disorder, and the Revolution a stage of
blood!   (XIII, 152–53)

Had he gone even half-way in such a description, Burke would not
have scrupled to interrupt himself with some pointed sarcasm, to assure the reader that a detached point of view was still being preserved. He might for example nickname the guillotine, *the little national window.*

What is weakest and most imitable in Burke's style is a quickness
of scorn that amounts at times to superciliousness. For this Hazlitt
has no use, and where the opportunity faces him he straightforwardly rejects it. In a later passage on the Terror, as he watches the
revolutionaries hitched from one drama to the next, and prompted
through each scene-change, he allows himself a single paragraph of
Burkean detachment, on the want of principle displayed in so many
transpositions of a new-found patriotism. Even here his tone never
approaches irony:

The French are a mercurial people, and pass with wonderful ease
"from grave to gay, from lively to severe." Nothing can engross
them long or wholly. The Committee of Public Safety devoted, at
the time we speak of, twenty hours out of the four-and-twenty to
business. They had to attend the Committee in the morning, the
Convention in the evening, and sat up nearly all night in examining papers and writing out reports. How they got through it they
knew not—except that their country's welfare required their ser-
vices! They thought themselves heroes, martyrs, and that they were
not only playing a conspicuous part on the stage of the world, but
entitling themselves to the gratitude and admiration of posterity.
They resembled men in a dream. Shortly after all this, the Parisians
danced in the Gardens of the Thuilleries as if nothing had happened; the guillotine was laid by as a child's plaything; and the
surviving actors in the scene lurked in obscure corners, like old
family-portraits, out of date and never thought of!

           (XIII, 156–57)

The illusions that the Committee hold respecting their work are given simply for the record, neither more nor less helpful to our understanding than Burke's probings into the heart of a pure-bred metaphysician, but here embalmed forever: "How they got through it they knew not." And beside those illusions, portraits of the same committee, stowed or littered in forgotten corners, the debris of a race for whom schemes of the present had replaced all inheritance from the past. No attitude is struck in this account, and no further appeal is offered. Burke's irony, after all, was an appropriate weapon of power in exile, or supposing itself in exile. But Hazlitt in the *Life of Napoleon* was trying to speak for power in possession of its own estate. At scenes like these, his ambition forbade him to alter his tone from that of the excited chronicler who has sworn to miss nothing, but his honesty allowed as a conclusive feeling only the bafflement he makes us share.

Of Hazlitt's relation to Burke, his own summary judgment is stated by allusion, in a passage on the death of King George the Third. The King's refusal to treat with Napoleon, and the consequent rupture of the Peace of Amiens, form the immediate background, but Hazlitt's phrasing assures us that he could hardly think of the monarchial residence without feeling the idea of Burke crowd his mind and alter the history he had set himself to tell. His prose in this instance might be read as an *experimentum crucis* for the sublimity of privation—a rubric under which Burke himself had ranked *Vacuity, Darkness, Solitude,* and *Silence.* But we are more acutely aware of a different sort of homage. Hazlitt means the description to serve as a palinode on his favorite stretch of Burke's mastery, the paragraph about the proud Keep of Windsor.

> Persons who are fond of dwelling on the work of retribution, might perhaps trace its finger here. The Monarch survived the accomplishment of all his wishes, but without knowing that they had been accomplished. To those who long after passed that way, at whatever hour of the night, a light shone from one of the watch-towers of Windsor Castle—it was from the chamber of a King, old, blind, bereft of reason, "with double darkness bound" of body and mind; nor was that film ever removed, nor those eyes or that understanding restored to hail the sacred triumph of Kings over mankind; but the light streamed and streamed (indicating no dawn

within) for long years after the celebration of that day which glad-
dened the hearts of Monarchs and of menial nations, and through
that second night of slavery which succeeded—the work of a single
breast, which it had dearly accomplished in darkness, in self-
oblivion, and in more than kingly solitude!   (XIV, 200–201)

The same "kindred and coeval towers" shadow the land, but now
emptied of their "frank-pledge," and of the mind of their inhabitant.
The arbitrary power which they once signified, and enhanced by association, has at last done its worst: the triumph of oppression is
complete. Yet the mind that hastened "that second night of slavery,"
could not survive the accomplishment of its own designs; gazing up
at the light from the windows, that "streamed and streamed (indicating no dawn within)," Hazlitt finds that the meaning of everything Burke saw has changed; but instead of searching for another
monumental structure to fill his story, he corrects the Burkean trope
and makes it answerable to the new circumstances. Before his eyes
the towers still loom, but what they recall is the moral law, and its
great principle of compensation, the soul of all structures when what
remains of a castle is its husk.

Nowhere more than in this inspired work of revision are we conscious of Burke as the genius of prose, a man of power operating at
the extremes and therefore a man of imagination. And yet, a discussion of what this meant to Hazlitt is incomplete without the contrasting figure that he sometimes sent instead of himself to contest
Burke—either out of respect for the dramatic principle or because he
wished for the moment to make a higher claim, and required a
proxy. This figure was Charles James Fox, whom Hazlitt exhibits as
a man of the understanding. The understanding-imagination division, I have pointed out in other contexts, was much less important
for Hazlitt than for some of his contemporaries; yet when he turned
his mind to Burke and the unstable companionship of knowledge
with power, it seemed to grow sharp again. The largest comparisons
between Fox and Burke occur more than twenty years apart, in *The
Eloquence of the British Senate* near the beginning of his journalistic career, and in the *Life of Napoleon* near the end. The first opposes Burke's susceptibility to every omen and Fox's habitual even-
ness of temper: where Burke refuses to assimilate any French event
after 1789 to the known terrors of the world, Fox by his coolness
denies the shared sense of a calamity beyond reckoning, for which
the standard terms of diplomacy will not do.

I can conceive of Burke, as the genius of the storm, perched over Paris, the centre and focus of anarchy, (so he would have us believe) hovering "with mighty wings outspread over the abyss, and rendering it pregnant," watching the passions of men gradually unfolding themselves in new situations, penetrating those hidden motives which hurried them from one extreme into another, arranging and analysing the principles that alternately pervaded the vast chaotic mass, and extracting the elements of order and the cement of social life from the decomposition of all society: while Charles Fox in the meantime dogged the heels of the Allies, (all the way calling out to them to stop) with his sutler's bag, his muster-roll, and army estimates at his back. He said, You have only fifty thousand troops, the enemy have a hundred thousand: this place is dismantled, it can make no resistance: your troops were beaten last year, they must therefore be disheartened this. This is excellent sense and sound reasoning, but I do not see what it has to do with philosophy.　　　　　　　　　　(VII, 319–20)

The picture of Burke "extracting the elements of order and the cement of social life from the decomposition of all society" is to my knowledge the only place Hazlitt ever showed him as an analyst. It explains why he would not have thought it hyperbolical to say that doing justice to Burke made it "necessary to quote all his works; the only specimen of Burke is, *all that he wrote.*"

Hazlitt starts this comparison with the aim of paying homage to Burke and Fox alike, as equally tenacious of their strategies, yet we feel that in the circumstances he would have found Burke's the mind more to be valued. Fox glances on the surface of events, and makes intelligent deductions, and that is all. Burke's observations mark an epoch in the moral education of man—Fox's are an episode in the history of practical politics. Burke's advantage comes from a love of power for this reason, that whether writing as the advocate or as the deprecator of a cause, he starts from an inward identification with the exertions of power in others. His counter-revolutionary sentiments owe much of their force to a prior understanding of the motives of revolutionaries. Hence the propriety of the word "reactionary" as applied to Burke in particular. Some such interpretation is now common among those who read Burke neither as scripture nor as a disembodied text in political theory, but as a great mind who resists being parcelled out in specimens; and the critic who has done most to advance this way of reading him, Conor Cruise O'Brien, seems to have begun with Hazlitt's insight. "Part of the secret," writes O'Brien, "of [Burke's] power to penetrate the processes of the revolution derives from a suppressed sympathy with revolutionaries." This has double truth for an Irishman who was also an artist, and in both capacities, as Hazlitt saw, "much of a theatrical man." Burke's sympathy with the oppressed, by an analogy between Ireland and France, interests O'Brien more than the sympathy of power with power; but his summary of Burke's predicament describes one set of feelings in a language fully appropriate to the other: a man like Burke "has reason to know how a revolutionary might feel; for him the forces of revolution . . . exist not only in the world at large but also within himself."[21] Our hatreds sprout up more violently in proportion as they are nourished by secret sympathies. That Burke was at the mercy of such sympathies is more than anyone can say, though Hazlitt appears from the first to have believed he was. But for Hazlitt to deplore motives like these, which he had spent a lifetime explaining as the source of everything good as well as everything wicked in human action, would have produced a very hollow victory.

So far, in the comparison of Burke with Fox, the understanding has played a derisory role. But as a difference in kind has never been admitted by Hazlitt between genius and common sense, one expects the balance to be righted sooner or later. The moment came for Hazlitt after Waterloo. Burke's policies had by then outlasted all rivals in knowledge or power, tried the patience of his sincerest admirers, and lived to be invoked (as a letter that kills) against every humane purpose they were designed to animate. The relevant passage in the *Life of Napoleon* is accordingly much more favorable to Fox.

> Mr. Fox, with that justness of thought which is the result of goodness of heart, saw or felt that the whole drift of Mr. Burke's theory went to make politics a question or department of the imagination, and that this could never be true, because politics treat of the public weal and the most general and wide-extended consequences, whereas the imagination can only be appealed to by individual objects and personal interests, and must give a false verdict in all other cases. It would never do, he saw, to make choice of half a dozen *dramatis personae,* to adorn them with tropes and figures, and sacrifice to this paltry foreground and meretricious embellishing the welfare of millions, who because they were millions could never be brought forward by the imaginative faculty and could only be weighed in the balance of abstract truth and reason.
>
> (XIV, 274)

This closes the record almost too neatly. One may even hesitate a little over the mention of Burke's theory: is it the theory of the sublime or the theory of society? Doubtless Hazlitt was thinking primarily of the *Reflections,* the "Letter to a Noble Lord," the *Letters on a Regicide Peace;* yet both the ambiguous reference and the return to "imagination" plead for the continuity between these works and the *Enquiry:* we are more impressed, more carried out of ourselves, by the fight of one man against a multitude, than by the struggle of a multitude to throw off their chains. On the modern stage, that man is a king, and he will always occupy the foreground: "That a thing *is,* is much easier to determine than whether *it is good or bad.*" By his understanding of this principle, Burke made himself the sublime poet of a counter-revolution. To Hazlitt, saying so would have been only another way of calling him an untoppable rhetorician, who moved his listeners even as he persuaded them, and robbed all contenders of speech. He tells a cautionary anecdote, in *The Spirit of the Age,* about Mackintosh's visit to Beaconsfield, where Burke had summoned him as a decent man of the opposite party. "In the course of three days' animated discussion of such subjects, Mr. Mackintosh became a convert not merely to the graces and levity of Mr. Burke's style, but to the liberality of his views, and the solidity of his opinions." Such, reflects Hazlitt, "is the influence exercised by men of genius and imaginative power over those who have nothing to oppose to their unforeseen flashes of thought and invention, but the dry, cold, formal deductions of the understanding." Hazlitt thought himself gifted with understanding, and yet in these lines one can hear him quietly affirm that he would have held out a good deal longer than Mackintosh. With Burke in his grave and no other man alive whom he could regard as an intellectual foe of comparable stature, what remained for him was to find a hero-in-action who adequately represented the idea of individual power, and who opposed the idea of aggregate power as embodied in an individual, "The right divine of kings to govern wrong." He strove mightily to convert Napoleon to these uses; but the liberator of Spain and Poland was a poor vessel for his hopes; and Hazlitt reposed them there as uneasily as any author of a four-volume biography can ever have done. Still, in person he retained the new loyalty out of hatred for the old enemies, and liked to say in his own defense that Napoleon was preferable to the Bourbons as a tyrant was preferable to tyranny.

CHAPTER IX

POETRY AND JUSTICE

CORIOLANUS

The foregoing account has involved a degree of anachronism. There was no way of avoiding it since Hazlitt's most disturbing meditations on power grew from his contest with Burke; it was Burke who gave the abiding impulse, and formed the inevitable point of reference, whatever the ostensible provocation to write. I have indicated the years 1808 and 1828 to suggest the periods, early and late, when his engagement was most productive. The *Characters of Shakespeare's Plays* appeared in 1815, when Hazlitt was thinking of Burke less directly. His chapter on *Coriolanus* nevertheless reflects the same preoccupations, and we are aware throughout that Hazlitt's idea of Coriolanus would have been impossible without the idea of Burke, whether solitary in the ranks of dissent, as he seemed in the debates over the American Revolution, or solitary as he later chose to be, with only the dead for fit company. However effectively he might serve as a propagandist for war, Burke in this last phase wrote from a personal fear that resisted assimilation, and made no party eager to attach his eloquence to a machine for governing. He himself quoted not Coriolanus, but Lear at a Coriolanus-like moment, when he thought of those who had betrayed him: "The little dogs and all, / Tray, Blanch, and Sweetheart—see, they bark at me."

Because the passage on Coriolanus seems to me too long to quote at one stretch but too extraordinary to miss any of, I will stop to comment where I think Hazlitt is breaking off to pursue a new train of thought. Something of his energy shows in the recoil from being harnessed into short paragraphs, and he often registers such movements by a dash.

> The cause of the people is indeed but little calculated as a subject for poetry: it admits of rhetoric, which goes into argument and ex-

planation, but it presents no immediate or distinct images to the mind, "no jutting frieze, buttress, or coigne of vantage" for poetry "to make its pendant bed and procreant cradle in." The language of poetry naturally falls in with the language of power. The imagination is an exaggerating and exclusive faculty: it takes from one thing to add to another: it accumulates circumstances together to give the greatest possible effect to a favourite object. The understanding is a dividing and measuring faculty: it judges of things not according to their immediate impression on the mind, but according to their relations to one another. The one is a monopolising faculty, which seeks the greatest quantity of present excitement by inequality and disproportion; the other is a distributive faculty, which seeks the greatest quantity of ultimate good, by justice and proportion. The one is an aristocratical, the other a republican faculty. The principle of poetry is a very anti-levelling principle. It aims at effect, it exists by contrast. It admits of no medium. It is every thing by excess. It rises above the ordinary standard of sufferings and crimes. It presents a dazzling appearance. It shows its head turretted, crowned, and crested. Its front is gilt and blood-stained. Before it, it "carries noise, and behind it leaves tears." It has its altars and its victims, sacrifices, human sacrifices. Kings, priests, nobles, are its trainbearers, tyrants and slaves its executioners.—"Carnage is its daughter." (IV, 214)

All the doubts about poetry that Hazlitt ever suggested as a reviewer of his contemporaries, in the essay "On Poetic Versatility" and the "Letter to William Gifford," in his reviews of *The Excursion* and *The Statesman's Manual,* come together here from his willingness to read *Coriolanus* as a play with a hero. "The language of poetry naturally falls in with the language of power" because English poets in the nineteenth century are adepts in the imagination of power, and so far kindred to the dramatic poet of the sixteenth century, or for that matter the epic poet of the first century B.C. One language falls in with another as a corollary to some proof may fall in with the main conclusion: every circumstance necessary to the combination was there from the start; only grant the premise common to both languages, and the rest follows. But it is the language of poetry that is subordinate, that *wants to serve;* and "falls in" is of all verbs in English the one least implying conscious or voluntary effort. When Hazlitt says that the imagination "takes from one thing to add to another," one thinks of the sense, familiar to any citizen, in which a leader somehow *is* the good fortune that has accrued to his name or that he has gathered about himself. This is a gift which the bearer of

power need never earn. It seems right to praise a king, or a member
of the nobility, or to a lesser extent any individual, for his lineage or
possessions or the intelligent persons who form his retinue. We find
it harder to feel sincere in ascribing this sort of merit to a collectiv-
ity, whether its name is the Brain Trust or the Proletariat. There is
thus awe as well as regret in Hazlitt's admission that the imagination "rises above the ordinary standard of sufferings and crimes."
And the same emotions are mingled in his quotation of the sentence, "Carnage is its daughter," which Wordsworth addressed as a
prayer (to Almighty God) but which Hazlitt, having read it as a
curse, now extends to poetry.

He continues with an example of the human love of power operating beyond politics, and indeed beyond any spectacle with human actors; his aim is to convince the most principled leveller among
his readers that our fascination with power does not end with these
things; yet if this is true, the emotions felt by those who applaud
Wordsworth's lines will be reducible to no political motive.

> —Poetry is right-royal. It puts the individual for the species, the
> one above the infinite many, might before right. A lion hunting a
> flock of sheep or a herd of wild asses is a more poetical object
> than they; and we even take part with the lordly beast, because
> our vanity or some other feeling makes us disposed to place our-
> selves in the situation of the strongest party. So we feel some con-
> cern for the poor citizens of Rome when they meet together to
> compare their wants and grievances, till Coriolanus comes in and
> with blows and big words drives this set of "poor rats," this rascal
> scum, to their homes and beggary before him. There is nothing
> heroical in a multitude of miserable rogues not wishing to be
> starved, or complaining that they are like to be so: but when a
> single man comes forward to brave their cries and to make them
> submit to the last indignities, from mere pride and self-will, our
> admiration of his prowess is immediately converted into contempt
> for their pusillanimity. The insolence of power is stronger than
> the plea of necessity. The tame submission to usurped authority or
> even the natural resistance to it has nothing to excite or flatter the
> imagination: it is the assumption of a right to insult or oppress
> others that carries an imposing air of superiority with it. We had
> rather be the oppressor than the oppressed. The love of power in
> ourselves and the admiration of it in others are both natural to
> man: the one makes him a tyrant, the other a slave. Wrong dressed
> out in pride, pomp, and circumstance, has more attraction than
> abstract right.   (IV, 214–15)

The romantic interest in the individual over the species, which has issued on the one hand in the egotistical sublime, on the other in the critical polemic against general nature, here turns against the revolutionary politics in which all romantic poetry and criticism had their source, and is found to be in principle opposed to them. We thus return to a point Hazlitt reached at the end of his *Essay:* only by an act of abstraction can the imaginative self-worshiper hold firm to his radical beliefs, and stop short of the easy transition to hero-worship. For if we want a hero, we shall not find him amidst "a multitude of miserable rogues not wishing to be starved." Far from joining cause with the multitude, he may insist on stamping his identity the more completely on our minds, by acting in defiance of every human plea to insure that they continue to starve. When we reject him in this role, we go against the natural tendency of the imagination, which loves nothing so much as to be excited or "flattered." Hazlitt uses this last word in an old and beautiful, and thoroughly Shakespearean sense, to mean *soothed, comforted,* or *enhanced by agreement,* instead of *falsely praised.* Also, with unconscious mastery, he turns a Burkean phrase against all that worked to soften its effect in the *Enquiry,* where Burke wrote that "the pleasure of resemblance is that which principally flatters the imagination." Even Burke knew better than he wrote: for it is contrast, the contrast between one and many—the former possessed of an identity, the latter by their incorporation deprived of one—which principally flatters the imagination.

This being granted in general, Hazlitt now applies his observations to the play in question.

—Coriolanus complains of the fickleness of the people: yet, the instant he cannot gratify his pride and obstinacy at their expense, he turns his arms against his country. If his country was not worth defending, why did he build his pride on its defence? He is a conqueror and a hero; he conquers other countries, and makes this a plea for enslaving his own; and when he is prevented from doing so, he leagues with its enemies to destroy his country. He rates the people "as if he were a God to punish, and not a man of their infirmity." He scoffs at one of their tribunes for maintaining their rights and franchises: "Mark you his absolute *shall?*" not marking his own absolute *will* to take every thing from them, his impatience of the slightest opposition to his own pretensions being in proportion to their arrogance and absurdity. If the great and powerful had the beneficence and wisdom of Gods, then all this would have been well: if with a greater knowledge of what is good for the people, they had as great a care for their interest as they have themselves, if they were seated above the world, sympathising with the welfare, but not feeling the passions of men, receiving neither good nor hurt from them, but bestowing their benefits as free gifts on them, they might then rule over them like another Providence. But this is not the case. Coriolanus is unwilling that the senate should shew their "cares" for the people, lest their "cares" should be construed into "fears," to the subversion of all due authority; and he is no sooner disappointed in his schemes to deprive the people not only of the cares of the state, but of all power to redress themselves, than Volumnia is made madly to exclaim,

> "Now the red pestilence strike all trades in Rome
> And occupations perish."   (IV, 215–16)

In reading this one is reminded that Edmund Kean came off badly when he played Coriolanus. To that part only John Kemble, with his more deliberate pace and aristocratic bearing, seemed capable of doing justice, even for an age in love with shocking performances. Kean's chief error was that by certain movements of voice and body he betrayed his inveterate sympathies. These were republican rather than aristocratic, but as Coriolanus he ought not to have "descended into the common arena of man, to make good his pretensions by the energy with which he contended for them." Of the readings special to this production, Hazlitt registered his strongest protest against the way Coriolanus's reply to the mob's banishment of him, his "I BANISH YOU," was given by Kean "with all the virulence of execration and rage of impotent despair, as if he had to strain every nerve and faculty of soul to shake off the contamination of their hated power over him, instead of being delivered with calm, majestic self-possession, as if he remained rooted to the spot, and his least motion, word, or look, must scatter them like chaff or scum from his presence." On the other hand, the speech Hazlitt singled out to recall Kemble's mastery, the "proud taunt" of Coriolanus to Aufidius— "like an eagle in a dove-cote, I / Flutter'd your Volscians in Corioli: / Alone I did it"—was, as he informs us, given "double force and beauty" by the action that accompanied it, probably a wave of the hand scattering the doves like chaff, as an emblem of one power setting itself above and sweeping away the claim of many rights.

We all prize such gestures, and Hazlitt concludes his general discussion with a comment on our reason for doing so.

This is but natural: it is but natural for a mother to have more regard for her son than for a whole city; but then the city should be left to take some care of itself. The care of the state cannot, we here see, be safely entrusted to maternal affection, or to the domestic charities of high life. The great have private feelings of their own, to which the interests of humanity and justice must courtesy. Their interests are so far from being the same as those of the community, that they are in direct and necessary opposition to them; their power is at the expense of *our* weakness; their riches of *our* poverty; their pride of *our* degradation; their splendour of *our* wretchedness; their tyranny of our servitude. If they had the superior knowledge ascribed to them (which they have not) it would only render them so much more formidable; and from Gods would convert them into Devils. The whole dramatic moral of CORIOLANUS is that those who have little shall have less, and that those who have much shall take all that others have left. The people are poor; therefore they ought to be starved. They are slaves; therefore they ought to be beaten. They work hard; therefore they ought to be treated like beasts of burden. They are ignorant; therefore they ought not to be allowed to feel that they want food, or clothing, or rest, that they are enslaved, oppressed, and miserable. This is the logic of the imagination and the passions; which seek to aggrandize what excites admiration and to heap contempt on misery, to raise power into tyranny, and to make tyranny absolute; to thrust down that which is low still lower, and to make wretches desperate: to exalt magistrates into kings, kings into gods; to degrade subjects to the rank of slaves, and slaves to the condition of brutes. The history of mankind is a romance, a mask, a tragedy, constructed upon the principles of *poetical justice;* it is a noble or royal hunt, in which what is sport to the few is death to the many, and in which the spectators halloo and encourage the strong to set upon the weak, and cry havoc in the chase though they do not share in the spoil. We may depend upon it that what men delight to read in books, they will put in practice in reality. (IV, 216)

It is a full-scale allegorical reading, much less provisional and more confident than that of *The Tempest*. Hazlitt asks us for the moment to consider the imagination and the understanding as completely separate, and locked in a battle to gain the exclusive sympathy of onlookers in all times and places. Coriolanus stands for power, "the cause of the people" for disinterested justice, and only the former commands the submission by evoking the awe of the imagination. The understanding, a "dividing faculty," comes into history later than the exaggerating faculty of imagination, and from the deference shown to all advances of the mind ought therefore to take precedence over its rival. But the motions of the understanding are critical, and divisive among themselves; those of the imagination are simple, unified, importunate. When a great hunt is promised, all clamor to take part in the unequal spectacle, and all on one side; nor do those whose bodies strew the path of the victor feel one instant's regret at their choice: between this costly excitement, and a life robbed of spectacle, they will choose the former. Hazlitt's recitation of what is really *theirs* and what *ours,* their power and our privation, through the whole curriculum of human woe, is carried off like a nursery lesson or catechism, and so it is: where the immediate drama of power is involved, the people look to their own interests with as little attentiveness as children. Yet "the people" here excludes none of us. We feel that selfishness, if only its movements are swift and sure, has somehow been disarmed of its sting: it may blind us with its glare, and we see only brilliance. As long as it towers above us, without descending into the common arena, we remain its natural servants and think nothing of causes or effects. The truth seems to be that any human grandeur sufficiently remote will be treated *as if* it were disinterested. Perhaps there is a love of justice even in the compulsion to make and remake history as "a romance, a mask, a tragedy, constructed upon the principles of *poetic justice.*" But the only hope for some good to mankind is that now and then we shall choose a hero whose way of keeping his distance is to become our benefactor.

Still, even if the slave hugs his chains the tighter because they give him a place in the system of things, he will not admire a tyrant while he is conscious of suffering from the cruelty of his edicts. The love of power can only be expressed by an act of abstraction: it does not emerge directly, but must be averted from, any terror of the immediate and practical consequences of power for our experience. Our admiration is in fact not of physical force and its effect of terror, but of energy of mind. It was because he thought of the matter in these terms that Hazlitt's praise of Napoleon never threatened to give over all criticism to a simple cult of force. Here, as in his remarks on Iago, he was able to regard the love of power as natural, but not necessarily prevalent; as involving unconscious affinity, more than will; and as potentially leagued with good as well as evil. If our love of power came into being in response to terror, there would be no doubt that it was conscious, and no limit to the evil it could do by confirming our respect for a policy of terror. This was a mistake which Burke—though free of it himself—had left open to others by the argument of his *Enquiry,* which subordinates the idea of power to the practical phenomena of terror. But if it is true that we need a certain detachment from these phenomena to admire the sublimity in any display of power, then we will admire power itself not as a terror-producing agency but as the most general name we have for energy of mind.

The phrase "energy of mind" was given currency by Richard Payne Knight's *Analytical Inquiry into the Principles of Taste* (1805), a work of recognized merit (reaching a fourth edition in 1808), by a clear-headed revisionist of Burke. Knight clearly separated where Burke had confounded the idea of power and the sensation of fear which anything terrible may evoke:

> As far as feeling or sentiment is concerned, and it is of feeling or sentiment only that we are speaking, *that* alone is terrible, which impresses some degree of fear. I may *know* an object to be terrible; that is, I may know it to possess the *power* of hurting or destroying: but this is *knowledge,* and not feeling or sentiment; and the *object* of that knowledge is *power,* and not terror; so that, if any sympathy results from it, it must be a sympathy with power only.[1]

Throughout his discussion of the sublime and the beautiful, Knight denies that such qualities have an invariable connection with particular sensations; and he ridicules Burke's appeal to the superior interest of the execution over the tragedy, as an extreme instance of the attraction we feel to physical terror itself.[2] This will not do, Knight sees, for we at once want to know: *whose* terror? It makes better sense to speak of an execution as an occasion of power, in which energy of mind is displayed; and in that case we have less trouble deciding whose energy, and why it claims attention: the spectators take an interest "not in proportion to the sufferings, but to the heroism and gallantry of the person executed."[3] Instead of a direct and sensational experience of fear, it is the ideas of strength, reserve, courage, and endurance, associated with the conduct of one sort of victim, which impart sublimity to the spectacle. More generally, when an object poses no threat to ourselves, our sympathy with power takes over: it may be sympathy with either the master or the slave, the condemned man or the signer of the death warrant, provided the "exertions of energy" that we see in action satisfy our

own quest for energy of mind. Knight is thus able to conclude that
"power itself" instead of terror is the source of our sympathies with
grand objects. If one imagines the crowd at an execution as no different in kind from the crowd at a political rally, the lesson Hazlitt
took from *Coriolanus* will seem a natural one, but with no implications for man's essential love of despotism. The following observation of Knight's applies to the play as I think Hazlitt read it:

> A despot may command the actions of men, but cannot command
> their sentiments or opinions: wherefore, as Longinus observes, it is
> not the tyrant diffusing terror, whose character is sublime; but
> the man, whose exalted soul looks down upon empire, and scorns
> the transitory possessions, which it can bestow. He displays a real
> energy of mind; and, with that energy, we sympathize; in whatever
> manner, or to whatever end, it be exerted. The tyrant therefore
> may show it, as well as the philosopher; and in that case, the char-
> acter of the tyrant will be sublime.[4]

Iago's indifference was a vice, and to Hazlitt not a sublime one, because from the start he had placed himself on a level with the other
characters, in order to deceive them. But the man "whose exalted
soul looks down upon empire" has an indifference unlike Iago's: his
view of things seems to exclude all pettiness, and by rewarding him
with our wonder we seek to gain for ourselves the strength of his "I
BANISH YOU."

Hazlitt writes of solitary power—free to its own favor, wanting nothing from others—in the same spirit in which he wrote of self-reliant
egotism. Yet this makes it look as if any power, for Hazlitt to praise
it, had better exert its claims against all worldly interests; whereas
the whole point of making Napoleon into an ideal had seemed to be
that he was a man in whom the solitary hero and cunning leader
were joined. There can be no escape from the contradiction; the
best that can be hoped, from a man trapped in it, is that he admit
its existence; but this seems to me the one movement of Hazlitt's
mind that he failed to treat consistently in "a true metaphysical
spirit." The result is visible in a number of passages where the egotist above the battle ends as the worldly conqueror, but Hazlitt praises
them in the same language and seems unaware of any transition.

A characteristic passage of this sort, from the *Journey through
France and Italy,* shows him moved by the chastening power of the
Alps, and then speculating on the greater man who passed there not

long before, only to pass through them expeditiously rather than pause for reflection. Was Napoleon nevertheless moved by what he saw?

> Any one, who is much of an egotist, ought not to travel through these districts; his vanity will not find its account in them; it will be chilled, mortified, shrunk up: but they are a noble treat to those who feel themselves raised in their own thoughts and in the scale of being by the immensity of other things and who can aggrandise and piece out their personal insignificance by the grandeur and eternal forms of nature! It gives one a vast idea of Buonaparte to think of him in these situations. He alone (the Rob Roy of the scene) seemed a match for the elements, and able to master "this fortress, built by nature for herself." Neither impeded nor turned aside by immoveable barriers, he smote the mountains with his iron glaive, and made them malleable; cut roads through them; transported armies over their ridgy steeps; and the rocks "nodded to him, and did him courtesies!" (X, 191)

It gives one a vast idea of Napoleon to imagine him face to face with the Alps. In this situation he shows himself thoroughly unmoved by what he sees; regarding every object as an obstacle to his will, he turns aside from the grandeur of the scene and treats it as so much brute matter for conquest; his impress is left on whatever stood in his path. (Logically, the preceding sentences require a *but* between them to register the disappointment with Napoleon; the exposition however goes on unalarmed, by its freedom from conjunctions denying the plausibility of doubts.) Unlike the common egotist—one might say to explain his conduct—Napoleon is not "chilled, mortified, shrunk up." Yet is not Hazlitt's account a portrait of an egotist all the same? For the response of the imaginative man is to feel "raised up," remain silent, and do nothing; certainly not to "cut roads through them." Indeed, for all the archaic dignity with which Hazlitt celebrates mountains being "smote," the weight of the "iron glaive," and armies moving across the "ridgy steeps" that separate them from their fate, these roads seem an efficient modern convenience and therefore beside the point.

One cannot dismiss this as an aberration: passages touched by a similar confusion are scattered throughout Hazlitt's work, and often seem to surprise him by their passion. It may therefore be helpful to surmise what Hazlitt feels at such moments but is on principle unwilling to say. It would seem that those who "feel raised up in their own thoughts and in the scale of being by the immensity of other things," whether this leads them to stand back in awe or put the immensity to some practical use, become admirable simply by virtue of the elevation they achieve. The exceptions Hazlitt makes in favor of Napoleon have given pause to his more genteel appreciators, and can hardly sit comfortably with those who respect him as a steadfast mind in politics. Nevertheless, such instances show how little there is of whim in the analogy he occasionally draws between Napoleon and Milton's Satan, which I illustrated in chapter 3. The comparison emerges very fully in his essay "On Means and Ends," where he argues that both heroes make us treat as a virtue, because they reveal in isolation, a conviction of self-worth that exists in all men but is sovereign in few.

> Pride scorns all alliance with natural frailty or indulgence; our wilful purposes regard every relaxation or moment's ease as a compromise of their very essence, which consists in violence and effort. . . . One of the chief traits of sublimity in Milton's character of Satan is this dreadful display of unrelenting pride and self-will—the sense of suffering joined with the sense of power and "courage never to submit or yield." . . . When Buonaparte fell, an English editor (of virulent memory) exhausted a great number of the finest passages in *Paradise Lost,* in applying them to his ill-fated ambition. This was an equal compliment to the poet and the conqueror: to the last, for having realised a conception of himself in the mind of his enemies on a par with the most stupendous creations of imagination; to the first, for having embodied in fiction what bore so strong a resemblance to, and was constantly brought to mind by, the fearful and imposing reality!   (XVII, 220–21)

Yet one feels that if pressed to choose between his idols, Hazlitt would without hesitation have picked Kean over Napoleon. For Kean, so unsuited to the part of Coriolanus, had given back to the world two Shakespearean characters in whom the sense of suffering is joined with the sense of power: Shylock and Othello. Even in these characters he had succeeded in bursts of discovery, and not through the long arc of performance; but then, as Hazlitt always acknowledged, Kean "must have opportunities to shine, and even (we may add) to fail as no other man can do, or he is not himself." His figure, of small stature, but roused to action in abrupt shocks and starts, and then striding with unmeasurely pace like the god of another kingdom than ours, resembles Hazlitt himself as he appears in most of the descriptions that have survived. Kean's inventions, which

were capable of turning a bit of stage business into theatrical metaphor—as when, to Hamlet's line "I'll make a ghost of him that follows me," he backed away *with* the ghost and pointed his sword at
Horatio—proceeded from a feeling for gesture and even gesticula-
tion, as part of the life of metaphor. He was not afraid to leave an
impression of jauntiness, if only it would tell; he was not afraid of
anything, if it would tell; criticisms of him as a man without art
usually started from this fact. When Hazlitt thought that Kean had
failed in his attempt to serve a greater master like Shakespeare, loyalty to a reputation he had helped to make did not stand in his way:
his point-by-point analysis of Kean's innovations as Lear, and the
condemnation that follows, present a self-confident triumph of the
critic's imagination over the performer's conceit, with no rival in
the dramatic criticism of our language.

But Kean, always disappointing the expectations he made Hazlitt
cherish of him, is always being redeemed, in his failure no less than
his success, by his potency as a figure of energy. He is "in general all
passion, all energy, all relentless will." For Othello, of which his version "is, we suppose, the finest piece of acting in the world," terms as
grand as these somehow do not suffice: "The energy of passion, as it
expresses itself in action, is not the most terrific part: it is the agony
of his soul, shewing itself in looks and tones of voice." Hazlitt had
never seen any actor match Kean in this part, being "so wrought
upon—so 'perplexed in the extreme.'" Such vulnerability implied
the actor's own stance as an outsider (like Othello and Shylock), his
unwilling isolation as a man of power, which he must nevertheless
preserve because his isolation and his power are uniquely bound to
each other. Where the power of Coriolanus was associated with an
unyielding aristocracy, the power of Kean is associated with a republicanism whose conquests are perpetually in question. His characteristic postures on stage therefore evoke an attitude at once proud and
defensive. He risked, Hazlitt believed, as much as actors or historical
personages of a higher tone of delivery, and by risking at the same
time our uneasy recognition that he was one of us, carried Shakespearean tragedy to its utmost scope of feeling. He united not only
suffering and power, but sympathy and power.

> Mr. Kean's acting is not of the patrician order; he is one of the
> people, what might be termed a *radical* performer. He can do all
> that may become a man "of our infirmity," "To relish all as sharply,
> passioned as we"; but he cannot play a God, or one who fancies

himself a God, and who is sublime, not in the strength of his own feelings, but in his contempt for those of others, and in his imaginary superiority to them. (XVIII, 290)

Only in the light of these qualities, as Hazlitt observed them even in Kean's unhappiest roles, can one appreciate the generous revision he made in his essay on "Free Admission," where having described Kean as "full of genius and full of errors," he struck the phrase and put in its place, "full of genius and free from errors."[5] To him, the sense of Kean as a "*radical* performer" would have been as important as his understanding that the spirit of poetry and the spirit of humanity were not the same. For this summing-up of Kean's power reaches far back into his memory—to Macbeth's "I dare do all that may become a man; / Who dares do more is none"—and has its events beyond counting, in all the bolder affirmations of his career in prose, down to the single sentence in "Common Places" which may stand as the imagined reply of one citizen to Coriolanus: "I am proud up to the point of equality."

BYRON AND THE PICTURESQUE

Hazlitt's ambivalence in praising a power beyond the reach of common humanity sometimes resolved itself into a set of pointed questions about aristocratic grandeur and aristocratic detachment, and the difficulty of freeing them from artifice and vanity. The author who served as a natural focus of such questions was Lord Byron. But Hazlitt's view of him was never simple: on the one hand, he cut a figure in society, above the run of modern lords and modern scribblers, and Hazlitt was capable of displaying an artless excitement when he thought he had identified Byron sitting near him at the theatre; on the other hand, all his powers seemed at the service of an overstimulated dandyism, or an irritable self-will. Hazlitt's interest in the most celebrated fact about Byron, namely his celebrity itself, was mingled with distrust of the man who had been placed so by the circumstances of his birth. In this, Byron formed a contrast with Burke, who had started his career and ended it as an outsider, and demanded admiration for nothing but what he had made of himself. Hazlitt's wariness of a title might reveal only a traditional Dissenter's attitude, were Burke not so important a guide to his reading of Byron. Yet reading alone cannot fully explain the response. It had in it an element of class antagonism, which he doubtless sharpened on the stories about Byron related by many who had come to know him. With middle-class friends, and Leigh Hunt particularly, Byron played a disconcerting game. He held the title above them and himself above the title. What Hazlitt felt about such conduct in a lord with republican pretensions, we know from his sketch of Byron for *The Spirit of the Age:* "He lounges with extravagance, and yawns so as to alarm the reader! Self-will, passion, the love of singularity, a disdain of himself and of others (with a conscious sense that this is among the ways and means of procuring admiration) are the proper categories of his mind: he is a lordly writer, is above his own reputation, and condescends to the Muses with a scornful grace!" The phrase, "above his own reputation," goes Byron himself one better: it speaks on behalf of a posterity that scales down every reputation, and may be still more indifferent to his work than he affects to be.

But Hazlitt in person was never indifferent to this sort of fame. Here, as usual, Hunt seems to me his best critic: he regrets Hazlitt's sanguineness (though admitting elsewhere that he shared it) about even the temporary alliance with Byron for the sake of publishing the *Liberal.*

> Mr. Hazlitt, habitually paradoxical, sometimes pastoral, and never without the self-love which he is fond of discerning in others, believed at the moment that a lord had a liking for him, and that a lord and a sophisticated poet would put up with his sincerities about the aristocratical and the primitive. It begat in him a love for the noble Bard; and I am not sure that he has [ever got rid of] the notion that it was returned. He was taken in, as others had been, and as all the world chose and delighted to be, as long as the flattering self-reflection was allowed a remnant to act upon. The mirror was pieced at Missolonghi, and then they could expatiate at large on the noble Lord's image and their own! . . . Lord Byron in truth was afraid of Mr. Hazlitt; he admitted him like a courtier, for fear he should be treated by him as an enemy; but when he beheld such articles as the "Spirit of Monarchy," where the "taint" of polite corruption was to be exposed, and the First Acquaintance with Poets, where Mr. Wordsworth was to be exalted above depreciation,
>
> "In spite of pride, in erring reason's spite—"
>
> (for such was Mr. Hazlitt's innocent quotation) his Lordship could only wish him out again, and take pains to show his polite friends that he had nothing in common with so inconsiderate a plebeian.[6]

Two points stand out in Hunt's analysis: that Hazlitt's love of Byron was an instance of paradoxical pastoralism; and that his defense of Wordsworth was a cause of Byron's realizing the irony always latent in his curiosity about aristocrats, and taking it as a pretext to "wish him out again." Hunt uses the word "pastoral" in what has become its strong modern sense, to imply a conjunction of high and low which may have at heart the inversion of high and low—whether in a representation of primitives as sophisticated, or of sophisticates as primitive. Of course, such a perspective is open to double ironies. Hazlitt interpreted *The Beggar's Opera* as exposing the viciousness of a pack of thieves whose vices mimic those of the gentlemen they aspire to become. (Nothing is commoner than a gentleman, as one can see by inspecting his apparent opposite.) Again, Hazlitt defined gentility as vulgarity in flight from itself and afraid of being caught. This was an antithesis that could not have made Byron happy, and several repetitions of it, in a few issues of the *Liberal,* convinced him of its personal application to himself. His understanding was correct though his response—the decision to terminate the magazine—was less original-minded than Hazlitt had wished.

While the *Liberal* was alive, I think Hazlitt half-expected to be welcomed as an influence on Byron's imagination. Byron was still getting the benefit of settled possessions: if he received it with a bad conscience he also disclaimed it in bad faith, and Hazlitt's function was to point out the error without embarrassment to either party. Another aspect of the same function was to persuade Byron that a rival, whose work showed men without fine clothes could have deep feelings, was to be exalted above depreciation. For Wordsworth's fame unlike Byron's had been achieved resolutely against the promptings of fashion; and he taught that a poet's task was to reform rather than maintain his inheritance. He ended by changing the lives of his readers because he was sublime in his humanity. This was perhaps beyond Byron's reach, owing to an inveterate sensationalism. At any rate Hazlitt's later reasons for thinking so may be guessed from two sentences which I take to have been written in reaction to *Cain,* in the essay "On Disagreeable People."

There are some objects that shock the sense, and cannot with propriety be mentioned: there are naked truths that offend the mind, and ought to be kept out of sight as much as possible. For human nature cannot bear to be too hardly pressed upon.   (XVII, 233)

For a moment in Byron's career, however, in the early 1820s, he seemed ready to become a poet of the sublime with something of Wordsworth's integrity. Whether he would succeed, as Hazlitt saw it, depended on how far he altered his conception of poetry; and a critic might assist him to the extent of offering an education in different principles.

Hazlitt regarded the imaginative fixities of Byron's work as entirely in keeping with the social certainties of a lord, and he connected both with a fondness for the picturesque. The picturesque frames the sublime, bounds it arbitrarily to make a complete picture, and cancels its energies to aid us in contemplating a finished product:[7] this appears as Byron's own characteristic activity, in Hazlitt's *London Magazine* article of June, 1821, on "Pope, Lord Byron, and Mr. Bowles." The article was written during the short interval of enchantment which Hunt's memoir has described, and yet it is a remarkably uningratiating performance. It begins as a review of Byron's *Letter* concerning Bowles's strictures on Pope, an energetic ramble of prose in which Byron took up the defense of Pope against all attacks on his character. But in twenty pages Hazlitt manages to show how a dispute between himself and Byron, on the merits of didactic poetry, bears upon a larger argument not only about the respective merits of the sublime and the picturesque, but about the power of genius to raise up and chasten all who share its vision, and the power of art to flatter those who share its premises.

In his opening paragraph Hazlitt calls Byron "a spoiled child of nature and fortune": what has gone on spoiling him as a grown-up person is the deference of men like Bowles. Thus a point of contention between them is whether a ship, launched into poetry by Thomas Campbell as "a beautiful and poetical artificial object," but loaded with "patriotic, natural, and foreign associations," is imaginative from its having been made by man, as Byron appears to believe, or because it has mingled in our minds with "the sun, the winds, and the waves," as Bowles asserts in reply. Here Bowles was trying to pamper Byron into a concession, and Hazlitt objects to his manner of doing so. " 'The sun,' says Mr. Bowles, 'is poetical, by your Lordship's admission.' We think it would have been so without it." Yet Byron seems to demand such treatment; and the objection is not that he uses advantages he was given as well as those he has made, but that he at once solicits and rebuffs the fulsome appreciation of his admirers.

Lord Byron has been twice as much talked of as he would have been, had he not been Lord Byron. His rank and genius have been happily placed "each other's beams to share," and both together, by their mutually reflected splendour, may be said to have melted the public coldness into the very wantonness of praise. . . . Whence, then, this repining, this ungracious cavilling, this *got-up* ill humour? We load his Lordship with ecstatic admiration, with unqualified ostentatious eulogies; and he throws them stifling back in our face: he thanks us with cool, cutting contempt: he asks us for our voices, "our sweet voices," like Coriolanus; and, like Coriolanus, disdains us for the unwholesome gift. Why, then does he ask for it? If, as a lord, he holds in contempt and abhorrence the willing, delighted homage, which the public pay to the poet, let him retire and feed the pride of birth in stately solitude, or take his place among his equals: but if he does not find this enough, and wants our wondering tribute of applause to satisfy his craving vanity, and make him something more than a mere vulgar lord among hundreds of other lords, why dash the cup of delicious poison, which at his uneasy request, we tender him, to the ground, with indignant reckless hands, and tell us he scorns equally our censure or our praise? If he looks upon both as equal impertinence, he can easily escape out of the reach of both by ceasing to write; we shall in that case soon cease to think of his Lordship.[8]

(XIX, 64–65)

This is an excellent diagnosis of Byron's affinity with Pope, and it closely echoes Johnson's criticism of Pope himself. Both critics expose the affectation of poets who are also thoroughly competent men of the world, but whose idea of a lofty character makes them wish to appear unworldly. To Johnson's many charges Hazlitt adds one that applies uniquely to Byron. He sees a psychological link between Byron's preference for received modes—he had announced in this *Letter* that the highest task of poetry was to impart moral precepts in verse—and his coming into possession of a received title, for which he need have done nothing but be born. A new generation of lords gets to be *distinguished* without any effort of its own, as easily as a new generation of couplets; both have their pedigree, and require only our inspection to be recognized for what they are. This double assumption Hazlitt discerns as the secret of the contempt shown throughout Byron's *Letter* for energy, invention, earned and individual power. Hazlitt speaks with an Augustan sanction far stronger than Byron's. For Johnson himself wrote, in the closing paragraph of his *Life of Milton*, "The highest praise of genius is original invention"; and he remarked of Pope's invention as a moralist, "Having exalted himself into the chair of wisdom he tells us much that every man knows, and much that he does not know himself. . . . Never were penury of knowledge and vulgarity of sentiment so happily disguised." When Byron says of imagination and invention that they are "the two commonest of qualities," Hazlitt is thus making a traditional reply when he observes:

> We will tell his Lordship what is commoner, the want of them. "An Irish peasant," he adds, "with a little whiskey in his head, will imagine and invent more than"—(What? Homer, Spenser, and Ariosto? No: but than)—"would furnish forth a modern poem." That we will not dispute. But at any rate, when sober next morning, he would be as "full of wise saws, and modern instances" as his Lordship; and in either case, equally positive, tetchy, and absurd!   (XIX, 68-69)

The absurdity is unconcealed when Byron writes that a poem expounding systematic doctrine, such as *De Rerum Natura*, "as mere poetry . . . is the first of Latin poems. What then has ruined it? His ethics. Pope has not this defect: his moral is as pure as his poetry is glorious." But a well-tested morality hardly permits an escape from the primary importance of invention: this, as Johnson realized, was precisely the difficulty confronting Pope, when he published in four steps the abstract of a system which he had not troubled to understand before putting it into verse. Hazlitt again causes the old objection to return on Byron, in an observation which for its play of terms requires an added emphasis: "The value of any moral truth depends on the *philosophic* invention implied in it. But this rests with the first author, and the general idea, which forms the basis of didactic poetry, remains the same, through all its mechanical transmissions afterwards." He then gives a reductive counter-example, but one that Byron has by no means guarded himself against: "The finding out the 48th proposition in Euclid made Pythagoras a great man. Shall we say that the putting this into a grave, didactic distich would make either a great mathematician or a great poet? It would do neither one nor the other; though, according to Lord Byron, this distich would belong to the highest class of poetry, 'because it would do that in verse, which one of the greatest of men had done in prose.' "

Byron's partly misleading sense of his affinity with Pope, on the ground of their shared concern for morality, had emerged from his

exasperation with the poetry of the present day, and especially with
the Lake school. To advance his own claims he identified Pope's
form with his subject, called both by a single name, "artificial," and
presented himself as Pope's sole legitimate heir. Again Hazlitt's criticism is unreserved: "Lord Byron's notions of art and poetry are sufficiently wild, romantic, far-fetched, obsolete; his taste is Oriental,
Gothic; his Muse is not domesticated; there is nothing *mimminee-
pimminee,* modern, polished, light, fluttering, in his standard of the
sublime and beautiful." In all these qualities he may be contrasted
with Pope's immediate and more obviously faithful successors: "He
is not a carpet poet. He does not sing the sofa, like poor Cowper."
Indeed Byron's ideas of the sublime and beautiful are just what
should take him beyond the derisive tone about invention which he
adopts in this letter.

> His Lordship likes the poetry, the imaginative part of art, and so
> do we. . . . He likes the *sombre* part of it, the thoughtful, the de-
> cayed, the ideal, the spectral shadow of human greatness, the de-
> parted spirit of human power. He sympathizes not with art as a dis-
> play of ingenuity, as the triumph of vanity or luxury, as it is con-
> nected with the idiot, superficial, petty self-complacency of the
> individual and the moment . . . but he sympathizes with the tri-
> umphs of Time and Fate over the proudest works of man—with
> the crumbling monuments of human glory—with the dim vestiges
> of countless generations of men—with that which claims alliance
> with the grave, or kindred with the elements of nature. This is
> what he calls art and artificial poetry. But this is not what any body
> else understands by the terms, commonly or critically speaking.
>
>   (XIX, 72)

"Crumbling monuments of human glory" belong to the accepted
vocabulary of the picturesque, as a middle ground of art softening
the contrast between the sublime and the beautiful. Yet Byron, as
Hazlitt reminds him, does not care for the nature of the "improvers," its scenes varied by ingenuity for the sake of "unexpectedness."
(What, pray tell, asks a skeptic in one of Peacock's novels, do you call
the unexpected when you see it a second time?) His poetry returns
again and again to "the triumphs of Time and Fate over the proud-
est works of man," in which emblems of destruction and survival are
mingled, and leave a record of the possible sublimity of the human
sentiments connected with a nature that transforms human monuments. What Byron has not yet recognized is that his elective affinities mark him as an enemy of the artificial school; and Hazlitt's arti-

cle is an effort to hasten the recognition. He takes liberties with
Byron, and may even seem to presume on his acquaintance, but only
because he supposes they are temperamentally allied. Hazlitt's version of the picturesque always moves toward the sublime, and always
implies the sense of "moral weight" that Martin Price finds characteristic of Ruskin, George Eliot, and others who wrote when the
vogue of the improvers had passed.

> The typical picturesque object or scene—the aged man, the old
> house, the road with cart-wheel tracks, the irregular village—carries
> within it the principle of change. All of them imply the passage of
> time and the slow working of its change upon them. A face in
> which one reads experience of suffering and endurance is seen in a
> moment that is earned by the long processes that have gone into its
> creation; it is a moment of dramatic resolution, in which we see
> some counterpoise of enduring substance and the accidents of
> time.[9]

Byron holds himself remote from such interests, and his own version
of the picturesque, with its characteristic tone, may be recalled by
Southey's quip about Manfred "bullying the Devil on the Jung-
frau." Hazlitt has a larger feeling for the accidents of time. By insisting that Byron shares it, he aims to convince him that the word
"artificial" can never explain his attachment, not so much to certain
favorite objects, as to those by which he has been moved to write
poetry.

Early in the essay Hazlitt had been hard on Byron's knowing-
ness, "all this *pribble-prabble*" about the wrecks and guidebook
relics of civilization, "the Venus, and Antinous, and the Acropolis,
and the Grand Canal at Venice, and the Turkish Fleet, and Falconer's
Shipwreck," on which Byron's observations, *aperçus,* and easy con-
fidences were only "what might be talked by any Bond-street lounger
of them all, after a last night's debauch, in the intervals between the
splashings of the soda-water and the acid taste of the port wine rising
in the mouth." But now these references to great objects, so few of
them artificial in anybody else's terms, are held strictly to account.

> What is the use of taking a work of art, from which "all the art of
> art is flown," a mouldering statue, or a fallen column in Tadmor's
> marble waste, that staggers and over-awes the mind, and gives birth
> to a thousand dim reflections, by seeing the power and pride of
> man prostrate, and laid low in the dust; what is there in this to
> prove the self-sufficiency of the upstart pride and power of man?
> A Ruin is poetical. Because it is a work of art, says Lord Byron. No,

but because it is a work of art o'erthrown. In it we see, as in a mirror, the life, the hopes, the labour of man defeated, and crumbling away under the slow hand of time; and all that he has done reduced to nothing, or to a useless mockery.   (XIX, 73)

The defeat of the hopes and labor of men *humanises,* as Hazlitt says elsewhere, by showing the impermanence of everything except feeling. This alone deepens even as it changes, and its power comes from the fact that "A man can make any thing, but he cannot make a sentiment!" Hazlitt believes that such objects as we ourselves make, and then call permanent from the attraction of idolatry, render us less than human.

Let Byron, he suggests, pick as the subject for a poem "not the pyramids of Egypt, but the pavilion at Brighton, and make a poetical description of it in prose or verse. We defy him." He then explains the grounds for his assurance:

As novels end with marriage, poetry ends with the consummation and success of art. And the reason (if Lord Byron would attend to it) is pretty obvious. Where all the wishes and wants are supplied, anticipated by art, there can be no strong cravings after ideal good, nor dread of unimaginable evils; the sources of terror and pity must be dried up: where the hand has done every thing, nothing is left for the imagination to do or to attempt: where all is regulated by conventional indifference, the full workings, the involuntary, uncontrollable emotions of the heart cease: property is not a poetical, but a practical prosaic idea, to those who possess and clutch it; and cuts off others from cordial sympathy; but nature is common property. . . . By *art* and *artificial,* as these terms are applied to poetry or human life, we mean those objects and feelings which depend for their subsistence and perfection on the will and arbitrary conventions of man and society; and by nature, and natural subjects, we mean those objects which exist in the universe at large, without, or in spite of, the interference of human power and contrivance, and those interests and affections which are not amenable to the human will. That we are to exclude art, or the operation of the human will, from poetry altogether, is what we do not affirm; but we mean to say, that where this operation is the most complete and manifest, as in the creation of given objects, or regulation of certain feelings, there the spring of poetry, *i.e.* of passion and imagination, is proportionably and much impaired. We are masters of Art, Nature is our master.   (XIX, 73-74)

As sublime indifference was before allied with the aristocratic privilege of Coriolanus and Byron, "conventional indifference" regulated by art is here allied with Pope and Byron. Against both qualities Hazlitt sets "the full workings, the involuntary, uncontrollable emotions of the heart." Instead of choosing among a set number of objects, prescribed in advance by habit and custom, the sublime imagination fixes upon whatever strikes it most, to which it anticipates the peculiar lustre that memory will give. We are thus recalled to the divided idea of imagination in Hazlitt's *Essay on Human Action,* and to the separate influences of sympathy and habit. The former Hazlitt now identifies with nature, the latter with art. But art in this sense has an ineradicable connection with the imposed norms of artificial society; and Hazlitt alludes again to its effect on Byron in a passage of his essay "On the Conversation of Lords": "all his ideas moulded themselves into stanzas, and all his ardour was carried off in rhyme. The channel of his pen was worn deep by habit and power; the current of his thoughts flowed strong in it, and nothing remained to supply the neighbouring flats and shallows of miscellaneous conversation, but a few sprinklings of wit or gushes of spleen." "On the Conversation of Lords" is an essay in which conversation, in actual life, as much as dramatic variety in poetry, is treated as the natural form of sympathy. Byron lacks the facility for either, the track of all his associations being "worn deep by habit and power." In the review Hazlitt turns "the channel of his pen" into something more resembling a moat, behind which lies the stately dwelling of the mind that owes all its power to place, and to an habitual deference.

Hazlitt's most extraordinary suggestion in this passage is the linking of art, habit, the power of received ideas and arbitrary conventions, with "property," that is, *private* property, which he calls "a practical prosaic idea, to those who possess and clutch." Against these he joins nature, sympathy, the power of impulse and an original self-will, and "common property." The first is what a few may own, and the rest envy: thus the majority elect to share in a power not their own. The second exists as part of the possibility of feeling: it is not there for any to claim, except as its power seems original to themselves; and yet, this is a feeling common to all. The opposition might be put more extravagantly, but with the sort of historical justice Hazlitt cares for, by saying: Byron cannot be loved as well as Wordsworth by those who love the imagination. His taste for Pope betrays a curious anachronism, and Hazlitt is not a naïve apologist for the *avant-garde* when he notices this. He is rather a critic distinctly placed in history, conscious that literature and politics belong to one world. Pope wrote when it was a poet's calling to adopt artificial manners, and cultivate the friendship of lords: his was the form power took in an age like that. But Byron can no longer invoke the same excuse from circumstances, being born himself a lord, and with the conviction besides of natural and common rights which everyone after Rousseau must have felt. It is no error to admire Pope, but it is somehow pointless, or merely quaint in the present state of things, to praise him for having written poetry of the highest class. Nature consists in the overcoming or supercession of the claims of this sort of art, as natural right was a usurpation of every distinction and contrivance that artificial society had erected in defense of inherited power. Manners are "in the power of the will to regulate or satisfy," and of these Pope is the unrivalled master. That is just why we feel the poet who shows us "the workings of the heart" to be superior to Pope. *We are masters of Art, Nature is our Master.*

Coriolanus, Timon of Athens, and *King Lear* were the plays Hazlitt praised for being written in earnest throughout, but of the three one understands, after testing the epigram, why his favorite was always *Lear.* In remarks like this, which stem from his comparison of Byron to Coriolanus, natural right seems in league with a poetry that keeps "nature" ever in view, while established or precedented right belongs to the poetry of "art." In the end art, and even the highest powers of an artificial society, are enemies of the imagination, for they lead us back to "the pavilion at Brighton," and the barriers separating the different classes of mankind. I have said that Hazlitt's objection to Byron is broadly historical, with "the rights of man" in politics and Wordsworth in poetry together making an antagonist whose strength Byron cannot recognize. But Hazlitt had already used this contrast of the natural with the artificial, in battle against the heirs-apparent of Burke, and with more general effect against the utilitarians, from Godwin to James Mill. It emerges again in his criticism of painting, as a preference of Raphael over Rubens, of the bold, naked, natural outline over the ramifying ornaments of conscious art—and, in his criticism of sculpture, as an ideal of the human form *as such,* not painted over or in any way improved. Anything of the sort struck him as an indulgence in illusionism. It was giving nature away to art, making the sublimely gratuitous into the insipidly useful.

Thus, when he discovered Flaxman calling usefulness "a property of beauty," he answered, in one of his annotations to the *Lectures on Sculpture,* that usefulness was *"always a bad reason"* for praising a work of art.[10] He elaborated the point in a review he eventually wrote of the *Lectures:*

> We certainly hate all wax-work, of whatever description; and the idea of colouring a statue gives us a nausea; but as is the case with most bigoted people, the clearness of our reasoning does not keep pace with the strength of our prejudices. It is easy to repeat that the object of painting is colour and form, while the object of sculpture is form alone; and to ring the changes on the purity, the severity, the abstract truth of sculpture. The question returns as before: Why should sculpture be more pure, more severe, more abstracted, than any thing else? . . . [Our] predominant feeling becomes an exclusive and unsociable one, and the mind rejects every addition of a more fleeting or superficial kind as an excrescence and an impertinence. The form is hewn out of solid rock; to tint and daub it over with a flimsy, perishable substance, is a mockery and a desecration, where the work itself is likely to last for ever. A statue is the utmost possible development of form; and that on which the whole powers and faculties of the artist have been bent: it has a right then, by the laws of intellectual creation, to stand alone in that simplicity and unsullied nakedness in which it has been wrought. *Tangible form* (the primary idea) is blind, averse to colour. A statue, if it were coloured at all, ought to be inlaid, that is, done in mosaic, where the colour would be part of the solid materials. But this would be an undertaking beyond human strength. Where art has performed all it can do, why require it to begin its task again? Or if the addition is to be made carelessly and slightly, it is unworthy of the subject. Colour is at best the mask of form: paint on a statue is like paint on a real face,—it is not of a piece with the work, it does not belong to the face, and justly obtains the epithet of *meretricious.*   (XVI, 361–62)

When one compares this with "We are masters of Art, Nature is our master," one sees Hazlitt's reason for calling the paint on statues meretricious. The practice of such "daubing" claims the first part of the epigram for a work which of all others has the glory of proving the truth of the second, in its purest and starkest form. For the sculptural ideal is what every human mind can feel from the nature of the senses: it presents us with *"tangible form."* To daub it over with something more perishable is to transform the appeal into something both higher and lower: painted ladies may compare its elegance with their own. The result may be successful, but the success is that of "wax-work."

Yet painted sculpture must, by Byron's canons of taste, stand a degree higher than mere tangible form, as polish and skill are higher things than invention and imagination. The same canons if applied to poetry would require us to rate very high not only poems that teach virtue in verse, but poems that praise good things, which may be conceived of as a kind of embodied virtue. One may recall here the lines from Pope's "Epistle to Burlington,"

> You show us, Rome was glorious, not profuse,
> And pompous buildings once were things of Use,

but that would be giving Byron too easy a time of it, for he has not ruled out the highest claims for poetry of a much humbler order. Hazlitt accordingly invokes the name of a more recent practitioner of the heroic couplet: "Dr. Darwin is among those, who have endeavoured to confound the distinctions of natural and artificial poetry, and indeed he is, perhaps, the only one who has gone the whole length of Lord Byron's hypercritical and super-artificial theory." As a touchstone of Darwin, he quotes several lines from an apostrophe to steel in *The Botanic Garden,* of which for our purposes the first two may suffice: "Hail, adamantine steel! magnetic lord, / King of the prow, the ploughshare, and the sword!" Hazlitt comments: "This is the true false gallop of the sublime. Yet steel is a very useful metal, and doubtless performs all these wonders. But it has not, among so many others, the virtue of amalgamating with the imagination." Use, habit, and art give us reflex associations, obvious at a glance, that need never be recalled because they seem inherent in the things themselves. Hence the comedy Hazlitt finds in the very idea of an *Apostrophe to Steel.* Where "the work itself is likely to last for ever," a well-turned compliment is as much an impertinence as a coat of paint. As for sentiments and associations, to last forever they must be of a different kind: adapted to the thing they relate to and modify, by the workings of the heart. It is beginning to be plain in what sense, when he wrote "A man can make any thing, but he cannot make a sentiment," Hazlitt could suppose he had exhibited once and for all the fallacy of Byron's attempt to start a Horatian revival.

The passage following that sentence in his review begins with an image from *The Merchant of Venice,* and exemplifies among other things the sort of close reading Hazlitt employed, as freely as Johnson and Ruskin, when a single passage seemed to him a focus of the possible relations between life and poetry, which no reader could fail to see in a similar light.

"How far that little candle throws its beams!
So shines a good deed in a naughty world."

The image here is one of artificial life; but it is connected with natural circumstances and romantic interests, with darkness, with silence, with distance, with privation, and uncertain danger: it is common, obvious, without pretension or boast, and therefore the poetry founded upon it is natural, because the feelings are so. It is not the splendour of the candle itself, but the contrast to the gloom without,—the comfort, the relief it holds out from afar to the benighted traveller,—the conflict between nature and the first and cheapest resources of art, that constitutes the romantic and imaginary, that is, the poetical interest, in that familiar but striking image. There is more art in the lamp or chandelier; but for that very reason, there is less poetry. A light in a watch-tower, a beacon at sea, is sublime for the same cause; because the natural circumstances and associations set it off; it warns us against danger, it reminds us of common calamity, it promises safety and hope: it has to do with the broad feelings and circumstances of human life, and its interest does not assuredly turn upon the vanity or pretensions of the maker or proprietor of it. This sort of art is co-ordinate with nature, and comes into the first-class of poetry, but no one ever dreamt of the contrary. The features of nature are great leading land-marks, not near and little, or confined to a spot, or an individual claimant; they are spread out everywhere the same, and are of universal interest. The true poet has therefore been described as

"Creation's tenant, he is nature's heir."

What has been thus said of the man of genius might be said of the man of no genius. The spirit of poetry, and the spirit of humanity are the same. (XIX, 75–76)

This seems to warrant an extension of the difference between natural and artificial poetry to one between two kinds of making. Artificial poetry enhances, and so augments without changing the idea of, the things men have made to flatter themselves. Natural poetry on the other hand is itself the thing it asks us to reflect on, which only one mind has made, but which once brought into the world must belong to all equally. There is a conflation of ends and means, which artificial poetry does not allow. When, hearing an object described in some passage of poetry, we feel that "the vanity or pretensions of the maker or proprieter" are involved in the interest we are supposed to feel, then the object is artificial in a way that excludes universal interest. Examples of such objects might be: coursers, carriages, titles, estates, nick-names. But what emerges from artificial life may still in the right circumstances be considered an object of natural poetry. This happens when associations connected with the object are open to all that read of it, from their exposure to the common fate of humanity. Such for example is the candle shining in the dark: though made by man, it brings to mind the invariable conditions of his life, as no strictly artificial object can. The matter becomes clearer when one admits an alternative use of the image, as life, shining in a world of death to which all equally are subject.

Now Byron, from his love of Pope, had committed himself to a view of poetry as dedicated to a record of manners, and asked in his *Letter:* "What is there of *human,* be it poetry, philosophy, wit, wisdom, science, power, glory, mind, matter, life, or death, which is *invariable?*" Hazlitt replies: "There is one of the particulars in this enumeration, which seems pretty invariable, which is death." Pope's use of a candle in a poem like *The Rape of the Lock* or even in the *Moral Essays,* would not have implicated it in "the broad feelings and circumstances of human life," as Shakespeare's does: it would have served as a stage prop, like the door-knocker at the start of the "Epistle to Arbuthnot"; and if not private property, in any but a trivial sense, it would nevertheless have remained an *occasional* object. To satisfy Hazlitt, the line, "Tye up the knocker, say I'm sick, I'm dead," must have the same meaning whether for those who are indoors or out; as must the candle for those whose way is in darkness or light. But there is no true parallel between the cases: Pope can write morally when he employs universals, like "light," "wit," or "good," yet his objects are never common in the sense that Shakespeare's are.

What the objects of great poetry signify for all readers, Hazlitt tells us in a phrase at the end. "The spirit of poetry, and the spirit of humanity are the same." It may seem a strange conclusion, from the author who five years before in an essay "On Poetical Versatility" had written, "The spirit of poetry is in itself favourable to humanity and liberty: but, we suspect, not when its aid is most wanted" —who, only two years before, had repeated this almost verbatim, in the "Letter to William Gifford"—and whom we have heard summing up all his doubts in the unsettling declaration prompted by a new production of *Coriolanus,* "The language of poetry naturally falls in with the language of power." But Hazlitt's impulse, from the *Essay* onward, has been to deny the language of power, if it owes its strength to artificial endowments, the final distinction of sublimity. His reasons must be connected with his estimate of the sublime as the highest class of poetry, his consequent vigilance on its behalf, and his suspicion that the various "sublime styles" which poetry and painting had inherited from the age of sensibility, were still giving a false standard to the productions of art. His repeated use of the word "common," to remind us of a quality true sublimity will always possess, also seems to me significant. One recalls Kant's idea of the sublime as that, the mere ability to think which shows a faculty of the mind surpassing every standard of sense; but one feels that Hazlitt would have added: it may not violate the *common* sense of what is possible to our affections. Wordsworth's shock at having crossed the Alps I quoted earlier as an instance of such surpassing. Yet there were other plausible sublimities in Byron's day, their sanction derived from an extension of the picturesque into the grand. Hazlitt's whole animus toward Byron in the review of the *Letter* arises from a belief that Byron was essentially a poet of "great objects," but tending toward a picturesque grandeur of this sort.

Byron's emphasis on the artificial thus seemed to Hazlitt merely a self-deceptive way of justifying his attraction to art on a more than human scale. His claim to be writing as Pope's successor was at this time founded on "English Bards and Scotch Reviewers," and perhaps the early cantos of *Don Juan,* while his serious productions were *Childe Harold, Manfred,* and *Marino Faliero.* The former could not yet sustain the comparison they evoked. In the latter Byron had been offering readers the long unbroken pageant of human suffering as their experience of the sublime, and here, as in other romantic trials of the unendurable, Hazlitt saw a corruption of purpose. He would have found it epitomized, I think, by some of De Quincey's essays, but he states a moderate version of his objection in examining an artist of more slender gifts, the landscape painter John Martin.

> [Martin] has no notion of the moral principle in all art, that a part may be greater than the whole. He reckons that if one range of lofty square hills is good, another range above that with clouds between must be better. He thus wearies the imagination, instead of exciting it. We see no end of the journey, and turn back in disgust. We are tired of [the same object]. . . . This craving after quantity is a morbid affectation. . . . You may build a house as high as you can lift up stones with pulleys and levers, but you cannot raise mountains into the sky merely with the pencil. They lose

probability and effect by striving at too much; and, with their ceaseless throes, oppress the imagination of the spectator, and bury the artist's fame under them. The only error of these pictures is, however, that art here puts on her seven-league boots, and thinks it possible to steal a march upon nature. (XVIII, 155)

The protest is not simply that Martin fails to raise the picturesque into the sublime by sufficiently mild gradations. It has to do rather with the close relation between sheer quantity and morbidness, and between the cultivation of a morbidly heightened state and the violence we feel done to our affections. So a writer like De Quincey, adapting Martin's tactics to prose, could extend a theatrical metaphor for the suffering of multitudes far beyond its Burkean scope, and with results the opposite of Burkean. In "The Revolt of the Tartars" he derives an exquisite horror from reciting the sheer facts of magnitude:

> It is remarkable that these sufferings of the Tartars, though under the moulding hands of accident, arrange themselves almost with a scenical propriety. They seem combined, as with the skill of an artist; the intensity of the misery advancing regularly with the advances of the march, and the stages of the calamity corresponding to the stages of the route; so that, upon raising the curtain which veils the great catastrophe, we behold one vast climax of anguish, towering upwards by regular gradations, as if constructed artificially for picturesque effect. . . . [Thus] the Russian armies did not begin to close in very fiercely upon the Kalmucks until after they had accomplished a distance of full 2000 miles: 1000 miles farther on the assaults became even more tumultuous and murderous: and already the great shadows of the Chinese Wall were dimly descried, when the frenzy and *acharnement* of the pursuers, and the bloody desperation of the miserable fugitives, had reached its uttermost extremity. Let us briefly rehearse the main stages of the misery, and trace the ascending steps of the tragedy, according to the great divisions of the route marked out by the central rivers of Asia.[11]

Examining a smaller scale of the picturesque, Ruskin would later speak of it as a "heartless" ideal, and say, of the warped sentiments of the typical adept: "Fallen cottage—deserted village—blasted heath—mouldering castle—to him, so that they do not show jagged angles of stone and timber, all are sights equally joyful."[12] In the same spirit Hazlitt criticizes the Byronic or De Quincean or Martinesque adept, for whom so many tens of thousands of dead are chiefly instructive as a nice piece of unexpectedness, for the way they dispose themselves evenly over an author's map of a desperate transcontinental migration.

Even at the end of Byron's career, when most of *Don Juan* was open to inspection, Hazlitt seems to have felt it right to connect his "artificiality" not with an instinct for satire, but with an attraction to this sort of misconceived sublimity. His analysis, refined for most of a decade, begins as early as the review of *Childe Harold* which I quoted in chapter 4, continues in the passage on Byron and Bowles describing the former's "notions of art and poetry" as "sufficiently wild, romantic, far-fetched, obsolete," and reaches its climax in *The Spirit of the Age,* with its decisive character of Byron as "often monotonous, extravagant, offensive" and its defense of a higher example: "He says of Mr. Wordsworth's poetry, that 'it is his aversion.' That may be: but whose fault is it? This is the satire of a lord, who is accustomed to have all his whims or dislikes taken for gospel." Hazlitt settled the estimate that he had been building all along, and the contrast with Wordsworth that formed its necessary groundwork, in an unsigned contribution to the *London Weekly Review* in April 1828. The occasion was an anecdote about Byron's having borrowed from Leigh Hunt, and returned with disparaging comments, a book of Spenser's poems. This led Hazlitt to reflect on the connection between duration in the works of man, and sentiments that last forever because they show the workings of the heart; between the capacity to respect the first, and to produce the second; between sublimity of utterance and sublimity of feeling. The one-paragraph note, called simply "Byron and Wordsworth," blends from Hazlitt's career so many of the strains of thought and feeling that I have been seeking to exhibit in ordered relation with each other—with an intensity of association that combines experience and reading so finely—that I give it without comment.

> I am much surprised at Lord Byron's haste to return a volume of Spenser, which was lent him by Mr. Hunt, and at his apparent indifference to the progress and (if he pleased) *advancement* of poetry up to the present day. Did he really think that all genius was concentrated in his own time, or in his own bosom? With his pride of ancestry, had he no curiosity to explore the heraldry of intellect? . . . I do not recollect, in all Lord Byron's writings, a single recurrence to a feeling or object that had ever excited an interest before; there is no display of natural affection—no twining of the heart round any object: all is the restless and disjointed effect of first im-

pressions, of novelty, contrast, surprise, grotesque costume, or sullen grandeur. *His* beauties are the *houris* of Paradise, the favourites of a seraglio, the changing visions of a feverish dream. His poetry, it is true, is stately and dazzling, arched like a rainbow, of bright and lovely hues, painted on the cloud of his own gloomy temper—perhaps to disappear as soon! It is easy to account for the antipathy between him and Mr. Wordsworth. Mr. Wordsworth's poetical mistress is a Pamela; Lord Byron's an Eastern princess or a Moorish maid. It is the extrinsic, the uncommon that captivates him, and all the rest he holds in sovereign contempt. This is the obvious result of pampered luxury and high-born sentiments. The mind, like the palace in which it has been brought up, admits none but new and costly furniture. . . . The author of the Lyrical Ballads describes the lichen on the rock, the withered fern, with some peculiar feeling that he has about them: the author of Childe Harold describes the stately cypress or the fallen column, with the feeling that every schoolboy has about them. The world is a grown schoolboy, and relishes the latter most. When Rousseau called out—"*Ah! Voila de la pervenche!*" in a transport of joy at sight of the periwinkle, because he had first seen this little blue flower in company with Madame Warens thirty years before, I cannot help thinking, that any astonishment expressed at the sight of a palm-tree, or even of Pompey's Pillar, is vulgar compared to this! Lord Byron, when he does not saunter down Bond-street, goes into the East: when he is not occupied with the passing topic, he goes back two thousand years, at one poetic gigantic stride! But instead of the sweeping mutations of empire and the vast lapses of duration, shrunk up into an antithesis, commend me to the "slow and creeping foot of time," in the commencement of Ivanhoe, where the jester and the swineherd watch the sun going down behind the low-stunted trees of the forest, and their loitering and impatience make the summer's day seem so long, that we wonder how we have ever got to the end of the six hundred years that have passed since! That where the face of nature has changed, time should have rolled on its course, is but a common-place discovery; but that where all seems the same (the long rank grass, and the stunted oaks, and the innocent pastoral landscape), all should have changed—this is to me the burthen and the mystery. The ruined pile is a memento and a monument to him that reared it—oblivion has here done but half its work; but what yearnings, what vain conflicts with its fate come over the soul in the other case, which makes man seem like a grasshopper—an insect of the hour, and all that he is, or that others have been—nothing!　　　　　　　　　　　　　　　　　(XX, 155–57)

CHAPTER X

FAMILIAR STYLE

THE VOCATION OF AN ESSAYIST

By 1820, Hazlitt had written most of his criticism of particular artists and works; in the decade that remained to him, he would be known chiefly as an essayist. Yet essay-writing was not a lighter employment for his intelligence, and it shared with criticism the same work of interpretation. To take only the most obvious common trait, Hazlitt's essays often proceed by a sequence of allegorical inventions. He may not name his characters as suggestively as Johnson did—Dick Minim (the Critic), Will Marvel (the Man of Susceptible Imaginings)—but the human qualities he picks out as topics embody characters just as distinctly, and they march through his pages with as little embarrassment: Vulgarity, Affectation, Toad-Eater, Tyrant. Here, as in his criticism, Hazlitt starts from a single truth about writing as persuasion. You cannot alter the understanding of a thing without first emphasizing certain of its features, and abstracting them from the rest; take the practice far enough and you will be accused of allegorizing; and yet, when an interpreter isolates one perspective in this way, he does just what he aimed to do. Hazlitt's essays communicate the author's tact for shifting inclinations, for negotiating between what "The Indian Jugglers" describes as different *languages* of action. The quip (in "On Genius and Common Sense") about the music-master who talked upon all subjects at sight, like the comparison (in "On a Landscape of Nicholas Poussin") of the painter with Milton for a certain inveterate pedantry, delights us as an act of rapid translation, though in the context it may seem merely an incidental stroke of wit. This chapter will center on a small group of essays where such moves are far from incidental; but first something must be said of the way Hazlitt chose to situate himself in a larger tradition.

Of his predecessors in essay-writing, Hazlitt reserved the highest

praise for Montaigne. Among English writers Johnson and Goldsmith were those who might have been supposed to strike him as fit
rivals. But in the *Rambler,* all the periods "are cast in the same
mould, are of the same size and shape, and consequently have little
fitness to the variety of things [Johnson] professes to treat of. His
subjects are familiar, but the author is always upon stilts," his style
"a species of rhyming in prose." Goldsmith, on the other hand,
though "more observing, more original, more natural" than Johnson, wrote the *Citizen of the World* in the ironic spirit of Montes-
quieu's *Persian Letters,* and Hazlitt says of its gradually ramifying
paradoxes that "the process is too ambiguous and full of intricacy to
be very amusing to my plain understanding." Hazlitt conceived of
an essay as an improvised process or trial, as the word by its etymology implies. In sincerity too there is always an element of performance: the writer seeks to show how great a store lies in his possession, as opposed to that of others; yet he makes not only his sense
of decorum, but his life and distinct experiences, answerable for the
result.

Hence the high position of Montaigne, and his worthiness as a
model in style as well as structure. He was "the first who had the
courage to say as an author what he felt as a man." Hazlitt adds a
long paragraph of elaboration, in which Montaigne's character as a
skeptic comes to seem a bulwark against all the temptations to appear a pedant or bigot, which beset the essayist's work: "He did not,
in the abstract character of an author, undertake to say all that could
be said upon a subject, but what in his capacity as an inquirer after
truth he happened to know about it." This alone might account for
our impression of a man steadily self-centered, yet never absorbing
back into the course of his thoughts the vapors of an irritable egotism
that his essays draw off: "There is an inexpressible frankness and
sincerity, as well as power, in what he writes." Inexpressible, in a
master of expression, because the variety of his topics, matched by
variety of treatment, leads us to suppose behind the work a mind
whose next inlet of knowledge or effusion of temperament can never
be predicted from the last. But it is Hazlitt's final words about Montaigne that assure us of the personal emphasis of the tribute, by
registering its cost to the writer who issues it.

> The same force and honesty of mind which urged him to throw
> off the shackles of custom and prejudice, would enable him to
> complete his triumph over them. He has left little for his suc-

cessors to achieve in the way of just and original speculation on human life. . . . He sowed the seed and cleared away the rubbish, even where others have reaped the fruit, or cultivated and decorated the soil to a greater degree of nicety and perfection. There is no one to whom the old Latin adage is more applicable than to Montaigne, *"Pereant isti qui ante nos nostra dixerunt."* There has been no new impulse given to thought since his time.   (VI, 93–94)

The Latin phrase, which might be freely rendered, "Away with those who said our best things before us," is in part an ironic injunction to read Montaigne, but it delivers Hazlitt further into debt than he must have wished to appear when he first undertook to lecture "On the Periodical Essayists."

Why should an essayist, who elsewhere seems aware of the need for some saving illusion of progress in any art whatever, have given away almost everything in writing the history of his own? Two answers recommend themselves to anyone familiar with Hazlitt's statements about his vocation. The first is that he never took it seriously—it was a stay against penury, that outlasted its intended span, and became habitual in spite of anything he could propose as an alternative form. This is a long way around to explain the existence of a hundred essays, more observing, original, and keen-witted than any others in the language. There are of course moods in which Hazlitt will speak of his essays as "abortions," but they are less frequent than those in which he consigns himself to the grave, and dispatches the essays to their permanent dwelling, with a hint of the *aere perennius* that is only the sweeter for its uninsistent good nature. Still, Hazlitt's famous statements about vocation figure him as a painter, a metaphysician, the first worthy biographer of Napoleon, much more than as an essayist. Of the clues that do indicate his seriousness about the profession he finally adopted, too little use has been made.

Hazlitt wrote extensive annotations in a copy of Bacon's *Advancement of Learning*, in which among other remarks he included suggestions to himself about possible essay-topics.[1] The presence, in this same copy, of notes in his hand giving only the initials R.T., appears to indicate that he read it while collecting quotations that would go into the articles of *The Round Table* (1814-1817); yet some notes mention the titles of essays written considerably later, in *Table-Talk* ("On the Ignorance of the Learned" is one); the copy also contains the beginning of a character of Bacon that would be fitted into his *Lectures on the Age of Elizabeth*. Many passages beside which he writes, "Quote," were never quoted, others seem to have joined his tact for a subject, to emerge later in paraphrase, or as an invention visibly different and his own. What interests me here is one note, on Bacon's reasons for "the preferment of the contemplative or active life": beside this, Hazlitt's comment is "mem. Essay on a man's living to himself R.T." One will search *The Round Table* in vain for such an essay, but it did appear several years later, in *Table-Talk* (1821). This is circumstantial evidence of a persuasive kind, and it will serve. He was, I think, in the habit of laying up essay topics, for use at some future date. He began the practice early, and was imagining himself an essayist early. This was the direction his mind took naturally when he thought of a future of writing. Further, there were for him no sure distinctions among certain essays that might appear in separate volumes, but were meant to be read as companions: *The Round Table,* for example, has a fine essay on the learnedness of the learned, "On Pedantry," whose lesson is that everyone is necessarily pedantic about what interests him most; and to this the later essay whose title he planned early was meant all along as a set-off. Again, he comments without specifying, "motto for essay," beside Bacon's observation "that some minds are proportioned to that which may be dispatched at once or within a short returne of time: others to that which begins afarre off, and is to be won with length of pursuite." Here the comment seems to mean: this thought has sometimes been mine also; I will make it the work of an essay. (Many touch the theme: "Why Distant Objects Please" is only the plainest instance.) Still another passage he scores with the notation, "motto for personal character": if one assumes that this too was done in the "R.T." period, he was looking forward to an essay then a decade ahead, which when it emerged would bear a motto from Montaigne instead of Bacon: "Men palliate and conceal their original qualities, but do not extirpate them." The thought is as old as Horace (*Naturam furca expelles, tamen usque recurret*), and would have been available to Hazlitt elsewhere in Bacon as well, from the first sentence of the essay "Of Nature in Men."

Once we have dismissed the idea that he thought himself only an amateur of the essay, a second possible reason for Hazlitt's ease with Montaigne is that for all their shared qualities of temperament, he did not consider himself Montaigne's kind of essayist, and could therefore regard him as a bearable predecessor. Every essayist has experienced a tension between two wishes, to be a Man of Wisdom or a Man of Genius. The former commands credence; the latter evokes awe; both sorts of attention are desirable, and as a result no essayist has quite gone over to one side. But with each role is parcelled out a suitable method. The Man of Wisdom proceeds by an accumulation of instances, and in the end hopes as the reward of his persuasiveness to be praised for his justice. The Man of Genius proceeds by a pointed selection of instances—will often, out of defiance, call attention to his omissions—and hopes to be praised for nothing but his insight. Even where the two styles are similar, the texture gives a clue to one role or the other; and without pressing a convenient distinction until it becomes an encumbrance, one may say that Hazlitt is always a little less than Montaigne the Man of Wisdom. The very look of a page of Montaigne tells part of the story: many quotations, and brief paragraphs because what is to be *learned* is best encountered in this way. Hazlitt's unbroken paragraphs of two pages or more, on the other hand, seem bent on earning Goldsmith's praise of Burke, with their graphic evidence of how genius *"winds* into the subject like a serpent." Hazlitt indeed uses the figure of a train of thought so often that he may fairly be said to have naturalized it in English. His essays were the highest discursive exercise conceivable, for the imaginative work of association he had described in the *Essay on Human Action.*

Another remarkable element of Hazlitt's procedure which sets him apart from Montaigne, is that as a rule he does not draw his quotations from the common stock of classic sententiae, though he employs them often enough to prevent our thinking they were not a live option for him. His quotations come instead from an idiosyncratic canon, in which recent figures such as Burke and Wordsworth are prominent. Something of his energy of mind is to be deduced from his originality of taste, and this energy involves a larger strategy of shifts, transpositions, sudden invasions from or excursions to a far reach of the world, or another mind. Montaigne's "I" is gentle, dignified, peripatetic, unpredictable. He plays host to himself, is polite though not effusive while the visit lasts, and gracious in his farewell. Hazlitt's "I" can enter the scene like a whirlwind, and leave the whole countenance of things altered by his departure. So too with their use of anecdotes. Montaigne's are well timed and have respect to their ends. Hazlitt's can get out of hand, and to have done so seems part of their pride in retrospect, a triumph just as useful as the trim virtue of appositeness. Montaigne never speaks of the strain of making his connections: they are there for him, the pride of the skeptic being not to forge them too brilliantly. But Hazlitt's essays register the strain in exclamations of disappointment or self-disgust,

as well as by the abruptness of transitions, or the abruptness of conclusions ("Are we not quits!").

Between the conduct of an argument for Hazlitt and for Montaigne, the difference will emerge more starkly if one considers a
fairly characteristic performance by the latter, and asks where the
affinity starts and stops. Thus the title of "On the Disadvantages of
Greatness" is echoed by Hazlitt's "On the Disadvantages of Intellectual Superiority"; and one might even say that the difference begins
there. Montaigne's phrase is rich with an irony not all of whose elements have yet been claimed: disadvantages for whom? greatness real
or pretended? But with Hazlitt the personal animus can be felt before one reads his first sentence. It may point the comparison to try
guessing how he would have changed the emphasis had he adopted
exactly the same topic. Montaigne's essay, as translated by Donald
Frame, starts off: "Since we cannot attain it, let us take our revenge
by speaking ill of it. Yet it is not absolutely speaking ill of something
to find some defects in it; there are some in all things, however beautiful or desirable they may be. In general greatness has this advantage, that it can step down whenever it pleases, and that it has almost
the choice of both conditions. For one does not fall from every
height; there are more from which one can descend without falling."
The self-disarming gesture of the opening sentence shows Montaigne's delicacy in the refinements of doubt, and it is a gesture that
would have been insupportable to Hazlitt. For its effect is that of an
ad hominem attack by the author on the author: resentment is
brought in from the start, as his possible motive for telling the truth,
so that we cease to credit Montaigne as a uniquely trustworthy observer, and believe his facts instead as the wisdom of observation. As
for the remaining sentences, they are chiefly concerned with the advantages of greatness. But Hazlitt, were he tempted to undertake an
essay on this topic, would reason as follows: (1) Greatness is a thing
we all acknowledge and can therefore treat as a fact of nature. (2) It
is difficult to separate those persons who seem impressive for a time
from those who will be so forever. (3) Anyway, I am not great, but
I have the sense to see that (4) Those who are esteemed my superiors
deceive the world only more deftly than I, as (5) Some examples will
show. Yet these remind us how pervasively (6) Our pleasure in individuality is predicated on our knowledge of limitation. There is
some comfort in this, once we have got over the mortification, which
we hardly ever do.

Though Montaigne seems to me the essayist most nearly related to Hazlitt, whether one considers tone, pace, rhetorical design, or intellectual temper, for all that he is not very close. In fact the best analogy for Hazlitt's essays is with Keats's verse-epistles, and in select cases with his odes. Before pursuing this in the next chapter, however, I need to state the associationist premise that Hazlitt and Keats evidently share. It is, that the stream of thought has its own coherence, flowing between alterable but determinate limits, from a particular source to a particular destination. The elements we discern of its composition will only be deducible from the place where we intercept it. In this sense the metaphor gives a peculiarly strong sanction for what the Man of Imagination has always wished to say about himself, that in encountering him the reader never quite steps into the same mind twice.

DEPTH, SURFACE, AND SITUATION

I will be discussing as examples of associative energy, three of Hazlitt's greatest essays, on which I have been drawing in any case for the exposition of his criticism. I select them not quite arbitrarily, one apiece from *Table-Talk, The Plain Speaker,* and the posthumous *Uncollected Essays:* in sequence, I think they illustrate a more than chronological progression. "The Indian Jugglers" defines the idea of genius against that of mechanical skill or dexterity; it compares them, first to the advantage of the latter (when Hazlitt's essays, as "trial" and therefore imperfect attempts, have to represent genius), and then to the advantage of the former (when the mortality of all feats of skill is compared with the unbounded future of the productions of genius); finally it subsumes both in the category of "greatness," and convinces us that this must be present wherever the power of any human exertion is communicated to the understandings of those who witness it. "On Depth and Superficiality" reveals the writer's genius as nothing other than his skill in making us suppose depths of causes and motives where we had glimpsed only the surface phenomena of behavior; the abstract-sounding topic becomes a special challenge to Hazlitt's gusto in working up a vivid illustration from a truth unflattering to the imagination. "On a Sun-dial" then isolates a particular chosen object, as an occasion for the writer to appear both spontaneous with the ease of the juggler, and permanent in his impressions, like the philosopher who shows how depths *are* surfaces.

"The Indian Jugglers" starts with Hazlitt's awe at the precision with which a spectacle is kept up, where "A single error of a hair's breadth, of the smallest conceivable portion of time, would be fatal." Our admiration for this is quickly made a test of our capacity to admire anything at all. "It is skill surmounting difficulty, and beauty triumphing over skill. It seems as if the difficulty once mastered naturally resolved itself into ease and grace, and as if to be overcome at all, it must be overcome without effort." Why in that case does not any habitual skill answer the same wish to be delighted by thorough mastery? Because it seldom answers visibly at the same time to the nature of things—it is not tried by the immediate test of failure. In the trick of the jugglers, we have a strange collaboration between the laws of gravity and the nervous system of a human being.

> The hearing of a speech in Parliament, drawled or stammered out by the Honourable Member or the Noble Lord, the ringing the changes on their common-places, which anyone could repeat after them as well as they, stirs me not a jot, shakes not my good opinion of myself: but the seeing the Indian Jugglers does. It makes me ashamed of myself. I ask what there is that I can do as well as this? Nothing. What have I been doing all my life? Have I been idle, or have I nothing to shew for all my labour and pains? Or have I passed my time in pouring words like water into empty sieves, rolling a stone up a hill and then down again, trying to prove an argument in the teeth of facts, and looking for causes in the dark, and not finding them?   (VIII, 78–79)

Yet the repeatability of all feats of mechanical skill also marks their limitation. "If the Indian Juggler were to play tricks in throwing up the three case-knives, which keep their positions like the leaves of a crocus in the air, he would cut his fingers. I can make a very bad antithesis without cutting my fingers. The tact of style is more ambiguous than that of double-edged instruments." Such ambiguity, Hazlitt now begins to show, is a necessary difficulty and also a richness, attendant on two facts about the artist's work that distinguish him from the juggler: he is involved in a contest ("If two persons play against each other at any game," Hazlitt observes in a footnote, "one of them necessarily fails"); and he is endeavoring to imitate nature, to "copy what she has set before us in the face of nature or 'human face divine.'" Remembering his own dictum that the artist imitates not things as they are but "as they are moulded by other thoughts and feelings, into an infinite variety of shapes and combinations of power," Hazlitt now revises his first response: the artist's work is essentially greater than the skilled mechanic's, for the same reason that it is off the scale of mechanical perfectibility. "Nature is also a language. Objects, like words, have a meaning; and the true artist is the interpreter of this language, which he can only do by knowing its application to a thousand other objects in a thousand other situations." That puts an end, not to our amazement in the presence of the jugglers, but to any lingering wish to describe their activity as great. It is one situation, given to us whole, which can be reproduced on command, and never need be interpreted. It cannot change, and it cannot change us. The following three-way distinction names the juggler's quality "talent," as against ingenuity and genius that is great.

> Talent is the capacity of doing any thing that depends on application and industry, such as writing a criticism, making a speech, studying the law. Talent differs from genius, as voluntary differs from involuntary power. Ingenuity is genius in trifles, greatness is genius in undertakings of much pith and moment. . . . Themistocles said he could not play on the flute, but that he could make of a small city a great one. This gives one a pretty good idea of the distinction in question.   (VIII, 84)

Greatness is defined as "great power, producing great effects"; power, in which we see both the striving to excel in a given situation, and the interest in revising our view of something important; effects, in which "we trace the master-mind, and can sympathise with the springs that urge him on." Contest remains Hazlitt's theme as much as interpretation, and he adds, "A really great man has always an idea of something greater than himself." But the essay now shifts unaccountably—so it must seem—to Hazlitt's transcription of his four-page obituary for "John Cavanagh, the famous hand fives-player," an article written as he says, "apparently between jest and earnest." By adopting this as his conclusion, Hazlitt brings back the puzzle the essay had seemed to leave unsolved, about the relation between contest as the athlete knows it and as the artist does. The individual athlete has a skill hardly trivial for the interest it commands, and adaptable to new situations, and involving him in contest with a risk of failure. Yet he does not interpret a language and extend his claim to the whole fabric of conduct, as the artist does. Where shall we place him?

Hazlitt begins Cavanagh's obituary: "the game of fives is what no one despises who has ever played at it." The comparison of this player's style with the lumbering, or wavering, or wide-shooting, or *let* balls that flaw the style of the age's more considerable literary gamesmen, I cited in chapter 3 as an instance of the mock epic of ordinary life. Yet the mockery could not exist without some presupposition of grandeur, and when Hazlitt arrives at his stories of Cavanagh's indomitability he has to confront the mystery of contemporary fame, both its apparent assurance and its real disobligingness as a token of immortality.

> In a word, there are hundreds at this day, who cannot mention [Cavanagh's] name without admiration, as the best fives-player that perhaps ever lived (the greatest excellence of which they have any notion)—and the noisy shout of the ring happily stood him in stead of the unheard voice of posterity! (VIII, 89)

And yet, Hazlitt has made of the "noisy shout" an echoing applause, which may in turn render the "unheard voice" articulate. He preserves Cavanagh's fame as Cavanagh could not himself, and when in conclusion he says of his tribute, "Let no rude hand deface it, / And his forlorn '*Hic Jacet*,'" the irony is grand and high-spirited, because this essay has stood in the way of defacement as no lapidary inscription could. "The Indian Jugglers" offers Cavanagh as a test case for distinguishing the artist from the mechanic. The truth is that only Hazlitt's ability to see the depth of art in the surface of mechanical skill—to plot the different situations that mark Cavanagh with the genius of "Cobbett and Junius together" (the sincere conviction of a slam repeated in the same spot, with the elegant refinement of the drop shot at uneven intervals)—has made the question an interesting one. The practiced eye more than finds, it invents the glory of the things that concern it. In this sense one might say that Hazlitt does for Cavanagh what the essayist does for his own experience all the time. His gift of immortality to one player marks his ascendancy over a limited contest, only as much as it marks his kinship with the contestant: the report would have been impossible had not the author himself been a fives-player, and the essay would have come to no conclusion but for Cavanagh. The trivial becomes the grand, when placed just so: "between jest and earnest," it becomes a picture nothing can deface, when drawn into the web of comparisons that present the characteristic workings of one mind.

"On Depth and Superficiality" seems to me one long series of meditations in the spirit of Cavanagh's obituary. Things familiar and definite become remote, and illustrate an unfamiliar principle, but the move is made plausible only by the conquering interpretation of the essayist, who appears as the master of experience. He can find a context in which many paradoxes make new sense: deep explanations turn into the obvious data of observation, and superficial phenomena come to seem the springs of a vast process. The essayist can find an original context for anything, and so place it that we are instantly persuaded of his explanation. Named things and natural kinds are to him interchangeable, depending on what the occasion and the whole movement of his mind require. Hazlitt confesses his purpose of upsetting our sense that the world yields one structure of explanation from top to bottom, in a short opening paragraph which concludes with a joke.

> I wish to make this Essay a sort of study of the meaning of several words, which have at different times a good deal puzzled me. Among these are the words, *wicked, false* and *true,* as applied to feeling; and lastly, *depth* and *shallowness.* It may amuse the reader to see the way in which I work out some of my conclusions underground, before throwing them up on the surface.   (XII, 346-47)

The first such conclusion is about the love of power in man, and comes from a question about fact.

> A great but useless thinker once asked me, if I had ever known a child of a naturally wicked disposition? and I answered, "Yes, that there was one in the house with me that cried from morning to night, *for spite."* I was laughed at for this answer, but still I do not repent it. It appeared to me that this child took a delight in tormenting itself and others; that the love of tyrannising over others and subjecting them to its caprices was a full compensation for the beating it received, that the screams it uttered soothed its peevish, turbulent spirit, and that it had a positive pleasure in pain from the sense of power accompanying it.   (XII, 347)

The underground from which that conclusion was thrown up has been the theme of my book. To credit Hazlitt's paradox of the moment, however, we need to be shown why the question, Whether the baby is the original form of the love of power (as depth) or merely manifests it involuntarily (as surface), is as unresolvable as the question, Whether we ought to consider the offender in its future. capacity as parent or its present capacity as offspring.

> If the child had been in pain or in fear, I should have said nothing, but it cried only to vent its passion and alarm the house, and I saw in its frantic screams and gestures that great baby, the world, tumbling about in its swaddling clothes, and tormenting itself and others for the last six thousand years.   (XII, 348)

"Itself and others" is the sort of comic touch available only to the essayist who is willing to transpose our habitual subordination of particular to general.

Hazlitt gives a second example of such a reversal proceeding from a commonplace incident, when he discusses Newton's invention of the law of gravity. Newton saw the apple fall, just as Hazlitt heard the baby cry; and an ordinary mortal would no more think of this in relation to some new principle of things, than he would call the baby wicked. Babies we suppose cry without motive, and apples fall downwards. But "Sir Isaac Newton by a bare effort of abstraction, or by a grasp of mind comprehending all the possible relations of things, got rid of this prejudice, turned the world as it were on its back, and saw the apple fall not *downwards,* but simply *towards* the earth, so that it would fall *upwards* on the same principle, if the earth were above it, or towards it at any rate in whatever direction it lay." This he accomplished by abstraction, but an effort of abstraction when sufficiently strange has the power to invert the former relationship of depth to surface: mass and attraction became the force to reckon with, instead of the directions up and down. In the same way one might cite Wordsworth's ability to make a mighty abstraction out of the word "common," or "things."

Hazlitt has nothing quite so striking to show for himself, but he follows the example from Newton with an example of what the essayist can do, to recover the laws of experience, or bring them into existence. In this passage he writes with the tact of the novelist, historian, and political orator, all contained in the author who could see power and spite in the apparently reflex cries of a child.

> I lately heard an anecdote related of an American lady (one of two sisters) who married young and well, and had several children; her sister, however, was married soon after herself to a richer hus-

band, and had a larger (if not finer) family, and after passing several years of constant repining and wretchedness, she died at length of pure envy. The circumstance was well known and generally talked of. Some one said on hearing this, that it was a thing that could only happen in America; that it was a trait of republican character and institutions, where alone the principle of mutual jealousy, having no high and distant objects to fix upon, and divert it from immediate and private mortifications, seized upon the happiness or outward advantages even of the nearest connexions as its natural food, and having them constantly before its eyes, gnawed itself to death upon them. I assented to this remark, and I confess it struck me as shewing a deep insight into human nature. Here was a sister envying a sister, and that not for objects that provoke strong passion, but for common and contentional advantages, till it ends in her death. (XII, 358-59)

The extravagance of anyone dying of *pure envy* thus has its reason in the character of the American republic, and one may assume Hazlitt would grant the person who made the connection a high degree of ingenuity. But the very word "insight" seems to imply sudden penetration to the depths of some matter, whereas Hazlitt wants to exhibit this as an observation available to the person of ordinary watchfulness, once he has freed himself from enough prejudices about the relations between abstraction and particularity. He speaks for that person in the rest of the paragraph, once again in a style that makes the passing insight of common sense—like the common awe for Cavanagh—a portion of genius that wants only an interpreter.

How then is this extraordinary development of an ordinary human frailty to be accounted for? From the peculiar circumstances? These were the country and state of society. It was in America that it happened. The democratic level, the flatness of imagery, the absence of those towering and artificial heights that in old and monarchial states act as conductors to attract and carry off the splenetic humours and rancorous hostilities of a whole people, and to make common and petty advantages sink into perfect insignificance, were full in the mind of the person who suggested the solution; and in this dearth of every other mark or vent for it, it was felt intuitively, that the natural spirit of envy and discontent would fasten upon those that were next to it, and whose advantages, there being no great difference in point of elevation, would gall in proportion to their proximity and repeated recurrence. . . . The fact, as stated in itself, is an anomaly: as thus explained, by combining it with a general state of feeling in a country, it seems to point out a great principle in society. Now this solution would not have been attained but for the deep impression which the operation of certain general causes of moral character had recently made, and the quickness with which the consequences of its removal were felt.

(XII, 359)

As, in "The Indian Jugglers," Hazlitt introduced his obituary as the work of someone else, which he happened across in the *Examiner,* so the *tour de force* of reasoning-in-manners is here introduced as what "some one said," to which he assented at the time. But the conjectural brilliance and headlong assurance of this passage could only have come from being midwife a second time to one's own thoughts. The remark was Hazlitt's, or what comes to the same thing, he makes it his, by the alacrity with which he undertakes its justification as a trial of genius, and allows its depth to appear after all just the surface of any profound experience of life in society. The scientist works with stories like this, as much as the artist; but Hazlitt would recognize one difference between them. The scientist, who invents a category of "death by pure envy," will tell you the story to persuade you of the reality of his category; whereas to the artist, whom for the moment Hazlitt exemplifies, the category was necessary only as a hint about what to put in and leave out of the story itself. Pure envy exists so long as it helps bring to life stories like this, and is made vivid by them. Imaginative prose for Hazlitt is no closer to science and the understanding, than poetry like Wordsworth's is. Nor however is it farther away. Art and science alike trace the work of laws—of character, of things—and are useful to us because they point out "levers that may move the world."[2]

"On a Sun-dial" is a meditation on the motto of a sundial near Venice, *Horas non numero nisi serenas,* which Hazlitt gives as "I count only the hours that are serene," but which his essay, by its care for light and shade, encourages us to read with the literal sense of serenity: "I count only the cloudless hours." The essay includes everything that Hazlitt can possibly connect with this sublime emblem of the passage of time: a catalogue of the clocks of Europe, reflections on the costume of society, and a warning to himself against the flight from nature in which all human life seems to conspire, in its effort to evade the thought of death. He starts by praising the sundial as, of all modes of counting time, "perhaps the most apposite and striking," yet even here he finds room for a personal bias.

It should be of iron to denote duration, and have a dull, leaden look. I hate a sun-dial made of wood, which is rather calculated to show the variations of the seasons, than the progress of time, slow, silent, imperceptible, chequered with light and shade. If our hours were all serene, we might probably take almost as little note of them, as the dial does of those that are clouded. It is the shadow thrown across, that gives us warning of their flight. Otherwise, our impressions would take the same undistinguishable hue; we should scarce be conscious of our existence. . . . The hour-glass is, I suspect, an older invention; and it is certainly the most defective of all. Its creeping sands are not indeed an unapt emblem of the minute, countless portions of our existence; and the manner in which they gradually slide through the hollow glass and diminish in number till not a single one is left, also illustrates the way in which our years slip from us by stealth. (XVII, 239)

The essay keeps returning to the sense in which all keepers of time bring us closer to our imperfections. The sand-clock is "defective" in that it leaves no room for incidental associations, to help us arrive at the reminder on our own. But it is better at least than a typical French device, "a figure of Time seated in a boat which Cupid is rowing along, with the motto, *L'Amour fait passer le Temps*." This style of ornamental wit, the once-clever joke on a subject of permanent gravity, suits a people who could never have conceived of the Latin motto, any more than they could of Shakespeare's "How sweet the moonlight sleeps upon that bank." Yet Hazlitt admits that the French here only conform to our more pervasive dandyism about time, and he gives an unhappy list of all the refinements of invention, "gold repeaters, watches with metal covers, clocks with hands to count the seconds," along with a complaint for the "pomposity and self-importance" of each. But another cause for protest lies nearer to hand:

There are two clocks which strike the hour in the room where I am. This I do not like. In the first place, I do not want to be reminded twice how the time goes (it is like the second tap of a saucy servant at your door when perhaps you have no wish to get up); in the next place, it is starting a difference of opinion on the subject, and I am averse to every appearance of wrangling and disputation. (XVII, 241)

To Virginia Woolf's remark that Hazlitt had no sense of humor, this passage seems a sufficient reply. We are to consider by whom the aversion is being confessed, and how odd a reversal of his known humor it would have appeared even to him. He admits, however, that clocks at any rate strike the hour, and thus make time "speak to us in an audible and warning voice."

The Miltonic note of prophecy is caught in a further sentence: "The clock that tells the coming, dread hour—the castle bell, that 'with its brazen throat and iron tongue, sounds one unto the drowsy ear of night'—the curfew, 'swinging slow with sullen roar' o'er wizard stream or fountain, are like a voice from other worlds, big with unknown events." As happens almost regularly at such moments in Hazlitt's writing, the prophetic gives way to a lyric strain, and the "other worlds" become the "worlds not realised" that Wordsworth found in childhood: "I confess, nothing at present interests me but what has been—the recollection of the impressions of my early life, or events long past, of which only the dim traces remain in a smouldering ruin or half-obsolete custom. That *things should be that are now no more,* creates in my mind the most unfeigned astonishment. I cannot solve the mystery of the past, nor exhaust my pleasure in it."

After a survey of European town clocks and village bells, which "impart a pensive, wayward pleasure to the mind"—including the clocks in Catholic countries, with their "everlasting tolling of bells to prayers or for the dead," and the delicate smaller sound of bells in the Apennines, and the "nuisance" of chimes in Holland—he arrives at his generic subject, those "stern, inflexible monitors, that nothing can prevent from discharging their duty." Apart from their common association with the "fearful summons" of an execution, something in the continuousness of the sound of bells tolling reminds us that every thought of time *is* also a thought of death. But this is an essay in the middle style, and accordingly Hazlitt refuses the opportunity an older essayist like Thomas Browne would have found here. He finds consolation instead in the unmonitored life of the savage, whose understanding is "a kind of natural almanac"; and in the thought of one hero of civilization, Robinson Crusoe, a man alone just as he is, "who lost his reckoning in the monotony of his life and that bewildering dream of solitude, and was fain to have recourse to the notches in a piece of wood. What a diary was his! And how time must have spread its circuit round him, vast and pathless as the ocean!"

Hazlitt now reveals what we hardly need to be told, that he has never owned a watch of any description.

When I am in a town, I can hear the clock; and when I am in the country, I can listen to the silence. What I like best is to lie whole mornings on a sunny bank on Salisbury Plain, without any object before me, neither knowing nor caring how time passes, and thus "with light-winged toys of feathered Idleness" to melt down hours to moments. Perhaps some such thoughts as I have here set down float before me like motes before my half-shut eyes, or some vivid image of the past by forcible contrast rushes by me—"Diana and her faun, and all the glories of the antique world"; then I start away to prevent the iron from entering my soul, and let fall some tears into that stream of time which separates me farther and farther from all I once loved! At length I rouse myself from my reverie, and home to dinner, proud of killing time with thought, nay even without thinking. Somewhat of this idle humour I inherit from my father, though he had not the same freedom from *ennui,* for he was not a metaphysician. (XVII, 245)

The essay, like a conversation poem, has begun fixed on a single object, rambled outward from that to kindred imaginings, and returning from its circuit at last settled into a new and long-earned repose of consciousness. It is Hazlitt's choice, among all the available objects, of an emblem of eternity—his unrelaxing pursuit of associations, as well as his assumption that the iron will have entered his soul if the circle of thought is not properly closed—that reminds one most of Keats's odes. They too speak of "killing time," taking the figure in a strong sense, and find a way to do so that enlarges the egotistical or Wordsworthian meditation on the things that are no more. Keats's inventions, like those of the critic he emulated, make the common sense of men a test of the genius of one man, by supplying the train of unfamiliar ideas through which the life of a writer may lastingly revisit the life of any reader.

CHAPTER XI

KEATS

ANOTHER SELF

In making large claims for a critic better known to his contemporaries than to posterity, one faces the question whether this is a task of antiquarian history or part of the history of the present. About any such writer one wants to know who read him then, that we should read him now. With Hazlitt the answer can be simple and satisfying. He was read by a genius of the next generation, who pronounced Hazlitt's "depth of taste" one of the three things to be prized in that age—alongside Haydon's paintings and *The Excursion*—and sought his company in person, for conversation, for practical suggestions, and for theoretical counsel. In the story of Keats's development, biographers have always needed some event to advance him from the novice who took Hunt and Byron as his patterns, to the author who taught himself to admire Shakespeare and Milton and to enter the lists with Wordsworth. That event was his reading of Hazlitt; to a lesser extent, the informal meetings in which Hazlitt did not disappoint the expectations Keats had formed of him; and finally, Hazlitt's lectures on poetry at the Surrey Institution. This suggestion is not new, but the record of Hazlitt's influence is much fuller, more convincing and more subtly connected with the practice of Keats's poetry, than anyone has yet shown.[1] The present chapter aims at an interpretation of the "Ode to a Nightingale" and "Ode on a Grecian Urn" in the light of Hazlitt's criticism. But I want first to exhibit several passages from Keats's letters, in the hope of demonstrating how his purpose and passion conspired with Hazlitt's. I need to admit at the outset that these imperfectly represent his letters as a whole: I chose the passages I thought would most plainly support my argument. Others could have served, however, with an emphasis very slightly different. Except Wordsworth, and the friends with whom he corresponded regularly, there was no contemporary who was more often in Keats's mind. The conclusion I will be working toward is this: that the odes test an idea of the imagination which Hazlitt had proposed in his lectures and critical essays; and that they afford, for power and for sympathy, a space as accommodating as that of the personal essays later collected in *Table-Talk,* which Hazlitt started writing about the same time.

In December 1814 Keats wrote an adoring sonnet "To Lord Byron," whom he then thought an incomparable poet, an expert unraveller of "The enchanting tale—the tale of pleasing woe." When one sets this poem against the letters of 1817, and considers that in the intervening months he had been studying Hazlitt, one can see what the first effect was. Keats had lacked a deep past, and this Hazlitt gave him. With it came the fear that he had arrived too late, but also the humility necessary to great work. In many instances he comes close to repeating Hazlitt's words from the *Round Table* essay "On Classical Education": "By conversing with the *mighty dead,* we imbibe sentiment with knowledge; we become strongly attached to those who can no longer either hurt or serve us, except through the influence which they exert over the mind. We feel the presence of that power which gives immortality to human thoughts and actions." Byron, though living, had never been a resource of this kind; and the tone in which Keats now praises the mighty dead is stronger and steadier, even if more deferential, than the tone in which he can praise any living poet. "I am," he writes to Haydon, "very near Agreeing with Hazlit that Shakespeare is enough for us."[2] In September 1817, three books into *Endymion,* he becomes aware of the connection between his progress as a poet and the close study of Shakespeare, and seeks a way of recording how much this has owed to Hazlitt. So he writes to a mutual friend, J. H. Reynolds: "How is Hazlitt? We were reading his [Round] Table last night—I know he thinks himself not estimated by ten People in the world—I wishe he knew he is."[3] Hazlitt's argument against egotism, which reached back to Shakespeare as a deeper source of poetic truth, seems to have calmed Keats's irritability and fortified his resolve in the pursuit of fame. It was always Hazlitt's lesson, from his abridgement of Tucker to "The Indian Jugglers," that genius works by unconscious exertions of power. Among the *Round Table* essays he had just been praising, Keats would have found the sentiment in "On Posthumous Fame": "Men of the greatest genius produce their works with too much facility (and, as it were, spontaneously) to require the

love of fame as a stimulus to their exertions, or to make them de-
serving of the admiration of mankind as their reward. It is, indeed,
one characteristic mark of the highest class of excellence to appear
to come naturally from the mind of the author, without consciousness or effort." From this Keats took one of his "Axioms" of poetry,
as sketched in a letter to John Taylor about revising *Endymion* for
publication: "if Poetry comes not as naturally as the Leaves to a tree
it had better not come at all."[4]

Two received ideas about Keats still limit both the specialist's
and the common reader's understanding of his character. First, that
he was a sensitive man, easily wounded, deficient perhaps in the
comic sense that can delight in smart repartees or revenges; and second, that he was skeptical about the intellect, and believed an "irritable reaching after fact & reason" was typical of the analytic
mind:[5] the part of him that laughed, and read books of philosophy,
did not write his poetry, and to prove it he gave us *Lamia,* with the
philosopher Apollonius who laughs into oblivion the thing of beauty
that poetry has been vouchsafed by myth. Two comments from
Keats's letters in the spring of 1818 will be of interest here. Writing
to Haydon on March 21, he applauds Hazlitt's strength as a good
hater—"Hazlitt has damned the bigotted and the blue—stockined
how durst the man?! he is your only good damner and if ever I am
damn'd—damn me if I shoul'nt like him to damn me"—and in a letter to Reynolds on April 27, he speaks of preparing "to ask Hazlitt
in about a years time the best metaphysical road I can take."[6] That
is, he has metaphysical ambitions like Hazlitt's own, and wants to
embark on a program of reading and speculation, but will not venture to present himself at the door of so admired a preceptor until
he feels sufficiently impressive.

A year later, in the winter and early spring of 1819, writing to
his brother George and sister-in-law Georgiana, he copies out for
their edification certain passages of Hazlitt's prose to set beside his
own. One of these is a considerable stretch (five pages in a modern
edition) of the "Letter to William Gifford." Hazlitt there exposed
to public opprobrium the slanderers of the "Cockney school," and
Keats would have seen it as an occasion of disinterested valor, at
which he as a beneficiary was permitted to rejoice. In his journal-
letter, even after laying down his pen for a day, Keats picks it up
with no thought more pressing than to continue with Hazlitt: it is
as important for George to hear from *him* as from the correspondent proper. The passage, copied out over two days, evokes Keats's

comment, "The manner in which this is managed: the force and innate power with which it yeasts and works up itself—the feeling for the costume of society; is in a style of genius—He hath a demon as he himself says of Lord Byron."[7] I quoted part of this earlier as an allusion to *gusto,* but I think "yeast" is explained as well by Keats's letter to Benjamin Bailey of January 28, 1818: the "portion of good" which is all that even the best of men have, is "a kind of spiritual yeast in their frames which creates the ferment of existence—by which a Man is propell'd to act and strive and buffet with Circumstance."[8] By 1819, when the "Letter to William Gifford" was published, Hazlitt seemed to Keats almost an embodiment of the modern idea of genius.

Even more intriguing than this journal-letter is a slightly earlier one, which quotes a shorter passage of Hazlitt's. It is from the *Lectures on the English Comic Writers,* which Keats did not attend but had contrived to borrow in manuscript, probably through J. H. Reynolds. He quotes from the portrait of St. Leon—a hero of Godwin's fiction whom the lecturer rated second only to Falkland in *Caleb Williams*—and he adds his own emphasis.

> He is a limb torn off from Society. In possession of eternal youth and beauty, he can feel no love; surrounded, tantalized and tormented with riches, he can do no good. The faces of Men pass before him as in a speculum; but he is attached to them by no common tie of sympathy or suffering. He is thrown back into himself and his own thoughts. He lives in the solitude of his own breast,—without wife or child or friend or Enemy in the world. *His is the solitude of the Soul, not of woods, or trees, or mountains*—but the desert of society—the waste and oblivion of the heart. He is himself alone. His existence is purely intellectual, and is therefore intolerable to one who has felt the rapture of affection, or the anguish of woe.[9]

Breaking off, with the idea of pursuing other matters, Keats then decides "as I am about it" to continue with Hazlitt's character of Godwin. It is followed by the comment, "This appears to me quite correct," and then by a transcription of Keats's "Bards of passion"—as the earlier quotation had been directly preceded by the poem, "Ever let the Fancy roam." Here again one is struck by the way Keats manages to interleave Hazlitt's thoughts and eloquence with his own. In the whole body of his letters he gives this sort of prominence to the words of no other writer. By itself, and without the passages he later quoted from "A Letter to William Gifford," there would still be something extraordinary about this quotation, flanked on either side by a poem from Keats himself, and presented to his brother as the work of a single hand. It is as if Hazlitt's description of St. Leon and his own new poetry had appeared to Keats, and were meant to appear to others, as a single continuous act of expression.

Hazlitt describes the solitude of one who finds "himself alone" intolerable, because his thoughts are still of society, the earth, all the common affections he has left behind. To such a figure egotism has become a *given* (however despised or regretted), and this Keats feared to be his situation as a poet. When in *The Fall of Hyperion* he set himself to endure whatever self-searchings were required to change his situation, he needed a second voice to dramatize the power of the accuser he faced, and it seems to have been his deliberate purpose to draw into the speech of the prophetess Moneta as many echoes as possible of Hazlitt's description. But the first echo is sounded by the poet himself. After his ascent to Moneta's shrine, he asks why the place of vision is deserted: "I sure should see / Other men here, but I am here alone." He is then told the strangeness of his fate:

> "Thou art a dreaming thing;
> A fever of thyself—think of the earth;
> What bliss, even in hope, is there for thee?
> What haven? Every creature hath its home;
> Every sole man hath days of joy and pain,
> Whether his labours be sublime or low—
> The pain alone; the joy alone; distinct:
> Only the dreamer venoms all his days,
> Bearing more woe than all his sins deserve."[10]

This is "the desert of society—the waste and oblivion of the heart," known to the man "thrown back into himself and his own thoughts," as Hazlitt had painted him. Keats's hope in *The Fall of Hyperion*, that something living may be salvaged from the desert, requires him to bear witness to a misery worse than his, that of the fallen Titans. What Hazlitt showed him was the interest of placing their drama within himself, and using it to open his sympathies. For he had found in writing the first *Hyperion* that as a tragic narrative, the story could not hold his attention. It touched him more nearly when he saw it as a motive for every exertion that the poet—like the Godwinian hero, always thrown back into himself—could undertake to heal the sickness of a "purely intellectual" existence. The character of St. Leon answers to the idea of himself which Keats cherished throughout his early life, as well as to the image of the artist, cast out by society to be preserved for immortality, which he bequeathed to a third and fourth generation of romantics. It is plain in his letters that this was also the way he saw Hazlitt. The discovery of a genius of criticism, isolated by genius as by politics, but possessed of a "demon" in all his trials, was for Keats the discovery of another self.

He first met Hazlitt in January 1818, and felt bold enough to call on him by December 1818. But Hazlitt would have known about Keats even before they met, not only from the poems Hunt showed him but from Keats's article "On Edmund Kean as a Shakespearean Actor," which appeared in the *Champion* of December 21, 1817, and contained a sentence easily mistakable for one of Hazlitt's: "There is an indescribable gusto in his voice, by which we feel that the utterer is thinking of the past and the future, while speaking of the instant."[11] Once they were acquainted, Hazlitt gave Keats advice about writing for magazines and, what was far more important, noticed him in a generous aside of his *Lectures on the English Poets*. We know how this came about, again from the evidence of Keats's letters. To Bailey, on January 23, 1818, Keats wrote that he would be attending the lectures as they were first delivered. In the event he missed some, but he certainly heard the sixth, "On Swift, Young, Gray, Collins, etc.," which included a judgment of Chatterton: "He did not show extraordinary powers of genius, but extraordinary precocity. Nor do I believe he would have written better, had he lived. He knew this himself, or he would have lived." How Keats was affected by this dismissal may be guessed from the circumstances of his life; and he spoke of his response in the letter to George and Tom Keats of February 21, 1818: "I hear Hazlitt's Lectures regularly—his last was on Grey Collins, Young &c. and he gave a very fine piece of discriminating criticism of Swift, Voltaire And Rabelais—I was very disappointed at his treatment of Chatterton—I generally meet with many I know there."[12] He arrived at an earlier lecture, as he told Tom and George, "just as they were coming out, when all these pounced upon me, Hazlitt, John Hunt & son, Wells, Bewick, all the Landseers, Bob Harris, Rox of the Burrough Aye & more."[13] Beside the casual phrase, "I generally meet with many I know there," this seems to show that Keats was in the habit of conversing freely after the lectures, with Hazlitt and his circle. Some such conversation after the sixth lecture will account for Hazlitt's recognition of him in the seventh.

> I am sorry that what I said in the conclusion of the last Lecture respecting Chatterton, should have given dissatisfaction to some persons, with whom I would willingly agree on all such matters. What I meant was less to call in question Chatterton's genius, than to object to the common mode of estimating its magnitude by its prematureness. The lists of fame are not filled with the dates of births or deaths; and the side mark of the age at which they were done, wears out in works destined for immortality. (V, 123)

Hazlitt's later appreciations of Keats are generally of two kinds. First, he recognizes him as an independent voice, one who can command the tones of genius and is leagued with himself against the mob of government critics and court bards. Keats's "fine fancy and powerful invention," he writes in the *Edinburgh Review* article on "The Periodical Press," "were too obvious to be treated with mere neglect; and as he had not been ushered into the world with the court stamp upon him, he was to be crushed as a warning to genius how it keeps company with honesty, and as a sure means of inoculating the ingenuous spirit and talent of the country with timely and systematic servility." Second, and in a very different key, he simply quotes Keats, as a touchstone of the original note in poetry after Wordsworth. In *The Spirit of the Age* for example, after illustrating the pedantic puerility of Gifford's *Baviad* and *Maeviad,* he quotes "The Eve of St. Agnes" for the pleasure of its "rich beauties and dim obscurities." In the essay "On Reading Old Books," he adds that "the reading of Mr. Keats's Eve of Saint Agnes lately made me regret that I was not young again." But the best homage he pays Keats is the impulse with which, to relieve an uneventful moment of his *Journey through France and Italy,* he launches into a one-line quotation from a poem then hardly five years in the world, as if everyone he cared to have as a reader would know it: "Oh for a beaker full of the warm South!" He had already published, in the essay "On Effeminacy of Character," a more stringent verdict on the poems than these gestures of loyalty seem to indicate.

> I cannot help thinking that the fault of Mr. Keats's poems was a deficiency in masculine energy of style. He had beauty, tenderness, delicacy, in an uncommon degree, but there was a want of strength and substance. His Endymion is a very delightful description of the illusions of a youthful imagination, given up to airy dreams—

we have flowers, clouds, rainbows, moonlight, all sweet sounds and smells, and Oreads and Dryads flitting by—but there is nothing tangible in it, nothing marked or palpable—we have none of the hardy spirit or rigid forms of antiquity. He painted his own thoughts and character; and did not transport himself into the fabulous and heroic ages. There is a want of action, or character, and so far, of imagination. . . . We see in him the youth, without the manhood of poetry.   (VIII, 254-55)

But I suspect he wrote this before looking closely at the 1820 volume, with *Hyperion* and the odes. Besides, he was saying no more than Keats himself had admitted in his Preface.

> [My Preface] is not written with the least atom of purpose to forestall criticisms of course, but from the desire I have to conciliate men who are competent to look, and who do look with a zealous eye, to the honour of English literature.
>
> The imagination of a boy is healthy, and the mature imagination of a man is healthy; but there is a space of life between, in which the soul is in a ferment, the character undecided, the way of life uncertain, the ambition thick-sighted: thence proceeds mawkishness, and all the thousand bitters which those men I speak of must necessarily taste in going over the following pages.[14]

Hazlitt's failure to review *Endymion* doubtless proceeded from a reluctance to say anything that might be wounding to its author. He kept the disappointment to himself while Keats was alive; gave his reputation several lifts following one skeptical delay after his death; and saved a final estimate for the section on Keats in *Select British Poets* (1824), where as Keats's first anthologist he had a chance to exhibit once more the depth of taste for which he had earned the lasting esteem of his subject. There are three passages from *Endymion*—including the Procession and Hymn in Honour of Pan (ending with the words "But in old marbles ever beautiful"), and the Indian Lady's Song—along with one from *Hyperion*, the "Ode to a Nightingale," "Fancy," and "Robin Hood." I have said that Keats found his second self in Hazlitt, and that he showed this particularly in the insistence that his brother read his verse beside Hazlitt's prose, as examples of kindred energies. Hazlitt was the older man in this friendship, and a comparable intensity of response could not be expected from him. But he wrote about Keats and appears also to have treated him as his equal in genius. No other encounter between poet and critic has been so fortunate for literature.

This does not strike me as the sort of influence—involving the spread of doctrine—which it has usually been supposed to exemplify. Keats understood Hazlitt's ideas till they became second nature to him; but the ideas were always inseparable from the tact of expression; Hazlitt's power, in every way, was *communicated*. This may be harder for us to see, and more paradoxical for us to ask questions about, than it would have seemed to romantic authors, for we find border-crossing expeditions between poetry and prose more difficult than they did. At any rate I think Hazlitt's effect on Keats can be traced to something so minute as the pace of his movement in verse, which is not the sinuous grace of Coleridge or the lapidary deliberation of Wordsworth, but the variable speed of uncommon thoughts, hurried along as each shift of subject permits a new accession of power. Keats has, in poetry as well as prose, the "fiery laconicism" he praised in Hazlitt—a very different thing from Byron's whirlwind truculence. *Lamia* is perhaps his closest approach to a middle style, and to Hazlitt's prose: its verse is lively, swift to digress and return, and at home in all the possible roles of a narrator.

> Love in a hut, with water and a crust,
> Is—Love, forgive us!—cinders, ashes, dust;
> Love in a palace is perhaps at last
> More grievous torment than a hermit's fast:—
> That is a doubtful tale from faery land,
> Hard for the non-elect to understand.
> Had Licius liv'd to hand his story down,
> He might have given the moral a fresh frown,
> Or clench'd it quite: but too short was their bliss
> To breed distrust and hate, that make the soft voice hiss.
> Besides, there, nightly, with terrific glare,
> Love, jealous grown of so complete a pair,
> Hover'd and buzz'd his wings, with fearful roar,
> Above the lintel of their chamber door,
> And down the passage cast a glow upon the floor.[15]

Though the opening two couplets make an observant and not uncritical homage to Byron's style of worldliness, the disclaimer, "Hard for the non-elect to understand," and "He might have given the moral a fresh frown, / Or clench'd it quite," are pure Hazlitt, in their self-confidence and gusto, and freedom from self-regard. Yet Keats speaks as a moral narrator not in his poems, but in the aphorisms of his letters. These have made him, in a few sayings, the single most widely quoted authority on the program of romanticism,

apart from Blake; and yet his aphorisms have the peculiarity that
they are useless to those who respect less than the whole of their context. This was a quality of Hazlitt's aphorisms too, and it seems to
belong more largely to the discursive genius of empiricism. Here I
want only to remind the reader of four well-known observations for
which Hazlitt's thought, as I have been tracing it, supplies a context
even more satisfying than Keats's *Letters*.

The first, from a letter to Bailey of November 22, 1817, concerns
the poet's freedom from the habitual or irritable demands of a single fixed identity, a set "character."

> Men of Genius are great as certain ethereal Chemicals operating
> on the Mass of neutral intellect—but they have not any individ-
> uality, any determined Character. I would call the top and head
> of those who have a proper self Men of Power.[16]

Men of Power are great because there is no telling what will strike
them: Wordsworth's attraction to the lichen on the rock, Rousseau's
care for the lustres of his remembered life, as epitomised by the
memory *"Ah, voilà de la pervenche,"* are equally unpredictable
from any individuality but theirs; whereas Byron is doubtless somewhere below the "top and head" of this class, having (only more
fluently) the strange and picturesque imaginings that come to most
men, when they put themselves in a strange and picturesque mood.
Shakespeare on the contrary would rank highest among the "Men of
Genius" whose individuality is dispersed through the invention of
dramatic characters. Keats refers to nothing more than the mystery
surrounding this dispersion, when he speaks of chemicals "operating
on the Mass of neutral intellect": he makes no claim for the poet's
detachment or impersonality.

John Middleton Murry thought the contrast between Shakespeare and Wordsworth must have been present to Keats's mind
whenever he set men of genius against men of power.[17] The special
importance of Shakespeare as a foil to the man of power, and as an
example of how the highest genius surpasses the egotistical, appears
more clearly by the proximity of the foregoing remarks to some
others about Wordsworth, offered after two months of further reflection, in the letter to Reynolds of February 3, 1818.

> It may be said that we ought to read our Contemporaries. that
> Wordsworth &c should have their due from us. but for the sake of
> a few fine imaginative or domestic passages, are we to be bullied
> into a certain Philosophy engendered in the whims of an Egotist—

Every man has his speculations, but every man does not brood and peacock over them till he makes a false coinage and deceives himself. . . . We hate poetry that has a palpable design upon us—and if we do not agree, seems to put its hands in its breeches pockets.[18]

Once again it was Hazlitt who gave Keats the polemical assurance one feels at work here. His review of *The Excursion* was the incitement without which we should hardly be reading Keats today, and this letter was written soon after the lecture "On Poetry in General."

The dramatic poet according to Hazlitt had a scope for his imaginative energies denied to the lyric poet—as the man of genius has a *range* of powers denied to the man of power. Keats is still pondering the difference in a letter to Haydon, of April 8, 1818, on the subject of heroic painting. What he can never know intimately about an artist of genius, but always believes in the existence of, are "the innumerable compositions and decompositions which take place between the intellect and its thousand materials before it arrives at that trembling delicate and snail-horn perception of Beauty," the result of much careful exploring in "your many havens of intenseness."[19] The immediate source is Hazlitt's lecture on Shakespeare, from a few weeks earlier, with its observation that in Shakespeare there is no "fixed essence of character" but "a continual composition and decomposition of its elements, a fermentation of every particle in the whole mass, by its alternate affinity and antipathy to other principles which are brought into contact with it." I have shown how Hazlitt adapted the same thought to a larger subject in the essay "On Imitation," where art "divides and decompounds objects into a thousand curious parts." The vocabulary of both Hazlitt and Keats in this instance, is pretty plainly Lockean, for Locke had spoken of the difficulty in "moral names" as peculiar to the associative process of composition and decomposition: "What need of a sign, when the thing signified is present and in view? But in moral names, that cannot be so easily and shortly done, because of the many decompositions that go to the making up the complex ideas of those modes."[20] One may see this as part of the same difficulty that interested Hazlitt and Keats, by reflecting that moral names are nothing but the signs for Hazlitt's "moral quantities," that is, for the stuff of character itself. Coleridge too had a way of employing this vocabulary, but generally with disgust, as a thing appropriate to the fallen labors of the understanding: "The leading differences," he writes in Appendix C of *The Statesman's Manual,* "between mechanic and vital philosophy may all be drawn from one point namely, that the former demanding for every mode and act of existence real or possible *visibility,* knows only of distance and nearness, composition (or rather juxtaposition) and decomposition, in short the relations of unproductive particles to each other. . . . This is the philosophy of death, and only of a dead nature can it hold good."[21] Keats, however, as much as Hazlitt, believed it was a philosophy of life. He would have expected Haydon as a painter to understand in advance that the compositions and decompositions can never confidently be numbered or classified; but in employing the phrase nevertheless he went out of his way to adopt an Enlightenment view of his experiments in poetry.

Their understanding of the mind's compositions and decompositions had broad implications for the politics of both Hazlitt and Keats. The same sympathies by which a reader of literature was taken out of his habitual self, allowed to inhabit other characters, and encouraged to revise the story of his own life by the alternate affinities and antipathies that he chose, made any system unnatural which supposed that the boundaries of self and of continuous identity were more permanent in society than in the individual mind, as it traveled from thought to thought. Only in the absence of such imposed boundaries could the man of genius and the man of power reside together in a single body. "Man," Keats tells Reynolds, in a letter of February 19, 1818, "should not dispute or assert but whisper results to his neighbour, and thus by every germ of Spirit sucking the Sap from mould ethereal every human might become great, and Humanity instead of being a wide heath of Furse and Briars with here and there a remote Oak or Pine, would become a grand democracy of Forest Trees."[22] Some days later, in the *Examiner* for March 7, 1818, Keats would have found a similar feeling in the first installment of Hazlitt's great manifesto, "What Is the People?"

> —And who are you that ask the question? One of the people. And yet you would be something! Then you would not have the People nothing. For what is the people? Millions of men, like you, with hearts beating in their bosoms, blood circulating in their veins, with wants and appetites, and passions and anxious cares, and busy purposes and affections for others and a respect for themselves, and a desire for happiness, and a right to freedom, and a will to be free.
>
> (VII, 259)

If the sound is fiercer than any we can imagine as native to Keats's grand democracy of forest trees, the reason is that Hazlitt was addressing those who must clamor and shout before they can be heard in whispers. But far from despising the quieter calling that Keats pursued, he was eager for its result, from the very start of a short career. The new voice was also an answering voice, and had for him the quality of a confirmation.

"ODE TO A NIGHTINGALE"

Negative capability was Keats's name for one elusive element that goes "to form a Man of Achievement especially in Literature, and which Shakespeare possessed so enormously."[23] The emphasis on Shakespeare owes much to Hazlitt's criticism; so does the unorthodox notion that art's task of selection and construction must begin with a negative sort of triumph: a purging away of the interfering self, and of all its particles of irritability. Apart from *The Round Table,* "A Letter to William Gifford," and Hazlitt's two books of lectures, he likely read the *Essay on Human Action;* and his thoughts about dramatic poetry were made keener by the *Characters of Shakespeare's Plays,* of which he praised the chapter on *King Lear* for its "hieroglyphic visioning." What he found most useful were Hazlitt's doubts about the predominance of the self in modern poetry: the egotistical, Hazlitt taught, was only one version of the sublime, and a limited one. The highest poetry makes us forget the identity of the poet in the many identities he assumes; thus Shakespeare had "only to think of any thing in order to become that thing, with all the circumstances belonging to it." He seems to us in dramatic works, as he passes from one character to another, "like the same soul successively animating different bodies."

In a letter to Richard Woodhouse of October 27, 1818, Keats adopted this idea for his own ends, and turned it against Wordsworth.

As to the poetical Character itself, (I mean that sort of which, if I am any thing, I am a Member; that sort distinguished from the wordsworthian or egotistical sublime; which is a thing per se and stands alone) it is not itself—it has no self—it is every thing and nothing—It has no character—it enjoys light and shade; it lives in gusto, be it foul or fair, high or low, rich or poor, mean or elevated—It has as much delight in conceiving an Iago as an Imogen. What shocks the virtuous philosopher, delights the camelion Poet. It does no harm from its relish of the dark side of things any more than from its taste for the bright one; because they both end in speculation. A Poet is the most unpoetical of any thing in existence; because he has no Identity—he is continually informing and filling some other Body.[24]

Keats here is curiously more polemical than Hazlitt. The main thing he wants the poet to avoid is any aspiration to the "wordsworthian or egotistical sublime": without the parenthesis his injunction would read, "As to the poetical character itself . . . it is not itself." Self, the "thing per se," Wordsworth (as Hazlitt described him) taking a personal interest in the universe, is the enemy whom the sentence rounds upon. Wordsworth remains himself entirely too much of the time. Yet why should Keats have made an antagonist of the poet who had created in *The Excursion* another of the "three things" he thought would survive the age? Keats too aimed to be a poet of the sublime, and perhaps that is reason enough. His sublimity, when he came to know it, would be closely related to Wordsworth's, but to invent it at all and discover the strength to pursue it, he had to believe the difference was going to be tremendous.

He hoped to attain a point of view from which sublime emotions could be his as a more than temporary privilege. At the same time he needed to be invulnerable to the charge of egotism that he had brought against Wordsworth. He was reconciled to seeing the self dominate his poetry as much as it had Wordsworth's; but unlike Wordsworth he would leave the way open to feel as someone or something else. The change has to do with dramatic situation. The narrator of a Keats ode is always on the verge of becoming not quite himself, and he makes us believe that to remain so is to widen experience. But this sounds like what English critics have sometimes called "empathy"—translating the German *Einfühlung*—and I need to say why it is closer to what Hazlitt all along had been calling "sympathy." Empathy is the process by which a mind so projects itself into its object that a transfer of qualities seems to take place. Keats, on the other hand, was looking for a capability of so heightening the imagination's response to anything that the identities of both the mind and its object would grow more vivid *as what they are*. Nor had Wordsworth failed utterly to advance this quest for an intenser sympathy. His poetry struck Keats as evidence that there was a "grand march of intellect"—even Milton "did not think into the human heart, as Wordsworth has done."[25] Yet the suspicion lingered with him that Wordsworth's poetry, though of a new kind, was not the most profound of its kind.

"To this point was Wordsworth come," Keats writes, in the letter I have just quoted: to this point, he means, and no further. For Wordsworth had remained content with what by Keats's lights was a constricting half-knowledge. He saw into his own heart only, and therefore the outward lesson of his poetry, which was the need for accommodation to the teachings of nature, made possible an inward deception. The accommodation really went the other way: nature, or a carefully selected aspect of it, was bent to the will of the poet. To a youthful admirer this could seem a betrayal of both poetry and nature, in the name of the human heart. Poetry, because Wordsworth by his choice of subjects and his limitation of tone, had contracted its scope so drastically; nature, because it now occupied the foreground of every poem, but was seen only through the distorting medium of poetry that had "a palpable design upon us." Keats's sense of disappointment is not what most readers can be expected to feel, when they read Wordsworth after Pope and Cowper, and beside Byron and Scott. But Keats had at this time a relentless narrowness of focus. He read Wordsworth after Shakespeare and beside Shakespeare.

Alison, and associationist critics generally, had argued that any object in nature could be expressive, because it had to be interpreted as an object of the mind, and would give back the mind's own expression as if from afar by awakening "trains of thought." If one takes this as a creed of individual life, and reads the associations of each mind as its signature, then associationism becomes a powerful sanction for the egotistical sublime. But if one supposes such trains of thought are interesting because they can be shared—if one concludes that the reader can be taught to recognize in them the workings of his own mind, and not encouraged to end in awe of the poet's—then associationism looks like the right intellectual groundwork for a poetry of sympathy. To the latter point Keats had come, by the time he wrote his odes: the reaction that his reading of Hazlitt fostered gives him more in common with Alison's American disciples like Bryant, than with Wordsworth after 1800. No single passage of Hazlitt's carries the force that the ideal of sympathy had to gather little by little in Keats's mind, through reading and reflection and the writing of new poems. Yet the conclusion of the essay "On Reason and Imagination"—written too late for Keats to have known it—gives an essence of the kind of understanding Keats was working toward, in his letters diffusely, and in his odes with an effect of such concentration that they make the ideal hard to name.

Man is (so to speak) an endless and infinitely varied repetition: and
if we know what one man feels, we so far know what a thousand
feel in the sanctuary of their being. . . . As is our perception of
this original truth, the root of our imagination, so will the force
and richness of the general impression proceeding from it be. The
boundary of our sympathy is a circle which enlarges itself according to its propulsion from the centre—the heart. If we are imbued
with a deep sense of individual weal or woe, we shall be awe-struck
at the idea of humanity in general. . . . If we understand the texture and vital feeling, we then can fill up the outline, but we cannot supply the former from having the latter given. Moral and
poetical truth is like expression in a picture—the one is not to be
attained by smearing over a large canvas, nor the other by bestriding
a vague topic. . . . I defy any great tragic writer to despise that
nature which he understands, or that heart which he has probed,
with all its rich bleeding materials of joy and sorrow. The subject
may not be a source of much triumph to him, from its alternate
light and shade, but it can never become one of supercilious indifference. He must feel a strong reflex interest in it, corresponding
to that which he has depicted in the characters of others. Indeed,
the object and end of playing, "both at the first and now, is to hold
the mirror up to nature," to enable us to feel for others as for ourselves, or to embody a distinct interest out of ourselves by the force
of imagination and passion.[26]   (XII, 54-55)

Hazlitt's "light and shade" necessary to a work of art—an associationist trope for the whole that is implied by the coexistence of
opposite parts—appear also in Keats's sketch of the poetical character, and they will reappear in his last letter: "the knowledge of contrast, feeling for light and shade, all that information (primitive
sense) necessary for a poem are great enemies of the stomach."[27] As
he prepared to write the "Ode to a Nightingale" in particular, he
was pondering what it meant to write from a sanctuary of being, such as Hazlitt speaks of, and what course the imagination
might trace from it. The "boundary of our sympathy," a "circle
which enlarges itself according to its propulsion from the centre—the
heart," was the region he hoped to explore in this poem.

Before discussing the poem I must add an unexpected link between the act of sympathy which it presents, and the argument for
disinterested action in Hazlitt's *Essay*. On March 19, 1819, in the
same journal-letter that had quoted the "Letter to William Gifford,"
Keats told his brother that the energies displayed in any natural
activity "though erroneous . . . may be fine—This is the very thing

in which consists poetry; and if so it is not so fine a thing as philosophy—For the same reason that an eagle is not so fine a thing as a truth.''[28] An eagle like a poem is beautiful quite apart from its moral qualities, moral truth not being understood here as a necessary condition of beauty. Yet it takes second place to a truth, as nature in our eyes takes second place to human society. The remark is partly explained by a passage earlier in the same letter which is not as well known.

> I perceive how far I am from any humble standard of disinterestedness—Yet this feeling ought to be carried to its highest pitch, as there is no fear of its ever injuring society—which it would do I fear pushed to an extremity—For in wild nature the Hawk would loose his Breakfast of Robins and the Robin his of Worms—The Lion must starve as well as the swallow.[29]

Disinterestedness ought to be kept up: it is a finer thing than self-interest, and as Hazlitt had shown it seems harder to act from only because we are trained by habit to look first to ourselves. It is of our very humanity to be disinterested, as much as it is to be self-centered. But when we move from human society to nature the matter alters. The possibility of disinterested action then turns out to be a result of artificial arrangements which society brings into being. Reduced to a practice by the hawk, it would oblige him to lose his meal. The hawk and eagle are not expected to act from disinterested motives, any more than they are expected to feel sympathy. Do they in this resemble the poet?

Keats wrote his letter in an experimental mood. It took the Ode to show us that poetry is more impressive than the eagle of his comparison would allow it to be. In their freedom from care and sympathy alike, the eagle and hawk resemble only one of the singers in Keats's poem: the nightingale. Keats aims to feel as it does. Yet the difference between them remains his necessary human inheritance. Having once recognized this, one may call his expansive gesture of identification by the name of empathy or, as seems more in keeping with Keats's own vocabulary, sympathy, but in either case it will be understood that the poet carries out an imaginative action of which the bird is incapable.[30] Indeed, the poet is only a poet by virtue of this gesture. He of all men feels in this way, even if he regrets the continual renewals of feeling and, with each wave, the sharper awareness that his subject is compounded of light and shade. So, in the course of the poem, those elements of the poet's character that belong to the irritable self, and can encounter nothing without palpable design, will vanish. The sort of personality that Keats still believes in is what Hazlitt described in his *Essay,* as "nothing more than conscious individuality: it is the power of perceiving that you are and what you are from the immediate reflection of the mind on its own operations, sensations, or ideas."

If one places those words from the *Essay* beside Keats's appreciation of a certain phase of Milton's poetry, where the reader feels the "Author's consolations coming thick upon him at a time when he complains most,"[31] one will have a fair sense of the intellectual allegiances he took for granted when he wrote.

> My heart aches, and a drowsy numbness pains
> 　My sense, as though of hemlock I had drunk,
> Or emptied some dull opiate to the drains
> 　One minute past, and Lethe-wards had sunk:
> 'Tis not through envy of thy happy lot,
> 　But being too happy in thine happiness,—
> 　　That thou, light-winged Dryad of the trees,
> 　　　In some melodious plot
> 　Of beechen green, and shadows numberless,
> 　Singest of summer in full-throated ease.

One recalls the aphorism from "The Indian Jugglers," that "greatness is great power, producing great effects." In the "Ode to Psyche" Keats's reader might have been conscious of the effects without feeling certain of the power: what kind it was, and from what source it claimed its authority. Even the identity of that poem's speaker is indefinite, until he comes upon Cupid and Psyche, and can assume their energy as his own.

> I wander'd in a forest thoughtlessly,
> 　And, on the sudden, fainting with surprise,
> 　Saw two fair creatures.

From this lucky diversion he gets his chance to make a poetry filled with sensations as well as thoughts. Still he draws all his strength from what he beholds; he cannot offer the sympathy of one distinct being for another, because he hardly exists before he unveils the lovers; he himself, it may be said, is created by the act of sympathy.

There is thus a quiet irony in the powerful line, "I see, and sing, by my own eyes inspir'd."

The reader who moves from this to the "Ode to a Nightingale" is startled by the presence of a feeling "I." One knows a good deal about this speaker after five lines: that he is acquainted with griefs and their numb aftermath; that envy (a twisted sympathy) is a motive he wants to rise above; that he is not quite conquered by cares, but acquires a strange vigilance from the pressure of having to contemplate them. The rest of the stanza opens an ambiguity which the rest of the poem will dramatize: "being too happy in thine happiness" may refer either to the poet or the bird; but the bird is never fully present except through the poet. Something must correspond to the "Thou," and yet it remains spectral without the "I," syntactically and grammatically tenuous. When the stanza achieves a finality of place and feeling, in "some melodious plot / Of beechen green, and shadows numberless," one feels that this could belong to the nightingale only with the spirit that inhabits it in conversation.

Keats's second stanza opens with a private joke against himself, "O, for a draught of vintage." Claret had appeared in his letters among the accessories proper to the full life of sensations. Now it is lovingly described, but with an awareness that its effect is to dull sensation, and to obscure identity. The effect can be felt especially in the Miltonic inversions of the last two lines—"That I might drink, and leave the world unseen, / And with thee fade away into the forest dim." The poet wishes to be unseen; but the world, given his present state, will also be unseen by him. Were the assimilative logic extended much beyond this, the second stanza would leave Keats in the situation of the knight in "La Belle Dame sans Merci." But any such ending is held back by a vision of ordinary suffering in a world less fortunate than the nightingale's, the world without motion in which Keats had nursed his brother Tom through the days just before his death. Its mood is dictated by powers offstage— in the poem itself, by the "fade away" that still governs from the last stanza—and the actions it permits are all subordinate.

> Here, where men sit and hear each other groan;
> Where palsy shakes a few, sad, last gray hairs,
>   Where youth grows pale, and spectre-thin, and dies;
>   Where but to think is to be full of sorrow
>   And leaden-eyed despairs,
>   Where Beauty cannot keep her lustrous eyes,
>   Or new Love pine at them beyond to-morrow.

Doubts of the real worth of poetry were crowding in upon Keats as he wrote this stanza; what at worst is done out of vanity may be judged by posterity to have been done in vain also. Is not every poet an egotist, compared to every nurse? How is Tom's death to be weighed in the balance with the composition of an ode?

From the burden of these questions Keats fancies for the moment that he can be released by an act of willed elation. The interjection, "Away! Away!" wards off the evil and, in the same breath, declares him bound for new regions. He is helped in this escape by the temporary artifice of a myth. Yet the language in which he presents it—"haply the Queen-Moon is on her throne, / Cluster'd around by all her starry Fays"—is facile in the worst style of *Endymion*. The effect I think is deliberate: Keats had to hear these particular notes ring false before he could be delivered back to himself. Unlike the bird he cannot join the night's tenderness simply by doing what is in his nature. He can join it nevertheless, by looking with different eyes on what has surrounded him all along. This is the major transition of the Ode, and as he enters it Keats's impression is that he is dazed, and for the first time must move slowly.

> I cannot see what flowers are at my feet,
>   Nor what soft incense hangs upon the boughs,
> But, in embalmed darkness, guess each sweet
>   Wherewith the seasonable month endows
> The grass, the thicket, and the fruit-tree wild;
>   White hawthorn, and the pastoral eglantine;
>   Fast fading violets cover'd up in leaves;
>   And mid-May's eldest child
> The coming musk-rose, full of dewy wine,
>   The murmurous haunt of flies on summer eves.

Here the poet is "cluster'd around" like the Queen-Moon: what she boded only he can fulfill humanly. As in "To Autumn," the catalogue here follows the course of a season, the early growths separable and a little plain, the late ones replete and intertwined. The effortless naturalism of the writing suggests that the hope Keats expressed in a letter to Bailey, of a kind of immortality from "having what we called happiness on Earth repeated in a finer tone and so repeated," was both sincere and pure of hermetic intent. That version of heaven was for those who delighted in sensation rather than hungered after truth. But Keats avoided the word "heaven"; he cared more for "havens of intenseness," wherever the artist might find them: his own life would arrive at a spiritual repetition from the effort of sympathy to compass ever vaster subjects. In this stanza he seems to have found the resting place from which the effort can begin.

He does not pause long. The sixth stanza will require his largest act of identification—the embrace of death—and Keats has too lively a sense of surprise, and even here too keen a love of the sheer sport of the exertion, to collect all his thoughts before us. Two associations seem to control his movement: "embalmed darkness" with its subtle shock had left the expectation that his mood would be explained, or more fully encountered; and the flower-catalogue had lightly echoed a similar description in "Lycidas," where the poet's bier was strewn with "The Musk-rose, and the well-attir'd woodbine, / With cowslips wan that hang the pensive head, / And every flower that sad embroidery wears." Keats must have discovered by these associations that he was composing an elegy after all. It remained for him to give it the shape of an elegy for himself, but without grief. The triumph of his movement from this to the next stanza is that he makes an apparently egotistical turn of the Ode coincide with its farthest stretch of imaginative sympathy.

> Darkling I listen; and, for many a time
> I have been half in love with easeful Death,
> Call'd him soft names in many a mused rhyme,
> To take into the air my quiet breath;
> Now more than ever seems it rich to die,
> To cease upon the midnight with no pain,
> While thou art pouring forth thy soul abroad
> In such an ecstasy!
> Still wouldst thou sing, and I have ears in vain—
> To thy high requiem become a sod.

With the phrase "Darkling I listen," an adjective probable only for the bird is appropriated by the poet; and it is understood that his readers will complete the exchange for themselves: "Thou wast not born for death, immortal Keats." Anti-sentimentalist critics have supposed that he was here confessing himself in love with death and, since there is something suspect in this, that he needed to shake free of the delusion before his poem was finished. Yet in calling death "easeful" he means, not "death, which is always easeful" but "one sort of death which has seemed easeful to me." This line, and all the lines that prepare for it, have an air neither of defiance nor of pas-

sive suffering and defeat. Death is in the poem, as a no longer ter-
rifying allegorical figure, because death is where the full diapason of
human identity must close. A sufficient motive for Keats's poise is the
untroubled connection he makes, however hard we may find it, between death and immortality. He finds nothing strange in asking
death to possess and continue his own wind of inspiration, "To take
into the air my quiet breath."

The most perfect gloss I can imagine for the seventh stanza is
Hazlitt's account of the dramatic strength in Shakespeare's poetry,
which Keats heard him say aloud in the lecture-hall and never forgot: "The passions are in a state of projection. Years are melted
down to moments, and every instant teems with fate. We know the
results, we see the process." At the conclusion of another lecture,
"On Thomson and Cowper," Hazlitt connected this "process" with
listening, and not merely thinking and speaking: "The cuckoo, 'that
wandering voice,' that comes and goes with the spring, mocks our
ears with one note from youth to age; and the lap-wing, screaming
around the traveler's path, repeats for ever the same sad story of
Tereus and Philomel." In Keats's mind these two passages had now
joined.

> Thou wast not born for death, immortal Bird!
>   No hungry generations tread thee down;
> The voice I hear this passing night was heard
>   In ancient days by emperor and clown:
> Perhaps the self-same song that found a path
>   Through the sad heart of Ruth, when, sick for home,
>   She stood in tears amid the alien corn;
>   The same that oft-times hath
> Charm'd magic casements, opening on the foam
>   Of perilous seas, in faery lands forlorn.

Listening to the "self-same song that found a path / Through the
sad heart of Ruth," he projects himself in imagination into the
prospect that stretched before her amid the alien corn. His success
here makes anything possible, and so the casement becomes magic.
Only after his venture into a human history, and by an effect best
described, in the anachronistic language of the cinema, as *montage,*
do we see the picture of Ruth give way to a kindred, equally generous but now visionary scene, opening "on the foam / Of perilous
seas, in faery lands forlorn."

Keats, as J. R. Caldwell demonstrated in *John Keats' Fancy,* wrote many of his poems in a kind of trance-state, which he believed congenial to the high argument of psychological romance. This practice would free him from habitual trains of thought—he might be bad but he would not be second-hand—and it would allow his imagination the unchanneled freedom which gave a promise of enduring invention. Some unhappy poems were produced as a result, but his greatest poems, the "Ode to a Nightingale" among them, were evidently written in much the same way. What may puzzle us is not the strangeness of his practice, since later poets have made it familiar, but rather Keats's implicit reliance on an exalted idea of the unconscious. There was no source for this in the associationist writers he knew, and we seem to be left with the true but primitive explanation that he invented the beliefs he needed to carry conviction. I prefer instead to enlist Hazlitt's aid again, by quoting from his essay "On Dreams," but with the same limitation I placed on the passage from "On Reason and Imagination." In these cases unlike the lectures and *The Round Table,* we cannot suppose that he showed Keats the way to his own thoughts. "On Dreams" was written after the Ode, and its interest is that it presents a genius of comparable sympathies working through a similar course of speculations.

Nevertheless I believe the essay brings some sort of order to the apparently lawless drift of fancy that Keats encouraged in himself; and the following passage may be read as a commentary on Keats's preferred manner of composition from *Endymion* to the odes.

> The *conscious* or connecting link between our ideas, which forms them into separate groups or compares different parts and views of a subject together, seems to be that which is principally wanting in sleep; so that any idea that presents itself in this anarchy of the mind is lord of the ascendant for the moment, and is driven out by the next straggling notion that comes across it. The bundles of thought are, as it were, untied, loosened from a common centre, and drift along the stream of fancy as it happens. . . . Thus we confound one person with another, merely from some accidental coincidence, the name or the place where we have seen them, or their having been concerned with us in some particular transaction the evening before. They lose and regain their proper identity perhaps half a dozen times in this rambling way; nor are we able (though we are somewhat incredulous and surprised at these compound creations) to detect the error, from not being prepared to trace the same connected subject of thought to a number of varying and successive ramifications, or to form the idea of a *whole.* . . . The difference, so far then, between sleeping and waking, seems to be

that in the latter we have a greater range of conscious recollections, a larger discourse of reason, and associate ideas in longer trains and more as they are connected with one another in the order of nature; whereas in the former, any two impressions, that meet or are alike, join company, and then are parted again, without notice, like the froth from the wave. So in madness, there is, I should apprehend, the same tyranny of the imagination over the judgment; that is, the mind has slipped its cable, and single images meet, and jostle, and unite suddenly together, without any power to arrange or compare them with others, with which they are connected in the world of reality. There is a continual phantasmagoria: whatever shapes and colours come together are by the heat and violence of the brain referred to external nature, without regard to the order of time, place, or circumstance. From the same want of continuity, we often forget our dreams so speedily: if we cannot catch them as they are passing out at the door, we never set eyes on them again. (XII, 20-21)

It is the conscious link between our ideas that organizes our experience into a consistent mass, and creates in us the abstract idea of self. We need this idea and this link if we are to be masters rather than servants of our associated ideas, and use the power of the imagination. Yet in sleep, or the kind of trance that slips the mind's cable, we are at the mercy of every chance link that may happen to connect our ideas, as they pass by each other and catch upon some salient point. We are thus robbed of the idea of a coherent self which seems to endow us with more than accidentally formed associations, and from which we gain the conviction of our power as agents. The waking imagination, no less than the judgment, requires the support of some such conviction, and Keats in his final stanza has to exorcise an impending tyranny of the dreaming imagination.

> Forlorn! the very word is like a bell
>   To toll me back from thee to my sole self!
> Adieu! the fancy cannot cheat so well
>   As she is fam'd to do, deceiving elf.
> Adieu! adieu! thy plaintive anthem fades
>   Past the near meadows, over the still stream,
>   Up the hill-side; and now 'tis buried deep
>   In the next valley-glades:
>   Was it a vision, or a waking dream?
>   Fled is that music:—Do I wake or sleep?

The contrast between waking and dreaming imagination, or between the "continual phantasmagoria" of sleep and the habitual relations of the self, had been given a different shading in Book II of *Endymion,* where the return from wandering thoughts was seen as a compelled tribute paid by fancy to the repressive self.

> There, when new wonders ceas'd to float before,
> And thoughts of self came on, how crude and sore
> The journey homeward to habitual self!
> A mad pursuing of the fog-born elf,
> Whose flitting lantern, through rude nettle-briar,
> Cheats us into a swamp, into a fire,
> Into the bosom of a hated thing.[32]

The recurrence in the Ode both of "cheat," and of the self-elf rhyme, persuades me that the old passage was still in Keats's mind, but he had set himself to revise it thoroughly. A great difference of tone separates the "habitual self" of *Endymion*—into which fancy betrays us by its excess, and is blamed for doing so—and the "sole self" of the Ode. The latter is a necessary thing, in charge of the daylight world which Keats no longer regrets, and which has its own sympathies to ask of us. It is fancy as such and not its "journey homeward," that Keats now describes as a cheat, exhibiting in this a self-possessed humor with some affection for his own errors: the "deceiving elf" only acts up to its name, but in the "fog-bound elf" of *Endymion* there had been something hellish. Keats in the Ode does not resent the obligation to reserve a space for less fanciful imaginings. As for the "sole self," it is what each of us has, in solitude, when for better or worse we do have the power to arrange and compare our ideas.

At the end of the Ode, dream images pass "out at the door," to adopt Hazlitt's words a last time. Keats himself remains fixed while the nightingale escapes "Past the near meadows, over the still stream, / Up the hill-side." The landscape has grown sober with the lucidity of daily things, and what survives the poem is a commitment to this mood as a final standard of comparison. And yet Keats is not oppressed by its demands, as he had seemed to be at the start of the poem. Out of the dream of truth in the middle stanzas has come the self-confidence of the egotist who is free of vanity because he has travelled outside himself for a time. "Do I wake or sleep"—it does not matter, because he is free to renew his journey, and to return again. The most nearly analogous emotion in literature is what one feels at certain moments of resolution in Shakespearean romance. One is made to believe that the ordinary must suffice but the ordinary too may be transfigured: as when, in *A Midsummer Night's Dream,* Helena speaks the lines that announce her contentment with what she can know but imperfectly, "And I have found Demetrius like a jewel, / Mine own and not mine own." Keats's poem ends like this not only because day follows night, but because the emotional extremes, being explored till they were exhausted, have at last left open a middle ground for the romance of realities.

One notices in rereading the Ode how deftly near the end it confirms Hazlitt's sense of the imagination's mastery over all associated impressions. Keats's use of the word "forlorn" has entered this poem at the suggestion of the same consonant group, f-l, which sounded in the phrase "faery lands." The adjective-noun pair was hopeful; the second adjective overcasts every hope: together, from the conformity of sounds alone, they exemplify the associative force of contrariety which was at work also in Keats's remarks about light and shade. By the end of the poem, however, he could afford to hear the low echo drawn out of high fancy, without contriving a miraculous escape. He is forlorn as a man untouched by irritations; his expansiveness and his skepticism here coincide. Imagination, he has seen, is the freedom to widen speculation; by making other things more vivid it contracts rather than expands the domain of self, though only for the moment; but what cannot ever be modified is the mind's liberty in forming new associations: to deny that would be, in Hazlitt's metaphor, "like supposing that you might tread on a nest of adders twined together, and provoke only one of them to sting you." Thus the narrowly sympathetic poetry of the Wordsworthian sermon and the Keatsian reverie have left room for a poetry that claims both the generosity and the privilege of a larger view. Long before this, in "Sleep and Poetry," in *Endymion,* and in sonnets dedicated to artists and art, Keats had written at the level he thought a modern could sustain. With the "Ode to a Nightingale" he had a poetry equal to what he loved.

"ODE ON A GRECIAN URN"

On this reading of the "Ode to a Nightingale," the poem has five distinct movements, the transitions being hard-won in each instance, and the constant sense of transition the necessary dramatic element in a poem that has one voice and yet means to shun the egotistical sublime. Keats begins by confessing his sickness of spirit; moves abruptly to dispel it, by his vow to "fly to thee" and join the Queen-Moon and her company, in what turns out to be a false effort of transcendence; finds nevertheless that this has led to an act of true imagination, with his embrace of death in "embalmed darkness"; by death is then reminded of the dead, and of another human sufferer of history or legend, whom the nightingale once soothed; and at last returns to life and the world of common realities, larger-spirited than the man who had begun, "My heart aches. . . ." These particulars need to be remembered because there has been a tendency among critics to read the "Ode on a Grecian Urn" as a companion poem, with a similar plot. The poems do seem to me to work together, but they were evidently written from very different impulses, and in the later poem it would be hard to trace any movement comparable to the one I have just proposed. Even the formal differences which separate them are not trivial. The urn is silent where the nightingale poured forth its song; static, where the nightingale was free to move and finally to depart from the poem. Keats might allow himself to "be intense upon" a creature he knew could not be captured. But the urn *can* perhaps be captured and somehow contained, whether by description or moralizing commentary, and Keats's effort to avoid doing so begins with his title. To address his poem "to" the urn would imply a degree of presumption about its identity; he writes merely "on" it. His tone through most of the poem, in keeping with the same downward modulation, is tentative and coaxing, and the exclamations of the "Ode to a Nightingale" are replaced by questions. The scenes depicted on the urn interest him to the point of excluding the artist who fashioned it, and this emphasis accounts for some of Keats's uneasiness about the sort of answer he wants. His ideas about the "poetical character" were by this time very clear, his ideas about the character of a poem much less so, as his abortive experiments with *Hyperion* had lately shown. The "Ode to a Nightingale" was a poem about the poet (warm, and adaptable to many identities) whereas the "Ode on a Grecian Urn" is about the poem (cold, and beyond interrogation). To Keats himself the first must have seemed an act of sympathy, and the second an act of power.

What readers most honor in the "Ode on a Grecian Urn," and are at the same time made uneasy by, is its dividedness of purpose. In spite of the task it assumes, it does not manage to exclude the warm strivings of life, or the troubled sympathies of the poet: he cannot finish the poem without trying to imprint on the urn the pathos of these things. By doing so he reduces the distance between himself and a chosen object of power, and implies that there are special dangers in our admiration for its cold remoteness and its grandeur above humanity. Since the object itself seemed to warn him of such dangers, Keats felt nothing wrong in allowing the object to instruct us concerning them, with a motto about the right use of art. Hence the inscription "Beauty is truth, truth beauty" which has perplexed much commentary on the poem. It is the third and fourth stanzas, with their scenes of "breathing human passion," that disturb commentators as not quite belonging there; but the weight of the protest falls on the concluding motto, which in retrospect seems answerable for every awkward fact. If he had written the poem without those stanzas, offering as complete stanzas 1, 2, and 5, we would regard it as a well-managed sublime poem on the order of Collins's "Ode to Evening." It would be more perfect and it would move us less. A recent critic of the Ode, Patrick Parrinder, writes that Keats "expresses the full allure of aestheticism, without quite taking the leap into vulgar commitment."[33] This is just perceptive enough to be irritating. Keats registers the allure only to reject it firmly, and to show an appreciation of art in which there is no want of keeping between art and humanity.

What did Keats feel when he saw before him an urn several centuries old? We have his testimony from one comparable occasion, the visit to the Elgin Marbles about which he wrote two sonnets in the spring of 1817. "On Seeing the Elgin Marbles for the First Time" seems to me the more conclusive in its statement of awestruck deference.

> My spirit is too weak—mortality
>   Weighs heavily on me like unwilling sleep,
>   And each imagined pinnacle and steep
> Of godlike hardship tells me I must die
> Like a sick eagle looking at the sky.
>   Yet 'tis a gentle luxury to weep
>   That I have not the cloudy winds to keep
> Fresh for the opening of the morning's eye.
> Such dim-conceived glories of the brain
>   Bring round the heart an undescribable feud;
> So do these wonders a most dizzy pain,
>   That mingles Grecian grandeur with the rude
> Wasting of old time—with a billowy main—
> A sun—a shadow of a magnitude.

The poem exhibits a poet's aspiration to compete with the grandeur of an art different from his, and greater by virtue of its duration. He hopes to find in himself a spirit as sublime as what he contemplates, yet the picture he gives of his failure is not sublime but pathetic, almost maudlin—"Like a sick eagle looking at the sky." Instead of the energy of mind that ought to reveal the poet's high contest with a nature informed by just such energy, he can show only "an undescribable feud," "a most dizzy pain." It looks as if, from a poem that began with the stock materials of the sublime—imagined pinnacles, cloudy winds—Keats were backing into a confession of defeat, which aims to move us by its sincerity. And yet the poem ends with impressive dignity in spite of its loss of heart. The new quality emerges from the sudden awareness of distance, in a mood so unexpected by Keats that he can approach it only by telegraphic dashes, and the reticence of the indefinite article: "a billowy main— / A sun—a shadow of a magnitude." The movement from an undescribable feud round the heart, to the acknowledgement of an alien strength, already suggests what Keats would mean in the "Ode on a Grecian Urn," when he spoke of being teased out of thought. His unhappier thoughts are of the soul's incompetence to gain these heights while the body still lives. But such thoughts come from our inability to be the contemporaries of our own greatness—which Keats, until the end of the poem, confuses with our inability to match the greatness of a past age. The last lines present the clearing away of that confusion. Nothing in the marbles themselves, Keats realizes, but rather the abyss that time has wrought between them and himself, brings the sensation of an incommensurable grandeur that he feels in looking at them. Cured of his weakness, he is able to participate in their glory at last, though it is experienced as something cold and inhuman. We may ponder this a moment longer in the light of all the elements that compose the resolution of the "Ode on a Grecian Urn." Here as in the later poem, the character of his feeling changes with the recognition that time itself creates sublimity, by robbing art of its signature and making it mysteriously natural. So old marbles can affect us "as doth eternity." Here too, mingled admiration and horror is a natural response to an object about which one can feel with a half-resentful certainty that "When old age shall this generation waste, / Thou shalt remain." Notwithstanding the strength of these associated feelings, there is no sense here that the sublime object could ever be "a friend to man."

Between the composition of this poem and the "Ode" two years later, Hazlitt had given his lecture "On Poetry in General," which we have good reason to suppose Keats read. The lecture included a comment on the relations between painting and poetry, and the remoteness of painting from human affections which only language can suggest. Raphael's cartoons are mentioned as proof of the rule, since their effect is inconceivable without our knowledge of the biblical texts; for contrast, Hazlitt calls to mind the "pure" beauty of Greek statues, and the phrase "marble to the touch" extends his criticism to the Elgin Marbles.

> Painting embodies what a thing contains in itself: poetry suggests what exists out of it, in any manner connected with it. But this last is the proper province of the imagination. Again, as it relates to passion, painting gives the event, poetry the progress of events: but it is during the progress, in the interval of expectation and suspense, while our hopes and fears are strained to the highest pitch of breathless agony, that the pinch of interest lies. . . . It is for want of some such resting place for the imagination that the Greek statues are little else than specious forms. They are marble to the touch and to the heart. They have not an informing principle within them. In their faultless excellence they appear sufficient to themselves. By their beauty they are raised above the frailties of passion or suffering. By their beauty they are deified. But they are not objects of religious faith to us, and their forms are a reproach to common humanity. They seem to have no sympathy with us, and not to want our admiration.[34]   (V, 10-11)

Hazlitt concludes by regarding the marbles as instances of power rather than sympathy: they are a kind of Coriolanus among art-objects. This, with an attendant sense of their cold self-sufficiency, was the conclusion Keats had reached in the last lines of his sonnet. He reaches it once more in the "Ode on a Grecian Urn," and one's suspicion that his reading of Hazlitt strengthened an earlier sentiment of his own is confirmed by the paraphrase, "All breathing human passion far above," which he makes of Hazlitt's "they are raised above the frailties of passion or suffering." The sharp "hopes and fears" that Hazlitt sees as special to poetry, "strained to the highest pitch of breathless agony," also have their answering interval in Keats, whose lovers are "For ever panting" and strained to the pitch of "A burning forehead, and a parching tongue."

In such intervals alone lies the hidden story that interests us when we look at works of art. But can an unspeaking object be relied on to tell the story unaided? Hazlitt thought not, and made his objection the more memorable by an allusion to Wordsworth's great line, "By our own spirits are we deified." As said by the poet in "Resolution and Independence," this had meant that only human sympathies give us a human immortality, in the minds of others. Yet as repeated by Hazlitt, and in its new form, "By their beauty they are deified," it bears witness to everything about the marbles that makes them gods above our humanity. Because the only religion we care for is the religion of humanity, this beauty renders them "not objects of religious faith to us." The irony of the allusion is directed against the marbles, and puts Hazlitt for the moment in accord with Wordsworth. When he came to write this Ode, Keats was searching for a more generous view of such objects, in which they would appear necessarily as a friend to the common affections. His problem was to do that in a poem which first acknowledged the coldness and strangeness of the object. He would thus be required to expand the interval in which, as Hazlitt said, "the pinch of interest lies," but without cheating, or somehow crediting the object with a pathos only language can express. Judged in these terms, the end of the Ode is a victory for art, but not for the urn; it is much closer to Hazlitt's distinction between poetic and plastic expression than Keats would have liked to come; for it shows the urn being rescued into meaning by the poet who speaks. The Ode is a marriage between the urn, plastic art, beauty, the "unravished bride of quietness"—and the poem, poetic art, truth, the master of verbal expression. At its consummation the urn is released into words, though of a sort possible only to writing or inscription, and not to oral speech. Decorum is thus preserved, but one feels that the poem's final weight of authority belongs with truth, without which beauty would remain cold to the touch as to the heart.

To test the argument beyond these preliminaries I have to quote the poem.

I

Thou still unravish'd bride of quietness,
   Thou foster-child of silence and slow time,
Sylvan historian, who canst thus express
   A flowery tale more sweetly than our rhyme:
What leaf-fring'd legend haunts about thy shape

Of deities or mortals, or of both,
    In Tempe or the dales of Arcady?
What men or gods are these? What maidens loth?
What mad pursuit? What struggle to escape?
    What pipes and timbrels? What wild ecstasy?

II

Heard melodies are sweet, but those unheard
    Are sweeter; therefore, ye soft pipes, play on;
Not to the sensual ear, but, more endear'd,
    Pipe to the spirit ditties of no tone:
Fair youth, beneath the trees, thou canst not leave
    Thy song, nor ever can those trees be bare;
    Bold Lover, never, never canst thou kiss,
Though winning near the goal—yet, do not grieve;
    She cannot fade, though thou hast not thy bliss,
For ever will thou love, and she be fair!

A poem written entirely in the key of the first four lines of these stanzas—the key of temperate and paradoxical satisfaction—would be very tedious to the merely human reader. But the relation which obtains here between the first four lines and the last six will be carried through the entire poem. First, the paradox is stated, with an air of ironic calm and good cheer; but in every case a deep distress has been held back, which needs the rest of the stanza to bring out its painful character. The relation between the two parts of each stanza is this, that the thought of immortality leads to the thought of death: the transition will be most astonishing in the final stanza, where the fourth line is not set off from the fifth by an end-stop—"Thou, silent form, dost tease us out of thought / As doth eternity," which I would paraphrase: "Your cold stillness shows us what silence all our thoughts end in, as for that matter our own deaths will show us." The not wholly agreeable surprise that Keats feels almost electrically across the line break is registered by the exclamation mark at "Cold Pastoral!" But about this phrase I will say more presently.

The thought which the opening lines of the first stanza hope to suppress, is that the urn was not always an orphaned thing. It now seems the "foster child of silence and slow time" because, though it had its human parentage, all trace of this has disappeared. Its silence, the absence of a signature, imparts mystery to the urn, and that mystery by the passage of time is transformed into sublimity. But the loss of any known author, and with it the loss of personal pathos, trouble Keats more than calling the urn its own author, "Sylvan Historian," would seem to imply. One has some sense of the violence of the exclusion in the queer pun on "express": as if the figures on the urn were straining against their condition, and pressed outward toward articulate life, in spite of the formal constraint that forbids them any verbal expression. The questions that follow are not a bit complacent—not content as rhetorical questions are, to be subdued to the silence that is their element—but rather tongue-tied, with the stammering of children not yet sure of their right to speak. In the last lines of the second stanza, Keats moves to reconcile the lover to the frozen gesture in which he finds himself trapped so near the goal. The over-insistent concern which he feels on the lover's account is chiefly evident in his repeated denials: "canst not," "nor ever," and to close off the last hope, "never, never." But Keats has to add, "do not grieve": poetry by its nature deals in "the flowing, not the fixed," as Hazlitt put it; and if sculpture deals in the fixed, may it not offer the consolation that its permanence is that of a paradise without death? The unfamiliarity of this thought provokes him to write two more stanzas confirming its beauty, and they are among the saddest he ever wrote.

III

Ah, happy, happy boughs! that cannot shed
  Your leaves, nor ever bid the spring adieu
And, happy melodist, unwearied,
  For ever piping songs for ever new;
More happy love! more happy, happy love!
  For ever warm and still to be enjoyed,
    For ever panting and for ever young;
All breathing human passion far above,
  That leaves a heart high-sorrowful and cloy'd,
    A burning forehead, and a parching tongue.

IV

Who are these coming to the sacrifice?
  To what green altar, O mysterious priest
Lead'st thou that heifer lowing at the skies,
  And all her silken flanks with garlands drest?
What little town by river or sea shore,
  Or mountain-built with peaceful citadel,
    Is emptied of this folk, this pious morn?

> And, little town, thy streets for evermore
> Will silent be; and not a soul to tell
> Why thou art desolate, can e'er return.

It is Keats himself whose cries of "happy, happy" must end in a breathless panting. And it is this happiness, more cloying than any sorrow, that makes us think of "breathing human passion" with relief. The ambiguous syntax, too, appears temporarily to set breathing human passion above anything the urn can depict; even when we read the syntactical inversion correctly—"These things, being above all human passion"—we may still be struck by the logical inversion that follows; for it would have been sounder practice, if the poem really wished us to forget the burning forehead and parching tongue, to place them somewhere other than the strong rhetorical position they now occupy at the end of the stanza.

But Keats at this period of his life must have counted himself among the lovers coming to the sacrifice, and sincerity compelled him to mention their pains in close conjunction with the question about their identity which opens the next stanza. The opening four lines describing the life of the town, however, are free of personal concern. In his effort to describe it without sympathy, and bounded by the speechless decorum of the urn itself, he approaches a Byronic pleasure in the picturesque. He writes of what is sublime, not because it is a work of man, but because it is a work of man overthrown; and yet he writes as if art alone, without any communion between the creating mind and the human passions it regards, could supply the terms in which we feel enlarged by such sublimity. If the poem had ended in this style, it might be included in Ruskin's general protest against the picturesque as a heartless ideal. In the second part of this stanza, however, Keats associates the urn's choice of an empty town to depict with his own readiness to empty the poem of all that concerns the town's inhabitants. The connection is between the urn-maker's choice to free his representation of persons, and what it would be for Keats to deprive his poem of feelings: the poem he thought he should aspire to make would be in this sense desolating. Keats was incapable of arriving at such a recognition without tremendous regret; and with his regret comes pity: "And, little town, thy streets for evermore / Will silent be." This is the only sentence, of all those following his questions, that even sounds like an answer. No soul can return, of course, except someone like Keats, a poet who does not accept the limits of the picture-making historian.

After the implicit equations have settled, of silence with apathy, and speech with pathos, the way open for the Ode as a poem was the way Keats took: to coax the urn, by compliment and salutation to conjure it into speech, and so to give it the sympathies of poetry. Yet he had to accomplish this in a manner that would reassure the urn that its condition as a silent and anonymous thing was not being violated.

V

O Attic shape! Fair attitude! with brede
   Of marble men and maidens overwrought,
With forest branches and the trodden weed;
   Thou, silent form, dost tease us out of thought
As doth eternity: Cold Pastoral!
   When old age shall this generation waste,
     Thou shalt remain, in midst of other woe
   Than ours, a friend to man, to whom thou say'st,
"Beauty is truth, truth beauty,"—that is all
   Ye know on earth, and all ye need to know.

Of many readers who felt uncomfortable with this ending, Robert Bridges was the first to object to "Attic Shape! Fair attitude!" as an embarrassing pun.[35] Others have followed him; and yet this is the language of conjuring: it is not more forced than "Abra Cadabra." The stanza affords much other evidence of a workmanship of style the reverse of negligent. The use of "overwrought" is the loveliest single instance, where the several meanings—"elaborately worked over"; "inlaid and intertwined"; "excited to the point of forgetting one's manners"—all converge in our sense of the maker's pains, the visible signs of his labor, and the vivid intensity of men and maidens on the brink of going too far. This was the sort of idiomatic play on words, incorporating both etymology and common usage, which Keats could manage like nobody else. Wordsworth can return to and revive the power of a word's origin, while allowing us to read it in some commoner way at first, as in his use of "consecration" and "distress" in the Peele Castle elegy; Coleridge is adept at finding grotesque juxtapositions for a word's original and colloquial meanings, though he often turns out to have half-invented one of them, as in his etymology of "atonement" (at-one-ment); but Keats sometimes liberates all the suspended senses of a word, to the advantage of all, with a lack of fuss that would cause equal delight to a parliamentary orator and a coffee-house politician. The implications of this freedom for a poem that has affected to renounce speech entirely will be felt in the progress of the stanza.

The great turn occurs at "Cold Pastoral!" H. W. Garrod argued that it need imply no change of heart, because Keats's admiration for such coldness has in fact been less pronounced all along than the reader supposes.[36] Some of Hazlitt's strictures on Benjamin West are pertinent to the difficulty: in particular his objection that Death in West's painting had "not the calm, still, majestic form of Death, killing by a look,—withering by a touch. His presence does not make the still air cold." Coldness like this, a possible attribute of the sublime and also of death, would have governed Keats's understanding of the word in the context he was building; and he had prepared readers to admire the sublime chill in just the way Garrod warns them against, in a whole series of passages. One recalls especially, from "Sleep and Poetry," the immortals on display at the home of Leigh Hunt:

> Round about were hung
> The glorious features of the bards who sung
> In other ages—cold and sacred busts
> Smiled at each other. Happy he who trusts
> To clear futurity his darling fame!

In the more skeptical mood of *The Fall of Hyperion,* shortly after the Ode, there is the chill Keats feels on the steps of Moneta's temple, and her cold lips, and her face "deathwards progressing / To no death": monitory sensations, but assisting the poet on his quest, with a privation that starves his illusions. It may be difficult to admire but we can reasonably expect that Keats, when he describes the urn as cold, will be saying so in a tone of admiration. Yet "Cold Pastoral!" is said much more in a tone of shock, and even of rebuke. This comes partly of the *memento mori* that has just startled him across a line-break. Eternity does not tease us out of thought into something finer (a life of sensations) but rather out of thought and out of life.

"Tease us out of thought" therefore seems to me the real enigma. An earlier use of the phrase, from the verse epistle "To J. H. Reynolds, Esq."—"Things cannot to the will / Be settled, but they tease us out of thought"—promises much but turns out to be no solution. It asserts that the insights of art have nothing to do with acts of the will, and about this one is hardly in doubt after four stanzas of the Ode. The urn is silent; it is we alone who have thoughts, and must be teased out of them: the poem still leaves us to guess what our thought is here. Yet, for the sense of vocation which chiefly interests us, there seem to be just two alternatives: (1) We are thinking of art's superiority to life and nature, its freedom from their pains, and its satisfying permanence; (2) We are thinking of the debt art owes to life and nature, which can never be repaid, but which it can sufficiently acknowledge in an expressive moment of sympathy.

In the poem Keats set out to write—about an ancient relic sublimely above our humanity, and indifferent to our pains—we would have been teased out of the second thought, and into a point of view congenial to the first though without being obliged to think it. But the effort to be honestly inclusive has worked into the poem so fully, and so shaken its structure with the climactic phrase "Cold pastoral!", that the teasing moves us in the opposite direction. It is the purist defense of plastic art that now seems merely abstract and speculative, a matter of thought rather than of sensation; while the communicative work of language, with all its associations, shows us how art can be "a friend to man." The urn teases us out of thought as art makes us go beyond art. Keats needed a reversal this strong and this assured to support the magnanimity that he almost hides with the ease of his qualifying syntax, when he says "Thou shalt remain, in midst of other woe / Than ours, a friend to man." In that other woe, a future poet will be looking at Keats himself as one of the figures on the urn, coming to the sacrifice, with a burning forehead and a parching tongue—and the apology for art which he in turn composes had better not be too fluent, or find too happy a retreat in the paradox of a career perpetually arrested before the goal. Nor ought it to deify as a thing of beauty what was once also a thing of pain. The poet of "other woe than ours" will be using the urn as a friend to man if he imagines Keats much as Keats in the "Ode to a Nightingale" had imagined Ruth.

"What the imagination seizes as Beauty must be truth": this, from a letter of November 1817—nine months after the Elgin Marbles sonnet, but eighteen months before the Ode and several strata earlier in the story of Keats's development—has often seemed an irresistible help in deciphering the Ode's conclusion. But even then it was only one of Keats's "favorite speculations," and on its most obvious construction I do not think the great poem will admit it: what strikes us as beautiful for the moment is not, even for the moment, the sum of all we need to know. I have given what seems to me a useful aid from Hazlitt's essay "On Imitation," in the statement that "to the genuine artist, truth, nature, beauty, are almost different names for the same thing"; but another statement by Hazlitt, from the "Letter to William Gifford" which Keats was copying out for his brother a few weeks before the Ode, seems to me an even stronger source. Replying to the objection that he was a florid writer, Hazlitt said: "As to my style, I thought little about it. I only used the word which seemed to me to signify the idea I wanted to convey, and I did not rest till I had got it. In seeking for truth, I sometimes found beauty." Here truth carries the main stress, as it must also in the poem Keats's Ode has become by its penultimate line.[37] But there is a special logic in the *sequence,* "Beauty is truth, truth beauty," which Hazlitt's writings on associationism help to explain. One needs to recall the tendency of any association to evoke its opposite: so light suggests shade; pleasure suggests pain; heat suggests cold; life suggests death. The process may always be reversed to conform to a different mood, as when Hazlitt writes in his essay "On the Fear of Death": "Perhaps the best cure for the fear of death is to reflect that life has a beginning as well as an end." If one grants the associationist premise that all our ideas are interrelated, it follows that by certain trains of thought, each of our experiences may imply every other, and that we come to know an experience not in itself but by its relation to every other.

When he imagined reading on the urn, "Beauty is truth, truth beauty," I think Keats was committing himself to the kind of sentiment that the urn, after his experience of it, might be supposed to say by inscription.[38] And yet he was doing more than that. Truth, in the associationist chain that he was exploring, meant "Everything that is the case," the sum of our experience; beauty meant the part of experience that art selects to represent the whole: but "is" still plays fast work with his purposes unless we read it discriminatingly. *Beauty implies truth, truth entails beauty.*[39] Or, to adapt Emerson's more responsive paraphrase, "There is no fact in nature which does not carry the whole sense of nature,"[40] and no fact of which our understanding is not modified by the whole sense of nature: this seems to me the expression of faith on which Keats's poem came to rest. We are asked to recognize that art excludes nothing of our experience, but finds in any part a sufficient clue to the whole, and in the whole the necessary modifications of each part. Keats thus ends by declaring that he values in art what Hazlitt valued in a "second nature." Beauty, truth, art, are to him almost different names for the same thing. Nor does the shift of a term imply any substantial dissent. Keats only refuses—as Hazlitt after "On Imitation" would generally refuse—to employ nature itself as an honorific name for the highest sort of art. He is, one may say, still surer than Hazlitt in his awareness of, and still more emphatic in communicating, the *work* art must do to make its selection.

Keats's sonnet on the Elgin Marbles came in spring 1817, Hazlitt's passage on them in "On Poetry in General" in spring 1818, and the "Ode on a Grecian Urn" in spring 1819. But the sequence is nicely progressive in something other than the dates. The sonnet had tried to find the marbles admirable precisely because they do not sympathize with us, and found the strain almost insupportable. Hazlitt replied in his criticism that one ought to search elsewhere for the effects of a human beauty and grandeur, because the marbles excluded on principle the moment of "breathless agony," the interval of suspended progress in which "the pinch of interest lies." The Ode deviated from its apparent theme to include that moment, and to consider it unstintingly, at the expense of concluding with an utterance more pertinent to English poetry, and what happens in this poem, than to the urn or Greek marbles for anything they show in themselves. The record would be incomplete without a final piece of evidence, from the same 1822 articles on the Elgin Marbles which I quoted in chapter 5. Hazlitt is more generous about them now, and I believe one thing that made him generous was Keats's poem. At all events he closes his account, as he had closed the chapter on *King Lear* several years earlier, with a set of propositions on the morality of art. There are ten of them, mostly too elementary in the assertion, and too elaborate in the justification, to add anything to the argument. But excerpts from the fifth, sixth, and tenth will certainly interest the reader who has come this far.

> *Grandeur consists in connecting a number of parts into a whole, and not leaving out the parts.*

> · · ·

> *As grandeur is the principle of connexion between different parts; beauty is the principle of affinity between different forms, or their gradual conversion into each other.*

> · · ·

> *Truth is, to a certain degree, beauty and grandeur, since all things are connected, and all things modify one another in nature.*
> (XVIII, 162-66)

If Keats's apology for art seems to apply more directly to poetry than to sculpture or ceramics, still the sympathy and power with which, in looking at an object, he widened speculation about its ground in human life, showed a way for the right use of any art. Hazlitt in this article was availing himself both of what he had taught Keats, and of what Keats had taught him in return.

More broadly, by helping Keats to revise his own idea of the imagination, Hazlitt altered the course of modern poetry. Keats opened up the romantic lyric from within, and by doing so lengthened its endurance. With *Hyperion,* mastered by an epic ideal, he had ended in disappointment, with an abrupt dismissal of his Miltonic experiment: "English ought to be kept up." All along Hazlitt had been moving him in the direction of Shakespeare, and if one looks in romantic poetry for a Shakespearean fullness, and a Shakespearean gusto in dialogue, the place to find them is nowhere in the poetic drama of the period, but in Keats's odes. For the odes have answering voices that are not merely echoes: Keats had come to a new understanding of how a writer's voice might implicate a reader's fate. When one considers his immense influence on the Victorians, and counts the long poems they wrote in any case, one may wonder whether the lyric need in fact have become their dominant mode, and whether it could have done so had he not enlarged its scope. Besides, there was another element of Keats's genius that made him attractive to his successors: he had found a place in poetry for the disagreeables. Not to be dispelled, evaporated, or reconciled, but to be named as part of truth, and belonging to a larger part. Hazlitt alone could have attached him to this faith, for though Keats might have sought it from Coleridge, there was, as Empson says in his essay on "Beauty is Truth," "remarkably little agony in Coleridge's theory of Imagination . . . whereas Keats was trying to work the disagreeables into the theory."[41] Keats's aims in poetry and Hazlitt's in criticism place both in accord with a concern for dramatic form that modern poets have been unwilling to disclaim.[42] Other forces, other personalities, of course intervened, but the periods of literary history are never as inviolable as we make them to speed our thinking, and one reason we read lyric poems today, and not epics or romances of solitary life, is that between 1815 and 1820 Hazlitt convinced a very young man born into a great age of poetry that something still remained to be done.

CONCLUSION

I started this book with Hazlitt's defense of Shylock, because its interest is easy to explain. It makes us feel that a truth is being told which has awaited utterance—that a kind of justice is being done, for the first time. What are we to make of the fact that the interpretation to which we owe these feelings came into being at a certain time, thanks to a certain writer? Hazlitt tells of the change when he observes that a character who had once been "a popular bugbear" was becoming "a half-favourite with the philosophical part of the audience." He does not say why some people became "disposed to think that Jewish revenge is at least as good as Christian injuries," and his reticence is understandable. The philosophical part of the audience were not yet *there:* he himself was setting out to create them. Spectators of *The Merchant of Venice* who gave their applause to a less dignified Shylock in the centuries before Hazlitt wrote, would have felt themselves properly responsive to the play, and would have been right to feel so. The reason is that truth and justice in criticism are historical virtues. They seem immediately intelligible to the audience of any period not because they are stationary but because like the audience they exist in time. One can seldom say just how a change comes about in their application to a given work, but Hazlitt's revision of Shylock is perhaps as close as one can get to a clear-cut instance.

Another person was necessary to the accomplishment, a performer in his first months in London, whose future would depend on his success in this character. Hazlitt's own reminiscences give Kean much of the credit for the interpretation and recall a few line-readings vividly. For example, Shylock's outcry at having lost the jewel he received from Leah, "I would not have parted with it for a wilderness of monkeys," was pronounced by Kean with an emphasis on *wilderness* that turned it into "a fine Hebraism." But the great moment that first evening had been Shylock's entrance, by which "a vague expectation was excited," for there was "a lightness in his step, an airy buoyancy and self-possession different from the sullen, dogged, gaol-delivery look of the traditional Shylocks of the stage." When Kean told "the tale of Jacob and his flock with the garrulous ease of old age and with an animation of spirit, that seem borne back to the olden time, and to the privileged example in which he exults"—it was plain that "a man of genius had lighted on the stage." So at any rate Hazlitt later implied.

The impression at the time was by no means universal, and for several months Hazlitt had to endure the charge of writing up Kean. He had watched him from the pit rather than a box, and traced all contention on the subject to the incorrigibility of those who would not descend to see him as the public did. From the "elevated sphere" above the stage, Hazlitt noted, in an estimate of Kean's performance as Sir Giles Overreach, an actor of genius can only appear to be "a little man in a great passion. . . . Without seeing the workings of his face, through which you read the movements of his soul, and anticipate their violent effects on his utterance and action, it is impossible to understand or feel pleasure in the part. All strong expression, deprived of its gradations and connecting motives, unavoidably degenerates into caricature." The other characters associated with Kean's popular success, particularly Sir Giles Overreach and Richard III, give a fair idea of the equipment he brought to Shylock. Buoyancy, vitality, a quick masculine resourcefulness, he would certainly have shown, and he took away the red beard and the long nose required by tradition. Yet the black beard he substituted, the nose an inch more human, and all his range of expressive power, still do not account for Hazlitt's response.

Shylock, as Kean played him, was a serious revenger, a good hater, "a man brooding over one idea." As Hazlitt presents him, in the *Characters of Shakespeare's Plays* and elsewhere, he has become more than that. He is, in a quotation Hazlitt borrows shockingly, "a man more sinned against than sinning." He is "more than half a Christian," and "our sympathies are much oftener with him than with his enemies. He is honest in his vices; they are hypocrites in their virtues." Between Kean's performance and Hazlitt's description, an evil character whose humanity had at last been shown, was transformed into one whose wrongs outweigh his faults, the most nearly heroic character in a play without a hero. And this reading both of the play and of the character has triumphed in the only way that can matter: any reversion to the older Shylock we would now find quaint and incredible; when we try to imagine the character at all we find ourselves somehow influenced by Hazlitt. Reviewers in the decades since 1814 have steadily echoed his words, to characterize Shylocks who cannot all have been facsimiles of what he saw, and the repetitions can be accounted for simply. Hazlitt's words have taken possession of what the reviewer sees, no matter what is before him. A comment on a 1960 performance by Peter O'Toole will serve to illustrate the tendency: "His courtesy is impeccable, his resolution steely; the result is extremely impressive, and against the appalling arrogance of Antonio and his caddish hangers-on he appears to be almost the only gentleman in Venice."[1] It is impossible today to propose without self-consciousness a conception of Shylock that makes him appear ignoble.

Historical reconstructions of what Shakespeare would have wanted us to think about Shylock of course have their own worth, but they cannot hope to challenge this view as an interpretation. Thus one may plausibly argue that by Shylock's religion, but also by certain signs apart from his religion, an Elizabethan reader would have known him as an outsider who must be kept out; that the play does nothing more than depict, with evident approval, the transition from the old law of Justice (as urged by Shylock) to the new law of Mercy (as urged by Portia); and that Shakespeare's art, while registering the cost of the exclusion, presents it as a necessary sacrifice to an ideal of Christian harmony.[2] Signs of this sort, though the concern of accurate scholarship, do not therefore appeal to the imagination. Hazlitt has construed the play too powerfully for us to respond to such reconstructions, and they strike us as an impracticable translation of a museum piece to a region where it cannot survive. Yet Hazlitt's view of Shylock is commonly described as a *mis*interpretation; so we may find something paradoxical in the admission that it is the only vivid idea of the character now available to us.[3] I think the paradox vanishes when one understands that Hazlitt's revision, whether or not we decide to call the result a misinterpretation, is a typical case of an *interesting* interpretation.

What does an analysis like his do for us? It changes one perspective for another; it makes us hear certain lines differently. The plainest instances are the speeches beginning, "You call me misbeliever, cut-throat dog," and "Hath not a Jew eyes." For an actor to say these, without communicating some sense that they have a claim on us—to deliver them instead in the accents of an insincere rhetorician, with the pure malignity of a Machiavel, or the whining ineffectuality of a comic butt—is not even to tempt fortune, it is to assure the nullity of the performance. There are many less celebrated passages where the actor faces a similar choice that is no longer between two live options. A line like "These be the Christian husbands!"—said by Shylock when a contest of self-sacrifice between Bassanio and Gratiano prompts each to outdo the other until both have wished their wives dead—calls our attention to an unpleasant shading which may once have been absent from the trial scene, but which has entered our experience of it beyond recall. It adds to the impression of a man honest in his vices while others are hypocrites in their virtues, and it cannot be said merely as the routine jeering of a villain. Hazlitt's sympathies have made a difference to ours. They have placed a new emphasis here, removed an habitual one there, in a pattern multiplied as many times over as a reader's or an actor's ingenuity can suggest.

Whether Hazlitt's play is really the same as Shakespeare's is a fair question, but one that cannot lead to fruitful answers. If we were informed on unquestionable authority that Shakespeare agreed with Hazlitt, it would scarcely strengthen the feelings we had already. If we were informed that he disagreed, we would have to admit (however regretfully) that we preferred Hazlitt's play to Shakespeare's. What in that case would be our loss? We read the play because we were in search of a story, and when the critic tells the story better than the author we are none the poorer for that. Once we assent to the economy of good stories, there seems nothing strange about what it implies for our practice of reading. Interpretations are not true or false, in any sense we can verify by consulting the work; rather they succeed or they fail; they carry the day, or they leave things where they were. But when the sentiments at issue are deep enough, the day may last more than a century.

This does not mean that Hazlitt's revision of Shylock is an advance on the older view, any more than the scholarly rehabilitation of Antonio and his friends is an advance on Hazlitt's. Criticism is not progressive, and progress, as a gradually tightening conformity of interpretation, is not what we seek in any event. We care for a new interpretation like Hazlitt's for the same reason he said we care for imitations, because they belong to the most interesting part of natural history, the history of man. An interpretation's power is measured by its consequences, not only for future readings and performances but for the discussion of other works. I have in mind specifically Bradley's observations on *King Lear,* analyzing the way that play's characters embody degrees of evil finely differentiated from each other. The unexpected valor of Edmund is important to the argument, and I do not see how a critic could even have noticed this without a readiness to grant the presence of justice, in a wicked character, as satisfying something of our sympathy with the good. Here the way had been prepared by Hazlitt.

Criticism must have much to do with history; but what the connection is may seem elusive. Questions like this about art Hazlitt always met with an uncompromising reply, most memorably in his chapter on *Coriolanus: what men delight to read in an artist's story they will put into practice.* With his writing as evidence, one may assert the same sort of connection betwen a critic's story and what men put into practice. Yet for most readers—less extreme than Hazlitt in our view of the effect words can have, because we are unlikely to have read any author as he read Burke, Rousseau, and Wordsworth— a more modest formulation will be more sincere. It seems enough to say that a story, whether an artist or a critic tells it, is apt to influence our lives in ways that we cannot imagine ever being able to define. It is the reader who connects the author's story with history, from the motives he comes to share by his sympathy with expression. But Hazlitt goes further than most critics in helping the reader to do that work. His pamphlet on the "Emancipation of the Jews," for example—the last article he is known to have written—does much to inform one's sympathy with his chapter on *The Merchant of Venice.*

The English in 1830 no longer forced Jews to give up their possessions or convert to Christianity, because the prejudice no longer existed which allowed them to do such things with a good conscience. Still, they were denying Jews the full rights of citizens, and Hazlitt begins the article by offering a revision of Burke's dictum about the permanence of sentiments: it is, he concedes, true that sentiments are and ought to be the basis of human institutions, but they turn out at the present time to be more liberal than those institutions. "The Emancipation of the Jews is but a natural step in the progress of civilization. Laws and institutions are positive things: opinions and sentiments are variable; and it is in conforming the stubbornness and perversity of the former to the freedom and boldness of the latter, that the harmony and beauty of the social order consist." He answers several lingering complaints against the Jews, and several apologies for maintaining a limited persecution of them. Their intimacy with "sordid vices" he admits, without discovering in the fact anything specially Jewish and therefore blameable: "If they are vicious it is we who have made them so. Shut out any class of people from the path to fair fame, and you reduce them to grovel in the pursuit of riches and the means to live." Their vices are a consequence rather than the cause of their persecution. Nor is Hazlitt impressed by the extenuating appeal that the Jews after all expect the coming of their Messiah, and so deserve no rights in a Christian kingdom: "this objection comes with but an ill grace from the followers of him who has declared, 'My kingdom is not of this world.'" He grants for the sake of argument the oldest and severest charge against the Jews, that they are guilty of the death of Christ and ought to be punished for it even now. If the report is true, Hazlitt says, then they must be reckoned faithful to their error: "That the Jews, as a people, persist in their blindness and obstinacy is to be lamented; but it is at least, under the circumstances, a proof of their sincerity; and as adherents to a losing cause, they are entitled to respect and not contempt." The article ends with an echo of his passage on Shylock: "It is the test of reason to be able to subsist without bugbears," and now that it is generally known that Jews do not eat children, the prejudice ought to cease, as it has long ceased "amongst the more reflecting part of the community." The theatre is England. The philosophical part of the audience are again evoked for the instruction of the rest, and the outcome will decide the fate of real and not imaginary persons.

My explanation of story and history—not as blending imperceptibly into each other, but as calling on the same motives, for the same kind of effect, with a continuous mutual influence—does not seem to me peculiarly modern. It is a paraphrase of Hazlitt's description of the art of a critic, in his essay "On the Prose-Style of Poets."

> The principle which guides his pen is truth, not beauty—not pleasure, but power. He has no choice, no selection of subject to flatter the reader's idle taste, or assist his own fancy: he must take what comes, and make the most of it. He works the most striking effects out of the most unpromising materials, by the mere activity of his mind. He rises with the lofty, descends with the mean, luxuriates in beauty, gloats over deformity. It is all the same to him, so that he loses no particle of the exact, characteristic, extreme impression of the thing he writes about, and that he communicates this to the reader, after exhausting every possible mode of illustration, plain or abstracted, figurative or literal. Whatever stamps the original

image more distinctly on the mind is welcome. . . . In prose, the
professed object is to impart conviction, and nothing can be admitted by way of ornament or relief, that does not add new force
or clearness to the original conception. The two classes of ideas
brought together by the orator or impassioned prose-writer, to wit,
the general subject and the particular image, are so far incompatible, and the identity must be more strict, more marked, more determinate, to make them coalesce to any practical purpose. Every
word should be a blow: every thought should instantly grapple
with its fellow. There must be a weight, a precision, a conformity
from association in the tropes and figures of animated prose to fit
them to their place in the argument, and make them *tell*.

                                                        (XII, 10-11)

The model for the writer portrayed here seems to be at times Burke,
at times any great and serious writer of prose, and at times Hazlitt
himself (though he will not say so). However one chooses to identify
him, he is not a collector of facts, a hired advocate, or a rhapsodist.
He is simply a master of persuasion. He is great when he succeeds in
imparting conviction, and the truth he cares for is a truth established by his effect on the audience, which they themselves disclose
by their words and actions. Such a writer may be great for better or
for worse, and in most instances both, as Hazlitt's portraits of Bentham, Godwin, Wordsworth, and Scott, in *The Spirit of the Age,* all
exist to remind us.

To regard criticism as an act of persuasive eloquence is to give it
value, in the literal sense of giving it weight in our lives. Yet everything Hazlitt says about sentiment, interest, and the imagination has
the aim of showing us that we are mistaken if we suppose that the
weight is ours to give. It is there anyway, from our condition as
members of a community of speech, and our only choice has to do
with how we recognize it, and what we want to do about it. As early
as 1806, in "Free Thoughts on Public Affairs," Hazlitt wrote: "I
know it is a general maxim, that we are not to war with the dead.
We ought not, indeed, to trample on their bodies; but with their
minds we may and must make war, unless we would be governed by
them after they are dead." That our community always extends into
the past is a critic's contribution to knowledge; that we ourselves invent our difference from the past is his contribution to wisdom. "We
stop too often," writes Nietzsche in *The Use and Abuse of History,*
"at knowing the good without doing it, because we also know the
better and cannot do it. Here and there a victory is won, which gives

a strange consolation to the fighters, to those who use critical history for the sake of life. The consolation is the knowledge that this 'first nature' was once a second, and that every conquering 'second nature' becomes a first."[4] Hazlitt's criticism offers the conquering second nature he believed all great writing must offer. His advantage as a fighter was that he had few illusions of permanent consolation. He knew that posterity alone decides what to ignore as a defeat, and that its finding is subject to revision. To a critic this may seem a hopeful circumstance or a catastrophic one, but the burden of his knowledge and wisdom together is only that this is what happens to works of the mind, from one generation to the next. Many of Hazlitt's victories are still to be declared.

NOTES

INTRODUCTION

1. Quoted by W. K. Wimsatt, Jr., *The Prose Style of Samuel Johnson* (New Haven, 1941), p. 54. His list is taken from the 1928 monograph on the styles of Addison, Johnson, Hazlitt, and Pater, by Zilpha E. Chandler.

2. John Flaxman, *Lectures on Sculpture* (London, 1829), pp. 199, 265. Quoted by permission of Gordon N. Ray.

3. Catherine Macdonald Maclean, *Born Under Saturn* (London, 1943), p. 339.

4. E. P. Thompson, *The Making of the English Working Class* (New York, 1963), p. 748.

5. *Henry Crabb Robinson on Books and Their Writers*, ed. Edith J. Morley, 3 vols. (London, 1938), I, 25.

6. Virginia Woolf, *The Moment and Other Essays* (Harvest edition, New York, 1974), p. 72.

7. Both phrases come from Coleridge's letter to Tom Wedgwood of September 16, 1803. Quoted by P. P. Howe, *The Life of William Hazlitt* (New York, 1922), pp. 75-76.

8. Wordsworth's version to Haydon, in *Diary of Benjamin Robert Haydon*, ed. Willard B. Pope, 5 vols. (Cambridge, Mass., 1960-1963), II, 470.

9. Samuel Taylor Coleridge, *Letters*, ed. E. L. Griggs, 6 vols. (Oxford, 1956-1971), IV, 735. Wordsworth and Southey likewise took credit for having rescued Hazlitt from the mob, contrived his escape-route, and so forth. Howe comments: "What is clear to us, I think, is that in after years, when Hazlitt had begun to write against them, each of the poets was equally anxious to appear in the character of his benefactor" (*Life of Hazlitt*, p. 81).

10. From Hazlitt's diary notes on Sarah Walker, in *The Letters of William Hazlitt*, ed. Herschel Sikes, W. H. Bonner, and Gerald Lahey (New York, 1978), p. 385.

11. Thomas De Quincey, "William Hazlitt," in *Works*, 16 vols. (Author's Edition, Edinburgh, 1863), XI, 303.

12. Quoted by Walter Benjamin, "Karl Kraus," in *Reflections*, ed. Peter Demetz, trans. Edmund Jephcott (New York, 1978), p. 253.

13. T. S. Eliot, "John Dryden" (1921), in *Selected Essays* (New York, 1932), p. 268.

14. W. K. Wimsatt, Jr. and Cleanth Brooks, *Criticism* (New York, 1957), p. 308. For another view of Hazlitt as the reliable medium of ideas-in-circulation,

see M. H. Abrams, *The Mirror and the Lamp* (New York, 1953). W. J. Bate in *From Classic to Romantic* (Cambridge, Mass., 1946) and other works, assigns him a more nearly central position among romantic critics.

15. William Empson, *Seven Types of Ambiguity* (2nd edition, London, 1947), p. 4.

16. John Kinnaird, *William Hazlitt: Critic of Power* (New York, 1978), especially chs. III-VI.

17. David Hume, *Treatise of Human Nature,* ed. L. A. Selby-Bigge (Oxford, 1888), I.iv.7, p. 265.

18. Coleridge, *Letters,* II, 672.

19. Hazlitt, *Works,* VII, 125. Compare "My First Acquaintance with Poets": "we found a little worn-out copy of the *Seasons,* lying in a window-seat, on which Coleridge exclaimed, '*That* is true fame!' " (XVII, 120). The concealment of the "friend's" identity would be poignant to those who knew it; others would not be conscious of having missed anything.

20. I owe the coinage to D. A. N. Jones, "Preachers in the Post" (*The Listener,* December 6, 1979), who derives it from an essay on "The Exclusionists in Taste" (XX, 262-63).

21. Carl R. Woodring, Introduction to *Leigh Hunt's Political and Occasional Essays* (New York, 1962), p. 36.

22. Kenneth Clark, *The Romantic Rebellion* (New York, 1977), p. 248.

23. Elisabeth Schneider, *The Aesthetics of William Hazlitt* (London, 1933), p. 86.

Chapter I. Imagination

1. In reading Hazlitt's attacks on Burke one must remember that the two causes—of civil liberty, and sympathy with a revolution abroad—were linked to each other in the mind of every radical, and that it was Burke who had bound them together. When, in his "Speech on the Petition of the Unitarians" (1792), he spoke out on the Test and Corporation Acts, he had in mind French Jacobins as much as English Dissenters: "The principle of your petitioners is no passive conscientious dissent, on account of an overscrupulous habit of mind: the dissent on their part is fundamental, goes to the very root; and it is at issue not upon this rite or that ceremony, on this or that school opinion, but upon this one question of an Establishment, as unchristian, unlawful, contrary to the Gospel and to natural right, Popish and idolatrous. These are the principles violently and fanatically held and pursued,—taught to their children, who are sworn at the altar like Hannibal. The war is with the Establishment itself,—no quarter, no compromise. As a party, they are infinitely mischievous: see the declarations of Priestley and Price,—declarations, you will say, of *hot* men. Likely enough: but who are the *cool* men who have disclaimed them? Not one,—no, not one!" (*Works,* 12 vols. (3rd edition, Boston, 1869), VII, 56-57). Priestley had been among Hazlitt's teachers at Hackney; Price had assisted in devising the school's curriculum.

2. Hazlitt was cheerful, not alarmed, in the company of political visionaries, but from having met them early in life and known them long, he was easily aroused to an uncongenial irony. He had kept within his father's milieu even after quitting his studies at Hackney, when he went to London, met Horne Tooke and Thomas Holcroft, and contracted for his first books with his father's publisher,

Joseph Johnson. He seems always to have honored the motives of the older, less doubt-ridden, and so far *purer* generation of Dissenters; while regretting the vanity by which they conceived that good theories would project them beyond the claims of history. The glimpse he offers of their speculative life, in a paragraph of "On Reading New Books," concludes with an objection that did not take Hazlitt a lifetime to mature, but was forming itself from his earliest sessions in their company:

> About the time of the French Revolution, it was agreed that the world had hitherto been in its dotage or its infancy; and that Mr. Godwin, Condorcet, and others were to begin a new race of men—a new epoch in society. Every thing up to that period was to be set aside as puerile or barbarous; or, if there were any traces of thought and manliness now and then discoverable, they were to be regarded with wonder as prodigies—as irregular and fitful starts in that long sleep of reason and night of philosophy. . . . The past was barren of interest—had neither thought nor object worthy to arrest our attention; and the future would be equally a senseless void, except as we projected ourselves and our theories into it. There is nothing I hate more than I do this exclusive, upstart spirit. (XVII, 209)

3. Roy Park argues that Hazlitt condemned abstraction in the usual meaning of the word, but saw the necessity of abstraction *as a process of individuation (Hazlitt and the Spirit of the Age* (Oxford, 1971)). The first part of this argument is a reductive account of Hazlitt's empiricism. The second part seems to me true and important: but, by describing Hazlitt's position in a vocabulary Hazlitt rejected—the vocabulary of universals and individuals, general and particular, with the first of each pair condemned as vicious—Park strains beyond intelligibility what ought to have been a routine point about the history of usage. In fact, Hazlitt was able to view abstraction as a necessary stage in every inquiry, because he read the word etymologically, as the detachment of drawing-away of one quality from a mass of others, for the sake of a certain emphasis and result. John Dewey's *Reconstruction in Philosophy* (1920; enlg. edition, Boston, 1948) has an excellent account of how the same word came to be used for two sorts of activity: "What is called false or vicious abstraction signifies that the *function* of the detached fragment is forgotten and neglected, so that it is esteemed barely in itself as something of a higher order than the muddy and irregular concrete from which it was wrenched. [However,] looked at functionally, not structurally and statically, abstraction means that something has been released from one experience for transfer to another. [In this sense] abstraction is liberation" (p. 150). Dewey offers an example: "The trait of flying is detached from the concrete bird. This abstraction is then carried over to the bat, and it is expected in view of the application of the quality to have some of the other traits of the bird. This trivial instance indicates the essence of generalization, and also illustrates the riskiness of the proceeding" (p. 151).

Hazlitt supposed that nothing is by its nature either abstract or concrete. Our counting it as one or the other depends on whether we use it as an organizing instrument to pick out traits from our experience, or as one of the traits themcasion. A musical note like middle C serves at different times in both categories. selves. And in every instance our choice will depend on the character of the ocSo does a metaphor like "the seat of authority." The difference between a "liberating" and a "vicious" abstraction is only that the former brings familiar objects into a new relation, whereas the latter mistakes an established relation for an object somehow more legitimate than others. In all our use of language, how we measure a word on the abstract-to-concrete scale is a matter not of certain properties of the word itself, but of its history and present context.

4. On Blake's argument against Locke, see Northrop Frye, *Fearful Symmetry* (Princeton, 1947), ch. 1.

5. Schneider, *The Aesthetics of William Hazlitt,* has a useful appendix on Hazlitt's reading in philosophy and criticism.

6. John Locke, *Essay concerning Human Understanding,* ed. Peter H. Nidditch (Oxford, 1975), II.xxi.21, p. 244.

7. Ibid., II.xxi.24, p. 246.

8. Ibid.

9. Ibid., II.xxi.46, p. 262.

10. Ibid., II.xxi.38, p. 256.

11. Ibid., II.xxi.47, pp. 263-64.

12. I reduce and paraphrase an argument advanced by Hans Aarsleff, "The State of Nature and the Nature of Man in Locke," in John W. Yolton, ed., *Locke: Problems and Perspectives* (Cambridge, 1969), pp. 99-136, to which I am indebted for qualifying my interpretation of the idea of power. He singles out as especially pertinent to "Of Power" Locke's earlier remarks in "Of Ethics in General," with emphasis on the sentence: "there is nothing morally good which does not produce pleasure to a man, nor nothing morally evil that does not bring pain to him" (p. 121). It seems to me that this sentence indeed merges the two ideas from "Of Power," but without in the process clarifying either. If Locke's claim here were obviously true, he would have felt no need in writing the *Essay* to supplement a power responsive to sensations with a power of suspense and reflection, for they would have been understood as the same. But it is hard to see how our moral choices could ever be experienced thus sensationally and immediately, unless the pleasures and pains we had in mind always included the ultimate rewards and punishments of God. Even if they did, most readers would still find the result a deeply unsatisfying way to end a discussion of motives.

Hazlitt's objection appears to have been that by power Locke meant both physical necessity (the will responding to a pressing uneasiness) and rational virtue (the mind taking stock of its choices). He believed that Locke's illustrations of power by inanimate objects—as with the billiard ball that takes its motion from the stick—only blurred the distinction between those meanings; and he commented in the *Lectures on English Philosophy*: "It were to be wished that [Locke] had given [the idea of power] as simple a source as possible, *viz.* the feeling we have of it in our minds, which he sometimes seems half inclined to do" (II, 160). In view of this sentence, I do not think Hazlitt deserves his place among the careless nineteenth-century readers of Locke, in Hans Aarsleff, "Locke's Reputation in Nineteenth-Century England" (*From Locke to Saussure* (Minneapolis, 1982), pp. 120-45). The standard nineteenth-century misreading of the chapter on power was that it argued consistently against the freedom of the will. But Hazlitt sees that Locke was "half inclined" to propose an idea of power clearly independent of our response to sensations.

Thus he cannot be accused of repeating, or helping to invent, the commonplace about Locke as a simple necessitarian. His objection has been shared by many careful readers before and since, who wished that "Of Power," *as an account of action,* were a little less rich in ambiguities. Shelley's notes to *Queen Mab* betray a similar frustration, and resolve it by affirming a necessitarianism more rigorous than Locke's: "What is power?—*id quod potest,* that which can produce any given effect. To deny power, is to say that nothing can or has the power to be or act. In the only true sense of the word power, it applies with equal force to the loadstone as to the human will. . . . The advocates of free-will assert that the will has the power of refusing to be determined by the strongest motive [i.e. the power of suspense]: but the strongest motive is that which, overcoming all others, ultimately prevails; this assertion therefore amounts to a denial of the will being ultimately determined by that motive which does determine it, which is absurd" (*Complete Works,* ed. Roger Ingpen and Walter E. Peck, 10 vols. (London, 1926-1928), I, 145).

13. Locke, *Essay,* II.xxi.72, p. 286.

14. From "Expostulation and Reply": "Nor less I deem that there are Powers/ Which of themselves our minds impress;/ That we can feed this mind of ours/ In a wise passiveness."

15. David Hartley, *Observations on Man,* 2 vols. (4th edition, London, 1801), I.iii.22.cor. IV.v.1., p. 114.

16. Ibid., I.ii.14.cor. IX.v.1, p. 83.

17. Leigh Hunt, "On the Realities of the Imagination," in *Essays by Leigh Hunt,* ed. Arthur Symons (London, 1887), p. 69.

18. Thomas Hobbes, *Leviathan,* ed. Michael Oakeshott (Oxford, 1946), ch. 11, p. 64.

19. *An Abridgement of The Light of Nature Pursued* was published by Joseph Johnson in 1807. Hazlitt's edition of Tucker is more than an abridgement though less than an original work by Hazlitt: it gives a vigorous rephrasing of Tucker's work, not without some rethinking. This has not been remarked by any scholar writing on Hazlitt or Tucker.

In a typical passage Hazlitt may contract three paragraphs of Tucker's to one of his own; tighten and improve the rhythm of sentences; and transpose the usage of Tucker's period into that of the early 1800s. For example, where Tucker speaks of the mind's assimilating "her *trains*" to "patterns she cannot *follow,*" Hazlitt makes the mind "assimilate her *feelings* to others she cannot *enter into*" (emphasis added). Hazlitt found the work of abridging another philosopher easier than writing as a philosopher himself; but he says of his effort to make Tucker manageable: "As to the pains and labour it has cost me, or the time I have devoted to it, I shall say nothing. However, if any one should be scrupulous on that head, I might answer, as Sir Joshua Reynolds is said to have done to some person who cavilled at the price of a picture, and desired to know how long he had been doing it, 'All my life' " (I, 123).

20. Abraham Tucker, *The Light of Nature Pursued,* 7 vols. (London, 1768-1777), I, Part 1, pp. 86-87.

21. Ibid., Part 2, pp. 314-15. Compare Hazlitt: "The love or affection excited by any general idea existing in my mind, can no more be said to be the love of myself, than the idea of another person is the idea of myself, because it is I who perceive it. . . . By the same rule it would follow that in hating another person I hate myself" (II, 231). A similar objection is advanced in the chapter "Of Self-Love" in Jonathan Edwards's *The Nature of True Virtue.*

22. On Tucker and Paley, see Sir Leslie Stephen, *History of English Thought in the Eighteenth Century* (1876; reprinted 2 vols., New York, 1962), II, 92-102. Hazlitt anticipates Stephen's verdict: "All that is good in Paley is taken from Tucker" (I, 346). On Tucker as a forerunner of utilitarianism, see Henry Sidgwick, *Outlines of the History of Ethics* (1886; Beacon edition, Boston, 1968), pp. 236-37.

23. Joseph Priestley gave currency to the "superfluous act" paradox in replying to Thomas Reid's *Inquiry into the Human Mind*: Reid had made his description of the mind as an unextended and invisible substance depend upon "common sense"; Priestley asked how, if this were so, the mind could be affected by anything that had extension, since things act upon each other only by means of a common property.

24. Brief quotations may be traced in the chapters on "Vehicular State," "Mundane Soul," and "The Vision," in volume II of Tucker. An analogy between Tucker's Mundane Soul and the "plastic natures" of the Cambridge Platonists is suggested by the discussion of the latter in Ernst Cassirer, *The Philosophy of the Enlightenment*, trans. Fritz C. A. Koelln and James P. Pettegrove (1932; Princeton, 1951), pp. 81-85.

25. Tucker, *Light of Nature*, II, Part 2, pp. 96-98.

26. It is possible that Blake conceived his Mundane Shell as a satire on Tucker's Mundane Soul, for he would have regarded the idea as one more equivocal consolation awarded by Natural Religion to itself. Urizen (a very Lockean figure) builds the Mundane Shell in Night the Second of *The Four Zoas;* the whole passage bears close comparison with Tucker's on the Mundane Soul; the result for Blake is that "The heavens were closd and spirits mournd their bondage night and day" (*The Poetry and Prose of William Blake,* ed. David V. Erdman (Garden City, 1965), p. 315). Yet the Mundane Shell is also "the fixed limit to the Fall, the protection against Non-Existence" (S. Foster Damon, *William Blake: His Philosophy and Symbols* (Boston, 1924), p. 370). Blake would thus be saying to Tucker: "Your compromise with materialism leads you into a grotesque misapprehension of nature. What you take to be a seeding-place of spirits is only an empty and imprisoning shell. No spirit that dwells there can be free: it is that *from which* creation moves, as from zero-level."

27. Tucker, *Light of Nature*, I, Part 1, p. 330.

28. Brief quotations may be traced in *An Essay on the Principles of Human Action* (I, 1-49).

29. On Hazlitt's view only two persons are required for a sympathetic action to take place. Smith evidently requires a third. This "impartial spectator" represents the conduct approved by society, and is internalized as "the man in the breast" or conscience. Yet Smith tells us that there are times when society is remote from all our thoughts, and when the impartial spectator can only be God. The spectator stands outside the scene of suffering or glory—the occasion for praise, blame, or some degree of sympathetic action—and moderates between the indifference of the agent and the entreaties of his object. The spectator thus gives the criterion for "keeping time" with the emotions and experiences of another, so as to produce approbation or solicitude in exactly the proper manner. For example, by referring the situation to "the man in the breast," any sufferer will learn how to depress his manifestations of pain, while any witness will learn to increase his sensibility to them, to the point where an acknowledgment of each

other's position can pass between the two: they come to feel that they are on common ground, and the law of propriety binds them both to a certain course of action.

In the background of Smith's idea of sympathy is a theory of justice, as in the background of Hazlitt's is a theory of the imagination in art. Smith regards all moral judgments as social *in origin,* whereas for Hazlitt it is in our nature to make such judgments, as much as it is to act sympathetically: society comes in after the fact, and decides only how sympathetic action and principled judgment are to be encouraged or deformed. In an important passage at the conclusion of his chapter "Of Utility," where Smith imagines a being cut off from all society, he says that as perceptions of right and wrong conduct "are merely a matter of taste . . . they probably would not be much attended to" by a solitary being, and adds: "All such sentiments suppose the idea of some other being, who is the natural judge of the person that feels them" (*The Theory of Moral Sentiments,* ed. D. D. Raphael and A. L. Macfie (Oxford, 1976), IV.2, 12, p. 193). The final clause especially Hazlitt calls into question. To predict how a solitary being would, while still in solitude, conduct himself toward another, is of course merely paradoxical. But all that Hazlitt's theory needs, to supply such a being with an idea of right and wrong, is the presence of a second being, with whom to enter into sympathy by analogy with himself. Smith's phrase about "the natural judge" makes it plain that for him a second would not suffice. Sympathy is the feeling that results from our adjustment to the demands of a second person, *and* to the internalized judgments of a third: hence his assurance that "What is called affection, is in reality nothing but habitual sympathy" (VI.ii.1, p. 220).

Intimations of Hazlitt's discovery much closer than anything in Smith can be found in Joseph Butler's *Sermons Delivered at Rolls' Chapel* (1729). Hazlitt was willing to call them "something like" his own argument "but not the same" (IX, 4). He had in mind particularly Butler's eleventh sermon, which considers how a weakness of will may divert even the most resolute pursuit of self-interest. For what do we say of the "prudence" of the man who gambles away a fortune in the hope of making one? Is he acting in his own interest? It may be wiser simply to suppose that many instances of apparent self-interest conflict with real self-interest more than benevolence does. "It appears," in Butler's words, "that private interest is so far from being likely to be promoted in proportion to the degree in which self-love engrosses us . . . that *the contracted affection may be so prevalent as to disappoint itself, and even contradict its own end, private good";* so that "however much a paradox it may appear," we must reconcile ourselves to the necessity "even from self-love . . . to get over all inordinate regard to, and consideration of ourselves" (*Sermons* (Oxford, 1874), p. 140).

Butler returned to the question of self-interest in the Preface to his *Sermons,* and the following passage was among Hazlitt's favorite in the history of philosophy:

> Every thing is what it is, and not another thing. The goodness or badness of actions does not arise from hence, that the epithet, interested or disinterested, may be applied to them, any more than that any other indifferent epithet, suppose inquisitive or jealous, may or may not be applied to them; not from their being attended with present or future pleasure or pain; but from their being what they are; namely, what becomes creatures such as we are. . . . Or in other words, we may judge and determine, that an

action is morally good or evil, before we so much as consider, whether it be interested or disinterested. This consideration no more comes in to determine whether an action be virtuous, than to determine whether it be resentful. Self-love in its due degree is as just and morally good, as any affection whatever. Benevolence towards particular persons may be to a degree of weakness, and so be blamable: and disinterestedness is so far from being in itself commendable, that the utmost possible depravity which we can in imagination conceive, is that of disinterested cruelty. (p. xxv)

The final sentence reveals why any writer in the tradition that Hazlitt wished to extend, would have been suspicious of the categorical imperative of Kant. For Kant in the *Groundwork of the Metaphysic of Morals* asserts that the performance of a disinterested and universalizable duty is praiseworthy only when not prompted by personal affections; and that such affections, to the degree that they contribute to an action, compromise its disinterestedness. Kant regards duty as utterly severed from inclination, and an action done from constraint cannot be done from love. It follows that if I sacrifice my own imagined interest to act in the interest of another person, *because of the affection I bear to him,* I fail to act in accordance with the imperative. To Hazlitt this sort of commandment was absurd. For better or worse the mind is the seat of rooted affections, and all moral speculation must begin by recognizing that fact.

For an argument reminiscent of Hazlitt's on the grounding of morality in persons and their situation, with remarks on the tension between moral reflection and habit and on the role of art in breaking up closed systems of habit, see Stuart Hampshire, *Thought and Action* (1959; Viking edition, New York, 1967), ch. 1, *passim;* pp. 208-10; pp. 244-47.

30. Hume, *Treatise,* I.iv.6, p. 260. The argument is in fact clinched several pages earlier, with a celebrated metaphor: "The mind is a kind of theatre, where several perceptions successively make their appearance; pass, re-pass, glide away, and mingle in an infinite variety of postures and situations. There is properly no *simplicity* in it at one time, nor *identity* in different. . . . They are successive perceptions only, that constitute the mind; nor have we the most distant notion of the place, where these scenes are represented, or of the materials, of which it is compos'd" (p. 253).

31. Ibid., II.ii.9, pp. 385-86.

32. A position comparable to Hazlitt's is outlined in an essay by Arnold Zuboff, who treats the "moment" of conscious experience as an Aristotelian universal discrete from other such moments ("Moment Universals and Personal Identity" in *Proceedings of the Aristotelian Society 1977-1978* (Tilsbury, 1978), pp. 147-54). Zuboff illustrates the bearing of any present moment on the future sequences or combinations to which it may lead, with the analogy of a single chess position which may belong to any of several possible games. Compare Hazlitt: "this self may be multiplied in as many different beings as the Deity may think proper to endue with the same consciousness, which if it can be renewed at will in any one instance, may clearly be so in an hundred others. Am I to regard all these as equally myself? Am I equally interested in the fate of all?" (I, 47). To the question, "How am I to know that I am not imposed upon by a false claim of identity," Zuboff gives a skeptical reply, without proposing consequences for ethical theory. Hazlitt's point, on the contrary, when he asked the question in those words, was to move by an irrefutable "as-if" to a conclusion about the reasons we give for

our actions: the justification I get from personal identity is such that *I might as well be about to turn into somebody else.*

One modern discussion of self-interest, Thomas Nagel's *The Possibility of Altruism* (1970; reprinted, Princeton, 1978), recovers something of Hazlitt's understanding of the family resemblance between egoism and altruism, as kinds of attention: "Altruistic reasons are parasitic upon self-interested ones; the circumstances in the lives of others which altruism requires us to consider are circumstances which those others already have reason to consider from a self-interested point of view" (p. 16). But Nagel writes without reference to Hutcheson, Smith, and the very full eighteenth-century debate on this subject which culminates in the *Essay on Human Action*. His belief that our reasons for action are the bearers of "timeless values," and his identification of altruism with an impersonal viewpoint, would I think have been rejected by every party to the debate until Kant.

33. The effort to establish a change of heart unacknowledged by Hazlitt as the crucial fact of his moral life, began in earnest with the Victorian revulsion from *Liber Amoris,* and is still going strong. See, e.g., Herschel Baker, *William Hazlitt* (Cambridge, Mass., 1962).

34. That Hazlitt "found himself" only as an essayist is an assumption common to Baker, *William Hazlitt,* and a good many shorter studies, of which the finest is a chapter in Laurence Stapleton's *The Elected Circle* (Princeton, 1973).

35. Samuel Taylor Coleridge, *Lectures 1795 on Politics and Religion* (Princeton, 1971), p. 12.

36. W. Carew Hazlitt, *Memoirs of William Hazlitt,* 2 vols. (London, 1867), I, 112.

CHAPTER II. INTEREST, HABIT, ASSOCIATION

1. Hazlitt, *The Eloquence of the British Senate,* 2 vols. (London, 1807), II, 297. This note was omitted (apparently by accident) from Howe's edition of Hazlitt's *Works.* It contains an important echo of Hume: "Reason is, and ought only to be the slave of the passions, and can never pretend to any other office than to serve and obey them" (*Treatise,* II.iii.3, p. 415).

2. William Wordsworth, *Poems,* ed. John O. Hayden, 2 vols. (Penguin edition, 1977), II, 975.

3. I find a perception like Hazlitt's in the conclusion of David Ferry's *The Limits of Mortality* (Middletown, 1959): "[Wordsworth] says a 'deep distress' 'humanized' his soul, and is this not at once a kind of confession that the love of nature had not led him to the love of man, and the declaration of a new aim and new interest which his imagination was not equipped to sustain? . . . The imagination—Wordsworth's imagination—could by no means attach itself to human life in other ways nor detach itself from its old interests; and its old interests, whether he knew it consciously or not, had failed. His genius was his enmity to man, which he mistook for love, and his mistake led him into confusions which he could not bear. But when he banished the confusions, he banished his distinctive greatness as well."

4. Brief quotations may be traced in Hazlitt's appendix, "Some Remarks on the Systems of Hartley and Helvetius" (I, 50-91).

5. For Hartley similarity is a "partial sameness"; that is, an exact sameness in the parts of two otherwise different wholes; that is, their overlapping or contiguity.

6. I deliberately adopt the Coleridgean word: on this he and Hazlitt are in accord, and it would be pointless to claim priority for one or the other. Coleridge remarks in a notebook entry that association is "as the force of gravity to leaping at any given point—without gravitation this would be impossible, and yet equally impossible to leap except by a *power* counteracting first, and then using the *force* of gravitation." Quoted by Humphry House, *Coleridge* (1953; reprinted, Philadelphia, 1965), p. 146. The analogy belongs to a larger distinction between the stuff "*out* of which we make our conceptions & perceptions" and that "*by* which we make them."

7. The *reductio ad absurdum* shows that Hartley, in his misplaced emphasis, was committing something akin to a "category-mistake." See Gilbert Ryle, *The Concept of Mind* (1949; reprinted, New York, 1959), pp. 15-18, especially the example of the foreigner to England who takes stock of the batter, bowler, and so forth, in a game of cricket, but wonders whose job it is to supply the *esprit de corps*. So might the foreigner to Hartleyan associationism put the question: "I see the associations of pleasure and pain; but where are those of change?" Hartley would require the third kind of association to inhabit the same level of mind as the first two.

8. Hazlitt, *Works*, XIV, 115. The whole paragraph is a *tour de force,* and the standard of internal worth—associated in Hazlitt's mind with the Rousseau of *The Confessions*—is introduced with the remark: "virtue and merit are in the end reduced to a piece of red ribbon, which is made their inadequate symbol. If a man of merit looks meanly in the street, you cannot say to the passengers, 'Respect this man;' they will rather learn to despise personal merit which is not corroborated by personal appearance. It is a translation from one language to another; and all things suffer by translation." On the relation of progress to abstraction, Hazlitt was from the first a consistent follower of Bacon: "as hieroglyphics were before letters, so parables were before arguments" (*Advancement of Learning,* II.iv.3).

9. Edmund Burke, *Reflections on the Revolution in France,* ed. Conor Cruise O'Brien (Penguin edition, Baltimore, 1968), pp. 89-90. Burke is refusing to speak of a "liberty" abstracted from the circumstances of the French and English nations.

10. I share P. N. Furbank's revulsion from the journalistic stand-by, "This author gives us his own world," with its implied endorsement of extreme mannerism (*Reflections on the Word "Image,"* (London, 1970), pp. 113-24). But I think Hazlitt did mean the suggestion of a world which was not *the* world of nature and society. At the same time, he kept clear of the apologetics to which this way of speaking naturally lends itself, and never maintained that all points of view were equally admirable. He comes nearest to a full-scale debate on the question in his sketch of Crabbe for *The Spirit of the Age.*

11. Bate in *From Classic to Romantic* cites these examples from Tucker, and his chapter on "Association of Ideas" is notable for the first clear assertion that Tucker's "psychology, as it applies to aesthetics, permeates most of Hazlitt's literary criticism" (p. 115). See also Stuart M. Sperry, *Keats the Poet* (Princeton, 1973), pp. 23-27; though I do not agree with Sperry that a distinction between the imagination and the understanding is enforced by Tucker in any consistent way.

12. John Kinnaird mentions the Mundane Soul in a similar context, as one precursor of Hazlitt's idea of nature (*William Hazlitt: Critic,* pp. 74-75). But he

makes much of Hazlitt's search for an "ultimate unity of nature," whereas this seems to me an after-effect of his idea of the imagination, and one that left no deep mark on his habits of thought. The notion of "elective affinity" is more important, and of this Kinnaird gives a somewhat confused account. He quotes a sentence from the essay "On Personal Character"—"The will selects the impressions by which it chooses to be governed with great dexterity and perseverence"—and comments: "Here is emphatic recognition of the 'unconscious' factor in motivation" (p. 75). Yet the sentence deals with the conscious selection of the will and not the unconscious affinity of the imagination; besides, Hazlitt never incorporated the imagination as an unconscious "factor in motivation": it was a *principle* requiring nothing to supplement it. The interpretation of statements about the will as statements about the imagination has broad consequences for Kinnaird's reading of Hazlitt.

That the very idea of "elective affinity" implied the unconsciousness of genius was Hazlitt's answer to a question he posed in the title of his essay, "Whether Genius Is Conscious of Its Powers?" The greater the genius, the more emphatically negative his answer. His English source for the phrase, *elective affinity*, casts further doubt on any effort to connect genius with will; for it is almost certainly the following sentence from Bacon's *Natural History*: "All bodies whatsoever, though they have no sense, yet have perception; for when one body is applied to another, there is a kind of election to embrace that which is agreeable, and to exclude that which is ingrate; and whether the body be alterant or altered, evermore a perception precedeth operation; for else all bodies would be like to one another." The whole passage is quoted by Alfred North Whitehead, in *Science and the Modern World* (1925; reprinted, New York, 1967), pp. 41-42. Bacon's opposition of sense to something "far more subtle," and the example of the loadstone drawing iron, are both repeated in the essay "On Genius and Common Sense."

13. On objects of the mind and "mental discourse," see Ian Hacking, *Why Does Language Matter to Philosophy?* (Cambridge, 1975), chs. 1-5.

14. W. P. Albrecht gives a concise account of association and the symbol, in *Hazlitt and the Creative Imagination* (Lawrence, 1965), ch. III, from which I have profited.

15. William Godwin, *An Enquiry Concerning Political Justice*, 2 vols. (Dublin, 1793), I, 239 and I, 114.

16. Ibid., I, 234 and I, 285-87.

17. Ibid., I, 114.

18. Ibid., I, 287.

19. Quoted in Francis E. Mineka, *The Dissidence of Dissent: The Monthly Repository, 1806-1838* (Chapel Hill, 1944), p. 161. The sentence comes from a pamphlet against Malthus by John Bone.

20. Godwin, *Political Justice*, I, 140.

21. Ibid., I, 144.

22. Ibid., II, 375.

23. Ibid., I, 69.

24. Ibid., II, 255.

25. On the anthropological point of view which qualifies Hume's skepticism, see Alasdair MacIntyre, "Hume on 'is' and 'ought'," in *Against the Self-Images of the Age: Essays on Ideology and Philosophy* (Notre Dame, 1978), pp. 109-24.

26. Godwin, *Political Justice*, II, 235.

27. Bentham's position on capital punishment was complex. He wrote against the misguided sentimentality that had prompted Cesare Beccaria and other reformers to plead for life-imprisonment as a milder punishment than death: one punishment, as Bentham pointed out, had greater intensity, but the other had longer duration, so that on Utilitarian principles one could not conclude that either was plainly the more severe. On the same principles Bentham was obliged to admit capital punishment was difficult to justify since some lives are worth more than others. I have relied on Elie Halévy's discussion, in *The Growth of Philosophic Radicalism* (Beacon edition, Boston, 1955), pp. 54-87, in comparing Hazlitt's position with the range of opinions that emerge from early Utilitarian debates.

28. William James, *The Principles of Psychology*, 2 vols. (1890; Dover reprint, New York, 1950), I, 225.

29. Ibid., I, 234.

30. Ibid.

31. Ibid., I, 278.

32. Ibid., I, 323.

33. Ibid.

34. Ibid., I, 325.

35. James's most extensive consideration of Fechner appears in Lecture IV of *A Pluralistic Universe* (New York, 1909); the following passage may have familiar resonances for the reader of Tucker's "Vision": "Fechner likens our individual persons on the earth unto so many sense-organs of the earth's soul. We add to its perceptive life so long as our own life lasts. It absorbs our perceptions, just as they occur, into the larger sphere of knowledge, and combines them with the other data there. When one of us dies, it is as if an eye of the world were closed, for all *perceptive* contributions from that particular quarter cease. But the memories and conceptual relations that have spun themselves round the perceptions of that person remain in the larger earth-life as distinct as ever, and form new relations and grow and develop throughout all the future, in the same way in which our own distinct objects of thought, once stored in memory, form new relations and develop throughout our whole finite life" (pp. 170-71).

36. James, *Principles of Psychology*, I, 594.

37. It is a pity we have no comment from Hazlitt on the heroine of *Mansfield Park*.

38. Hazlitt, *Works*, IX, 177. From this, Hazlitt's view of Falstaff is easily surmised: "we are not offended but delighted with him. . . . We only consider the number of pleasant lights in which he puts certain foibles (the more pleasant as they are opposed to the received rules and necessary restraints of society) and do not trouble ourselves about the consequences resulting from them" (IV, 279).

39. Baker, *William Hazlitt*, pp. 424-25. "Mainly," according to Baker, "the maxims gloss his love-affair with Sarah Walker."

40. Compare Nietzsche: "Once the decision has been made, close your ear even to the best counterargument: sign of a strong character" (*Beyond Good and Evil*, trans. Walter Kaufmann (Vintage edition, New York, 1966), section 107).

41. Nietzsche, *Beyond Good and Evil*, section 126.

42. Because sympathy may be painful, Smith makes it part of his system of propriety that the sufferer ought to disguise his pain. By doing so he may hope to render sympathy a lighter task to the spectator. Smith seems to imply a stage

of reconnaissance preparatory to sympathy, in which we gain some foreknowledge of how far a given act of sympathy will take us, and consciously decide whether to assume that portion of the sufferer's pain which sympathy will make us share. Virtue, Smith says, will evoke the greatest appreciation when it is silent about its suffering. The spectator will then sympathize, not only with the virtuous sufferer's pain, but with his effort to observe propriety in disguising it. Of such propriety Cato is the pattern (*The Theory of Moral Sentiments,* I.iii.1, pp. 46-48).

While admitting the pains with the pleasure of sympathy, Hazlitt has no use for the act of will that Smith connects with propriety. If we are capable of feeling sympathy, he believes, then we shall feel it willy-nilly; and neither an effort of self-control on our part, nor of disguise on the sufferer's, can prevent the feeling from running its course. Understandably, given this premise, he is unmoved by Cato: he notes that virtue is difficult both to contemplate and to sympathize with, in proportion as it is untouched by weakness. This would apply with still greater force to *suffering* virtue. His key phrase is: "Virtue costs the spectator, as well as the performer, something" (IX, 173).

43. The Preface points to the absurdity of a physiological ground of self-interest, and affirms that the imagination is a single unified faculty as easily adapted to the future interests of others as to our own: "Our ideas and feelings act in concert." The dialogue on "Self-Love and Benevolence" is a nearly verbatim transcription of parts of the *Essay.*

Chapter III. Why the Arts Are Not Progressive

1. *Byron's Letters and Journals,* 12 vols., ed. Leslie A. Marchand (Cambridge, Mass., 1973-1982), III, 219-20.

2. From the *Blackwood's* arsenal, quoted in Alexander Ireland, *List of the Writings of William Hazlitt, Leigh Hunt, and Charles Lamb* (1868; reprinted, New York, 1970), p. 230.

3. Ibid., p. 78.

4. The phrase occurs in the draft of a letter from Hunt to Hazlitt. Quoted by permission of the Huntington Library, San Marino, California (HM 20601). Most of the final version of this letter appears in Howe, *Life of Hazlitt,* pp. 318-20.

5. Ibid.

6. Hazlitt, *Letters,* p. 204.

7. Hunt, *Political and Occasional Essays,* p. 20.

8. P. G. Patmore, *My Friends and Acquaintances,* 2 vols. (London, 1854), II, 57.

9. Hunt, *Essays,* pp. 52-53.

10. Ibid., p. 61.

11. *The Works of Charles and Mary Lamb,* ed. E. V. Lucas, 7 vols. (London, 1903-1905), I, 233-34.

12. *The Letters of John Keats,* ed. Hyder E. Rollins, 2 vols. (Cambridge, 1958), I, 282.

13. Archibald Alison, *Essays on the Nature and Principles of Taste,* 2 vols. (4th edition, Edinburgh, 1815), II, 351.

14. David Hume, *Essays: Moral, Political, and Literary,* ed. T. H. Green and T. H. Grose, 2 vols. (London, 1875), I, 195.

15. Ibid., p. 197.

16. Quoted in Ralph Wardle, *William Hazlitt* (Lincoln, 1971), pp. 76-77.

17. Nietzsche, *The Use and Abuse of History,* trans. Adrian Collins (New York, 1957), p. 17.

18. Flannery O'Connor, *Mystery and Manners* (New York, 1969), p. 84.

19. I have in mind Wordsworth's "Essay, Supplementary to the Preface" of 1815, and especially the following paragraph:

> And where lies the real difficulty of creating that taste by which a truly original poet is to be relished? Is it in breaking the bonds of custom, in overcoming the prejudices of false refinement, and displacing the aversions of inexperience? Or, if he labour for an object which here and elsewhere I have proposed to myself, does it consist in divesting the reader of the pride that induces him to dwell upon those points wherein men differ from each other, to the exclusion of those in which all men are alike, or the same; and in making him ashamed of the vanity that renders him insensible of the appropriate excellence which civil arrangements, less unjust than might appear, and Nature illimitable in her bounty, have conferred on men who may stand below him in the level of society? Finally, does it lie in establishing that dominion over the spirits of readers by which they are to be humbled and humanised, in order that they may be purified and exalted?

(*Prose Works,* ed. W.J.B. Owen and J. W. Smyser, 3 vols. (Oxford, 1974), III, 80-81.) The reader is here stripped and given correction, and made to see justice in the laws of man and society, so that he may be humbled and humanized, and then purified and exalted by the poet. Wordsworth's criticism contains no plainer acknowledgment than this of the completeness of those powers with which the poet is entrusted by "contract" with the reader. For my purposes, the most important claim is the negative one: that the reader's own feelings do not matter until the poet makes them submit to a new control. A century later this would become part of an international *avant-garde* creed: in 1815 Wordsworth felt the extremeness of his position acutely enough to take refuge in the frame of three successive rhetorical questions.

20. Eliot, *Selected Essays,* p. 247.

21. On "open and closed sequences" in the history of art, see George Kubler, *The Shape of Time* (New Haven, 1962), pp. 35-39.

22. Eliot, *Selected Essays,* p. 5.

23. A function Eliot is seldom adequately praised for having performed; though a salutary exception is E. M. Forster's essay in *Abinger Harvest.*

24. Kinnaird, *William Hazlitt: Critic,* pp. 179-80.

25. Ibid., p. 188.

26. Hazlitt speaks only of Iago's "love of" mischief and power. It seems to me unfair to substitute the words "will to" for "love of," without offering some justification.

27. Maclean, *Born Under Saturn* (pp. 315-17) dismisses the whole episode as the by-product of an uncommonly wild fit of misogyny. It is notable for us only because Hazlitt tried, on the whole so successfully, to secure his criticism from the irruptions of his "headstrong humours and tormenting passions." The relevant passage on Desdemona is in *A View of the English Stage* (V, 217).

28. Thomas Barnes commented acutely on this passage: "in his able portrait . . . was [Hazlitt] not delineating some ideal being rather than the Iago of the poet? Perhaps he had some existing character before him: at any rate the picture

bears a stronger resemblance to Bonaparte than to Shakespeare's Ancient." Quoted in Edmund Blunden, *Leigh Hunt's "Examiner" Examined* (London, 1928), p. 43.

29. For an interpretation of the play strongly allied to Hazlitt's, see John Bayley. *The Characters of Love* (New York, 1960), pp. 127-201.

30. A landscape "full of associations" Hazlitt commonly described as "romantic."

31. Hazlitt's revolt against any necessitarian doctrine in religion appears nowhere more boldly than in a late *Examiner* article called "The Reverend Edward Irving: An Hypothesis." Since, in the romantic age, there seems to be no literary figure about whom the claim will not sooner or later be advanced, that after all he was religious *in some sense,* I append the following passage and ask that it be weighed in future deliberations about Hazlitt.

> Even human frailty refuses to transmit painful and distressing maladies to future generations,—how much more impossible, then, for the Father of all to entail wilful and endless misery on his creation! The argument amounts to a contradiction in terms, and requires us to suppose that infinite truth and rectitude, being shocked at the smallest possible evil, in order to remedy it, proceeds remorselessly to inflict the greatest possible evil, *to which it is perfectly indifferent.* . . . To compare small things with great, and be familiar after the manner of the Methodists—can any one suppose that Sir Isaac Newton, with the accessions of knowledge which his mild spirit may have acquired in the starry sphere, would be thrown into convulsions of rage and agony on beholding some mistake which a poor village schoolmaster had committed in a sum in arithmetic?—and shall we suppose the Divine Being, who is the great geometer of the universe, to be unable to endure or witness without emotions of intolerable loathing, those mixed results which he has contemplated from the beginning to the end of time, and ordained in their eternal and immutable progression? Forbid it, decency and common sense! (XX, 225)

CHAPTER IV. THE EGOTISTICAL SUBLIME

1. Hazlitt's references to the "exclusive excellence" of Wordsworth frequently echo Johnson's *Life of Pope:* "In the letters both of Swift and Pope, there appears such narrowness of mind as makes them insensible of any excellence that has not some affinity with their own. . . ."

2. My sense of Wordsworth's role in "Hart-Leap Well," as a self-aggrandizing guide to the monuments he surveys, owes much to an unpublished paper by Samuel Schulman of Boston University.

3. Ralph Waldo Emerson, "The Poet," *Works,* 12 vols. (Boston, 1903), III, 11.

4. Francis Jeffrey, *Contributions to the Edinburgh Review,* 4 vols. (London, 1844), II, 343. Stanley Jones, in "Some New Hazlitt Letters," *N&Q* 222 (1977), pp. 336-42, gives evidence for the assertion that much of this review is Hazlitt's, and reproduces the letter to Jeffrey in which, as Jones says, Hazlitt appears to have "given his editor *carte blanche* to do what he wanted with his contribution" (p. 337).

5. The sharp contrast between fancy and imagination which Coleridge brought into English criticism, and of which Wordsworth in his *Preface* of 1815 became a

useful publicist, has been so important to modern critics that a decent skepticism is no longer maintained about the degree of its contemporary influence. "Fancy, or the aggregating faculty of the mind—not Imagination, or the *modifying,* and *co-adunating* Faculty" (Coleridge, *Letters,* II, 459-60)—this seems to us the natural way for romantic criticism to behave. But it did not always seem so. Hazlitt in calling the imagination "an exaggerating faculty" identifies it as something very close to Coleridge's fancy. Nothing more exalted is at stake than resistance to the generation of new terminologies: if Coleridge's resistance was unusually low I suspect Hazlitt's was unusually high; he needed to be very sure he could see the boundary dividing two things before he would admit the second name. In this instance his usage was almost certainly more representative of the age than Coleridge's. At any rate one cannot assume that after 1820 or so, anybody who talks about fancy must be using the word as a follower of Coleridge would, with just a trace of condescension.

Keats liked both words and used them variously. Having read their Coleridge, the leading American critics of the next age, Poe and Emerson, became the one a fancy- the other an imagination-man. And, partly owing to the special character of Keats's influence on the Victorians, fancy and imagination kept up a competitive vitality well into our century. Until the mid-1920s at the earliest, I do not think a journalistic critic could go on about a poet's "fancy" and expect his audience to register a demotion. A great deal more work needs to be done on the history of both words throughout the nineteenth century, with some such model as Jean Hagstrum's discussion of "the beautiful, the pathetic, and the sublime" in *Samuel Johnson's Literary Criticism.* The results I think will show that Coleridge's distinction, though finally as influential as Burke's between the sublime and the beautiful, and no less bold in driving apart what had once been kindred terms, had to wait much longer for its effect to be fully absorbed.

6. Together with a revision already noticed—"understanding" for "imagination" in the sentence that quotes Milton—two others contribute to the different shading of this passage in the *Round Table* version. "He sees all things in his own mind" becomes "He sees all things in himself"; and "striking subjects or remarkable combinations of events" becomes "remarkable objects or situations." With the first revision, the perfect heterocosm is admitted to be selfish; Wilde's epigram ("He found in stones the sermons he had already hidden there") is not far off; whereas "all things in his own mind" had preserved something of the Wordsworthian generosity about "mind" ("And the round ocean, and the living air,/ And the blue sky, and in the mind of man"). The second revision again limits Wordsworth's claim to imagination. The debate really centers on Wordsworth's "disposition," as the Preface to *Lyrical Ballads* had described it, "to be affected more than other men by absent things as if they were present." This Hazlitt accepts, but with severe restrictions. Wordsworth revives things that were once present to himself, and makes them present to us.

The paragraph concludes by reflecting on a further claim of the *Preface,* "to throw over [the chosen incidents and situations] a certain colouring of the imagination, whereby ordinary things should be presented to the mind in an unusual aspect." Wordsworth's own language brings him uncomfortably close to eighteenth-century notions about the adaptation of style to subject, and needs somehow to be squared with the rest of his program. So Hazlitt in fact restores the expressive emphasis which in a single phrase Wordsworth seemed to have forfeited: the garment of "certain colouring" becomes an atmosphere or "haze," the medium through which alone the Wordsworthian object may be seen. We must lose it before we can know it.

7. Of Hazlitt's view of Wordsworth a fine if involuntary summary can be found in R. H. Horne's *A New Spirit of the Age* (1844). Horne wrote as a disciple of Hazlitt, but in dealing with the same subjects he was also, at times, an interpreter. He says in his successor-sketch of Wordsworth: "This is the sublime of egotism, *disinterested as extreme*" (emphasis mine). In another phrase reminiscent of the *Excursion* review he remarks that Wordsworth's "Sonnets in favour of the punishment of death, chiefly on the ground of not venturing to meddle with an old law, are the tomb of his prophet-title. He is a prophet of the Past."

8. See especially Letter XXIII of Junius (to the Duke of Bedford): "Can grey hairs make folly venerable? and is there no period to be reserved for meditation and retirement? For shame! my Lord: let it not be recorded of you, that the latest moments of your life were dedicated to the same unworthy pursuits, the same busy agitations, in which your youth and manhood were exhausted. Consider that, although you cannot disgrace your former life, you are violating the character of age, and exposing the impotent imbecility, after you have lost the vigour of the passions" (John Cannon, ed., *The Letters of Junius* (Oxford, 1978), p. 123).

Compare Hazlitt reviewing Southey's "Letter to William Smith": "As some persons bequeath their bodies to the surgeons to be dissected after their death, Mr. Southey publicly exposes his mind to be anatomized while he is living. He lays open his character to the scalping-knife, guides the philosophic hand in its painful researches, and on the bald crown of our *petit tondu,* in vain concealed under withered bay-leaves and a few contemptible grey hairs, you see the organ of vanity triumphant—sleek, smooth, round, perfect, polished, horned, and shining, as it were in transparency" (VII, 187).

9. "Disenchantment or Default," in Conor Cruise O'Brien and William Dean Vanech, ed., *Power and Consciousness* (New York, 1969), pp. 174-75.

10. Ibid., pp. 177-78.

11. *Edinburgh Review* (January 1830), p. 565.

12. Hazlitt, *Letters*, p. 372.

13. DeQuincey, *Works*, V, 246-51.

14. From the Ode, "Laodamia," "The World Is Too Much with Us," and "Lines Written While Sailing in a Boat at Evening." On the Wordsworthian element of Hazlitt's "time-sense," with some excellent comments on this essay, see Christopher Salvesen, *The Landscape of Memory* (London, 1965), pp. 185-97.

15. Longinus, *On the Sublime,* trans. W. Rhys Roberts (New York, 1930), section 33, p. 109.

16. *Crabb Robinson on Books,* ed. Morley I, 89.

17. Coleridge, *Anima Poetae,* entry of November 27, 1799, in I. A. Richards, ed., *The Viking Portable Coleridge* (New York, 1950), p. 304.

18. I borrow the phrase from Thomas Weiskel, *The Romantic Sublime* (Baltimore, 1976), chs. 1, 2, 4, though my use of it differs somewhat from his. In general I have found Weiskel's book suggestive. His related but imperfectly parallel dichotomies—between the metonymic and the metaphorical sublime, the writer's and the reader's sublime—seem to me less clearly made out than they need to be. The difference between Burke and Kant is of course at the bottom of all such refinements, and I am therefore puzzled by the tendency of Weiskel and other

commentators to treat them as adequate glosses of each other. Coleridge was I think a Kantian here even before he discovered the *Critique of Judgment*—a fact of temperament that makes one reliable master-clue to the antipathy between his mode of criticism and Hazlitt's.

The matter comes to this: whether you stand most in admiration of the mind's halt before what it cannot fathom; or of the eloquence by which it consoles itself with its own capacity to make something grand of that halt. In Hazlitt's terms you use words either to reveal the abyss or to throw a bridge over it. Of the gradual accommodation to the second, and unifying, gesture in the *Critique of Judgment,* Weiskel observes: "it is difficult to avoid the conclusion that . . . reason posits its own sensible or imaginative frustration in order to discover itself freshly in an attitude of awe" (pp. 40-41). The sentence is a good abstract of Wordsworth's progression in Book VI of *The Prelude,* from sudden privation to a sense of glory and enhancement so well-managed that the discovery has in retrospect a premeditated look. Yet Weiskel never quite allows his key distinction to take the form "Burke vs. Kant"; he comes closest when he rechristens it "sublime vs. beautiful *in Kant*": "the sublime . . . at least the negative sublime—leads to alienation in all its forms. The beautiful . . . leads to a reconciliation in which the critical, 'negative' power of art is in danger of melting away" (p. 46). But the Hegelian sense here given to the words "alienation" and "negative" is of doubtful value to a reader of Hazlitt or Wordsworth.

CHAPTER V. FROM IMITATION TO EXPRESSION

1. Coleridge makes a similar point in the essay fragment "Shakespeare's Judgment Equal to His Genius" in *Shakespearean Criticism,* ed. T. M. Raysor, 2 vols. (London, 1960), I, 194-98.

2. Ibid., I, 64.

3. In all this part of his criticism, Hazlitt has so much in common with Blake— whose annotations to Reynolds he could not have known—that the reader may be curious for a more exact verbal comparison. The following examples suggest the depth of the affinity: (1) answering a phrase of Reynolds's about the "minute accidental discriminations" of particulars, Blake writes, "Minute Discrimination is Not Accidental All Sublimity is founded on Minute Discrimination"; (2) answering "any endeavour to copy the exact peculiar colour . . . of another man's mind . . . must always be . . . ridiculous," he writes, "Why then Imitate at all?"; (3) answering "Art in its perfection is not ostentatious; it lies hid, and works its effect, itself unseen," he writes, "This is a Very Clever Sentence who wrote it God knows"; (4) answering "violent passions will naturally emit harsh and disagreeable tones," he writes, "Violent Passions Emit the Real Good & Perfect Tones"; (5) answering "to preserve the most perfect beauty IN ITS MOST PERFECT STATE, you cannot express the passions, all of which produce distortion and deformity, more or less, in the most beautiful faces," he writes, "What Nonsense Passion & Expression is Beauty Itself—The Face that is Incapable of Passion & Expression is Deformity Itself Let it be Painted & Patched & Praised & Advertised for Ever it will only be admired by Fools." See Erdman, ed., *Poetry and Prose of Blake,* pp. 625-51.

4. *Spectator,* No. 412 is pertinent: Addison there divides the imagination's pleasures into its experience of the great, the uncommon, and the beautiful, the

first two serving as his versions of the sublime and the picturesque; and he remarks that "our imagination loves to be filled with an object," thus anticipating
Burke's physiological emphasis as well as Johnson's praise of images that crowd
the mind. But almost in the next phrase, he domesticates his thought: "We are
flung into a pleasing astonishment at such unbounded views." *Pleasing astonishment,* with its many possible variants, e.g. "agreeable surprise," presents an oxy-
moron which Addison can regard complacently, as affording the same sort of
diversion he ascribes to new or uncommon scenes. Burke's challenge was to make
readers doubt whether they could ever lose sight of the violent contrast implied
by pleasing astonishment: if those words *were* adequate to the emotion, the pleasure in question would take a great deal of explaining. Astonishment has its root
in a Latin word meaning "to thunder; to strike with lightning"; the implications
of this metaphor Addison hoped to keep buried by giving it a thoroughly pleasant resting-place. On Burke's sensationalism as an advance beyond Addison's idea
of pleasure, see Ernest Tuveson, *The Imagination as a Means of Grace* (Berkeley,
1960), chs. V-VII.

5. Hazlitt suspected Burke of having "suggested the train of thought" for the
best sections of Reynolds's *Discourses*. He offers the conjecture, and by doing so
half-revokes the credit for a long quotation he agrees with, in the essay "On
Genius and Common Sense"; a more complete record of his sensitivity to Burke's
influence can be traced in his marginal annotations to the *Discourses*: see Frederick W. Hilles, "Reynolds among the Romantics," in Frank Brady, John Palmer,
and Martin Price, ed., *Literary Theory and Structure* (New Haven, 1973), pp.
267-83, which compares these with Haydon's annotations in the same copy, and
with Blake's. Among the notes which Hazlitt never saw fit to publish is perhaps
the most vehement dismissal of general nature in all of romantic criticism. To
Reynolds's "perfect beauty in any species must combine all the characters which
are beautiful in that species," he replies: "These discourses seem written by an
Hermaphrodite."

6. Burke writes, in the section of his *Enquiry* entitled "Power" (II.v): "the
idea of pain, in its highest degree, is much stronger than the highest degree of
pleasure; and . . . it preserves the same superiority through all the subordinate
gradations. From hence it is, that where the chances for equal degrees of suffering
or enjoyment are in any sort equal, the idea of suffering must always be prevalant.
And indeed the ideas of pain, and, above all, death, are so very affecting, that
whilst we remain in the presence of whatever is supposed to have the power of
inflicting either, it is impossible to be perfectly free from terror" (*Works*, I, 138).
Milton's sublime portrait of Death gives Burke the primary illustration for his
section on "Obscurity."

7. Coleridge, *Shakespearean Criticism*, II, 103-104.

8. Ibid.

9. Keats, *Letters*, I, 192.

10. Two sonnets of *Astrophil and Stella* which bear out this description of
Sidney with a special emphasis are 35 ("What may words say, or what may words
not say") and 45 ("*Stella* oft sees the verie face of wo"). Even if we had no other
evidence, Hazlitt would have placed himself in the anti-rhetorical camp simply by
the force of his preferences as a reader of Elizabethan literature. *The Advancement of Learning* was his favorite book of that period, outside Shakespeare. And
he says in his *Lectures on the Age of Elizabeth*: "Sir Philip Sidney is a writer for

whom I cannot acquire a taste. As Mr. Burke said, 'he could not love the French Republic'—so I may say, that I cannot love the Countess of Pembroke's Arcadia, with all my good-will to it" (VI, 318). On rhetoric in Sidney's criticism, see Ronald Levao, "Sidney's Feigned *Apology*," *PMLA* 94 (1979), pp. 223-33.

11. Samuel Taylor Coleridge, *Biographia Literaria*, ed. George Watson (London, 1965), ch. 17, pp. 189-90.

12. I. A. Richards justified the last line of the Ode as a pseudo-statement. T. S. Eliot saw this as a way out of serious criticism of the relations between poetry and belief, and implied that Richards had got the discussion on a wrong footing from having chosen a poor example. Keats's formula struck Eliot as a "blemish" on the poem, "and the reason must be either that I fail to understand it, or that it is a statement which is untrue. And I suppose that Keats must have meant something by it, however remote his truth and his beauty may have been from these words in ordinary use" (*Selected Essays*, p. 231). Eliot was right in his suspicion that Keats meant something, wrong in his assumption that "ordinary use" had stayed about the same for these words between Keats's time and his own. In this controversy both critics show a remarkable want of historical tact, but they have managed nevertheless to set the terms of subsequent argument about the poem, so that to understand it readers feel they must regard Keats as temporarily (a) mystical, or (b) ironic. A good corrective is J. R. Caldwell, *John Keats' Fancy* (Ithaca, 1945), ch. 5.

13. Hume, "Of the Standard of Taste," in *Essays*, I, 268; and Burke, *Works*, I, 95.

14. Burke, *Works*, I, 98.

15. Hume, *Essays*, I, 282.

16. On Alison and the romantic psychology of associationism, I have profited from Caldwell, *John Keats' Fancy*, pp. 64-78.

17. Alison, *Essays on Taste*, I, 37.

18. Ibid.

19. Burke, *Works*, I, 97.

20. Alison, *Essays on Taste*, I, 91.

21. Ibid., I, 195.

22. Ibid., I, 205.

23. Hume, *Essays*, I, 270-71.

24. Alison, *Essays on Taste*, II, 21-22.

25. See W. J. Bate, *Samuel Johnson* (New York, 1977), pp. 286-88.

26. Keats, *Letters*, II, 76.

CHAPTER VI. AGAINST AESTHETICS

1. The point is assumed rather than argued in most books on Coleridge. A temperate version of the standard Coleridgean view respecting Hazlitt's strength as a writer, and defects as a pretender to advanced thought, can be found in Kathleen Coburn, "Hazlitt on the Disinterested Imagination," in James V. Logan, John E. Jordan, and Northrop Frye, ed., *Some British Romantics* (Columbus, 1966). For a more generous account of Hazlitt's originality, see René Wellek, *A History of Modern Criticism: 1750-1950*, 4 vols. (London, 1955-), II, 151-215.

2. Kant, *Critique of Judgment*, trans. J. H. Bernard (New York, 1951), section 51, p. 165.

3. *The Novels of Thomas Love Peacock,* ed. David Garnett, 2 vols. (1948; 2nd edition, London, 1963), I, 280-81.

4. Samuel Taylor Coleridge, *Lay Sermons,* ed. R. J. White (Princeton, 1972), pp. 38, 40.

5. Keats, *Letters,* II, 189.

6. Coleridge, *Shakespearean Criticism,* I, 79.

7. Ibid., I, 76.

8. Coleridge, *Lay Sermons,* p. 30. The symbol in this sense was necessary to Coleridge's reading of the Bible as still sacred even if neither literally nor metaphorically the word of God. His phrasing at one point brings his idea of the symbol very close to his idea of secondary imagination: "Hence by a derivative, indeed, but not a divided influence, and though in a secondary, yet in more than a metaphorical sense, the Sacred Book is worthily entitled the Word of God." Quoting the sentence in his review for the *Examiner,* Hazlitt concluded: "Of all the cants that ever were canted in this canting world, this is the worst!"

9. On the connection between symbol and synecdoche, I am indebted to Kenneth Burke, *The Philosophy of Literary Form* (1941; 3rd edition, Berkeley, 1973), pp. 18-33.

10. On symbol, allegory, type and *figura,* see Erich Auerbach, "Figura," in *Scenes from the Drama of European Literature* (New York, 1959): the quotation comes from his discussion of the symbol, pp. 56-57. For Coleridge's discussion of metaphor and allegory, see *The Viking Coleridge,* pp. 398-401. A. D. Nuttall's *Two Concepts of Allegory* (New York, 1967) and Paul de Man's "The Rhetoric of Temporality," in Charles Singleton, ed., *Interpretation: Theory and Practice* (Baltimore, 1969), both illustrate the tendency of symbol and allegory, under the slightest pressure of narrative intelligence, to lose most of the clear features by which Coleridge hoped to distinguish them from each other.

11. W. B. Yeats, "Pages from a Diary in 1930," in *Explorations* (New York, 1963), pp. 304, 325.

12. Quoted in G. N. G. Orsini, *Coleridge and German Idealism* (Carbondale, 1969), p. 80.

13. James, *Principles of Psychology,* I, 160.

14. Kant, *Critique of Judgment,* section 58, p. 195.

15. Ibid., sections 45-46, pp. 149-50.

16. Longinus, *On the Sublime,* section 22, p. 96.

17. Ibid., section 7, p. 66.

18. Kant, *Critique of Judgment,* section 30, p. 121.

19. I here summarize the solution advanced in section 57 of the *Critique.*

20. Richard Rorty, *Philosophy and the Mirror of Nature* (Princeton, 1979), pp. 152-54. In general, my understanding of the relations between idealism and romanticism has been influenced by Rorty; by Charles Taylor, *Hegel* (Cambridge, 1975), ch. I; and by Josiah Royce, *The Spirit of Modern Philosophy* (Boston, 1892), chs. III-VI.

21. Kant, *Critique of Judgment,* section 17, p. 69.

22. The "it is"—"I am" opposition I borrow from Thomas McFarland, *Coleridge and the Pantheist Tradition* (Oxford, 1969), where "it is" figures as the necessitarianism that Coleridge associated with Spinoza, and "I am" as the idealism that he associated with Kant.

23. Rorty, *Philosophy and the Mirror of Nature,* p. 353.

24. John Stuart Mill, "Coleridge," in *Collected Works*, 19 vols. (Toronto, 1963-1981), X, 119-20.

25. Quoted by Mill, ibid., p. 148.

26. Quoted by Mill, ibid., p. 151.

27. Ernst Cassirer traces Rousseau's influence on the philosophy of Kant in *The Question of Jean-Jacques Rousseau,* trans. Peter Gay (Bloomington, 1963), where he argues that to Rousseau "freedom did not mean arbitrariness but the overcoming and elimination of all arbitrariness, the submission to a strict and inviolable law which the individual erects over himself. Not renunciation and release from this law but free consent to it determines the genuine and true character of freedom. And that character is realized in the *volonté generale,* the will of the state" (p. 55). In support of this interpretation, Cassirer cites from the *Social Contract* Rousseau's claim that "Each man, by giving himself to all, gives himself to nobody"—commenting that it was precisely this belief in the law and "its unconditional universal validity" that made Kant his "admiring disciple."

28. Coleridge, *Biographia Literaria,* ch. 14, pp. 173-74.

29. Mary Warnock, *Imagination* (Berkeley, 1976), p. 93. Of the confused balance and antithesis of the famous definition, she writes: "It simply adds to the impression, which is hard to resist, that Coleridge was here writing without thinking, just playing about with the remembered counters. And this impression is confirmed by the fact that immediately after . . . he goes on in a different manner, apparently talking not about transcendental psychology but about style." She justifies the impression by remarking that Coleridge "sometimes spoke of the categories, or pure concepts of the understanding, as conceptions *formed from materials furnished by the senses;* that is to say, he did not grasp the difference, absolutely crucial to Kant's theory, between the *a priori* and the *a posteriori,* between what we bring to the world, and what we collect from it. He thought of the understanding as forming rules *from* given sensible examples (in Kant the function of the judgment not the understanding). The whole nature of Kant's Copernican Revolution, according to which he argues that the understanding *applies* concepts *a priori* to the materials of the senses, seems to have escaped him" (pp. 95-96).

I would add that some of the confusion results from an unannounced shift of terms: Coleridge makes his Imagination cover the activity of Kant's understanding as well as judgment; whereas his own Understanding deals in the mere counters or data of sense-experience. At the same time I think Warnock is right that nothing in Coleridge's vocabulary quite corresponds to, or leaves adequate room for, the faculty of practical reason by which we apply laws to our own experience of freedom.

An ecstatic defense of Coleridge's sketch of "the poet, described in ideal perfection," takes up several pages of Richards's Introduction to *The Viking Coleridge,* and is worth consulting as an instance of apologetic paraphrase. Coleridge's language is often vague enough to permit great latitude of invention to his interpreters, and to render any dispute on matters of detail almost unresolvable. Thus Richards's "Appendix on Value" in *Principles of Literary Criticism* seems to confess that he reads poetry to satisfy different needs, and with a different end in view, than Coleridge: "The purpose of [my] theory is just to enable us to compare . . . experiences in respect of their value; and their value, I suggest, is a quantitative matter. To put it very briefly the best life is that in which as much as possible of our possible personality is engaged. And of two personalities that one is the better in which there is more which can be engaged without confusion." Applied to great poetry, this would issue in a Benthamite determination of merit on the basis of personality-pulses or engagement-quotients, and make value reckonable by the Understanding. Yet Richards, in a later study of *Coleridge on Imagination*, plainly demonstrates that he supposed he had derived his own views from Coleridge. Of his misreading of Coleridge the best discussion is D. G. James's, in *Scepticism and Poetry* (London, 1937), chs. 2 and 4, though it fixes too much of the blame on Richards.

30. Abrams, *The Mirror and the Lamp*, p. 154.
31. Coleridge, *Shakespearean Criticism*, II, 66-67.
32. Ibid., I, 198.
33. Coleridge, *Biographia Literaria*, ch. 7, p. 72.
34. To Wordsworth too the allegory of the Castle of Indolence seemed to fit Coleridge, and the description of him in "Stanzas Written in my Pocket-Copy of Thomson's *Castle of Indolence*" adapts, almost to the point of paraphrase, the following stanzas from Thomson's original (I, 57-59).

> Of all the gentle tenants of the place,
> There was a man of special grave remark:
> A certain tender gloom o'erspread his face,
> Pensive, not sad; in thought involved, not dark:
> As soote this man could sing as morning-lark,
> And teach the noblest morals of the heart;
> But these his talents were yburied stark;
> Of the fine stores he nothing would impart,
> Which or boon nature gave or nature-painting art.
>
> To noontide shades incontinent he ran
> Where purls the brook with sleep-inviting sound;
> Or, when Dan Sol to slope his wheels began,
> Amid the broom he basked him on the ground,
> Where the wild thyme and camomil are found;
> There would he linger till the latest ray
> Of light sat quivering on the welkin's bound;
> Then homeward through the twilight shadows stray
> Sauntering and slow. So had he passed many a day.
>
> Yet not in thoughtless slumber were they past:
> For oft the heavenly fire, that lay concealed
> Emongst the sleeping embers, mounted fast
> And all its native light anew revealed.
> Oft as he traversed the cerulean field
> And marked the clouds that drove before the wind,
> Ten thousand glorious systems would he build,
> Ten thousand great ideas filled his mind;
> But with the clouds they fled, and left no trace behind.

The first several lines have a particularly strong echo in Wordsworth's picture of "A noticeable man with large grey eyes,/ And a pale face that seemed undoubtedly/ As if a blooming face it ought to be." Coleridge's enticements in the later poem are again those of ten thousand things never to be done, and when Hazlitt misquotes Thomson in "My First Acquaintance with Poets"—"A certain tender bloom has face o'erspread"—he gives Wordsworth's revision precedence over its model.

Chapter VII. Critical Temperament

1. Quoted in Howe, *Life of Hazlitt,* pp. 318-19. A manuscript draft of the letter contains one passage of some interest which Hunt omitted from the version he sent Hazlitt. In self-defense Hunt writes: "What is it that annoys you so with a love of innovation which you have yourself, or with that gayer + superficial part of character which you have not? People will think that you want a monopoly rather than improvement of the one; + that you pay a homage to the other, as little humble as it well can be, in thus resenting the possession of a trifling quality or so, which you do not happen to number among your own." Quoted by permission of the Huntington Library, San Marino, California (HM 20601).

2. Hazlitt, *Letters,* p. 206.

3. Ibid., p. 204.

4. The phrase appears in Hazlitt's *Letters,* p. 206, as "a parcel of small grievances"; I have changed it to accord with the manuscript. Quoted by permission of the Huntington Library, San Marino, California (HM 20600).

5. *Crabb Robinson on Books,* ed. Morley, I, 201.

6. Blunden, *Leigh Hunt's "Examiner" Examined,* p. 59.

7. *The Rambler,* ed. W. J. Bate and Albrecht B. Strauss, 3 vols. (New Haven, 1969), I, 323.

8. Coleridge, *Letters,* II, 990-91.

9. On Junius's identity I have been persuaded by the "Note on Authorship" in John Cannon's edition of the *Letters.* A private letter from Philip Francis could not, however, have been known to Burke as a letter from Junius, and my point in merging the private with the public character is that both exemplified a kind of refinement for which Hazlitt's admiration is scarcely predictable. On Francis as a critic of Burke, see O'Brien's Introduction to *Reflections on the Revolution in France,* pp. 49-50.

10. *Crabb Robinson on Books,* ed. Morley, I, 24.

11. Coleridge, *Shakespearean Criticism,* II, 154-55.

12. Ibid., II, 238.

13. Ibid., I, 206.

14. Hazlitt would have had special fun making Cobbett and Caliban a pair, from the recentness of Cobbett's attack on Shakespeare. He answered Cobbett at greater length in the *Examiner* under the heading "Cobbett and Shakespeare: A Postscript" (XX, 58-60).

Chapter VIII. The Politics of Allusion

1. De Quincey, "Charles Lamb," in *Works,* VIII, 126-36; especially the following remarks: "Hazlitt was not eloquent, because he was discontinuous. . . . Eloquence resides not in separate or fractional ideas, but in the relations of manifold ideas, and in the mode of their evolution from each other. It is not indeed

enough that the ideas should be many, and their relations coherent; the main condition lies in the *key* of evolution, in the *law* of succession. The elements are nothing without the atmosphere that moulds, and the dynamic forces that combine. Now Hazlitt's brilliancy is seen chiefly in separate splinterings of phrase or image which throw upon the eye a vitreous scintillation for a moment, but spread no deep suffusions of colour, and distribute no masses of mighty shadow. A flash, a solitary flash, and all is gone. . . . Hazlitt's thoughts were of the same fractured and discontinuous order as his illustrative images—seldom or never self-diffusive; and *that* is a sufficient argument that he had never cultivated philosophic thinking" (pp. 128-29). De Quincey's thought as well as his diction—"evolution," "the atmosphere that moulds," "self-diffusive"—betrays how far he was committed to seek in prose what Coleridge had taught him to admire in all works of the mind. But when he mentions the discontinuousness of Hazlitt's rhetoric, and the abruptness of its solitary flashings-forth, he seems to deplore it for just the qualities that a critic who followed Longinus more nearly than Coleridge would admire.

Between Hazlitt's discontinuousness and his practice of quoting, De Quincey finds an explicit relation: "The reason for resisting the example and practice of Hazlitt lies in this—that essentially it is at war with sincerity, the foundation of all good writing, to express one's own thoughts by another man's words. . . . Simply to back one's own view by a similar view derived from another, may be useful; a quotation that repeats one's own sentiment, but in a varied form, has the grace which belongs to the *idem in alio,* the same radical idea expressed with a difference—similarity in dissimilarity; but to throw one's own thoughts, matter, and form, through alien organs so absolutely as to make another man one's interpreter for evil and good, is either to confess a singular laxity of thinking that can so flexibly adapt itself to any casual form of words, or else to confess that sort of carelessness about the expression which draws its real origin from a sense of indifference about the things to be expressed" (pp. 135-36). This is unimaginative criticism, and very strange to come from a good quoter. The third possibility which De Quincey omits from his either-or formulation, is that by quoting one makes another man one's interpreter *while guiding the interpretation, as if from afar.* The farther the reader must travel to fetch the quotation from memory, the more he shares the author's energy of mind in having placed it so, and the more he will be struck by its foreignness and rightness—the dissimilarity and similarity, each inhabiting his consciousness of the other—which alone justify the peculiar choice of two men's words instead of one. Incidentally, De Quincey's emphasis on quotation as a bad habit that pervasively mars Hazlitt's writing would seem to complicate any future assertion of his earlier charge that "Hazlitt had read nothing." But his argument is perhaps evolutionary, being freed in its higher developments from any self-conscious reflection on its past, and he lets both points stand.

2. Ibid., p. 128.

3. Quoted in James T. Boulton, *The Language of Politics in the Age of Wilkes and Burke* (London, 1963), p. 57.

4. Johnson, "Life of Savage," in *Lives of the English Poets,* 3 vols. (London, 1896), II, 217; Henry James, *What Maisie Knew* (Anchor edition, New York, 1954), p. 176.

5. Baker, *William Hazlitt,* p. 42.

6. For this use of "itinerary" to mean the probable history of an allusion (the family of anterior instances which the present instance seems to evoke), I am in-

debted to Thomas Greene, whose own elaborations of the idea appear in *The Light in Troy: Imitation and Discovery in Renaissance Poetry* (New Haven, 1982).

7. John Hollander, *The Figure of Echo* (Berkeley, 1981), p. 64.

8. Walter Benjamin, "What Is Epic Theatre," in *Illuminations*, trans. Harry Zohn (New York, 1968), p. 151. On the relation between quoting and the sublime pathos of distance which Benjamin calls "aura," see his "Karl Kraus," in *Reflections*. Benjamin himself quotes Kraus, "The more closely you look at a word the more distantly it looks back," and explains: "To quote a word is to call it by its name. . . . In the quotation that both saves and chastises, language proves the matrix of justice. It summons the word by its name, wrenches it destructively from its context, but precisely thereby calls it back to its origin" (pp. 268-69). The description seems to me apt for all Hazlitt's practice of quotation, but especially for his use of the Immortality Ode to enforce justice against Wordsworth in the name of the poem itself, or a supposed original sense of the poem.

9. Keats, *Letters*, I, 138.

10. *Liber Amoris* is of all Hazlitt's works perhaps the richest in evidence of how seriously he lived out the drama of his allusions. Throughout the published romance, he appears as Othello, and there are even hints of a catastrophe similar to his prototype's, narrowly averted. The reader who suspects me of exaggerating is invited to consider his many echoes of "Othello's occupation's gone"; his speech to Sarah Walker's father, informing him of "the whole story, 'what conjurations, and what mighty magic I won his daughter with'"; and his address to her in the closing lines as "thou poor hapless weed," after Othello's epithet "fair weed" for Desdemona.

Playing Othello also involved him in an identification with Richardson's Lovelace. One is apt to assign as a motive for this second set of allusions nothing more than the filthy boarding-house which Hazlitt shared with Lovelace as his setting; until one recalls Lovelace's all-important quotation of the lines from *Othello*, "Perdition catch my soul/ But I do love thee! And when I love thee not,/ Chaos is come again." Unquoted, these lines make so constant an undercurrent in *Liber Amoris* that they hardly need to surface. Stewart C. Wilcox's manuscript-study of "The Fight," *Hazlitt in the Workshop* (Baltimore, 1943), shows his thoughts, even during the composition of that essay, turning irresistibly to Sarah Walker, and the mirror he stares into once again disclosing the baffled countenance of Lovelace. The revealing sentences in Hazlitt's manuscript—deleted from the published essay—occur in the third paragraph, after "I passed Hyde Park Corner (my Rubicon), and trusted to fortune." Between that sentence and the next, "Suddenly I heard the clattering of a Brentford stage, and the fight rushed full upon my fancy," he wrote the following:

> Oh! thou dumb heart, lonely, sad, shut up in the prison house of this rude form, that hast never found a fellow but for an hour & in very mockery of thy misery, speak, find bleeding words to express thy thoughts, break thy dungeon-gloom, pronouncing the name of thy [Clarissa] [infelice] or die & wither of pure scorn! I thought of the time when I was a little happy [thoughtless] [careless] child, of my father's house, of my early lessons, of my brother's picture of me when a boy, of all that had since happened & of the waste of years to come—I stopped, faultered, & was going to turn back once more to make a longer truce with wretchedness & patch up a hollow

league with love—when suddenly the clattering of a Brentford-stage reminded me where I was.

I preserve the final transition to the essay as we know it, to exhibit how far, in its original conception, it seems to have told the story of a forced recovery. But the under-plot of "The Fight" is disclosed more plainly here than in any comparable stretch of the published version. Hazlitt's motive for going to see the boxers was by a single stroke, through his absorption in some violent spectacle, to throw off the load of tormenting jealousies which for months had kept him a haunted man. The impetuous pace of the essay and the arbitrary high spirits he imposes from the start, with "Where there's a will, there's a way," are finer when one sees them as a *fit* of remedy for immedicable woes, and I think Hazlitt deleted the passage for strictly prudential reasons.

11. Chiefly De Quincey, whose essay on "The Poetry of Pope" deviates for several paragraphs into a sympathetic rehearsal of the canons of taste by which Pope had been denied the highest poetic merit. The essay here can be read as a more general defense of romantic habits of reading, with results so satisfactory that the digression has commonly been printed as a separate fragment, under the title "The Literature of Knowledge and the Literature of Power." De Quincey repeats the contrast of "Why the Arts are not Progressive?" while adding a metaphor that confuses the distinction: "There is, first, the literature of *knowledge;* and, secondly, the literature of *power*. The function of the first is—to *teach;* the function of the second is—to *move:* the first is a rudder; the second an oar or a sail. The first speaks to the *mere* discursive understanding; the second speaks ultimately, it may happen, to the higher understanding or reason, but always *through* affections of pleasure and sympathy" (De Quincey, *Works,* VIII, 5).

The thought is Hazlitt's, but in style De Quincey writes as a total disciple of Coleridge: those who find his metaphor enlightening, and can assent to the supposition that the rudder has a function somehow more passive than that of sails and oars, are born lovers of the *Biographia Literaria*. Having recognized the distinction, De Quincey goes on to urge its use as a way of separating classics of science like Newton's *Principia,* which for a time influence readers as books *"militant* on earth," but then desert their eminence leaving behind only the luminous name of their authors—and classics of poetry, like *Paradise Lost,* which conquer not for the sake of a scheme to improve the understanding but by the integrity and permanence of their imaginings, and are therefore "triumphant for ever." This second contrast, and these excellent phrases, De Quincey invented, and for them he deserves the credit. For the rest, this fragment would have struck the more advanced of his readers as a commonplace, or at best a summing-up by a master of paraphrase. His essay on Pope appeared in 1848, "Why the Arts are not Progressive?" in 1814.

12. *Rambler,* No. 4, I, 22.

13. Burke, *Reflections,* ed. O'Brien, pp. 169-70. Here as elsewhere I have used this edition as preferable to Volume III of the *Works*. It corresponds to the tenth and final 1790 edition, the last supervised by Burke himself, and the one Hazlitt is likely to have known.

14. James Mackintosh, *Vindiciae Gallicae* (2nd edition, London, 1791), p. vii.

15. Mary Wollstonecraft, *A Vindication of the Rights of Men* (2nd edition, London, 1790), p. 110.

16. *Leigh Hunt's Literary Criticism,* ed. L. H. Houtchens and C. W. Houtchens (New York, 1956), pp. 244, 253.

17. Burke, *Works,* V, 210-11. But I quote Hazlitt's version of the passage, in "On the Prose-Style of Poets."

18. *Leigh Hunt's Literary Criticism,* ed. Houtchens and Houtchens, p. 244.

19. Burke, *Works,* V, 187.

20. Ibid., VI, 47-48. Even his first reaction to news of the revolution—"What Spectators and what Actors!"—has this sort of assurance for the *outside* spectator whom Burke addresses. Quoted by Conor Cruise O'Brien in "Imagination and Politics," O'Brien and Vanech, ed., *Power and Consciousness.*

21. O'Brien, Introduction to Burke's *Reflections,* pp. 75-76.

Chapter IX. Poetry and Justice

1. Richard Payne Knight, *Analytical Inquiry into the Principles of Taste* (4th edition, London, 1808), pp. 370-71.

2. Knight saw to what absurdities Burke's example might lead, with its insistence on terror as an emotion both *immediate* and *physically present* to the spectator. To kill the argument forever, he gave a ludicrous counter-example: if Burke himself had condescended to test his theory, by suddenly appearing "among the managers in Westminster-hall without his wig or coat; or had walked up St. James's Street without his breeches, it would have occasioned great and universal *astonishment;* and if he had, at the same time, carried a loaded blunderbuss in his hands, the astonishment would have been mixed with no small portion of *terror;* but I do not believe that the united effects of these two powerful passions would have produced any sensation or sentiment approaching to sublime, even in the breasts of those, who had the strongest sense of self-preservation, and the quickest sensibility to danger" (*Analytical Inquiry,* pp. 383-84).

3. Ibid., p. 329.

4. Ibid., pp. 366-67.

5. The change is in Hazlitt's hand, cited with the permission of the Poetry/ Rare Book Collection of the University Libraries, State University of New York at Buffalo.

6. Leigh Hunt, *Lord Byron and Some of his Contemporaries* (Philadelphia, 1828), pp. 60-61.

7. On the picturesque as a framing of the sublime, see Angus Fletcher, *Allegory* (Ithaca, 1964), pp. 252-78. Fletcher is interested in these categories as two names for a single kind of "ambivalence," which leaves us suspended between attraction and repulsion, pleasure and pain, awe in the unbounded and satisfaction in the mind's effort to bound whatever it confronts, with the threat of damnation (or utter destruction) as a counter-weight to every impulse of salvation (or original construction). He regards the sublime and the picturesque as essentially the same phenomenon seen under different aspects, and argues that what distinguishes the picturesque is its greater attentiveness to "textural" quality and details. My treatment in the following pages is more conservative. It exhibits the picturesque as a domestication—a rendering more accessible to habit—of the objects associated with sublime emotions. On this account the whole language of "scenery" is a development of the picturesque: it illustrates both a complacency and a trust in reliable taxonomies, alien to the sublime. At least one of Fletcher's quotations—

from Mrs. Inchbald's *Memoirs,* about her view from a safe distance of the burning of Drury Lane theatre—seems to confirm this division of the subject, and Fletcher comments: "there is a degree of sublimity in which the ambivalence is too great to be supported, but the picturesque diminishes this tension to an acceptable level" (p. 259).

I agree that the sublime and the picturesque are in a sense the double face of one phenomenon, and that they get no interesting help from the addition of a third term, the beautiful. I summarize elsewhere in this chapter a more common-place view which Hazlitt sometimes credits, that the picturesque "softens the contrast" between the extremes of the sublime and the beautiful: but this makes sense only in measuring the three on the uninteresting continuum of the scale-of-ideas (where the sublime is always incommensurable, the picturesque just within our grasp, and the beautiful no trouble at all). Ultimately the beautiful occupies a separate place because it makes no pretense of dealing with the un-bounded. For the remaining pair, Fletcher offers some convenient differentiae: "Both sublime and picturesque scenes share the power of eliciting ambivalent fascination, but they may perhaps finally be distinguished in two major charac-teristics, (1) the magnitude of the elements in each, the immense versus the mi-nute, and (2) in consequence of the picturesque's reduction of sublime grandeur to minute textural intricacy, the more approachable, more charming, more com-fortable effect of picturesque scenes" (pp. 257-58).

For the reasons just cited, this seems to me an unsatisfying conclusion: it in-troduces the beautiful once again—which is small, intricate, charming—and de-fines the picturesque by its comparative closeness to the third term. The implica-tion is that the difference between sublimity and picturesqueness has something to do with the actual size of the objects. Yet what Hazlitt saw, when he described as "picturesque" Byron's tourism across continents and centuries, was that the difference has to do with the sort of purchase the mind wants on its objects: if settling into an easy grip, then picturesque; if ever reaching *toward,* then sublime. Fletcher may after all be summarizing Uvedale Price, but if one needs a contem-porary guide to the subject Hazlitt is subtler and more rewarding than Price. He echoes the Kantian language of ambivalence, without ever incorporating, or being encumbered by, the explicit Kantian theory.

8. Johnson has a parallel description of a poet's self-deceiving hauteur in re-lation to his audience, in the *Life of Pope:* "Pope, in one of his letters, complain-ing of the treatment which his poem had found, 'owns that such criticks can in-timidate him, nay almost persuade him to write no more, which is a compliment this age deserves.' The man who threatens the world is always ridiculous; for the world can easily go on without him, and in a short time will cease to miss him. . . . Pope had been flattered till he thought himself one of the moving powers in the system of life. When he talked of laying down his pen, those who sat round him intreated and implored, and self-love did not suffer him to suspect that they went away and laughed." To Hazlitt the whole tone of Byron's *Letter*—satire alter-nating with petulant complaint—was wrong for a poet, because it made too little of the high office every poet is granted by his readers. He saw nothing wrong in a poet's seizing even the slightest occasion to recall, by some gesture or effect, the significance of his function, and there was no mockery in his recollection three decades afterwards of the way Wordsworth recited *Peter Bell:* "Whatever might be thought of the poem, 'his face was a book where men might read strange mat-

ters,' and he announced the fate of his hero in prophetic tones." Hazlitt's protest against Byron was that his affected carelessness finally went deeper than affectation. Again one may recall Johnson: "One of his favorite topicks is contempt of his own poetry. For this, if it had been real, he would deserve no commendation, and in this he was certainly not sincere; for his high value of himself was sufficiently observed, and of what could he be proud but of his poetry?" Byron was making Wordsworthian claims in his poetry, with a Popean air of indifference: the result, Hazlitt thought, was a pose of irritability which betrayed a more deeply-lying unsteadiness of temper. Could Byron ever read out "the fate of his hero in prophetic tones"?

9. Martin Price, "The Picturesque Moment," in Frederick W. Hilles and Harold Bloom, ed., *From Sensibility to Romanticism* (New York, 1965), p. 285.

10. Flaxman, *Lectures on Sculpture*, p. 199. Quoted by permission of Gordon N. Ray.

11. De Quincey, "The Revolt of the Tartars," *Works*, IV, 141.

12. Quoted by Price, "The Picturesque Moment," p. 264.

Chapter X. Familiar Style

1. The following notes are transcribed from Hazlitt's copy of the *Advancement* (1629), and reproduced by permission of the London Borough of Camden, from the Collections at Keats House, Hampstead. They were first attributed to Hazlitt by Payson G. Gates, "Bacon, Keats and Hazlitt," *South Atlantic Quarterly*, 46 (1947), 238-51.

2. This metaphor belongs to Hazlitt's qualified appreciation of Malthus, at the beginning of his sketch in *The Spirit of the Age* (XI, 104).

Chapter XI. Keats

1. Of the many critics and scholars who have surveyed the influence of Hazlitt on Keats, I am chiefly indebted to Hyder Rollins, for his notes to Keats's *Letters*; W. J. Bate, *John Keats* (1963; Oxford University Press edition, New York, 1966), pp. 255-63; Caldwell, *John Keats' Fancy*, pp. 172-86; and C. D. Thorpe, "Keats and Hazlitt," *PMLA* 42 (1947), 487-502. Bate and Caldwell are particularly admirable for exhibiting Keats as part of the mind of the age. On the other hand, my record of the Keats-Hazlitt friendship may be read as an antidote to Baker, *William Hazlitt*, pp. 247-51. In portraying Hazlitt as a recalcitrant party to this friendship, it seems to me that Baker makes the worst of appearances wherever possible.

2. Keats, *Letters*, I, 143.

3. Ibid., I, 166.

4. Ibid., I, 238-39.

5. Of Keats's biographers only Robert Gittings is sufficiently wary of these ideas.

6. Keats, *Letters*, I, 252, 274.

7. Ibid., II, 76.

8. Ibid., I, 210.

9. Ibid., II, 24.

10. *Fall of Hyperion*, canto I, lines 168-176, *The Poems of John Keats,* ed. Jack Stillinger (Cambridge, Mass., 1978), p. 482.

11. Printed as Appendix 5 in Keats' *Complete Poems,* ed. John Barnard (1973; 2nd Penguin edition, New York, 1977), p. 528.

12. Keats, *Letters,* I, 237.

13. Ibid., I, 214.

14. Keats, *Poems,* ed. Stillinger, pp. 102-103.

15. Part II, lines 1-15, *Poems,* pp. 463-64.

16. Keats, *Letters,* I, 184.

17. John Middleton Murry, *Keats and Shakespeare* (London, 1925), ch. 4.

18. Keats, *Letters,* I, 223-24.

19. Ibid., I, 264-65.

20. Locke, *Essay concerning Human Understanding,* IV.iv.9, p. 567.

21. Coleridge, *The Statesman's Manual,* in *Lay Sermons,* p. 89.

22. Keats, *Letters,* I, 232.

23. Ibid., I, 193.

24. Ibid., I, 386-87. I here adopt a textual change suggested by George Beaumont in *TLS,* February 27, May 1, 1930, pp. 166, 370: "informing" in place of "in for —." The word is characteristic of Keats as of Hazlitt, and it fits his sense.

25. Keats, *Letters,* I, 282.

26. A companion aphorism may be found in *Characteristics:* "The pleasure derived from tragedy is to be accounted for in this way, that, by painting the extremes of human calamity, it by contrast kindles the affections, and raises the most intense imagination and desire of the contrary good" (IX, 209).

27. Keats, *Letters,* II, 360. In *Characteristics* Hazlitt writes: "Good and ill seem as necessary to human life as light and shade to a picture" (IX, 208). On the associative relation of contrast and its tendency to imply a whole, see Caldwell, *John Keats' Fancy.*

28. Keats, *Letters,* II, 80-81.

29. Ibid., II, 79.

30. The opposite—that poet and bird intermingle as equals—has been asserted by Earl Wasserman, in *The Finer Tone* (Baltimore, 1953). Wasserman supposed an "antithesis of the two empathies, the poet's and the nightingale's" (p. 185), and argued that "the bird has entered into the essence of nature, and the poet into the essence of the bird" (p. 187). I believe on the contrary that Keats, as the poem starts, is burdened by an excess of consciousness and of susceptibility, whereas the bird possesses neither. Its song fits no known definition of empathy, and I am not aware that Keats ever wrote of "essence" quite in Wasserman's sense (the "fellowship with essence" passage of *Endymion* will not do). A nightingale that entered into the essence of nature would have to be outside it to begin with, and that was not the way Keats looked at things, as his descriptions in letters of the hawk, the eagle, the robin, and the swallow all indicate.

31. From Keats's annotations to *Paradise Lost,* in J. A. Wittreich, Jr., ed., *The Romantics on Milton* (Cleveland, 1970), p. 558.

32. Keats, *Endymion,* Book II, lines 274-280, in *Poems,* p. 140. In pointing out a connection between the two passages, I have been anticipated by M. R. Ridley, *Keats' Craftsmanship* (1933; reprinted, Lincoln, 1963), p. 231.

33. Patrick Parrinder, *Authors and Authority: A Study of English Literary Criticism and Its Relation to Culture 1750-1900* (London, 1977), p. 97.

34. The history of interpreting these comments of Hazlitt's as a clue to the "Ode on a Grecian Urn" is as follows. Ian Jack quoted the last few sentences, beginning with "the Greek statues are little more than specious forms," in *Keats and the Mirror of Art* (Oxford, 1967) and observed: "It would be curious to have the comment of Keats on this passage" (p. 72). Patrick Parrinder replied in *Authors and Authority* that "we have that comment; it is the 'Ode on a Grecian Urn,'" but said nothing further about Hazlitt; to Jack's quotation he added the beginning of the sentence Jack had picked up in the middle: "It is for want of some such resting place for the imagination. . . ." I give the entire passage, of which the first half seems to me quite as pertinent as the second, and propose that Hazlitt influenced not only the sentiment of the poem, but a good deal of its dramatic movement.

35. *Collected Essays, Papers, etc. of Robert Bridges,* 10 vols. (London, 1927-1936), III, 132.

36. H. W. Garrod, *Keats* (London, 1926), pp. 107-108.

37. As a corrective to the cant of "ironic distancing" at the end of Keats's poem, I recommend Pratap Biswas, "Keats's Cold Pastoral," *University of Toronto Quarterly,* 47 (Winter 1977-1978), 95-111. The article, though not always tactful, seems to me admirably clear in its formulations, and is the most emphatic argument I know for Keats's sympathy with truth over beauty.

38. I have profited from Geoffrey Hartman's treatment of the saying as part of the romantic tradition of nature-inscriptions, in "Wordsworth, Inscriptions, and Romantic Nature Poetry," reprinted in *Beyond Formalism* (New Haven, 1970); and from Leo Spitzer's reading of the final lines as spoken by the urn, in "The 'Ode on a Grecian Urn,' or Content vs. Metagrammar," reprinted in *Essays on English and American Literature* (Princeton, 1962).

39. This paraphrase borrows from, and simplifies, William Empson's remarks on the "A is B" family of logical assertions, to which Keats's sentence belongs. See *The Structure of Complex Words* (Ann Arbor, paperback edition, 1967), pp. 350-74. Empson's seems to me much the best twentieth-century commentary on the Ode, and his summing up of Keats's feelings about the "little town" strikes the note I have tried to sustain: "These people's homes will be left desolate because they have gone to make a piece of art-work, and so will Keats' home because he is spending his life on art. Beauty is both a cause of and an escape from suffering, and in either way suffering is deeply involved in its production" (p. 370).

40. Emerson, "The Poet," in *Works,* III, 17.

41. Empson, *Structure of Complex Words,* p. 370. But I do not think Keats for any stretch of his life was "working on the ideas of Coleridge." His references to Coleridge—including the description of their walk about Highgate, and the phrase from the "negative capability" letter, about letting go "by a fine isolated verisimilitude caught from the Penetralium of mystery"—are as a rule lightly mocking in tone. The matter is easy to check because the references are so few.

42. Of the continuity between the romantic and modern lyric, by way of Keats's dramatic sympathies, the invention of the dramatic monologue by Browning and Tennyson, and the modern need to balance the speaker's song with his situation, the best account is Robert Langbaum's *The Poetry of Experience* (1957; 2nd Norton edition, New York, 1971). His treatment of the romantic criticism of Shakespeare (ch. 5) with its new emphasis on character, as the single most important connection between the self-announcing lyric of the romantics and the

self-defining monologue of the Victorians, strikes me as especially subtle, and is for obvious reasons congenial to my argument about Hazlitt. My disagreements are slight and have mainly to do with Langbaum's tendency to make Keats in his odes stand for the same tendencies as Wordsworth in a poem like "Resolution and Independence." To Keats, the dramatic encounter which Wordsworth seemed concerned to record, and for which he raised high expectations in his reader, was always being lost in the magnetic field of the egotistical narrator. In this respect Keats thought of his own poetry as attempting nearly the opposite of Words-worth's.

Conclusion

1. Quoted from a review in *Punch,* in Toby Lelyveld, *Shylock on the Stage* (Cleveland, 1960), p. 132.

2. See C. L. Barber, *Shakespeare's Festive Comedy* (Princeton, 1959), ch. 7; and Lawrence Danson, *The Harmonies of the Merchant of Venice* (New Haven, 1978).

3. Langbaum summarizes this judgment concisely: "The alternative to the modern misinterpretation would seem to be an historically accurate but dead document" (*Poetry of Experience,* p. 169). Of the incompatibility of such documents with the concerns of any period, H.-G. Gadamer, *Truth and Method,* Part I (English translation, New York, 1975), offers a thorough account. *What can be believed in performance* emerges for Gadamer as one index of an historically satisfying interpretation: "the compelling quality of the representation is not lessened by the fact that it cannot have any fixed criterion. Thus we do not allow the interpretation of a piece of music or a drama the freedom to take the 'text' as a basis for a lot of ad-lib effects, and yet we would regard the canonisation of a particular interpretation, e.g. in a gramaphone recording conducted by the composer, or the detailed notes on performance which come from the canonised first performance, as a failure to understand the actual task of interpretation" (p. 107).

4. Nietzsche, *Use and Abuse of History,* p. 22.

INDEX

445